Corporate Financial Analysis:

A Comprehensive Guide to Real-World Approaches for Financial Managers

John D. Finnerty
Vice President
Lazard Frères & Co.

McGraw-Hill Book Company

New York   St. Louis   San Francisco   Auckland   Bogotá
Hamburg   Johannesburg   London   Madrid   Mexico
Montreal   New Delhi   Panama   Paris   São Paulo
Singapore   Sydney   Tokyo   Toronto

To   John Patrick Finnerty
     Patricia Conover Finnerty
     O.K. Taylor

LIBRARY OF CONGRESS CATALOGING IN PUBLICATION DATA

Finnerty, John D.

Corporate Financial Analysis.
   Includes index.
      1. Corporations—Finance. I. Title.
HG4026.F524   1986   658.1'5   85-13255
ISBN 0-07-021040-3

234567890   DOC/DOC   89876

ISBN 0-07-021040-3

The editors for this book were William Sabin and Rita Margolies, the designer was Dennis Sharkey, and the production supervisor was Thomas G. Kowalczyk. It was set in Baskerville by McGraw-Hill Information Systems and Technology.

Printed and bound by R. R. Donnelley & Sons Company.

Contents

v

Preface

Financial analysis is the process of collecting and refining financial data and presenting the refined financial information in summary format suitable for effective decision making. Whether the problem involves the choice of a project in which to invest corporate funds and the means of financing it, the selection of an appropriate capital structure for the firm, or the choice of an appropriate dividend policy, to name but a few of the types of financial problems with which this book deals, the quality of the financial analysis that is available to the decision maker will determine to a great extent whether the decision is truly the best one under the circumstances. Sound financial analysis lies at the heart of effective decision making.

Corporate Financial Analysis provides a comprehensive survey of the techniques of modern corporate financial analysis. Part 1 develops a unified analytical framework based on discounted cash flow analysis and sets the stage for the balance of the book. Part 2 deals with the analysis of capital investment projects. Part 3 explains how a company decides upon the most appropriate mix of debt and equity funds with which to finance itself. Part 4 discusses how a company can decide what portion of its available cash flow to pay out as dividends to its common stockholders. Part 5 explains how a company can determine what mix of current assets and current liabilities is most appropriate. Part 6 provides a comprehensive discussion of the alternative sources of long-term financing. Part 7 discusses a variety of bond refunding situations, and explains and illustrates analytical techniques appropriate to each. Part 8 deals with four issues relating to financial planning and strategy: corporate financial planning, venture capital and going public, mergers and acquisitions, and reorganization and liquidation. Part 9 reviews the principal sources of financial information. I know of no other book that provides coverage as comprehensive as this one of the range of financial problems with which financial managers must deal in their day-to-day work.

Each part of the book begins with a practical example to motivate the discussion. Each part presents techniques that corporate financial managers, investment bankers, commercial bankers, and financial consultants actually use to solve problems of the type discussed in that part. Each technique is carefully explained so that the reader can understand the "theoretical" justification for it *and* can appreciate the practical value of the technique. The book is liberally illustrated with practical examples, which makes it easy to use as a reference work. The emphasis throughout the book is on how to apply the techniques of financial analysis to solve problems of the type financial managers regularly encounter.

As most readers are aware, financial analysis is becoming increasingly quantitative. Fortunately, for those who are not mathematically inclined, computers and calculators have assumed most of the computational burden. Consequently, the emphasis in this book can be placed where it belongs: on explaining the techniques and interpreting the results, rather than on how to perform the calculations.

I decided to write this book after I failed to find a book on financial analysis that I felt adequately covered the subject. Despite a long and varied academic career, I never found time for business school. Nevertheless, I was fortunate enough to be able to pursue a career in investment banking—first at Morgan Stanley & Co. and currently with Lazard Frères & Co. Prior to joining Morgan Stanley, I tried to prepare for my chosen career by reading what I had been assured were the leading books in the fields of financial management and the techniques of financial analysis. It was only after I began working as an investment banker that I discovered how wide the gulf between "textbook" financial analysis and "real-world" financial analysis really was. For example, textbooks talk about selecting the "optimal," or best, dividend policy, the best capital structure, and so on. But, in practice, a company cannot afford the resources required to determine what is truly the optimal dividend policy or what is truly the best capital structure. The best it can do is to determine a reasonable dividend policy and reasonable capital structure. And to reach these decisions, much simpler techniques are available than the ones described in textbooks on financial management and financial analysis. In particular, by analyzing a carefully chosen group of comparable companies, a company can infer from market and other financial data a reasonable set of dividend, capital structure, and other financial policies. This book describes how to perform this type of financial analysis and how to apply a variety of other useful practical approaches.

The book should appeal to a broad audience. Financial managers who need to understand the techniques of financial analysis and the financial analysts who need to apply these techniques in their everyday work will find the book indispensable. Engineers and other nonfinancial people who are appointed to a corporate financial position for the first time will find it a particularly helpful introduction to the range of financial issues they will have to confront on a day-to-day basis. Investment bankers, commercial bankers, and financial consultants will find it a very useful foundation for their work. Corporate finance lawyers will find it of interest in order to learn something about "how the other half lives." Last but not least, the book is also compatible with textbooks on financial management; students will find the "how-to" approach to financial problem solving a refreshing departure from the typically more highbrow textbook approaches.

There are a number of people whom I would like to thank for their contributions to the book. First and foremost, Bill Sabin, my sponsoring editor, provided just the right mix of coaxing and prodding to keep me from turning the writing of the book into an interminable project. Rita Margolies, the editing supervisor for the manuscript, and the production staff at McGraw-Hill did an excellent job of turning the raw manuscript into a polished product. Mitchell Brock and Willard Taylor, partners of Sullivan & Cromwell, and Peter Lasusa, partner of Arthur Andersen & Co., provided expert assistance with certain portions of the book dealing with legal, tax, and accounting issues. Anne Mintz of Lazard Frères & Co. helped me prepare the lists of financial sources in Chapter 29. I also owe a great debt of gratitude to my former colleagues at Morgan Stanley and my current colleagues at Lazard Frères & Co. who have helped me learn and refine the techniques described in the book. Finally, I would like to thank Christine Watt Finnerty and Alexandra Weir who prepared the index; Tom Robinson of Alacrity Typing Service who expertly typed several drafts and, unlike the author, never missed a deadline; and Geraldine McInerney who assisted in the final, most critical stages of the project.

I think it is appropriate to close the preface by offering a few words of encouragement to the reader. Once you have learned the techniques of financial analysis, you will, hopefully, find yourself able to deal more effectively with the financial problems you encounter in your job. You might even become motivated to consult the financial periodicals regularly in order to keep abreast of the development of more sophisticated analytical techniques. In any case, I hope you find your study fruitful and derive as much satisfaction from reading this book and using the techniques described in it as I did from writing it.

Weehawken, N.J. John D. Finnerty
April, 1985

Corporate Financial Analysis

Part 1

Basic Techniques of Financial Analysis

This book describes a variety of problem-solving techniques that corporate financial managers and analysts will find useful. These techniques have certain features in common. Part 1 describes the basic techniques of financial analysis, which underlie the somewhat more specialized techniques described and illustrated in Parts 2 through 8.

Chapter 1 discusses the purpose and scope of financial analysis and the role of the analyst in helping to solve financial problems. Chapter 2 introduces the firm's financial statements, which are the primary source of financial information about a company, and shows how to use financial ratio analysis to make more meaningful the information these statements contain. Chapter 3 develops a flow of funds framework for evaluating the financial implications of business decisions. The essential element of this flow of funds framework is the firm's cash flow. Chapter 4 describes the basic techniques of discounted cash flow analysis, and Chapter 5 discusses how to take risk into account in discounted cash flow analysis.

Purpose and Scope of Financial Analysis

Chapter 1

What do the following problems have in common?

- Washington Chemical Corporation, a manufacturer of specialty chemicals, is considering whether to build a new plant in New York at a cost of $90.5 million or a new plant in New Jersey at a cost of $85 million or, instead, to expand its existing New Jersey plant at a cost of $58 million. It cannot undertake all three capital investment projects simultaneously.

- Washington Chemical has financed itself with one-third debt and two-thirds common equity. Its board of directors has asked the company's management whether this degree of leverage is appropriate in view of the company's desire to maintain its single-A senior debt rating.

- Major Pharmaceutical Company's board of directors has asked the company's treasurer to recommend an appropriate dividend action at the board's next meeting. Major's treasurer would like to present to the board a dividend policy study supporting the dividend recommendation.

- Diversified Chemical Company has maintained a 2:1 ratio of current assets to current liabilities. Diversified's president has asked the treasurer whether the company should change this target in order to protect the prime-quality rating of its commercial paper.

- Western Metals and Mining Corporation plans to undertake a mining project that it expects will cost $100 million, and Western's board of directors has asked Western's vice-president of finance to prepare a financing plan for the project.

- In 1976, New Jersey Bell Telephone Company paid bondholders a premium of 7.74% to redeem $100 million of long-term debt bearing a 9.35% coupon

3

and issued $100 million of new debt bearing an 8.00% coupon. How can a company decide whether to refund an outstanding debt issue?

- Eastern Foods Company is considering purchasing Zeus Frozen Foods Company, whose common stock is publicly traded. Eastern's board of directors has asked the company's financial staff to recommend the price that Eastern should offer to pay for Zeus' shares, to determine the maximum price Eastern could afford to pay, and to recommend the financial package that Eastern should offer Zeus' shareholders.

All these problems are similar to the types of financial problems companies regularly face. All require the selection of one of various alternatives. All therefore require an analysis of the financial implications of pursuing each alternative. Later chapters describe methods for conducting these analyses and then apply these techniques to the aforementioned problems. This chapter sets the stage for the entire book and, specifically, discusses the purpose and scope of financial analysis and the role of the financial analyst in helping to solve problems like those just described.

PURPOSE OF FINANCIAL ANALYSIS

Financial analysis is the process of collecting and refining financial data and presenting the refined financial information in summary format suitable for effective decision making. Its primary purpose is to aid the decision maker; in order to be able to make an informed decision, the decision maker must have reviewed the relevant information. But information in raw form may not reveal clearly the important underlying relationships. For example, suppose a company is considering whether to increase the quarterly dividend rate on its common stock. Simply gathering dividend-related statistics on all companies in the same industry would probably not prove very illuminating, particularly if the number of firms in the industry is large. But by narrowing the sample of companies to a group that is most nearly comparable in terms of size, product mix, growth prospects, and other important business and financial characteristics and by providing the relevant dividend-related statistics for each, such as current dividend yield, payout ratio, historical dividend growth rate, and percentage of cash flow paid out as dividends, the analyst can separate the most useful information from that which is less useful and then place it at the decision maker's disposal.

Practical financial analysis is generally directed toward identifying an *appropriate policy* rather than the *optimal policy*. To continue the dividend policy example, an analysis of the relevant information would be more likely to suggest an appropriate range of payout ratios, e.g., 35 to 40% of earnings, than to indicate that a 37% payout ratio would lead to the highest market price for the company's shares. Conceptual models often lead to such choices of an "optimal" policy; but in actual financial analysis, the cost of obtaining and processing the required information, the importance of nonquantifiable variables, and other mitigating factors normally prevent such precision.

It deserves to be emphasized that financial analysis is a means to an end rather than an end in itself. The data should be gathered and refined, and the summary information should be presented with a clear view toward illuminating the problem that is under study. Unnecessary detail and complexity should be avoided. Most importantly, care must be taken to ensure that the results of the analysis are presented in a clear and understandable fashion.

SCOPE OF FINANCIAL ANALYSIS

Financial analysis consists of two branches, *corporate financial analysis* and *securities analysis*. Corporate financial analysis is designed to aid the professional manager and the entrepreneur in arriving at capital investment, financing, and other decisions that have a bearing on the financial state of the company. The corporate financial analyst is concerned with a broad range of problems because virtually every decision company executives make has some sort of financial implication. Corporate financial analysis is intended to determine those implications, at least qualitatively if not quantitatively, before the decision is made. As such, it is one crucially important aspect of corporate financial management.

Securities analysis is intended to aid the investor and the portfolio manager in the evaluation of alternative investment opportunities. These include proposed purchases of securities as well as proposed purchases of real estate and other assets.

This book is concerned with corporate financial analysis. Nevertheless, certain basic principles and techniques are common to both branches of financial analysis. The reader who has studied securities analysis will consequently find that certain concepts that are useful in securities analysis, such as the capital asset pricing model, are also useful in corporate financial analysis.

It is useful to distinguish several different, though related, aspects of corporate financial analysis. A glance at the table of contents will reveal these areas:

- *Analysis of capital investment projects.* Do the returns expected from a proposed capital investment project, when considered in the light of the project's risks and alternative uses for the funds, justify the investment?
- *Capital structure analysis.* What is the appropriate financing mix for a particular company in view of its business(es) and its business objectives?
- *Dividend policy analysis.* What percentage of a company's available earnings and cash flow should it distribute to its shareholders—and what percentage should it retain in its business—and how should it distribute the cash: through dividend payments or through share repurchases?

- *Working capital management.* What are the appropriate levels of current assets and current liabilities, and what is the most profitable mix of current assets and the least costly mix of short-term funds sources?
- *Selection of sources of long-term funds.* What is the most appropriate source of funds for a particular capital investment project, and how should these securities issue(s) be designed so as to facilitate minimum cost while preserving the desired degree of financial flexibility for the company?
- *Liabilities management.* What opportunities exist for refunding profitably a company's outstanding fixed income obligations and for profitably managing the sinking funds contained in outstanding fixed income issues?
- *Financial planning and strategy.* Are there opportunities for profitably redeploying the firm's assets, for example, by disposing of unwanted assets and using the proceeds to acquire other assets or whole companies?

ROLE OF THE ANALYST

The analyst is charged with the responsibility for collecting the relevant information, selecting the most appropriate analytical techniques for processing the data, carrying out the required calculations correctly, and summarizing the results in an appropriate format. The analyst is also often called upon to draw conclusions and make recommendations based on the analysis; in some cases, he or she may also serve as the decision maker.

Because financial analysis is directed toward a particular problem (or set of problems), it is incumbent upon the analyst to answer the following questions at the initial stage of any analysis:

1. What is the problem (or set of problems) toward which the analysis is directed? Has the problem been clearly defined, or are there certain aspects that require further clarification?
2. What types of financial information are required by the decision maker? Which information is most essential?
3. How exact does the information provided the decision maker have to be? How much time and effort can be devoted to refining the information to enhance its accuracy?
4. What are the major sources of the required financial data? How reliable are these data? How sensitive is the information provided the decision maker likely to be to the less reliable data? Are there ways of verifying the less reliable data?
5. What means are available for supplementing the data available from conventional sources?
6. What are the limitations of the analytical tools to be used? How will these limitations affect the accuracy of the results obtained?

In order to be able to answer these questions and then proceed with the analysis, the analyst must be thoroughly familiar with the techniques of financial analysis. This book is dedicated to that goal.

SUMMARY

This chapter discussed the purpose and scope of corporate financial analysis. Financial analysis is the process of collecting and refining financial data and presenting the refined financial information in summary format suitable for effective decision making. Corporate financial analysis is designed to aid the professional manager and the entrepreneur in their financial decision making. The financial analyst plays an important role in this process: collecting the relevant information, selecting the most appropriate analytical techniques for processing it, carrying out the calculations, and summarizing the results in an appropriate format.

The Firm's Financial Statements and Financial Ratio Analysis

Chapter 2

The primary source of financial information concerning a company is its financial statements. The information contained in these statements summarizes the financial performance and financial position of the business enterprise. This chapter reviews the principal financial statements and their use in financial analysis.

The firm's financial statements alone are generally not sufficient to provide a complete picture of the financial performance and financial condition of the firm. Financial managers and investors also require certain yardsticks as a basis for comparison. The yardsticks most frequently used are a collection of relatively standardized *financial ratios*. By comparing the values of selected financial ratios for a particular firm with values of the same ratios calculated on an equivalent basis for comparable firms, the financial analyst can achieve a better understanding of the financial health of the firm than the financial data alone could provide. Also, by studying changes in key financial ratios over time, the analyst is better able to discern improvement or deterioration in the firm's financial condition and performance.

THE FIRM'S FINANCIAL STATEMENTS

The firm's published financial statements include, at a minimum, an *income statement*, a *balance sheet*, a *statement of changes in financial position*, and accompanying notes.

Income Statement
The income statement reports the profit (or loss) performance of a business entity for a specific period of time, usually a year or some portion thereof.

Profit, or net income, is the difference between total revenue and total cost for the period. The income statement for Lincoln Manufacturing Corporation is shown in Table 2-1. For a manufacturing company, the income statement provides a breakdown of costs into (1) the direct cost of producing the goods that are sold (chiefly labor and raw materials), (2) the other expenses incurred in operating the company, including taxes, and (3) the expenses related to financing it, including interest and the dividends paid to the holders of the

Table 2-1
Income Statement
Lincoln Manufacturing Corporation and Consolidated
Subsidiaries for the Years Ended December 31, 1984 and 1983
(Millions of Dollars Except Per Share Amounts)

	1984	1983
Revenue:		
Net sales	$744.0	$662.3
Other income	7.0	6.6
Total revenue	751.0	668.9
Costs and Expenses:		
Cost of goods sold (excluding depreciation and amortization)	532.0	484.8
Selling, general, and administrative expense	65.3	57.9
Depreciation and amortization	39.0	35.4
Interest expense	25.7	24.5
Capitalized interest	(1.8)	(2.3)
Minority interest in earnings of consolidated subsidiaries	0.3	0.4
Total	660.5	600.7
Net income before taxes and extraordinary items	90.5	68.2
Federal and state income taxes	37.7	29.3
Net income before extraordinary items	52.8	38.9
Preferred stock dividends	2.0	2.4
Earnings available for common stock before extraordinary items	50.8	36.5
Extraordinary gains (losses) net of taxes	(10.1)	—
Earnings available for common stock	$ 40.7	$ 36.5
Average number of common shares outstanding (thousands)	9300	8800
Earnings per common share before extraordinary items	$ 5.46	$ 4.15
Extraordinary gains (losses) per common share	(1.08)	—
Earnings per common share	$ 4.38	$ 4.15
Dividends per common share	$ 1.92	$ 1.80

company's preferred stock. Note that certain noncash items, such as depreciation and amortization, are deducted from revenue in arriving at net income. The residual, earnings available for common stock, is available for payment to common shareholders as dividends or for reinvestment in the business.

Figures for earnings per share and, in some cases, dividends per share are provided at the foot of the income statement. The owners of the outstanding shares of the company's common stock are the residual claimants on the firm's profit; they are paid dividends out of the firm's earnings net of interest payments and net of dividends to holders of preferred stock. The per-share figures indicate how large the residual pool of net income is relative to the number of common shares, or claims, against it. The number of common shares used in this calculation should be the weighted average number of common shares outstanding during the period adjusted, in accordance with generally accepted accounting principles, for any *common stock equivalents* in the company's capital structure. A common stock equivalent is described under Accounting Principles Board Opinion No. 15 as a security whose common equity characteristics are reflected in its market value to such an extent that the security is the "substantial equivalent" of common stock. In addition, if the conversion of convertible securities or the exercise of warrants or options not treated as common stock equivalents would result in a significant reduction in reported earnings per share, such *dilution* must be disclosed in accordance with generally accepted accounting principles in the form of a *fully diluted earnings-per-share* figure. This fully diluted figure gives the analyst a better feel for how large each outstanding share's residual claim on the earnings of the business really is than could the nondiluted figure alone. Earnings per common share before extraordinary items should be distinguished from the earnings per common share (net of these items), because the former figure is the more meaningful measure of the firm's sustainable profit.

The income statement in Table 2-1 seems to highlight the company's earnings per share. Indeed that figure and its rate of growth over time are the most widely used measures of a company's performance and, hence, the investment potential of its common stock. It is worth emphasizing, therefore, that generally accepted accounting principles permit companies some latitude in calculating net income and, hence, earnings per share. For example, the last-in–first-out (LIFO) and the first-in–first-out (FIFO) methods are acceptable methods of inventory valuation, but in periods of high inflation, LIFO accounting will produce significantly lower earnings than FIFO accounting. In addition, there are accounting methods followed by particular industries, such as the practice of recognizing allowance for funds used during construction in the utility industry, that can distort interindustry comparisons based solely on earnings per share. The reader should be warned, then, that the earnings per share figure, in spite of the significance some would attach to it, should not be relied upon exclusively to measure a company's performance or the attractiveness of its common stock for investment purposes.

Balance Sheet

The balance sheet reports the financial condition of a business entity at a particular point in time. It is a critical indicator of the fundamental credit strength of a company and, therefore, of the company's capability of financing itself. The balance sheet shows, on a historical cost basis, the *assets* of the enterprise, which are the productive resources utilized in its operations, and the *liabilities* and *stockholders' equity* of the enterprise, which are the total claims—divided between the claims of creditors and those of the owners—against those assets.

A typical balance sheet for a manufacturing company is shown in Table 2-2. Note that the basic balance sheet identity,

$$\text{Assets} = \text{liabilities} + \text{stockholders' equity} \tag{2-1}$$

is satisfied. Note also that assets and liabilities are each broken down into a current component that, in the case of assets, matures or is expected to be realized as cash within 1 year and, in the case of liabilities, comes due or is expected to be paid out in cash within 1 year, and a long-term component. The size of current assets in relation to current liabilities indicates the company's ability to meet its short-term obligations as they come due.

Statement of Changes in Financial Position

The purpose of the statement of changes in financial position is to indicate how the financial position of the company has changed during the period covered by the income statement. As such, it complements the income statement and the balance sheet. The financial position changes not only as a result of the net income generated from operations that is retained in the business but also because of additional borrowings or repayments of debt (both short-term and long-term), additional issues or retirements of capital stock (both common and preferred), additions to or disposals of fixed assets, and several other factors. The flows of funds between a business enterprise and investors, creditors, workers, customers, etc., serves as the fundamental starting point for the financial analysis of the firm.

A typical statement of changes in financial position is shown in Table 2-3. Such statements are typically prepared on either of two bases: a working capital basis, as illustrated by the table, or a cash basis. In either case, the basic overall structure is the same. The sources of funds (and the resource inflow associated with each) and the applications of funds (and the resource

Table 2-2
Balance Sheet

Lincoln Manufacturing Corporation and Consolidated
Subsidiaries at December 31, 1984 and 1983

(Millions of Dollars)

	1984	1983
Current Assets:		
Cash	$ 6.8	$ 9.9
Marketable securities	51.5	45.4
Accounts receivable	47.6	42.5
Inventories	150.6	122.1
Prepaid taxes and other expenses	11.3	8.6
Total current assets	267.8	228.5
Investments:		
Equity in assets of nonconsolidated subsidiaries	32.3	25.9
Other investments—at cost	43.1	49.4
Total investments	75.4	75.3
Plant, Property, and Equipment:		
At cost	769.0	688.5
Less accumulated depreciation and amortization	290.2	261.2
Net property, plant, and equipment	478.8	427.2
Other assets	5.8	5.7
Total assets	$827.8	$736.7
Current Liabilities:		
Notes and loans payable	$ 41.0	$ 32.1
Current portion of long-term debt	16.3	10.3
Accounts payable and accrued liabilities	115.2	94.2
Income taxes payable	38.6	31.0
Total current liabilities	211.1	167.6
Long-term debt (less current portion)	203.3	198.1
Capitalized lease obligations due after 1 year	35.8	34.5
Deferred credits	67.2	55.0
Total liabilities	517.4	455.2
Minority interest in subsidiaries	2.4	3.7
Preferred stock not subject to mandatory redemption		
(229,000 and 255,000 shares issued and outstanding)	22.9	25.5
Common Stockholders' Equity:		
Common stock (15,000,000 shares authorized;		
9,400,000 and 9,000,000 shares outstanding)	48.1	46.1
Capital surplus	76.1	68.2
Retained earnings	164.1	141.2
Less treasury stock—at cost (128,000 shares)	(3.2)	(3.2)
Total common stockholders' equity	285.1	252.3
Total liabilities and stockholders' equity	$827.8	$736.7

Table 2-3
Statement of Changes in Financial Position
Lincoln Manufacturing Corporation and Consolidated
Subsidiaries for the Years Ended December 31, 1984 and 1983

(Millions of Dollars)

	1984	1983
Net income before extraordinary items	$ 52.8	$ 38.9
Depreciation and amortization	39.0	35.4
Deferred income taxes	9.4	5.2
Minority interest in earnings of consolidated subsidiaries	0.3	0.4
Equity in undistributed earnings of nonconsolidated subsidiaries	(3.0)	(1.3)
Interest capitalized	(1.8)	(2.3)
Funds generated from operations	96.7	76.3
Proceeds from disposal of property	1.5	5.3
Proceeds from issuance of long-term debt	35.3	20.8
Proceeds from issuance of common stock	9.9	8.5
Other—net	0.5	3.2
Total funds generated	$147.8	$114.1
Dividends paid to stockholders: Preferred	$ 2.0	$ 2.4
Common	17.8	15.8
Additions to property, plant, and equipment	99.5	62.0
Reacquisition and retirement of preferred stock	2.6	—
Reduction of long-term debt	30.1	25.7
Total funds applied	152.0	105.9
Increase in working capital	$ (4.2)	$ 8.2
Cash	$ (3.1)	$ 10.1
Marketable securities	6.1	12.7
Accounts receivable	5.1	3.2
Inventories	28.5	8.1
Prepaid taxes and other expenses	2.7	(2.1)
Notes and loans payable	(8.9)	(10.1)
Current portion of long-term debt	(6.0)	3.2
Accounts payable and accrued liabilities	(21.0)	(10.5)
Income taxes payable	(7.6)	(6.4)
Increase (decrease) in working capital	$ (4.2)	$ 8.2

outflow associated with each) are itemized. Note that the basic accounting identity

$$\text{Resource inflows} - \text{resource outflows} = \text{change in resources} \qquad (2\text{-}2)$$

is satisfied, with *change in resources* being the net increase (decrease) in working capital or cash, depending on the basis on which the statement is prepared. A particularly important quantity in the statement of changes in financial position is *funds generated from operations* or, more simply, *cash flow*. Because noncash items can significantly affect reported earnings, cash flow has been given increased emphasis in recent years as a measure of a company's ability to meet its financial obligations and to fund its growth.

Notes to the Financial Statements

The notes to a firm's financial statements are an integral part of those statements. The notes reveal the significant accounting policies utilized in the preparation of the financial statements and provide additional detail concerning several of the items in the financial statements. This normally includes more detailed information concerning investments in nonconsolidated subsidiaries, schedules of long-term debt obligations, lease obligations, provision for income taxes, unfunded pension liabilities, commitments and contingent liabilities, quarterly operating results, financial results by business segment, and replacement cost information. In addition, companies engaged in oil and gas production are required to provide supplemental information concerning their hydrocarbon reserves, the cost of obtaining and developing those reserves, and an estimate of the present value of future net revenues to be derived therefrom. The notes section also normally includes a discussion by management of recent operating results and a 5- or 10-year summary of the company's operating performance. The notes to a firm's financial statements thus contain a wealth of information that is useful to the financial analyst.

RECASTING THE FIRM'S FINANCIAL STATEMENTS

The firm's financial statements contained in Tables 2-1 and 2-2 can be recast into a form that makes them more amenable to careful analysis. In particular, the components of the income statement and balance sheet can be supplemented with ratios that help to highlight changes over time in the financial performance and financial condition of the firm.

Income Statement

Table 2-4 contains the income statements for Lincoln Manufacturing Corporation for the years 1983 and 1984, which were provided in Table 2-1,

Table 2-4
Recast Income Statements
Lincoln Manufacturing Corporation and
Consolidated Subsidiaries, 1980–1984

(Millions of Dollars Except Per Share Amounts)

For the 12 Months Ended December 31

	1984		1983		1982		1981		1980		Four-Year Growth Rate, %
	Amount	%	Amount	%	Amount	%	Amount	%	Amount	%	
Net sales	$744.0	100.0	$662.3	100.0	$579.3	100.0	$509.3	100.0	$406.1	100.0	14.74
Cost of goods sold	532.0	71.5	484.8	73.2	414.2	71.5	371.8	73.0	294.8	72.6	14.46
Gross profit	212.0	28.5	177.5	26.8	165.1	28.5	137.5	27.0	111.3	27.4	15.44
Operating Expenses:											
S, G, & A	65.3	8.8	57.9	8.7	60.3	10.4	39.2	7.7	42.0	10.3	12.73
Depreciation and amortization	39.0	5.2	35.4	5.4	32.4	5.6	27.9	5.5	22.6	5.6	13.29
Total operating expenses	104.3	14.0	93.3	14.1	92.7	16.0	67.1	13.2	64.6	15.9	12.88
Operating income	107.7	14.5	84.2	12.7	72.4	12.5	70.4	13.8	46.7	11.5	18.50
Other income	7.0	0.9	6.6	1.0	10.9	1.9	6.7	1.3	3.4	0.8	
Interest expense—net	(23.9)	(3.2)	(22.2)	(3.4)	(22.9)	(4.0)	(21.0)	(4.1)	(17.2)	(4.2)	
Minority interest	(0.3)	—	(0.4)	—	(0.4)	—	(0.5)	(0.1)	(0.5)	(0.1)	
Pretax income	90.5	12.2	68.2	10.3	60.0	10.4	55.6	10.9	32.4	8.0	22.59
Income taxes	37.7	5.1	29.3	4.4	25.4	4.4	23.3	4.6	8.3	2.1	32.56
Net income before extraordinary items	52.8	7.1	38.9	5.9	34.6	6.0	32.3	6.3	24.1	5.9	17.55

Preferred stock dividends	$ 2.0	0.3	$ 2.4	0.4	$ 2.9	0.5	$ 3.6	0.7	$ 3.7	0.9	
Earnings available for common stock before extraordinary items	50.8	6.8	36.5	5.5	31.7	5.5	28.7	5.6	20.4	5.0	20.65
Extraordinary gains (losses) net of taxes	(10.1)	(1.3)	—	—	—	—	3.5	0.7	—	—	
Earnings available for common stock	$ 40.7	5.5	$ 36.5	5.5	$ 31.7	5.5	$ 32.2	6.3	$ 20.4	5.0	15.07
Earnings per Common Share:											
Before extraordinary items	$5.46		$4.15		$3.92		$3.82		$2.79		14.26
Extraordinary items	1.08		—		—		0.46		—		
Net	$4.38		$4.15		$3.92		$4.28		$2.79		8.71
Dividends per common share	$1.92		$1.80		$1.56		$1.52		$1.32		9.18

and, in addition, income statements for the years 1980 to 1982. Note that operating revenue (net sales) and operating income have been distinguished from nonoperating income (other income), which includes such items as equity in the earnings of nonconsolidated affiliates, interest, and dividends earned on the company's portfolio of marketable securities and income from other sources that are incidental to Lincoln's principal (manufacturing) lines of business. Each of the major-line items is then expressed as a percentage of yearly sales, which produces certain measures of profitability that are discussed below. Also, growth rates for certain variables of interest have been calculated. By comparing the ratios from one year to the next and by comparing the growth rates, the financial analyst can obtain a clearer picture of how the performance of Lincoln has changed over the past 5 years than could be provided by an examination of the absolute quanitities alone. For example, between 1980 and 1984, operating income, net income before extraordinary items, and earnings available for common stock before extraordinary items increased significantly in absolute amount and, more importantly, increased significantly as a percentage of net sales.

The calculation of the growth rates in Table 2-4 deserves comment. Two methods are widely used, the *simple compound growth method* and the *log-linear least-squares method.* Both are discussed at the end of the chapter. It is sufficient to note here that the log-linear least-squares method is generally preferred because it takes all the observations, and not just those at the beginning and the end of the period, into account.

Balance Sheet

Table 2-5 contains the recast balance sheets for Lincoln Manufacturing Corporation for the years 1983 and 1984. Many summary formats are possible, and Table 2-5 provides one that many analysts have found convenient. The components of assets and liabilities are presented in summary form, and each is expressed as a percentage of net assets (or equivalently, total capitalization). In Table 2-5, cash and cash equivalents on the one hand and inventories on the other are distinguished from other current assets while short-term debt is distinguished from other current liabilities. Under certain circumstances, it would also be appropriate to show some of the other components of current assets and current liabilities separately, as for example, if receivables had increased dramatically. The difference between current assets and current liabilities represents *net working capital*:

$$\text{Net working capital} = \text{current assets} - \text{current liabilities} \qquad (2\text{-}3)$$

which provides a measure of the business's liquidity, or its ability to meet its short-term obligations as they come due. Next shown are the business's noncurrent assets and noncapitalized long-term liabilities. Adding plant, property,

Table 2-5
Recast Balance Sheets
Lincoln Manufacturing Corporation and Consolidated
Subsidiaries at December 31, 1983 and 1984
(Millions of Dollars Except Per Share Amounts)

	At 12/31/84		At 12/31/83	
	Amount	%	Amount	%
Cash and marketable securities	$ 58.3	10.6	$ 55.3	10.8
Inventories	150.6	27.4	122.1	23.7
Other current assets	58.9	10.7	51.1	9.9
Total current assets	267.8	48.7	228.5	44.4
Short-term debt	57.3	10.4	42.4	8.2
Other current liabilities	153.8	28.0	125.2	24.4
Total current liabilities	211.1	38.4	167.6	32.6
Net working capital	56.7	10.3	60.9	11.8
Plant, property, and equipment—net	478.8	87.1	427.2	83.1
Investments	75.4	13.7	75.3	14.7
Other	5.8	1.1	5.7	1.1
Total other assets	81.2	14.8	81.0	15.8
Deferred credits	67.2	12.2	55.0	10.7
Net assets*	$549.5	100.0%	$514.1	100.0%
Long-term debt	$203.3	37.0%	$198.1	38.6%
Capitalized lease obligations	35.8	6.5	34.5	6.7
Minority interest	2.4	0.4	3.7	0.7
Preferred stock (involuntary liquidation value of $105 per share)	24.0	4.4	26.8	5.2
Common stockholders' equity	284.0	51.7	251.0	48.8
Total capitalization	$549.5	100.0%	$514.1	100.0%
Book value per common share	$30.21		$27.89	

*Calculated from Formula 2-4.

19

and equipment and other assets to working capital and subtracting the noncapitalized long-term liabilities gives *net assets*, which also equals the sum of the amounts of long-term financing by which the business has been capitalized.

$$
\text{Net assets} = \begin{matrix} \text{net} \\ \text{working} \\ \text{capital} \end{matrix} + \begin{matrix} \text{plant,} \\ \text{property,} \\ \text{and equipment} \end{matrix} + \begin{matrix} \text{other} \\ \text{assets} \end{matrix} - \begin{matrix} \text{noncapitalized} \\ \text{long-term} \\ \text{liabilities} \end{matrix}
$$

$$
= \begin{matrix} \text{total} \\ \text{assets} \end{matrix} - \begin{matrix} \text{current} \\ \text{liabilities} \end{matrix} - \begin{matrix} \text{noncapitalized} \\ \text{long-term} \\ \text{liabilities} \end{matrix}
$$

$$
= \text{total capitalization} \tag{2-4}
$$

Some analysts prefer to think of deferred income taxes and other deferred credits as "cost-free capital" and to define net assets more simply as the difference between total assets and current liabilities. Because these deferred credits do not represent financing in any conventional sense, but rather result from tax timing differences, Formula 2-4 seems more appropriate.

The total capitalization of the business summarizes the distribution of the claims on its net assets among its long-term creditors (including lessors), the holders of minority interests in its consolidated subsidiaries, its preferred stockholders, and its common stockholders. In some cases, a company's charter specifies that upon liquidation of the business, the preferred shareholders must be paid a premium before any liquidation proceeds can be paid to common stockholders. In that case, it is more appropriate to list the preferred stock at its liquidation value and to adjust common stockholders' equity accordingly (as has been done in Table 2-5). Lincoln Manufacturing Corporation's preferred stock has an involuntary liquidation preference of $105 per share, which represents a 5% premium over its $100 par value. Therefore, $5 × 229,000 = $1.1 million has had to be added to the book value of the preferred stock in 1984 and subtracted from the book value of common stockholders' equity in 1984 to reflect this liquidation preference.

The adjusted value of common stockholders' equity is divided by the number of common shares outstanding on the balance sheet date to obtain the book value per common share:

$$
\begin{matrix} \text{Book value} \\ \text{per} \\ \text{common share} \end{matrix} = \begin{matrix} \text{common} \\ \text{stockholders'} \\ \text{equity} \end{matrix} \div \begin{matrix} \text{common} \\ \text{shares} \\ \text{outstanding} \end{matrix} \tag{2-5}
$$

This calculation for Lincoln for 1984 is performed in the following manner:

$$
\begin{matrix} \text{Book value} \\ \text{per} \\ \text{common share} \end{matrix} = \frac{284.0}{9.4} = \underline{\underline{\$30.21}}
$$

The book value per common share represents the residual value per share if the corporation is liquidated, i.e., its assets are sold for the amounts shown on the balance sheet, its debt is repaid at its principal amount (as shown on the balance sheet), its capitalized lease obligations and minority interest are paid their respective book amounts, and preferred stock is redeemed at its involuntary liquidation value.

RATIO ANALYSIS

Financial analysts find it helpful to calculate *financial ratios* when interpreting a firm's financial statements. The number of financial ratios that might be calculated is virtually limitless, but there are certain basic ratios that are frequently used. These fall into four classes: *liquidity ratios, profitability ratios, leverage ratios,* and *common stock ratios.* The calculation and interpretation of ratios belonging to the first three classes are discussed below. Those belonging to the fourth class are discussed in Chapters 13 and 19.

LIQUIDITY RATIOS

Liquidity ratios are designed to measure the firm's ability to meet its financial obligations on time. Such measures are of three basic types: measures of overall liquidity, turnover ratios, and coverage ratios.

Measures of Overall Liquidity

The most widely used measure of overall liquidity is the *current ratio*, which is computed as follows:

$$\text{Current ratio} \;=\; \text{current assets} \div \text{current liabilities} \qquad (2\text{-}6)$$

The current ratio measures the number of times that the firm's current assets cover its current liabilities. The higher the current ratio, the greater the firm's ability to meet its short-term obligations as they come due. A rough rule of thumb holds that a 2:1 current ratio is an appropriate target for most firms.

Current assets include inventories, which are normally more difficult than marketable securities and receivables to turn into cash on short notice in order to pay off current liabilities. Thus, analysts often exclude inventories from the numerator in Formula 2-6 and calculate the *acid test ratio*:

$$\begin{array}{c}\text{Acid test}\\\text{ratio}\end{array} \;=\; \left(\begin{array}{c}\text{current}\\\text{assets}\end{array} - \text{inventories}\right) \div \begin{array}{c}\text{current}\\\text{liabilities}\end{array} \qquad (2\text{-}7)$$

Illustration of Current Ratio and Acid Test Ratio Calculations

Using the financial statements provided in Table 2-5, the current ratio and acid test ratio for 1984 for Lincoln Manufacturing Corporation are:

$$\text{Current ratio} = \frac{267.8}{211.1} = 1.27$$

$$\text{Acid test ratio} = \frac{267.8 - 150.6}{211.1} = 0.56$$

Turnover Ratios

Turnover ratios can be calculated to measure the degree of liquidity associated with specific current assets. The *receivable turnover ratio*, calculated as

$$\begin{matrix} \text{Receivable} \\ \text{turnover} \\ \text{ratio} \end{matrix} = \begin{matrix} \text{annual} \\ \text{credit} \\ \text{sales} \end{matrix} \div \begin{matrix} \text{average} \\ \text{accounts} \\ \text{receivable} \end{matrix} \qquad (2\text{-}8)$$

measures the number of times the average accounts receivable balance turns over during the year. Note that annual credit sales, which give rise to receivables, are used in the numerator. If a figure for annual credit sales is not available, the firm's net sales is used instead. The average accounts receivable is the average of the beginning-of-year and end-of-year amounts.

A measure of liquidity for inventories that is similar to Formula 2-8 is the *inventory turnover ratio*, which is calculated as follows:

$$\begin{matrix} \text{Inventory} \\ \text{turnover} \\ \text{ratio} \end{matrix} = \begin{matrix} \text{cost of} \\ \text{goods sold} \end{matrix} \div \begin{matrix} \text{average} \\ \text{inventory} \end{matrix} \qquad (2\text{-}9)$$

Net sales may also be used in the numerator of Formula 2-9, although that introduces the possibility that differences in how firms choose to mark up costs of goods sold, rather than inventory policy alone, would affect a comparison based on inventory turnover ratios.

Illustration of Turnover Ratio Calculations

The turnover ratios for Lincoln Manufacturing Corporation for 1984 are:

$$\text{Receivable turnover ratio} = \frac{744.0}{(47.6 + 42.5)/2} = 16.51$$

$$\text{Inventory turnover ratio} = \frac{532.0}{(150.6 + 122.1)/2} = 3.90$$

Note that because receivables turn over 16.51 times per year, the average collection period is $365/16.51 = 22$ days. Thus, Formula 2-8 can be converted easily into a measure of the average collection period. A more accurate picture of the firm's accounts receivable could be obtained by preparing an *aging schedule for accounts receivable*, which would show the amounts of receivables that have been outstanding for different periods, e.g., 0 to 15 days, 16 to 30 days, more than 30 days. An external analyst typically lacks such detailed information; so the rougher calculation embodied in Formula 2-8 must be used instead.

Coverage Ratios

Coverage ratios are designed to measure the firm's ability to cover its financing charges. The *interest coverage ratio* measures the number of times the income available to pay interest charges covers the firm's interest expense. It is calculated as

$$\begin{matrix} \text{Interest} \\ \text{coverage} \\ \text{ratio} \end{matrix} = \begin{matrix} \text{earnings before} \\ \text{interest and} \\ \text{income taxes} \end{matrix} \div \begin{matrix} \text{interest} \\ \text{expense} \end{matrix} \qquad (2\text{-}10)$$

Because lease payments contain an interest component, the Securities and Exchange Commission prefers the following modified calculation:

$$\begin{matrix} \text{Fixed charge} \\ \text{coverage ratio} \end{matrix} = \left(\text{EBIT} + \begin{matrix} \tfrac{1}{3} \text{ of} \\ \text{rentals} \end{matrix} \right) \div \left(\begin{matrix} \text{interest} \\ \text{expense} \end{matrix} + \begin{matrix} \tfrac{1}{3} \text{ of} \\ \text{rentals} \end{matrix} \right) \qquad (2\text{-}11)$$

where EBIT is *earnings before interest and income taxes. Interest expense* in Formulas 2-10 and 2-11 includes the amortization of debt discount or premium (if any) and the amortization of debt issuance expense. The $\frac{1}{3}$ *of rentals* in Formula 2-11 approximates the interest component of total rental expense. If the exact interest component is known, that figure should be used instead.[1] The numerators in Formulas 2-10 and 2-11 are pretax figures because interest is a tax-deductible expense.

Calculating the *interest coverage ratio* and *fixed charge coverage ratio* requires the calculation of EBIT. The SEC specifies the following formula:

EBIT = net income before (1) income taxes, (2) extraordinary items, (3) income (loss) from discontinued operations, and (4) minority interest
   + interest expense net of capitalized interest
   − equity in undistributed earnings of nonconsolidated subsidiaries

Capitalized interest is excluded from EBIT unless the company is a regulated utility company, which will recover capitalized interest through future customer charges.

Preferred dividends are also a financing charge. The associated coverage ratio is

$$\text{Preferred stock dividend coverage} = \left(\text{EBIT} + \frac{1}{3} \text{ of rentals}\right)$$

$$\div \left(\frac{\text{interest}}{\text{expense}} + \frac{1}{3} \text{ of rentals} + \frac{\text{preferred dividends}}{1 - \text{tax rate}}\right)$$

(2-12)

where *tax rate* is the company's average income tax rate. Formula 2-12 reflects the facts that interest expense must be met before preferred stock dividends can be paid and that preferred stock dividends are an after-tax expense.

The coverage calculations in Formulas 2-10 to 2-12 are based on pretax amounts. Alternatively, the calculations could be done on an after-tax basis. For example, charter tests for the issuance of additional preferred stock are often based on after-tax amounts.

Illustration of Coverage Ratio Calculations

Suppose the footnotes to Lincoln Manufacturing Corporation's financial statements for 1984 reveal annual rental expense of $4.2 million. Lincoln's EBIT would be calculated in the following manner:

$$\text{EBIT} = 90.5 + 0.3 + (25.7 - 1.8) - 3.0 = 111.7$$

since the statement of changes in financial position in Table 2-3 reveals equity in undistributed earnings of nonconsolidated subsidiaries amounting to $3.0 million. Lincoln's coverage figures would be calculated in the following manner:

$$\text{Interest coverage ratio} = \frac{111.7}{25.7} = 4.35\times$$

$$\text{Fixed charge coverage ratio} = \frac{111.7 + 4.2/3}{25.7 + 4.2/3} = 4.17\times$$

$$\text{Preferred stock dividend coverage} = (111.7 + 1.4)$$

$$\div \left[25.7 + 1.4 + \frac{2.0}{1 - (37.7/90.5)}\right] = 3.70\times$$

PROFITABILITY RATIOS

Profitability ratios serve as measures of the firm's financial performance. Performance can be measured in relation to either sales or investment or it can be measured on a per-share basis.

Profit Margins

Profit margins measure the firm's profitability in relation to sales. Three measures are commonly used.

The *gross profit margin* measures the firm's ability to control expenses. It is calculated as follows:

$$\begin{matrix} \text{Gross} \\ \text{profit} \\ \text{margin} \end{matrix} = \begin{matrix} \text{gross} \\ \text{profit} \end{matrix} \div \begin{matrix} \text{net} \\ \text{sales} \end{matrix}$$

$$= \left(\begin{matrix} \text{net} \\ \text{sales} \end{matrix} - \begin{matrix} \text{cost of} \\ \text{goods sold} \end{matrix} \right) \div \begin{matrix} \text{net} \\ \text{sales} \end{matrix} \qquad (2\text{-}13)$$

The *operating profit margin* measures the surplus that is available after meeting the firm's operating expenses in addition to the cost of goods sold:

$$\begin{matrix} \text{Operating} \\ \text{profit} \\ \text{margin} \end{matrix} = \begin{matrix} \text{operating} \\ \text{income} \end{matrix} \div \begin{matrix} \text{net} \\ \text{sales} \end{matrix}$$

$$= \left(\begin{matrix} \text{net} \\ \text{sales} \end{matrix} - \begin{matrix} \text{cost of} \\ \text{goods sold} \end{matrix} - \begin{matrix} \text{operating} \\ \text{expenses} \end{matrix} \right) \div \begin{matrix} \text{net} \\ \text{sales} \end{matrix} \qquad (2\text{-}14)$$

Finally, the *net profit margin* measures the surplus that is available to equity holders after all expenses, including interest and taxes, have been paid:

$$\begin{matrix} \text{Net} \\ \text{profit} \\ \text{margin} \end{matrix} = \begin{matrix} \text{net income} \\ \text{before} \\ \text{extraordinary items} \end{matrix} \div \begin{matrix} \text{net} \\ \text{sales} \end{matrix} \qquad (2\text{-}15)$$

Illustration of Profit Margin Calculations

Lincoln Manufacturing Corporation's profit margins for 1984 are calculated in the following manner:

$$\text{Gross profit margin} = \frac{212.0}{744.0} = 28.5\%$$

$$\text{Operating profit margin} = \frac{107.7}{744.0} = 14.5\%$$

$$\text{Net profit margin} = \frac{52.8}{744.0} = 7.1\%$$

all of which appear in the recast income statement in Table 2-4.

Rates of Return

The *rate of return* measures express profitability in relation to various measures of funds invested in the firm. As such, they measure the effectiveness with which the firm's assets are deployed. Three measures are commonly used.

The *return on assets* corresponds to the operating profit margin; by replacing net sales with average total tangible assets (total assets less intangibles, such as goodwill) and adding other income to the numerator:

$$\text{Return on assets} = \left(\text{operating income} + \text{other income}\right) \div \text{average total tangible assets} \qquad (2\text{-}16)$$

where *average total tangible assets* is calculated as the average of the beginning-of-year and end-of-year amounts. Return on assets is also often calculated on an after-tax and after-interest-expense basis by using net income in the numerator of Formula 2-16.

The *return on invested capital* measures the percentage return realized on the long-term funds invested in the business:

$$\text{Return on invested capital} = \left(\text{operating income} + \text{other income} - \text{income taxes}\right) \div \text{average net tangible assets} \qquad (2\text{-}17)$$

where

Net tangible assets = total assets − intangibles − current liabilities
= capitalization + deferred taxes
= long-term funds invested in the business

Return on invested capital is also often calculated on a pretax basis by not subtracting taxes in the numerator of Formula 2-17. However, by subtracting taxes, the firm's leverage (its chosen mix of debt and equity capital) is explicitly taken into account. Also, some analysts prefer to exclude deferred taxes from the denominator in Formula 2-17.

Finally, the *return on common equity* measures the percentage return to the firm's common stockholders:

$$\text{Return on common equity} = \text{earnings available for common stock before extraordinary items} \div \text{average common stockholders' equity} \qquad (2\text{-}18)$$

where *common stockholders' equity* includes common stock (at par value), capital surplus, and retained earnings.

Illustration of Rate of Return Calculations

Suppose Lincoln's 1984 annual report indicates that Lincoln had no intangible assets at year-end 1983 or year-end 1984. The 1984 rates of return for Lincoln are calculated as follows:

$$\text{Return on assets} = \frac{107.7 + 7.0}{(827.8 + 736.7)/2} = 14.7\%$$

$$\text{Return on invested capital} = \frac{107.7 + 7.0 - 37.7}{(616.7 + 569.1)/2} = 13.0\%$$

$$\text{Return on common equity} = \frac{50.8}{(284.0 + 251.0)/2} = 19.0\%$$

Per-Share Measures

The two most widely used per-share measures of profitability are *earnings per share*, which has historically enjoyed a high degree of prominence, and *cash flow per share*, which seems to be attracting increasing attention from professional managers and investors. As discussed further in Chapter 3, cash flow per share is, in some important respects, a more meaningful figure than earnings per share. To illustrate the difference between the two, Lincoln's earnings per share (before extraordinary items) for 1984 was

$$\text{Earnings per share} = \frac{50.8}{9.3} = \$5.46$$

while its cash flow per share was

$$\text{Cash flow per share} = \frac{96.7}{9.3} = \$10.40$$

the difference reflecting noncash expense items that decrease reported earnings per share but, by providing a tax shield, enhance cash flow per share.

LEVERAGE RATIOS

Leverage ratios indicate how the firm has financed itself. Leverage ratios are of two principal types: *capitalization ratios*, which measure each type of capital relative to the firm's total capitalization, and *debt ratios*, which relate long-term debt or total debt to certain balance sheet and flow of funds quantities.

Capitalization Ratios

The recast balance sheet in Table 2-5 contains, among other things, a *capitalization table*, which breaks down the total long-term capital invested in the firm (total capitalization) into its constituent parts. Some analysts would include deferred taxes among the sources of long-term funds and calculate the capitalization ratios accordingly. Also, long-term debt would be divided into senior debt and subordinated debt, and convertible debt would be shown separately if Lincoln had such classes of debt outstanding. Finally, Table 2-5 breaks down capitalization on a book-value basis. Alternatively, each component could be listed on the basis of its market value, which might provide a very different impression depending on the firm's share price and the level of interest rates.

Debt Ratios

Because interest is tax-deductible, the use of debt financing offers certain tax advantages to the firm and its shareholders. But because debt involves

and common stockholders will emphasize return on common equity (and the profitability ratios generally).

Discriminant Analysis

Among the many applications of financial ratio analysis, the detection of company operating and financial difficulties, the prediction of bond rating changes, and the evaluation of the likelihood of a borrower's defaulting seem to have attracted the greatest interest. All three problems have been approached using *discriminant analysis*, a statistical procedure that uses the values of certain selected financial ratios and, possibly, other variables to classify an observation into one of various groupings. The predicted classification is then compared with the actual classification. For example, a discriminant analysis of bonds rated either "A" or "BBB" by Standard & Poor's might reveal that a particular company whose bonds are currently rated "BBB" has financial characteristics more similar to those companies whose bonds are rated "A." This would suggest that the bonds are a candidate for upgrading to the higher "A" rating, which would make them more valuable to investors.

As a second example, one can use discriminant analysis to assess a firm's bankruptcy potential. Edward Altman's 1968 study of bankruptcy prediction is one of the classics in this area.[3] Altman collected data for the 1946–1965 time period from two populations of firms, one bankrupt and the other not. He selected a paired sample and estimated the following discriminant function for 1 year prior to bankruptcy:

$$Z = 0.012X_1 + 0.014X_2 + 0.033X_3 + 0.006X_4 + 0.999X_5 \qquad (2\text{-}24)$$

where X_1 = working capital/total assets
X_2 = retained earnings/total assets
X_3 = earnings before interest and taxes/total assets
X_4 = market value of equity/book value of total debt
X_5 = sales/total assets
Z = overall index (discriminant score for the observation)

Altman found that $Z = 2.675$ discriminated best between bankrupt and non-bankrupt firms (in the sense that it minimized the number of misclassifications) and that Formula 2-24 correctly predicted the bankruptcy of 94% of the firms that went bankrupt 1 year later and correctly predicted that 97% of those that did not fail within the next year would survive.

PRO FORMA FINANCIAL STATEMENTS

Prior to undertaking a major financial transaction, a company will want to consider the impact the proposed transaction would have on the company's reported financial results. A company can gauge the impact by preparing a *pro forma income statement* and a *pro forma balance sheet* (or, more simply, a *pro forma capitalization table*). Pro forma financial statements provide a very useful tool for financial planning. This section describes how to prepare a pro forma income statement and a pro forma balance sheet to isolate the financial impact of individual transactions. Part 8 describes how to prepare a full set of pro forma statements to reflect the combined future impact of the transaction and policies embodied in the company's strategic and operating plans.

Preparation of Pro Forma Financial Statements

Preparation of pro forma financial statements normally involves making the appropriate adjustments to the company's most recent balance sheet and its income statement for the most recently completed fiscal year (or latest 12 months). Also, in many cases, the same adjustments are applied to the company's projected year-end balance sheet and projected full-year income statement. Then the analyst can recalculate the financial ratios that are affected by the proposed transaction. By comparing the adjusted and unadjusted financial statements and by also comparing the financial ratios before and after the proposed transaction, the analyst will gain some indication of the transaction's financial impact.

Illustration of Preparation of Pro Forma
Financial Statements

Suppose that it is early in 1985 and that Lincoln Manufacturing Corporation is considering selling $50 million of either (1) long-term debt bearing a 12% coupon or (2) its common stock, which is currently selling for $25 per share.

Pro Forma Income Statement. Table 2-6 illustrates pro forma income statements for the proposed financing transactions. To simplify the calculations, the income statement is presented in summary form. For example, neither financing transaction will affect Lincoln's revenue. Consequently, it is not necessary to show net sales and other income separately.

Issuing debt would increase Lincoln's interest expense but would decrease income tax expense to the extent of the tax shields the interest expense produces. Borrowing would reduce coverages. The after-tax interest expense would also reduce earnings per common share. Issuing common stock would not alter coverages but would have a greater dilutive impact on earnings per common share than would issuing debt.

In Table 2-6, the proceeds of the securities issues do not produce any income. This would be the case, for example, if the cash were invested immediately in plant and equipment that would not begin generating revenue until after year-end. If instead, Lincoln invested some or all of the cash temporarily in interest-bearing securities, the income so realized would increase earnings before interest and taxes accordingly and would also increase income tax expense. Alternatively, if Lincoln used the proceeds from the securities issue to repay short-term debt, the reduction in interest expense on short-term debt

Table 2-6
Pro Forma Income Statement
Lincoln Manufacturing Corporation
and Consolidated Subsidiaries
(Millions of Dollars Except Per Share Amounts)

	Actual for the Year Ended 12/31/84	Pro Forma the Issuance of $50 million of 12% Bonds	Pro Forma the Issuance of 2,000,000 Common Shares at $25/Share
Revenue	$751.0	$751.0	$751.0
Operating costs and expenses	636.3	636.3	636.3
Earnings before interest and taxes	114.7	114.7	114.7
Interest expense—net	23.9	29.9	23.9
Minority interest	0.3	0.3	0.3
Income taxes*	37.7	34.7	37.7
Net income before extraordinary items	52.8	49.8	52.8
Preferred stock dividends	2.0	2.0	2.0
Earnings available for common before extraordinary items	50.8	47.8	50.8
Extraordinary gains (losses) net of taxes	(10.1)	(10.1)	(10.1)
Earnings available for common stock	$ 40.7	$ 37.7	$ 40.7
Earnings per common share before extraordinary items†	$ 5.46	$ 5.14	$ 4.50
Percent dilution	—	5.9	17.6
Interest coverage	4.35×	3.52×	4.35×
Fixed charge coverage‡	4.17	3.42	4.17

*Calculation assumes a marginal income tax rate (combined federal and state) of 50%.

†Based on 9,300,000 average shares outstanding during 1984.

‡Fixed charges include $1.4 million interest component of rental expense.

would be subtracted from net interest expense. In that case, if Lincoln issued long-term debt, the pro forma figure for net interest expense would reflect two adjustments: the increase in interest expense due to the issuance of long-term debt and the reduction in interest expense due to the repayment of short-term debt. If the interest cost of short-term debt exceeded the interest cost of long-term debt, pro forma coverages and earnings per common share would exceed the unadjusted amounts.

Pro Forma Balance Sheet. Table 2-7 illustrates the pro forma balance sheets for the two financing alternatives just considered using the balance sheet in Table 2-2 as the basis for these calculations. Note that net property, plant, and equipment increases by $50 million.

Issuing debt rather than common stock would increase Lincoln's debt ratios and would decrease the cash-flow-to-debt ratios. Issuing common stock would decrease book value per common share because Lincoln would have to sell the common stock below book value ($25.00 per share versus $30.21 per common share).

Which alternative Lincoln would prefer would depend on a variety of considerations in addition to the pro forma impact illustrated in Tables 2-6 and 2-7. Particularly important among these considerations would be Lincoln's desired capital structure, or mix of debt and equity. Part 3 deals with the factors that affect the capital structure decision.

Table 2-7
Pro Forma Balance Sheet
Lincoln Manufacturing Corporation
and Consolidated Subsidiaries
(Millions of Dollars Except Per Share Amounts)

	Actual at 12/31/84	Pro Forma the Issuance of $50 million of 12% Bonds	Pro Forma the Issuance of 2,000,000 Common Shares at $25/Share
Current assets	$267.8	$267.8	$267.8
Investments	75.4	75.4	75.4
Net property, plant, and equipment	478.8	528.8	528.8
Other assets	5.8	5.8	5.8
Total assets	$827.8	$877.8	$877.8
Short-term debt	$ 57.3	$ 57.3	$ 57.3
Other current liabilities	153.8	153.8	153.8
Total current liabilities	211.1	211.1	211.1
Long-term debt	203.3	253.3	203.3
Capitalized lease obligations	35.8	35.8	35.8
Deferred credits	67.2	67.2	67.2
Total liabilities	517.4	567.4	517.4
Minority interest	2.4	2.4	2.4
Preferred equity	22.9	22.9	22.9
Common equity	285.1	285.1	335.1
Total liabilities and stockholders' equity	$827.8	$877.8	$877.8
Book value per common share	$ 30.21	$ 30.21	$ 29.30
Long-term debt ratio	43.5%	48.2%	39.9%
Total debt to adjusted capitalization	48.8	52.7	45.1
Cash flow to long-term debt	40.4	33.4	40.4
Cash flow to total debt	32.6	27.0	32.6

METHODS FOR CALCULATING GROWTH RATES

There are two widely used methods for calculating growth rates: the *simple compound growth method* and the *log-linear least-squares method*.

Simple Compound Growth Rate

Suppose a quantity grows at a constant annual percentage rate. Let A_0 denote the initial amount and let g denote the constant annual percentage growth rate (expressed as a decimal). The quantity in question grows to $A_1 = A_0 \times (1 + g)$ after 1 year, to $A_2 = A_0 \times (1 + g)^2$ at the end of 2 years, and so on to

$$A_t = A_0 \times (1 + g)^t \qquad (2\text{-}25)$$

at the end of t years.

If A_0, A_t, and t are given, Formula 2-25 can be solved for g:

$$g = \left(\frac{A_t}{A_0}\right)^{1/t} - 1 \qquad (2\text{-}26)$$

The value of g so obtained is called the *simple compound growth rate*.

Illustration of Calculation of Simple Compound Growth Rate

A securities analyst would like to calculate the average annual growth rate of earnings per share between 1980 and 1984 for the Monroe Bottling Company. Monroe had earnings per share of $2.75, $2.48, $2.85, $3.15, and $3.55 in 1980, 1981, 1982, 1983, and 1984, respectively.

First note that the growth rate is a 4-year growth rate. Substituting $t = 4$, $A_0 = \$2.75$, and $A_4 = \$3.55$ into Formula 2-26 gives

$$g = \left(\frac{3.55}{2.75}\right)^{0.25} - 1 = 0.0659 \qquad \text{or } 6.59\% \text{ per annum}$$

Formula 2-26 ignores the intermediate values of A. When the observed values do not all lie along a smooth growth path (as in the preceding example, where earnings per share decreased significantly between 1980 and 1981), these intermediate values should not be ignored.

Log-Linear Least-Squares Growth Rate

The log-linear least-squares method uses all the observed values of the quantity of interest in calculating the average annual growth rate. Suppose that growth occurs continuously so that the quantity A_t satisfies the equation[4]

$$A_t = A_0 e^{gt} \qquad (2\text{-}27)$$

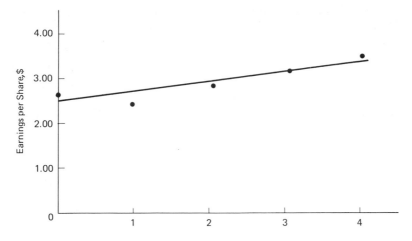

Figure 2-1. Trend in earnings per share.

where e is a number approximately equal to 2.71828. Taking the natural logarithm of the expression on each side of Formula 2-27 leads to the equivalent equation:

$$\ln A_t \;=\; \ln A_0 \,+\, \ln e^{gt} \;=\; \ln A_0 \,+\, gt \qquad\qquad (2\text{-}28)$$

But by defining the new variable $Y_t = \ln A_t$, Formula 2-28 can be rewritten as

$$Y_t \;=\; \ln A_0 \,+\, gt$$

which is called a *linear equation* because its graph is a straight line. Least-squares regression is a technique for estimating the constants in a linear equation, in this case $\ln A_0$ and g. The log-linear least-squares regression method can thus be used to estimate the growth rate g in Formula 2-27. The term *log-linear* describes the process of taking logarithms to convert the given Formula 2-27 into an equivalent linear form, Formula 2-28.

Illustration of Calculation of Log-Linear Least-Squares Growth Rate

Consider again the problem posed in the preceding example. Using a hand-held calculator gives

$$\ln A_0 \;=\; 0.9263 \qquad \text{and} \qquad g \;=\; 0.0750 \qquad \text{or } 7.50\% \text{ per annum}$$

Interpreting the Log-Linear Least-Squares Growth Rate. The earnings-per-share figures in this example are graphed in Figure 2-1. Since $A = \ln A_0$, it follows that

$$A_0 = e^{0.9263} = 2.5251$$

Substituting into Formula 2-27, the earnings-per-share growth path is

$$A_t = 2.5251e^{0.0750t} \tag{2-29}$$

which has also been graphed in Figure 2-1.

The log-linear least-squares growth rate measures the *trend* rate of growth; that is, the growth path described by Formula 2-29 is "fitted to" the observed values in such a way that it mirrors the actual growth in the quantity of interest. In the preceding example, the trend rate of growth of earnings per share is 7.50% per annum. Actual earnings-per-share growth may have been more or less than this amount (the actual observations do not lie on the growth path in Figure 2-1), but between 1980 and 1984 there was an "average" tendency for earnings per share to increase by 7.50% from one year to the next.

SUMMARY

The primary source of financial information is the firm's financial statements. These include, at a minimum, income statements, balance sheets, and statements of changes in financial position. The information contained in these statements is often supplemented by financial ratios, which bring out more clearly the changes over time in the firm's financial performance and financial condition.

Financial ratios are of four principal types: liquidity ratios, profitability ratios, leverage ratios, and common stock ratios. Several examples of ratios belonging to each of the first three classes were described and their calculation illustrated in this chapter. Financial ratio analysis can be applied to a wide range of financial problems. Various uses of financial ratio analysis are presented in later chapters.

The Business Enterprise from a Flow of Funds Standpoint

Chapter 3

A business enterprise purchases land and capital goods (or rents their services) and hires labor and uses these real resources to produce goods that it expects to be able to sell at a profit. One can view the operations of the business enterprise either in terms of the movements of the real resources into the firm and goods out of the firm or, equivalently, in terms of the offsetting flows of cash or credit, collectively called *funds*, to which the movements of resources and goods give rise. Financial analysts find it more meaningful to work with funds flows. They also find changes in the firm's funds position more meaningful in many applications than the firm's profit or loss. There are two reasons for this. First, there are noncash expenses, such as depreciation, which decrease reported net income but enhance the inflow of funds because of the tax shield effect. Second, there are many transactions that affect the financial position of the firm, such as sales of securities and purchases of assets, but have little or no immediate impact on the income statement. The analytical framework they use for this purpose is called *flow of funds analysis*.

NATURE OF FLOW OF FUNDS

If the firm operated strictly on a cash basis, paying for all its expenses in cash as they are incurred and being paid in cash upon delivery of goods, the flow of funds would correspond exactly to the flow of cash into and out of the firm. But the term *funds* has a wider meaning because not all resources are hired and not all goods are sold on the basis of cash transactions.

Flow of funds analysis distinguishes between *sources of funds* and *uses of funds*. Transactions such as the issuance of long-term securities, the sale of assets, and increases in accounts payable, which either *produce an inflow of cash* (the issuance of securities or the sale of assets) or *postpone or are made in lieu of an outflow of cash* (the increase in accounts payable since payment in cash will not be made until a later date), represent sources of funds. Transactions such as the payment of dividends, the purchase of assets, and increases in accounts receivable, which either *require an outflow of cash* (the payment of dividends or the purchase of assets) or *postpone or are received in lieu of an inflow of cash* (the increase in accounts receivable since payment in cash will not be received until a later date), represent uses of funds. By including an increase in the amount of cash the firm has on hand as a use of funds, a flow of funds model can be constructed in which

$$\text{Total sources of funds } = \text{ total uses of funds} \qquad (3\text{-}1)$$

holds as an identity. The next section develops a simple flow of funds model around this identity.

FLOW OF FUNDS MODEL

The flow of funds model is most easily described by means of an example. Consider the business of two flower vendors. The vendors purchase fresh flowers each morning from a wholesale supplier and sell them to passers-by from their location on the corner of Avenue of the Americas and Forty-sixth Street in New York City. All flowers not sold by the end of the day must be discarded. Initially at least, the vendors operate without a stand. In this simple business, the vendors require some cash with which to purchase the flowers each morning and then realize cash as flowers are sold.

All Transactions on Cash Basis

The flow of funds model is illustrated in Table 3-1. The vendors invest $100 to start the business, which is the business's initial cash balance. Each commitment of resources has associated with it a source of funds and a use of funds which, as illustrated in Table 3-1, can be recorded in double-entry-bookkeeping fashion. Early in the day the vendors purchase flowers for $87, which decreases the cash balance by that amount. During the day the vendors realize $131 from the sale of flowers, which increases the cash balance by that amount.

At the end of the day the vendors have a cash balance of $144 (= $100 − 87 + 131). Owners' equity is also $144, representing the sum of the initial investment ($100) and earnings of $44 (= revenue of $131 less expenses of $87), which are retained for use in the business. The flow of funds statement for the start-up of the business would indicate owners' investment as a source of funds providing $100 and an increase in cash balance (the business's working

Table 3-1
Flow of Funds Model: All Transactions on Cash Basis

Commitment of Resources	Sources of Funds		Uses of Funds	
	Source	Amount	Use	Amount
Owners invest $100 to start business	Owners' investment	$100	Increase in cash balance	$100
Purchase flowers	Decrease in cash balance	87	Operating expenses	87
Sale of flowers	Operating revenue	131	Increase in cash balance	131

Balance Sheet

	Start of Business	End of Day	Difference
Assets			
Cash	$100	$144	+$44
Liabilities and Owners' Equity			
Owners' equity	$100	$100	—
Retained earnings	—	44	+$44
Total	$100	$144	+$44

Income Statement

Revenue	$131
Expenses	87
Profit	$ 44

Flow of Funds

	To Start the Business	From Operations	Total
Sources of funds:			
Profit from operations	—	$44	$ 44
Owners' investment	$100	—	100
Total sources of funds	$100	$44	$144
Uses of funds:			
Increase in cash balance	$100	$44	$144

capital) as the use to which the $100 was put. For the first day, funds amounting to $144 were provided from two sources: earnings and owners' investment. The funds were used to increase the business's cash balance.

Two points should be noted. First, the impact of operations on the business's flow of funds is summarized as a single-line item. When revenues exceed expenses, a profit is realized, and the operations of the business represent a source of funds. When expenses exceed revenues, a loss is realized, and the operations of the business represent a use of funds (since cash is drained from the business). This must be true when a business is operated on a purely cash basis.

Second, total sources of funds must equal total uses of funds. The double-entry bookkeeping in Table 3-1 reveals why this must be so. Even as the flow of funds model becomes more complex, the basic identity (3-1) must continue to hold.

Noncash Transactions

When all transactions are on a cash basis, the flow of funds model simply reflects sources and uses of cash. There are, however, a variety of noncash transactions that can affect a business's flow of funds. The impact of two of these, accounts receivable and accounts payable, are illustrated in this section. The flow of funds statement and related statements are provided in Table 3-2.

The flower vendors invest an additional $35 and purchase flowers for $149. In addition, the vendors decide to broaden the business's product line by purchasing and offering flower pots for sale. The flower vendors have been able to work out an arrangement with the seller of the pots, which involves a $30 immediate cash payment and an understanding that another $30 will be repaid later (presumably after the flower pots have been sold). Because the flower pots can be held until they are sold, their purchase is recorded as an addition to inventory. As flower pots are sold, operating expense will be recorded as inventory is reduced.

During the second day, the flower vendors sell flowers worth $203, receiving $181 in cash and extending credit of $22 to a number of customers who promise to pay what they owe later in the week. As a result of the day's activities, the flower vendors realize a profit of $57 (= $181 + 22 + 13 − 149 − 10). Profit from operations, which includes profit realized on flowers sold on credit, provides $57 of funds. Note that the $22 in accounts receivable appears as a use of funds, in a sense offsetting $22 of the $57 realized from operations. The $22 in accounts receivable represents a use of funds inasmuch as it was received in lieu of cash. In the use of funds section of the flow of funds statement, the $30 in accounts payable represents a source of funds inasmuch as it permitted the vendors to receive $30 worth of flower pots without the expenditure of cash. The increases in both accounts receivable and accounts

Table 3-2
Flow of Funds Model: Some Transactions
on Noncash Basis

Commitment of Resources	Sources of Funds		Uses of Funds	
	Source	Amount	Use	Amount
Owners invest $35	Owners' investment	$ 35	Increase in cash balance	$ 35
Purchase flowers	Decrease in cash balance	149	Operating expenses	149
Purchase flower pots	Decrease in cash balance	30	Increase in inventory	60
	Increase in accounts payable	30		
Sales of flowers for cash	Operating revenue	181	Increase in cash balance	181
Sales of flowers on credit	Operating revenue	22	Increase in accounts receivable	22
Sales of flower pots	Decrease in inventory	10	Operating expense	10
	Operating revenue	13	Increase in cash balance	13

Balance Sheet

	Beginning of Day	End of Day	Difference
Assets			
Cash	$144	$194	+$ 50
Accounts receivable	—	22	+ 22
Inventory	—	50	+ 50
Total	$144	$266	+$122
Liabilities and Owners' Equity			
Accounts payable	—	$ 30	+$ 30
Owners' equity	$100	135	+ 35
Retained earnings	44	101	+ 57
Total	$144	$266	+$122

Income Statement

Revenue	$216
Expenses	159
Profit	$ 57

Flow of Funds

Sources of Funds:

Profit from operations	$ 57
Increase in accounts payable	30
Increase in owners' investment	35
Total sources of funds	$122

Uses of Funds:

Increase in accounts receivable	$ 22
Increase in inventories	50
Increase in cash balance	50
Total uses of funds	$122

payable are associated then with commitments of real resources; both affect the funds position of the business even though cash is not involved.

Long-Term Financing and Investment

On the third day, the owners, now flush from 2 days of successful operation, decide to order a flower stand. Lacking sufficient cash, the vendors borrow $300 from a friend (and issue a long-term note) to pay for the stand. During the day, they sell for $225 cash flowers that cost them $165 and for $13 cash flower pots that cost $10, which reduces their inventory accordingly. In addition to cash receipts from the day's sales, the vendors are repaid $11 of the $22 owed from the previous day's sales. The owners also decide to draw a salary of $40 (to go out to dinner to celebrate the success of the new venture), to set aside $20 with which to pay income taxes and to purchase for $50 an insurance policy (to insure against the destruction of the new stand), which is recorded under prepaid expenses. As an exercise, the reader should itemize the sources and uses of funds, as in Tables 3-1 and 3-2, and verify that the financial results of all these actions are as reported in Table 3-3. Note that the line items in the flow of funds statement can be traced directly to changes in balance sheet items between the beginning and the end of the day.

PRINCIPAL ELEMENTS OF FLOW OF FUNDS ANALYSIS

The preceding example illustrates certain principal elements that underlie all flow of funds analyses.

Summary of Sources and Uses of Funds

Looking at the flow of funds statements in Tables 3-1 to 3-3, one begins to see a pattern emerge. A *decrease in assets* (decreases in cash balances, accounts receivable, and inventories in Table 3-3) represents a *source of funds*, whereas an *increase in assets* (an increase in cash balances in Tables 3-1 and 3-2, increases in accounts receivable and inventories in Table 3-2, and an increase in prepaid expenses in Table 3-3) represents a *use of funds*. Correspondingly, an *increase in liabilities* (increase in accounts payable in Table 3-2 and increases in accrued taxes and long-term debt in Table 3-3) represents a *source of funds*, whereas a *decrease in liabilities* (e.g., if the vendors had paid a portion of the accounts payable) represents a *use of funds*. Finally, an *increase in equity* (owners' investment in Tables 3-1 and 3-2) represents a *source of funds*, whereas a *decrease in equity* (e.g., if the vendors had decreased their investment by $40 rather than by taking the sum out as salary) represents a *use of funds*.

Table 3-3
Flow of Funds Model: Long-Term
Financing and Investment

Balance Sheet

	Beginning of Day	End of Day	Difference
Assets			
Cash	$194	$188	−$ 6
Accounts receivable	22	11	− 11
Inventory	50	40	− 10
Prepaid expenses	—	50	+ 50
Current assets	266	289	+ 23
Fixed assets	—	300	+ 300
Total	$266	$589	+$323
Liabilities and Owners' Equity			
Accounts payable	$ 30	$ 30	—
Accrued taxes	—	20	+$ 20
Current liabilities	30	50	+ 20
Long-term debt	—	300	+ 300
Owners' equity	135	135	—
Retained earnings	101	104	+ 3
Total	$266	$589	+$323

Flow of Funds

Sources of Funds:

Profit from operations	$ 3
Decrease in cash balance	6
Decrease in accounts receivable	11
Decrease in inventories	10
Increase in accrued taxes	20
Increase in long-term debt	300
Total sources of funds	$350

Uses of Funds:

Increase in prepaid expenses	$ 50
Increase in fixed assets	300
Total uses of funds	$350

Income Statement

Revenue	$238
Expenses	215
Pretax income	23
Taxes	20
Profit	$ 3

Table 3-4
Sources and Uses of Funds
in the Flow of Funds Model

Sources of Funds		Uses of Funds
Profit from operations, as		Loss from operations, as
adjusted for nonfund items*		adjusted for nonfund items*
Continuing operations		Continuing operations
Discontinued operations		Discontinued operations
Extraordinary gains†		Extraordinary charges†
Decrease in assets		Increase in assets
Increase in liabilities		Decrease in liabilities
Increase in equity		Decrease in equity
Total sources of funds	≡	Total uses of funds

*As adjusted to offset the impact of items included in the calculation of
net income that did not provide funds or require the use of funds.
†As adjusted for nonfund items.

Table 3-4 summarizes the principal sources and uses of funds. The reader
should verify that the flow of funds statements in Tables 3-1 to 3-3 are consistent
with Table 3-4. The reader should also note the important connection between
the flow of funds statement in Table 3-4 and the firm's income statement and
balance sheet. First, the profit (or loss) from operations (before adjustments)
comes directly from the firm's income statement. Second, each change in a
balance sheet item corresponds to a particular source or use of funds.

Adjustments to Profit from Operations
for Nonfund Items

The calculation of (reported) profit from operations typically includes certain
noncash expenses, such as depreciation, amortization, and depletion. It is
therefore necessary to adjust reported net income so as to reexpress it in terms
of the funds generated from the firm's operations. The principal adjustments
are summarized below.

> Profit from operations (before extraordinary items)
> + depreciation, depletion, and amortization
> + deferred income taxes
> + accruals for other noncurrent liabilities
> + minority interests in earnings of consolidated subsidiaries
> − gain (loss) on disposal of property
> − equity in undistributed earnings of nonconsolidated
>   subsidiaries and affiliates
> − capitalized interest
> _____
> funds generated from operations   (3-2)

Funds generated from operations is generally broken down into *funds generated from continuing operations* and *funds generated from discontinued operations*. The above format can be used in both calculations.

The four additions in Formula 3-2 are explained as follows. Depreciation, depletion, and amortization; deferred income taxes and accruals for other noncurrent liabilities are noncash expenses, so they must be added back to profit from operations. Such accruals include additions to bank loan loss reserves, allocations to loss reserves for disposal of facilities, provision for noncurrent employee benefits, etc. Similarly, minority interests in the earnings of consolidated subsidiaries is a noncash item, which is subtracted out when net income is calculated; it should thus be added back. Some analysts prefer, however, to add back only that portion of minority interests not paid out as dividends, arguing that only that portion is available for use by the parent corporation.

The three subtractions in Formula 3-2 are explained as follows. When gain or loss on the disposal of property is included in the calculation of net income, the effect of this should be reversed (unless the company is normally in the business of buying and selling property) because, strictly speaking, such funds are not generated by the company's *operations*. Similarly, equity in the undistributed earnings of nonconsolidated subsidiaries and affiliates, which is included in the net income calculation, should be netted out; only the dividends actually received from such subsidiaries and affiliates are included. Finally, capitalized interest is excluded from net income under Statement of Financial Accounting Standards No. 34. Because this cash expense must be met currently, the amount of interest that has been capitalized is subtracted out in Formula 3-2.

The resulting figure, *funds generated from operations*, or *cash flow*, represents a measure of the ability of the firm's operations to generate funds to meet securities redemption requirements, pay dividends, and provide for the firm's working capital and capital investment requirements.

Free Cash Flow

Cash flow, as conventionally defined, is calculated net of interest expense but before dividend payments and expenditures for increases in working capital; property, plant, and equipment; and other investments required to support the firm's existing operations and to provide for normal growth. In certain applications, a measure of cash flow is required that (1) recognizes that a portion of the funds generated by a healthy and growing business will have to be set aside for investment purposes and will not be available for dividend payments and (2) distinguishes the financing policy of the firm from its investment policy. The firm's free cash flow is calculated for this purpose.

Free cash flow is defined in the following manner:

Funds generated from operations (cash flow)
+ interest expense (after-tax)
_____
operating cash flow
− required net investment (disinvestment) in working capital
− investment in property, plant, and equipment
− other investment expenditures
_____
free cash flow   (3-3)

A company's operating cash flow represents the funds generated by the company's operations that are available to fund the firm's capital investment program and to make payments (interest, dividends, and principal repayments) to the providers of capital. Free cash flow is that portion that remains after the company has funded its capital expenditure program. Free cash flow thus separates the firm's investment policy, which together with operating cash flow determines the amount of funds left over to make payments to the firm's securities holders, from its financing policy, which determines how this sum will be apportioned among the providers of debt and equity.

To highlight the residual cash flow available to common stockholders, many analysts calculate

Free cash flow
− interest expense (after-tax)
− preferred stock dividends
− debt and preferred stock repayments
_____
discretionary cash flow   (3-4)

Discretionary cash flow is most useful in setting corporate dividend policy, as discussed in Chapter 13.

The interest payments added to funds generated from operations in Formula 3-3 are the after-tax amount. Because the tax savings resulting from the interest deduction are netted out, the value of free cash flow will not vary with the firm's debt-equity ratio. Free cash flow, as defined by Formula 3-3, is used in the analysis of capital investment projects in Part 2 and in the discussion of corporate financial planning and strategy in Part 8.

The *required* net investment in working capital in Formula 3-3 requires some explanation. As sales expand, a company will have to make additional investments in inventories and receivables to support the higher level of sales. *Required net investment (disinvestment) in working capital* is calculated in the following manner:

$$
\begin{array}{l}
\text{Increase (decrease) in current inventories and receivables} \\
\text{— excess investment (deficiency in investment) in inventories} \\
\text{\quad and receivables} \\
\underline{\text{— increase (decrease) in non-interest-bearing current liabilities}} \\
\text{required net investment (disinvestment) in working capital}
\end{array} \qquad (3\text{-}5)
$$

At times, a company may find itself in an excess or shortage position with respect to its inventories or receivables. Because excess current assets do not contribute to future cash flow, increases in such excess amounts should not be included in the firm's investment in working capital. Measuring the excess amount can be difficult, however. As illustrated in the example below, a rough estimate of the excess amount can be obtained by assuming that the ratio of the quantity in question to sales should be equal to the average value for the industry. Similarly, shortfalls will have to be made up and so should be subtracted when calculating free cash flow.

The net investment in working capital is calculated in Formula 3-3, and in Formula 3-5 net of the increase or decrease in non-interest-bearing current liabilities. Any increase in payables, for example, reduces the cash required to finance the increase in inventories and receivables. Note, however, that because a company typically enjoys some degree of flexibility in substituting long-term debt for short-term debt and, vice versa, any change in short-term debt (including the current portion of long-term debt) is best viewed as an aspect of the firm's financing policy, rather than its investment policy, and so is not subtracted in Formulas 3-3 and 3-5.

Illustration of Calculation of Free Cash Flow and Discretionary Cash Flow

Madison Steel Corporation, a manufacturer of steel wire and related products, reported funds generated from operations for 1984 amounting to $169 million. Analysis of Madison's financial statements for 1983 and 1984 reveals the following information (dollar amounts in millions):

Year	Sales	Working Capital	Inventories	Short-Term Debt
1984	$936	$135	$119	$ 45
1983	873	121	99	41

(Continued on next page)

Expended for property, plant, and equipment in 1984	$110
Other investments (purchase of steel wire distributor accounted for as a pooling of interests)	55
Interest expense in 1984 (pretax)	30
Dividends declared on preferred stock in 1984	8
1984 tax rate	50%

Madison's public disclosures indicate that sales were below expectations. A comparison of similar steel companies reveals that the average ratio of sales to inventory is 9×. Based on this average, the 1983 inventory level should have been approximately $873/9 = 97$, and the 1984 inventory level should have been approximately $936/9 = 104$. Thus, the excess investment in inventory is $(119 - 99) - (104 - 99) = 15$. Similar comparisons suggest that the other components of current assets do not appear to be in excess or shortage positions (but if any had been, adjustments similar to the inventory adjustment would have been made).

Calculating operating cash flow and then applying Formulas 3-3 and 3-4 gives:

$$\text{Operating cash flow} = \$169 + (0.5 \times 30) = \$184 \text{ million}$$

$$\text{Free cash flow} = \$184 - (14 + 20 - 15 - 4) - 110 - 55 = \$4 \text{ million}$$

$$\text{Discretionary cash flow} = \$4 - (0.5 \times 30) - 8 = -\$19 \text{ million}$$

The concept of free cash flow proves to be very important in a wide range of problems in later chapters and, in particular, in the analysis of capital investment projects and in the analysis of corporate acquisitions.

PRESENTATION OF FLOW OF FUNDS ANALYSIS

As the reader will recall from Chapter 2, publicly traded firms report, as a fundamental part of their financial statements, a statement of changes in financial position. This statement is the form in which a business enterprise provides a flow of funds analysis to investors. An example of a statement of changes in financial position was provided in Table 2-3.

The statement of changes in financial position in Table 2-3 presents the flow of funds analysis on a working capital basis:

$$\begin{array}{l} \text{Sources of funds} \\ \underline{- \text{ uses of funds}} \\ \text{net change in working capital} \end{array}$$

Alternatively, companies are permitted to present the statement of changes in financial position on a cash basis:

Sources of funds
— uses of funds

net change in cash and marketable securities

Most companies prefer to use the cash-basis format.

The flow of funds statement involves a reworking of the components of Table 3-4. As previously noted, in an overall sense total sources of funds must be equal to total uses of funds. It is more meaningful, however, to focus specifically on how either the cash position or the working capital position of the business enterprise has been affected by its operating, financing, investment, and dividend decisions. The statement of changes in financial position is constructed in such a way that changes in the items other than current assets and current liabilities (which determine working capital), in the case of Table 2-3, or changes in the items other than cash and cash equivalents, in the case of the alternative method of presentation, are netted out to provide the desired net change. The two approaches are very similar, and a flow of funds statement presented on a cash basis could easily be transformed into one on a working capital basis and vice versa.

SUMMARY

One can view the operations of the business enterprise either in terms of the movements of real resources into the firm and goods out of the firm or, equivalently, in terms of the offsetting flows of cash or credit to which the movements of resources and goods give rise. A means of portraying these movements of real resources and goods in terms of flows of funds was described and illustrated in this chapter.

The concept of funds has a wider meaning than cash because not all transactions are carried out on a cash basis. Transactions that either produce an inflow of cash or postpone an outflow of cash represent sources of funds. Transactions that either require an outflow of cash or postpone an inflow of cash represent uses of funds. Decreases in assets and increases in liabilities or equity represent sources of funds, and increases in assets and decreases in liabilities or equity represent uses of funds. By definition, the total sources of funds must equal the total uses of funds.

The statement of changes in financial position is the framework within which publicly held companies present a flow of funds analysis to investors. These statements are generally constructed on either a cash basis or a working capital basis. In both cases, the starting point is funds generated from operations, or cash flow, which is obtained by adjusting net income (before extraordinary items) for cost items that do not require the use of funds and revenue or income items that do not generate funds. Cash flow is a quantity that has taken on increasing significance as a measure of the firm's financial performance.

Discounted Cash Flow Analysis

Chapter 4

When a business enterprise invests in a piece of equipment or purchases a security, an asset is purchased that is expected to yield a stream of future returns. In order to be able to evaluate the relative attractiveness of alternative investment opportunities, the financial manager needs a means of collapsing the stream of values to a single number. But because the promise of a dollar to be received a year from now is not equivalent in value to a dollar received today, the elements of each stream of future returns cannot simply be added. Each payment must be weighted according to when it will be received; only then will the sums be comparable. *Discounted cash flow analysis* provides the framework for accomplishing this.

TIME VALUE OF MONEY, COMPOUND AMOUNT, AND PRESENT VALUE

The promise of $1.00 to be received 1 year from today is not equivalent in value to the receipt of that $1.00 today. A dollar received today can be invested. If it is deposited into a savings account earning 6% interest, it will grow to $1.06 (ignoring compounding for the moment) 1 year from today. Similarly, if $0.94 is deposited into the same account, it will grow to $1.00. The promise of a dollar to be received 1 year from today is equivalent in value to $0.94 received today when the interest rate is 6%. This illustrates what is called the *time value of money*. The value of money to be received or to be disbursed is directly related to the *timing* of its receipt or disbursement.

Compound Amount

In the foregoing example, $1.00 deposited today grew to $1.06 after 1 year. Interest is generally *compounded*, that is, interest left in an account itself earns interest the following period. Thus, if the $1.06 was left in the account and the interest rate did not change, the $1.06 would grow to $1.12 two years from today. This simple example can be generalized.

If $1 is deposited today at *interest rate* × 100%, it will grow to 1 + interest rate after 1 year, to 1 + interest rate + interest rate (1 + interest rate) = (1 + interest rate)^2 after 2 years, (1 + interest rate)^3 after 3 years, and so on. The amount in the account will grow to

$$\text{Compound amount} = (1 + \text{interest rate})^N \tag{4-1}$$

after N years. *Compound amount* represents the amount in the account when $1 is deposited and left for N years to earn interest at interest rate × 100%. Note that interest rates are normally expressed in percent per annum but are expressed in decimal form when used in calculations. For example, an interest rate of 6% would be expressed in decimal form as interest rate = 0.06 when used in Formula 4-1 and in the other formulas presented in this chapter.

Note that Formula 4-1 is also valid if interest rate and N are expressed in terms of some other unit of time. For example, suppose that $1 is deposited into an account that earns interest that is paid quarterly at the rate of 1.5% per quarter. The amount in the account will grow to

$$\text{Compound amount} = (1.015)^6 = \$1.09344 \cong \$1.09$$

after six quarters, or 1 $\frac{1}{2}$ years. As long as interest rate and N are expressed in terms of the *same unit of time*, Formula 4-1 can be used whether interest is paid yearly, quarterly, monthly, or at some other frequency interval. The analyst can consult a standard compound amount table or use a hand-held calculator to perform the calculation once interest rate and N have been specified properly.

Even when interest is compounded more frequently than once per year, the interest rate is customarily expressed as a *nominal interest rate per annum* and the length of time is expressed as a fraction or multiple of a year. In that case, interest rate and N must be reexpressed so as to conform to the frequency of compounding in Formula 4-1. Suppose that interest is paid at the nominal rate of 6% per annum compounded quarterly. Interest is thus paid with frequency = 4 times per year. The interest rate per quarter is interest rate ÷ frequency = 0.06/4 = 0.015, or 1.5% per quarter. Suppose that the $1 is left to accumulate interest for a period of 1 $\frac{1}{2}$ years. The money is thus left for a total of N × frequency = 1.5 × 4 = 6 periods. The compound amount of $1 deposited for 1 $\frac{1}{2}$ years into an account earning interest at the rate of 6% per annum compounded quarterly is, once again, $1.09.

When interest rate is expressed as a nominal annual interest rate and N is expressed as a fraction or multiple of a year, Formula 4-1 becomes

$$\text{Compound amount} = [1 + (\text{interest rate} \div \text{frequency})]^{N \times \text{freq}} \qquad (4\text{-}2)$$

where *frequency*(freq) denotes the number of interest periods per year. In Formula 4-2, interest rate must be divided by frequency and N must be multiplied by frequency so that they conform to the frequency with which interest is compounded.

Formulas 4-1 and 4-2 can be used to find the compound amount of any initial sum.

Illustration of Compound Amount Calculation:
Constant Interest Rate

An individual invests $5000 in a money market fund that pays interest at the rate of 12% per annum compounded monthly. How much is the individual's investment worth after 18 months?

Because interest is compounded monthly, the interest rate must be expressed as a monthly rate and N must be measured in months. The compound amount of each dollar is

$$\text{Compound amount} = \left(1 + \frac{0.12}{12}\right)^{18} = \$1.19612$$

after 18 months. The investment is therefore worth

$$\text{Compound amount} = \$5000 \times 1.19612 = \$5980.60 \quad 5980.24?$$

after 18 months.

The compound amount of any initial sum invested for N years is

$$\underset{\text{amount}}{\text{Compound}} = \underset{\text{sum}}{\text{inital}} \times [1 + (\text{interest rate} \div \text{frequency})]^{N \times \text{freq}} \qquad (4\text{-}3)$$

when (1) interest is paid at the nominal rate of *interest rate* × 100% per annum at the end of each period and (2) there are frequency interest periods per year.

Formulas 4-1 to 4-3 require that interest be paid at the *same* rate (interest rate or interest rate ÷ frequency as appropriate) per period at the *end* of *each* of the $N \times$ frequency periods. If the interest rate varies, the formulas must be modified. We illustrate the modification of Formula 4-1 for arbitrary initial sum; Formulas 4-2 and 4-3 are adjusted in a similar manner. If interest is paid at the rate *interest rate*(1) × 100% the first period, interest rate(2) × 100% the second period, interest rate(3) × 100% the third period, and so on, the amount *initial sum* compounded over N periods is

$$\text{Compound amount} = \text{inital sum} \times [1 + \text{interest rate}(1)]$$
$$\times [1 + \text{interest rate}(2)]$$
$$\times [1 + \text{interest rate}(3)]$$
$$\times \cdots \times [1 + \text{interest rate}(N)] \qquad (4\text{-}4)$$

where the dots denote the intermediate terms.

Illustration of Compound Amount Calculation: Changing Interest Rate

If the money market fund in the preceding example pays interest at the rates of 10, 8, 9, 13, and 14% over a 5-month period, the $5000 investment will be worth

$$\text{Compound amount} = \$5000 \times \left(1 + \frac{0.10}{12}\right) \times \left(1 + \frac{0.08}{12}\right)$$
$$\times \left(1 + \frac{0.09}{12}\right) \times \left(1 + \frac{0.13}{12}\right) \times \left(1 + \frac{0.14}{12}\right)$$
$$= \$5229.04$$

after 5 months.

Present Value

A dollar deposited into an account that earns interest at the rate of 6% per annum compounded quarterly will increase in amount to

$$\text{Compound amount} = \left(1 + \frac{0.06}{4}\right)^{N \times \text{freq}} = (1.015)^{N \times \text{freq}}$$

after N × frequency quarters. Correspondingly, the amount that would have to be deposited into that account to have (the compound amount) $1.00 in the account after N × frequency quarters is $1/(1.015)^{N \times \text{freq}}$ because then, by Formula 4-3 with initial sum = $1/(1.015)^{N \times \text{freq}}$,

$$\text{Compound amount} = \left[1 \div (1.015)^{N \times \text{freq}}\right] \times (1.015)^{N \times \text{freq}} = \$1.00$$

The amount $1/(1.015)^{N \times \text{freq}}$ is called the *present value* of the $1.00 to be received N × frequency quarters hence.

As the foregoing example suggests, Formula 4-3 can be rearranged to obtain a formula for *present value*:

$$\text{Present value} = \text{amount} \div \left(1 + \frac{\text{interest rate}}{\text{frequency}}\right)^{N \times \text{freq}} \qquad (4\text{-}5)$$

when (1) interest is paid at the nominal rate of *interest rate* × 100% per annum at the end of each period for N years and (2) there are frequency interest periods per year. Present value is the *present value* of *amount* in the sense that the promise of receiving *amount* (with certainty) N years hence is equivalent in value to receiving the sum present value in Formula 4-5 immediately. Formula 4-5 proves extremely useful in financial analysis because it provides a means of measuring the value of a sum to be received or a disbursement to be made in the future in terms of an equivalent sum received or disbursed immediately. This process becomes crucial when several sums at different points in time are involved.

The interest rate used in present value calculations is called the *discount rate*. Henceforth we use *discount rate* in place of *interest rate* in present value calculations in order to conform with financial convention. It is important for the reader to appreciate that, depending on the problem, it may or may not be obvious what the appropriate discount rate is. Since the discount rate chosen obviously has an important effect on present value in Formula 4-5, the discussion in subsequent chapters of each of the applications includes some guidance as to how the discount rate or an appropriate range of discount rates should be chosen.

Illustration of Present Value Calculation:
Constant Discount Rate

An investor has just purchased a bond that matures in 20 years. The bond has a principal amount of $1000 and pays interest semiannually at the rate of 10% per annum. What is the present value of the principal repayment? Formula 4-5 gives

$$\text{Present value} = \$1000 \div \left(1 + \frac{0.1}{2}\right)^{20 \times 2} = \$142.05$$

Changing Discount Rate

When the discount rate varies, Formula 4-4 can be rearranged to obtain the appropriate formula for the present value of a dollar to be received N periods hence:

$$\text{Present value} = 1 \div \{[1 + \text{discount rate}(1)] \times [1 + \text{discount rate}(2)]$$
$$\times [1 + \text{discount rate}(3)] \cdots [1 + \text{discount rate}(N)]\}$$
$$(4\text{-}6)$$

where *discount rate* (1) denotes the rate at which a payment to be received at the end of period 1 is discounted back to the beginning of the same period. The other discount rates are interpreted similarly.

Illustration of Present Value Calculation: Changing Discount Rate

A leasing agreement gives the lessee the option to purchase the equipment under lease for $1000 at the end of 5 years. If the lessor expects to be able to invest funds at the rate of 9% per annum over the next 2 years and at the rate of 10% per annum thereafter, the present value (to the lessor) of the $1000 payment is

$$\text{Present value} = \$1000 / \left[(1.09)^2 \times (1.10)^3 \right] = \$632.37$$

Effective Annual Rate of Interest

When two or more investments that pay interest with different frequencies (for example, bonds issued domestically by U.S. corporations pay interest semi-annually, but Eurobonds pay interest annually) are being compared, analysts often find it helpful to calculate for each the *effective annual rate of interest*, which takes into account the frequency of compounding. The effective annual rate of interest is that rate of interest that would have to be paid if interest were paid only once at the end of the year to produce the compound amount that results when interest is paid at the nominal rate of interest rate × 100% per annum compounded frequency times per year. The effective annual rate of interest *effective annual rate* × 100% solves the equation

$$\text{Amount} = 1 + \frac{\text{effective}}{\text{annual rate}} = \left[1 + \left(\frac{\text{interest}}{\text{rate}} \div \text{frequency} \right) \right]^{\text{freq}}$$

which gives

$$\frac{\text{Effective}}{\text{annual rate}} = \left[1 + \left(\frac{\text{interest}}{\text{rate}} \div \text{frequency} \right) \right]^{\text{freq}} - 1 \qquad (4\text{-}7)$$

Illustration of Calculation of Effective Annual Rate

Interest is paid at the nominal rate of 8% per annum compounded quarterly. The effective annual rate of interest is

$$\text{Effective annual rate} = \left(1 + \frac{0.08}{4} \right)^4 - 1 = 0.0824, \text{ or } 8.24\%$$

The sum of $100 deposited at 8.24% per annum *compounded annually* and the sum of $100 deposited at 8% per annum *compounded quarterly* both grow to $108.24 after 1 year.

PRESENT VALUE OF
A STREAM OF PAYMENTS

Many financial problems involve streams of two or more payments for which a present value calculation must be carried out. For example, the net present value of a capital investment project will be defined in Part 2 as the present value of the stream of benefits less the present value of the stream of costs. As a second example, the value of a bond can be calculated as the present value of the stream of interest payments and principal repayment(s). These present value calculations can be carried out by applying Formula 4-5 or Formula 4-6 to each payment in the stream and then summing the present value amounts. It is typically assumed that the discount rate is constant over time. In that case, the present value calculation is

$$
\begin{aligned}
\text{Present value} = {}& \sum_{t=1}^{N} \text{payment}(t) \div \left(1 + \frac{\text{discount}}{\text{rate}}\right)^{t} \\
= {}& \left[\text{payment}(1) \div \left(1 + \frac{\text{discount}}{\text{rate}}\right)\right] \\
& + \left[\text{payment}(2) \div \left(1 + \frac{\text{discount}}{\text{rate}}\right)^{2}\right] \\
& + \cdots + \left[\text{payment}(N) \div \left(1 + \frac{\text{discount}}{\text{rate}}\right)^{N}\right] \quad (4\text{-}8)
\end{aligned}
$$

where *payment (t)* denotes the payment received at the end of t periods. There are a total of N payments, one per period.

Illustration of Calculation of Present Value of
a Stream of Payments

An equipment supplier is to receive $1000, $1200, $1500, $1500, and $2000 payments 1, 2, 3, 4, and 5 years from now, respectively, under an installment sales contract. If the equipment supplier can earn interest at the rate of 16% per annum compounded quarterly on investments in receivables, what is the present value of the payments stream?

Year	Interest Rate ÷ Frequency	$N \times$ Frequency	Present Value Factor	Payment	Present Value
1	0.04	4	0.85481	$1000	$ 854.81
2	0.04	8	0.73069	1200	876.83
3	0.04	12	0.62460	1500	936.90
4	0.04	16	0.53391	1500	800.87
5	0.04	20	0.45639	2000	912.78
			Total	$7200	$4382.19

Valuation of Common Stock

Formula 4-8 has a variety of useful applications in the valuation of securities. For example, suppose an individual is considering purchasing a share of a particular common stock, which he or she expects to hold for 1 year. Suppose the investor expects the company to pay dividends at the rate of *dividends(t)* per share per quarter at the end of quarter t and that he or she expects to be able to sell the share for *sale price* at the end of the holding period. What is the share worth to the individual? Ignoring transaction costs and taxes, the value of the share, *current value*, is equal to the discounted value of the dividends plus the proceeds to be received when the share is sold:

$$\text{Current value} = \left[\text{dividends}(1) \div \left(1 + \frac{\text{discount}}{\text{rate}}\right)\right]$$

$$+ \left[\text{dividends}(2) \div \left(1 + \frac{\text{discount}}{\text{rate}}\right)^2\right]$$

$$+ \left[\text{dividends}(3) \div \left(1 + \frac{\text{discount}}{\text{rate}}\right)^3\right]$$

$$+ \left[\text{dividends}(4) + \frac{\text{sale}}{\text{price}}\right] \div \left(1 + \frac{\text{discount}}{\text{rate}}\right)^4$$

where *discount rate* denotes the rate at which the shareholder discounts these payments.

If the individual instead plans to hold the shares for a total of H quarters, the above formula is easily extended. In the more general case, the value of the share is given by the formula

$$\begin{aligned}\frac{\text{Current}}{\text{value}} = \sum_{t=1}^{H} &\left[\text{dividends}(t) \div \left(1 + \frac{\text{discount}}{\text{rate}}\right)^t\right] \\ &+ \left[\frac{\text{sale}}{\text{price}} \div \left(1 + \frac{\text{discount}}{\text{rate}}\right)^H\right]\end{aligned} \qquad (4\text{-}9)$$

where *sale price* denotes the proceeds received when the share is sold. Because dividends are paid quarterly, *dividends(t)* and *discount rate* should be expressed on a quarterly basis in Formula 4-9. In practice, however, analysts typically use annual dividend rates and an annualized discount rate. The uncertainty surrounding the estimates of future dividend rates and the required rate of return is such that probably little accuracy is lost when annual rather than quarterly figures are used.

If the discount rate used in Formula 4-9 is the one applied by the investors "at the margin" who, in effect, determine the prevailing share price, then *current value* in Formula 4-9 represents the company's share price for that particular choice of discount rate.

Finally, suppose instead that the prospective holder is a perpetual trust which would hold the shares forever. In that case, the value of the share would equal the discounted value of an infinite stream of dividends:

$$\begin{array}{c} \text{Share} \\ \text{price} \end{array} = \sum_{t=1}^{\infty} \text{dividends}(t) \div \left(1 + \frac{\text{discount}}{\text{rate}}\right)^{t} \qquad (4\text{-}10)$$

where the symbol ∞, which stands for "infinity," indicates that the stream of dividends lasts forever.

Constant Growth Model

Formula 4-10 does not lend itself to calculations, and even Formula 4-9 is cumbersome if the expected holding period extends over several years. Fortunately, a simpler approach exists. Suppose that dividends are expected to grow at a constant *growth rate* (expressed as a decimal). In that case, the dividend grows over time according to Formula 4-1:

$$\text{Dividends}(t) = \text{dividends}(0) \times (1 + \text{growth rate})^{t}$$

where dividends(0) denotes the initial dividend rate. Substituting into Formula 4-10 and simplifying gives the formula

$$\begin{array}{c} \text{Share} \\ \text{price} \end{array} = \text{dividends}(1) \div \left(\frac{\text{discount}}{\text{rate}} - \frac{\text{growth}}{\text{rate}}\right) \qquad (4\text{-}11)$$

Formula 4-11 assumes that dividends grow at a constant growth rate. In practice, analysts interpret growth rate as the long-term average annual rate at which dividends are expected to grow. This estimated growth rate is used together with the estimated annual dividend rate for the coming year [dividends (1)] and the (annualized) required rate of return, denoted by *discount rate*, to determine the share price. Note that, as a special case,

$$\text{Share price} = \text{dividends}(1) \div \text{discount rate} \qquad (4\text{-}12)$$

if the dividend rate is expected to remain *dividends*(1) forever. In the case of zero dividend growth, the share price is equal to the *capitalized* (at the investors' discount rate) value of the constant annual dividend rate.

Illustration of Share Price Calculation

A potential investor determines that National Oil Company's annual dividend rate has grown at an average annual rate of 10% over the past 5 years. The investor expects this rate of growth to continue. Securities analysts predict that National will pay out $2.40 in dividends per share during the coming year. The investor can earn a 16% rate of return on comparable investments. A share of National Oil is thus worth

$$\text{Share price} = \frac{\$2.40}{0.16 - 0.10} = \$40$$

to this investor. If the shareholder expected dividend growth to fall to zero, however, a share of National Oil would be worth only

$$\text{Share price} = \frac{\$2.40}{0.16} = \$15$$

to the investor.

FUTURE VALUE AND PRESENT VALUE OF AN ANNUITY

In the previous section the payments in the stream consisted of different amounts. There are some situations in which the payments are equal in amount. In that case, a formula can be developed that makes possible a much simpler calculation than Formula 4-8.

A stream of payments in which the payments are equal in amount and occur at regular intervals is called an *annuity*. For example, the stream of interest payments associated with a bond is an annuity consisting of equal semiannual interest payments (paid in arrears) over the life of the bond. When each payment occurs at the end of a period, the annuity is called an *ordinary annuity*.

Consider the ordinary annuity consisting of N equal payments each in the amount *payment*. Suppose interest is paid at the rate of *interest rate* $\times$ 100% per annum. Two quantities associated with such a stream of payments are of particular interest. The *future value of an annuity* is the amount that would be available at the end of N periods if each of the N payments was deposited into an account and left there to accumulate interest. The *present value of an annuity* is the minimum amount that would have to be deposited into such an account today to permit someone to withdraw exactly the amount *payment* from the account at the *end* of each of the next N periods.

Future Value of an Annuity

The future value of an annuity for an ordinary annuity is equal to the compound amount of the first payment, *payment* $\times$ [1 + (*interest rate* $\div$ *frequency*)]$^{N \times \text{freq} - 1}$, plus the compound amount of the second, *payment* $\times$ [1 + (*interest rate* $\div$ *frequency*)]$^{N \times \text{freq} - 2}$, ..., plus the compound amount of the next to last, *payment* × [1 + (*interest rate* ÷ *frequency*)], plus the last payment. Through the magic of mathematics, this sum simplifies to

$$
\begin{array}{l}
\text{Future value} \\
\quad \text{of an} \\
\quad \text{annuity}
\end{array}
= \text{payment} \times \left[\left(1 + \frac{\text{interest rate}}{\text{frequency}} \right)^{-N \times \text{freq}} - 1 \right]
$$

$$
\times \frac{\text{frequency}}{\text{interest rate}} \tag{4-13}
$$

which is easily evaluated with the aid of a hand-held calculator.

Illustration of Future Value Calculation

The Adams family plans to set up a college fund. They will deposit $200 quarterly for 10 years into an account that will earn interest at the rate of 6% per annum compounded quarterly. They wish to calculate how much will be in the account after 10 years when their daughter will be ready for college. Formula 4-13 gives

$$
\begin{array}{l}
\text{Future value} \\
\quad \text{of an} \\
\quad \text{annuity}
\end{array}
= \$200 \times \left[\left(1 + \frac{0.06}{4} \right)^{10 \times 4} - 1 \right] \times \frac{4}{0.06} = \$10{,}853.58
$$

Present Value of an Annuity

The future value of an annuity is the value of the stream of payments figured as of a point in time N periods in the future. The present value of that same annuity is its value as of the present. It can be calculated as the present value of the future value of an annuity in Formula 4-13:

$$
\begin{array}{l}
\text{Present value} \\
\quad \text{of an} \\
\quad \text{annuity}
\end{array}
=
\begin{array}{l}
\text{future value} \\
\quad \text{of an} \\
\quad \text{annuity}
\end{array}
\div \left(1 + \frac{\text{interest rate}}{\text{frequency}} \right)^{N \times \text{freq}}
$$

$$
= \text{payment} \times \left[1 - \left(1 + \frac{\text{interest rate}}{\text{frequency}} \right)^{-N \times \text{freq}} \right]
$$

$$
\times \frac{\text{frequency}}{\text{interest rate}} \tag{4-14}
$$

Illustration of Calculation of Present Value
of an Annuity

The present value of the interest payments to be received by the purchaser of the 20-year bond discussed in the first section is

$$
\begin{array}{l}
\text{Present value of} \\
\quad \text{an annuity}
\end{array}
= \$50 \times \left[1 - \left(1 + \frac{0.1}{2} \right)^{-20 \times 2} \right] \times \frac{2}{0.1} = \$857.95
$$

Note that the sum of the present value of the interest payments and the present value of the principal repayment is $1000.00, the purchase price of the bond.

An annuity in which the stream of payments continues forever is called a *perpetual annuity*. The stream of dividend payments associated with a share of perpetual preferred stock is an example of such a stream. A formula for the present value of a perpetual annuity can be obtained from Formula 4-14 by recognizing that $[1 + (\text{interest rate} \div \text{frequency})]^{-N \times \text{freq}}$ approaches zero as N becomes very large. The desired formula is thus

$$\frac{\text{Present value of}}{\text{perpetual annuity}} = (\text{payment} \times \text{frequency}) \div \text{interest rate} \qquad (4\text{-}15)$$

Note that Formula 4-15 is very similar to Formula 4-12. Each expresses the present value of a perpetual annuity in terms of the capitalized value of the constant annual payment. Thus, a share of common stock that pays a constant dividend rate forever is an example of a perpetual annuity.

Illustration of Calculation of Present Value
of Perpetual Annuity

The market value of a share of perpetual preferred stock that pays dividends at the rate of $2.25 per quarter when the current dividend rate on new issues of comparable quality is 12% is

$$\text{Share price} = \frac{\$2.25 \times 4}{0.12} = \$75.00$$

CONTINUOUS COMPOUNDING

Formula 4-2 provides the compound amount when interest is compounded frequency times per year. Consider the investment of $1000 at a nominal interest rate of 8% per annum. If interest is compounded annually, the compound amount at the end of 1 year is

$$\text{Compound amount} = \$1000 \times 1.08 = \$1080.00$$

Under quarterly compounding, the compound amount after 1 year is

$$\text{Compound amount} = \$1000 \times \left(1 + \frac{0.08}{4}\right)^4 = \$1082.43$$

Under daily compounding, the compound amount after 1 year is

$$\text{Compound amount} = \$1000 \times \left(1 + \frac{0.08}{365}\right)^{365} = \$1083.28$$

Table 4-1
The Effect on Compound Amount of Compounding
Interest with Greater Frequency
Nominal interest rate: 8% per annum
Amount deposited: $1000

Frequency of Compounding	Compound Amount after 1 Year	Effective Annual Interest Rate, %	Frequency of Compounding	Compound Amount after 1 Year	Effective Annual Rate of Interest, %
Annually	$1080.00	8.00	Monthly	$1083.00	8.30
Semiannually	1081.60	8.16	Daily	1083.28	8.33
Quarterly	1082.43	8.24	Continuously	1083.29	8.33

Table 4-1 indicates the compound amount for various frequencies of compounding. If we were to increase the frequency of compounding to hourly, then every minute, then every second, and so on, we would find that the compound amount would approach more and more closely, but never exceed, $1083.29. In the extreme, interest is said to *compound continuously.* For any particular nominal interest rate, compounding with greater frequency produces a greater compound amount and a higher effective annual rate of interest. An investor facing several investment alternatives that compound interest at different frequencies should not simply compare nominal interest rates but should compare effective annual rates of interest.

Compound Amount and Present Value
The compound amount of *payment* after N years when interest is paid at the nominal rate of *interest rate* per year compounded continuously is

$$\frac{\text{Compound}}{\text{amount}} = \text{payment} \times \exp\left(N \times \frac{\text{interest}}{\text{rate}}\right) \qquad (4\text{-}16)$$

where "exp" denotes the function "raise to the power of the number e (approximately 2.71828)," which can be found on many hand-held calculators. For example, when *payment* = $1000, *interest rate* = 0.08, and $N = 1$,

$$\frac{\text{Compound}}{\text{amount}} = \$1000 \times \exp(1 \times 0.08) = \$1083.29$$

As before, the compound amount formula can be turned around to produce a present value formula:

$$\frac{\text{Present}}{\text{value}} = \text{payment} \times \exp\left(-N \times \frac{\text{interest}}{\text{rate}}\right) \qquad (4\text{-}17)$$

Equivalent Continuously Compounded Rate of Interest

In certain problems, such as the application of the Black-Scholes model to option pricing in Chapter 21, it proves useful to be able to reexpress a particular nominal interest rate with some specified frequency of compounding in terms of an *equivalent continuously compounded rate of interest*.

Consider the following problem. One dollar is deposited into an account that pays *interest rate* = 0.10 per annum and that compounds interest frequency = 4 times per year. At the end of 1 year,

$$\text{Compound amount} = \left(1 + \frac{0.10}{4}\right)^4 = \$1.10381$$

by Formula 4-2. If instead interest were compounded continuously, Formula 4-16 can be used to find the continuously compounded rate of interest that would provide the same compound amount. This interest rate is called the *equivalent continuously compounded rate of interest*. Equating the two compound amounts leads to the formula:

$$\begin{array}{l}\text{Equivalent} \\ \text{continuously} \\ \text{compounded rate}\end{array} = \ln\,[1 + (\text{interest rate} \div \text{frequency})]^{\text{freq}} \qquad (4\text{-}18)$$

where "ln" denotes the function "find the power of the number e," which can be found on many hand-held calculators. To continue the preceding example,

$$\text{Equivalent continuously compounded rate} = 0.09877, \text{ or } 9.877\%$$

which gives $1.10381 when substituted into Formula 4-16.

YIELD

The present value of a series of cash flows is calculated by discounting each element of the flow at the given discount rate. Many applications involve a reversal of this process; the present value is known and the implicit discount rate, or *yield*, must be calculated. For example, a capital investment project involves the purchase of an asset (the current outlay) that will yield a stream of future cash returns. As a second example, the purchaser of a bond pays the current price of the bond and becomes entitled to the stream of future interest payments and the repayment of principal when the bond matures. The financial analysis of each of these investments involves the calculation of an implicit discount rate; this implicit discount rate is called the *internal rate of return* in the case of a capital investment project and the *yield (to maturity* or *to average life*, depending on the time horizon chosen) in the case of bond investments. The two calculations are performed in the same manner.

The yield associated with a particular current outlay and a particular cash flow stream is the solution yield (or solutions, if there are more than one) to the equation

$$
\begin{aligned}
\text{Current outlay} &= \sum_{t=1}^{N} \left[\text{payment}(t) \div (1 + \text{yield})^t \right] \\
&= \left[\text{payment}(1) \div (1 + \text{yield}) \right] \\
&\quad + \left[\text{payment}(2) \div (1 + \text{yield})^2 \right] \\
&\quad + \cdots + \left[\text{payment}(N) \div (1 + \text{yield})^N \right] \quad (4\text{-}19)
\end{aligned}
$$

where *current outlay* denotes the purchase price of the bond or the initial capital investment, as appropriate, and *payment(t)* denotes the payment or cash flow during period t. In general, there is no formula for calculating yield, but most hand-held financial calculators have been programmed to find the solution.

Illustration of Yield Calculation

An investor is considering whether to purchase a short-term note ($1000 principal amount) that will mature in 2 years. The current price is $93\frac{1}{2}$ (i.e., $935 per $1000 principal amount). The note bears interest at the rate of $11\frac{1}{4}\%$ per annum paid semiannually. The cash flows in Formula 4-19 are current outlay = $935, payment(1) = payment(2) = payment(3) = $56.25 and payment(4) = $1056.25. With the aid of a hand-held calculator, the note's yield to maturity is found to be yield = 15.14%.

SUMMARY

The promise of $1.00 to be received 1 year from today is not equivalent in value to the receipt of $1.00 today. Money has a time value, which is measured by the rate of interest, and interest is generally compounded. Formulas were developed for calculating the compound amount of a single sum and the future value of an ordinary annuity. The frequency of compounding may vary; more frequent compounding results in higher compound amount and future value.

Financial analysis often involves a comparison of two or more cash flow streams. Because money has a time value, the elements of each stream cannot simply be added. Each element must be discounted from the point in time at which it will be received. Formulas were developed for calculating present value that can be applied to a wide range of problems, including the analysis of capital investment projects and securities valuation.

The methods of discounted cash flow analysis developed in this chapter play a crucial role in the analytical techniques discussed throughout the book. The reader must therefore understand the basic techniques described in this chapter in order to appreciate and use effectively the techniques presented in the chapters that follow.

Risk Analysis Chapter 5

In Chapter 4, we assumed that all future events (in particular, future interest rates) were known with certainty. In practice, however, the amounts of future payments that will actually be received and other relevant factors will not be known beforehand with certainty. This lack of certainty should be reflected in financial analyses.

Because the future financial flows that will result from any decision, for example, the decision to build a new plant, cannot be known beforehand, the decision maker must trade off what he or she *expects* to happen on the one hand and the *risk* that the actual result may differ substantially from what she or he expects on the other. Suppose that project A promises "slightly higher" expected returns than project B but that the decision maker is concerned that if project A fails it might bankrupt the firm whereas project B involves no risk of bankruptcy. A prudent decision maker could be expected to pursue project B. This is admittedly an extreme case. Nevertheless, it bears out the point that one must be concerned with more than just what one expects to happen. This is the purpose of risk analysis.

This chapter describes various approaches to quantifying the *expected* outcome and the *risk* or *uncertainty* associated with the various possible outcomes. There is, unfortunately, no formula for determining the appropriate risk-return trade-off in any particular situation. That necessarily involves a degree of subjectivity. But quantifying the variables involved can help the decision maker evaluate how much greater the expected returns and how much greater the risks are between one alternative and another. Provided with such information, the decision maker can more confidently weigh the alternatives.

UNCERTAINTY AND RISK

Statisticians frequently distinguish risk from uncertainty. An event is said to be subject to *risk* when there is more than one possible outcome but all possible outcomes and the relative likelihood of each are known. An event is said to be subject to *uncertainty* when neither all the possible outcomes nor their relative likelihoods are known. Uncertainty is clearly unsatisfactory from a decision-making standpoint. In most cases, the range of possible outcomes can be approximated meaningfully and a (possibly subjective) probability, or measure of the relative likelihood of occurrence, can be associated with each.

In this book we deal exclusively with situations involving risk, and the terms *risk* and *uncertainty* are used interchangeably to denote situations in which a set of outcomes can be associated with each possible course of action and a (possibly subjective) probability, or degree of relative likelihood, can be associated with each possible outcome.

PROBABILITIES

The *probability* that a certain outcome will occur is a measure of its relative likelihood. For example, one would say that the probability that a "5" will appear when a fair die is rolled is $1/6$ because there is one chance in six that such an outcome will occur. The probabilities associated with the possible outcomes of a particular event should exhibit the following two properties:

1. $0 < \text{probability}(I) \leq 1, I = 1, \ldots, \text{number of possible outcomes}$

    (Each event is possible; a zero probability would imply that the Ith outcome could not occur, in which case it could be deleted from the list of possible outcomes.)

2.
$$\sum_{I=1}^{\text{number of possible outcomes}} \text{probability}(I) = 1$$

    [The probabilities sum to 1; the number of possible outcomes exhausts the list of possible outcomes; at least one of these (but no other) must occur.]

where *probability*(I) measures the relative likelihood of occurrence associated with outcome number I. Note that assigning a probability of $1/6$ to each possible outcome on the roll of a fair die satisfies these properties.

Illustration of Probabilities

Johnson Glass Works is considering whether to build a new plant to manufacture bottles and other glass containers. Johnson's planning department has described five alternative future business environments, associated a probability with each, and calculated for each the net present value of the cash flows resulting from the construction of the new plant:

Future Business Environment	Probability	Net Present Value of Cash Flows
Optimistic	.05	$ 6,000,000
Favorable	.20	4,000,000
Base case	.40	3,000,000
Unfavorable	.30	1,000,000
Pessimistic	.05	−2,000,000
	1.00	

The collection of probabilities assigned to the possible outcome is said to define a *probability distribution* over those outcomes. The next two sections discuss certain measures of the "expected outcome" and "risk" that can be associated with a probability distribution.

MEASURES OF EXPECTATION

There are two basic measures that statisticians would associate with the distribution of possible outcomes in the Johnson Glass Works example. First, they would associate a measure of *central tendency*, that is, an "average value." Second, they would associate a measure of *dispersion*, that is, a measure of the variability of the possible outcomes around the "average value."

Expected Value, Median, and Mode

There are three principal measures of central tendency, the *mean*, the *median*, and the *mode*. The mean, or the *expected value*, is the most widely used measure. It is calculated as the weighted average of the possible outcomes, with the probabilities serving as the weights. Suppose there are a number of possible outcomes, denoted by $I = 1, \ldots, N$. Let *probability*(I) and *value*(I) denote the probability and value, respectively, associated with the Ith possible outcome. The *expected value* is defined by the formula:

$$\text{Expected value} = \sum_{I=1}^{\substack{\text{number of} \\ \text{possible outcomes}}} \text{probability}(I) \times \text{value}(I)$$

$$= [\text{probability}(1) \times \text{value}(1)]$$

$$+ [\text{probability}(2) \times \text{value}(2)]$$

$$+ \cdots + [\text{probability}(N) \times \text{value}(N)] \qquad (5\text{-}1)$$

The value associated with each possible occurrence is multiplied by the likelihood of its occurrence, and then these probability-weighted values are summed.

The *median* is the value of the outcome that divides the probability distribution into two equal parts: the probability that the actual outcome will be greater than or equal to the median value is at least .5 and the probability that it will be less than or equal to the median value is also at least .5.[1] The *mode* is the outcome (there may be more than one) for which the probability of occurrence is greatest.

Illustration of Calculation of Expected Value, Median, and Mode

For the probability distribution in the Johnson Glass Works example:

1. The expected value is

$$\text{Expected value} = .05(\$6{,}000{,}000) + .20(4{,}000{,}000)$$

$$+ .40(3{,}000{,}000) + .30(1{,}000{,}000)$$

$$+ .05(-2{,}000{,}000)$$

$$= \$2{,}500{,}000$$

2. The median is $3,000,000 because the probability that the net present value of the cash flows will be greater than or equal to $3,000,000 is .40 + .20 + .05 = .65, whereas the probability that it will be less than or equal to $3,000,000 is .40 + .30 + .05 = .75. (As an exercise, the reader should show that the other four possible outcomes fail to satisfy the definition of the median.)

3. The mode is $3,000,000.

The expected value is the most widely used measure of central tendency because its calculation takes into account directly both the value and the probability of each possible outcome. The expected value is not always the best measure of central tendency, however. As illustrated in Figure 5-1,

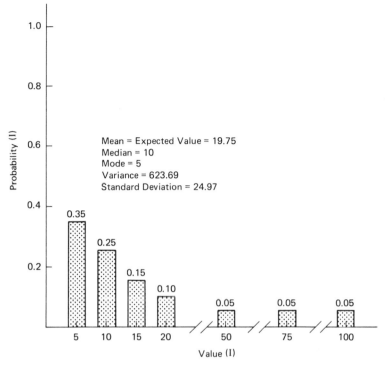

Figure 5-1. Expected value versus median.

the median is a better indicator of the "average" value when the probability distribution is highly skewed. The value = 100, even though it has a very low probability, affects the calculation of the expected value, but decreasing it to 25 or increasing it to 250, for example, would not affect the median. The analyst should calculate the median rather than the expected value when there is a danger that the latter would be misleading.

MEASURES OF RISK

There are four basic measures of risk that are widely used in general applications: variance, standard deviation, range, and interquartile range.

Variance and Standard Deviation

When expected value is used as the measure of central tendency, variance or its square root is used to measure dispersion. *Variance* is defined by the formula

$$\text{Variance} = \sum_{I=1}^{\substack{\text{number of} \\ \text{possible outcomes}}} \text{probability}(I) \times [\text{value}(I) - \text{expected value}]^2$$

$$= \text{probability}(1) \times [\text{value}(1) - \text{expected value}]^2$$

$$+ \text{probability}(2) \times [\text{value}(2) - \text{expected value}]^2$$

$$+ \cdots + \text{probability}(N) \times [\text{value}(N) - \text{expected value}]^2 \quad (5\text{-}2)$$

where *expected value* is calculated from Formula 5-1. It is the weighted average of the squared deviations of the possible outcomes around the expected value. The square root of variance in Formula 5-2 is called the *standard deviation*:

$$\text{Standard deviation} = +\sqrt{\text{variance}} \quad (5\text{-}3)$$

Illustration of Calculation of Variance

The *variance* of the probability distribution in the Johnson Glass Works example is

$$\text{Variance} = .05(6.0 - 2.5)^2 \times 10^{12} + .20(4.0 - 2.5)^2 \times 10^{12}$$

$$+ .40(3.0 - 2.5)^2 \times 10^{12} + .30(1.0 - 2.5)^2 \times 10^{12}$$

$$+ .05(-2.0 - 2.5)^2 \times 10^{12}$$

$$= 2.85 \times 10^{12}$$

The standard deviation is

$$\text{Standard deviation} = \sqrt{2.85 \times 10^{12}} = \$1,688,194$$

The significance of the value calculated for the standard deviation is illustrated for the bell-shaped *normal probability distribution* in Figure 5-2. Approximately two-thirds of the probability lies within one standard deviation of the mean, 95% lies within two standard deviations, and 99.7% lies within three standard deviations. A larger standard deviation thus implies greater dispersion; that is, the possible outcomes appear "more spread out."

Range and Interquartile Range

When the median is used as the measure of central tendency, either of two other measures of dispersion is frequently used. The *range* is the difference between the largest and smallest values among all the possible outcomes. The *interquartile range* is the range of outcomes that includes the middle half of the

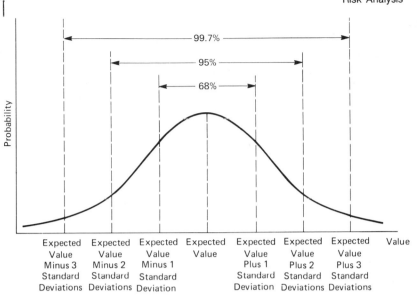

Figure 5-2. Distribution of probabilities for the bell-shaped normal probability distribution.

probability distribution; there is a probability of .25 that the actual outcome will exceed the upper end of this range and an equal probability that it will fall below its lower end.

Illustration of Calculation of Range

The range for the probability distribution in the Johnson Glass Works example is $6,000,000 - (-2,000,000) = \$8,000,000$.

The interquartile range is calculated in the following manner. The probability that the outcome will be greater than or equal to $4,000,000 is .25, and the probability that it will be less than or equal to $3,000,000 is .75. The upper boundary (the third or highest quartile) is thus not clearly determined. It is approximated by taking a weighted average of the two candidate values using their respective probabilities as weights:

$$(.2 \times \$4,000,000 + .4 \times 3,000,000)/.6 = \$3,333,333$$

The lower boundary (the first or lowest quartile) is $1,000,000. The interquartile range is

$$\$3,333,333 - 1,000,000 = \$2,333,333$$

Half the probability falls within a range of outcomes that is approximately $2,333,333 in width.

Beta

The capital asset pricing model provides a third type of risk measure that is used in the analysis of capital investment projects and common stock investments and for a variety of other purposes. In contrast to standard deviation and interquartile range, which represent absolute measures of risk, the capital asset pricing model measures risk relative to a market norm. This makes it more useful than the other two measures of risk in many applications. Chapter 9 explores the usefulness of the capital asset pricing model in discounted cash flow analysis.

METHODS OF RISK ANALYSIS

Under uncertainty, there are two or more possible cash flow streams. Two basic methods are available for dealing with this uncertainty in discounted cash flow analysis. These are:

1. First, calculate an expected cash flow for each period using Formula 5-1. Next, determine an appropriate risk-adjusted discount rate. Then substitute the expected cash flows for *payment(I)* and the risk-adjusted discount rate for *discount rate* in Formula 4-8, and evaluate present value.[2]

2. First, use Formula 4-8 to calculate present value for the cash flow stream associated with each of several possible business scenarios (for example, for each of the scenarios in the Johnson Glass Works example). Then display the present values together with the expected value and variance or standard deviation (or, if more appropriate, median and range or interquartile range) of the present values.

Method 1 adjusts for risk in the discounting process and yields a single risk-adjusted number. Method 2 takes risk into account after the present values of the (two or more) separate cash flow streams have been calculated.

Adjusting the Discount Rate for Uncertainty

Method 1 involves adjusting the discount rate in Formula 4-8 by adding an appropriate *risk premium*:

$$\text{Risk-adjusted present value} = \sum_{t=1}^{N} \text{expected payment}(t) \div \left(1 + \text{risk-adjusted discount rate}\right)^t \quad (5\text{-}4)$$

where the *risk-adjusted discount rate* is calculated by adding an appropriate *risk premium* to the *risk-free discount rate* (e.g., the yield on Treasury securities):

$$\text{Risk-adjusted discount rate} = \text{risk-free discount rate} + \text{risk premium}$$

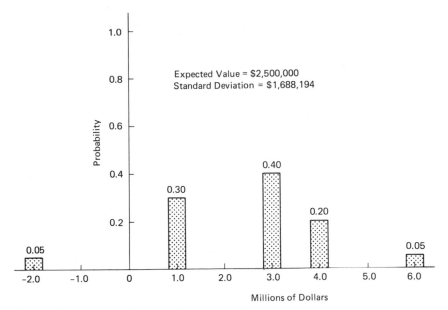

Figure 5-3. Histogram display of discounted cash flows.

Greater degrees of risk require greater risk premiums. The capital asset pricing model, which is discussed in Chapter 9, offers one approach in determining the appropriate risk premium.

Illustration of Discount Rate Adjustment

An investor is considering whether to purchase shares of a particular stock. Suppose that the current yield on 90-day Treasury bills is 11% and that the appropriate risk premium is 5% in view of the stock's volatility relative to share prices generally. The investor expects to receive quarterly dividends of $0.50 and to be able to sell the shares for $25.00 at the end of the projected 5-year holding period. Thus,

$$\text{Risk-adjusted discount rate} = 0.11 + 0.05 = 0.16, \text{ or } 0.04 \text{ per period}$$

Applying Formula 4-9 gives

$$\text{Current value} = \sum_{t=1}^{20} \frac{\$0.50}{(1.04)^t} + \frac{\$25.00}{(1.04)^{20}} = \$18.20$$

The investor should pay no more than $18.20 per share.

Histogram of Present Values

Method 2 involves treating the cash flow stream associated with each business scenario as if it were certain. The probability, or relative likelihood of occurrence, of the business scenario is then associated with the present value so calculated. The collection of discounted cash flows, each with associated probability measure, is displayed in a *histogram*, similar to those in Figure 5-1. The histogram for the discounted cash flows given in the Johnson Glass Works example is illustrated in Figure 5-3.

Choice of Methods

The two methods for adjusting for risk will not, in general, lead to precisely the same expected value. Both methods involve a certain degree of subjectivity because both require that the probabilities be estimated. In addition, method 1 requires that the appropriate risk-adjusted discount rate be estimated. Finally, method 2 furnishes the decision maker with more information than method 1 because the former indicates the degree of variability, or risk, associated with the possible outcomes. But method 1 also requires less information because, in practice, the expected cash flows required under method 1 are often estimated directly without first specifying a separate cash flow stream for each possible scenario. Moreover, method 1 can be supplemented with a *sensitivity analysis* in which the expected cash flows are adjusted upward or downward (with the discounting procedure repeated after each adjustment). The results of this sensitivity analysis can be summarized in a histogram like the one in Figure 5-3. Thus, although the two approaches do not lead to identical results, either one can be used effectively to adjust discounted cash flows for risk.

SUMMARY

Future cash flows are seldom known with certainty. It is therefore necessary to adjust for risk when performing discounted cash flow analysis. This is normally done either (1) by adding a suitable risk premium to the riskless interest rate and discounting the expected cash flow stream or (2) by discounting the alternative cash flow streams separately and displaying the resulting discounted cash flows together with appropriate summary statistical measures such as standard deviation or variance. The two procedures will produce similar results.

Analyzing Capital Investment Projects and Measuring the Required Rate of Return

Part 2

Most businesses utilize long-lived capital assets along with current inputs, such as labor and raw materials, to produce their goods and services. Capital assets differ from current inputs because of the time pattern of the cash flows associated with their purchase and use. Purchasing plant and equipment requires a long-term *capital investment*. The firm spends cash in the current period in anticipation of realizing inflows of cash in future periods as the capital assets are applied in production. This initial cash outlay is often substantial in relation to the firm's cash flow. *Capital budgeting* involves the evaluation of these future cash inflows in relation to the initial cash outlay in order to determine whether this capital investment is in the company's shareholders' interest. The purpose of Part 2 is to provide the financial analyst with a framework within which to make this determination. For the purposes of this discussion, the business enterprise's choice of the mix of debt and equity funds used to finance its investment is taken as given. This decision is taken up in Part 3.

The following example illustrates the type of problem with which we are concerned in Part 2. Washington Chemical Corporation, a specialty chemicals company, is considering three capital investment alternatives. The cash outlays required and the future streams of returns under best-case (B), expected-case (E), worst-case (W) scenarios are given in Table 6-1 (see page 81). Washington's board of directors has decided that the company can pursue only one of the three projects. Recently, Washington has been using a 15% cost of capital in its capital budgeting studies. The board has directed Washington's chief financial officer to reassess the appropriateness of the 15% cost of capital and then to undertake a capital investment analysis of the three projects and make a recommendation to the board.

It is not immediately evident from the patterns of the cash flows which alternative would be most advantageous to Washington's shareholders and, more importantly, whether any of them would be beneficial. Part 2 is dedicated to helping Washington Chemical solve its capital budgeting problem. Chapter 6 describes a basic discounted cash flow framework for capital investment analysis. Chapter 7 discusses how to utilize the basic framework to adjust for risk and uncertainty. Chapter 8 discusses how to measure a company's cost of capital for use in evaluating a particular project. Chapter 9 describes some more sophisticated approaches to capital budgeting. Equipped with these analytical tools, Washington Chemical's chief financial officer will be able to respond to the board's request.

Discounted Cash Flow Approaches to Analyzing Capital Investment Projects

Chapter 6

The analysis of a proposed capital investment project begins with the estimation of the incremental cash flows associated with the project. The analyst can then derive from these expected cash flows certain measures of the profitability of the proposed project.

CASH FLOW FRAMEWORK

The cash flows associated with a capital investment project are of essentially three types. First, there is an initial investment outlay. Second, there are future net cash benefits to be realized from the investment. Third, there may be a future benefit or cost associated with terminating the project (e.g., salvage value).

Three points deserve emphasis. First, the costs and benefits associated with a capital investment project are measured in terms of cash flow rather than earnings. Capital budgeting is concerned with cash flow rather than earnings because the former rather than the latter is required to meet the firm's debt obligations, to reinvest in other projects, and to pay dividends. Second, these cash flows should be measured on an *after-tax basis*. Third, the cash flows should be measured on an *incremental basis*, that is, as the difference between the firm's cash flows with and without the proposed project.

Calculation of Incremental Free Cash Flow

The incremental free cash flow for a capital investment project during any particular period is calculated in the following manner:

Change in cash revenue
- change in cash expenses (excluding financing charges)
- change in noncash expenses deductible for tax purposes

Change in pretax income (excluding financing charges)
- change in income taxes

Change in net income (excluding financing charges)
+ change in noncash expenses deductible for tax purposes
+ change in income taxes that are deferred

Incremental operating cash flow
- incremental capital expenditures for the project

Incremental free cash flow (6-1)

The *noncash expenses deductible for tax purposes* consist principally of depreciation, depletion, and amortization expenses, and incremental capital expenditures for the project include incremental investment in working capital and expenditures for capital improvements.

It is important to note in Formula 6-1 that financial charges are excluded from the calculation of incremental free cash flow. These financing charges—interest and preferred stock dividends—as well as the rate of return on equity required by the firm's owners, are taken into account separately in the analysis through the calculation of the required rate of return that is used to discount the incremental free cash flow stream. The method of discounting these cash flows is described below. The calculation of the required rate of return based on the firm's financing charges is discussed in Chapter 8.

Illustration of Calculation of Incremental Free Cash Flow

Consider Washington Chemical Corporation's proposed expansion of its New Jersey plant referred to in Table 6-1. For the moment, assume that this plant expansion is the only capital investment project Washington Chemical has under consideration. Assume also that the expected-case scenario actually unfolds. The initial investment is $58 million:

Cost of plant and equipment	$51,000,000
Increased investment in inventory	5,000,000
Increased investment in receivables	2,000,000
Total investment	$58,000,000

Table 6-1
Required Investment and Anticipated Returns
under Different Business Scenarios for
Three Alternative Chemical Projects
(Dollar Amounts in Millions)

Alternative	Scenario	Probability	Required Investment	Expected Annual Incremental Free Cash Flow in Years										
				1–2	3–4	5	6–8	9	10	11–15	16–20	21	22–24	25
Build new plant in New York	B	.25	$85.5	21.0	22.0	22.0	22.0	22.0	14.0	14.0	6.0	5.0	—	—
	E	.50	90.5	20.0	22.0	22.0	24.0	24.0	24.0	12.0	6.0	—	—	—
	W	.25	93.0	20.0	22.0	22.0	24.0	24.0	12.0	12.0	6.0	(5.0)	—	—
Build new plant in New Jersey	B	.20	82.0	21.0	22.0	22.0	22.0	25.0	25.0	15.0	15.0	6.0	6.0	15.0
	E	.70	85.0	20.0	22.0	22.0	22.0	24.0	24.0	12.0	12.0	6.0	6.0	10.0
	W	.10	89.5	20.0	20.0	20.0	20.0	16.0	16.0	12.0	12.0	6.0	6.0	—
Expand existing plant in New Jersey	B	.20	58.0	16.5	18.0	18.0	19.5	15.0	21.0	—	—	—	—	—
	E	.60	58.0	15.0	17.5	12.5	15.5	11.0	19.0	—	—	—	—	—
	W	.20	62.0	15.0	17.0	13.0	15.0	10.0	5.0	—	—	—	—	—

Table 6-2
Annual Cash Flows Associated with
Expansion of New Jersey Plant
(Dollar Amounts in Millions)

	Initial Cost	Years 1–2	Years 3–4	Year 5	Years 6–8	Year 9	Year 10
Investment	$ (58.0)	—	—	—	—	—	—
Cash revenue		$100.0	$120.0	$120.0	$100.0	$ 80.0	$ 80.0
Cash expenses		75.0	90.0	90.0	75.0	64.0	64.0
Depreciation (tax)		5.0	5.0	5.0	6.0	6.0	6.0
Pretax income		20.0	25.0	25.0	19.0	10.0	10.0
Taxes		10.0	12.5	12.5	9.5	5.0	5.0
Net income		10.0	12.5	12.5	9.5	5.0	5.0
Depreciation		5.0	5.0	5.0	6.0	6.0	6.0
Incremental operating cash flow		$ 15.0	$ 17.5	$ 17.5	$ 15.5	$ 11.0	$ 11.0
Nonoperating cash flows:							
Capital improvements		—	—	$ (5.0)	—	—	—
Total		—	—	$ (5.0)	—	—	—
Incremental free cash flow		$ 15.0	$ 17.5	$ 12.5	$ 15.5	$ 11.0	$ 11.0
Terminal value:							
Salvage value							$ 1.0
Release of working capital							7.0
Total							$ 8.0

The total investment includes the required *increases* in Washington's working capital as well as the cost of plant and equipment.

The expected annual incremental free cash flow stream is shown in Table 6-2. The additional plant and equipment are assumed to have a useful economic life of 10 years, at the end of which the equipment will have a salvage value of $1,000,000. The plant and equipment are assumed to be depreciable for tax purposes on a straight-line basis over the 10-year period, resulting in depreciation expenses of [1]

$$\frac{\$51,000,000 - 1,000,000}{10} = \$5,000,000 \text{ per year}$$

Additional modernization expenses of $5,000,000 will be required near the end of the fifth year, resulting in an additional $1,000,000 of depreciation expense in years 6 to 10. State and federal income taxes are assumed to be 50% of pretax income.

Replacement Capital Investments

The foregoing example illustrates the calculation of the incremental free cash flow stream associated with the purchase of additional assets. Capital budgeting is also concerned with the improvement and replacement of existing assets. Indeed, most firms periodically reevaluate their capital investments to determine which assets should be modernized or upgraded, which assets need to be replaced, and which investments should be discontinued.

Illustration of Calculation of Replacement's Incremental Free Cash Flow

Washington Chemical Corporation is considering whether to replace the conveyor system in its New Mexico plant. The existing system has a tax basis of $500,000, which can be depreciated for tax purposes over 5 years. The plant engineer estimates that the existing system could be used for up to an additional 9 years. The new system will cost $2,700,000, which can be depreciated for tax purposes over a 9-year period, and will result in expected pretax operating savings of $900,000 per year. If the existing system is replaced, Washington estimates that it could sell it for only $150,000.

The initial cash outlay in this case is equal to the purchase price of the new conveyor system less the after-tax cash flow associated with the disposal of the existing system. Assuming a 50% tax rate, the $350,000 loss on disposal of the existing system results in tax savings of $175,000 (provided Washington Chemical's pretax income is at least $350,000). Washington Chemical's investment is:

Purchase price of new conveyor system	$2,700,000
Minus cash inflow from sale of existing system	150,000
Minus tax savings from loss on disposal	175,000
Total investment	$2,375,000

Note that the original purchase price of the existing conveyor system does not enter into this calculation. This original cost is a *sunk cost*; it was incurred in the past and, hence, cannot be affected by the decision to replace or not to replace the existing conveyor system.

The annual incremental free cash flow stream resulting from this investment is calculated by modifying Formula 6-1 in the following manner:

	Years 1–5 ($000)		Years 6–9 ($000)
Pretax cash operating savings		$900	$900
Depreciation on new system	$300		$300
Less depreciation on old system	100		—
Changes in depreciation		200	300
Changes in pretax income		700	600
Changes in taxes (at 50% marginal tax rate)		350	300
Changes in net income		350	300
Changes in depreciation		200	300
Incremental free cash flow		$550	$600

Mutually Exclusive Projects and Independent Projects

The techniques discussed in Part 2 are designed to be applied to a collection of proposals, each of which is independent with respect to some and mutually exclusive with respect to the others. A collection of investment proposals is *mutually exclusive* if acceptance of one precludes acceptance of any of the others. For example, the firm may have decided that for strategic reasons it can invest in only one of three plants it has under consideration.

An investment proposal is *dependent* on another if its acceptance is contingent on another project's acceptance. For example, investment in a particular machine may be dependent on expansion of a particular plant. When two or more proposed projects are dependent on one another, the range of alternatives should be redefined so that each dependent proposal is included in a larger project of which its dependency makes it a part. This eliminates the dependencies. To continue the example, the machine would not be considered a separate investment; the machine and plant expansion would be considered as one proposal.

PAYBACK PERIOD

The *payback period* is the length of time required for the firm to recover its initial cash investment. The payback period is calculated by summing the annual incremental free cash flows for years 1, 2, etc., until the sum equals the initial outlay. In the special case in which the incremental free cash flow is the same each year,

$$\frac{\text{Payback}}{\text{period}} = \frac{\text{initial cash}}{\text{investment}} \div \frac{\text{incremental}}{\text{free cash flow}}{\text{per year}} \tag{6-2}$$

For example, a capital investment project requiring an initial cash investment of $1,000,000 and providing an incremental free cash flow of $200,000 per year has a payback period of $1,000,000/200,000 = 5 years.

Illustration of Payback Calculation

The payback period for the plant expansion considered earlier in this chapter is approximately 3.6 years because

$$58 = 15 + 15 + 17.5 + 0.6 \times 17.5$$

The payback period for the new conveyor system is

$$\frac{\$2,375,000}{\$550,000} = 4.32 \text{ years}$$

Application of Payback Period to Capital Investment Analysis

The payback period can be used to evaluate capital investment projects in the following manner. Management can establish a maximum acceptable payback period. Only projects that meet this test are accepted. For example, if Washington Chemical's management requires a payback period of 4 years or less, the plant expansion is acceptable but the new conveyor system is not.

Payback period could, in theory, be used to select from among a set of mutually exclusive investment projects. The firm would pursue the project having the shortest payback period. But, obviously, use of this criterion is likely to produce poor results. The payback period calculation ignores free cash flow that occurs after the corporation has recovered its initial investment. The payback calculation also ignores the magnitude and timing of cash flows during the payback period. For example, consider two investment projects that have the following free cash flows:

	Invest- ment	Free Cash Flow				
		Year 1	Year 2	Year 3	Year 4	Year 5
Project A	100	50	50	—	—	—
Project B	100	75	25	50	50	50

Each has a 2-year payback period but project B is clearly more desirable.

As this example illustrates, an investment project's payback period cannot be regarded as a measure of its profitability.

In practice, payback period is often used in conjunction with the measures of a project's profitability that are discussed below. Because it provides management with some insight into the liquidity and riskiness of a project, cash-poor companies often find it a useful measure. As long as the firm expects to be able to borrow or to sell stock in the future, however, profitability rather than liquidity should be the primary concern. Because of its weaknesses, payback period seems more appropriate as a constraint to be satisfied than as an objective to be minimized.

AVERAGE RATE OF RETURN ON INVESTMENT

The *average rate of return on investment* (ROI) measures the profitability of a proposed capital investment project as the ratio of the average annual incremental free cash flow to the average investment:

$$\text{ROI} = \frac{\text{average annual incremental free cash flow}}{} \div \text{average investment} \tag{6-3}$$

For example, assuming straight-line depreciation, the average rate of return on investment for a capital investment project requiring an initial cash investment of $1,000,000 and providing an incremental free cash flow of $200,000 per year is

$$\text{ROI} = \frac{\$200,000}{\$1,000,000/2} = 40.0\%$$

Some analysts prefer to use the initial cash investment in the denominator of Formula 6-3. Others prefer to use net income instead of average annual free cash flow in the numerator, although that approach suffers from the disadvantage inherent in using accounting income rather than cash flow to measure investment returns.

The average rate of return on investment is widely used at least in part because of its simplicity. The ROI of a proposed project is easily calculated and compared with a minimum required rate of return, or *hurdle rate*, to determine whether the firm should accept the proposal. The ROI measure has some significant shortcomings, however. The averaging of annual incremental free cash flows in the numerator of Formula 6-3 ignores the time value of money. For example, consider two projects having the following free cash flows:

	Invest- ment	Free Cash Flow							
		Year 1	Year 2	Year 3	Year 4	Year 5	Year 6	Year 7	Year 8
Project A	120	20	15	10	20	20	25	25	25
Project B	120	0	15	30	20	20	20	20	35

Both projects have an ROI of 33% (= 20/60), but project A is clearly more profitable. In addition, the ROI calculation does not take into account the length of a project's life. For example, suppose there is a project C that requires the same investment as projects A and B and that yields the same free cash flow as project A through the eighth year but yields an additional 20 in the ninth year. Project C also has a 33% ROI, although it is clearly preferable to the other two projects.

NET PRESENT VALUE

The payback-period approach and the average-rate-of-return-on-investment approach to evaluating proposed capital investment projects both ignore the time value of money. The discounted cash flow approaches to evaluating capital investment projects do take the time value of money into account.

Net-Present-Value Calculation

The *net present value* (NPV) of a capital investment project equals the present value of the incremental free cash flow stream plus the present value of the terminal value of the project less the original investment:

$$
\text{NPV} = \sum_{t=1}^{\text{life}} \left[\begin{array}{l} \text{incremental} \\ \text{free cash flow}(t) \end{array} \div \left(1 + \frac{\text{discount}}{\text{rate}} \right)^t \right]
$$
$$
+ \left[\begin{array}{l} \text{terminal} \\ \text{value} \end{array} \div \left(1 + \frac{\text{discount}}{\text{rate}} \right)^{\text{life}} \right] - \text{investment} \qquad (6\text{-}4)
$$

where *incremental free cash flow*(t) is the net cash benefit (possibly negative) during period t, *terminal value* is the salvage value less disposal costs upon termination of the project, *investment* denotes the initial cash outlay, and *life* denotes the useful economic life of the project.

The *discount rate* in Formula 6-4 deserves special mention. Each expected incremental free cash flow is discounted at the discount rate, which is the firm's *hurdle rate*, or minimum acceptable rate of return. The hurdle rate should be the rate of return the firm could realize on other investments having the same degree of risk as the project under consideration. The calculation of this rate is discussed in Chapter 8. For now, assume that the discount rate is given.

Application of Net-Present-Value Criterion

Independent capital investment projects are acceptable if and only if net present value is positive, $NPV > 0$, and are rejected if net present value is negative, $NPV < 0$. In the in-between case, $NPV = 0$, and the firm is indifferent about undertaking or not undertaking the project. In the case of mutually exclusive proposals, the one with the largest net present value is accepted (provided at least one of the NPVs is nonnegative) and the others are rejected.

This criterion is easily interpreted. If net present value is positive, the present value of the cash inflows exceeds the present value of the cash outflows; on a time-weighted basis, investing in the project would enhance the wealth of the firm's shareholders.

Illustration of Net-Present-Value Calculation

Washington Chemical's hurdle rate for the plant expansion discussed earlier is 15%. The net present value of the proposed project is

$$NPV = -58.0 + \frac{15.0}{1.15} + \frac{15.0}{(1.15)^2} + \frac{17.5}{(1.15)^3} + \frac{17.5}{(1.15)^4}$$

$$+ \frac{12.5}{(1.15)^5} + \frac{15.5}{(1.15)^6} + \frac{15.5}{(1.15)^7} + \frac{15.5}{(1.15)^8}$$

$$+ \frac{11.0}{(1.15)^9} + \frac{19.0}{(1.15)^{10}}$$

$$= \$19.53 \text{ million}$$

The hurdle rate for the less risky investment in a new conveyor system is 12%. The net present value of this investment is

$$NPV = -2375 + \frac{550}{1.12} + \frac{550}{(1.12)^2} + \frac{550}{(1.12)^3}$$

$$+ \frac{550}{(1.12)^4} + \frac{550}{(1.12)^5} + \frac{600}{(1.12)^6}$$

$$+ \frac{600}{(1.12)^7} + \frac{600}{(1.12)^8} + \frac{600}{(1.12)^9}$$

$$= \$641,700$$

Because the net present value of both projects is positive, both would be accepted if they were independent of other possible projects.

Sensitivity of Net Present Value to the Discount Rate

It should be evident from Formula 6-4 that a larger value for *discount rate* reduces NPV when *incremental free cash flow(t)* and *terminal value* are all positive. Also, when two or more proposals are compared, a larger value for the discount rate tends to work in favor of projects whose cash inflows are concentrated in the early years. For example, consider two projects with associated cash flows:

	Invest-ment	Net Cash Benefit			
		Year 1	Year 2	Year 3	Year 4
Project A	−100	50	50	20	20
Project B	−100	20	20	60	60

The net present value of each varies with the hurdle rate in the following manner:

	Net Present Value at Discount Rate of					
	0%	4%	8%	12%	16%	20%
Project A	40.00	29.18	19.74	11.45	4.12	−2.39
Project B	60.00	42.35	27.40	14.64	3.68	−5.79

Not only the net present value of each project but also the rankings of the projects can vary with changes in the hurdle rate. For example, project A is preferred if the discount rate is 16%, but project B is preferred if it is only 12%. Consequently, the choice of an appropriate discount rate is crucially important to the usefulness of the net-present-value criterion.

INTERNAL RATE OF RETURN

The *internal rate of return* (IRR) of an investment project is the discount rate that equates the net present value of the project's aggregate cash flow stream to zero:

$$0 = \text{NPV} = \sum_{t=1}^{\text{life}} \left[\begin{matrix} \text{incremental} \\ \text{free cash flow}(t) \end{matrix} \div (1 + \text{IRR})^t \right]$$

$$+ \left[\text{terminal value} \div (1 + \text{IRR})^{\text{life}} \right] - \text{investment} \quad (6\text{-}5)$$

A financial hand-held calculator can be used to find IRR.

Relationship to Net-Present-Value Criterion

In Formula 6-5, $\text{NPV} = 0$ is given and the discount rate is to be calculated. In contrast, in Formula 6-4, the discount rate is given and NPV is to be calculated. NPV and IRR are related in a much more fundamental way, however, as shown in Figure 6-1. Note that if *discount rate* < IRR, then NPV > 0; and if *discount rate* > IRR, then NPV < 0.

It is therefore possible to extend the acceptance criterion from the previous section. Independent capital investment projects for which all cash flows other than the initial outlay are positive are accepted (rejected) if the internal rate of return is greater than (less than) the hurdle rate. In the case of mutually

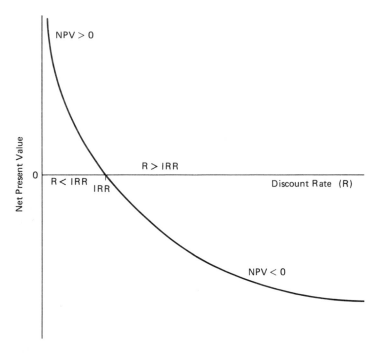

Figure 6-1.   Relationship between net present value and internal rate of return.

exclusive proposals, the one with the highest internal rate of return is normally accepted (provided at least one of the IRRs exceeds the hurdle rate) and the others are rejected. These criteria are applicable to most projects. However, the internal-rate-of-return method breaks down when some of the later incremental free cash flows are negative. Complexities can also arise when two or more mutually exclusive projects are compared.

Illustration of Internal-Rate-of-Return Calculation

Consider the proposed investment in a new conveyor system discussed earlier in the chapter. With the aid of a hand-held calculator, the internal rate of return is found to be IRR = 20.94%, which exceeds Washington Chemical's 12% hurdle rate.

Complications

The internal rate of return in the preceding example is unique. This is usually but not always the case. To illustrate, consider an investment involving the following cash flows:

Year	0	1	2
Cash flow	−$10,000	$26,000	−$16,800

Solving for the internal rate of return produces two values: 20 and 40%. The problem is due mathematically to the two reversals of sign in the cash flow stream. When more than one reversal in sign occurs, more than one solution, or "root," is possible.

When more than one root occurs, which one is "the" internal rate of return? Actually, neither one. The firm has effectively borrowed $16,800 from the project at the end of year 1 and will repay it at the end of year 2. The proposal consists, then, of an investment at time 0 with payback in year 1 coupled with a disinvestment in year 1 with repayment in year 2. Analysis of such a proposal using the internal-rate-of-return method is cumbersome and is more easily accomplished using the net-present-value method.

COMPARISON OF ANALYTICAL TECHNIQUES

In general, the two time-adjusted approaches lead to the same accept/reject decision for independent investment proposals and, because they take into account the time value of money, these approaches are generally regarded as superior to the non-time-adjusted approaches. There are, however, important differences between the methods and, in the case of mutually exclusive proposals, the two methods may give contradictory results. For this reason, many analysts prefer the net-present-value method over the internal-rate-of-return method.

Independent Proposals

The accept/reject criteria for the two time-adjusted approaches are summarized below:

Method	Accept Proposal	Reject Proposal	Indifferent
Net present value	NPV > 0	NPV < 0	NPV = 0
Internal rate of return	IRR > R	IRR < R	IRR = R

where R denotes the firm's hurdle rate. The relationships are illustrated in Figure 6-1.

Mutually Exclusive Proposals

Consider two proposals A and B that have the following expected cash flows:

	Expected Cash Flows, Thousands of Dollars						
	Year 0	Year 1	Year 2	Year 3	Year 4	Year 5	Year 6
Project A	−150	60	60	60	60	60	60
Project B	−150	40	40	60	80	80	100

Proposals A and B have internal rates of return of 32.66 and 30.53%, respectively. If the firm's hurdle rate is 15%, however, the net present values of the two proposals are $77,069 and $83,226, respectively. Thus, proposal A is preferred over proposal B if the internal-rate-of-return method is used, but the ordering is reversed if the net-present-value method is used. As illustrated in Figure 6-2, the hurdle rate would have to be greater than 20.56% in order for proposal A to have a higher net present value than proposal B. If the hurdle rate is less than 20.56% and if the proposals are mutually exclusive, some way must be found to resolve this conflict.

Resolution of this conflict becomes even more crucial when the sizes of the investment projects differ. For example, suppose the expected internal rate of

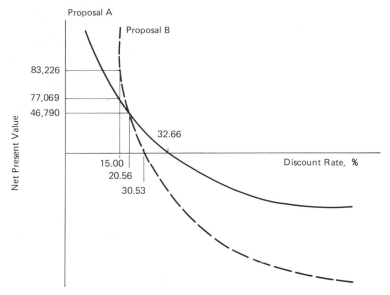

Figure 6-2. Comparison of mutually exclusive proposals using the net-present-value and internal-rate-of-return methods.

return from a $10,000 project is 30% and the expected internal rate of return from a $100,000 project is 29%. One must determine that the implicit returns on the incremental $90,000 investment are inadequate before rejecting the $100,000 project.

The conflict results from the different rates at which the two methods implicitly assume that the incremental free cash flows are compounded. The internal-rate-of-return method implicitly assumes that incremental free cash flows are reinvested at the internal rate of return, whereas the net-present-value method implicitly assumes that they are reinvested at the hurdle rate. To illustrate, suppose that $10,000 is invested in a project that produces no income the first year, $15,000 the second year, and no income thereafter. The project's internal rate of return is 22.474%. If the firm's hurdle rate is 15%, the project's net present value is $1342. Note that if $11,342 (= $10,000 investment + $1342 NPV) is invested at 15% interest (annually compounded), the compound amount at the end of 2 years is $15,000 by Formula 4-3, which is the payout at the end of the project's useful life. Alternatively, if $10,000 (= $10,000 investment + $0 NPV) is invested at 22.474% interest, the compound amount at the end of 2 years is, once again, $15,000.

Which method is better thus depends on the firm's reinvestment rate. Which is the closer approximation—the internal rate of return or the hurdle rate? If neither, then one could use the expected reinvestment rate for each period and use Formula 4-4 to calculate the compound amount of each year's incremental free cash flows as of the end of the project's useful life. These could be summed to obtain a future value for each project. Unfortunately, this would require estimating a reinvestment rate for each period. If one must choose between the internal-rate-of-return and the net-present-value methods, the latter is generally considered to be superior.[2]

Modified Internal-Rate-of-Return Method

In practice, the internal-rate-of-return method is probably the more widely used of the two methods. Many financial managers find it easier to interpret. Because of this, it is useful to consider how the method can be modified to accommodate mutually exclusive proposals. This is done in the following manner:

1. Calculate the differential cash flows.
2. Calculate the internal rate of return for the differential cash flows.
3. If this internal rate of return exceeds the firm's hurdle rate, accept the project that has the greater aggregate nondiscounted cash flow.

Illustration of Modified
Internal-Rate-of-Return Calculation

Consider again the proposals A and B introduced earlier in this section. The differential cash flows are:

	Expected Cash Flows, Thousands of Dollars						
	Year 0	Year 1	Year 2	Year 3	Year 4	Year 5	Year 6
Proposal A	−150	60	60	60	60	60	60
Proposal B	−150	40	40	60	80	80	100
Differential	0	20	20	0	−20	−20	−40

The internal rate of return of the differential cash flows is 20.56%. Since 20.56% > 15%, proposal B, which has the greater aggregate nondiscounted cash flow, is preferred. Applied properly, the modified internal-rate-of-return method leads to the same decision as the net-present-value method.

SUMMARY

Capital budgeting involves evaluating the profitability of spending what are often large sums on a capital investment project when the returns are distant and uncertain and when investing in that project may preclude investing in other (mutually exclusive) projects. This chapter discussed four techniques analysts use to assess the economics of proposed capital investments: payback period, average rate of return on investment, net present value, and internal rate of return. The payback-period and average-rate-of-return-on-investment methods both ignore the time value of money. The net-present-value and internal-rate-of-return methods do not and are thus more reliable tools for assessing a capital investment project's worth to the firm's shareholders.

The net-present-value and internal-rate-of-return methods make different assumptions concerning the reinvestment rate. Because of this, the two techniques can lead to inconsistent rankings of mutually exclusive proposals. Nevertheless, as a practical matter, the two normally provide consistent results, and the internal-rate-of-return method appears to be the most widely used capital budgeting tool.

Corporations should accept all independent investment proposals that have a positive net present value or, equivalently in most cases, an internal rate of return that exceeds the corporation's hurdle rate. They should invest in the project from among a set of mutually exclusive projects that has the highest net present value.

Evaluating Risky Capital Investment Projects

The future cash flows associated with a proposed capital investment are not known with certainty. They are, at best, estimates. These estimates may be subject to a high degree of uncertainty, for example, as in the case of an investment in new plant and equipment to produce a new product. Or they may be subject to only a modest degree of uncertainty, for example, as in the case of the replacement of equipment to produce a firmly established product.

Uncertainty, or risk, is an important factor in the capital budgeting process. A firm should undertake a capital investment project only if the *risk-adjusted* after-tax returns are greater than those the firm could realize by investing in some alternative project. This chapter describes procedures for modifying the basic analytical techniques presented in Chapter 6 to account for project risks. It also discusses certain other refinements to the incremental free cash flow calculations to reflect taxes and other factors that can affect future incremental free cash flow.

INCREMENTAL CASH FLOWS RECONSIDERED

Certain provisions of the tax code, notably accelerated depreciation and the investment tax credit, enhance the economics of capital investment projects.

Accelerated Depreciation

The Internal Revenue Code has traditionally permitted businesses to claim depreciation deductions for tax purposes on an accelerated basis. The precise method has changed from time to time. Table 7-1 describes three methods the Code has permitted businesses to use at one time or another. To illustrate

97

the difference between these accelerated methods and the straight-line method, consider the purchase for $50,000 of tools and special equipment with a depreciable life of 5 years. The amounts of depreciation expense calculated under the four methods are:

Year	Straight-Line Method	Sum-of-the-Years'-Digits Method	Double-Declining-Balance Method	150% Declining-Balance Method
1	$10,000	$16,667	$20,000	$15,000
2	10,000	13,333	12,000	10,500
3	10,000	10,000	7,200	8,167
4	10,000	6,667	5,400	8,167
5	10,000	3,333	5,400	8,166
Total	$50,000	$50,000	$50,000	$50,000

Total depreciation expense is the same under all four methods but the accelerated methods permit greater depreciation deductions in the early years. The sum-of-the-years'-digits method permits deductions of $5/15$ of the value of the investment the first year, $4/15$ the second year, and so on. (Note that the denominator in these fractions is the sum $1 + 2 + 3 + 4 + 5 = 15$.) The double-declining-balance method permits deductions amounting to 40% of the undepreciated balance each year switching to the straight-line method

Table 7-1
Description of Accelerated Depreciation Methods

Method	Description
Sum-of-the-years'-digits method	Depreciation expense each year equals the number of years remaining in the asset's useful life divided by the sum of the years' digits and multiplied by the cost of the asset net of its salvage value.
Double-declining-balance method	Depreciation expense equals twice the straight-line rate applied each year to the net asset balance (original cost minus accumulated depreciation) with a switch to the straight-line method around or sometime after (depending on salvage value) the midpoint of the life of the asset.
150% declining-balance method	Same as double-declining-balance method except that 150% rather than 200% of the straight-line depreciation rate is used (before the switchover).

in the fourth year. The 150% declining-balance method permits deductions amounting to 30% of the undepreciated balance each year with the switch to the straight-line method occurring in the third year.

The greater depreciation expense in the early years leads to lower income tax expense and, hence, enhanced cash flow in those years. Of course, depreciation expense is lower and, as a result, cash flow is lower in the later years. But because money has a time value, shifting cash flow from the later years to the early years is advantageous to the firm. The net present value and the internal . rate of return of an investment project are higher and the payback period is shorter when the accelerated methods are used.

Illustration of Impact of Accelerated Depreciation. Suppose the tools and special equipment mentioned above have incremental cash flows in years 1 to 5 of $20,000 per year when depreciation is calculated on a straight-line basis. Suppose also that the firm's marginal tax rate is 46% and that its hurdle rate is 15%. Using accelerated depreciation significantly enhances the investment's attractiveness.

Year	Straight-Line Method; Incremental Free Cash Flow	Sum-of-the-Years'-Digits Method		Double-Declining-Balance Method	
		Additional Depreciation	Incremental Free Cash Flow	Additional Depreciation	Incremental Free Cash Flow
0	−$50,000	—	−$50,000	—	−$50,000
1	20,000	$6667	23,067	$10,000	24,600
2	20,000	3333	21,533	2,000	20,920
3	20,000	—	20,000	−2,800	18,712
4	20,000	−3333	18,467	−4,600	17,884
5	20,000	−6667	16,933	−4,600	17,884
Total	$50,000	$ 0	$50,000	$ 0	$50,000
NPV	$17,043		$18,468		$18,630
IRR	28.65%		30.68%		31.00%
Payback period	2.50 years		2.27 years		2.24 years

Depreciable Life. It was assumed in the preceding example that the asset's useful economic life was the same as its depreciable life. The Code establishes depreciable lives that are, in many cases, substantially shorter than the useful economic lives of assets used by businesses. This further accelerates depreciation tax deductions.

Taxes

Incremental free cash flow is calculated on an after-tax basis. In addition to accelerated depreciation, the Code at various times has permitted companies to claim an investment tax credit, sometimes supplemented by other special tax credits such as an energy tax credit, for certain qualifying capital investments. The amount of the credit available has often been as high as 10% of the asset's cost. The amount of the credit effectively reduces the size of the initial investment outlay. For example, suppose the tools and special equipment in the example presented earlier qualify for an investment tax credit of 6%. On the assumption that the firm's tax bill was large enough to allow the full credit, $3000 (6% of $50,000) would be subtracted from the amount of taxes owed in the year the tools and equipment are put into use.[1] The firm's investment is thus effectively reduced to $47,000.[2]

There is one other important tax factor. If the salvage value at the end of a depreciable asset's useful life is greater (less) than the firm's tax basis in the asset, the firm will have to recognize a gain (loss) for tax purposes. In general, the firm can deduct such a loss from ordinary income but must include the gain, to the extent of the depreciation deductions claimed in the past, in ordinary income. Any excess of gain over previous depreciation deductions is taxed as a capital gain.

ECONOMIC LIFE RECONSIDERED

Two refinements in the treatment of useful economic life are required. First, it may be desirable to abandon a project before the end of its economic life. Second, mutually exclusive alternatives should be analyzed over the same time span.

Abandonment and Asset Replacement

An investment project's useful economic life is the period over which it is expected to produce incremental annual free cash flow. Depending on the magnitude of these cash flows and the abandonment values that are realizable, it may be more advantageous for the firm to abandon the project before the end of its useful life. This is the case when the present value of the abandonment value exceeds the present value of the incremental free cash flow stream foregone as a result of abandonment.

With the exception of the special case of like-for-like replacement, which is treated below, the date of abandonment can be estimated in the following manner. Reexpress Formula 6-4 as

$$\text{NPV}(J) = \sum_{t=0}^{J} \left[\text{incremental free cash flow}(t) \div (1 + \text{discount rate})^t\right]$$

$$+ \left[\text{abandonment value in year } J \div (1 + \text{discount rate})^J\right]$$

$$(7\text{-}1)$$

Discount rate is the firm's hurdle rate, *abandonment value in year J* denotes the abandonment value of the project (net of abandonment expenses and related taxes) at the end of year J, and $NPV(J)$ is the sum of the present value of the annual incremental free cash flows through the year of abandonment plus the present value of the net cash proceeds from abandonment. The planned date of abandonment is the year J that maximizes $NPV(J)$.[3]

Illustration of Abandonment Calculation

A firm estimates the following expected annual incremental free cash flows and year-end abandonment values for a proposed investment project:

	Thousands of Dollars						
	Year 0	Year 1	Year 2	Year 3	Year 4	Year 5	Year 6
Expected cash flow	−$25.0	$10.0	$15.0	$12.0	$10.0	$ 5.0	$ 3.0
Abandonment value	—	12.0	10.0	8.0	6.0	5.0	—
NPV(J) (at 15%)	—	5.9	2.6	8.2	12.1	13.6	12.4

If the firm's hurdle rate is 15%, the project should be abandoned after 5 years because $NPV(J)$ is then maximized. This is the case because the present value of the abandonment proceeds ($2486) exceeds the present value of the expected cash flow that would have to be foregone as a result of abandonment ($1297). Five years rather than 6 years would therefore be used as the project's "useful life."

Like-for-Like Replacement

In the special case of like-for-like replacement, the net-present-value calculation summarized in Formula 7-1 must be modified to take the replacement of assets directly into account. A study by Gaumnitz and Emery[4] concludes that if the asset is to be replaced at regular intervals forever, this can be done by dividing each of the $NPV(J)$'s in Formula 7-1 by the quantity $1 - \exp(-J \times$ discount rate):

$$\text{Adjusted } NPV(J) = NPV(J) \div [1 - \exp(-J \times \text{discount rate})]$$

$$= \left[\sum_{t=0}^{J} \frac{\text{incremental free cash flow}(t)}{\left(1 + \frac{\text{discount}}{\text{rate}}\right)^t} + \frac{\text{abandonment value in year } J}{\left(1 + \frac{\text{discount}}{\text{rate}}\right)^J} \right]$$

$$\div \left[1 - \exp\left(-J \times \frac{\text{discount}}{\text{rate}}\right) \right] \quad (7\text{-}2)$$

where exp $(-J \times$ discount rate) denotes the number e raised to the power $(-J \times$ discount rate), which can be performed on a hand-held calculator. The optimal replacement period is found by determining the value of J for which *adjusted NPV(J)* is maximized.

Illustration of Abandonment Calculation Continued

Suppose now that the investment project in question involves an asset that the firm expects to replace at regular intervals forever. It follows from Formula 7-2 that

	Thousands of Dollars					
	Year 1	Year 2	Year 3	Year 4	Year 5	Year 6
Adjusted NPV(J)	−$42.4	$10.0	$22.6	$26.8	$25.8	$20.9

The firm should thus replace the asset every 4 years. Note that the holding period in this case is shorter than if the asset were not to be replaced. Even though the firm could increase the net present value of benefits realized during the initial cycle by holding the asset for a fifth year, that would postpone the start of the next holding period by 1 year. In this case, the costs of such postponement outweigh the near-term benefits of holding the asset for a fifth year.

If an investment proposal involves an asset that the firm expects to replace regularly, the optimal replacement period and the associated value of adjusted NPV(J) should be used in its evaluation.

Comparable Time Span

Mutually exclusive investment proposals should be evaluated over the same time span. For example, suppose one is considering replacing a machine that has 3 years remaining in its useful economic life. It would be unusual for the replacement item to have a useful economic life of only 3 years. The useful lives must be made comparable, however, before the net replacement savings can be calculated. If incremental free cash flow after the expiration of the useful life of the machine to be replaced were included in the calculation without regard for the rate at which cash flows can be reinvested over the period spanning the ends of their useful economic lives, the decision would be biased.

To handle such problems, one can assume (for analytical purposes only) that the replacement asset would be abandoned after 3 years. There are three ways this could be done. One could estimate an abandonment value, calculate the net present value of replacement, and replace the asset if this value is positive. Another way would be to use the incremental free cash flows to calculate the abandonment value at which the firm would be indifferent between holding and replacing the asset in question, and then base the replacement decision on whether the expected abandonment value exceeds this break-even abandonment value. A third way would be to assume that the cash flows from the two assets are reinvested over a period equal to the longer of the assets' useful economic lives and select the proposal that promises the greater terminal value.

Unequal economic lives are also troublesome when the modified internal-rate-of-return method is used to select from among a collection of mutually exclusive projects. In such cases, it is normally easier to use the net-present-value method than to modify further the internal-rate-of-return method.

Illustration of Adjustment for Unequal Useful Lives

Suppose project A with a useful economic life of 7 years and costing $150,000 has a net present value of $100,000 and project B with a useful economic life of 10 years and also costing $150,000 has a net present value of $120,000. Suppose further that the firm's hurdle rate is 15% and that the firm can earn a 15% annual return on investments between years 7 and 10. Project A has a terminal value of $100,000 \times (1.15)^7$. That sum invested for 3 years yields $100,000 \times (1.15)^7 \times (1.15)^3 = \$100,000 \times (1.15)^{10}$, which has a present value of $100,000 \times (1.15)^{10}/(1.15)^{10} = \$100,000$. Thus, $100,000 is also the net present value of project A extended to a 10-year life. The firm would prefer project B. Note that as long as the firm's hurdle rate measures the opportunity cost of funds tied up in one project beyond the end of a competing project's useful economic life, the projects' net present values do not need to be adjusted; the project with the highest net present value is selected. But if the $100,000 \times (1.15)^7$ sum could not be invested at the firm's hurdle rate, then the net present value of project A would have to be adjusted accordingly before the two projects' net present values could be compared meaningfully.

CAPITAL RATIONING

Some firms arbitrarily impose a constraint on capital spending. This most often takes one of two forms: a policy of financing all capital expenditures internally or capital budget ceilings imposed on the firm's operating divisions. With such a constraint, the firm may be unable to invest in all projects whose expected net present value is positive. In that case, profitable opportunities would be eschewed and the firm would not maximize its share price.

When a capital spending contraint exists, the firm attempts to select the combination of proposals that provides the greatest net present value consistent with satisfying the constraint. This may require accepting a number of smaller, less profitable projects rather than the largest, most profitable project. For example, consider a division that faces a $1,000,000 capital budget constraint and has available the following investment opportunities:

	Proposal 1	Proposal 2	Proposal 3
Initial outlay	$750,000	$600,000	$400,000
Net present value	$225,000	$156,000	$ 92,000

The division would have to select proposals 2 and 3 in order to stay within the constraint, even though proposal 1 is the most profitable.

The foregoing example is somewhat oversimplified; such rigid one-period constraints are unusual, and the division would undoubtedly consider other possible uses for the $250,000 remaining if proposal 1 were selected. Usually, there is some flexibility in the constraint; capital costs can be spread over two or more periods; investment projects can be postponed rather than fore-gone entirely; and differences in project payback periods will affect the cash flow available for future projects. Capital rationing, if done at all, should be carried out in a multiperiod context.[5] Despite this shortcoming, the example nevertheless demonstrates that self-imposed capital rationing tends to produce a less-than-optimal investment policy. The firm should accept all independent capital investment projects that yield returns in excess of its hurdle rates for those projects. To do otherwise interferes with the financial markets' rationing of capital among firms.

RISK CONSIDERATIONS

The future cash inflows from a project are inherently unpredictable. This makes returns variable and projects risky. The managers of a corporation can make an educated guess as to the cash inflows it might realize from a project. But this educated guess is necessarily based on certain assumptions regarding the future business and economic environment, and these assumptions may not be borne out by future events.

The analyst can quantify in two ways some of the risks the corporation takes when it invests in a project. First, the analyst can measure the sensitivity of net present value (or internal rate of return) to variation in key parameters such as the price of output, volume of output, price of each key input, capital cost of the project, and so on. Second, the analyst can adjust the net-present-value or internal-rate-of-return calculation to take project risks explicitly into account.

Sensitivity Analysis

Testing the sensitivity of investment returns to variation in key parameters is called *sensitivity analysis*. Normally, the analyst begins with a base case analysis. The base case reflects the cash flows anticipated in what the firm regards as the most likely future operating climate for the investment project. The analyst calculates the net present value, internal rate of return, or value of whatever other profitability measure is desired that the base case implies for the project. The analyst then varies each of the parameters one at a time by some specified increment or decrement and calculates the net present value (or value of whatever profitability measure the firm has chosen) that would result from the new cash flow stream.

Illustration of Sensitivity Analysis

Table 7-2 reports the results of a sensitivity analysis for a proposed copper mine and smelter in Africa, the copper output from which would be transported to Europe for sale. The table shows the impact of variations of plus or minus 10% and plus or minus 25% on the base case net present value of variation in each of the parameters the project's sponsors identified as having an important influence on project economics. The table is constructed such that the two right-most columns report the impact on net present value of a 10 or 25% increase, respectively, in each particular revenue item during each year of the project's

Table 7-2
Sensitivity Analysis for a Proposed
Copper Mine and Smelter
(Dollar Amounts in Millions)
Base Case Net Present Value $87.6

	Net Present Value when Parameter Changes by*			
Sensitivity to	−25%†	−10%†	+10%‡	+25%‡
Increase in price of copper	$(110.9)	$10.7	$162.6	$248.5
Increase in annual rate of output	(65.4)	25.3	142.1	231.9
Increase in size of ore reserves	(20.7)	43.8	125.2	189.3
Decrease in capital cost	50.5	71.5	103.2	125.9
Decrease in construction period	65.1	78.2	95.3	107.9
Decrease in operating cost	(15.3)	44.5	132.1	199.3
Decrease in cost of labor	42.8	69.2	105.4	131.5
Decrease in cost of electricity	21.0	60.9	114.3	161.1
Decrease in transportation cost	27.7	64.1	110.9	148.3

*Numbers in parentheses denote decreases.
†Denotes decrease in revenue item or increase in expense item.
‡Denotes increase in revenue item or decrease in expense item.

useful life and of a 10 or 25% decrease, respectively, in each particular cost item during each year of the project's useful life. The two left-most columns indicate the impact of changes in the opposite direction. Similar tables could have been constructed for internal rate of return, payback period, or some other quantity.

The project's expected net present value is $87.6 million. The net present value is most sensitive to variation in the price of copper. A 10% increase in the projected price of copper during each year of the project's projected economic life would increase net present value by 85.6% to $162.6 million. This would suggest that if the project sponsor wishes to reduce the degree of risk associated with investing in the project, the sponsor should first consider possible means of reducing price uncertainty (e.g., by hedging or by entering into long-term copper sale contracts), then the means to reduce uncertainty as to output levels (e.g., by examining more closely the operating reliability of the smelter and the mine), then the means of reducing operating cost uncertainty (e.g., by entering into long-term supply contracts covering electricity or other inputs), and so on.

Sensitivity analysis like that in the preceding example also provides some guidance to the analyst concerning how to go about defining future business scenarios for use in project risk analysis.

Project Risk Analysis

The analyst can also accommodate risk and uncertainty by modifying the formulas for net present value or internal rate of return appropriately. In the case of net present value, the analyst can risk adjust the incremental free cash flows and then discount the risk-adjusted incremental free cash flows at the riskless rate of interest. Alternatively, he or she can risk adjust the discount rate and then discount the expected cash flows at the risk-adjusted discount rate. Chapter 9 describes procedures for risk adjusting the discount rate to reflect the risks that are specific to the project under consideration.

The first approach mentioned, adjusting the cash flows, is discussed here. One particularly useful approach is to define scenarios that represent alternative future states of the business and economic climate surrounding the project and then specify an incremental free cash flow stream for each. The relative likelihoods of occurrence of these scenarios determine the variability of project cash flows and hence project returns.

The variability of a project's possible returns indicates the riskiness of the project. *Risk analysis* involves measuring this variability. By calculating the variance (or standard deviation) of the net present value (or variance or standard deviation of internal rate of return) of a project and comparing this value with the variances (or standard deviations) calculated for other projects, the analyst can gauge the relative riskiness of the project in question relative to that of other projects the corporation is pursuing or has under consideration.

An analyst can measure the riskiness of a proposed project in the following manner. With the aid of top management, the analyst specifies certain future business scenarios for each project. For example, three scenarios have been specified for each project in Table 6-1. These have been labeled simply B for best case, E for expected case, and W for worst case. Also with the aid of top management, the analyst can assign a probability to each scenario for each proposal.

Once a scenario has been specified, the analyst can calculate the net present value for the proposed project under that scenario. However, in this case the analyst should discount the future cash flows at the riskless interest rate. According to this approach, uncertainty is accommodated by assigning probabilities to the scenarios that are possible. But once a scenario has been specified, the future cash flows *for that scenario* are treated as though they were certain to occur. Discounting at a risk-adjusted rate would double count the effects of uncertainty: first when the cash flow stream in each scenario is discounted and then again when the probabilities are attached to the scenarios.

For any particular project, the expected net present value, denoted by *expected NPV*, is just the probability-weighted average of the net present values for the different scenarios:

$$\text{Expected} \atop \text{NPV} = \sum_{n=1}^{\substack{\text{number} \\ \text{of scenarios}}} {\text{NPV in} \atop \text{scenario } n} \times {\text{probability of} \atop \text{scenario } n} \qquad (7\text{-}3)$$

NPV in scenario n denotes the present value of the project under scenario n calculated by discounting at the riskless rate of interest. *Probability of scenario n* denotes the relative likelihood that scenario n will occur. *Number of scenarios* denotes the number of distinct scenarios (e.g., number of scenarios = 3 in Table 6-1).

The standard deviation of the net present value, denoted by *standard deviation of NPV*, is just the square root of the probability-weighted average of the squared deviations around the expected net present value:

$$\text{Standard} \atop {\text{deviation} = \atop \text{of NPV}} \sqrt{\sum_{n=1}^{\substack{\text{number} \\ \text{of scenarios}}} \left({\text{NPV in} \atop \text{scenario } n} - {\text{expected} \atop \text{NPV}} \right)^2 \times {\text{probability of} \atop \text{scenario } n}}$$

$$(7\text{-}4)$$

The greater the standard deviation of NPV, the greater the degree of dispersion of possible (net present value) returns, and hence risk.

When the expected NPV given by Formula 7-3 or standard deviation of NPV given by Formula 7-4 vary substantially from one project to another, financial managers often find it more meaningful to use a measure of relative dispersion so as to adjust for this. The coefficient of variation is one such measure:

$$\begin{matrix}\text{Coefficient}\\\text{of variation}\end{matrix} = \begin{matrix}\text{standard}\\\text{deviation}\\\text{of NPV}\end{matrix} \div \begin{matrix}\text{expected}\\\text{NPV}\end{matrix} \qquad (7\text{-}5)$$

For example, if two projects each have standard deviation of 1000 but the expected net present value of the first is 500 and the expected net present value of the second is 5000, the second is relatively less risky than the first.

Illustration of Project Risk Analysis

Table 7-3 summarizes the risk analysis for the three projects in Table 6-1. The riskless interest rate is assumed to be 10%. It is further assumed that Washington Chemical can reinvest annual cash flows at a rate of return equal to the 10% riskless rate so that the cash flow streams do not have to be adjusted before discounting.

The proposed new New Jersey plant has an expected net present value that is more than twice as large as the expected net present value of the plant expansion. The coefficient of variation for the new New Jersey plant is less than half that of the plant expansion. Thus, the new New Jersey plant involves twice the return for half the risk of the expansion and is thus clearly a superior project.

The comparison of the new New York and New Jersey plants is less clearcut. The New York plant promises roughly three-quarters of the New Jersey plant's expected net present value but also involves substantially lower risk. However, the New Jersey plant promises substantially better returns in its expected case than the New York plant does in its best case. Thus unless

Table 7-3
Project Risk Analysis for Three
Alternative Chemical Projects
(Dollar Amounts in Millions)

	Build New York Plant	Build New Jersey Plant	Expand New Jersey Plant
Net present value (probability)			
Best case	$71.44 (.25)	$93.62 (.20)	$52.20 (.20)
Expected case	68.90 (.50)	80.51 (.70)	36.82 (.60)
Worst case	61.10 (.25)	61.41 (.10)	25.82 (.20)
Expected net present value	$67.59	$81.22	$37.70
Standard deviation of net present value	3.89	8.39	8.41
Coefficient of variation	.06	.10	.22

the decision maker is very risk averse, he or she would probably prefer the New Jersey plant over the New York plant.

Probability of Negative NPV

One other measure of risk that can prove useful is the probability that the net present value of future returns discounted at the riskless interest rate will be negative. The inverse of coefficient of variation in Formula 7-5 represents the number of standard deviations that expected NPV lies to the right of zero. If it is assumed that the net present values for a particular project corresponding to the different scenarios follow the bell-shaped normal probability distribution, a table of standard normal probabilities can be used to find the probability that the net present value of the project will be negative.

Illustration of Probability Calculation

An analysis of the proposed new conveyor system discussed in Chapter 6 suggests net present value savings of $850,000 in the best case (probability .30); $500,000 in the expected case (probability .40); and zero savings in the worst case (probability .30). The expected net present value savings are

$$\text{Expected} \atop \text{NPV} \ - \ \$850,000 \times .3 + 500,000 \times .4 + 0 \times .3 = \$455,000$$

and the standard deviation of the net present value savings is

$$\text{Standard} \atop \text{deviation} \ = \ \sqrt{(395,000)^2 \times .3 + (45,000)^2 \times .4 + (-455,000)^2 \times .3} \atop \text{of NPV}$$

$$= \$331,248$$

The value of the expected net present value savings lies

$$\frac{\$455,000}{\$331,248} = 1.37$$

standard deviations to the right of zero. The area under a standard normal probability curve to the left of −1.37 thus represents the probability that the net present value might be less than zero. A standard normal probability table indicates that this probability is .0853. Thus, there is less than a 10% chance that the present value of the incremental free cash flows from the new conveyor system would fall short of the investment's $2,375,000 cost.

SUMMARY

In evaluating proposed capital investment projects, it is important to reflect taxes and abandonment values accurately and to adjust the analysis for unequal useful economic lives. The investment tax credit and accelerated depreciation provisions of the Internal Revenue Code enhance the incremental annual free cash flows during the early years of a project's life and thus increase the profitability of capital investments to the firm.

Capital budgeting analyses should also take project risks explicitly into account. This can be done by measuring the sensitivity of investment returns to variation in key parameters or by adjusting for risk in the calculation of net present value and internal rate of return. Firms typically employ both techniques.

The survey of capital budgeting methods presented in Chapters 6 and 7 gives the analyst a set of well-defined procedures to use in evaluating capital investment projects. Nevertheless, capital budgeting, particularly when it comes to risk analysis, is more art than science. Estimating future cash flows and assessing probabilities are necessarily inexact. Notwithstanding these problems, careful consideration of a reasonable range of future operating scenarios coupled with the correct application of capital budgeting techniques can play an important role in helping the firm make informed and intelligent capital investment decisions.

Measuring a Company's Cost of Capital

In Chapters 6 and 7 we took as given the firm's cost of capital. This chapter describes techniques for measuring the cost of capital as the weighted average of the costs of funds the firm raises from different sources.

WHAT IS THE COST OF CAPITAL?

A company raises the funds it needs to finance a capital investment project from various sources. These include principally debt, preferred (and preference) equity, and common equity. These classes of funds differ in their fundamental financial characteristics. For example, the interest payments on debt are deductible for tax purposes, whereas dividends on preferred stock and common stock are not. On the other hand, if a company misses a debt interest payment or principal repayment, the holders of its debt can force it into bankruptcy; the holders of preferred stock and common stock do not enjoy this right.

Because of these and other differing risk-return characteristics, the particular blend of debt and equity financing can affect the firm's overall cost of capital. The *cost of capital* is the minimum rate of return that the firm must earn on a capital investment project, given the firm's chosen mix of funds sources, in order for the firm's share price to remain unchanged. If the firm realizes a higher rate of return, the share price should increase. If the realized rate of return is less than the cost of capital, the share price should decrease.

The cost of capital can be calculated by first determining separately the cost of funds from each source and then combining these component costs of funds into an overall "weighted average cost of capital." This cost calculation is not the whole story, of course. We must also explore how the firm chooses the most appropriate mix of funds sources—because this mix determines the "weights" in the cost of capital calculation—but we defer the discussion of this issue until Part 3.

MEASURING THE COST OF LONG-TERM DEBT

Corporations issue a variety of long-term debt instruments. Some are *convertible*, offering the holder the option to exchange the debt instrument for a specified number of shares of the corporation's common stock during some specified period. In this section we are concerned with *straight*, or nonconvertible, debt.

Long-term debt instruments have certain features in common. Each calls for the payment of interest at a specified coupon rate at regular intervals. Each also has a specified maturity date at which time the issuer makes the final mandatory redemption payment. Many issues have a *bullet* maturity at which the issuer repays the entire principal amount in one lump sum; others provide for a *sinking fund* consisting of two or more mandatory redemption payments. Because of these common features, the same basic approach, based on discounted cash flow analysis, serves to calculate the cost of any straight debt issue.

The *cost of long-term debt*, or the *cost of borrowing* (associated with long-term debt), is the unit cost a company must pay for the use of borrowed funds. Equivalently, it is the rate of return the company would have to earn upon investment of the borrowed funds in its business in order to generate sufficient cash to pay interest on the borrowed funds and repay principal on time. The calculation of this cost must take two important factors into account. First, the issuer has available for its use the offering price of the issue *net* of the costs of issuance (gross spread plus expenses). Second, because the net cash flows expected from an investment project are calculated on an after-tax basis, the cost of funds utilized to finance the project should also be expressed net of tax in the weighted average cost of capital calculation in order to make costs and benefits comparable.

The cost of long-term debt is calculated in the following manner. Let *price* denote the aggregate dollar price at which the issue is sold to investors, and let *amount* denote the aggregate principal amount of the issue. (The principal amount of each bond is typically $1000.) Amount is also the sum the company must repay bond holders. Price may differ from amount. If price < amount, the bonds are said to be sold at a *discount*; if price > amount, the bonds are said to be sold at a *premium*.

The issuer must also pay certain issuance expenses, such as printing and engraving charges, legal fees, and fees paid to securities firms to market the issue. Denote the aggregate amount (for the entire issue) of these expenses plus spread or commission by *expenses*. The issuer thus realizes *net proceeds* = price − expenses.

The issuer incurs after-tax interest expense amounting to $(1 - tax\ rate) \times interest(t)$ during each of the t years the issue remains outstanding, where tax rate denotes the issuer's marginal ordinary income tax rate. If there is no sinking fund, this expense is the same each year: $Interest(t) = coupon \times amount$ for all years t. In addition, the issuer can amortize the expenses for tax purposes over the life of the issue, which provides a tax shield. The tax effect is similar to that which depreciation affords: a noncash expense that reduces the taxes that the firm would otherwise have to pay. If there is no sinking fund, the issuer can then amortize these expenses on a straight-line basis. The tax shield amounts to *tax rate × expenses ÷ maturity in years* each year. When there is a sinking fund, the issuer can (1) allocate the expenses pro rata among the sinking fund payments and then (2) for each such payment, allocate the pro rata amount over the period the sinking fund amount remains outstanding on a straight-line basis. Finally, when bonds are not issued at their par value, the discount or premium that results is amortized for tax purposes under the effective interest method, that is, as interest implicitly compounds. The issuer uses the bonds' yield to maturity to make this allocation. Amortizing a discount provides an additional tax shield, while amortizing a premium produces noncash income that is taxable. Let *amortization(t)* denote the amount of expenses plus discount (or less premium) allocated to year t.

If there is no sinking fund, the issuer repays *amount* at maturity. When there is a sinking fund, the issuer of the debt must make payments amounting to *sinking fund(t)* during year t. Because these payments must in the aggregate retire the entire issue,

$$\sum_{t=1}^{\substack{\text{maturity} \\ \text{in years}}} \text{sinking fund}(t) = \text{amount}$$

The after-tax cost of debt, expressed on an annual basis, satisfies the equation:

$$\begin{aligned} \text{Net} \atop \text{proceeds} = &\sum_{t=1}^{\substack{\text{maturity} \\ \text{in years}}} \left[\left(1 - \frac{\text{tax}}{\text{rate}}\right) \times \text{interest}(t) + \frac{\text{sinking}}{\text{fund}(t)} \right. \\ &\left. - \frac{\text{tax}}{\text{rate}} \times \text{amortization}(t) \right] \\ &\div (1 + \text{cost of debt})^t \end{aligned} \qquad (8\text{-}1)$$

For an issue that does not have a sinking fund, set sinking fund$(t) = 0$ for all years but the last, and set sinking fund$(t) =$ amount for the last year. For such issues Formula 8-1 can be easier to work with when it is reexpressed on a per-bond basis by dividing each side of the equation by amount. The cost of debt is just the internal rate of return of the stream of after-tax debt service payments, which can be obtained with the aid of any hand-held calculator that contains an internal rate of return routine. Note that the cost of debt calculation assumes that the issuer does not redeem the debt prior to its scheduled maturity.

Formula 8-1 leads to the cost of debt only if interest is paid annually, as is the case with Eurobond issues. Domestic debt issues require semiannual interest payments: $(1 - \text{tax rate}) \times \text{coupon} \times \text{amount}/2$ every 6 months when there is no sinking fund. In addition, the amortization per semiannual period is amortization(t). When interest is paid semiannually, the semiannually compounded after-tax cost of debt solves the equation:

$$
\begin{aligned}
\frac{\text{Net}}{\text{proceeds}} = \sum_{t=1}^{\substack{\text{number of} \\ \text{periods}}} & \left[\left(1 - \frac{\text{tax}}{\text{rate}} \right) \times \text{interest}(t) + \frac{\text{sinking}}{\text{fund}(t)} \right. \\
& \left. - \frac{\text{tax}}{\text{rate}} \times \text{amortization}(t) \right] \\
& \div \left(1 + \frac{\text{cost of debt}}{2} \right)^t
\end{aligned}
\tag{8-2}
$$

Note that *cost of debt* is expressed on an annualized basis (i.e., percent per annum), as is customary. Note also that if the pretax cost of borrowing is desired, we simply set tax rate $= 0$ in Formulas 8-1 or 8-2, as appropriate.

Illustration of Cost of Discounted Non-Sinking Fund Debt Calculation

On June 7, 1979, Duke Power Company sold $150,000,000 principal amount of $10\frac{1}{8}\%$ first and refunding mortgage bonds due 2009 at a price of 99.50%. The issue has a bullet maturity. Issuance expenses consisted of an underwriting spread of 0.875% and out-of-pocket expenses of $205,000. Thus, Duke Power realized net proceeds of

Gross proceeds	$0.995 \times 150{,}000{,}000 =$	$149,250,000
Less U/W commission	$0.00875 \times 150{,}000{,}000 =$	1,312,500
Less misc. expenses		205,000
Net proceeds		$147,732,500

Semiannual interest expense amounts to

$$\frac{\$(1 - 0.46) \times 0.10125 \times 150,000,000}{2} = \$4,100,625$$

assuming a 46% tax rate. The aggregate discount is \$750,000 (= 0.005 × \$150,000,000). When the percentage discount is 1% or less, little accuracy is lost by assuming straight-line amortization of the discount for tax purposes. Under this treatment, the semiannual amortization tax shield is

$$\frac{\$(0.46) \times [(205,000 + 1,312,500) + 750,000]}{60} = \$17,384$$

Duke Power's after-tax cost of borrowing solves the equation

$$147,732,500 = \sum_{t=1}^{60} \left[(4,100,625 - 17,384) \div \left(1 + \frac{\text{cost of debt}}{2} \right)^t \right]$$
$$+ \left[150,000,000 \div \left(1 + \frac{\text{cost of debt}}{2} \right)^{60} \right]$$

or

$$\text{Cost of debt} = 0.0555, \text{ or } 5.55\%$$

Following the same sequence of steps with tax rate = 0 gives

$$\text{Pretax cost of debt} = 0.1029, \text{ or } 10.29\%$$

Illustration of Cost of Sinking Fund Debt Calculation

On June 21, 1979, Cordis Corporation sold \$20,000,000 principal amount of $12\frac{1}{4}\%$ subordinated sinking fund debentures due 1999 at a price of 99.50%. The gross underwriting spread was 3.00% and out-of-pocket expenses were \$200,000. Table 8-1 provides the after-tax cash flow debt service stream.

Applying Formula 8-2, Cordis Corporation's

$$\text{Cost of debt} = 0.0705, \text{ or } 7.05\%$$

A Special Case

Note that if price = amount and there are no issuance expenses or other cash inflows or cash outflows associated with the debt issue:

$$\text{Cost of debt} = (1 - \text{tax rate}) \times \text{coupon} \tag{8-3}$$

Table 8-1
After-Tax Cash Flows Associated With Cordis Corporation's 12¼% Debt Issue*

Period	Net Proceeds	After-Tax Interest	Expense Amortization†	Amortization of Discount‡	Amortization Tax Shields	Sinking Fund Payment	Net Cash Flow§
0	$19,100,000	—	—	—	—	—	−$19,100,000
1	—	$ 661,500	$ 6,531	$ 1,158	$ 3,537	—	657,963
2	—	661,500	6,532	1,230	3,571	—	657,929
3	—	661,500	6,531	1,306	3,605	—	657,895
4	—	661,500	6,532	1,386	3,642	—	657,858
5	—	661,500	6,531	1,471	3,681	—	657,819
6	—	661,500	6,531	1,562	3,723	—	657,777
7	—	661,500	6,532	1,658	3,767	—	657,733
8	—	661,500	6,531	1,760	3,814	—	657,686
9	—	661,500	6,532	1,869	3,864	—	657,636
10	—	661,500	6,531	1,984	3,917	—	657,583
11	—	661,500	6,531	2,113	3,976	—	657,524
12	—	661,500	6,532	2,243	4,037	—	657,463
13	—	661,500	6,531	2,381	4,100	—	657,400
14	—	661,500	6,532	2,527	4,167	—	657,333
15	—	661,500	6,531	2,682	4,238	—	657,262
16	—	661,500	6,531	2,847	4,314	—	657,186
17	—	661,500	6,532	3,022	4,395	—	657,105
18	—	661,500	6,531	3,208	4,480	—	657,020
19	—	661,500	6,532	3,405	4,571	—	656,929
20	—	661,500	6,531	3,616	4,668	$ 1,400,000	2,056,832
21	—	615,195	5,831	3,332	4,215	—	610,980
22	—	615,195	5,832	3,536	4,309	1,400,000	2,010,886
23	—	568,890	5,195	3,241	3,881	—	565,009
24	—	568,890	5,195	3,440	3,972	1,400,000	1,964,918
25	—	522,585	4,612	3,139	3,565	—	519,020
26	—	522,585	4,612	3,332	3,654	1,400,000	1,918,931

27	—	476,280	4,073	3,023	3,264	—	473,016
28	—	476,280	4,073	3,208	3,349	1,400,000	1,872,931
29	—	429,975	3,573	2,892	2,974	—	427,001
30	—	429,975	3,573	3,070	3,056	1,400,000	1,826,919
31	—	383,670	3,107	2,740	2,690	—	380,980
32	—	383,670	3,107	2,907	2,766	1,400,000	1,780,904
33	—	337,365	2,669	2,573	2,411	—	334,954
34	—	337,365	2,669	2,731	2,484	1,400,000	1,734,881
35	—	291,060	2,257	2,387	2,136	—	288,924
36	—	291,060	2,257	2,534	2,204	1,400,000	1,688,856
37	—	244,755	1,868	2,177	1,861	—	242,894
38	—	244,755	1,869	2,311	1,923	1,400,000	1,642,832
39	—	198,450	1,500	1,940	1,582	—	196,868
40	—	198,450	1,500	2,059	1,637	6,000,000	6,196,813
Total	$19,100,000	$21,366,450	$200,000	$100,000	$138,000	$20,000,000	$22,128,450

* Assumes a 46% marginal ordinary income tax rate.

† The $200,000 of out-of-pocket expenses are allocated pro rata among the 11 sinking fund payments. Each of the first 10 payments represents 7% of the issue and has 7% of the expenses ($14,000) allocated to it. The final payment represents 30% of the issue and has 30% of the expenses ($60,000) allocated to it. The expenses so attributable to each sinking fund amount are allocated on a straight-line basis over the period the sinking fund amount remains outstanding. For each semiannual period, the respective portions of expenses associated with the sinking fund amounts that are outstanding that period are summed and then rounded to the nearest dollar. Fractional amounts are allocated to nearby periods so that total expense amortization equals $200,000.

‡ The discount is amortized under the effective interest method. The effective interest rate used in this calculation is the debt issue's offering yield, 12.3232% on a semiannually compounded basis, which can be calculated by applying Formula 8-2 with $19,900,000 (principal amount net of discount) in place of net proceeds and tax rate = 0. The offering yield is applied to the unamortized balance at the beginning of a period to get the amount of actual interest plus imputed interest (i.e. amortization of the discount) consistent with a yield of 12.3232%. Then the amount of interest actually paid that period is subtracted to obtain the portion of the aggregate discount that corresponds to the amount of imputed interest for that period. For the first period, the beginning balance is $19,900,000. Applying the 12.3232% yield gives interest plus amortization of $1,226,158.40. Subtracting the $1,225,000 interest payment gives amortization of $1158.40, which is added to the unamortized balance. For the second period, the unamortized balance is $19,901,158.40. Applying the 12.3232% yield gives interest plus amortization of $1,226,229.78. Subtracting the $1,225,000 interest payment gives amortization of $1229.78. And so on. The unamortized balance is also reduced in later periods for sinking fund payments.

§ Negative sign indicates a cash inflow, and a positive sign indicates a cash outflow

For example, if Duke Power had sold the $10\frac{1}{8}\%$ bonds at par without incurring any issuance expenses, it would have realized

$$\text{Cost of debt} = (1 - 0.46) \times 0.10125 = 0.0547, \text{ or } 5.47\%$$

Note that Formulas 8-1 to 8-3 assume that the issuer expects to earn sufficient revenue to be able to claim the full interest deduction for tax purposes each interest period over the entire life of the issue. If it does not, for example, because substantial accelerated depreciation deductions will reduce taxable income to zero during certain periods, then tax rate = 0 should be used for those periods in which the corporation expects to lose the interest tax deduction forever, and a present value tax rate should be used for those periods for which the corporation expects to have to defer the interest deduction to a later period.

MEASURING THE COST OF PREFERRED STOCK

In general, dividend payments are declared at the discretion of the company's board of directors, and dividend payments and principal repayments, if any, are contingent on sufficient funds being legally available therefor. In practice, most issuers view these dividend and sinking fund payment obligations as fixed obligations because making the payments required on outstanding issues is necessary for continued access to the market.

Cost of Sinking Fund Preferred Stock

If the issuer makes uninterrupted dividend payments and the preferred stock issue has a sinking fund, Formula 8-2 is easily modified to obtain a formula for calculating the cost of preferred stock. This requires three adjustments. Dividends on preferred stock issues are customarily paid quarterly; these payments are not tax deductible; and the issuance expenses and new issue discount, if any, on preferred stock are also not tax deductible.

Let *dividends(t)* denote the amount of dividends paid during quarter t, and let *sinking fund(t)* denote the aggregate sinking fund requirement during quarter t. The cost of sinking fund preferred stock, expressed on a quarterly compounded basis, is the solution to the equation:

$$\begin{aligned}
\text{Net proceeds} = &\sum_{t=1}^{\substack{\text{number} \\ \text{of periods}}} \left[\text{dividends}(t) + \frac{\text{sinking}}{\text{fund}(t)}\right] \\
&\div \left(1 + \frac{\text{cost of sinking fund preferred stock}}{4}\right)^t
\end{aligned} \quad (8\text{-}4)$$

Table 8-2
Quarterly Cash Flows Associated With Aerospace
Corporation's Sinking Fund Preferred Stock Issue

Quarter	Net Proceeds	Dividend Payments	Sinking Fund Payment	Net Cash Flow*
0	$47,023,000	—	—	−$47,023,000
1–64	—	$1,400,000	—	1,400,000
65	—	1,400,000	$5,000,000	6,400,000
66–68	—	1,260,000	—	1,260,000
69	—	1,260,000	5,000,000	6,260,000
70–72	—	1,120,000	—	1,120,000
73	—	1,120,000	5,000,000	6,120,000
74–76	—	980,000	—	980,000
77	—	980,000	5,000,000	5,980,000
78–80	—	840,000	—	840,000
81	—	840,000	5,000,000	5,840,000
82–84	—	700,000	—	700,000
85	—	700,000	5,000,000	5,700,000
86–88	—	560,000	—	560,000
89	—	560,000	5,000,000	5,560,000
90–92	—	420,000	—	420,000
93	—	420,000	5,000,000	5,420,000
94–96	—	280,000	—	280,000
97	—	280,000	5,000,000	5,280,000
98–100	—	140,000	—	140,000
101	—	140,000	5,000,000	5,140,000

*Negative sign indicates a cash inflow, and a positive sign indicates a cash outflow.

Illustration of Cost of Sinking Fund Preferred
Stock Calculation

On August 23, 1979, Aerospace Corporation sold 2,000,000 shares of sinking fund preferred stock at a price of $25.00 per share. The issue will mature 25.25 years from the date of issue (if not called for redemption prior to that date). It carries a $2.80 annual dividend rate and provides for an annual sinking fund that becomes active at the end of the sixteenth year.

Table 8-2 provides the dividend and principal repayment streams associated with the issue. The 2,000,000 shares yielded net proceeds amounting to $47,023,000 after underwriting discounts of $1.35 per share and out-of-pocket expenses of $277,000. The cost of sinking fund preferred stock for the issue was 11.99%.

Companies also issue *preference stock*, typically when charter restrictions on the company's ability to issue additional preferred stock cannot be met. Preference stock is junior to preferred stock, but its provisions are otherwise substantially the same as those of preferred stock. For this reason, Formula 8-4 is also applicable to preference stock.

Cost of Perpetual Preferred Stock

While most of the preferred stock issued in recent years has provided for a sinking fund, most older issues are perpetual, just like common stock. An expression for the cost of perpetual preferred stock can be obtained by manipulating Formula 4-12. This formula expresses the price of a share of stock that makes annual cash dividend payments at a constant dividend rate forever as the ratio of the dividend rate to the appropriate discount rate. From the standpoint of the issuer of preferred stock, this discount rate is the *cost of perpetual preferred stock*, and the present value of the stream of dividend payments it promises to make is the *net proceeds* of the share issue. Manipulating Formula 4-12 gives

$$\begin{matrix} \text{Cost of perpetual} \\ \text{preferred stock} \end{matrix} = \begin{matrix} \text{annual} \\ \text{dividend rate} \\ \text{per share} \end{matrix} \div \begin{matrix} \text{net proceeds} \\ \text{per share} \end{matrix} \qquad (8\text{-}5)$$

Cost of perpetual preferred stock is an after-tax cost because neither dividends nor issuance expenses on preferred stock are tax deductible.

Illustration of Cost of Perpetual Preferred Stock Calculation

On February 21, 1979, Georgia Power Company sold 2,000,000 shares of perpetual preferred stock bearing a dividend rate of $2.56 per share per annum at a price of $25.10 per share. The underwriters charged $0.849 per share, and out-of-pocket expenses amounted to $135,000, or $.0675 per share. The cost of this issue was

$$\begin{matrix} \text{Cost of perpetual} \\ \text{preferred stock} \end{matrix} = \frac{\$2.56}{\$25.10 - (0.849 + 0.0675)} = 0.1059, \text{ or } 10.59\%$$

MEASURING THE COST OF COMMON EQUITY

A company's *cost of common equity* can be defined as the minimum rate of return on common equity the firm must earn at the margin in order to keep its share price from falling; it is the rate of return that investors expect to realize on their investment in the company's common stock. In theory, this cost is the rate at which holders of the firm's common stock discount the future cash returns they expect to receive during the period they hold the stock. These future returns consist of two components: (1) the dividends, if any, the investor will receive during the period the investor holds the shares and (2) the capital gain (or loss) the investor will realize when the investor sells the shares. Unlike debt or preferred stock, the required rate of return cannot be calculated directly because investors' rate of return expectations are not observable directly; instead this required rate of return must be inferred from stock market data.

In principle, a careful analysis of a company's long-term earnings and cash flow prospects would suggest what pattern of cash returns an investor in the company's common stock could reasonably expect to receive. This cash return stream could then be used to calculate the discount rate required to equate the present value of those returns to the company's current share price. However, in order to be workable, such an approach requires certain simplifying assumptions and careful judgement.

Retained Earnings versus New Issues
There are two sources of common equity capital: retained earnings and new issues of shares. Retained earnings entail a lower cost because a new issue involves added expenses, such as an underwriting spread and legal, printing, and other costs. Measurement of the cost of equity capital thus requires that we distinguish between these two sources of funds.

Perpetual Dividend Growth Model
Several discounted cash flow models have been developed for estimating the cost of common equity capital. One of the more frequently applied models is Gordon's perpetual dividend growth model.[1] In this model, the cost of common equity is estimated as the discount rate which equates the present value of the expected future stream of dividends to the current share price.

Cost of Retained Earnings. Recall from Formula 4-11 that the price of a share of common stock can be expressed as the present value of the future dividend stream:

$$\frac{\text{Share}}{\text{price}} = \text{dividends}(1) \div \left(\frac{\text{discount}}{\text{rate}} - \frac{\text{growth}}{\text{rate}}\right)$$

where dividends(1) denotes the estimated annual dividend rate for the coming year and discount rate measures common stock investors' risk-adjusted required rate of return. That is, discount rate is the company's cost of common equity (in particular, its cost of retained earnings). Rearranging terms gives

$$\begin{array}{l} \text{Cost of} \\ \text{retained} \\ \text{earnings} \end{array} = \begin{array}{c} \text{current} \\ \text{indicated annual} \\ \text{dividend yield} \end{array} + \begin{array}{c} \text{projected} \\ \text{dividend} \\ \text{growth rate} \end{array}$$

$$= \left(\begin{array}{c} \text{indicated} \\ \text{annual} \\ \text{dividend rate} \end{array} \div \begin{array}{c} \text{current} \\ \text{share price} \end{array}\right) + \begin{array}{c} \text{projected} \\ \text{dividend} \\ \text{growth rate} \end{array} \qquad (8\text{-}6)$$

In Formula 8-6, the *current indicated annual dividend yield* is calculated by multiplying the most recently declared quarterly dividend rate per share by 4 and dividing by the *current share price*. The most recent closing price for the company's shares or, because share prices are affected by a variety of factors that may distort any one closing price, an average of closing share prices over a recent short period can serve as current share price. Many analysts use the average of the closing prices on the 10 most recent trading days. However, if factors such as merger rumors have distorted the share price over an extended time period, the analyst should gauge the impact of these distortions and adjust the 10-day average share price accordingly when calculating current share price. The *projected dividend growth rate* is the average annual rate at which the company's annual dividend rate per share is expected to grow into the foreseeable future.

It deserves to be emphasized that the *cost of retained earnings* equals the current dividend yield only if projected dividend growth rate = 0. For example, if a stock sells at a 2% dividend yield, this does not mean that investors will be satisfied if the company realizes a 2% return on its equity investments. The low yield reflects investors' expectations that the equity funds will be invested in ventures sufficiently profitable that the firm will be able to increase the dividend rate rapidly in the future. If such growth is not forthcoming, the dividend yield will not remain at 2% for long.

A few words of caution on the use of Formula 8-6 are in order. In order for cost of retained earnings in Formula 8-6 to be a reasonable approximation to the true cost, projected dividend growth rate must be consistent with the expectations of investors at the margin. Second, Formula 8-6 assumes that the dividend rate will grow at a constant (average annual) rate forever. It may be more realistic in some cases to assume that the growth rate of dividends will decrease significantly beyond some point. More exotic models based on different assumed dividend growth patterns exist. In practice, then, projected dividend growth rate represents a projected long-run average. Reports prepared by securities analysts who cover the company under study or its industry often provide information that is helpful in estimating investors' projected dividend growth rate.

The third limitation of Formula 8-6 concerns companies that do not pay a cash dividend on their common stock and cannot be expected to do so in the foreseeable future. Smaller, rapidly growing companies, such as those currently in various high-technology businesses, are typically in this position. Such stocks can nevertheless sell at lofty prices. Investors expect, of course, that these companies will reinvest the retained earnings profitably and so are willing to value the shares with the expectation that the company will eventually be able to pay handsome dividends. It is probably best to use the capital asset pricing model, which is described in Chapter 9, to estimate the cost of common equity for such companies.

Cost of a New Common Stock Issue. The costs of issuing common stock reduce the firm's net proceeds. These costs include the underwriting spread and expenses mentioned in connection with debt and preferred stock issues. In addition, the market price of a company's common stock typically declines on the announcement of an upcoming public offering.

Let *expenses* denote the aggregate underwriting spread and out-of-pocket expenses expressed as a percentage of the offering price, and let *market impact* denote the percentage decrease in the share price that is expected to occur in response to the announcement of the offering. The *cost of a new common stock issue* is obtained by using the share price adjusted for these price effects, current share price × (1 − expenses − market impact), in place of share price in Formula 8-6:

$$
\begin{aligned}
\text{Cost of a new} \atop \text{common stock issue} =\ & \left\{ \text{indicated annual} \atop \text{dividend rate} \right. \\[1em]
& \div \left[\text{current} \atop \text{share price} \times \left(1 - \text{expenses} - \text{market} \atop \text{impact} \right) \right] \Big\} \\[1em]
& + \ \text{projected dividend} \atop \text{growth rate}
\end{aligned}
\tag{8-7}
$$

The market impact can be estimated by measuring the market impact of comparable offerings (percentage decline in share price relative to a suitable stock market index).

Comparison of Formulas 8-6 and 8-7 reveals that the cost of a new common stock issue will always exceed the cost of retained earnings. Thus, it is to the firm's advantage to finance its equity investments internally to the maximum extent possible. The cost premium associated with a new share issue, obtained by subtracting the cost of retained earnings in Formula 8-6 from the cost of a new common stock issue in Formula 8-7, is

$$
\begin{aligned}
\text{New issue} \atop \text{cost premium} =\ & \left[\text{indicated annual} \atop \text{dividend rate} \times \left(\text{expenses} + \text{market} \atop \text{impact} \right) \right] \\[1em]
& \div \left[\text{current} \atop \text{share price} \times \left(1 - \text{expenses} - \text{market} \atop \text{impact} \right) \right] > 0
\end{aligned}
\tag{8-8}
$$

Illustration of Calculation of Cost of Retained Earnings and New Issues. Buchanan Industries' common stock price has averaged $30 over the past 10 trading days, and the stock has traded at around this level for the past month. The current dividend rate is $0.45 per share per quarter. Thus, the indicated annual dividend rate is $1.80 per share. Buchanan projects a long-term rate of growth of earnings per share of 10% per annum, and several securities analysts have quoted this rate in their reports on Buchanan's earnings prospects. Buchanan expects to pay out a constant percentage of its earnings. Projected long-term dividend growth is thus 10% per annum, and Buchanan's approximate cost of retained earnings is

$$\text{Cost of retained earnings} = \frac{1.80}{30.00} + 0.10 = 0.16, \text{ or } 16.00\%$$

Because of a substantial projected increase in its capital budget, Buchanan plans a common stock offering. Buchanan's financial staff has found that recent common stock offerings by Buchanan's principal competitors have required an underwriting spread and issuance expenses per share equal to approximately 6% of the public offering price. These issues suffered a 4% market impact on average (measured as the difference between the issuer's closing share price on the day prior to the announcement date and the public offering price, adjusted for the change in the Standard & Poor's 500 index over the same period). The cost of a new issue is thus

$$\begin{array}{l}\text{Cost of a}\\\text{new common}\\\text{stock issue}\end{array} = \frac{1.80}{30.00\,(1\,-\,0.06\,-\,0.04)} + 0.10 = 0.1667, \text{ or } 16.67\%$$

Combined Cost of Common Equity. Suppose that over time the firm expects to raise a proportion p of its common equity capital internally (and therefore a proportion $1 - p$ through new issues). The combined *cost of common equity* is calculated as the weighted average:

$$\begin{array}{l}\text{Cost of}\\\text{common}\\\text{equity}\end{array} = p \times \begin{array}{l}\text{cost of}\\\text{retained}\\\text{earnings}\end{array} + (1 - p) \times \begin{array}{l}\text{cost of a}\\\text{new common}\\\text{stock issue}\end{array} \qquad (8\text{-}9)$$

Suppose that Buchanan Industries projects that 80% of its common equity capital will be furnished by retained earnings. Buchanan's cost of common equity is thus

$$\begin{array}{l}\text{Cost of}\\\text{common}\\\text{equity}\end{array} = (0.8 \times 0.16) + (0.2 \times 0.1667) = 0.1613, \text{ or } 16.13\%$$

Chapter 9 describes an alternative technique, based on the capital asset pricing model, for estimating a company's cost of common equity, which ties the cost of common equity calculation directly to the actual historical performance of the company's share price.

MEASURING THE COST OF ISSUING CONVERTIBLE SECURITIES

Corporations frequently issue debt securities and preferred (or preference) stock that contain a *conversion option* in addition to the customary features of debt and preferred stock, respectively. The conversion option typically gives the security holder the option to exchange each convertible bond (or each share of convertible preferred stock) for a predetermined number of shares of the issuer's common stock. For example, on April 3, 1980, Hughes Tool Company issued $100 million of $8 \frac{1}{2}\%$ Convertible Subordinated Debentures due April 1, 2005. Each debenture is convertible into 16.0321 shares of Hughes Tool common stock, which represents a conversion price of $\$62\frac{3}{8}$ per Hughes Tool common share. Hughes Tool's common stock closed at a price of $\$52\frac{7}{8}$ on April 2, 1980, implying a *conversion premium* of $(62\frac{3}{8} - 52\frac{7}{8})/52\frac{7}{8} = 0.1797$, or 17.97%.

As discussed in Chapter 21, convertible securities are best viewed as delayed common equity financing. Issuers expect them to be converted at some point and are willing to pay a convertible bond coupon rate or convertible preferred stock dividend rate that exceeds the common stock dividend yield in order to be able to sell deferred common equity at a conversion price that exceeds the prevailing common stock price. Because of this delayed equity feature, measuring the cost of issuing convertible securities should reflect the issuer's expected cost of common equity beyond the expected conversion date.

Measuring the Cost of Issuing Convertible Debt

Convertible debt securities are bought and sold principally on the basis of a payback relationship between the conversion premium on the one hand and the difference between the interest income the convertible debt security provides and the dividend income the underlying common stock would provide on the other. The magnitude of the conversion premium investors will find acceptable depends on the extent to which the convertible debt security provides higher current income to the expected date of conversion.

The payback calculation takes any one of a number of forms, of which the most widely used currently is:

$$\text{Break-even} = \frac{\text{conversion premium}}{\left(1 + \frac{\text{conversion}}{\text{premium}}\right)} \div \left(\begin{array}{c}\text{current annual} \\ \text{interest yield}\end{array} - \begin{array}{c}\text{indicated annual} \\ \text{dividend yield on} \\ \text{common stock}\end{array}\right)$$

$$(8\text{-}10)$$

where the *current annual interest yield* equals the ratio of the annual interest income the bondholder receives to the price he or she paid for the bond. The *break-even* (in years) represents the number of years investors expect to have to hold the convertible debt instrument prior to being able to convert it profitably. The break-even for a newly issued convertible debt security generally varies within a band from 2.0 to 4.0 years.

The break-even can be used in the following manner in estimating the *cost of convertible debt*. Assume the convertible issue is converted on the future date that corresponds to the break-even. Prior to that date, the issuer will make interest payments at the stated coupon rate. Following that date, the issuer will make dividend payments on the common stock issued upon conversion. We may assume that conversion takes place (immediately after the payment of interest) on the interest payment date nearest the break-even date.

The cost of issuing convertible debt can be calculated as the internal rate of return of the stream consisting of after-tax interest payments and amortization tax shields prior to the break-even date and dividend payments after the break-even date. If it is assumed that dividends will grow forever at a constant average annual projected dividend growth rate beyond the break-even date, the following equation can be solved for the cost of convertible debt:

$$
\begin{aligned}
\begin{matrix} \text{Net} \\ \text{proceeds} \\ \text{per bond} \end{matrix} = \sum_{t=1}^{B} & \left[\left(1 - \frac{\text{tax}}{\text{rate}}\right) \times \begin{matrix} \text{interest} \\ \text{per} \\ \text{bond}(t) \end{matrix} \right] \div \left(1 + \frac{\begin{matrix}\text{cost of} \\ \text{convertible debt}\end{matrix}}{2}\right)^{t} \\[2em]
- \sum_{t=1}^{B} & \left[\begin{matrix}\text{tax} \\ \text{rate}\end{matrix} \times \begin{matrix}\text{amort.} \\ \text{per bond}(t)\end{matrix} \right] \div \left(1 + \frac{\begin{matrix}\text{cost of} \\ \text{convertible debt}\end{matrix}}{2}\right)^{t} \\[2em]
+ \ & \frac{\left[\begin{matrix}\text{conversion} \\ \text{ratio}\end{matrix} \times \begin{matrix}\text{indicated annual} \\ \text{dividend rate at} \\ \text{break-even date}\end{matrix} \right]}{\left(\begin{matrix}\text{cost of} \\ \text{convertible} \\ \text{debt}\end{matrix} - \begin{matrix}\text{projected} \\ \text{dividend} \\ \text{growth rate}\end{matrix} \right)} \\[2em]
\div \ & \left(1 + \frac{\begin{matrix}\text{cost of} \\ \text{convertible debt}\end{matrix}}{2}\right)^{B}
\end{aligned}
\tag{8-11}
$$

where *conversion ratio* denotes the number of shares into which each bond is convertible and B denotes break-even. The numerator of the last term represents the present value of the dividend stream beyond the break-even date discounted back to the break-even date at the cost of convertible debt.

Formula 8-11 assumes that the convertible debt issue's sinking fund, if the issue has one, does not become active prior to conversion. This is a reasonable assumption when break-even is in the range from 2.0 to 4.0 years (and even if it were to be somewhat longer). In the second term, the issuer can amortize the costs and expenses and new issue discount, if any, on the convertible issue for tax purposes, on the same basis as a nonconvertible bond up to the conversion date. Any unamortized balance as of the conversion date is treated as part of the cost of issuing the common stock and is thus not tax deductible. The third term in Formula 8-11 effectively attributes the company's cost of retained earnings to the convertible debt issue following the break-even date.[2]

A trial-and-error procedure must be used to find the cost of convertible debt. However, this is not terribly onerous because the relatively short break-even period means that the cash flow stream that must be discounted typically contains a relatively small number of terms.

Illustration of Calculation of Cost of Issuing Convertible Debt

Let us reconsider the Hughes Tool Company convertible debt issue mentioned previously. The conversion premium was 17.97%. The coupon rate on the issue was $8^1/_2\%$, and the current indicated annual dividend yield on Hughes Tool's common stock at the time it issued the convertible debt was $4 \times \$0.21/\$52^7/_8 = 1.59\%$. Applying Formula 8-10 gives

$$\text{Break-even} = \frac{0.1797/1.1797}{0.085 - 0.0159} = 2.20 \text{ years}$$

Thus, we will assume that the bonds are converted at the end of the fourth semiannual interest period.

Assuming that Hughes Tool's marginal tax rate was projected to be 46% for at least the ensuing 2 years, the convertible issue would require after-tax interest payments of $(1 - 0.46) \times 0.085 \times \$1000/2 = \$22.95$ per bond per semiannual period.

The conversion ratio is 16.0321 shares per bond. Over the period 1975 to 1979, Hughes Tool's annual dividend rate per share had grown at an average annual rate of 30.6% per annum. However, earnings per share grew at an average annual rate of 16.6% per annum during the same period. Thus, it is questionable whether the high rate of dividend growth is sustainable. Suppose that a more careful analysis of Hughes Tool's growth prospects suggested an average annual rate of dividend growth of 20% per annum over the next 2 years and of 15% per annum thereafter into the foreseeable future. In that case,

$$\begin{array}{c}\text{Indicated annual} \\ \text{dividend rate at} \\ \text{break-even date}\end{array} = 0.84 \times (1.20)^2 = \$1.21$$

and

$$\begin{array}{c}\text{Projected dividend} \\ \text{growth rate}\end{array} = 0.15$$

Table 8-3
Cash Flows and Cost of Hughes Tool
Company's Convertible Debt Issue

Period	Net Proceeds*	After-Tax Interest	Subsequent Dividend Payments	Net Cash Flow†
0	$986.32	—	—	−$986.32
1–3	—	$22.95	—	22.95
4	—	22.95	$19.399/C‡	22.95 + 19.399/C‡

$$\$986.32 = \sum_{t=1}^{4}\left[22.95 \div \left(1 + \frac{\text{cost of convertible debt}}{2}\right)^t\right]$$

$$+ \left[\frac{19.399}{(\text{cost of convertible debt} - 0.15)}\right.$$

$$\left. \div \left(1 + \frac{\text{cost of convertible debt}}{2}\right)^4\right]$$

Cost of Convertible Debt	Value of Right-Hand Side of Equation
0.1659	$ 962.57
0.1650	1017.43
0.1650	1017.43
Cost	986.32
0.1659	962.57

$$\left.\begin{array}{l}1017.43\\986.32\end{array}\right\}31.11 \quad \left.\begin{array}{l}\\\\\end{array}\right\}54.46 \qquad \frac{31.11}{54.86} \times 0.0009 = 0.0005$$

Cost of convertible debt = 0.1650 + 0.0005 = 0.1655, or 16.55%.

---

*Net proceeds per bond amounted to $1000 issue price less underwriting spread of 1.125% ($11.25 per bond) less also out-of-pocket expenses of $2.43 per bond.
†Negative sign indicates a cash inflow, and a positive sign indicates a cash outflow.
‡C = cost of convertible debt −0.15.

Table 8-3 provides the periodic cash flows and shows the details of the cost calculation. To simplify the example, we have ignored the amortization of issuance costs and expenses. We proceed iteratively beginning with a rough estimate of the cost of retained earnings, 0.0159 + 0.15 = 0.1659, and interpolate at the last step. Cost of convertible debt is roughly 31.11/54.86 of the way from 16.50 to 16.59%, or

$$\text{Cost of convertible debt } = \ 16.55\%$$

Measuring the Cost of Issuing Convertible Preferred Stock

The cost of issuing convertible preferred stock is measured in the same manner as the cost of issuing convertible debt. However, dividends on convertible preferred stock, like dividends on preferred stock generally, are not tax deductible and are paid quarterly. Hence, *dividends per convertible preferred share(t)* replaces *(1 − tax rate) × interest per bond(t)*, *cost of convertible preferred stock ÷ 4* replaces *cost of convertible debt ÷ 2*, and the amortization term disappears.

CALCULATING THE WEIGHTED AVERAGE COST OF CAPITAL

We now blend the separate costs of funds into an overall *cost of capital* for the firm. First we present the procedure. Then we provide a justification for it.

Weighted Average Cost of Capital Formula

The *weighted average cost of capital* for a company is calculated as the weighted average of the costs of the separate sources of funds:

$$
\begin{aligned}
\text{Weighted} \\
\text{average cost} \\
\text{of capital}
\end{aligned} =
\left(
\begin{aligned}
&\text{proportion} \\
&\text{of debt} \\
&\text{financing}
\end{aligned}
\times
\begin{aligned}
&\text{cost of} \\
&\text{debt}
\end{aligned}
\right)
+
\left(
\begin{aligned}
&\text{proportion of} \\
&\text{preferred} \\
&\text{stock financing}
\end{aligned}
\times
\begin{aligned}
&\text{cost of} \\
&\text{preferred} \\
&\text{stock}
\end{aligned}
\right)
$$

$$
+
\left(
\begin{aligned}
&\text{proportion} \\
&\text{of retained} \\
&\text{earnings}
\end{aligned}
\times
\begin{aligned}
&\text{cost of} \\
&\text{retained} \\
&\text{earnings}
\end{aligned}
\right)
$$

$$
+
\left(
\begin{aligned}
&\text{proportion new} \\
&\text{equity issue} \\
&\text{financing}
\end{aligned}
\times
\begin{aligned}
&\text{cost of a} \\
&\text{new common} \\
&\text{stock issue}
\end{aligned}
\right)
+
\left(
\begin{aligned}
&\text{proportion} \\
&\text{conv. debt} \\
&\text{financing}
\end{aligned}
\times
\begin{aligned}
&\text{cost of} \\
&\text{convertible} \\
&\text{debt}
\end{aligned}
\right)
$$

$$
+
\left(
\begin{aligned}
&\text{proportion} \\
&\text{conv. preferred} \\
&\text{financing}
\end{aligned}
\times
\begin{aligned}
&\text{cost of} \\
&\text{convertible} \\
&\text{preferred stock}
\end{aligned}
\right)
$$

$$(8\text{-}12)$$

By definition, the weights in the weighted average cost of capital formula always sum to 1.

The weighted average cost of capital formula provides a measure of the cost of capital for those projects that are a mirror image of the firm. This involves two requirements. First, the project must have the same business risk (or operating risk) profile as the company as a whole. Second, the project must support the same degree of leverage (and hence involve the same degree of financial risk) as the firm as a whole; there are no special debt capacity side effects. When either assumption is not satisfied, the hurdle rate for the project may differ from the company's weighted average cost of capital. Later in this section and in Chapter 9 we describe techniques for handling this problem. For now, it is sufficient to note that if a company is involved in one basic business or in more than one business all of which involve the same basic business risk profile, the weighted average cost of capital formula normally yields reliable hurdle rates for projects that fall within the company's basic line(s) of business.

Calculating the Weights

The weights in Formula 8-12 represent the relative proportions of funds the firm intends to raise from straight debt financing, straight preferred stock financing, retained earnings, new common stock financing, convertible debt financing, and convertible preferred stock financing, respectively, to finance its capital investment projects. The weights must represent the relative proportions based on *relative market values* rather than *relative book values*.

For example, suppose a company intends to maintain its current capital structure and that its capital structure contains $100 million face amount of debt with a market value of $80 million and common equity with a book value of $100 million and a market value of $160 million. The relative proportions of debt and common equity are one-half and one-half, respectively, on a book value basis and $1/3$ (= 80/240) and $2/3$ (= 160/240), respectively, on a market value basis. The market value weights, $1/3$ and $2/3$, should be used in the weighted average cost of capital calculation.

The reason why market value weights should be used instead of book value weights is easily explained. Suppose common stock investors require a 20% rate of return. If a company raised $80 million through an equity issue, and the market value of this equity subsequently increased to $160 million because of profitable investments, would investors expect a 20% return on the original $80 million (implying a 10% return on the $160 million of market value) or a 20% return on the $160 million? They would expect a 20% return on the $160 million market value of equity. Hence, if a company's current capitalization ratios are to be used as weights, they should be calculated on the basis of market values. Moreover, the existing ratios should be used only if they represent the relative proportions in which the firm will raise capital from these sources for future projects. If they differ, the relative proportions in which the firm intends to raise funds *over the longer term* in the future (and *not* just for one particular project) should be used in the weighted average cost of capital calculation.

Illustration of Calculation of Weighted Average Cost of Capital

Let us return to the problem confronting Washington Chemical Corporation. Washington Chemical intends to finance its chemical plant construction one-third with debt and two-thirds with common equity. Washington Chemical can issue new long-term debt bearing a 12% coupon rate. Washington's marginal income tax rate is 50%. Allowing for underwriting spread and issuance expenses, Washington Chemical's treasurer estimates

$$\text{Cost of debt} = 6.10\%$$

with the aid of Formula 8-2. This 6.10% cost has been calculated on a semiannually compounded basis. Washington Chemical wished to discount annual cash flows. The 6.10% cost expressed on an equivalent annually compounded basis is

$$\text{Cost of debt} = \left(1 + \frac{0.0610}{2}\right)^2 - 1 = 0.0619, \text{ or } 6.19\%$$

Washington Chemical's common stock currently provides an indicated annual dividend yield of 3.14%. Washington Chemical's financial planning staff projects long-term quarterly earnings per share growth of 15% per annum with a stable payout ratio. Washington Chemical intends to finance the equity portion of the new plants internally. By Formula 8-6, its

$$\begin{matrix}\text{Cost of} \\ \text{retained earnings}\end{matrix} = 0.0314 + 0.1500 = 0.1814, \text{ or } 18.14\%$$

expressed on a quarterly compounded basis (because dividends are paid quarterly and earnings growth was calculated on a quarterly basis). The 18.14% cost expressed on an equivalent annually compounded basis is

$$\begin{matrix}\text{Cost of} \\ \text{retained earnings}\end{matrix} = \left(1 + \frac{0.1814}{4}\right)^4 - 1 = 0.1941, \text{ or } 19.41\%$$

Washington Chemical's weighted average cost of capital is, by Formula 8-12:

$$\begin{matrix}\text{Weighted average} \\ \text{cost of capital}\end{matrix} = \frac{1}{3} \times 6.19\% + \frac{2}{3} \times 19.41\% = 15.00\%$$

expressed on an annually compounded basis. This is, of course, the hurdle rate we used to evaluate the proposed plant expansion and new plant investments in Chapter 6.

This calculation illustrates two important points. First, the component costs are the expected future costs. A common mistake is to use historical costs, for example, the average cost of debt the firm already has on its books. This historical cost is irrelevant; what matters is the company's cost of incurring additional debt. Second, the component costs should be expressed on a consistent basis, e.g., all expressed on an annually compounded basis or all expressed on some other common basis, which matches the periodicity of the cash flows to be discounted.

Rationale Underlying Weighted Average Cost of Capital Calculation

We have noted that the weighted average cost of capital is desired as a hurdle rate for project evaluation. We noted in Chapter 6 that if a project's internal rate of return just equals its hurdle rate, the project's net present value will be zero, and the firm will be indifferent between undertaking and not undertaking it.

To appreciate the significance of the 15.00% weighted average cost of capital, suppose Washington Chemical's proposed New Jersey plant expansion, which is expected to cost $58.0 million, would produce operating income of $17.4 million per year before taxes. After taxes (at a 50% rate), $8.7 million is left to service debt and to provide a return to Washington Chemical's stockholders. This $8.7 million represents an after-tax rate of return of 15% on capital invested in the project. Washington Chemical has raised $19,333,333 (= $58,000,000/3) of debt, which costs 6.19% per annum to service on an after-tax basis. This utilizes $1,196,733 (= $19,333,333 × 0.0619) of the after-tax operating income, leaving $7,503,267 for shareholders. Washington Chemical provided $38,666,667 (= $58,000,000 × $2/3$) of internally generated funds. Thus, it realizes a rate of return of

$$\frac{\$7,503,267}{\$38,666,667} = 0.1941, \text{ or } 19.41\%$$

on equity, which we calculated earlier as Washington Chemical's cost of equity capital.

If Washington Chemical earns its 15% hurdle rate on its $58 million investment, it will be able to service the debt it has raised and have just enough of a surplus to provide the minimum rate of return shareholders require. This is, quite simply, precisely what the weighted average cost of capital formula is designed to accomplish.

Cost of Capital for a Division or a Project

A company's weighted average cost of capital should be used as the hurdle rate for a project only if the project's business risk profile mirrors the business risk profile of the firm and the project will support exactly the same degree of financial leverage as the firm. In particular, if the proposed project is not in the company's main line of business or if the company is in two or more unrelated lines of business (with different business risk profiles), it is inappropriate to use a single hurdle rate for all projects. However, if each line of business is contained in a different division, a separate cost of capital can be calculated for each division. Chapter 9 describes a procedure for accomplishing this.

The weighted average cost of capital formula also breaks down when the firm's capital investment and financing decisions are not independent. If a project involves debt capacity side effects, such as the ability to support higher leverage than the firm customarily maintains, the cost or benefit of these side effects is not reflected in the weighted average cost of capital calculation. In such situations, the adjusted present value method, which is discussed in Chapter 9, is more appropriate than discounting expected future cash flows from the project at the firm's (or any division's) weighted average cost of capital.

SUMMARY

A company's cost of capital for a project is the minimum rate of return that the company must earn on capital invested in that project in order not to suffer a fall in its share price. Under certain circumstances, this cost of capital, or hurdle rate, can be calculated simply as a weighted average of the separate costs the company must pay to raise debt, preferred equity, or common equity, or to sell convertible securities. This weighted average cost of capital can serve meaningfully as the hurdle rate for a proposed capital investment project so long as the business risk profile of a project mirrors the company's overall business risk profile and the project will support precisely the same degree of leverage that the firm wishes to maintain overall.

This chapter developed procedures for measuring the incremental cost of money from each of the principal funds sources on an after-tax basis using discounted cash flow analysis. The cost of funds in each case is the discount rate that equates the present value of the after-tax payments to security holders to the net proceeds the issuer realizes upon issuing the securities.

Capital-Asset-Pricing-Model-and Adjusted-Present-Value Approaches to Capital Budgeting

Chapter 9

The *capital asset pricing model* (CAPM) represented a major breakthrough in explaining how risk considerations affect the valuation of securities. Developed by Sharpe and Lintner in the 1960s, the CAPM explains how the market place values securities on the basis of the degree of riskiness that investors cannot eliminate through diversifying their portfolios.[1] The greater the unavoidable risks associated with a particular security, the higher the rate of return investors will demand before investing in that security.

This basic principle also applies to capital investment projects. The CAPM provides a technique for estimating a company's risk-adjusted cost of capital for a project in which the risk adjustment is based on the "unavoidable" or "nondiversifiable" risks of the project and the rate of return "premium" investors require because of these risks.

The CAPM also proves useful in applying another important technique in capital budgeting. The weighted-average-cost-of-capital approach does not take into account the possible interaction between the firm's investment and financing decisions. The *adjusted-present-value (APV) method* does. The last two sections of the chapter describe how to use the APV method to figure into the net present value calculation the benefits and costs of project-related debt capacity side effects.

CAPITAL ASSET PRICING MODEL

The CAPM provides a framework for valuing an asset—a share of stock, a bond, or a capital investment project—based on how that asset's risk-return characteristics compare with the risk-return profile of (1) a "riskless" security

135

and (2) the "market portfolio" of common stocks.[2] In practice, U.S. Treasury bills serve as the riskless security and Standard & Poor's 500-Stock Index serves as the proxy for the market portfolio.

Measuring Excess Returns

An investor who purchases a share of stock in a company will normally expect to earn a rate of return in excess of the riskless rate, i.e., the Treasury bill rate. Similarly, a portfolio of common stocks should yield an average rate of return that exceeds the riskless rate. In both cases, the "excess rate of return" compensates for the riskiness of the common stock investment relative to an investment in Treasury bills. Studies of the relationship between the excess rate of return for a particular stock on the one hand and the excess rate of return on the market portfolio on the other have generally revealed a relationship like the one depicted in Figure 9-1.

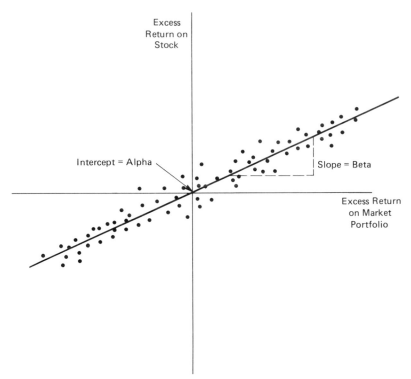

Figure 9-1. Relationship between excess return on particular stock and excess return on market portfolio.

Measuring Risk

The relationship between excess returns approximates a straight line. The fit is not exact, however. A variety of factors affect the returns a holder of an asset actually realizes. This variability can be attributed to two sets of factors.

First, the factors that affect the excess returns on the market portfolio also affect the returns earned on individual stocks. As depicted by the line in Figure 9-1, the excess return associated with a particular stock will vary systematically with the excess return on the market portfolio. This systematic variability, or *systematic risk*, plays a pivotal role in valuing stocks in the CAPM.

Second, other factors cause the excess return actually realized on a particular stock to deviate from the straight-line relationship. The dispersion of points above and below the line in Figure 9-1 reflects *nonsystematic risk*. An investor could substantially reduce the degree of nonsystematic risk in his or her portfolio by purchasing a broadly diversified portfolio of stocks. In the extreme case, if the investor could duplicate the market portfolio, he or she could eliminate nonsystematic risk entirely.

The existence of transaction costs limits the extent to which investors can diversify their portfolios economically. Nevertheless, even with transaction costs, diversification can substantially reduce the degree of nonsystematic risk.[3] Consequently, systematic risk, which they cannot diversify away, is the crucial element in calculating risk-adjusted returns in the CAPM.

Beta as the Measure of Systematic Risk

The line in Figure 9-1 is called the *characteristic line* of the stock. A line can be characterized uniquely by its slope and intercept. The equation of the line takes the form

$$\begin{matrix} \text{Return} \\ \text{on stock} \end{matrix} - \begin{matrix} \text{risk-free} \\ \text{rate} \end{matrix} = \text{alpha} + \text{beta}$$

$$\times \left(\begin{matrix} \text{return on} \\ \text{market portfolio} \end{matrix} - \begin{matrix} \text{risk-free} \\ \text{rate} \end{matrix} \right) \quad (9\text{-}1)$$

where *return on stock − risk-free rate* denotes the excess return on the stock and *return on market portfolio − risk-free rate* denotes the excess return on the market portfolio.

The slope of the characteristic line is called the stock's *beta*. It measures the strength of the relationship between excess return on the stock and excess return on the market portfolio. The steeper this slope, the greater the variability of excess return on the stock in response to changes in the rate of return on the market portfolio and the higher the degree of systematic risk. If a stock's beta is greater than 1, its systematic risk exceeds that of the market; total return increases or decreases by a greater percentage than the total return on the market portfolio. The opposite is true when beta is less than 1. Most common stock betas fall within the range from 0.5 to 1.5.

The intercept of the characteristic line is known as *alpha*. The characteristic line in Figure 9-1 passes through the point where the two axes cross so that alpha is zero. Under the CAPM, if the expected excess return on the market portfolio is zero, the expected excess return on an individual stock, and hence the stock's alpha, should also be zero. However, empirical studies often indicate nonzero alpha for at least some stocks. This may result from market imperfections, temporary disequilibrium, or other factors.

Example of Beta Calculation

Table 9-1 illustrates the calculation of beta for the common stock of Exxon Corporation. Beta is usually estimated from monthly excess returns over a period of between 4 and 7 years.[4] To simplify the computations, quarterly data are used in Table 9-1.

Because quarterly data are used, riskless rate of return, *risk-free rate*, is measured as the new issue annually compounded coupon equivalent yield on 91-day Treasury bills at the beginning of each quarter.[5] All other variables are also expressed on an annualized basis in order to maintain consistency. The *return on market portfolio* is measured as the percentage change in the value of Standard & Poor's 500-Stock Index during the quarter, expressed on an annualized basis:

$$\begin{aligned} \text{Return on} \atop \text{market portfolio} = 4 \times \left(\begin{array}{c} \text{value of S\&P} \\ \text{500 at end} \\ \text{of quarter} \end{array} - \begin{array}{c} \text{value of S\&P} \\ \text{500 at beginning} \\ \text{of quarter} \end{array} \right) \\ \div \begin{array}{c} \text{value of S\&P} \\ \text{500 at beginning} \\ \text{of quarter} \end{array} \end{aligned} \tag{9-2}$$

More correctly, return on market portfolio includes dividends paid during the quarter on the stocks that comprise the Standard & Poor's 500-Stock Index. However, prior studies have determined that alpha and beta in Formula 9-1 can be estimated with virtually the same degree of accuracy if the simpler measure in Formula 9-2 is used in the analysis. The rate of return on the stock, *return on stock*, is measured as the investor's total percentage return from holding the stock over the quarter, also expressed on an annualized basis:

$$\begin{aligned} \text{Return} \atop \text{on stock} = 4 \times \left(\begin{array}{c} \text{share price} \\ \text{at end of} \\ \text{quarter} \end{array} - \begin{array}{c} \text{share price} \\ \text{at beginning of} \\ \text{quarter} \end{array} + \begin{array}{c} \text{dividend} \\ \text{paid during} \\ \text{quarter} \end{array} \right) \\ \div \begin{array}{c} \text{share price} \\ \text{at beginning of} \\ \text{quarter} \end{array} \end{aligned} \tag{9-3}$$

Table 9-1
Calculation of Beta for the Common
Stock of Exxon Corporation

Quarter	Return on Stock	Risk-Free Rate	Excess Return on Stock	Return on Market Portfolio	Excess Return on Market Portfolio
1979-I	0.0959	0.3684	0.2725	0.2281	0.1322
1979-II	0.0987	0.1536	0.0549	0.0520	−0.0467
1979-III	0.0920	0.4547	0.3627	0.2492	0.1572
1979-IV	0.1078	−0.1881	−0.2959	−0.0505	−0.1583
1980-I	0.1262	0.2866	0.1604	−0.2168	−0.3430
1980-II	0.1749	0.6686	0.4937	0.4761	0.3012
1980-III	0.0731	0.2958	0.2227	0.3929	0.3198
1980-IV	0.1203	0.7097	0.5894	0.3284	0.2081
1981-I	0.1461	−0.5209	−0.6670	0.0071	−0.1390
1981-II	0.1309	0.0801	−0.0508	−0.1409	−0.2718
1981-III	0.1461	−0.2774	−0.4235	−0.4582	−0.6043
1981-IV	0.1492	0.1125	−0.0367	0.2193	0.0701
1982-I	0.1221	−0.3040	−0.4261	−0.3457	−0.4678
1982-II	0.1405	0.0533	0.0872	0.0840	−0.2245
1982-III	0.1391	0.1441	0.0050	0.3945	0.2554
1982-IV	0.0807	0.3571	0.2764	0.6716	0.5909

$$\text{Excess return on stock} = \text{alpha} + \text{beta} \times \text{excess return on market portfolio}$$

$$\text{Alpha} = 0.05$$
$$\text{Beta} = 0.74$$
$$R^2 = 0.48$$

The excess returns were then calculated, and a standard linear regression routine (which is available on many hand-held calculators) was used to calculate alpha and beta. The estimated value of beta is 0.74. This implies, for example, that if the value of the Standard & Poor's 500-Stock Index should increase by 10% during a particular quarter, the price of Exxon common stock should increase so as to provide a 7.4% (= 0.74 × 10%) rate of return during the same period.

The R^2 figure indicates that the variation in excess market portfolio return explained roughly 48% of the observed variation in the excess return on Exxon common stock over the 1979 to 1982 period. The remainder of the variation was due to nonsystematic risk.

Fortunately, a number of financial service organizations provide estimates of beta on a regular basis, at least for the stocks of the largest companies, so that it is often not necessary to perform the calculation illustrated in Table 9-1. These services include Value Line, Wells Fargo Bank, and several brokerage firms.

Expected Rate of Return for a Particular Stock

The particular objective in using the CAPM is to calculate the expected *future* rate of return. If historical data provide a reliable guide, then we can use a historical relationship like the ones depicted in Figure 9-1 and Table 9-1 as the basis for estimating the required rates of return on capital investment projects.

If all nonsystematic risk is diversified away, alpha = 0. Then Formula 9-1 can be expressed as

$$\begin{matrix} \text{Return} \\ \text{on stock} \end{matrix} = \begin{matrix} \text{risk-free} \\ \text{rate} \end{matrix} + \text{beta} \times \left(\begin{matrix} \text{return} \\ \text{on market} \\ \text{portfolio} \end{matrix} - \begin{matrix} \text{risk-free} \\ \text{rate} \end{matrix} \right) \qquad (9\text{-}4)$$

Formula 9-4 is just as valid for expected future returns as for historical returns:

$$\begin{matrix} \text{Expected return} \\ \text{on stock} \end{matrix} = \begin{matrix} \text{expected risk-} \\ \text{free rate} \end{matrix} + \text{beta}$$

$$\times \left(\begin{matrix} \text{expected return} \\ \text{on market portfolio} \end{matrix} - \begin{matrix} \text{expected risk-} \\ \text{free rate} \end{matrix} \right) \qquad (9\text{-}5)$$

In Formula 9-5, the expected rate of return for a particular stock over some specified holding period equals the (average) *expected risk-free rate* over that same period plus an appropriate risk premium. This risk premium is equal to the stock's beta, which serves as a measure of its riskiness, multiplied by the expected excess return on the market portfolio, *expected return on market portfolio − expected risk-free rate*, which might be thought of as the "market price of risk." The risk premium thus varies directly with the security's beta. Figure 9-2 illustrates this relationship. A higher beta necessitates a greater expected rate of return.

The *expected return on stock* in Formula 9-5 is also the rate of return investors would require of comparable stocks in order to be willing to invest in them. It is also the return on equity investors would require on the equity capital that the firm invests in capital investment projects that have the same risk-return profile as the company as a whole. Consequently, Formula 9-5 gives the CAPM estimate of the cost of equity capital. However, it really represents the CAPM estimate of the cost of retained earnings. Adding the new issue cost premium given by Formula 8-8 gives the CAPM cost of a new common stock issue.

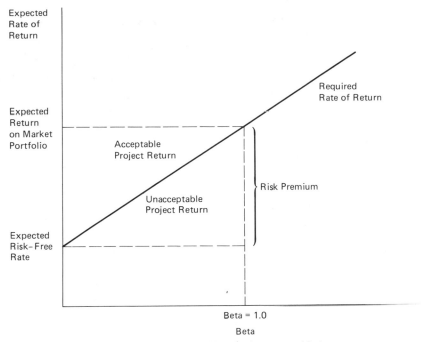

Figure 9-2. Relationship between expected rate of return and beta.

The usefulness of Formula 9-5 depends on the reliability of historical beta as an indicator of future beta and on the values used for the expected risk-free rate and for the expected return on market portfolio. All should be the best available estimates for the future. Various econometric services project future interest rates. An average of these projected Treasury bill rates may be used. However, because of the long-lived nature of most projects and the hazards of trying to make distant projections, many experts recommend simply using the current 3-month Treasury bill rate as the risk-free rate.

The expected excess return on the market portfolio is frequently estimated from historical information. A study by Ibbotson and Sinquefield found that the excess return on the market portfolio during the period 1926 to 1981 averaged 5.95% on an annually compounded basis, based on Standard & Poor's 500-Stock Index, and that investors required an additional risk premium of 4.12% in the case of smaller companies.[6]

Returning to the Exxon example discussed earlier, suppose that securities analysts expect the quarterly Treasury bill rate to average 10% over the next 5 years. The expected 5-year holding period annual rate of return on Exxon common stock would then be

$$\begin{matrix}\text{Expected}\\ \text{return on}\\ \text{Exxon stock}\end{matrix} = 0.10 + 0.74 \times 0.0595 = 0.1440, \text{ or } 14.40\% \text{ per annum}$$

using 5.95% as the expected excess portfolio return.

The CAPM implies that investors assess the riskiness of a security solely on the basis of that security's contribution to the riskiness of a fully diversified portfolio of stocks. It also rests on the assumptions that capital markets are efficient and frictionless (i.e., no taxes, no transaction costs, and no bankruptcy penalties) and that investors' expectations are homogeneous. Nevertheless, studies indicate that the CAPM provides a useful share valuation framework.

APPLICATION OF CAPITAL ASSET PRICING MODEL TO CAPITAL BUDGETING

The CAPM offers a framework for risk adjusting, on the basis of market-determined risk premiums, the rates of return required on equity invested in capital investment projects. This section assumes all-equity financing, and the next one shows how to accommodate debt financing.

Required Rate of Return on Equity Invested in a Project

According to the CAPM, the required rate of return on equity invested in a particular capital investment project varies with the degree of systematic risk associated with the project according to the relationship:

$$\begin{matrix}\text{Required return}\\ \text{on project equity}\end{matrix} = \begin{matrix}\text{expected risk-}\\ \text{free rate}\end{matrix} + \begin{matrix}\text{project}\\ \text{beta}\end{matrix}$$
$$\times \left(\begin{matrix}\text{expected return on}\\ \text{market portfolio}\end{matrix} - \begin{matrix}\text{expected risk-}\\ \text{free rate}\end{matrix}\right) \quad (9\text{-}6)$$

Formula 9-6 is perfectly analogous to Formulas 9-4 and 9-5. Note that beta in Formula 9-6 is specific to the project. It is important in calculating project beta to be sure that it reflects as accurately as possible the *business risk* associated with comparable investment opportunities. Only if the risk-return profile of a proposed project mirrors that of the company will the company's common stock beta also be the appropriate project beta.

The required return on project equity reflects the rate of return equity investors expect on comparable investments. As illustrated in Figure 9-2, if the project in question promises to provide a higher rate of return than comparable investments, the project's internal rate of return will exceed the required return given by Formula 9-6, and the company should accept the project. If the project in question promises a lower rate of return than the required return given by Formula 9-6, it should be rejected.

An important implication of Formula 9-6 is that required return on project equity does not depend directly on the company undertaking the project.[7] A project may be more valuable to one company than to another because of differences in management expertise, operating economies, or other factors. But the required return on project equity required by the capital market depends on the risk-return profile of the project rather than on the risk-return profile of the company undertaking the project.

Measuring the Required Rate of Return on Equity

There are two procedures available for estimating project beta when the company's and the project's risk-return profiles differ. Which is more useful depends on whether there exist companies whose risk-return profiles match that of the project under consideration.

Comparable-Company Approach. In many cases, it is possible to find one or more publicly traded companies each with a business that, in its entirety, closely resembles the project. When one or more comparable companies can be found, their betas can be used in the manner described below to infer a beta for the project.

For example, suppose a chemical company is considering forming an oil and gas exploration, development, and production company. The chemical company can estimate project beta from the betas of publicly traded oil and gas companies that have no other operations outside the industry. However, it would have to be careful to choose those oil and gas companies whose mix of exploration, development, and production activities reflects most closely the mix of operations it intends for its own oil and gas business.

Surrogate Period-by-Period Returns Approach. If a closely comparable publicly traded company cannot be found, it may be possible to use period-by-period cash flows and asset values from similar projects the company has pursued in the past to estimate beta.

For example, suppose that a publishing company is considering purchasing a new printing press and that it has owned its own printing presses for a number of years. Its own records will enable it to determine the net after-tax cash flow realized from such a machine during each accounting period. Because used printing presses are often sold, the publishing company can estimate the market value of one of its existing presses at the end of each accounting period.

The publishing company can use this information to calculate beta for the proposed new investment. It first calculates the period-by-period total returns associated with one of its existing presses:

$$\begin{aligned}\text{Return per} \atop \text{period} = \bigg(&\text{value of machine} \atop \text{at end of period} - \text{value of machine at} \atop \text{beginning of period}\\ &+ \text{net after-tax cash} \atop \text{flow during period}\bigg) \div \text{value of machine at} \atop \text{beginning of period}\end{aligned} \quad (9\text{-}7)$$

The period-by-period returns obtained from Formula 9-7 are substituted into Formula 9-1 to estimate an unleveraged beta for the asset. The resulting beta, which measures the riskiness of the asset's total returns relative to the riskiness of a fully diversified portfolio of common stocks, when substituted into Formula 9-6 gives the required rate of return on an all-equity-financed investment in the asset. This approach would work for any asset or project for which reasonable period-by-period market values could be obtained. However, the markets for used assets are generally less liquid and less efficient than the markets for most stocks. Consequently, the comparable-company approach, when workable, is almost always preferable to the surrogate period-by-period returns approach.

A Note of Caution Concerning Historical Data. The critical assumptions in the approaches just described are that comparable situations can be identified and that the past serves as a reliable proxy for the future. Comparable companies or comparable assets must be chosen with care. To minimize error, it is best to try to identify a number of comparable situations, calculate a beta value for each, and then average these values.

Even when closely comparable companies and assets are identified, the relationship between asset returns and the rate of return on the market portfolio may have changed over time, for example, as the industry matured or as its technology evolved. In that case, the past relationship may not be a reliable indicator of the future relationship. To allow for this possibility, the analyst can estimate beta over periods of varying length to determine whether a significant change in beta might have taken place. If it has, then the future cash flows expected from the proposed capital investment project could be discounted at different discount rates that reflect the past variability of beta. If the proposed project's net present value is positive for all of these discount rates, it should be undertaken. If it is positive for some but negative for others, the company will have to make a determination as to which value(s) of beta are more reasonable.

ESTIMATING THE COST OF CAPITAL FOR AN INVESTMENT PROJECT

This section describes the adjustments necessary to reflect appropriately the degree of financial leverage a company intends for its project. The higher the proportion of debt financing, the greater is the project's financial risk. The required rate of return for the project must reflect an appropriate premium for the financial risk in addition to an appropriate premium for the project's business risk. The higher the degree of leverage, the greater must be the financial risk premium.

In describing how to take financial leverage into account, it is useful to consider the following three cases separately:

1. The company's common stock is publicly traded, the project is in the company's basic line of business (and involves business risks similar to those of the company as a whole), and the project can appropriately be financed with the same proportions of debt and equity as the company as a whole.
2. Same as item 1 except that the project's leverage ratio differs from that of the company.
3. The comparable-company approach must be used, and the leverage ratios of the comparable companies differ from the leverage ratio intended for the project.

Matching Business and Financial Risks
This represents the simplest case. The company's beta also serves as the beta for the project. This is often possible when the company is involved predominantly in one business, the project is long-lived and involves new production capacity, and it is appropriate to finance it in the same manner as the company as a whole.

Differing Financial Risk
When a company decides to finance a project with different proportions of debt and equity than the company as a whole, the required rate of return calculation must reflect this. Suppose that a particular project will support a higher degree of leverage than the company as a whole. In that case, a required rate of return on equity calculated on the basis of company beta would *understate* the required financial risk premium because beta increases with increasing leverage (to reflect the higher risk). Consequently, the required rate of return on equity so calculated would be smaller than is really justified, and the capital investment analysis would be *biased in favor* of accepting the project.

Adjusting for Leverage. Beta can be adjusted for this leverage effect using the following equation:

$$\begin{array}{l} \text{Leveraged} \\ \text{beta} \end{array} = \begin{array}{l} \text{unleveraged} \\ \text{beta} \end{array}$$
$$\times \left[1 + \left(1 - \begin{array}{l} \text{corporate} \\ \text{tax rate} \end{array} \right) \times \begin{array}{l} \text{debt-to-} \\ \text{equity ratio} \end{array} \right] \qquad (9\text{-}8)$$

Leveraged beta is the beta actually calculated when Formula 9-1 is used. The *unleveraged beta* is the beta the company would have if it were all-equity financed. The *debt-to-equity ratio* should be based on market values but, in practice, book values are normally used.

If we have calculated the actual leveraged beta and wish to find the unleveraged beta, we can do so by rearranging Formula 9-8:

$$\frac{\text{Unleveraged}}{\text{beta}} = \frac{\text{leveraged}}{\text{beta}}$$

$$\div \left[1 + \left(1 - \frac{\text{corporate}}{\text{tax rate}} \right) \times \frac{\text{debt-to-}}{\text{equity ratio}} \right] \qquad (9\text{-}9)$$

Illustration of Required Rate of Return Calculation. Calculation of the required rate of return for a project that involves similar business risk but differing financial risk from that of a company as a whole involves the following steps:

1. Calculate the actual leveraged beta for the company.
2. Use Formula 9-9 to calculate the unleveraged beta for the *company* by adjusting on the basis of the *company's* debt-to-equity ratio.
3. Use Formula 9-8 to calculate the leveraged beta for the *project* by adjusting on the basis of the *project's* debt-to-equity ratio.
4. Use the beta calculated at step 3 in Formula 9-6 to calculate the required return on project equity.
5. Use the proportions of debt and equity financing for the project together with the required return on project equity calculated at step 4 and the cost of debt for the project to calculate the weighted average cost of capital for the project:

$$\frac{\text{Hurdle rate}}{\text{for project}} \equiv \frac{\text{cost of capital}}{\text{for project}}$$

$$= \frac{\text{proportion of}}{\text{debt financing}} \times \frac{\text{after-tax}}{\text{cost of debt}}$$

$$+ \frac{\text{proportion of}}{\text{equity financing}} \times \frac{\text{required return}}{\text{on project equity}} \qquad (9\text{-}10)$$

To illustrate this procedure, suppose that a company that is currently levered $1:3$ can finance a project with 50% debt and 50% equity because of the project's relatively low operating risk. Suppose further that the risk-free rate is 10%, that the company pays tax at corporate tax rate = 0.46, and that the pretax cost of debt for the project is 12%. Suppose also that upon applying the method illustrated in Table 9-1, the analyst estimates the company's beta to be 1.10.

Using Formula 9-9, the unleveraged beta for the company is

$$\text{Unleveraged company beta} = \frac{1.10}{1 + (1 - 0.46) \times \frac{1}{3}} = 0.9322$$

The leveraged beta for the project is, by Formula 9-8,

$$\text{Leveraged project beta} = 0.9322 \times [1 + (1 - 0.46) \times 1] = 1.4356$$

Using Formula 9-6, the required return on equity for the project is

$$\text{Required return on project equity} = 0.10 + 1.4356 \times 0.0595 = 0.1854, \text{ or } 18.54\%$$

where the risk premium on the market portfolio is assumed to be 5.95%. Finally, the hurdle rate for the project is, by Formula 9-10,

$$\text{Hurdle rate for project} = 0.5 \times 0.54 \times 0.12 + 0.5 \times 0.1854$$

$$= 0.1251, \text{ or } 12.51\%$$

The company should accept the project if the net present value of its incremental cash flow stream is positive when the flows are discounted at 12.51% or, equivalently, if the internal rate of return for these same cash flows is greater than 12.51%.

Note that the company's overall cost of equity capital is $0.10 + 1.10 \times 0.0595 = 0.1655$, or 16.55%, and that its overall cost of capital is $0.25 \times 0.54 \times 0.12 + 0.75 \times 0.1655 = 0.1403$, or 14.03%. The project's required return on equity exceeds the company's cost of equity capital because the project is more highly leveraged than the company. However, the hurdle rate for the project is lower than the company's cost of capital because the project will support greater leverage.

Two points of caution are in order. First, as we just saw, a higher assumed degree of leverage will generally lower a project's hurdle rate. However, a degree of leverage greater than that of the company is only justified if it is consistent with the company's overall capital structure policy. For example, if financing the aforementioned project with 50% debt means that other comparable projects will have to be financed with substantially less than 25% debt so as not to jeopardize the company's debt rating, the company should use 14.03% rather than 12.51% as the hurdle rate for the project. The 12.51% hurdle rate is justified only if financing the project with 50% debt in no way affects how the company finances its other projects.

Second, project cash flows are generally estimated on an annual basis, whereas beta is often estimated using monthly Treasury bill rates and monthly stock return data. In such cases, the required rate of return is really being calculated

Table 9-2

Calculation of Hurdle Rate for a New Chemical Plant

Company	Actual Beta	Debt/Equity*	Unleveraged Beta†	Company	Actual Beta	Debt/Equity*	Unleveraged Beta†
Betz Laboratories, Inc.	1.00	0.001	1.00	The Lubrizol Corporation	1.10	0.026	1.08
Cabot Corp.	1.40	0.278	1.22	Morton Thiokol, Inc.	0.95	0.071	0.91
Chemed Corp.	0.80	0.253	0.70	NCH Corp.	0.80	0.036	0.78
Crompton & Knowles Corp.	0.85	0.297	0.73	Nalco Chemical Co.	0.90	0.014	0.89
DeSoto Inc.	0.85	0.125	0.80	Oakite Products, Inc.	0.55	0.045	0.54
Economics Laboratory, Inc.	1.10	0.290	0.95	Pennwalt Corp.	0.85	0.375	0.71
H. B. Fuller Co.	1.05	0.290	0.91	Petrolite Corporation	0.75	0.026	0.74
Great Lakes Chemical Corp.	0.95	0.117	0.89	Products Research & Chemical Corp.	0.95	0.042	0.93
Grow Group, Inc.	0.90	0.459	0.72	Reichhold Chemicals, Inc.	0.90	0.325	0.77
Phillip A. Hunt Chemical Corp.	0.80	0.127	0.75	The Sherwin-Williams Co.	1.00	0.335	0.85
International Flavors & Fragrances Inc.	1.00	—	1.00	Sun Chemical Corp.	1.00	1.268	0.59
Lawter International, Inc.	0.85	0.006	0.85	Witco Chemical Corp.	0.95	0.470	0.76
Loctite Corporation	1.00	0.042	0.98	Average	0.93	0.213	0.84

Leveraged beta for project $= 0.84 \times [1 + (1 - 0.46) \times {}^1/_2] = 1.07$

Required return on project equity $= 0.1000 + 1.07 \times 0.0595 = 0.1637$‡

Cost of capital for project $= {}^1/_3 \times 0.0550 + {}^2/_3 \times 0.1637 = 0.1275$, or $\underline{12.75\%}$§

*Ratio of approximate market value of long-term debt (including capitalized leases) to market value of common and preferred equity.

†Calculation assumes each company's marginal tax rate is 46%.

‡Assumes 91-day Treasury bill rate of 10.00% on an annually compounded coupon equivalent yield basis.

§Assumes a pretax cost of conventional debt of 12% and a pretax cost of pollution control debt of 8%, both on a semiannually compounded basis; a mix of $10 million of pollution control debt and $9.33 (= $^{58}/_3 - 10$) million of conventional debt; and a 46% marginal tax rate.

Source: Value Line, Inc., *The Value Line Investment Survey*, April 15, 1983, pp. 515–539.

on the basis of monthly compounding. It should be converted to an equivalent annually compounded basis before being used to discount annual cash flows. For example, a 12.51% monthly compounded rate of return is equivalent to a

$$\begin{matrix} \text{Equivalent annually} \\ \text{compounded cost} \\ \text{of capital} \end{matrix} = \left(1 + \frac{0.1251}{12}\right)^{12} - 1 = 0.1325, \text{ or } 13.25\%$$

annually compounded rate of return.

Adjusting for Leverage in
Comparable-Company Approach

When it is necessary or desirable to look to publicly traded companies in the industry to which a particular project belongs in order to calculate the appropriate hurdle rate, the approach just outlined should be modified slightly:

1. Calculate the actual beta for each comparable company.
2. Use Formula 9-9 to calculate the unleveraged beta for each company.
3. Calculate the average of unleveraged betas calculated at step 2.
4. Use Formula 9-8 and the chosen debt-to-equity ratio for the project to calculate the leveraged beta that corresponds to the average unleveraged beta calculated at step 3.
5. Use the beta calculated at step 4 and Formula 9-6 to calculate the required return on project equity.
6. Use Formula 9-10 to calculate the hurdle rate for the project.

ILLUSTRATION OF CAPITAL-
ASSET-PRICING-MODEL APPROACH

This section shows how to use the capital-asset-pricing-model approach to calculate a hurdle rate for the new plants and the plant expansion that Washington Chemical Corporation is considering building.

Washington Chemical's proposed plants would be used for the production of specialty chemicals. Table 9-2 provides a list of specialty chemicals producers. The actual common stock beta for each was obtained from *The Value Line Investment Survey* dated April 15, 1983. The companies' respective debt-to-equity ratios as of that date were used to calculate the unleveraged betas in Table 9-2.

Washington Chemical intends to finance the projects it selects in the company's customary ratio of one-third debt and two-thirds common equity. This implies a leveraged beta for the new projects amounting to 1.07. The projected average 91-day Treasury bill rate, expressed on an annually compounded coupon equivalent yield basis, is 10%. Consider the proposed expansion of the New Jersey plant. The project is expected to cost $58.0 million. Suppose that

$10.0 million of this cost will qualify for pollution control financing at an interest rate of 8%. Assume that any other debt Washington Chemical issues must bear interest at a rate of 12% and that Washington Chemical pays income tax at a 46% marginal rate. Under these assumptions, hurdle rate for project = 12.75% on an annually compounded basis.

ADJUSTED-PRESENT-VALUE METHOD

The adjusted-present-value method represents an alternative to the weighted-average-cost-of-capital approach. It is specifically designed to handle large projects that might affect the debt capacity of the firm. It is particularly useful in analyzing proposed merger transactions. Chapter 27 discusses that special application.

The starting point for the adjusted-present-value method is the concept of *value additivity*. Simply put, value additivity asserts that the whole is equal to the sum of the parts: The market value of a company can be expressed as the sum of (1) the present values of all the assets the company owns, intangible as well as tangible, as though each were financed on an all-equity basis plus (2) the present value of the interest tax shields on the firm's outstanding debt. Accordingly, the *adjusted present value* (APV) of a proposed capital investment project can be calculated as

$$
\begin{array}{l}
\text{Adjusted present} \\
\text{value of project}
\end{array}
= \text{APV} =
\begin{array}{c}
\text{net present value} \\
\text{of project on} \\
\text{all-equity basis}
\end{array}
$$

$$
+
\begin{array}{c}
\text{present value of} \\
\text{interest tax shields on} \\
\text{project-related debt}
\end{array}
+
\begin{array}{c}
\text{net present value} \\
\text{of project-related} \\
\text{side effects}
\end{array}
$$

$$(9\text{-}11)$$

The APV method values separately each of the components of the value of a project. These separate values are then added to obtain the APV of the project. In contrast, the discounted cash flow methods discussed previously in Part 2 attempt to capture all these valuation effects in a single calculation by adjusting the discount rate. As we have found, adjusting the discount rate is not always easy. This is particularly true when an investment project has substantial debt capacity and other financial side effects. In such cases, the APV method can prove very helpful.

Net Present Value of Project on All-Equity Basis

First, the value of a project is calculated as though the project were financed on an all-equity basis by applying Formula 6-4:

$$\begin{array}{c} \text{Net present value} \\ \text{of project on} \\ \text{all-equity basis} \end{array} = \sum_{t=0}^{\text{life}} \frac{\text{net cash}}{\text{flow}(t)} \div (1 + \text{discount rate})^t \qquad (9\text{-}12)$$

where *life* denotes the useful economic life of the project and *net cash flow*(0) = $-$investment. The final period's *net cash flow* includes the project's terminal value. For all intermediate periods, *net cash flow*(t) = incremental free cash flow(t). The discount rate in Formula 9-12 is the rate of return investors would require if the project were financed on an all-equity basis. Thus, Formula 9-12 is just the customary net present value calculation with one important modification: The discount rate in the denominator is not adjusted for how the company chooses to finance the project. The other terms in Formula 9-11 take these effects into account.

Present Value of Interest Tax Shields

A capital investment project, except in extreme cases, will support some level of new debt financing that is in keeping with the company's senior debt rating objective. This amount of debt, expressed as a percentage of project cost, may be more or less than the proportion of debt in the company's desired capital structure, depending on the business risks of the project. The amount of additional debt the project will support will generate tax shields of *tax shield in year t*, the present value of which is:

$$\begin{array}{c} \text{Present value} \\ \text{of interest} \\ \text{tax shields} \end{array} = \sum_{t=1}^{\text{life}} \frac{\text{tax shield}}{\text{in year } t} \div \left(1 + \frac{\text{interest rate}}{\text{on debt}}\right)^t \qquad (9\text{-}13)$$

The appropriate discount rate in this calculation is the interest rate on the new debt. This assumes that the interest tax shields are equally as risky as the interest payments that produce them.

It is important that the amount of debt assumed in calculating the present value of the tax shields should be the incremental borrowing capacity to which the project gives rise. A company might borrow the entire amount it needs for a project. But if the assets will support only, say, 50% debt financing and if the project has the same business risk profile as the company's existing portfolio of assets, then the tax shields that would result from 50% debt financing should be used in Formula 9-13.

Net Present Value of Project-Related Side Effects

The third category of valuation effects includes project-related side effects. Two that are particularly important are the subsidies available on certain types of debt financing, such as pollution control financing and industrial development

Table 9-3
Application of APV Method to Washington Chemical's Proposed New Jersey Plant Expansion

Year	Expected Net Cash Flow[a]	Present Value of Remaining Cash Flows[b]	Debt-to-Value Ratio of 1:3[c]			Debt Service Coverage of 3.00×[d]				Pollution Control Issue	
			Beginning-of-Year Debt	Interest Paid	Interest Tax Shield[a]	Beginning-of-Year Debt	Debt Repayment	After-Tax Interest[a]	Interest Tax Shield[a]	Beginning-of-Year Debt	Interest Subsidy[e]
1	$15.0	$77.53	$27.95	$3.35	$1.54	$36.98	$2.60	$2.40	$2.04	$10.00	$0.22
2	15.0	74.16	26.57	3.19	1.47	34.38	2.77	2.23	1.90	9.51	0.21
3	17.5	70.28	25.01	3.00	1.38	31.61	3.79	2.05	1.74	8.95	0.19
4	17.5	63.33	22.42	2.69	1.24	27.82	4.03	1.80	1.54	8.02	0.17
5	12.5	55.33	19.50	2.34	1.08	23.79	2.62	1.54	1.31	6.98	0.15
6	15.5	51.13	17.87	2.14	0.99	21.17	3.80	1.37	1.17	6.39	0.14
7	15.5	43.29	15.02	1.80	0.83	17.37	4.04	1.13	0.96	5.37	0.12
8	15.5	34.29	11.82	1.42	0.65	13.33	4.30	0.86	0.74	4.23	0.09
9	11.0	23.93	8.19	0.98	0.45	9.03	3.08	0.59	0.50	2.93	0.06
10	19.0	16.52	5.60	0.67	0.31	5.95	5.95	0.39	0.33	2.00	0.04

[a] Assuming a 46% marginal income tax rate.

[b] Present value of expected annual net cash flows beginning in the year indicated through the tenth year discounted at 15.00%.

[c] The beginning-of-year debt each year represents one-third of the sum of (1) the present value of remaining cash flows and (2) the present value of remaining interest tax shields (discounted at the pretax interest rate on the debt).

[d] The ratio of the expected annual net cash flow to annual debt service equals 3.00× each year.

[e] Calculated as 0.0216 times the amount of pollution control debt outstanding at the beginning of the year.

bond financing, and new issue expenses associated with securities issued (or loans arranged) to finance the project.

Value of Interest Subsidy. If certain project expenditures qualify for tax-exempt financing or some other form of interest subsidy, the value of these subsidies increases the project's adjusted present value by the amount:

$$\begin{matrix} \text{Value of} \\ \text{subsidy} \end{matrix} = \sum_{t=1}^{\text{life}} \begin{matrix} \text{after-tax} \\ \text{subsidy in} \\ \text{year } t \end{matrix} \div \left(1 + \begin{matrix} \text{after-tax cost} \\ \text{of conventional} \\ \text{debt issue} \end{matrix} \right)^t \qquad (9\text{-}14)$$

For example, if \$5,000,000 of project expenditures qualify for pollution control financing, life = 10 years, the issuer's tax rate is 50% and the pretax costs of issuing 10-year conventional debt and pollution control debt are 12 and 8%, respectively, then:

$$\text{Value of subsidy} = \sum_{t=1}^{10} \frac{0.5 \times 5{,}000{,}000 \times 0.04}{(1.06)^t} = \$736{,}009$$

Because this debt is specific to the project (it must be under current tax regulations), the subsidy is fully attributable to the project. The value of the subsidy represents the amount of new debt, \$736,009, the company could service using the after-tax cash flow of \$100,000 per annum for 10 years.

New Issue Expenses. Issuance expenses, net of the present value of any tax savings resulting therefrom, reduce the project's adjusted present value.

ILLUSTRATION OF ADJUSTED-PRESENT-VALUE APPROACH

Once again consider Washington Chemical's proposed expansion of its New Jersey plant. Table 9-3 provides the expected annual net cash flows for this project as well as details concerning the calculation of the amount of debt the project can support.

Beginning with the first component of Formula 9-11, the appropriate unleveraged beta was found in Table 9-2 to be 0.84. Thus, the required rate of return for the project on an all-equity basis is

$$\begin{matrix} \text{Required return} \\ \text{on project equity} \end{matrix} = 0.10 + 0.84 \times 0.0595 = 0.1500, \text{ or } 15.00\%$$

assuming that the prevailing rate on 91-day Treasury bills (converted to an annually compounded coupon equivalent yield basis) is 10%. Then the net present value of the project on an all-equity basis is

$$\begin{array}{c}\text{Net present value}\\\text{of project on}\\\text{all-equity basis}\end{array} = -\$58.0 + \sum_{t=1}^{10} \frac{\text{net cash flow}(t)}{(1.15)^t} = \$19.53 \text{ million}$$

Next we find the present value of the tax shields that would result from fully utilizing the increased debt capacity to which the project will give rise. Table 9-3 indicates two possible approaches to figuring the amount of indebtedness a project can support. One approach employs the company's target debt-to-equity ratio (or, equivalently, its debt-to-total-value ratio). The other uses a debt service coverage test. Both are described below.

Washington Chemical's target debt-to-equity ratio is $1:2$. Consequently, over the long run, Washington Chemical would like the market value of its outstanding debt to represent one-third of the company's total market value. By working backward from year 10, we can calculate how much debt Washington Chemical can have outstanding at the beginning of each year in order to satisfy this one-third test. For example, the present value of the year 10 expected net cash flow is $16.52 million as of the beginning of year 10. The combined market value of the assets and the present value of the tax shields on the left-hand side of the company's balance sheet will support an equal combined amount of debt and equity on the right-hand side of the company's balance sheet. Consequently, the proposed project will create the capacity to support debt at the beginning of year 10 amounting to

$$\begin{array}{c}\text{Market value of}\\\text{project assets}\end{array} + \begin{array}{c}\text{present value of}\\\text{interest tax shields}\end{array} = \begin{array}{c}\text{year 10}\\\text{debt}\end{array} + \left(\begin{array}{c}\text{year 10}\\\text{debt}\\[4pt]\div\ \begin{array}{c}\text{debt-to-equity}\\\text{ratio}\end{array}\end{array}\right)$$

$$16.52 + \frac{0.46 \times 0.12 \times \text{year 10 debt}}{1.12} = \begin{array}{c}\text{year 10}\\\text{debt}\end{array} + \left(\begin{array}{c}\text{year 10}\\\text{debt}\end{array} \div\ ^1\!/_2\right)$$

$$(9\text{-}15)$$

Washington Chemical can have year 10 debt = $5.60 million outstanding at the beginning of the year. In that case, the total value of the project is $16.80 (= $16.52 + 0.31 ÷ 1.12) million, which is three times the amount of outstanding debt.

Proceeding in the same manner, the present value of year 9 and year 10 expected net cash flows as of the beginning of year 9 is $23.93 million. Given the amount of debt outstanding at the beginning of year 10 (i.e., also the end of year 9), how much debt can Washington Chemical have outstanding at the beginning of year 9 in order to still satisfy the one-third test? By modifying Formula 9-15 slightly, we find that the amount of debt Washington Chemical can have outstanding at the beginning of year 9 must satisfy the equation

$$\left[23.93 + \frac{0.31}{(1.12)^2} + \frac{0.46 \times 0.12 \times \text{year 9 debt}}{1.12}\right] \div 3 = \text{year 9 debt}$$

or

$$\text{Year 9 debt} = \$8.19 \text{ million}$$

The term in brackets represents simply the sum of (1) the present value of future expected net cash flows plus (2) the present value of future interest tax shields.

Proceeding in this manner iteratively from year 10 to year 1 reveals the amount of new debt the proposed plant expansion will support. Washington Chemical could thus issue $27.95 million of new debt bearing a 12% interest rate. The amortization schedule would involve debt repayments amounting to $1.38 million in year 1 ($27.95 million outstanding at the beginning of the year less $26.57 million outstanding at the beginning of year 2), $1.56 million in year 2, and so on, with all the debt incurred in connection with the project being fully repaid by the project's year 10 termination date. The resulting present value of the interest tax shields is

$$\begin{array}{l}\text{Present value} \\ \text{of interest} \\ \text{tax shields}\end{array} = \sum_{t=1}^{10} \frac{\text{interest tax shield in year } t}{(1.12)^t} = \$6.33 \text{ million}$$

The foregoing calculation assumes that the debt-to-total-value ratio is the principal determinant of Washington Chemical's debt capacity. Actually, it is but one of several factors that must be taken into account. Suppose that Washington Chemical has studied companies closely comparable to itself and discovered that over the past 5 years these companies have, on average, maintained total debt service coverage of approximately three times annual debt service.[8]

Beginning with year 10, we can calculate the maximum amount of debt Washington Chemical could have outstanding at the beginning of the period that is consistent with 3.00× debt service coverage:

$$\begin{array}{l}\text{Debt service} \\ \text{coverage ratio}\end{array} = 3.00 = \frac{19.0/(1 - 0.46)}{0.12 \times \begin{array}{l}\text{year 10} \\ \text{debt}\end{array} + \left[\begin{array}{l}\text{year 10} \\ \text{debt}\end{array}\middle/(1 - 0.46)\right]}$$

or

$$\text{Year 10 debt} = \$5.95 \text{ million}$$

Note that expected net cash flow is stated after taxes so that earnings before interest and taxes in year 10 is $19.0/(1 - 0.46) = 35.19$. Note also that all debt outstanding at the beginning of year 10 must be repaid at the end of the year. Proceeding recursively, the maximum amount of year 9 debt, given the amount of year 10 debt outstanding at the end of year 9 (and beginning of year 10), solves

$$\frac{\text{Debt service}}{\text{coverage ratio}} - 3.00$$

$$= \frac{11.0/(1 - 0.46)}{0.12 \times \frac{\text{year 9}}{\text{debt}} + \left[\left(\frac{\text{year 9}}{\text{debt}} - \frac{\text{year 10}}{\text{debt}}\right)/(1 - 0.46)\right]}$$

Note that the amount *year 9 debt − year 10 debt* is repaid at the end of year 9.

Proceeding in the same manner back to year 1 leads to the amounts of debt Washington Chemical can have outstanding each year, from which the annual interest tax shields can be calculated. The present value of the tax shields that result when 3.00× debt service coverage is the constraint is

$$\begin{array}{c}\text{Present value}\\ \text{of interest}\\ \text{tax shields}\end{array} = \sum_{t=1}^{10} \frac{\text{interest tax shield in year } t}{(1.12)^t} = \$7.91 \text{ million}$$

Thus, the present value of the tax shields realized from the project is between $6.33 million and $7.91 million. The lower of these is the more conservative estimate.

If Washington Chemical issues $10 million of pollution control debt at 8% interest, it will realize a 2.16% after-tax interest subsidy. To value this subsidy, it seems reasonable to assume that the amortization schedule for the pollution control debt will mirror the amortization schedule that corresponds to the more conservative of the two debt service streams in Table 9-3. This leads to the amortization schedule and schedule of annual subsidies shown in the two right-most columns in Table 9-3. The present value of this subsidy is, by Formula 9-14,

$$\begin{array}{c}\text{Value}\\ \text{of}\\ \text{subsidy}\end{array} = \sum_{t=1}^{10} \frac{\text{after-tax subsidy in year } t}{(1.0648)^t} = \$1.07 \text{ million}$$

Finally, the debt involves various issuance expenses. Suppose these amount to 1% of the gross proceeds of the debt issued to finance the plant expansion, or $0.15 million (= $27.95 × 0.01 × 0.54) after taxes (assuming, for convenience only, immediate deductibility).

Combining the various sources of value, the APV of the proposed New Jersey plant expansion is

$$\text{APV} = \$19.53 + 6.33 + 1.07 - 0.15 = \$26.78 \text{ million}$$

If the plant expansion were independent of the other two specialty chemicals projects Washington Chemical has under consideration, an APV of $26.78 million would indicate that Washington Chemical should proceed with the plant expansion project. However, because the three projects are mutually exclusive, Washington Chemical must calculate the APV for each of the other two projects in order to determine whether either of them has a greater APV. When selecting from among a set of mutually exclusive capital investment projects, a company should pursue the project that has the largest APV (assuming that at least one of the APVs is positive). As noted in Chapter 6, the NPV criterion is applied in the same manner.

Relationship between APV and Average-Cost-of-Capital Approaches

The APV method and the weighted-average-cost-of-capital method offer alternative approaches to calculating the net present value of a proposed capital investment project. Which method is preferable depends on the nature of the project. For example, as calculated in Table 9-2, the hurdle rate for the proposed New Jersey plant expansion using the weighted-average-cost-of-capital approach is 12.75%. Thus, the net present value of the project is:

$$NPV = \sum_{t=1}^{10} \frac{\text{expected net cash flow}}{(1.1275)^t} - 58.0 = \$26.63 \text{ million}$$

Before issuance expenses, the APV of $26.93 (= 26.78 + 0.15) million exceeds the NPV of $26.63 million because the project expands Washington Chemical's debt capacity by more than $19.33 (= 58/3) million. The APV calculation reflects the actual period-by-period changes in project-related debt capacity, as Table 9-3 illustrates, whereas the NPV calculation assumes simply that Washington Chemical borrows $19.33 million and leaves that debt outstanding throughout the life of the project. The difference between the present value of the interest tax shields under these two assumptions is $0.3 million. The weighted-average-cost-of-capital approach understates in this case the effect of the project on Washington Chemical's debt capacity. However, the difference between the two present value figures is really rather small (the $0.3 million difference represents 1.1% of APV), and either criterion would indicate that the proposed project should be accepted.

The APV method thus allows the analyst to account explicitly for debt capacity side effects that are expected to result from a proposed capital investment project. When these expected side effects are insignificant—and the project represents essentially a mirror image of either the sponsor or some comparable company—the weighted-average-cost-of-capital approach is probably the simpler of the two approaches. However, when a project is expected to have significant debt capacity side effects, the APV method will give the more accurate estimate of the project's true net present value to the firm's shareholders.

SUMMARY

This chapter described two approaches that utilize the capital asset pricing model to evaluate the economics of risky capital investment projects. The first involves using the CAPM to calculate the cost of equity capital and the weighted-average-cost-of-capital formula to calculate the hurdle rate and then discounting expected net cash flows at that rate to compute the project's net present value. The second involves utilizing the CAPM to calculate the cost of capital for an all-equity-financed firm, discounting the expected future net cash flows at that rate and using Formula 9-11 to compute the project's adjusted present value. Both procedures enable the financial analyst to evaluate the returns a project is expected to yield in relation to the risk-adjusted returns investors currently require of comparable projects and securities. They differ, however, in that the APV method explicitly takes into account any interaction between the capital investment decision and the project financing decision.

The CAPM measures the riskiness of a security or of a project relative to the riskiness of a "market portfolio," typically a fully diversified portfolio of common stocks. It is useful in capital budgeting because it offers a method of calculating risk-adjusted discount rates for projects that reflect market-determined rate premiums. The CAPM has become more widely used in capital budgeting analyses in recent years. Similarly, the APV approach is also likely to gain wider use as more and more analysts become familiar with it. We shall return to the subject of the CAPM and the APV method in Chapter 27 where we take up a second particularly important application of these techniques, namely, the evaluation of corporate acquisitions.

The Capital Structure Decision

Part 3

In Part 2, we calculated Washington Chemical's cost of capital assuming that Washington Chemical's desired mix of funds is one-third debt and two-thirds common equity. We postponed, until now, any discussion concerning the appropriateness of this policy decision.

A company's mix of long-term funds sources is known as its *capital structure*. A critically important question in corporate finance is how (if at all) a company's choice of capital structure affects its true cost of capital. Chapter 10 reviews the debate that has raged for years over the relevance (or lack thereof) of capital structure choice. In practice, a firm's choice of capital structure does matter. Reviewing the debate will bring out more clearly the reasons why it matters.

Chapter 11 describes and illustrates the application of analytical procedures for determining an appropriate capital structure for a company. The arguments presented in Chapter 10 imply that there exists a capital structure that is truly best for each company in the sense that it maximizes the total value of the company and, equivalently, minimizes its overall cost of capital. In practice, however, finding the "best" capital structure for a particular company would normally prove to be a very expensive exercise. Obtaining the information required to make this determination is just too expensive. So, instead, a company typically strives to identify a capital structure that is appropriate, or reasonable, in light of its objectives. The target capital structure is intended to, at least, come "close to" the value-maximizing capital structure. Chapter 11 describes how a company can make such a choice and then illustrates the procedure by showing how Washington Chemical's top management chose its one-third debt and two-thirds common equity capital structure objective.

Does the Choice of Capital Structure Affect a Company's Share Price?

Chapter 10

A company applies its assets in its business to generate a stream of operating cash flows. After paying taxes, the firm makes distributions to the providers of its capital and retains the balance for use in its business. If the company is all-equity financed, the entire after-tax operating cash flow each period accrues to the benefit of its shareholders (in the form of dividends and retained earnings). If instead the company has borrowed a portion of its capital, it must dedicate a portion of the cash flow stream to service this debt. Moreover, debtholders have the senior claim to a company's cash flow; shareholders are only entitled to the residual. The company's choice of capital structure determines the allocation of its operating cash flow each period between debtholders and shareholders.

The debate over the significance of a company's choice of capital structure is esoteric. But, in essence, it concerns the impact on the total market value of the company (i.e., the combined value of its debt and its equity) of splitting the cash flow stream into a debt component and an equity component. Financial experts traditionally believed that increasing a company's *leverage*, that is, increasing the proportion of debt in the company's capital structure, would increase value up to a point. But beyond that point, further increases in leverage would increase the company's overall cost of capital and decrease its total market value.

Modigliani and Miller challenged that view in their famous 1958 article.[1] They argued that the market values the earning power of a company's real assets and that if the company's capital investment program is held fixed and certain other assumptions are satisfied, the combined market value of a company's debt and equity is independent of its choice of capital structure. Since Modigliani and Miller published their capital structure irrelevancy paper, much attention has focused on the reasonableness of these "other assumptions," which include the absence of taxes, bankruptcy costs, and other imperfections that exist in the real world. Because of these imperfections, a company's choice of capital structure undoubtedly does affect its total market value. The significance of corporate leverage is reflected in the articles that have appeared in the financial press following periods like the 1970s when leverage increased significantly. However, the extent to which a company's choice of capital structure affects its market value is still debated.

This chapter summarizes the issues involved in the debate over the relevancy of capital structure choice. To keep the discussion simple, we assume a simplified capital structure consisting solely of "debt" and "equity." The conclusions to be drawn will still be valid for more complex capital structures.

THE TRADITIONAL VIEW OF THE SIGNIFICANCE OF CAPITAL STRUCTURE

The traditional view holds that there is an optimal capital structure. Accordingly, an unleveraged firm could increase its total market value by leveraging itself judiciously.

Figure 10-1 illustrates the traditional view. As a company increases its leverage, its cost of equity and its cost of debt both increase because of the increase in financial risk. But for low degrees of leverage, the cost of debt increases very little with increasing leverage. As a result, substituting debt for equity initially leads to a lower weighted average cost of capital. The savings resulting from substituting a cheaper source of funds for equity more than offset the increase in the cost of equity capital. But beyond some point—which determines the location of the optimal capital structure in Figure 10-1—the increase in the cost of equity capital more than offsets the savings resulting from substituting a cheaper source of funds for equity. By adopting the optimal capital structure, a company minimizes its weighted average cost of capital and maximizes its total market value.

A Closer Look at the Traditional View

Increasing a company's leverage generally has two effects on its return on equity. As long as the company's return on assets exceeds its cost of debt, increasing the company's leverage will increase its return on equity. In equation form,

$$\begin{matrix} \text{Return} \\ \text{on} \\ \text{equity} \end{matrix} = \begin{matrix} \text{return} \\ \text{on} \\ \text{assets} \end{matrix} + \left(\text{debt} \div \text{equity} \right) \times \left(\begin{matrix} \text{return} \\ \text{on} \\ \text{assets} \end{matrix} - \begin{matrix} \text{cost} \\ \text{of} \\ \text{debt} \end{matrix} \right) \qquad (10\text{-}1)$$

Table 10-1 illustrates the impact of increasing leverage on a company's expected return on equity. As leverage increases, the company will realize a

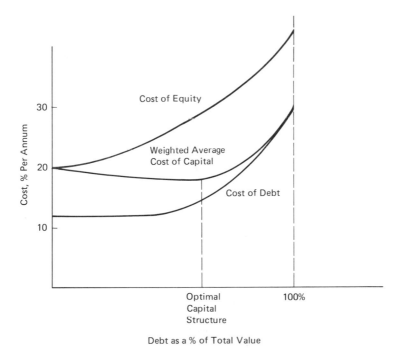

Figure 10-1. The traditional view of the significance of the firm's choice of capital structure.

higher return on equity as long as its return on assets exceeds its cost of debt. For example, if the company realized a 9% return on assets, its return on equity is 13% if its debt-to-equity ratio is 1 : 1 and is 17% if its debt-to-equity ratio is 2 : 1. But if its return on assets falls below its cost of debt, leverage reduces the company's return on equity, as happens in Table 10-1 when the company's return on assets is only 3%.

Leverage also magnifies the impact of changes in the return on assets on the company's return on equity. As noted in Chapter 5, the relative dispersion of return from an investment reflects the riskiness of the investment. In Table 10-1, the standard deviation of return on equity is used as a proxy for the riskiness of the company's equity. Note that riskiness increases as leverage increases. Thus, while increased leverage can raise a company's expected return on equity, it also increases the riskiness of the company's equity.

These two factors are capable of explaining the shape of the weighted average cost-of-capital curve in Figure 10-1. When leverage is low, substituting debt for equity has a proportionately greater impact on expected returns to equity investors than on the riskiness of their investment. The cost-of-equity capital

Table 10-1
Impact of Increased Leverage on Expected
Return and Risk of Equity

Debt-to- Equity	Cost of Debt	Return on Equity when Return on Assets Is					Expected Return on Equity*	Standard Deviation of Return on Equity*
		3%	6%	9%	12%	15%		
$1/4$	5%	2.50%	6.25%	10.00%	13.75%	17.50%	10.00%	5.30%
$1/3$	5	2.33	6.33	10.33	14.33	18.33	10.33	5.66
$1/2$	5	2.00	6.50	11.00	15.50	20.00	11.00	6.36
1	5	1.00	7.00	13.00	19.00	25.00	13.00	8.49
2	5	−1.00	8.00	17.00	26.00	35.00	17.00	12.73
3	5	−3.00	9.00	21.00	33.00	45.00	21.00	16.97
4	5	−5.00	10.00	25.00	40.00	55.00	25.00	21.21

*Calculation assumes that all five possible values for return on assets are equally likely.

increases, but not enough to offset the effect of the substitution of lower-cost debt for equity. But as leverage continues to increase, the riskiness of the company's equity increases at an accelerating rate. Note that as the company's leverage doubles from $1/2$ to 1, then from 1 to 2, and then from 2 to 4 in Table 10-1, risk increases first by one-third (to 8.49 from 6.36), then by one-half (to 12.73 from 8.49), and then by two-thirds (to 21.21 from 12.73). Equity investors require greater and greater risk premiums to compensate for the greater variability of their returns. This causes the cost-of-equity curve in Figure 10-1 to become more steeply sloped as leverage increases. Eventually, the increased riskiness more than offsets the favorable impact of increased leverage on expected returns. Beyond that point, the weighted average cost-of-capital curve turns upward.

Illustration of Impact of Leverage on Cost
of Capital
Consider a company that is currently not taxable. The company's new issue debt rate is 12%, and its cost of equity capital is 20% for modest degrees of leverage. The company's cost of capital would be

$$\text{Weighted average cost of capital} = 1 \times 0.20 + 0 \times 0.12 = 0.20, \text{ or } 20.00\%$$

if it were all-equity financed but would be

$$\text{Weighted average cost of capital} = 0.5 \times 0.20 + 0.5 \times 0.12 = 0.16, \text{ or } 16.00\%$$

if it were financed with equal amounts of debt and equity.

Suppose that if the company increased its debt-to-equity ratio to $3:1$, its new issue debt rate would be 15% and its cost of equity capital would be 25%. In that case, its

$$\text{Weighted average cost of capital} = 0.25 \times 0.25 + 0.75 \times 0.15 = 0.175, \text{ or } 17.50\%$$

The company's cost of capital would be higher with a $3:1$ debt-to-equity ratio than with a $1:1$ debt-to-equity ratio. If the company's operating income is $10,000,000 per year, its total market value is $50,000,000 in the unleveraged case; $62,500,000 ($31,250,000 of debt and $31,250,000 of equity) in the $1:1$ case; and $57,142,857 ($42,857,143 of debt and $14,285,714 of equity) in the $3:1$ case.

The variation in the weighted average cost of capital with respect to changing leverage in the preceding example is consistent with the shape of the weighted-average-cost-of-capital curve in Figure 10-1. But should the weighted average cost of capital vary in that manner? To answer this question, it is useful to consider first conditions under which the weighted-average-cost-of-capital curve would be flat. By examining why these conditions fail to hold in the real world, we can better appreciate why the weighted-average-cost-of-capital curve has the shape illustrated in Figure 10-1.

A REAPPRAISAL: DOES THE CHOICE OF CAPITAL STRUCTURE REALLY MATTER?

In their path-breaking article, Modigliani and Miller argued that investors value a company based on the operating profitability of its real assets. According to their view, investors apply a capitalization rate to operating income that does not vary with the company's degree of leverage. In other words, in the Modigliani-Miller world, the value of a company depends on the size of its operating income stream, not on how that stream is divided between debtholders and shareholders. If two companies have identical operating profitability but different capital structures, arbitrage among investors would ensure that the two companies have equal market values.

Illustration of Arbitrage Argument

Consider two companies that each generate $10 million of operating income and that are identical in every other aspect except that company A has debt in its capital structure and company B is debt-free. Suppose that investors currently value the two companies as indicated in Table 10-2. Company A has a higher value because of its leverage.

According to the Modigliani-Miller view, this situation cannot persist. Arbitrage activity would drive the values of the two companies to equality. They

Table 10-2
Illustration of the Impact of Arbitrage Activity
on the Value of Company A and Company B

	Prearbitrage		Postarbitrage	
	Company A	Company B	Company A	Company B
Target capital structure:				
% Debt	50	—	50	—
% Equity	50	100	50	100
Interest rate on debt	12%	—	12%	—
Operating income	$10,000,000	$10,000,000	$10,000,000	$10,000,000
− Interest expense	3,000,000	—	3,000,000	—
Net income	$ 7,000,000	$10,000,000	$ 7,000,000	$10,000,000
÷ Cost of equity capital	0.24	0.22	0.28	0.20
Market value of equity	$29,166,667	$45,454,545	$25,000,000	$50,000,000
+ market value of debt	25,000,000	—	25,000,000	—
Total market value of company	$54,166,667	$45,454,545	$50,000,000	$50,000,000
Weighted average cost of capital	18.46%	22.00%	20.00%	20.00%
Return to an investor who owns 1% of company A and who:	retains it	reinvests in B	retains it	reinvests in B
Composition of investor's funds:				
% Debt	—	50	—	50
% Equity	100	50	100	50
Total investment	$ 291,667	$ 583,334	$ 250,000	$ 500,00
Gross return*	70,000	128,333	70,000	100,000
Less interest†	—	35,000	—	30,000
Net return	$ 70,000	$ 93,333	$ 70,000	$ 70,000

*Calculated as the total investment multiplied by the company's cost of equity capital. It is thus assumed that each company realizes a return on equity equal to its cost of equity capital.
†Assumes an interest rate of 12% on the investor's loan.

would argue along the following lines. A shareholder of company A could realize a greater return on his or her investment with no increase in the amount
of funds invested by selling shares of company A, borrowing enough funds to
create his or her own personal 50% leverage to conform to company A's target
capital structure, and using the proceeds from the share sale and the personal
loan to purchase shares of company B.

Consider an investor who owns 1% of the shares of company A. He or she
can sell these shares for $291,667 (= 0.01 × $29,166,667). The investor then

borrows $291,667. This creates 50% leverage at the investor level, which is identical to the leverage of company A. The investor can purchase 0.0128 (= $583,334/45,454,545), or 1.28% of company B's equity. If the interest rate on the investor's loan is 12%, the investor realizes a return net of interest expense amounting to $93,333 (= $583,334 × 0.22 − 291,667 × 0.12). If the investor had continued to hold the shares of company A, his or her return would have been only $70,000 (= $291,667 × 0.24). Arbitrageurs would thus sell the shares of the leveraged firm, borrow, and purchase shares of the unleveraged firm in order to reap a profit of $23,333 (= $93,333 − 70,000).

Arbitrage activity would continue until there was no longer any opportunity for profit. At that point, under the Modigliani-Miller assumptions, an investor who purchases 1% of company A with nonborrowed funds would realize exactly the same returns as an investor who purchases 1% of company B and borrows half the funds at an interest rate of 12% to make this investment. This is illustrated in Table 10-2. In the "postarbitrage" case, the investor realizes a total return of $70,000 whether he or she creates his or her own leverage and invests in company B or invests in company A and lets the company create the leverage. Under either alternative, the individual investor's investment is 50% leveraged.

Note also that in the postarbitrage case the two companies have the same weighted average cost of capital. Under the Modigliani-Miller assumptions, investors discount each company's operating cash flow at the same rate, in this case 20%:

$$\begin{array}{l} \text{Market value} \\ \text{of company A} \end{array} = \$10,000,000/0.2 = \$50,000,000 = \begin{array}{l} \text{market value} \\ \text{of company B} \end{array}$$

$$= \$25,000,000 + 25,000,000 = \$50,000,000 + 0$$

A company's choice of capital structure in such an environment is irrelevant to its valuation. The use of supposedly "less expensive" debt is exactly offset by the increase in the cost of equity capital (to 28% from 20% in Table 10-2) that results from the increase in leverage. This is illustrated in Figure 10-2. The weighted-average-cost-of-capital curve is horizontal. There is no optimal capital structure.

Conditions Needed to Ensure Irrelevance

Modigliani and Miller's conclusion that capital structure does not affect valuation rests upon a number of simplifying assumptions. First, investors must be able to substitute their own leverage for the corporation's leverage. If they are able to do this at no additional cost, then corporate leverage is not a thing of value. The nature of the investment alternatives available to each investor is not altered by changes in corporate capital structure.

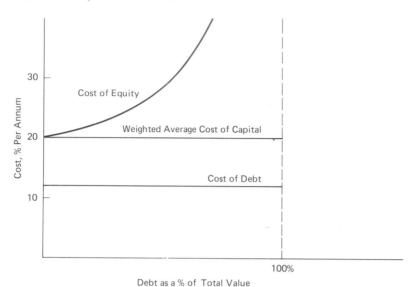

Figure 10-2. The Modigliani-Miller view as to the irrelevance of the firm's choice of capital structure.

This so-called "homemade leverage" is crucial to the irrelevance argument. But can individuals really borrow as cheaply as corporations? Could the share-holders of Exxon Corporation, for example, issue personal 30-year debentures as cheaply as Exxon could? Of course not. Exxon, because of its size and greater financial sophistication, can borrow more cheaply than its individual shareholders. In general, the higher the percentage of individual shareholders and the smaller the percentage of larger, more sophisticated (taxable) institu-tional investors within a company's shareholder body, the greater the advantage of corporate leverage vis-à-vis homemade leverage.

Second, in order for the arbitrage mechanism to work properly, securities markets must be free of imperfections such as transaction costs. Third, in order for investors to be unconcerned about high degrees of leverage, there can be no cost of financial distress, such as bankruptcy penalties. In reality, there are market imperfections of various sorts and there are bankruptcy penalties such as legal fees and the cost of disposing of assets at distress prices.

WHY THE CHOICE OF
CAPITAL STRUCTURE MIGHT MATTER

The irrelevance of capital structure depends on the absence of market imper-fections, such as taxes and bankruptcy penalties. The balance of this chapter discusses how these and other capital market imperfections can cause the firm's choice of capital structure to affect its valuation.

Corporate Income Taxes

Interest payments are tax deductible but dividend payments and retained earnings are not. Thus, the system of corporate taxation imparts a bias in favor of debt financing; interest payments escape taxation at the corporate level.

Table 10-3 illustrates the advantage resulting from the deductibility of interest payments for corporate tax purposes. Companies A and B are identical except that company B is leveraged and has annual interest expense of $200. If neither company paid taxes, each would have $1000 available to distribute to bondholders and stockholders regardless of the mix of debt and equity it employed. But if each company pays taxes at a 46% rate, the interest deductions reduce company B's tax bill by $92 (= $200 × 0.46). Combined income to stockholders and bondholders is greater for the leveraged company by the

Table 10-3
Lower Tax Rate on Personal Equity Income Partially
Offsets the Advantage of Debt Financing

	Company A	Company B
Earnings before interest and taxes	$1,000	$1,000
Interest	—	200
Pretax income	1,000	800
Income taxes (at 46%)	460	368
Income available to common stockholders	540	432
Interest	—	200
Combined income to stockholders and bondholders	$ 540	$ 632
Interest tax shield*	—	$ 92
Combined after-tax income to stockholders and bondholders:		
Interest	—	$ 200
Less personal tax (at 30%)	—	(60)
Equity-related income	$ 540	432
Less personal tax (at 18%)†	(97)	(78)
Combined after-tax income‡	$ 443	$ 494

*Calculated as the tax rate multiplied by the amount of interest paid.

†Assumes one-third of income available to common stockholders is paid out as dividends and taxed at a 30% rate and the other two-thirds are reinvested in the business and realized as long-term capital gains which are taxed at a 12% rate (40% of the ordinary income tax rate). Calculation assumes that the present value of the after-tax long-term capital gain equals the amount of reinvested earnings multiplied by 0.12.

‡Expressed on a present value basis.

amount of the interest tax shield. In effect, the U.S. government pays a subsidy to company B for the use of debt.

Interest tax shields increase the value of a leveraged company over an otherwise identical unleveraged company. As illustrated in Table 10-3,

$$
\begin{array}{l}
\text{Income available} \\
\text{to security holders} \\
\text{of leveraged company}
\end{array}
=
\begin{array}{l}
\text{income available} \\
\text{if company were} \\
\text{unleveraged}
\end{array}
+ \text{ tax shield}
$$

This relationship holds for each accounting period so that

$$
\begin{array}{l}
\text{Total market} \\
\text{value of company}
\end{array}
=
\begin{array}{l}
\text{value if} \\
\text{unleveraged}
\end{array}
+
\begin{array}{l}
\text{present value} \\
\text{of tax shields}
\end{array}
\qquad (10\text{-}2)
$$

Formula 10-2 implies that the total market value of a company increases steadily with increasing leverage because of the greater tax shields. A company should adopt 100% debt financing in order to maximize its value![2] Clearly, this conclusion is sharply at variance with corporate behavior. At year-end 1982, debt represented only approximately 27% of the capitalization of U.S. corporations.[3] It is hard to believe that corporations are so far off the mark. The problem is that the valuation Formula 10-2 is incomplete. It omits factors and, as a result, overstates the value of corporate leverage.

Corporate and Personal Income Taxes

Personal income taxation would not eliminate the advantage of corporate borrowing if the income to bondholders and the income to stockholders were taxed at the same rate. For example, suppose interest income and the income to stockholders are each taxed at a 30% rate. The combined income to stockholders and bondholders of the two companies in Table 10-3 is $378 [= $540 × (1 − 0.3)] in the case of company A and $442 [= $632 × (1 − 0.3)] in the case of company B. The added income resulting from corporate leverage is reduced by the 30% tax rate on personal income, but the net advantage to corporate leverage remains.

The system of personal income taxation treats interest income and equity-related income differently. In particular, long-term capital gains are taxed at a lower rate than interest and dividends, and capital gains tax is deferred until the gain is realized.[4] Table 10-3 also illustrates the combined impact of corporate and personal income taxation. Individual investors are assumed to pay tax on interest income at a 30% rate and on equity-related income at an effective tax rate of 18% (after allowing for the lower tax rate on capital gains). The increase in combined income net of all taxes that results from leveraging is reduced to $51 from $92 because of the higher taxation of personal interest income. The system of personal taxation reduces but does not eliminate the net advantage of corporate borrowing.

It is possible to construct numerical examples in which the higher taxation of interest income completely offsets the value of corporate interest tax shields. Merton Miller put forward this argument in his 1976 presidential address to the American Finance Association.[5] But Miller's argument rests on the assumptions that the tax rate on personal equity-related income is zero and that the personal tax rate on interest income equals the tax rate on corporate income. These assumptions are suspect. Companies do pay dividends, and Treasury tax data indicate that a high percentage of individuals realize more dividend income than the personal dividend exclusion can shelter and consequently have taxable dividend income.[6] In addition, the yield on longer term municipal debt has historically been about 70% of the yield on taxable corporate debt of the same credit rating, which implies a 30% tax rate for the marginal investor. But this 30% tax rate is substantially less than the statutory 46% federal corporate income tax rate. Personal taxation diminishes but does not eliminate the advantage of corporate borrowing.[7]

Financial Distress

There is a tax advantage to corporate borrowing; yet corporations are judicious in their use of leverage. There is a good reason for this. Higher leverage increases the risk of financial distress. In the extreme case, a company that is too highly leveraged and, as a result, finds itself unable to meet its debt service obligations can be forced into bankruptcy by disappointed creditors. This often leads to substantial legal and administrative expenses as well as the costs implicit in selling assets at distress prices. But even if the firm is not forced into bankruptcy, high leverage can impose significant costs. Investors are likely to find the company's stock less attractive as the probability of financial distress increases. The company will find it more difficult to raise funds quickly on terms it finds acceptable. Lenders will require a higher interest rate—if they are willing to lend at all—and trade creditors will normally require more stringent terms. In addition, competitors may become more aggressive in order to exploit the company's perceived financial weakness.

The value relationship (10-2) must be modified to reflect these costs of financial distress:

$$
\begin{array}{c}\text{Total market}\\\text{value of}\\\text{company}\end{array} = \begin{array}{c}\text{value if}\\\text{unleveraged}\end{array} + \begin{array}{c}\text{present}\\\text{value of}\\\text{tax shields}\end{array} - \begin{array}{c}\text{present value}\\\text{of costs of}\\\text{financial distress}\end{array} \quad (10\text{-}3)
$$

Figure 10-3 illustrates the trade-off between tax shield benefits and the costs of financial distress implied in this relationship. The *present value of costs of financial distress* depends on both the likelihood of distress and the costs associated with financial distress. As leverage increases, so does *present value of tax shields* at a more or less steady rate. But the present value of the costs

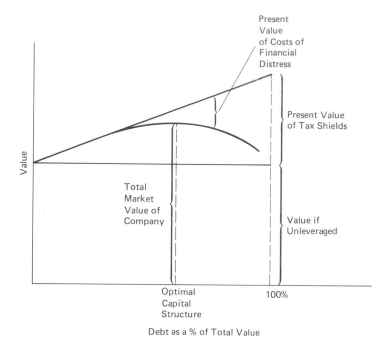

Figure 10-3. The total market value of a corporation in the presence of taxes and costs of financial distress.

of financial distress increases at an increasing rate. At low leverage ratios, increasing leverage increases tax shield benefits more rapidly than the present value of financial distress costs. As a result, increasing leverage enhances value.

If the firm tried to increase its leverage beyond the optimal capital structure indicated in Figure 10-3, it would find that the present value of the costs of financial distress would increase more rapidly than the present value of tax shields. As a result, its total market value would decrease. Thus, the trade-off between the added tax shield benefits and the added costs of financial distress that result from increased leverage determines the optimal capital structure for a company. As a special case, note that Formula 10-3 implies that a company that does not expect to be in a tax-paying position (because it has other means of sheltering its income) should not do any debt financing until it expects to become a taxpayer.

Other Market Imperfections

At least three other market imperfections affect the degree of leverage in the optimal capital structure. First, personal leverage and corporate leverage are not perfect substitutes. When a corporation borrows, its shareholders enjoy limited liability. If a corporation goes bankrupt, its shareholders' losses are limited to their respective investments in the corporation. But if an investor borrows personally and pledges the stock as collateral, the investor faces margin calls if the value of the collateral declines significantly. Even worse, in most instances, if the company goes bankrupt and the stock becomes worthless, the investor would still be liable for the loan.

Second, the effective cost of borrowing tends to be lower the larger the borrower and the more diversified its sources of income. In general, then, corporations can borrow more cheaply than individual investors. In addition, pension funds and certain other institutional investors are not permitted to borrow to finance their investments. For them, homemade leverage is an impossibility.

The foregoing factors provide an impetus to corporate borrowing in lieu of personal borrowing. The third factor works in the opposite direction. Many institutional investors, particularly pension funds, are restricted concerning the stock and bond investments they are permitted to make. For example, most government pension funds can purchase only those bonds that are rated single-A or better by at least one of the major rating agencies. The credit rating assigned to a company's bonds depends to a large extent on the company's leverage. Consequently, if a company raises its leverage to too high a level, its senior debt rating will suffer and the potential market for its bonds will shrink.

During some market periods, there is only a limited market for bonds that are not of investment-grade quality. During difficult market periods, such as 1974 to 1975, the market for non-investment-grade bonds all but vanishes, and even the issuers of bonds that are rated toward the lower end of the investment-grade scale have to agree to reduced maturities, sinking fund schedules, or covenant restrictions that would not be required during normal market periods in order to sell their bonds. In order to enjoy relatively uninterrupted access to the debt market, companies should strive to maintain a degree of leverage consistent with a single-A debt rating.[8] Chapter 11 describes a procedure for setting specific financial ratio targets consistent with this rating objective.

Covenant Restrictions

Higher leverage also increases the likelihood that lenders will require tight covenant restrictions to protect their interests. The various types of covenant restrictions lenders typically require are discussed in Chapter 20. It is sufficient to note here that they can include limitations on the disposition of assets, payment of cash dividends, and additional borrowing, as well as other restrictions that can limit the corporation's operating and financing flexibility. These restrictions become tighter, and the costs consequently become higher, the higher the degree of leverage. But, in general, lenders will not impose meaningful covenant restrictions on a corporation whose senior debt is rated at least single-A.

SUMMARY

The extent to which the firm's choice of capital structure affects the combined valuation of its debt and equity continues to be one of the more controversial subjects in finance. It was traditionally believed that a company could lower its cost of capital and increase its share price by leveraging itself judiciously.

In two now-famous studies, Modigliani and Miller challenged that view. In the first, they argued that the firm's choice of capital structure is irrelevant to its valuation. Investors value the real assets of the corporation and the overall operating income stream these assets generate, and this valuation is not affected by how the income stream is divided between bondholders and stockholders. Accordingly, changes in capital structure cannot affect the size of the pie but only how it is sliced. But that argument rests on the twin assumptions of no taxes and frictionless markets. In the second study, they introduced corporate income taxes and arrived at the startling conclusion that companies should leverage themselves 100% in order to maximize value. In a third study, Miller tried to reestablish irrelevancy by introducing personal taxation and arguing that opportunities for personal leverage eliminate fully the advantage of corporate leverage.

The consensus view currently is that leverage does indeed matter. Opportunities for personal leverage offset partially, but not fully, the advantage of corporate leverage. Several studies have documented the contribution that increased corporate leverage makes to the value of the firm. However, the increased danger of financial distress and reduced marketability of a company's bonds that come with higher leverage place a limit on the degree of leverage that is prudent.

Thus, for any particular company, there would appear to be an optimal capital structure that is determined by the trade-off between the net tax advantage of additional corporate leverage on the one hand and the costs associated with the increased likelihood of financial distress and reduced marketability of corporate debt that would result from additional leverage on the other. Unfortunately, quantifying the various aspects of this trade-off and fixing precisely the optimal capital structure is a very difficult, if not impossible, task. Chapter 11 describes an approach for attempting to deal with it.

Selecting an Appropriate Capital Structure

Chapter 11

Corporations exercise great care in choosing an appropriate capital structure. The choice is difficult because the factors involved are complex and the impact of each on the value of the firm is not clearcut. In principle, a corporation should balance the net advantage of additional leverage against the additional costs that would result. Unfortunately, the net advantage to a particular company's shareholders of an increase in corporate leverage, the change in the present value of the expected costs of financial distress, and the cost of reduced marketability of the corporation's debt do not lend themselves to precise measurement.

A number of methods exist for analyzing the impact of alternative capital structures. But in the end the choice of capital structure requires expert judgment. The analytical models suggest a range of reasonable capital structures rather than pinpoint the optimal one. This chapter describes how a company can take into account the various factors relevant to the capital structure decision in order to select an appropriate (as distinguished from "the" best) capital structure.

INDUSTRY DIFFERENCES IN CAPITAL STRUCTURE

The capital structure choices of comparable companies provide useful guidance to a company that is reconsidering its capital structure or formulating a capitalization policy for the first time. Several studies have detected systematic differences in capital structure across industries.[1]

Table 11-1 is based on the results of one such study. Bowen, Daley, and Huber measured the ratio of long-term debt plus short-term debt to total assets at 3-year intervals between 1951 and 1969 for companies in nine

Table 11-1
Industry Differences in Leverage, 1951–1969

Industry (SIC Code)	1951		1960		1969		Average 1951–1969‡	
	Leverage*	Rank†	Leverage*	Rank†	Leverage*	Rank†	Leverage*	Rank†
Auto parts and accessories (3714)	0.38	5§	0.26	1	0.34	1	0.29	1
Steel (3310)	0.37	3§	0.32	3	0.35	2	0.33	2
Oil-integrated domestic (2912)	0.32	2	0.31	2	0.37	3	0.34	3
Textile products (2200)	0.29	1	0.38	4§	0.47	6	0.38	4
Chemicals (2800)	0.38	5§	0.38	4§	0.42	4	0.40	5
Retail department stores (5311)	0.37	3§	0.41	6	0.48	7	0.42	6
Retail food chains (5411)	0.45	8	0.42	7	0.46	5	0.44	7
Aerospace (3721)	0.52	9	0.48	8	0.54	8	0.50	8
Air transportation (4511)	0.44	7	0.63	9	0.60	9	0.55	9

*Leverage measured as long-term debt plus short-term debt divided by total assets.

†Annual ranking from lowest leverage (1) to highest leverage (9).

‡Average of the annual industry averages for 1951, 1954, 1957, 1960, 1963, 1966, and 1969.

§Denotes tie.

Source: Robert M. Bowen, Lane A. Daley, and Charles C. Huber, Jr., "Evidence on the Existence and Determinants of Inter-Industry Differences in Leverage," *Financial Management,* vol. 11, Winter 1982, pp. 10–20.

industries (defined by four-digit SIC codes).[2] Table 11-1 provides their results for 1951, 1960, and 1969, and provides industry rankings for each year. The rankings did not remain fixed over the 19-year period, but the rankings do appear fairly stable, particularly between 1960 and 1969. Auto parts manufacturers, steel companies, and domestic integrated oil companies were the least highly leveraged throughout the 19-year period. Aerospace and air transportation companies were the most highly leveraged. Bowen, Daley, and Huber performed a variety of statistical tests that established more rigorously that the differences in capital structure illustrated in Table 11-1 were truly significant (in a strict statistical sense) and that these differences persisted over time.

The systematic differences in industry capital structure can be attributed to two principal factors: differences in the degree of operating risk and differences in the extent of tax shelter provided by accelerated depreciation, investment tax credit, and operating tax loss carryforwards. Both factors are easy to explain.

Differences in Operating Risk

We found in Chapter 10 that increasing the degree of leverage in a company's capital structure increases the variability of the returns to its shareholders. Increasing leverage increases the degree of financial risk. But it increases the financial risk to the bondholder as well as to the shareholder. Table 11-2 illustrates this point.

Table 11-2 shows how the company's interest coverage varies with its return on assets and the degree of leverage in its capital structure. From Formula 2-10, interest coverage is measured as:

$$\text{Interest coverage ratio} = \text{EBIT} \div \text{interest expense} \qquad (11\text{-}1)$$

where EBIT denotes earnings before interest and income taxes. In the high operating risk case, for example a manufacturing company in a very competitive industry, the company's expected return on assets is 12%, but the actual return it realizes might be as low as 5% or as high as 17%. In the low operating risk case, for example an electric utility company, the company's expected return on assets is still 12%, but the realized return varies within the narrower band from 10 to 14%.

If the company belongs to an industry characterized by high operating risk, its interest coverage might fall to 2.00 times if its leverage ratio is 0.25 or only 1.00 time if its leverage ratio is 0.50. With higher leverage, it would fail in the worst case to cover its interest charges. But if the company belongs to an industry characterized by low operating risk, even in the worst case it would cover its interest charges at least 2.00 times as long as its leverage ratio does not exceed 0.50. Thus, the low operating risk company could support greater leverage; the company is capable of taking on a higher degree of financial risk

Table 11-2
**Degree of Operating Risk Affects the Capacity
to Support Additional Leverage**
(Dollar Amounts in Millions)

High Operating Risk

	5% Return on Assets			12% Return on Assets			17% Return on Assets		
	Low Leverage	Modest Leverage	High Leverage	Low Leverage	Modest Leverage	High Leverage	Low Leverage	Modest Leverage	High Leverage
Total assets	$100	$100	$100	$100	$100	$100	$100	$100	$100
Total debt/total assets	0.25	0.50	0.75	0.25	0.50	0.75	0.25	0.50	0.75
Total debt	$ 25	$ 50	$ 75	$ 25	$ 50	$ 75	$ 25	$ 50	$ 75
Earnings before interest and taxes	$ 5.0	$ 5.0	$ 5.0	$12.0	$12.0	$12.0	$17.0	$17.0	$17.0
Interest (at 10%)	2.5	5.0	7.5	2.5	5.0	7.5	2.5	5.0	7.5
Interest coverage	2.00X	1.00X	0.67X	4.80X	2.40X	1.60X	6.80X	3.40X	2.67X

Low Operating Risk

	10% Return on Assets			12% Return on Assets			14% Return on Assets		
	Low Leverage	Modest Leverage	High Leverage	Low Leverage	Modest Leverage	High Leverage	Low Leverage	Modest Leverage	High Leverage
Total assets	$100	$100	$100	$100	$100	$100	$100	$100	$100
Total debt/total assets	0.25	0.50	0.75	0.25	0.50	0.75	0.25	0.50	0.75
Total debt	$ 25	$ 50	$ 75	$ 25	$ 50	$ 75	$ 25	$ 50	$ 75
Earnings before interest and taxes	$10.0	$10.0	$10.0	$12.0	$12.0	$12.0	$14.0	$14.0	$14.0
Interest (at 10%)	2.5	5.0	7.5	2.5	5.0	7.5	2.5	5.0	7.5
Interest coverage	4.00X	2.00X	1.33X	4.80X	2.40X	1.60X	5.60X	2.80X	1.87X

than the high operating risk company because of the lower degree of operating risk. Because operating risks do vary from one industry to another, it is not surprising that capital structures do also.

Differences in Capacity to Utilize Tax Benefits

The Bowen, Daley, and Huber study mentioned earlier furnished evidence that the relative (to company size) amount of tax shelter provided by accelerated depreciation, investment tax credit, and operating tax loss carryforwards was negatively related to the average degree of leverage in the capital structures of companies in the nine industries listed in Table 11-1. One would expect that because of differences in capital intensity across industries, there would be differences in the availability of other sources of tax shelter. These operating sources of tax shelter reduce a company's ability to utilize the tax shelter benefits that would result from increased leverage. Greater availability of operations-related tax shelter should therefore reduce the degree of leverage that is optimal. Interindustry differences in the availability of operations-related tax shelter should therefore produce systematic differences in capital structure, which is just what Bowen, Daley, and Huber found. In addition, they found a tendency for the capital structures of individual firms in an industry to gravitate toward the industry mean over a 5- to 10-year period.

DEBT RATINGS AND CAPITAL STRUCTURE

Interindustry differences in capital structure are only part of the story. There are differences among firms within any particular industry with respect to tax position, size, competitive position, operating risk, business prospects, and so on. There also appear to be important differences among firms with respect to their desired level of financial risk and degree of access to the capital markets, as reflected in the ratings they strive to achieve for their debt obligations. Bond rating is, in practice, a very important factor affecting a company's choice of capital structure.

Significance of Bond Rating

Rating agencies, notably Moody's Investors Service, Inc., and Standard & Poor's Corporation, publish debt ratings that reflect their assessment of the relative likelihood that the issuer will experience financial distress during the life of the issue. The highest four rating categories (Moody's Aaa, Aa, A, and Baa and Standard & Poor's AAA, AA, A, and BBB) constitute the range of *investment grade ratings*. The lower ratings represent *speculative grade ratings*. Each agency distinguishes different levels of credit quality within each rating category below triple-A. Moody's attaches numbers 1 (high), 2 (medium), and 3 (low) whereas Standard & Poor's attaches "+" for the highest and "−" for the lowest. Thus, for example, a medium-grade single-A credit would be rated (Moody's/Standard & Poor's) A2/A and would be of somewhat lower quality than one rated A1/A+.

Bonds rated among the top three investment-grade categories have investment attributes that range from "favorable" to "gilt edge" and a capacity to pay interest that ranges from "strong" to "extremely strong" according to the rating definitions these agencies have adopted. Bonds rated in the lowest investment-grade category (Baa/BBB) offer investors less protection than higher-rated bonds; that is, the risk of financial distress prior to maturity is greater than in the case of higher-rated bonds. Bonds rated speculative grade are significantly riskier, at best offering bondholders only "very moderate" protection and at worst being already in default.

The distinction between investment-grade ratings and speculative-grade ratings is important because of restrictions placed on certain classes of institutional investors. Under regulations issued by the Comptroller of the Currency, bonds must generally be of investment-grade quality in order to qualify as *legal investments* for commercial banks. In addition, various state laws impose minimum-rating and other standards that debt obligations (or their issuers) must satisfy in order for the bonds to qualify as legal investments for savings banks, trust companies, public pension funds, and insurance companies. In general, bonds rated speculative grade do not qualify as legal investments and, in many cases, state regulators require ratings no lower than single-A for legal investment purposes.

If a company's bonds fail to qualify as a legal investment, the market for them narrows. The institutions just mentioned are severely restricted in terms of their ability to purchase bonds that fail to qualify as legal investments, and many face an absolute prohibition. Bond rating is very important, then, to a company that wants to ensure its uninterrupted access to the capital markets on acceptable terms.

The choice of a bond rating objective by a company thus involves a decision as to (1) the relative degree of risk of future financial distress it is willing to bear and (2) the relative degree of future access to the capital markets it would like to achieve. A single-A rating would seem to be a reasonable rating target, but companies might prefer to be more or less conservative than this standard implies.

Bond Rating and the Choice of Financial Objectives

Once a company has chosen its rating target, how can it decide what financial objectives are most consistent with achieving this target? The rating agencies apply a large number of criteria in reaching a judgment concerning the most appropriate rating. For example, in the case of industrial companies, Standard

& Poor's evaluates the following nine factors: (1) degree of operating risk in the company's principal businesses, (2) the company's market position in these businesses, (3) the company's margins and other measures of its profitability, (4) quality of the company's management, (5) conservatism of the company's accounting policies, (6) fixed charge coverage, (7) leverage (including off-balance-sheet debt) in relation to the liquidation value of the company's assets, (8) adequacy of cash flow to meet future debt service obligations, and (9) the company's future financial flexibility in the light of its future debt service obligations and planned capital expenditure requirements.[3] While there is no all-purpose formula that expresses bond rating as a function of these factors, the values of certain key credit statistics for comparable companies whose debt carries the target debt rating offer useful guidance.

Table 11-3 shows how the values of 10 key credit statistics vary across the six highest rating categories assigned by Standard & Poor's. Note how pretax interest coverage, pretax fixed charge coverage, cash flow to long-term debt, and cash flow to total debt are all progressively better the higher the company's senior debt rating. These four measures of a company's ability to continue to service its debt on a current basis are probably more important than the other six indicators of credit quality. Taken together, the 10 measures would go a long way toward distinguishing a stronger credit from a weaker one.

Having selected a rating target, a company can use the values of the key credit statistics of comparable companies whose debt has been assigned the target rating as a rough guide to the ratio targets it should set for itself. A method for accomplishing this is described later in the chapter. For now, three points of caution should be emphasized:

1. Quantitative factors are not the entire story. A deteriorating market position or perceived weaknesses in management will require above-average credit statistics.
2. Achieving an improved credit rating requires a proven track record. Simply achieving improved credit statistics will not necessarily guarantee a higher credit rating; the company must demonstrate that it can maintain them.
3. The averages may change over time. There was a noticeable deterioration in credit quality between 1978 and 1982. In view of this, a company would be well-advised to strive for better-than-average financial ratios, particularly if it is trying to improve its debt rating.

ANALYZING THE EFFECT OF ALTERNATIVE CAPITAL STRUCTURES

There are at least three basic considerations involved in the choice of capital structure.

Table 11-3
Senior Debt Ratings as Indicators of Credit Quality*

Senior Debt Rating†	"AAA"	"AA"	"A"	"BBB"	"BB"	"B"
Interest coverage ratio	14.44×	7.61×	5.47×	3.26×	2.43×	1.53×
Fixed charge coverage ratio‡	7.46	4.42	3.33	2.31	2.06	1.34
Cash flow/long-term debt	250.94%	109.54%	68.18%	39.01%	27.73%	13.90%
Cash flow/total debt	138.56	75.13	55.68	33.60	24.55	11.18
Pretax return on average long-term capital employed	29.04	24.93	19.73	15.95	17.23	12.58
Operating income/sales	16.65	14.45	12.44	9.57	12.62	9.14
Long-term debt/capitalization	11.56	19.61	25.66	35.95	42.43	56.11
Total debt/capitalization including short-term debt	16.98	24.88	30.06	38.02	47.81	60.33
Total debt/capitalization including short-term debt (including 8× rents)	29.45	37.86	40.81	48.59	55.41	66.70
Total liabilities/tangible shareholders' equity and minority interest	76.43	97.31	104.11	127.86	182.02	276.66

*Median of the 3-year simple arithmetic averages for the period 1980–1982 for companies whose senior debt had the indicated rating.

†As assigned by Standard & Poor's Corporation.

‡Based on full rental charges, rather than the one-third of rental charges used in the SEC fixed charge coverage calculation.

Source: Credit Overview: Industrial Ratings, Standard & Poor's Corporation, New York, November 1983, p. 26.

Ability to Service Debt

A prudent financial manager will not recommend that his or her company incur additional debt unless he or she is confident that the company will be able to generate sufficient cash, even under adverse conditions, to be able to service it, that is, to pay interest and repay principal on schedule.

Various measures of debt servicing capacity are available. One is the interest coverage ratio defined by Formula 11-1. A more comprehensive measure of a company's ability to service its debt obligations, which reflects the interest component of rentals and the need to repay debt, is the ratio:

$$
\begin{aligned}
\text{Debt service} \atop \text{coverage ratio} &= \left(\text{EBIT} + \tfrac{1}{3} \text{ of rentals} \right) \\
&\div \left(\text{interest expense} + \tfrac{1}{3} \text{ of rentals} + \frac{\text{principal repayments}}{1 - \text{tax rate}} \right)
\end{aligned}
\tag{11-2}
$$

Principal repayments must be divided by $1 -$ tax rate because principal repayments are not tax deductible; they are paid out of after-tax dollars.

A company can evaluate the impact of alternative capital structures by calculating the interest coverage ratio, fixed charge coverage ratio, debt service coverage ratio, etc., for each capital structure under different projected business scenarios and then comparing the calculated values with benchmarks that reflect the company's desired credit quality. Table 11-3 suggests the following rough benchmarks. If a company in an industry characterized by average cyclicality, or operating risk, wishes to meet minimum investment-grade standards, it should strive for annual pretax interest coverage of no less than 3.26 times and annual pretax fixed charge coverage of no less than 2.31 times under reasonably conservative "expected case" assumptions. It must also strive for, at a minimum, debt service coverage of no less than 1.00 time under "pessimistic" assumptions.

A company in a highly cyclical industry should set higher interest coverage and fixed charge coverage ratio standards in order to compensate for the higher level of operating risk, while one in an acyclic industry can prudently set lower standards. For example, an electric utility company can set lower coverage ratio standards than a manufacturing company in a highly competitive industry. A company that wishes to maintain single-A ratios would aim toward pretax interest coverage of at least 5.47 times and pretax fixed charge coverage of at least 3.33 times if it is in an industry of "average" operating risk. Higher or lower standards would be appropriate for companies in more cyclical or less cyclical industries, respectively. More precise benchmarks can be obtained by calculating the three ratios for companies in the same industry that are of the desired credit quality.

In addition, the risk of insolvency will depend on the company's ability to generate cash through additional borrowing, sale of equity securities, or sale of assets. With regard to the latter, the more liquid a company's assets, the higher the degree of leverage they are generally capable of supporting. Thus, a real estate company or a credit company can generally support relatively high degrees of leverage.

Ability to Utilize Tax Shield Benefits Fully

The principal benefit of debt is the tax deductibility of interest payments. The U.S. government provides a de facto subsidy when a company uses debt financing. But the company will be able to turn this subsidy into cash only if it generates sufficient income from operations to be able to claim the tax deductions.

A company that does not pay taxes and does not expect to become a taxpayer should not incur additional debt. The added debt would increase the risk of financial distress. In the absence of any tax shield benefits, the added debt would thus be harmful to shareholders. Note that a company that is not currently in a tax-paying position but expects to be sometime in the future must also think twice before incurring additional debt. It can carry tax losses forward, but the added debt will be beneficial only if the expected present value of these tax shield benefits exceeds the expected present value of the costs of financial distress.

Desired Degree of Access to the Capital Markets

A company that plans to undertake a substantial capital expenditure program will want to ensure its uninterrupted access to the capital markets on acceptable terms. To do so, it will have to maintain adequate credit strength. A company that is large enough to sell debt publicly can ensure reasonably uninterrupted access to this market on acceptable terms by maintaining a strong single-A credit standing. If it is not large enough to tap the public debt market, it will still find it important to maintain single-A financial ratios in order to reduce the likelihood that lenders will require covenant restrictions that might seriously impair the company's operating and financial flexibility.

SELECTING AN APPROPRIATE CAPITAL STRUCTURE

The basic framework for determining an appropriate capital structure consists of a *comparative credit analysis*, which suggests a range of target capital structures that might be appropriate, and a *pro forma financial structure analysis*, which shows the impact of the alternatives within the target range on the company's credit statistics and reported financial results and indicates whether the company will be able to utilize tax shield benefits fully.

Comparative Credit Analysis

In practice, the most widely used technique for selecting an appropriate capital structure utilizes comparative credit analysis. This approach bases the choice of capital structure on the capital structures exhibited by comparable companies whose senior debt carries the desired bond rating. The approach involves the following steps:

1. Select the desired bond rating objective.
2. Identify a set of comparable companies and select from among these the companies whose senior debt has the desired senior debt rating.
3. Perform a comparative credit analysis of these companies in order to define the capital structure (or range of capital structures) most consistent with this rating objective.

Selection of Rating Objective. As noted earlier, a bond rating of single-A seems a reasonable compromise on ensuring continued ability to service the company's debt and relatively uninterrupted capital market access on the one hand and realizing the full tax-saving potential of added leverage on the other. However, more conservative companies and companies that have very heavy future financing programs might strive for a higher debt rating while other companies that are willing to bear greater financial risk might set a lower rating target.

Illustration of Comparative Credit Analysis

Table 11-4 illustrates a comparative credit analysis of specialty chemicals companies that are comparable to Washington Chemical Corporation. There are six specialty chemicals companies with rated debt outstanding. The senior debt ratings (Moody's/Standard & Poor's) range from a low of Ba1/BB to a high of A2/A.

Choice of Financial Ratio Targets. Washington Chemical's top management, upon the recommendation of the company's chief financial officer, who had carefully reviewed Part 3 of this book, decided that a senior debt rating "comfortably within" the single-A range would be appropriate. Three of the companies in Table 11-4 have at least one senior debt rating in the single-A category, and Jackson Chemical Inc. and Western Chemical Corp. are rated in the middle of the single-A category by both major agencies.

Washington Chemical's financial staff prepared the comparative credit analysis. The various credit statistics and financial ratios were calculated in accordance with the formulas presented in Chapter 2. The analysis shows that Washington Chemical is significantly more profitable than one of the A2/A-rated issuers and only slightly less profitable than the other. Washington Chemical's debt-to-capitalization, cash-flow-to-debt, and fixed charge coverage ratios fall

Table 11-4
Comparative Credit Analysis of Specialty Chemicals
Companies with Rated Debt Outstanding*
(Dollar Amounts in Millions)

	Washington Chemical Corp.	Midwest Chemicals Corp.	National Chemicals Inc.	Delaware Chemical Corp.	Wisconsin Industries	Jackson Chemical Inc.	Western Chemical Corp.
Senior Debt Rating (Moody's/ Standard & Poor's)	—	A3/BBB+	Ba1/BBB−	Baa2/BBB−	Ba1/BB†	A2/A	A2/A
Profitability:							
Operating profit margin (2–14)	7.5%	5.7%	1.8%	4.5%	8.9%	4.1%	9.2%
Net profit margin (2–15)	3.9	2.6	1.0	2.3	2.2	2.3	4.1
Return on assets (2–16)	4.7	3.2	2.2	4.9	2.8	4.3	4.9
Return on common equity (2–18)	10.3	9.2	5.0	13.9	8.8	10.8	10.0
Capitalization:							
Short-term debt	$ 15.8	$ 60.2	$ 9.9	$ 10.2	$ 16.4	$ 8.3	$ 36.5
Senior long-term debt	$158.3	$144.3	$ 48.5	$163.0	$110.0	$139.8	$245.5
Subordinated long-term debt	—	—	—	13.3	80.0	8.1	—
Total long-term debt	158.3	144.3	48.5	176.3	190.0	147.9	245.5
Capitalized lease obligations	—	22.2	10.1	19.9	—	—	0.5
Minority interest	—	—	3.2	1.6	—	—	—
Preferred equity	—	2.2	35.0	5.4	—	—	—
Common equity	321.4	253.4	165.5	333.5	162.1	278.2	658.8
Total capitalization	$479.7	$422.1	$262.3	$536.7	$352.1	$426.1	$904.8

Debt Ratios:							
Long-term debt ratio (2–19)	33.0%	34.2%	18.5%	32.8%	54.0%	34.7%	27.1%
Total-debt-to-adjusted-capitalization ratio (2–20)	35.1	47.0	25.2	37.7	56.0	36.0	30.0
Cash-flow-to-long-term-debt ratio (2–22)	60.1	43.7	46.1	36.3	26.8	51.5	62.9
Cash-flow-to-total-debt ratio (2–23)	54.6	32.1	39.4	34.5	24.6	48.8	54.8
Liquicity:							
Current ratio (2–6)	2.4×	1.9×	2.7×	2.1×	1.9×	2.2×	2.6×
Fixed Charge Coverage Ratio (2–11):							
Latest 12 months	3.5×	2.3×	2.4×	3.3×	1.9×	3.3×	3.7×
Latest fiscal year	4.3	4.0	3.8	2.9	2.2	4.4	4.2
One year prior	5.6	3.1	3.2	2.6	2.8	5.4	5.9
Two years prior	6.3	4.0	2.9	2.2	3.9	7.8	4.9

*Numbers within parentheses indicate the number of the formula in Chapter 2 that defines the ratio.
†Based on subordinated debt rating of Ba3/B+.

between the higher and lower of the two values for each ratio exhibited by the two A2/A-rated specialty chemicals companies. Washington Chemical's ratios are substantially better than those of Midwest Chemicals Corp., which is a borderline triple-B–single-A credit. Washington Chemical concluded from this analysis that its financial condition is of medium-grade single-A quality.

Two points regarding the ratios in Table 11-4 require clarification. This book has emphasized the importance of basing financial decisions on market values; yet the financial ratios in Table 11-4, as well as those in Table 11-3, are based on book values. Market values and the factors that create market values are not being ignored, but it is simply impractical to attempt to calculate the ratios in Table 11-4 on the basis of market values. However, the rating agencies do consider the market value of a company's assets in assessing its leverage. But they view these assets on a liquidating basis rather than on a going-concern basis.[4] Thus, the true debt-to-capitalization ratio should value the common equity component on the basis of the liquidation value of the assets rather than on the basis of either the current book value of equity or the prevailing share price of the company's common stock (which reflects the value of the company on a going-concern basis). Assets, such as proven oil and gas reserves, that are relatively liquid will support a higher degree of leverage than less liquid assets. New plant and equipment will tend to support greater leverage than an equal book value amount of antiquated plant. But determining these liquidating values is necessarily subjective because liquid markets for fixed assets generally do not exist and appraisals generally are not available.

Second, the rating agencies evaluate issuers' accounting methods in order to adjust the reported profit measures to a reasonably comparable basis for the issuers in each industry. They also use information reported in the footnotes to the financial statements to adjust reported long-term debt to include "off-balance-sheet liabilities" such as unfunded pension fund liabilities, non-capitalized lease obligations, and take-or-pay contract obligations and other project-financing-related liabilities.

Based on its careful consideration of the comparative credit analysis in Table 11-4, Washington Chemical established the following financial ratio ranges:

Annual fixed charge coverage ratio	3.50–4.00×
Annual cash-flow-to-total-debt ratio	50–60%
Long-term debt ratio	30–35%

In arriving at the third of these ranges, Washington Chemical included the permanent component of short-term debt in long-term debt.

Pro Forma Financial Structure Analysis

Before deciding where to aim within each of these ranges (or whether to be more conservative in its use of leverage), Washington Chemical thought it important to confirm its ability to utilize fully the implied volume of tax shield benefits, particularly under somewhat adverse conditions, and determine what impact, if any, this capital structure policy might have on its dividend policy.

Table 11-5 contains a pro forma financial structure analysis. If Washington Chemical is to achieve and maintain a long-term debt ratio within its target range, it will have to finance itself 30 to 35% with long-term debt. Also, Washington Chemical realized the importance of considering a reasonably pessimistic case as well as its expected case projected operating results. Consequently, there are four cases considered in Table 11-5 that correspond to two different degrees of leverage (long-term debt ratio of 30 and 35%) and two different operating scenarios (10% growth and 5% growth).

It is evident from cases 1 and 2 that Washington Chemical could justify a 35% long-term debt ratio in the expected case scenario. Fixed charge coverage and cash flow to total debt both increase steadily and remain comfortably within their respective target ranges. Moreover, Washington Chemical can utilize fully the tax benefits of ownership and can claim fully all interest deductions, and its external equity financing requirement would be very modest ($10.3 million if the long-term debt ratio is 35% and $21.9 million if it is only 30%). Such modest requirements would probably not jeopardize its dividend policy.

Under a more pessimistic operating scenario, cases 3 and 4 illustrate that Washington Chemical's fixed charge coverage and cash-flow-to-total-debt ratios would eventually fall below their respective target ranges. The deterioration is less severe in case 4 because the long-term debt ratio is only 30%. However, the external equity financing requirement is greater. Because it attaches some positive likelihood to the pessimistic case, Washington Chemical decided to "hedge" itself and finance itself in the ratio of one-third debt to two-thirds equity. Because Washington Chemical can fully utilize all available tax deductions even in the pessimistic case, the company has no plans to use leveraged lease or preferred stock financing. Thus, its financing ratios will be one-third conventional long-term debt and two-thirds common equity.

Other Aspects of the Capital Structure Decision

Companies often adopt more complex capital structures that include one or more layers of subordinated debt, convertible debt, capitalized lease obligations, preferred equity, or other forms of capital.

Subordinated Debt. Holders of subordinated debt rank behind senior debtholders in the event of default. If strict priority were preserved in bankruptcy, a layer of subordinated debt would be just as beneficial as additional equity to senior debtholders. In addition, the interest payments to subordinated debtholders

Table 11-5
Pro Forma Financial Structure Analysis
for Washington Chemical Corporation
(Dollar Amounts in Millions)

	Initial	Projected Ahead				
		1 Year	2 Years	3 Years	4 Years	5 Years
Case 1: Leverage at Upper End of Range/Expected Case Operating Results						
Pretax income × 0.46*	$ 19.8	$ 22.1	$ 24.3	$ 26.7	$ 29.4	$ 32.6
Investment tax credit†	12.5	10.0	12.5	13.5	15.0	15.0
Surplus	$ 7.3	$ 12.1	$ 11.8	$ 13.2	$ 14.4	$ 17.6
Fixed charge coverage	3.5×	3.6×	3.7×	3.7×	3.7×	3.8×
Cash flow‡	$ 95.1	$104.6	$115.1	$126.6	$139.2	$153.2
External equity requirement§	$ 19.0	$ (3.6)	$ 5.8	$ 4.8	$ 6.2	$ (2.9)
Cash flow to total debt	54.6%	56.8%	57.3%	58.0%	58.6%	60.3%
Case 2: Leverage at Lower End of Range/Expected Case Operating Results						
Pretax income × 0.46*	$ 19.8	$ 22.2	$ 24.5	$ 27.1	$ 29.9	$ 33.3
Investment tax credit†	12.5	10.0	12.5	13.5	15.0	15.0
Surplus	$ 7.3	$ 12.2	$ 12.0	$ 13.6	$ 14.9	$ 18.3
Fixed charge coverage	3.5×	3.7×	3.7×	3.8×	3.9×	4.0×
Cash flow‡	$ 95.1	$104.6	$115.1	$126.6	$139.2	$153.2
External equity requirement¶	$ 19.0	$ (2.0)	$ 8.2	$ 7.2	$ 9.1	$ (0.6)
Cash flow to total debt	54.6%	57.2%	58.4%	59.7%	60.8%	62.9%

Case 3: Leverage at Upper End of Range/Pessimistic Case Operating Results

Pretax income × 0.46*	$ 19.8	$ 20.7	$ 21.1	$ 21.6	$ 21.9	$ 22.4
Investment tax credit†	12.5	10.0	12.5	13.5	15.0	15.0
Surplus	$ 7.3	$ 10.7	$ 8.6	$ 8.1	$ 6.9	$ 7.4
Fixed charge coverage	3.5×	3.5×	3.3×	3.1×	3.0×	2.8×
Cash flow‡	$ 95.1	$ 99.9	$104.8	$110.1	$115.6	$121.4
External equity requirement§	$ 19.0	$ (0.5)	$ 12.6	$ 15.6	$ 21.7	$ 18.0
Cash flow to total debt	54.6%	53.9%	51.5%	49.2%	46.6%	44.9%

Case 4: Leverage at Lower End of Range/Pessimistic Case Operating Results

Pretax income × 0.46*	$ 19.8	$ 20.7	$ 21.3	$ 21.9	$ 22.4	$ 23.1
Investment tax credit†	12.5	10.0	12.5	13.5	15.0	15.0
Surplus	$ 7.3	$ 10.7	$ 8.8	$ 8.4	$ 7.4	$ 8.1
Fixed charge coverage	3.5×	3.5×	3.4×	3.2×	3.1×	3.0×
Cash flow‡	$ 95.1	$ 99.9	$104.8	$110.1	$115.6	$121.4
External equity requirement¶	$ 19.0	$ 1.1	$ 15.2	$ 18.6	$ 25.3	$ 21.2
Cash flow to total debt	54.6%	54.4%	52.5%	50.7%	48.6%	47.2%

* Assumes an income tax rate of 46%.
†Calculated as 10% of capital expenditures.
‡Estimated to grow at 10% per annum in the "expected case" and 5% per annum in the "pessimistic case."
§Calculated so as to preserve a ratio of 35% long-term debt financing to 65% common equity financing when company pays out as dividends one-third of earnings available for common.
¶Calculated so as to preserve a ratio of 30% long-term debt financing to 70% common equity financing when company pays out as dividends one-third of earnings available for common.

are tax deductible, whereas payments to equity holders are not, which benefits the issuer. However, interest payments and principal repayments must be made in a timely fashion on subordinated debt as well as on senior debt in order for the issuer to avoid default.

In view of the greater exposure to default risk, the rating agencies generally rate subordinated debt one step below senior debt if the senior debt is rated investment-grade and two steps below senior debt if the senior debt is rated speculative-grade.[5] The rating differential adds about 25 basis points (or more in the case of speculative-grade issues) to the cost of a new debt issue. Moreover, because strict priority is not always preserved in bankruptcy, the rating agencies will generally add nonconvertible subordinated debt to senior debt for purposes of their ratio calculations. In view of the higher interest cost, $1 of subordinated debt has a more severe impact than $1 of senior debt on a company's coverage and cash-flow-to-debt ratios. Consequently, investment-grade industrial companies seldom issue nonconvertible subordinated debt.

Finance companies typically do issue subordinated debt. Because of the comparatively close matching of the maturity structures of their assets and their liabilities, finance companies can support a high degree of leverage. Because the bulk of their business consists of lending funds at a favorable spread over their funding costs, a well-run finance company will have the capacity to utilize fully the interest tax shields even when it is very highly leveraged. The subordinated debt will provide comfort to senior lenders, just as equity does, and tax deductions to the issuer.

Companies customarily do issue convertible debt on a subordinated basis. This is appropriate because both issuers and investors expect the issue to be converted into common equity, an even more junior security, within a matter of years. Hence, issuing convertible debt on a senior basis would not normally lead to significant cost savings.

Capitalized Lease Obligations. Companies that cannot fully utilize the tax benefits of ownership often find it advantageous to lease assets from entities that can claim these tax deductions and that are willing to pay something for them in the form of reduced lease payments. But failure to make a timely lease payment places a company in default under the lease agreement. Consequently, lease obligations are really a form of debt obligation. The rating agencies customarily include capitalized lease obligations in long-term debt. The decision as to whether to take on capitalized lease obligations or to borrow on a conventional basis thus hinges principally on tax considerations.

Preferred Equity. Preferred stock is a hybrid security, incorporating certain debt features and certain equity features. For a nonregulated company, preferred equity financing can be an economical alternative to debt financing when the company does not expect to have to pay income taxes for several years because corporate holders receive 85% of the dividends tax-free. The issuer benefits to the extent holders effectively pass part of the tax savings back to the issuer by accepting a dividend rate that is lower than the interest rate they would require on a similarly structured debt issue.

Failure to make a timely preferred dividend or preferred sinking fund payment will not put the issuer into default. Consequently, substituting preferred stock for a portion of a company's debt will enhance the position of debtholders. However, companies normally treat their preferred stock payment obligations as though they were fixed. Consequently, if a company issues a significant amount of preferred stock, particularly if it contains a sinking fund, these payment obligations can impair the credit standing of the company's debt securities.[6]

Captive Finance Subsidiary. A large number of companies have formed captive finance subsidiaries. Under generally accepted accounting principles, an industrial company normally does not have to consolidate a captive finance subsidiary for financial reporting purposes, even if the captive's business and financial condition are inextricably tied to those of the parent.

The rating agencies generally analyze the credit quality of a company that has a captive finance subsidiary by examining the company both with and without the finance subsidiary fully consolidated.[7] When the financial support mechanisms that run from the parent to the captive are extremely tight (as they usually are) the avoidance of consolidation per se probably has little, if any, real impact on the parent's debt capacity. However, if the captive conducts a significant portion of its business away from its parent and is also capable of standing alone should its parent have to file for bankruptcy, having a separate finance subsidiary—regardless of the accounting treatment—could benefit a company if that enables it to leverage the assets in the subsidiary more highly than it could if the subsidiary's assets were owned directly by the parent.

EFFECTING CHANGES IN CAPITAL STRUCTURE

Following a change in management or a change in management philosophy, a company might reassess its capital structure. Suppose that it finds that its desired capital structure differs significantly from its current capital structure. What should the company do?

The company has two basic choices. It could alter its capital structure slowly by adjusting its future financing mix. For example, suppose a company's target capital structure consists of one-third long-term debt and two-thirds common equity while its current capital structure contains one-quarter long-term debt and three-quarters common equity. The company could cure this underleveraged condition by financing with, say, 50% long-term debt and 50%

common equity until its long-term debt ratio reaches one-third. However, this would mean that the company's capital structure would continue to be suboptimal for as long as it took the company to over-debt-finance and correct the condition. Moreover, the company's future financing mix would deviate from the desired one-third and two-thirds.

Alternatively, the company could alter its capital structure more quickly through an exchange offer, a recapitalization, or a debt or share repurchase. This would enable the company to begin employing immediately a mix of financing that conforms to its desired capital structure. This approach involves various transaction costs, however.

If a company's capital structure deviates from its target capital structure to the extent that the company is one full category or more away from its rating objective, an exchange offer or some other type of transaction designed to effect an immediate change in capital structure is probably warranted. If the company is less than one full category away from its rating objective (e.g., it is a weak single-A credit and it wants to become a strong single-A credit), altering its retention ratio and its external financing mix is probably more appropriate. If it does alter its financing mix, however, it should use its new target capitalization ratios in calculating its weighted average cost of capital.

SUMMARY

Choosing an appropriate capital structure involves balancing the net tax advantage of additional leverage against the additional risk of insolvency and the cost of reduced financial flexibility that can result from increased leverage. Unfortunately, these cost factors do not lend themselves to precise measurement. As a result, a company cannot pinpoint the truly "best" capital structure. From a practical standpoint, the best the firm can do under present circumstances is infer an appropriate capital structure from the senior debt ratings and capital structure choices of closely comparable companies. This basic approach is reasonable in view of the evidence regarding systematic differences in capital structure across industries.

This chapter described and illustrated a procedure a company can use to select an appropriate capital structure. The procedure involves two important steps. First, the company conducts a comparative credit analysis. This involves identifying a set of closely comparable companies from an operating standpoint. These companies will have comparable operating risk profiles and, because corporate tax positions also tend to vary systematically across industries, reasonably comparable tax situations. The company's finance staff then calculates the values of the key financial ratios for each company in the set in order to determine the relationship between senior debt rating and financial structure within the set of comparable companies.

Bond rating serves as a surrogate for both the relative risk of financial distress and the relative degree of free access to the capital markets. A senior debt rating in the single-A range connotes very modest risk of financial distress and is usually sufficient to ensure uninterrupted access to the capital markets on acceptable terms. The choice of debt rating together with the results of the comparative credit analysis permit a company to specify reasonable ranges of variation of the key financial ratios that define its capital structure.

The second step in the procedure involves conducting a pro forma financial structure analysis. This tests, among other things, the company's ability to utilize fully both the tax benefits of ownership under its planned capital expenditure program and the interest tax shields if it finances itself in accordance with its target capital structure. If it cannot, then it should reduce its target debt ratio. The result of this two-step process is a target capital structure that balances the tax advantages against the costs of a further increase in financial leverage.

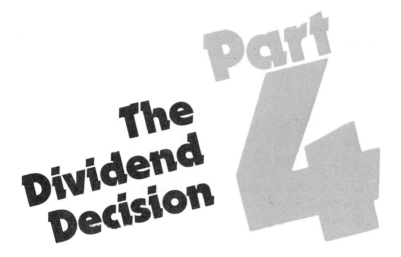

The Dividend Decision

Part 4

Part 4 deals with a financial policy decision that is typically of considerable concern to shareholders: the corporation's dividend policy. The dividend decision involves a number of interrelated considerations that are illustrated by the following example.

The Board of Directors of Major Pharmaceutical Company will discuss at its February meeting whether to increase Major's quarterly per-share dividend. In preparation for that meeting, Major's board chairperson has asked the company's treasurer to study the company's dividend policy and to recommend appropriate dividend action to the board.

Table 13-5 provides Major's 10-year dividend history. Major's *payout ratio*, the ratio of dividends per share to its earnings per share, has decreased slightly over the 10-year period, whereas the average payout ratio of the companies that comprise Standard & Poor's Corporation's drug industry group has increased more or less steadily from roughly 40% to roughly 50% during the same period. In addition, Major paid out a slightly lower percentage of available cash flow in the form of dividends during the past 5 years than it had during the prior 5-year period.

Major projects earnings per share of $5, $6, and $7.20 in the next 3 years, respectively. However, Major will have to increase its capital expenditure budget substantially above historical levels in two of those years in order to complete the development of its new arthritic pain killer and to purchase additional plant and equipment to accommodate production of the new drug.

Major's treasurer has prepared the following list of questions for study:

- Is a dividend increase likely to increase Major's share price?
- Is Major's current payout ratio appropriate?
- Would a share repurchase program benefit Major's shareholders more than a cash dividend?
- In view of Major's heavy capital expenditure requirements, should Major temporarily cut the dividend or should it pay a stock dividend instead of a cash dividend in order to conserve cash?

The responses to these and related questions will determine a company's *dividend policy*: What percentage of its earnings and cash flow should a company distribute to its shareholders; in what forms should it distribute the cash; and how should it time these distributions? Chapter 12 deals principally with the somewhat controversial question of whether there is any connection between a company's dividend policy and its share price. Chapter 13 discusses from a practical standpoint how a company can go about selecting an appropriate dividend policy. Chapter 14 explores the relative attractiveness to shareholders of cash dividends and share repurchases, the two principal means by which a corporation can distribute cash to its shareholders.

During the course of these discussions, we will help the treasurer of Major Pharmaceutical Company prepare the recommendation to the company's board.

Does Dividend Policy Affect a Company's Share Price?

Chapter 12

The critical question in the area of dividend policy is whether a company's choice of dividend policy can affect its share price. As often happens in finance, there are conflicting points of view.

One school of thought, the traditional one, advocates high payout ratios. According to the traditional view, shareholders prefer immediate dividends over less certain and more distant capital gains, which would presumably result if the cash were reinvested in the business instead of being paid out as dividends. For obvious reasons, finance textbooks have dubbed this view the "bird-in-the-hand argument."

A second school of thought takes the opposite stance. According to that view, shareholders prefer capital gains over dividends, and hence low payout ratios, because capital gains are taxed at a lower rate than dividends (at least to individual shareholders).

A third school of thought, which owes its origin to Merton Miller and Franco Modigliani's classic article on dividend policy, maintains that a company's stock market value is relatively insensitive to its choice of dividend policy.[1] Their article demonstrated that under somewhat idealized conditions and with a company's capital expenditure program held fixed, changes in the company's payout ratio would not affect its stock market value. According to this view, dividend policy is a passive rather than an active decision; each period a company should first determine its capital investment program and then pay out as dividends whatever cash is left over. However, this so-called "dividend irrelevance" does depend on Miller and Modigliani's assumptions.

A fourth school of thought, which has attracted growing support in recent years, has brought the dividend policy debate full circle. According to this

199

view, dividend changes represent an important signal to investors regarding changes in management's expectations as to the company's future earnings. In particular, a dividend increase signals the expectation of higher future earnings. It is widely acknowledged that, at least in this particular sense, dividend policy is relevant to share valuation.

Most important from a practical standpoint, companies actually behave as though dividends do matter. For example, it is not uncommon to find rapidly growing companies with funds needs that are growing more rapidly than earnings but which nevertheless pay small dividends. Also, there are many companies, such as electric utilities, that have relatively high payout ratios and that sell new issues of common stock from time to time. If dividend policy really did not matter, it would be cheaper for these companies to pay out smaller dividends and finance capital investment with retained earnings rather than more expensive new issues.

It is the author's view that a company's choice of dividend policy can affect its stock market value, even though the precise impact can generally not be quantified. In order to provide a perspective on why dividend policy might matter, this chapter discusses the various points of view concerning the relevance (or lack thereof) of dividend policy and explores the reasons why a company should exercise care in establishing dividend policy and, particularly, in changing its dividend rate.

THE TRADITIONAL VIEW OF THE SIGNIFICANCE OF DIVIDEND POLICY

If the amount of dividends a company pays affects its share price, there exists some optimum level of dividends that maximizes the company's stock market value. In the extreme, if one believes that shareholders always prefer more dividends to less, the company should pay out all its earnings. However, few would take the argument that far.

Several models have been developed to assist in determining the optimal dividend policy. One of the earliest, which has served as a foundation for later models, was presented in Benjamin Graham and D. L. Dodd's classic book on securities analysis[2]:

$$\frac{\text{Share}}{\text{price}} = \frac{\text{price-earnings}}{\text{multiple}} \times \left(\frac{\text{dividends}}{\text{per share}} + \frac{\text{1/3 of earnings}}{\text{per share}}\right) \qquad (12\text{-}1)$$

Graham and Dodd calculated the *price-earnings multiple* as the multiplier that would be applied to earnings alone if the company paid a "normal" dividend, representing two-thirds of its earnings.[3] They intended Formula 12-1 to apply principally to the stocks of nongrowing, non-blue chip companies, but others have tried to apply it more broadly.

The Graham-Dodd model implies that an additional dollar of dividends is four times as valuable to stockholders as an additional dollar of retained earnings. For example, if a company whose multiple is 12 earns an extra dollar, paying out that entire dollar increases the share price by $12 \times (\$1 + \$ \frac{1}{3}) = \$16$, whereas retaining that dollar increases the share price by only $12 \times (\$ \frac{1}{3}) = \$4$, i.e., only one-fourth as much.

James Walter later developed a model that can lead to the opposite conclusion[4]:

$$\text{Share price} = \left(\frac{\text{dividends}}{\text{per share}} + \frac{\text{retained}}{\substack{\text{earnings} \\ \text{per share}}} \times \frac{\text{return on common equity}}{\text{market capitalization rate}} \right) \div \substack{\text{market} \\ \text{capitalization} \\ \text{rate}} \tag{12-2}$$

where the *market capitalization rate* is calculated as the inverse of the price-earnings ratio that would apply if the company paid out 100% of its earnings. If a company can earn a return on common equity that exceeds its market capitalization rate, then an additional dollar of retained earnings increases the share price by an amount greater than an additional dollar of dividends. For example, if a company can earn 25% on an additional dollar per share of reinvested earnings and its market capitalization rate is 20%, a dollar of additional earnings per share will result in an increase of $\$1 \times (0.25/0.20)/0.20 = \$6.25$ in the share price if it is retained but only $\$1/0.20 = \$5$ if it is paid out. On the other hand, if the market capitalization rate exceeds the return the firm can realize by reinvesting the earnings, it should pay out the additional earnings.

Other examples could be given but, hopefully, these two have given the reader a flavor for the traditional view. Unfortunately, statistical studies designed to test the validity of the traditional models have reached conflicting conclusions. The reasons for the significance of dividend policy are more complex than the traditional view suggests. Clues as to why this is so can be gleaned from reviewing Miller and Modigliani's irrelevancy proposition. Where this proposition breaks down provides the very reasons why dividend policy might matter.

A REAPPRAISAL: DO DIVIDENDS REALLY MATTER?

A company's dividend decision is often mixed up with its capital investment and financing decisions. For example, in the Walter model discussed in the previous section, the firm should retain earnings provided the return on equity in the incremental investment project exceeds the company's cost of equity capital. If a company adheres to this policy, its dividend decision is a by-product of its capital investment decision. If its investment opportunities diminish suddenly and it announces a dividend increase, and as a consequence its share price falls, should the fall in share price be attributed to the diminished investment opportunities or to the dividend increase? It is unclear in this case because the two policies are inseparable.

The debate regarding the significance of dividend policy concerns the significance of a dividend change when a company's capital investment program and capital structure are held fixed. What the Miller and Modigliani article mentioned earlier really demonstrated was that under certain idealized conditions—essentially a frictionless world in which there are no impediments to share transactions such as brokerage commissions and taxes—a company that has selected its desired capital investment program and its desired capital structure cannot affect its share price by paying out either more or less than its residual cash flow.[5] The company should still pay dividends, but only to the extent of any retained earnings that it cannot invest profitably. In such a situation, the dividend decision is a passive one, being dictated by the capital investment decision.

When Dividend Policy Is Irrelevant

Suppose that a company has determined its desired capital investment program and its desired capital structure. It can then calculate the residual earnings that are available for distribution as dividends. Paying out more than this residual would require a new share issue.

The crux of the Miller and Modigliani argument is that the payment of a cash dividend that is financed by a new share issue leaves the stock market value of the firm unchanged. The aggregate value of the shares that were outstanding prior to the dividend distribution decreases by the amount of the dividends paid. The value of the new shares must equal the amount of the dividend distribution in order to leave the firm's capital investment program and capital structure unaffected. Consequently, the aggregate stock market value of the firm is the same before and after the dividend-distribution-cum-new-issue. Value has neither been created nor destroyed; it has simply been transferred from new shareholders to the existing shareholders.

The astute reader will have recognized that the payment of a cash dividend will reduce each shareholder's capital gain (or increase his or her capital loss) by the amount of the dividend per share because the share price should fall by that amount.[6] Would not this make a difference to shareholders whose capital gains are taxed at a lower rate than dividends? Also, would not the cash dividend payment be beneficial to shareowners who desire liquidity and who would have to pay rather large percentage commission charges if they were to try to "manufacture" their own dividends by selling portions of their shareholdings? As discussed below, both concerns are valid in practice; however, in building their argument, Miller and Modigliani assume that frictions such as taxes, transaction costs, and other market imperfections do not exist. Consequently, in their model, an investor is indifferent about receiving a cash dividend payment on the one hand and creating his or her own "homemade dividends" by selling shares on the other.

Illustration of Dividend Irrelevance

Consider a company that has 1 million shares outstanding that are selling at $19 each immediately prior to the announcement of a major capital investment project. The capital investment project will cost $1 million and will have a net present value of $2 million. The company's aggregate stock market value would be $19 million (= $19 × 1 million) prior to this announcement and $21 million (= $19 million + $2 million) following the announcement.

Suppose that the company has $1 million in cash available to finance the capital investment project. If it did so, rather than pay the cash out as a dividend, each share would be worth $21 (= $21 million/1 million). If shareholders wish to raise $1 million of cash, they can do so by selling 47,619 (= 1 million/21) of their own shares.

If instead the company announces a cash dividend of $1 per share, it must find some other source for the $1 million it needs for the project. In order to keep its capital structure fixed, it would have to raise $1 million through the sale of new shares in order (1) to raise sufficient cash and (2) to replace the $1 million reduction in equity that will occur when it pays the dividend.

Suppose the company decides to declare the $1 million dividend and to raise $1 million of new equity immediately after paying the dividend. Immediately after paying the dividend, each share will be worth the predividend share price ($21) less the amount of the dividend ($1), or $20. Note that paying the dividend does not affect shareholder wealth. Prior to the dividend a holder of one share owned a security worth $21; following the dividend payment, the holder of one share has a security worth $20 plus $1 of cash, or $21 in all.

The company must sell 50,000 = (1,000,000/20) new shares, assuming these shares are fairly priced, in order to raise the $1 million it needs. Immediately following the new share issue, the company will have 1,050,000 shares outstanding trading at $20 each, giving it an aggregate stock market value of $21 million (= 1,050,000 × $20), just the value it had prior to the dividend-distribution-cum-new-share-issue. Thus, the mere payment of the dividend has not altered the company's aggregate stock market value or the wealth of its shareholders.

WHY DIVIDEND POLICY MIGHT MATTER

It is difficult to quarrel with the logic of the Miller and Modigliani argument. However, the unrealistic assumptions on which it rests should give little comfort to financial managers. Because new share issues involve flotation costs and capital gains possess a tax advantage over dividends, financial managers generally believe that an additional dollar of retained earnings is mutually better for the corporation and its shareholders than an additional dollar of dividends. Nevertheless, shareholders can be quite outspoken in their desire for dividends. Let us examine briefly the reasons why a corporation might wish to manage its dividend policy actively rather than passively.

Informational Content of Dividend Changes

Dividend changes could have an impact on the price of a company's stock if such changes convey useful information to investors concerning a company's future earnings prospects. For example, if a company sets a long-term payout ratio target and changes this target infrequently, then a change in the dividend rate would signal a corresponding change in management's assessment of the company's earnings prospects. If, in addition, management is loath to cut the dividend rate, a dividend decrease would signal a substantial worsening of the company's earnings prospects while a dividend increase would signal an improvement in the company's minimum sustainable level of earnings.

The available evidence generally supports the view that managers typically adopt a target payout ratio objective and that they are reluctant to cut the dividend rate.[7] Tests of the significance of dividend changes generally have found that the stock market reacts favorably to announcements of dividend increases and adversely to announcements of dividend decreases, supporting the view that dividend changes do have informational content.[8]

If dividend announcements do indeed convey useful information, as the preponderance of the evidence suggests, it is reasonable to expect that the quality of the information these announcements convey would depend on the degree to which dividend changes conform to, or deviate from, an established dividend pattern. Such a pattern would have two important attributes: (1) the amount of each dividend change and (2) the timing of each change. For example, if a company has established a pattern consisting of regular annual increases in its dividend rate and has demonstrated that this pattern of increases is sustainable by keeping its payout ratio stable, any deviation from that pattern—i.e., an increase that differs from the preceding year's increase—would signal to investors a change in the firm's earnings prospects. Moreover, it would signal that it had achieved a higher sustainable *dividend growth rate*, rather than just a higher sustainable *dividend level*.

Because of the informational content of dividend changes, simply paying out residual cash flow on a year-by-year basis would not appear to be in the shareholders' best interest. Such a policy would lead to a dividend level and a payout ratio that could fluctuate wildly, depending on year-to-year changes in the availability of attractive capital investment projects. A company should therefore manage its dividend policy in such a way that dividend changes are orderly and consistent with changes in its earnings prospects.

Shareholder Preference for Current Income

There are natural clienteles for high-payout stocks on the one hand and for high-growth low-payout stocks on the other. For example, electric utility common stocks are among the highest yielding common stocks, and they have undoubtedly attracted a natural clientele of investors who look to the dividend stream as an important source of income.

Shareholders who have a preference for current income could, of course, sell shares on a periodic basis to generate income. However, most investors would probably regard this alternative as less attractive than receiving regular dividend checks. Regular dividend checks relieve investors of the inconvenience and significant brokerage charges involved in making frequent small odd-lot share sales. Thus, it is really market imperfections, rather than a shareholder preference for current income per se, that explains why certain investors prefer high-payout stocks.

Difference in Taxation of Dividends and Capital Gains

Dividends are generally taxed more heavily than capital gains, at least for individual investors. Under the Internal Revenue Code, cash dividends in excess of $100 ($200 for a joint return) are taxed as ordinary income, which means that they can be taxed at marginal rates of up to 50% (as of year-end 1984). In contrast, only 40% of the capital gain realized upon the sale of a share of common stock an investor has held more than 6 months is subject to tax (as of year-end 1984). The balance is tax-free. Hence, the maximum tax rate on long-term capital gains is only 20%. Consequently, for individual investors with high incomes, the tax system creates a bias in favor of capital gains.[9]

There is no such bias in the case of tax-exempt institutions, such as pension funds. Moreover, there is a reverse bias in the case of corporate shareholders and also individuals who receive no more than $100 of dividend income in any year because of the $100 individual dividend exclusion. Under the Code, corporate shareholders are permitted to claim an 85% dividends received deduction. A fully taxable corporate shareholder would therefore pay tax on dividend income at a rate no greater than 6.9% (= 0.15 × 46%) because only 15% of the dividends it receives are taxable. In contrast, corporate shareholders pay tax on long-term capital gains at rates of up to 28%.

Corporate investors thus prefer dividends over capital gains from a purely tax standpoint.

Table 12-1 illustrates the impact that the differential taxation of dividends and capital gains can have on a company's share price. It is assumed that firm 1 and firm 2 are identical except for dividend policy, that a shareholder of either company would have wealth of $30 per share on a pretax basis at the end of the year, and that the 1-year investment would provide a 10% after-tax rate of return.

If dividends and capital gains were not taxed (or if both were always taxed at the same rate), the shares of firms 1 and 2 would have the same value. However, if dividends are taxed at a higher rate, as is currently the case, the shares of the dividend-paying company (firm 2) would have to provide a higher pretax rate of return, and therefore trade at a lower price, in order to compensate for the greater taxes for which its shareholders would be liable. Note that the $0.28 (= $26.94 − $26.66) difference in share prices simply represents the present value of the shareholder's added tax liability that results from owning a share of firm 2 instead of a share of firm 1.[10]

Table 12-1
Implications of Tax Bias in Favor of Capital
Gains for Choice of Dividend Policy

	Dividends and Capital Gains Not Taxed		Dividends Taxed at 30% and Capital Gains Taxed at 12%*	
	Firm 1 (Nondividend Paying)	Firm 2 (Dividend Paying)	Firm 1 (Nondividend Paying)	Firm 2 (Dividend Paying)
After-tax rate of return	10.0%	10.0%	10.0%	10.0%
Year-end dividend	—	$ 1.50	—	$ 1.50
Year-end share price	$ 30.00	28.50	$ 30.00	28.50
Total per share	$ 30.00	$ 30.00	$ 30.00	$ 30.00
Current share price†	$ 27.27	$ 27.27	$ 26.94	$ 26.66
Capital gain:				
Before-tax	2.73	1.23	3.06	1.84
After-tax	2.73	1.23	2.69	1.62
After-tax dividend	—	1.50	—	1.05
Pretax rate of return‡	10.0%	10.0%	11.4%	12.5%

*Assuming the capital gain qualifies as a long-term gain, it is taxed at a rate of $0.4 \times 30\% = 12\%$.

†Calculated so as to provide an after-tax rate of return of 10%.

‡The sum of the year-end dividend, if any, plus before-tax capital gain divided by the current share price.

Flotation Costs and Commission Charges

Shareholders who desire a stream of share-related income could sell portions of their holdings and create "homemade" dividends in lieu of the corporation paying a cash dividend. However, they will incur brokerage commissions. Alternatively, if the corporation pays a cash dividend and issues shares in order to preserve both its capital structure and planned capital investment program (as Miller and Modigliani assume), it will incur the costs of floating the new issue. Thus, the existence of brokerage commissions tends to favor dividend payments over share sales for shareholders who prefer current income; however, brokerage commissions favor retained earnings over dividends for shareholders who prefer reinvestments. Similarly, the existence of flotation costs tends to favor retained earnings over new issues as a means of raising equity capital for capital investment purposes.

A shareholder who desires an increased income stream would prefer real cash dividend payments over homemade dividends if the firm could sell new shares more cheaply than shareholders could but would prefer homemade dividends if shareholders could sell shares more cheaply. In general, brokerage commissions and flotation costs both vary inversely with the size of the transaction. These economies of scale would make it cheaper for the company to sell a large block of shares than for individual shareholders to make small odd-lot sales. Consequently, it is generally cheaper for the company to pay dividends than for shareholders to manufacture homemade dividends. Table 12-2 illustrates this point.

The shareholders of both firms desire $1,500,000 of "dividend" income. Each company initially has 1 million shares outstanding, which trade at a price of $30 per share. If there were no flotation costs or brokerage commissions, shareholders would find the two firms equally attractive because the shareholders could duplicate any dividend stream a company pays out by manufacturing homemade dividends. However, if brokerage commissions on average (for selling shareholders) exceed flotation costs, a company can "manufacture" dividends (through a new issue) more cheaply than shareholders can (through share sales). Consequently, if firm 2 continued to pay dividends but firm 1 did not, income-oriented investors would tend to gravitate toward firm 2 because of the greater wealth they could realize thereby. Note that the $32,000 difference in the total wealth of original shareholders (adjusted for rounding error) equals the difference in transaction costs ($1,500,000 × 0.04 − $1,500,000 × 0.02).

Two developments have affected the difference between flotation costs and brokerage commissions in recent years. The growth of the discount brokerage industry has reduced brokerage commissions; however, the greatest commission reductions have occurred in connection with larger share transactions, for example, those involving several hundred shares or more. In addition, the

Table 12-2
Implications of Flotation Costs and Brokerage
Commissions for Choice of Dividend Policy
(Thousands of Dollars Except Per-Share Amounts)

	No Flotation Costs or Brokerage Commissions		Flotation Costs of 2% and Brokerage Commissions of 4%	
	Firm 1, Homemade Dividends	Firm 2, Company Distribution	Firm 1, Homemade Dividends	Firm 2, Company Distribution
Desired dividend income	$ 1500	$ 1500	$ 1500	$ 1500
Company's Shares:				
Number initially	1,000,000	1,000,000	1,000,000	1,000,000
Predividend share price	$ 30.00	$ 30.00	$ 30.00	$ 30.00
Dividend per share	—	1.50	—	1.50
Share Sales:				
Price per share	$ 30.00	$ 28.50*	$ 30.00	$ 28.50*
Flotation/ brokerage, %	—	—	4	2
Net proceeds per share	$ 30.00	$ 28.50	$ 28.80	$ 27.93
Number of shares†	50,000	52,632	52,083	53,706
Original Shareholders:				
Remaining shares	950,000	1,000,000	947,917	1,000,000
Value per share	$ 30.00	$ 28.50	$ 30.00	$ 28.47‡
Aggregate value	$ 28,500	$ 28,500	$ 28,438	$ 28,470
Net dividends	1,500	1,500	1,500	1,500
Total wealth	$ 30,000	$ 30,000	$ 29,938	$ 29,970

*Share sales are assumed to take place immediately after the dividend is paid.

†Designed to produce net proceeds of $1,500,000 (rounded to the nearest thousand).

‡Adjusted for dilution resulting from the additional shares that must be sold to cover the 2% flotation cost, i.e., $30,000,000 total value divided by 1,053,706 total shares.

proliferation of new issue dividend reinvestment plans has permitted companies to reduce issuance costs substantially, perhaps to as little as 2% (vs 4 to 5% for normal-size public offerings). Dividend reinvestment plans offer shareholders the option to reinvest their dividends at little or no brokerage commission. This reduces the penalty a high-dividend-payout policy would otherwise impose on shareholders who wish to reinvest dividends.

Legal and Policy Restrictions

Certain institutions are prohibited, either by law or by policy, from investing in the common stocks of companies that have not established a history of regular dividend payments over a sufficiently long period. Other investors, such as many trust and endowment funds, can only spend dividend income as a matter of policy. These investors exhibit a preference for at least some minimum level of regular dividend income.

Net Effect of Taxes and Transaction Costs

Financial experts generally regard the tax bias in favor of capital gains as exerting a stronger influence on what a company's dividend policy ought to be than transaction cost considerations or the legal and policy restrictions that are responsible for certain investors having a dividend preference. Consequently, they believe that the combined effect of the factors discussed in this section favors retentions over dividends to some degree. The extent of this bias depends largely on the shareholder mix and on the tax positions and liquidity preferences of shareholders.

If individual shareholders predominate and consist chiefly of upper-income higher-tax-paying individuals, there is likely to be a net preference for retained earnings over dividends. (In fact, these shareholders would prefer that the firm make cash distributions through share repurchases rather than cash dividends.) But financial institutions, many of which are tax-exempt, have greatly increased the percentage of outstanding common stock they own.[11] If some combination of corporate shareholders, older retired individuals, and tax-exempt institutions predominates, there is likely to be a net preference for dividends. In that case, a company should establish a somewhat higher payout ratio than would otherwise be appropriate. A dividend reinvestment plan would lessen the impact of this higher-payout policy on shareholders who wish to reinvest their dividends.

Need for Stability in Dividend Policy

While some investors prefer high-payout stocks, others prefer capital gains. As one would expect, dividend-oriented common stock investors generally gravitate toward high-payout common stocks, such as electric utility stocks, and capital-gain-oriented common stock investors generally gravitate toward more rapidly growing companies that distribute little or no dividends. Thus, a significant change in dividend policy would tend to induce a shift in shareholder mix. Following a period of transition, there might be little, if any, change in the company's stock market value because former shareholders who objected to the new dividend policy would simply have sold out to new shareholders who found the new policy to their liking. In this way, changes in shareholder mix would tend to lessen the longer-term impact of a change in a company's dividend policy on its share price.

Even though a company's shareholder mix can shift in response to a change in dividend policy, a sudden shift may be disruptive to its share price in the near term and frequent major shifts may be disruptive over the longer term because transaction costs make it expensive for investors to buy and sell shares. A company should strive to maintain a stable dividend policy, departing from an established dividend policy only when significant changes in its investment opportunities or earnings prospects dictate.

SUMMARY

A company should establish its dividend policy with a view to maximizing shareholder wealth. It should set its payout policy chiefly in keeping with its investment opportunities and internal funds needs. But also important are (1) the relative preferences of its shareholders for capital gains and dividends, (2) their liquidity preferences and the relative costs to the firm and to shareholders of selling shares, and (3) legal or policy restrictions on substantial shareholders that may create a preference for dividend income.

The critical issue in dividend policy is whether a company should take the dividend decision actively or passively. It was traditionally believed that shareholders placed a higher value on dividends than on more distant, less certain capital gains. The traditional view argued for high payout ratios, perhaps even approaching 100% of earnings. In their classic article on dividend policy, Miller and Modigliani challenged the traditional view. They held the firm's capital investment program fixed and specified conditions under which the firm's choice of dividend policy would not affect its stock market value. Under their assumptions, dividend policy does not matter because homemade dividends are a perfect substitute for real dividends. Consequently, dividend policy would be passive: Companies would simply distribute excess funds.

But, in contrast to the idealized conditions Miller and Modigliani assumed, the financial system contains some significant "imperfections." The system of individual taxation imposes a bias in favor of capital gains and against dividends. The system of corporate taxation does just the opposite. Flotation costs impose a bias in favor of retained earnings over new share issues. On the other hand, certain investors do want at least some minimum level of dividend income, and brokerage commissions impose a bias in favor of actual dividends over homemade dividends.

Dividend changes are also important as a signaling device. Thus, simply paying out residual earnings year by year would be inadvisable. Such a policy would in most cases cause the dividend rate to fluctuate wildly and thus lose its information value.

The discussion in this chapter suggests the following dividend policy guidelines. First, a company should determine what percentage of its earnings it expects to have available for distribution over its planning horizon (typically 5 years). This percentage will depend on its earnings prospects, the availability of attractive investment opportunities, and its chosen capital structure policy. Second, the company should determine whether a higher or a lower payout ratio is warranted in view of the company's particular shareholder mix. The payout ratios of comparable companies provide a useful guide in this regard. Generally, a shareholder mix dominated by upper-income individual share-holders would argue for a payout ratio somewhat below that justified solely on the basis of residual earnings considerations, whereas a shareholder mix dominated by corporate shareholders, retired individuals, and tax-exempt insti-tutions would argue for the opposite. Third, a company should make orderly changes in its dividend rate. In particular, a company should determine at each decision point whether it should continue its current quarterly dividend rate or whether it expects to be able to sustain a higher rate into the foreseeable future. Of course, if earnings prospects have materially worsened since the last decision point, the company must consider cutting the dividend rate to a lower but sustainable level. The next chapter describes and illustrates procedures companies can use to implement these guidelines.

Selecting an Appropriate Dividend Policy

Chapter 13

Chapter 12 discussed reasons why a firm's choice of and implementation of its dividend policy might affect its share price. This chapter explains how companies can select an appropriate dividend policy and determine how best to implement it.

OVERVIEW OF CORPORATE DIVIDEND POLICIES

The actual dividend policies of corporations provide a useful backdrop for our discussion of how a corporation can select an appropriate dividend policy. Actual dividend policies of publicly traded companies exhibit a number of common fundamental characteristics.

Predilection for Paying Common Dividends

Smaller and younger companies generally do not pay cash dividends to their common stockholders. However, at some point in the life cycle of a company, it begins paying common dividends. Among larger companies, a very high percentage make regular cash dividend payments. Over the past 40 years, between 80 and 90% of the common stocks listed on the New York Stock Exchange in any year paid cash dividends during the year.[1] It seems reasonable to conclude that something other than merely paying out residual earnings accounts for this dividend-paying behavior.

Dividends More Stable than Earnings

Figure 13-1 illustrates the pattern of corporate earnings and dividends during the postwar period and the corresponding movement in the average annual

213

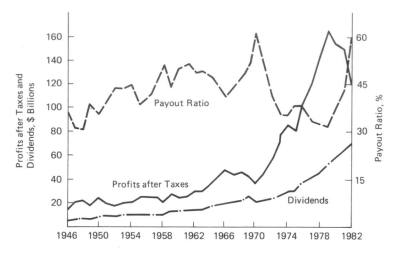

Figure 13-1. Corporate dividends and earnings over the business cycle.
Source: Economic Indicators, U. S. Government Printing Office, Washington, D.C.

payout ratio. Dividends are generally more stable than earnings; this is true for individual firms as well as in the aggregate.

Regularity of Dividend Payments

Dividend-paying companies typically make quarterly payments. Some companies make semiannual or annual payments, and no more than a handful of operating companies make monthly distributions. Once they begin paying common dividends, companies strive to continue making regular payments and frequently highlight the lengths of their uninterrupted dividend records when issuing dividend declarations. Table 13-1 illustrates the longevity of the dividend payment records of companies listed on the New York Stock Exchange as of year-end 1983. Roughly half had made quarterly payments on an uninterrupted basis for 20 years or longer. Regularity of dividend distributions thus appears to be an important corporate objective.

Reluctance to Cut the Dividend Rate

Companies exhibit a strong aversion to cutting the dividend rate. Investors generally interpret dividend reductions as a signal that the company's earnings prospects have worsened. This can adversely affect a company's share price and, in some cases, the share prices of other companies in the same industry. For example, Consolidated Edison Company of New York announced on April 23, 1974 that it would omit its second quarter 1974 dividend. Its share price fell by 43% between April 22, 1974, and May 15, 1974. During the same period, many other electric utility stocks decreased in price as investors feared that other electric companies would reduce their dividend rates.

Table 13-2 illustrates the corporate reluctance to reduce dividends. During the period 1968 to 1982, dividend increases and resumptions outnumbered dividend decreases and omissions more than 7:1. The numbers of dividend decreases and omissions increased sharply during the recessionary periods 1970, 1974 to 1975, and 1980 to 1982. Companies generally cut the dividend rate only during periods of adversity.

Regular versus Extra or Special Dividends

Table 13-2 also indicates the number of companies that declared "extra" or "special" dividends during the period 1968 to 1982. During the early part of this period, roughly 1 company in 10 declared either an extra dividend or a special dividend during the year. The number of companies declaring an extra or special dividend fell sharply, to only 1 in 20, during the 1980 to 1982 recessionary period. In any case, the number of companies paying an extra or special dividend is substantially smaller than the number of companies paying a regular dividend.

Extra or special dividends, as their names suggest, do not connote regularity. Extra dividends are generally paid during periods of temporarily higher earnings to bring a company's payout ratio up to its target level. Many companies in cyclical businesses, as for example General Motors Corporation, declare extra or special dividends during periods when earnings are at a cyclical peak and increase the regular dividend rate only when they have reached a higher level of sustainable earnings. A company might also pay a special dividend when it has substantial excess cash that it wishes to distribute to its shareholders.[2] Consequently, neither an extra dividend nor a special dividend serves as an effective device for signaling a change in a company's earnings prospects.

Table 13-1
Longevity of Dividend Payment Records of New York Stock Exchange–Listed Common Stocks

	Number of Companies That Have Paid Dividends over a Period of Consecutive Years of Length								Number of Companies Listed Year–End 1983
	100 or More	75–99	50–74	25–49	20–24	20 or More	10–19	Less than 10*	
Quarterly payments	6	41	134	448	86	715	201	602	1518
Annual payments	37	85	232	403	84	841	201	476†	1518

*Includes stocks that do not pay dividends.
†Includes stocks that do not make quarterly dividend payments.

Source: New York Stock Exchange Fact Book, 1984, p. 35.

Table 13-2
Dividend Changes Announced by Publicly
Owned U.S. Companies, 1968–1982

Year	Number of Companies Taking Dividend Action	Dividend Increased	Dividend Resumed	Dividend Decreased	Dividend Omitted	Extra or Special Dividend Declared
1968	Approx. 9800	1582	101	117	130	993
1969	Approx. 9800	1416	54	101	124	935
1970	Approx. 9800	828	75	201	284	910
1971	Approx. 9800	885	111	154	213	841
1972	Approx. 9800	1563	107	73	103	980
1973	Approx. 9800	2197	116	37	114	1105
1974	Approx. 9800	2120	139	86	228	1097
1975	Approx. 9800	1648	129	186	266	1013
1976	Approx. 9800	2624	137	74	117	1047
1977	Over 10,000	2984	120	68	138	968
1978	Over 10,000	3211	105	46	105	997
1979	Over 10,000	2968	71	46	131	829
1980	Over 10,000	2445	51	88	160	719
1981	Over 10,000	2160	45	103	198	640
1982	Over 10,000	1530	46	253	307	459

Source: Standard & Poor's Corporation, *Annual Dividend Record*, 1974–1982 issues.

Timing of Dividend Announcements

Most companies review their dividend policies at least once annually, often during the same quarter each year. Many companies review their dividend policies around fiscal year-end when they are reviewing the past year's results and budgeting for the following year. Companies in highly seasonal businesses often choose the quarter least affected by seasonal factors in order not to let such factors affect the dividend decision.

In contrast to the timing of regular dividend payments, extra and special dividend announcements occur predominantly in the October to December quarter. Companies tend to wait until year-end to declare such dividends. This suggests that companies pay extra (or special) dividends when the year-end review reveals unexpectedly high or unsustainably high earnings for the year, and the company wishes to pay out its target percentage of earnings but does not wish to signal falsely a higher sustainable level of earnings.

Industry Differences in Payout Ratio

An interesting study of corporate dividend policies by Allen Michel, the results of which are summarized in Table 13-3, revealed systematic differences in company payout ratios across industries.[3] Because of these systematic differences in payout ratio—and also the reasonable presumption that systematic differences in profitable investment opportunities are at least partly responsible—the payout ratios of firms in the same industry offer a useful guide in selecting an appropriate payout ratio for a publicly traded company.

DIVIDEND POLICY GUIDELINES

Establishing its dividend policy requires a company to take into account a variety of complex and conflicting considerations. Chapter 12 discussed reasons why almost any dividend decision a company with a diversified shareholder mix reaches will disappoint at least some of its shareholders. Nevertheless, a company must strive to balance the desires of all of its shareholders against one another.

Is There a Unique "Best" Dividend Policy?

In concept, a company could commission a detailed study of its shareholder mix and of the relationship between past dividend changes by companies in its industry on the one hand and resulting share price changes on the other. However, shareholder mixes change, particularly as institutions have come to play an ever larger role in the equity markets, and past statistical studies of the relationship between dividend changes and share price changes have been largely inconclusive.

Table 13-3
Industry Differences in Payout Ratio

Industry	Five-Year Industry Average		Ten-Year Average, 1967–1976
	1967–1971	1972–1976	
Life insurance	20.1%	25.5%	22.8%
Aerospace and aircraft	32.8	25.4	29.1
Building materials	41.5	31.1	36.3
Business equipment	34.9	38.5	36.7
Paper and paper products	45.7	32.2	38.9
Oil	47.9	34.6	41.2
Drugs and health care	49.7	38.9	44.3
Metals and mining	49.9	38.9	44.4
Steel	53.8	37.3	45.6
Textiles	48.5	44.9	46.7
Chemicals	55.3	42.3	48.8
Foods	57.0	47.3	52.1
Electric utilities	68.5	69.5	69.0
Average	46.6	39.0	42.8

Source: Allen Michel, "Industry Influence on Dividend Policy," *Financial Management*, vol. 8 (autumn 1979), p. 26.

In Figure 13-2, the optimal payout ratio is P^*. That payout ratio leads to the maximum shareholder wealth W^*. A higher or lower payout ratio leads to lower shareholder wealth. But payout ratios "near" P^* lead to values of shareholder wealth "near" W^*. The shape of the curve determines the size of the penalty that results from paying out more or less than P^*. In practice, if we had the ability to draw the curve in Figure 13-2, we would probably find that for most companies there is a range of payout ratios within which the curve is relatively flat. Once inside that range, the cost of obtaining the information required to change the payout ratio from, say, P to P^* would exceed the benefit shareholders could realize as a result of that change.

The payout ratios of comparable companies provide the best clue as to the boundaries of the target payout range in Figure 13-2. Factoring in the company-related and investor-related considerations discussed in Chapter 12 then enables a company to decide where its long-term target payout ratio should lie. The goal, then, is to determine an appropriate long-term target payout ratio rather than a unique optimal payout ratio.

Three-Step Approach to the Dividend Decision

Determining an appropriate dividend policy for a company involves a three-step approach.

Estimating Future Residual Funds. The starting point for any analysis leading up to the dividend decision is the company's cash flow projection over a

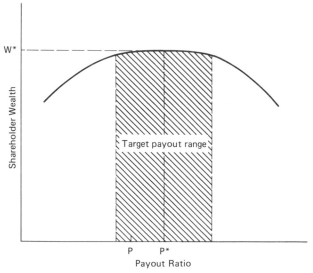

Figure 13-2. Target payout range.

reasonable time horizon, typically 5 years. The projected levels of capital expenditures and operating cash flow are most important in this regard. At a minimum, a company should pay out, over time, that portion of its cash flow which it is unable to reinvest profitably. Based on investor-related considerations, a company may decide to pay out more than this minimum level. However, because of the costs associated with floating new issues, it is generally inadvisable for a company to pay out so much more than the minimum that the dividend decision per se triggers the need for a new equity issue.

Several factors complicate this analysis. The company must ensure that bond indenture or other legal restrictions on dividend distributions are satisfied. Capital expenditure projects often come in large units and are subject to delays and cost overruns. As business conditions change so will the desired portfolio of capital expenditure projects. Similarly, future operating cash flow is not entirely predictable. Thus, analyzing even the most carefully prepared cash flow projections will suggest a range of distributable amounts, a range of funds needs, and hence a range of *feasible target payout ratios*.

Determining an Appropriate Target Payout Ratio. An analysis of the payout ratios of comparable companies, essentially those in the same industry and of nearly the same size and with similar product mix and other operating characteristics, will suggest a range of *customary payout ratios* for (that segment of) the industry. A company should consider the range of feasible target payout ratios together with the range of customary payout ratios and any special shareholder mix considerations in setting its long-term target payout ratio.

Setting the Quarterly Dividend Rate. Because of the informational content of dividend changes, a fluctuating regular dividend rate is generally undesirable. Investors would find the dividend signals confusing, and the conflicting signals could lead to gyrations in the company's share price. Such a policy might also lead to shifts in the shareholder clientele. Because share transactions are costly, an unstable dividend rate would undoubtedly penalize a company's share price.

A company should increase its dividend rate, then, only if it can sustain the higher rate. Similarly, if earnings prospects worsen materially, at some point the company will have to cut its dividend rate or else compromise its capital spending plans or capital structure objective or else trigger the need for a new equity issue. If an increase in the dividend rate is deemed appropriate, investment bankers generally counsel companies to make a significant increase in lieu of several tiny increases and accordingly advise that any change be no smaller than 5% of the previous rate.

Given its target payout ratio and its earnings projections, a company should establish its quarterly dividend rate at the highest *comfortably sustainable* level. That is, the dividend rate should be sustainable at least over the planning horizon, and prudence dictates setting the actual rate somewhat below the

Table 13-4
Setting Dividend Policy for a Company
in a Relatively Noncyclical Business
(Dollar Amounts in Millions Except Per-Share Amounts)

	Current Year	Projected Ahead				
		1 Year	2 Years	3 Years	4 Years	5 Years
Earnings per common share		$ 5.00	$ 6.00	$ 7.20	$ 8.50	$10.00
Number of common shares, millions		10	10	10	10	10
Earnings available for common		$ 50.0	$ 60.0	$ 72.0	$ 85.0	$100.0
Depreciation		10.0	12.0	14.0	17.0	20.0
Other noncash charges		2.0	2.0	2.0	2.0	2.0
Cash flow available for reinvestment		62.0	74.0	88.0	104.0	122.0
Capital investment requirement—net[a]		40.0	60.0	80.0	72.0	60.0
Target debt-to-equity ratio		1 : 3	1 : 3	1 : 3	1 :3	1 : 3
To Maintain Target Debt-to-Equity Ratio:						
Additional borrowing to fund capital expenditures—net[b]		$ 10.0	$ 15.0	$ 20.0	$ 18.0	$ 15.0
Required retained earnings[c]		30.0	45.0	60.0	54.0	45.0
Residual earnings		20.0	15.0	12.0	31.0	55.0
Discretionary cash flow[d]		22.0	17.0	14.0	33.0	57.0
Alternative Policy 1						
Dividend per share	$ 1.36	$ 1.48	$ 1.60	$ 1.72	$ 3.24	$ 4.76
Payout ratio		0.30	0.27	0.24	0.38	0.48
Year-end debt[e]	$ 80.0	$ 82.8	$ 96.8	$120.0	$137.4	$143.0
Year-end equity[f]	240.0	275.2	319.2	374.0	426.6	479.0
Debt-to-equity ratio	0.33	0.30	0.30	0.32	0.32	0.30
Cash flow coverage[g]		4.19×	4.63×	5.12×	3.21×	2.56×
Alternative Policy 2						
Dividend per share	$ 1.36	$ 1.60	$ 1.84	$ 2.08	$ 3.12	$ 4.16
Payout ratio		0.32	0.31	0.29	0.37	0.42
Year-end debt[e]	$ 80.0	$ 84.0	$100.4	$127.2	$143.4	$143.0
Year-end equity[f]	240.0	274.0	315.6	366.8	420.6	479.0
Debt-to-equity ratio	0.33	0.31	0.32	0.35	0.34	0.30
Cash flow coverage[g]		3.88×	4.02×	4.23×	3.33×	2.93×

**Table 13-4
Setting Dividend Policy for a Company
in a Relatively Noncyclical Business** *(Continued)*

	Current Year	Projected Ahead				
		1 Year	2 Years	3 Years	4 Years	5 Years
Alternative Policy 3						
Dividend per share	$ 1.36	$ 1.76	$ 2.16	$ 2.56	$ 2.96	$ 3.36
Payout ratio		0.35	0.36	0.36	0.35	0.34
Year-end debt[e]	$ 80.0	$ 85.6	$105.2	$136.8	$151.4	$143.0
Year-end equity[f]	240.0	272.4	310.8	357.2	412.6	479.0
Debt-to-equity ratio	0.33	0.31	0.34	0.38	0.37	0.30
Cash flow coverage[g]		3.52×	3.43×	2.81×	2.87×	3.63×

[a] Gross capital expenditures less depreciation expense.

[b] Calculated as one-fourth of capital investment requirement—net; preserves debt-to-equity ratio of 1 : 3.

[c] Calculated as three-fourths of capital investment requirement—net; preserves debt-to-equity ratio of 1 : 3.

[d] Calculated as cash flow available for reinvestment plus additional borrowing to fund capital expenditures—net less (capital investment requirement—net plus depreciation).

[e] Calculated as beginning-of-year debt plus additional borrowing to fund capital expenditures—net plus (aggregate dividends paid less discretionary cash flow). As a result, it is assumed that excess cash is used to reduce debt (e.g., pay down bank lines).

[f] Calculated as beginning-of-year equity plus earnings available for common less aggregate dividends paid.

[g] Calculated as cash flow available for reinvestment divided by aggregate dividends paid.

expected maximum in order to compensate for the uncertainty of the earnings and funds forecasts.

SELECTING AN APPROPRIATE DIVIDEND POLICY

This section applies the three-step approach to dividend policy to Major Pharmaceutical Company. Major's Financial Planning Group has prepared a 5-year plan, which Major's board of directors has tentatively approved. Table 13-4 provides the projected values of certain financial variables drawn from the 5-year plan.

Satisfying the Funds Needs of the Business

Major's board of directors has tentatively approved a 5-year capital expenditure budget of $385 million. Major's board approved this budget after Major's chief financial officer informed it that the budget included only projects promising a positive net present value. After allowing for depreciation, this budget provides for net capital investment amounting to $40.0 million, $60.0 million, $80.0 million, $72.0 million, and $60.0 million 1, 2, 3, 4, and 5 years into the future, respectively.

Table 13-5
Ten-Year Dividend History for Major Pharmaceutical Company*

Years Prior	Dividends per Share	Earnings per Share	Payout Ratio Company	Payout Ratio Standard & Poor's Drug Companies	Cash Flow per Share Available for Common Dividends	Cash Flow Coverage of Common Dividends	Quarterly Common Dividend Increased In Quarter	Quarterly Common Dividend Increased From	Quarterly Common Dividend Increased To
10	$0.42	$1.20	35.0%	39.4%	$1.53	3.64×	I	$0.09	$0.105
9	0.465	1.32	35.2	41.0	1.58	3.40	II	0.105	0.12
8	0.54	1.50	36.0	40.9	1.87	3.46	II	0.12	0.14
7	0.68	1.85	36.8	41.7	2.50	3.68	I	0.14	0.17
6	0.76	2.07	36.7	43.2	2.69	3.54	I	0.17	0.19
5-year growth rate	15.7%	14.3%			15.9%				
5-year average			35.9	41.2		3.54			
5	0.88	2.45	35.9	42.4	3.06	3.48	I	0.19	0.22
4	1.00	3.10	32.3	44.6	4.19	4.19	I	0.22	0.25
3	1.12	3.73	30.0	45.6	4.66	4.16	I	0.25	0.28
2	1.24	4.01	30.9	51.6	4.83	3.90	I	0.28	0.31
1	1.36	4.25	32.0	48.0	5.51	4.05	I	0.31	0.34
5-year growth rate	10.9%	13.6%			13.2%				
5-year average			32.2	46.4		3.96			
10-year growth rate	13.6%	15.4%			15.5%				
10-year average			34.1	43.8		3.75			

*Adjusted for stock splits.

Source: Standard & Poor's Corporation, *Analyst's Handbook.*

Major's chief financial officer has previously determined that a 1 : 3 debt-to-equity ratio is appropriate in view of Major's desire to maintain its Aa3/AA− senior debt rating. Major's board has approved that policy decision. Maintaining this 1 : 3 debt-to-equity ratio would require the additional borrowing levels and the required retained earnings figures shown in Table 13-4. Residual earnings, simply the difference between forecasted earnings and required retained earnings, are projected to decrease slightly 2 and 3 years ahead and to increase sharply thereafter. Over the 5-year period, Major projects aggregate residual earnings of $133.0 million and aggregate discretionary cash flow of $143.0 million.

Target Payout Ratio
The projected residual earnings of $133.0 million represent 36.2% of projected earnings available for common, which are $367.0 million for the 5-year period. From having read Chapter 12, Major's treasurer is reluctant to recommend this target without first taking other relevant factors into consideration.

As illustrated in Table 13-5, Major's payout ratio has averaged 34.1% over the past 10 years and 32.2% over the past 5, both tracking the average payout ratio for Standard & Poor's drug industry group. Major's financial staff has also analyzed the payout policies of Major's closest 10 competitors in the ethical drug segment of the pharmaceutical industry from which Major derives more than 90% of its sales revenue and operating income. The average payout ratios for these companies were 37.8% last year within a range from 21.1 to 50.2% and 40.6% this year within a range from 18.6 to 53.7%. Based on this analysis, Major's treasurer believes that a payout ratio in the range from 30 to 40% would be appropriate for Major. Because of Major's heavy capital expenditure program over the next 3 years, he believes it appropriate that Major's payout ratio continue to be below the industry average during that period.

**Analyzing the Impact of Alternative
Dividend Policies**
Table 13-4 also examines the impact of three alternative dividend policies. A company would normally wish to examine a larger number of alternatives before deciding on the appropriate dividend action, but these three alternatives illustrate how a company can weigh the various dividend policy trade-offs.

The current indicated annual dividend rate is $1.36 per share. Policy 1 continues the pattern of 12 cents per share per annum increases for 3 years in order to conserve cash for Major's capital expenditure program and then provides for increases of $1.52 in each of the next 2 years in order to pay out in the aggregate approximately 35% of aggregate earnings projected for the 5-year period. That percentage, of course, represents the midpoint of what Major's treasurer believes is the appropriate target payout range. Policy 3 provides for equal annual dividend increases amounting to 40 cents per share per annum in order to signal Major's prospects for greater sustained earnings growth. Policy 2 represents a middle ground, with each year's dividend level roughly halfway between the respective year's dividend levels under Policies 1 and 3. For comparability, each policy results in the same aggregate dividend payout over the 5-year period. Consequently, each policy would result in the same end-of-planning-horizon balance sheet. However, there are major differences in financial statement impact during the 5-year period.

Policy 1 conserves cash the first 3 years but results in the most variable payout ratio and cash flow coverage. The abnormally large dividend increases the last 2 years are probably not sustainable. Thus, policy 1 would probably send confusing signals to the marketplace.

Policy 3 would probably send the right dividend signal because it provides for a very stable payout ratio and it connotes sustained earnings growth. However, the debt-to-equity ratio is volatile. It exceeds Major's target debt-to-equity ratio by a significant margin in 2 of the 5 years.

Of the three policies, policy 2 would appear the most reasonable. The payout ratio is stable the first 3 years, and the aggregate payout would only slightly exceed discretionary cash flow for that period. While the payout ratio is at the lower end of the target range, it is in line with Major's historical payout ratios. Policy 2 also provides for larger dividend increases the next 3 years than in the past. Because Major's treasurer reviews Major's dividend policy annually, the projections for 4 and 5 years ahead are important in the current year's analysis only to the extent that Major's treasurer needs to know whether a dividend change effected this year is likely to be sustainable. The analysis in Table 13-4 implies that an annual dividend increase of $0.24 per share could be sustained at least through the planning horizon. Therefore Major's treasurer can be comfortable in recommending an increase of $0.24 per share per annum when Major's board reconsiders the dividend rate at the February board meeting.

As this example illustrates, determining the appropriate dividend action requires judgment. Seldom will a particular dividend action satisfy the target payout ratio and debt-to-equity ratio year by year. A company must weigh the trade-offs and settle on a dividend action that is consistent with (1) a reasonably stable payout ratio that lies within the target range, (2) a reasonably stable debt-to-equity ratio, and (3) a reasonably stable progression of dividend changes that appropriately reflects changes in the company's earnings and cash flow prospects.

Special Considerations for the Privately Held Firm

The preceding example applies only to publicly traded companies. Privately held firms do not have informational effects to worry about. However, tax considerations and the owners' liquidity needs are of great importance.

The maximum corporate tax rate is lower than the maximum individual tax rate. Thus, the owners of a closely held firm can benefit by having the corporation retain earnings and reinvest funds rather than paying them out as dividends. Double taxation is avoided, the investment income is taxed at a lower rate, and if the company is sold, the reinvested earnings will effectively be taxed at capital gains rates rather than at ordinary income tax rates. For this reason, Internal Revenue Service regulations prohibit "excessive" earnings retention. But what is truly "excessive" is seldom clear. Privately held firms are generally smaller than publicly traded companies. They consequently have less financial flexibility and somewhat more variable liquidity requirements. Somewhat greater retentions are therefore warranted to compensate for the higher risks privately held firms face. Minimizing dividend payouts may therefore be financially prudent as well as beneficial from a tax standpoint.

ADDITIONAL CONSIDERATIONS
FOR UTILITY COMPANIES

The appropriate dividend policy for a utility company poses a special problem. As illustrated in Table 13-3, electric utility companies pay out a much higher percentage of their earnings than U.S. corporations generally. But in the latter part of the 1970s and early 1980s electric utility companies were also frequent issuers of common stock. A high payout ratio coupled with frequent new issues would appear to conflict with the dividend policy guidelines outlined earlier in this chapter.

Utility Dividend Policy
It is important to distinguish utility company dividend policy from the dividend policy of nonregulated firms. Utility commissions authorize the rates utilities are permitted to charge. These rates are designed to allow the utility company to realize, under ideal circumstances, its authorized return on common equity. This authorized return is in turn determined in rate proceedings based on expert testimony regarding what constitutes a "fair" rate of return under capital market conditions prevailing around the time of the rate proceeding. As a result, the regulatory process really determines, among other things, a "fair" rate of return to equity holders based on market conditions, much like market participants determine a fair rate of return, called the yield to maturity, on a new issue of debt or preferred stock. Consequently, utility company common stocks, particularly those of electric utility companies, can be viewed as quasi-fixed income securities.

The appropriate payout ratio for a utility company is determined chiefly by the need to offer shareholders a competitive rate of return. Once again, the best indicator of the appropriate payout ratio is the range of payout ratios of comparable utility companies. If the utility company has abnormally large or unusually small future capital expenditure requirements, its payout ratio should be nearer the lower end or the upper end, respectively, of the relevant range.

Maximum Sustainable Rate of Dividend Growth

Many utility companies strive to provide regular annual dividend increases. A utility company's ability to increase its dividend rate is constrained by the returns its regulators will permit it to realize. A particular rate of dividend increase is *sustainable* as long as the regulated firm can realize the return on equity required to support it. If the rate of dividend increase is too high, attempting to sustain it will eventually require returns on equity above those the utility can reasonably expect to realize. To avoid this, the regulated firm can calculate the returns on equity implied in any particular rate of dividend increase and grant dividend increases no greater than those that expected future returns are capable of sustaining.

The following model provides the rate of return on common equity, ROE(T), required T years from the present to sustain a particular rate of dividend *growth* per annum (expressed as a decimal) over that period when the utility increases the number of shares outstanding at the rate of *shares* per annum (expressed as a decimal) and sells these new shares at a specified *market-to-book* ratio[4]:

$$\text{ROE}(T) \; = \; \text{div} \; \times \; (\text{factor})^{T} \; \div \; \left\{ \text{payout} \; \times \; \text{book} \; + \; (1 \; - \; \text{payout}) \right.$$

$$\left. \times \; \text{div} \; \times \; \left[\frac{(\text{factor})^{T} \; - \; 1}{\text{factor} \; - \; 1} \right] \right\}$$

$$\text{if growth} > 0 \text{ or shares} > 0 \qquad\qquad (13\text{-}1\text{a})$$

$$\text{ROE}(T) \; = \; \text{div} \; \div \; [\text{payout} \; \times \; \text{book} \; + \; (1 \; - \; \text{payout}) \; \times \; \text{div} \; \times \; T]$$

$$\text{if growth} = 0 \text{ and shares} = 0 \qquad\qquad (13\text{-}1\text{b})$$

In Formula 13-1, *div* denotes the current dividend rate per share per annum (in dollars per share), *payout* is the utility company's target payout ratio, and *book* is the current book value per share. (Factor)^{T} denotes the quantity *factor* being raised to the power T. The quantity factor reflects the impact of dividend increases and new share issues on required future returns on equity. It takes the following form:

$$\text{Factor} \; = \; (1 \; + \; \text{growth}) \; \times \; [1 + \text{shares} \; \times \; (1 \; - \; \text{market-to-book})] \qquad (13\text{-}2)$$

Although designed for utility companies, Formulas 13-1 and 13-2 could also be applied to nonregulated companies.

Formulas 13-1 and 13-2 have the following implications:

- A higher rate of dividend growth raises the returns on equity the utility must realize in the future in order to sustain its rate of dividend growth.
- The required rate of return increases as the volume of external equity financing increases when the utility sells new shares for less than their book value, but the reverse happens when it sells shares for more than their book value. When the utility sells shares below book value, new issues dilute the earning power behind each previously outstanding share and necessitate a higher rate of return to offset this.
- The required rate of return initially decreases as the payout ratio increases. But beyond some point, the required rate of return increases with increasing payout. Initially, a utility can increase its payout ratio in order to achieve a higher-than-sustainable rate of dividend growth. But if it fails to realize higher returns, this policy eventually becomes self-defeating because the higher payout ratio raises required future returns even higher.

The dependency of the required returns ROE on the rate of dividend growth is illustrated by the following example. Electric Company currently pays an annual dividend rate of div = \$2.00 per share on its common stock. Its target payout ratio is 70%, or payout = 0.7. Its common stock has a book value of \$25.00 per share.

The current rate of return is

$$\text{ROE}(0) = \frac{2.00}{0.7 \times 25.00} = 0.1143, \text{ or } 11.43\%$$

In the absence of new issues, a dividend growth rate of 5% per annum necessitates a rate of return of

$$\text{ROE}(5) = 2.00 \times (1.05)^5$$

$$\div \left\{ 0.7 \times 25.00 + 0.3 \times 2.00 \times \left[\frac{(1.05)^5 - 1}{(1.05 - 1)} \right] \right\}$$

$$= 0.1226, \text{ or } 12.26\%$$

5 years hence, but a 10% rate of dividend growth requires a 15.22% rate of return 5 years hence. But if Electric Company increases the number of shares outstanding by shares = 0.05 per annum and sells these shares at only 75% of book value (market-to-book = 0.75), the 10% dividend growth rate requires an even higher rate of return on equity 5 years hence:

$$\text{ROE}(5) = 2.00 \times (1.11375)^5$$

$$\div \left\{ 0.7 \times 25.00 + 0.3 \times 2.00 \times \left[\frac{(1.11375)^5 - 1}{(1.11375 - 1)} \right] \right\}$$

$$= 0.1612, \text{ or } 16.12\%$$

since

$$\text{Factor} = (1.10) \times [1 + 0.05 \times (1 - 0.75)] = 1.11375$$

A utility financial manager can use Formula 13-1a to gauge how large a rate of dividend increase his or her company can sustain over any particular time horizon given the rates of return on equity the utility expects to realize during that period. To continue the preceding example, suppose the projected realized return on equity is 14.00% each year for 5 years. The maximum sustainable rate of dividend increase over the next 5 years is approximately 8.0% per annum if shares = 0 or market-to-book = 1. At higher growth rates, the utility would have to realize a return on equity greater than 14% by the fifth year. For an infinite horizon, the maximum sustainable rate of dividend growth is approximately 4.2% per annum.[5] If shares = 0.1 and market-to-book = 0.75, the maximum sustainable rate of dividend growth over the next 5 years is approximately 5.4% per annum, significantly less than if Electric Company did not have to issue new shares.

DOES PAYING "SPECIAL" OR "EXTRA" DIVIDENDS ENHANCE VALUE?

Companies in cyclical businesses often pay extra or special dividends during periods when earnings are at a cyclical peak. Such a policy is prudent because it preserves the integrity of changes in the regular dividend rate as a signaling device while, at the same time, enabling the company to pay out a stable percentage of its earnings, which corresponds to the longer term ratio of residual earnings to total earnings.

Alternatively, a company could set a higher regular dividend rate in order to achieve the same aggregate dividend payout over time. This would require additional borrowing during cyclical troughs with the borrowings being repaid during cyclical peaks. Such a policy would worsen a company's liquidity position during cyclical troughs when it might already be strained for other reasons. For companies in highly cyclical businesses, a policy of regular dividend payments supplemented by occasional extra or special dividends is less risky from a financial standpoint than a policy consisting exclusively of regular dividend payments.

Table 13-6 illustrates how a company involved in a highly cyclical business might set its dividend policy. The table contrasts the financial impact of two alternative dividend policies. Policy A provides for regular dividend payments plus occasional extra dividend payments. The regular dividend is set at a level the company can sustain without triggering additional borrowing or a new equity issue. Policy B provides for regular dividend payments only. To compare the policies meaningfully, it is assumed that (1) a total of $21.0 million

Table 13-6
Setting Dividend Policy for a Company
in a Highly Cyclical Business
(Dollar Amounts in Millions)

	Projected Ahead					
	1 Year	2 Years	3 Years	4 Years	5 Years	5-Year Total
Earnings available for common[a]	$11.0	$15.0	$20.0	$16.0	$13.0	$75.0
Depreciation	2.0	2.0	2.0	2.0	2.0	10.0
Cash flow available for reinvestment	13.0	17.0	22.0	18.0	15.0	85.0
Capital investment requirement—net[b]	12.0	15.0	18.0	21.0	15.0	81.0
Target debt-to-equity ratio	1:2	1:2	1:2	1:2	1:2	1:2
To Maintain Target Debt-to-Equity Ratio:						
Additional borrowing to fund capital expenditures—net[c]	$ 4.0	$ 5.0	$ 6.0	$ 7.0	$ 5.0	$27.0
Cumulative borrowing	4.0	9.0	15.0	22.0	27.0	
Required retained earnings[d]	8.0	10.0	12.0	14.0	10.0	54.0
Residual earnings	3.0	5.0	8.0	2.0	3.0	21.0
Discretionary cash flow[e]	3.0	5.0	8.0	2.0	3.0	21.0
Target payout ratio						0.28[f]
Policy A: Regular and Extra						
Regular dividend payments	$ 3.0	$ 3.0	$ 3.0	$ 3.0	$ 3.0	$15.0
Extra dividend payments	—	2.0	4.0	—	—	6.0
Actual payout ratio	0.27	0.33	0.35	0.19	0.23	0.28
Actual retained earnings	$ 8.0	$10.0	$13.0	$13.0	$10.0	$54.0
Total borrowing[g]	4.0	5.0	5.0	8.0	5.0	27.0
Cumulative borrowing	4.0	9.0	14.0	22.0	27.0	
Actual debt-to-equity ratio[h]	0.50	0.50	0.48	0.50	0.50	
Policy B: Regular Only						
Regular dividend payments	$ 4.2	$ 4.2	$ 4.2	$ 4.2	$ 4.2	$21.0
Extra dividend payments	—	—	—	—	—	
Actual payout ratio	0.38	0.28	0.21	0.26	0.32	0.28
Actual retained earnings	$ 6.8	$10.8	$15.8	$11.8	$ 8.8	$54.0
Total borrowing[g]	5.2	4.2	2.2	9.2	6.2	27.0
Cumulative borrowing	5.2	9.4	11.6	20.8	27.0	
Actual debt-to-equity ratio[h]	0.52	0.51	0.45	0.48	0.50	

[a] Net income less preferred stock dividends, if any.

[b] Gross capital expenditures less depreciation expense.

[c] Calculated as one-third of capital investment requirement—net; preserves debt-to-equity ratio of 1:2.

[d] Calculated as two-thirds of capital investment requirement—net; preserves debt-to-equity ratio of 1:2.

[e] Calculated as cash flow available for reinvestment plus additional borrowing to fund capital expenditures—net less (capital investment requirement—net plus depreciation).

[f] Calculated as 5-year residual earnings divided by 5-year earnings available for common.

[g] Calculated as additional borrowing to fund capital expenditures—net plus (regular dividend payments less discretionary cash flow).

[h] Based on initial debt of $33 1/3 million and equity of $66 2/3 million.

is paid out under either policy over the 5-year period and (2) the company's debt-to-equity ratio is 1 : 2 at the end of the period under either policy.

Policy B requires additional borrowing in years 1, 4, and 5 but less borrowing in years 2 and 3. As a result, the company's debt-to-equity ratio is more variable under policy B than under policy A.

Table 13-6 assumes that free cash flow that is not paid out as common dividends is used to pay down debt. Alternatively, it could be assumed that the company builds up excess cash balances. Such a policy would make the debt-to-equity ratio more stable but would not be beneficial to shareholders if they could reinvest the funds at a higher rate of return than the company. Thus, paying extra dividends enables a company in a highly cyclical business to maintain a stable regular dividend rate consistent with (1) not building up excess cash balances and (2) not triggering net additional borrowing or securities issues. A company can use the framework illustrated in Table 13-6 to determine an appropriate mix of regular and extra dividend payments.

STOCK DIVIDENDS AND STOCK SPLITS

Companies do not always pay dividends in cash. Frequently companies pay *stock dividends*. For example, a company may declare a 5% stock dividend. That means that a common stockholder of the company will receive 5 new shares for each 100 shares of the company's common stock he or she already owns.

A company can achieve much the same financial effect as a stock dividend through a *stock split*. While there is a technical difference between the two, stock dividends and stock splits represent alternative means of recapitalizing a company's capital accounts. However, neither one affects the net worth of the company or the proportionate ownership interest of any of its shareholders.

Stock Dividends

A stock dividend increases the number of shares each shareholder owns proportionally. The fair market value of the shares distributed in the stock dividend payment is transferred from the retained earnings account to the "paid-in capital" and "capital contributed in excess of par value" accounts on the company's balance sheet.

Table 13-7 illustrates the balance sheet impact of a 100% stock dividend for a company whose shares are selling at $50. The $50 million fair market value of the 1 million shares that constitute the dividend is transferred out of retained earnings. The declaration of the stock dividend does not affect each share's par value. So $2,000,000 (= $2 × 1,000,000) is added to paid-in capital and the $48,000,000 balance is added to capital contributed in excess of par value. The company's net worth remains $85,000,000.

Table 13-7
Comparison of the Balance Sheet
Impact of a 100% Stock Dividend
and a Two-for-One Stock Split

Common Stockholders' Equity Initially

Paid-in capital ($2 par value, 1 million shares)	$ 2,000,000
Capital contributed in excess of par value	8,000,000
Retained earnings	75,000,000
Common stockholders' equity	$85,000,000

Common Stockholders' Equity Following
100% Stock Dividend

Paid-in capital ($2 par value, 2 million shares)	$ 4,000,000
Capital contributed in excess of par value	56,000,000
Retained earnings	25,000,000
Common stockholders' equity	$85,000,000

Common Stockholders' Equity Following
Two-for-One Stock Split

Paid-in capital ($1 par value, 2 million shares)	$ 2,000,000
Capital contributed in excess of par value	8,000,000
Retained earnings	75,000,000
Common stockholders' equity	$85,000,000

Stock Splits
Table 13-7 also illustrates the balance sheet impact of a comparable stock split, i.e., a two-for-one split. A stock split alters the par value of the shares but does not involve any transfer of balances between the components of common stockholders' equity. In the case of a two-for-one stock split, the par value of each share is halved. Thus, paid-in capital is unchanged.

Stock Dividends versus Stock Splits
Companies usually effect relatively small stock distributions through stock dividends and relatively large stock distributions through stock splits. Indeed, the rules of the New York Stock Exchange prescribe that companies should make share distributions of less than 25% through stock dividends rather than stock splits.

Financial Impact of Stock Dividends and
Stock Splits
The 100% stock dividend and two-for-one stock split in Table 13-7 each doubled the number of shares outstanding but did not affect the company's liquidity

Table 13-8
Distribution of Prices of New York Stock
Exchange—Listed Common Stocks, 1967–1984

Price Group	As of January 6, 1967		As of January 7, 1972		As of February 3, 1978		As of December 31, 1984	
	Number of Companies	Percentage of Total	Number of Companies	Percentage of Total	Number of Companies	Percentage of Total	Number of Companies	Percentage of Total
Under $10	77	6.1	105	7.4	283	18.0	219	14.5
$10–19 7/8	282	22.3	350	24.8	561	35.7	448	29.6
$20–29 7/8	327	25.8	355	25.2	457	29.0	384	25.3
$30–39 7/8	251	19.9	241	17.0	163	10.4	238	15.7
$40–49 7/8	139	10.9	173	12.3	64	4.1	112	7.4
$50–59 7/8	73	5.8	71	5.1	22	1.4	56	3.7
$60–99 7/8	102	8.0	91	6.5	18	1.1	50	3.3
$100 and Over	14	1.2	25	1.7	4	0.3	8	0.5
Total	1265	100.0%	1411	100.0%	1572	100.0%	1515	100.0%
Closing value of Dow Jones Industrial Average	808.74		910.37		770.96		1211.57	

Source: The Wall Street Journal, various issues.

position, capital expenditure program, leverage, or any operating variable. Consequently, barring any informational effects, which will be discussed in a moment, a stock dividend or a stock split should leave the stock market value of a company unchanged. Hence, a proportional reduction in the company's share price should occur.

Suppose the company in Table 13-7 earned $10 per share prior to the stock dividend or stock split, or $10 million in the aggregate. A 100% stock dividend or two-for-one stock split would double the number of shares outstanding but would not alter the $10 million aggregate earnings. Thus, earnings per share would be $5 per share following the dividend or split, and the share price would be halved to $25. The same earnings pie has simply been sliced into a greater number of pieces. So what is the value to shareholders of a stock dividend or of a stock split?

The principal benefit is probably the information a stock dividend or stock split conveys. Most of the shares listed on the New York Stock Exchange, for example, tend to trade in the range between $10 and $30 per share, as illustrated in Table 13-8. Companies frequently announce in connection with a stock split their desire to reduce the price of a share to within a "more popular trading range." Stock dividends and stock splits are therefore usually associated with growth companies. A stock split, in particular, may signal management's expectation that the company's share price would, in the absence of the split, move out of or farther above the top end of this customary trading range. If so, investors ought to react favorably to the news of an impending stock split, and there is evidence that they do.[6] A stock split, normally involving a greater reduction in share price than a stock dividend, is likely to have the greater informational content of the two.[7]

Second, companies often maintain the cash dividend per share following a stock dividend and maintain or reduce less than proportionately the cash dividend following a stock split. To the extent an increase in cash dividends per prestock dividend or presplit share is of value to investors, they would greet the announcement of a stock dividend or stock split favorably.

By reducing the share price to within a more popular trading range, a stock split and, to a lesser degree, a stock dividend may increase trading activity in a stock and thus improve its liquidity. By increasing the number of shares outstanding (and increasing the volume of trading activity), a stock split and, to a lesser degree, a stock dividend may broaden the ownership of a company's shares. However, the evidence on both points is not entirely conclusive.

Stock Dividend versus Cash Dividend

Companies sometimes declare a stock dividend in lieu of a cash dividend in order to conserve cash. Stockholders probably do not regard the sale of stock received in a stock dividend as a sale of their principal. At least some therefore derive some psychological benefit from receiving a stock dividend which they can sell rather than having to sell a portion of their original holdings to create their own cash dividend. However, a stock dividend is more expensive administratively than a cash dividend payment. Moreover, when a company substitutes a stock dividend for a cash dividend because of financial difficulty, it is very unlikely that many investors miss the real significance of the substitution.

SUMMARY

Corporate dividend policies exhibit a predilection toward paying at least some minimum level of dividends on a regular basis, a desire to maintain both a stable payout ratio and a stable regular dividend rate and to make orderly changes in the dividend rate, and a strong aversion to cutting the dividend rate. There also appear to be systematic industry differences in payout policies.

The chapter developed a three-step procedure for establishing dividend policy. A company should first project its expected residual earnings. It should then look to the payout ratios of comparable companies as well as to the fraction of projected earnings it expects to represent residual earnings in order to determine an appropriate long-term target payout ratio but should avoid setting the target payout ratio at a level that would trigger the need for an additional equity issue. It should then set its dividend rate at a level consistent with its financial policies and its earnings and cash flow prospects. Particularly important in this regard, the dividend rate should be sustainable into the foreseeable future in order to maximize its value as a signaling device. Companies often supplement regular dividend payments with extra dividend payments during peak earning periods so as to stabilize both the payout ratio and the regular dividend rate.

In the final analysis, striving for "the" optimal payout ratio and "the" optimal dividend rate at any particular point in time is probably unwise. A company should seek to pay out a reasonable and stable percentage of its earnings and to make orderly changes in its dividend rate. As with many other aspects of financial policy, "satisficing" rather than "optimizing" in the near term may indeed constitute the optimal policy, all things considered, over the longer term.

Repurchasing Shares versus Increasing the Dividend

Chapter 14

Corporations that wish to distribute cash to their shareholders typically declare cash dividends. Alternatively, a corporation can repurchase shares of its common stock. For example, International Business Machines Corporation announced a tender offer for up to 4 million shares of its common stock in February 1977. At the time, IBM had more than $6 billion of cash and marketable securities on its balance sheet. The tender offer resulted in IBM reacquiring 2,546,000 shares at a cost of $280 per share, an aggregate cost of approximately $713 million.

This chapter discusses why companies repurchase their shares, describes how a share repurchase program affects shareholder wealth, and reviews the alternative means by which a company can implement a share repurchase program.

WHY COMPANIES REPURCHASE THEIR SHARES

The IBM example illustrates but one of several reasons why corporations repurchase their shares. Surveys of corporate share repurchase programs, principally two Conference Board studies, indicate the following motives.[1]

Distribute Cash to Shareholders

The substitutability of share repurchases for cash dividend distributions is most vividly demonstrated by the sharp increase in the magnitude of share repurchases in 1973 and 1974. In connection with the wage and price controls program in 1973 to 1974, the government imposed limitations on dividend payments but not on share repurchases. New York Stock Exchange–listed companies, for example, increased their volume of share repurchases from 44 million shares in 1972 to 144 million in 1973 and 90 million in 1974.

Corporations that find themselves with a substantial amount of excess cash to distribute generally prefer to repurchase shares rather than declare a "special" or "extra" dividend. An individual shareholder who receives more than $100 per year in dividends is generally better off financially if a corporation distributes excess cash through stock repurchases rather than in the form of dividends because long-term capital gains are taxed to individuals at a lower rate than dividend income (in excess of $100). The share repurchase effectively converts dividend income into a long-term capital gain, provided the shareholder has owned the shares long enough to qualify the capital gain for long-term capital gain treatment.[2]

The Tandy Corporation has been one of the stronger proponents of the view that a company should repurchase shares rather than pay cash dividends. Tandy has never paid a cash common stock dividend, and between 1973 and 1984 it repurchased more than $700 million of its common stock, including $100 million and $355 million cash tender offers and two exchange offers worth approximately $125 million, all with the avowed intention of reducing its shareholders' tax liability on Tandy's cash distributions.[3]

The aforementioned tax advantage exists for one-time share repurchase programs. If a company substituted a program of regular share repurchases for periodic dividend payments, there is a danger that the Internal Revenue Service would treat as "essentially equivalent to a dividend" the proceeds realized by any shareholder who does not sell sufficient shares to reduce disproportionately his or her percentage ownership interest in the corporation and tax the sales proceeds as dividends.

As noted in Chapter 12, the tax position of corporate shareholders differs substantially from that of individuals because of the 85% dividends received deduction. From a purely tax standpoint, corporate shareholders prefer dividends over capital gains. Because of the differing tax positions of the different investment groups, it is important for a corporation that is contemplating a share repurchase program as a means of distributing excess cash to take into consideration its shareholder mix.

Buy Out Small Shareholdings

The cost of servicing a small shareholder account, e.g., printing and mailing annual and quarterly reports, proxy materials, dividend checks, etc., is proportionately greater than the cost of servicing a large shareholder account. Corporations frequently try to reduce the overall cost of servicing shareholders by offering to repurchase small shareholdings. For example, on August 2, 1982, LTV Corporation announced an offer to repurchase common shares from its shareholders who owned at the time 20 or fewer shares. LTV offered a premium of $1 over the closing price the day the shareholder's order was received plus a bonus of $5 for each tendering shareholder account.

Increase Leverage

A corporation that wishes to increase its leverage can either borrow funds and use the proceeds to repurchase shares or offer its shareholders the opportunity to exchange their shares for a new issue of debt. For example, Kaufman and Broad, Inc., offered on December 22, 1978, to exchange $10 principal amount of newly issued $12\frac{1}{4}\%$ debentures for each of up to 3 million shares of its common stock.

Company's Shares Are Undervalued

The company's common stock is undervalued and therefore provides an attractive investment opportunity is one of the reasons most frequently articulated by corporations when announcing a share repurchase program. Shareholders would benefit if the announcement caused the stock market to revalue the company's shares upward. Remaining shareholders might benefit further if management is unusually prescient. At least two major studies have provided evidence regarding management's ability to identify when their own companies' stocks are undervalued.[4]

Neutralize Dilutive Impact of Certain Transactions

Repurchasing shares to have them available for employee compensation plans, acquisition programs, the exercise of warrants, or the conversion of convertible securities was the principal motive according to The Conference Board surveys. Repurchasing shares neutralizes the dilutive impact of the subsequent share issue. Alternatively, of course, a corporation could use newly issued shares and use the cash initially earmarked for the share repurchase program to make a dividend distribution.

Increase Reported Earnings per Share

A share repurchase program can increase reported earnings per share. If the company's shares continue to trade at the same price-earnings multiple, the share price will be higher following the repurchase. However, a company should compare (1) the combined value of the dividend plus the value of a share immediately thereafter if the corporation makes a dividend distribution and (2) the value of a share immediately following the repurchase if the corporation uses an identical sum of cash to make share repurchases. If the corporation repurchases shares at a "fair" price, the two alternatives should leave (the remaining) shareholders in an identical position.

If the company pays a premium, however, the increase in earnings per share will not compensate fully for the dividend distribution (per share) that is foregone. In that case, selling shareholders would benefit at the expense of the remaining shareholders.

Consolidate Insiders' Control Position

Although it is seldom stated explicitly as an objective, it is apparent that some corporations have repurchased shares in order to consolidate the position of existing management or certain large shareholders (collectively "insiders"). This most often takes the form of block purchases from contentious minority shareholders, sometimes at a substantial premium to the prevailing market price (referred to in the financial press as "greenmail"), or open market purchases intended principally to reduce the percentage held by persons not affiliated with the insider group. In other cases, a company repurchases shares in order to reduce its liquidity and hence its attractiveness as an acquisition candidate and thereby enhance management's security. In each of these cases, however, the repurchase program is not necessarily consistent with the objective of maximizing the wealth of the company's shareholders generally.

Eliminate Market Overhang

One of the reasons stated in connection with the IBM tender offer mentioned at the beginning of the chapter was to eliminate "market overhang." A repurchase program provides liquidity to large holders who might otherwise have to dispose of their holdings at significant discounts.

IMPACT OF REPURCHASING SHARES ON SHAREHOLDER WEALTH

Whether a corporation can increase shareholder wealth by reacquiring shares remains a controversial subject within the financial community.

Dividend versus Repurchase: A Special Case

In order to appreciate better the possible advantages of repurchasing shares, it is useful to begin with a rather special case in which there is no such advantage. Suppose a company has $1 million available for distribution; that it has 1 million shares outstanding held entirely by individuals; that it projects earnings per share of $2.40; and that its current share price is $25. The company could pay a dividend of $1 per share, implying an exdividend share price of $24 per share, or 10 times projected earnings per share. Alternatively, the company could use the $1 million to repurchase 40,000 (= 1,000,000/25) shares. If markets are frictionless, the company's shares would continue to trade at a 10-times multiple because the dividend-vs-repurchase decision does not affect the company's capital investment or financing decisions. Projected earnings per share would increase to $2.50 (= $2.40 × 1,000,000/960,000), and each share would consequently be worth $25 (= $2.50 × 10). As long as the company repurchases shares at a fair price, a shareholder who does not sell realizes the same wealth per share, before taxes, as one who does, namely, $25 per share. Moreover, a shareholder who pays tax at the same rate on dividends and capital gains would realize the same after-tax wealth per share whether the company repurchased shares or instead paid a $1.00 dividend.

Tax Advantage to Repurchasing Shares

Because of the differential taxation of dividends and capital gains, individual shareholders would generally suffer a lesser tax liability, and hence realize greater wealth, if the corporation repurchases shares in lieu of making a cash dividend distribution. An individual shareholder in the 50% tax bracket would have to pay $0.50 per share in taxes on the $1 per share dividend but only $0.20 per share in capital gain taxes for each share he or she sold. Corporate holders, however, would pay only $0.069 per share in taxes on the $1 dividend but $0.28 per share in capital gain taxes if they sold shares.

Reaction of the Investment Community

The impact of a share repurchase program on shareholders who do not sell any shares depends on how the share repurchase program affects the company's share price. This depends chiefly on two factors: (1) how the investment community reacts to the repurchase announcement and (2) how the execution of the share repurchase program affects the share price.

Among the possible negative implications of a share repurchase announcement, securities analysts and investors might interpret the use of a company's liquid assets to reacquire a substantial number of shares as a tacit admission that the company lacks attractive business opportunities. If the investment community had not anticipated this reduction in attractive investment opportunities, the announcement would probably lead to a fall in the company's share price. Among the possible positive implications, the investment community might interpret the announcement of a share repurchase as a signal of management's confidence in the future of the company's business. If significant improvements in profitability had followed previous share repurchases by the company, the investment community might be more inclined to react favorably unless there were other negating factors.

A careful review of recent securities analysts' reports on a company will provide clues as to how the investment community might react to the announcement of a share repurchase program. When a company has a valid business purpose for undertaking a share repurchase program, announcing it minimizes the risk of an adverse reaction.

Evidence Regarding the Stock Market's Reaction

The stock market's reaction is probably influenced by the general profile of repurchasing firms that has emerged from studies of the financial and operating characteristics of these firms. These studies have revealed that firms that repurchase their shares are generally less leveraged, less profitable, and slower growing than comparable firms.[5] These results are broadly consistent with a lack of profitable investment opportunities.

The investment community's reaction also depends importantly on how the company decides to effect the share repurchases. In particular, recent evidence suggests that a tender offer is more likely to have a favorable market impact than an open market repurchase program. At least four studies have demonstrated that tender offers generally do have a favorable share price impact around the time the company announces the tender offer and that any price rollback that occurs when the tender offer terminates is generally not significant, except possibly when the tender offer is oversubscribed *and* the company elects to prorate its purchases among tendering shareholders.[6] In addition, one of these studies found that open market purchase programs had only a negligible share price impact.[7]

ANALYZING WHETHER TO BUY SHARES OR PAY A DIVIDEND

The repurchase of common stock is a use of shareholder funds. It represents but one of several alternatives. It is the most advantageous alternative to shareholders only if it is the one that maximizes shareholder wealth. This involves a number of related considerations.

Evaluating the Share Repurchase Decision

Suppose the firm's capital expenditure program and its financial structure are held fixed. In that case, a share repurchase program is best viewed as an alternative to a dividend distribution as a means of returning excess liquid assets to shareholders. Next suppose that only the corporation's capital expenditure program is held fixed. If a corporation wishes to increase its leverage and borrows funds to finance a share repurchase, the transaction can be viewed as a composite of two transactions: (1) borrowing and reducing equity in order to increase leverage and (2) paying a dividend versus repurchasing shares as a means to reduce equity. Finally, suppose that only the corporation's financial structure is held fixed. The corporation should invest in all projects that the corporation expects to yield an internal rate of return at least equal to its hurdle rate. Any cash that it cannot invest profitably should be returned to shareholders—either as a dividend or as share repurchases.[8]

Thus, the alternatives of distributing cash to shareholders, "investing" the cash in the company's common stock, incurring debt and reducing equity in order to increase leverage, or investing the cash in real assets are interrelated to the extent that each involves the evaluation of alternative uses of cash, including the trade-off between making a dividend distribution on the one hand and repurchasing shares of the company's common stock on the other.

Repurchase/Dividend Decision

If the company believes it is in an excess cash position, it must determine in the light of future requirements for cash and future prospects for cash generation whether an excess position really exists and, if an excess exists, the amount of the excess. The second step involves deciding how best to distribute the cash.

Impact on Shareholder Wealth. The most important factor to consider is how the method of distribution is likely to affect shareholder wealth. A company should try to determine in light of the composition of its shareholder body which method will result in a greater distribution net of tax effects. In addition, it must weigh the costs of each type of distribution. Share repurchase programs are generally more expensive than dividend distributions, particularly if the company repurchases shares by tendering at a significant premium over the prevailing share price. Third, if management believes the company's shares are undervalued and it wishes to signal this to the investment community, it might wish to tender for shares rather than make a dividend distribution. Fourth, announcing a share repurchase program (or a large extra or special dividend) might have a negative impact on a company's share price if the investment community had previously believed the company had superior growth prospects. Companies may therefore be tempted to retain most of the excess cash and pay it out over time through increases in the regular dividend. However, this policy will prove harmful to shareholders if they can invest the funds more profitably.

Impact on Reported Financial Results. A share repurchase program reduces the number of outstanding common shares. Consequently, earnings per share, cash flow per share, and book value per share will be higher following a share repurchase program than following an equivalent dividend distribution. While it seems unlikely that simply altering per share figures can affect stock market value, many companies like to maintain a smooth progression in earnings per share.

Effect on the Company's Dividend Policy. A large dividend increase that the company could not sustain would send a false signal to the market. A large dividend increase followed by a dividend reduction might harm the company's credibility. Consequently, if a company does not expect the condition that gave rise to the excess cash to persist, it would be preferable for the company to repurchase shares (or perhaps declare an "extra" or "special" dividend) rather than to increase the regular dividend by the full amount of the excess cash.

Investor Preferences for Liquidity. Most common stock investors, particularly individuals, would prefer regular dividend payments over irregular cash distributions. Regular dividend payments facilitate individual financial planning by each shareowner, and certain institutions are limited by legal or policy constraints to stocks that pay regular dividends.

Effect on Accounting for Acquisitions. A share repurchase program can, under certain circumstances, prevent a company that acquires another company in an exchange of common stock that occurs within 2 years of the share repurchase program from accounting for the acquisition on a *pooling-of-interests* basis. This diminishes the flexibility of companies that prefer to account for acquisitions in this manner. However, the operating characteristics and tax position of the combined companies are not affected by the choice of financial accounting method. Accordingly, the choice of accounting method should not affect the stock price of the combined entity.[9] This suggests that accounting considerations are less important than companies generally believe.

Possible Impact on Debt Ratings. A share repurchase program might have an adverse ratings impact if in the rating agencies' view, the higher leverage would decrease the company's financial flexibility. However, this factor is likely to be important only if (1) the share repurchase program is large relative to the company's capitalization and (2) the rating is in jeopardy.

EVALUATING THE RELATIVE ADVANTAGE OF REPURCHASING SHARES

A company's shareholders would prefer a share repurchase program over a dividend distribution of equal (pretax) size if the share repurchase program results in a greater payment net of (1) shareholder taxes and (2) transaction costs. It is impractical for a company to poll its shareholders to determine their individual tax situations. However, a company can estimate the break-even tax rate that would make its shareholders, as a group, indifferent about a share repurchase program and a dividend distribution. It can then review its shareholder records to determine whether the bulk of the shares are held by institutions, which generally pay tax at a relatively low marginal rate, or individuals, who generally pay tax at a relatively high marginal rate. If the holders of a majority of the shares probably pay tax at a rate that is greater than the break-even rate, tax considerations would support the repurchase of shares rather than a dividend distribution; in the opposite situation, tax considerations would support a dividend distribution rather than a share repurchase program.

Determining the Most Tax Effective Alternative

The following approach can be used to estimate the break-even tax rate.[10] Let *cash available* denote the amount of cash the company has available for distribution, *stockholders* the number of stockholders of record, *administrative cost per stockholder* the incremental cost per shareholder of making the dividend distribution, and *dividend tax rate* the (composite) marginal tax rate the company's shareholders must pay on dividend income. A dividend distribution costs the company administrative cost per stockholder × stockholders so that shareholders realize an amount

$$\left(\begin{array}{c} \text{Cash} \\ \text{available} \end{array} - \begin{array}{c} \text{administrative} \\ \text{cost per} \\ \text{stockholder} \end{array} \times \text{stockholders} \right) \left(1 - \frac{\text{dividend}}{\text{tax rate}} \right) \qquad (14\text{-}1)$$

net of taxes.

Alternatively, the firm can repurchase shares. Let *transactions* denote the number of repurchase transactions required to complete the repurchase program, and *transaction cost* the incremental cost per transaction; let *solicitation cost* denote the incremental cost per shareholder for soliciting purchases (e.g., mailing), *tax basis* the holders' average tax basis, and *capital gain tax rate* the (composite) marginal tax rate shareholders must pay on capital gains. A repurchase program costs the company

$$\begin{array}{c} \text{Repurchase} \\ \text{program} \\ \text{cost} \end{array} = \frac{\text{solicitation}}{\text{cost}} \times \text{stockholders} + \frac{\text{transaction}}{\text{cost}} \times \text{transactions}$$

The company can distribute *cash available* less *repurchase program cost*. Shareholders would receive this amount and would allocate a proportionate share of their tax basis to the proceeds received, that is

$$\text{Tax basis} \times \left(\begin{array}{c} \text{cash} \\ \text{available} \end{array} - \begin{array}{c} \text{repurchase} \\ \text{program cost} \end{array} \right) \div \begin{array}{c} \text{prior market} \\ \text{value} \end{array}$$

where *prior market value* denotes the stock market value of the firm just prior to the repurchase program. After paying taxes, shareholders realize

$$\left(\begin{array}{c} \text{Cash} \\ \text{available} \end{array} - \begin{array}{c} \text{repurchase} \\ \text{program} \\ \text{cost} \end{array} \right) \left(1 - \begin{array}{c} \text{capital} \\ \text{gain} \\ \text{tax rate} \end{array} \right.$$

$$\left. \times \left\{ 1 - \frac{\text{tax basis}}{\text{prior market value}} \left[1 - (1 + R)^{-T} \right] \right\} \right) \qquad (14\text{-}2)$$

where the factor $1 - (1 + R)^{-T}$ reflects the fact that the portion of the shareholder's tax basis that is used to reduce taxes currently will not be available when the balance of the shares are sold (i.e., at some time T) and where R represents the time value of money to the company's shareholders.

For individuals, the ordinary income tax rate exceeds the capital gains tax rate. Let *fraction* denote the fraction of capital gains income that must be added to ordinary income when calculating the "average" shareholder's tax liability. The *break-even tax rate* is the dividend tax rate that equates Formulas 14-1 and 14-2 when fraction × dividend tax rate is substituted for capital gain tax rate:

$$
\begin{aligned}
\text{Break-even} \atop \text{tax rate} = \bigg[&{\text{transaction} \atop \text{cost}} \times \text{transactions} \\
&+ \left({\text{solicitation} \atop \text{cost}} - {\text{administrative cost} \atop \text{per stockholder}} \right) \times \text{stockholders} \bigg] \\
\div \bigg(&\left({\text{cash} \atop \text{available}} - {\text{administrative} \atop \text{cost per} \atop \text{stockholder}} \times \text{stockholders} \right) \\
- \text{fraction} \times &\left({\text{cash} \atop \text{available}} - {\text{repurchase} \atop \text{program} \atop \text{cost}} \right) \\
\times &\left\{ 1 - \frac{\text{tax basis}}{\text{prior market value}} \left[1 - (1 + R)^{-T} \right] \right\} \bigg)
\end{aligned} \quad (14\text{-}3)
$$

The higher the break-even tax rate, the smaller the net tax advantage to repurchasing shares rather than making a dividend distribution.

Example of Break-Even Tax Rate Calculation

Company A, which has 100,000 shareholders, wishes to distribute $1 million. Its records show that administrative cost per stockholder = $0.50. Based on an analysis of comparable repurchase transactions, it estimates solicitation cost = $2 and transaction cost = $10 for transactions = 4000. Its annual share volume equals one-fourth the number of shares outstanding, implying an average holding period of roughly 2 years. Company A's current share price is roughly twice the average share price during the past 4 years, and so company A decides to use tax basis ÷ prior market value = 0.5. In addition, the 2-year average holding period suggests $T = 2$. The 2-year high-grade municipal bond yield is $R = 0.10$. Substituting into Formula 14-3 gives

Break-even tax rate = 0.2826, or 28.26%

Individual shareholders who pay tax at a marginal rate in excess of 28.26%, depending on the shareholder's actual tax basis, would generally prefer that company A repurchase shares, whereas individual shareholders in lower tax brackets would generally prefer the company to pay the cash out as dividends instead. If company A has a high percentage of individual shareholders in low tax brackets (e.g., retirees) and/or a high percentage of corporate shareholders, it should seriously consider paying a dividend instead of buying back shares.

In general, a share repurchase program involves greater transaction costs than a dividend distribution. For small distributions, the tax savings may not offset the higher transaction costs associated with repurchasing shares (i.e., the situation in which company A finds itself). For large distributions, individual shareholders, at least, are generally better off under a share repurchase program than under a dividend distribution. Finally, the higher transaction costs associated with buying back shares imply that tax-exempt shareholders will generally prefer a dividend distribution. Thus, a high concentration of tax-exempt shareholders (e.g., pension funds, charitable institutions, and college endowments) would argue in favor of a dividend distribution.

ANALYZING THE FINANCIAL STATEMENT IMPACT OF A SHARE REPURCHASE PROGRAM

Companies contemplating share repurchase programs typically analyze the financial statement impact as well as the basic economics of alternative share repurchase programs. Table 14-1 illustrates the type of pro forma analysis that companies find useful.

Major Pharmaceutical has $80 million of excess cash and marketable securities. If Major Pharmaceutical wishes to spend more than $80 million on share repurchases, it will have to borrow the additional amount (at an assumed interest rate of 12%). In any case, applying the excess cash to repurchase shares will reduce investment income (a 10% yield on short-term investments is assumed in Table 14-1).

As long as the average price per share does not exceed $40, Major Pharmaceutical can purchase up to 2 million of its shares with excess cash. This reduces net income, but the number of shares outstanding decreases by a greater percentage so that earnings per share increase. Aggregate dividend expense decreases (at least on a pro forma basis) because the number of outstanding shares decreases. However, cash flow net of dividends decreases in this case because the foregone investment income would exceed the dividends saved as a result of the repurchase. Book value per share decreases in this case because shares are repurchased at a price that exceeds the pre-repurchase book value per share; book value per share would increase if shares were repurchased for less than book value per share. Finally, the credit statistics worsen slightly, reflecting the reduction in liquidity and increase in leverage due to the share repurchases.

Table 14-1
Pro Forma Analysis for Share Repurchase Program
for Major Pharmaceutical Company
(Amounts in Millions Except Per-Share Amounts)

		Pro Forma the Repurchase of			
		2 Million Shares at Average Cost of		3 Million Shares at Average Cost of	
	Actual at 12/31/XX	$30	$40	$30	$40
Effect on Shares Outstanding					
Number outstanding	60.0	58.0	58.0	57.0	57.0
% decrease		3.3%	3.3%	5.0%	5.0%
Value of shares repurchased		$ 60.00	$ 80.0	$ 90.0	$ 120.0
Effect on Earnings and Dividends					
Earnings before interest and taxes	$ 406.0	$ 400.0[e]	$ 398.0[e]	$ 398.0[e]	$ 398.0[e]
Interest expense	46.0	46.0	46.0	47.2[f]	50.8[f]
Pretax income	360.0	354.0	352.0	350.8	347.2
Income tax expense	180.0	177.0	176.0	175.4	173.6
Net income	$ 180.0	$ 177.0	$ 176.0	$ 175.4	$ 173.6
Earnings per share	$ 3.00	$ 3.05	$ 3.03	$ 3.08	$ 3.05
% Change		+1.7%	+1.0%	+2.7%	+1.7%
Common dividends:					
Per share	$ 0.75	$ 0.75	$ 0.75	$ 0.75	$ 0.75
Total	45.0	43.5	43.5	42.75	42.75
% Change		−3.3%	−3.3%	−5.0%	−5.0%
Cash flow net of dividends[a]	$ 255.0	$ 253.5	$ 252.5	$ 252.7	$ 250.9
% Change		−0.6%	−1.0%	−0.9%	−1.6%
Effect on Balance Sheet					
Cash and marketable securities[b]	$ 100.0	$ 40.0	$ 20.0	$ 20.0	$ 20.0
As % of total assets[c]	4.0%	1.6%	0.8%	0.8%	0.8%
As % of current liabilities[d]	50.0%	20.0%	10.0%	10.0%	10.0%
Net working capital[d]	$ 300.0	$ 240.0	$ 220.0	$ 220.0	$ 220.0
Book capitalization:					
Short-term debt	$ 60.0	$ 60.0	$ 60.0	$ 60.0	$ 60.0
Long-term debt	$ 400.0	$ 400.0	$ 400.0	$ 410.0	$ 440.0
Stockholders' equity	1,200.0	1,140.0	1,120.0	1,110.0	1,080.0
Total capitalization	$1,600.0	$1,540.0	$1,520.0	$1,520.0	$1,520.0

**Pro Forma Analysis for Share Repurchase Program
for Major Pharmaceutical Company** *(Continued)*
(Amounts in Millions Except Per-Share Amounts)

	Actual at 12/31/XX	Pro Forma the Repurchase of			
		2 Million Shares at Average Cost of		3 Million Shares at Average Cost of	
		$30	$40	$30	$40
Book value per share	$ 20.00	$ 19.66	$ 19.31	$ 19.47	$ 18.95
% Change		−1.7%	−3.5%	−2.7%	−5.3%
Selected Ratios					
Current ratio	2.50×	2.20×	2.10×	2.10×	2.10×
Long-term debt/ capitalization	25.0%	26.0%	26.3%	27.0%	28.9%
Total debt/(short-term debt and capitalization)	27.7%	28.8%	29.1%	29.7%	31.6%
Pretax interest coverage	8.83×	8.70×	8.65×	8.43×	7.83×
Return on average equity	15.9%	16.5%	16.7%	16.8%	17.1%
Cash flow/long-term debt[a]	75.0%	74.3%	74.0%	72.0%	66.7%

[a] Assumes $300 million cash flow from operations prior to repurchase.
[b] Assumes $80 million of cash and marketable securities available for share repurchase or dividend distribution.
[c] Assumes total assets of $2500 million prior to repurchase.
[d] Assumes current assets of $500 million and current liabilities of $200 million prior to repurchase.
[e] Assumes short-term investments would yield a pretax annual return of 10%.
[f] Assumes additional borrowings at a 12% interest rate.

If instead Major Pharmaceutical were to repurchase 3 million of its shares, the larger program would have a greater impact on earnings per share but would also have a more severe impact on Major Pharmaceutical's credit statistics.

EVALUATING THE ECONOMICS OF BUYING OUT SMALL SHAREHOLDINGS

Companies frequently decide to repurchase small shareholdings in order to reduce their overall shareholder servicing costs. Such a transaction benefits the larger shareholders who remain behind when the present value of the resulting reduction in future shareholder servicing costs exceeds the immediate cost of the repurchase program.

Measuring the Net Savings[11]

Let *threshold size* denote the largest shareholding a company is considering tendering for. That is, the company will offer to repurchase any or all shares held by a holder who owns threshold size or fewer shares. Let *number of accounts* denote the aggregate number of accounts that each contain threshold size or fewer shares, and let *number of shares* denote the aggregate number of shares these accounts hold.

The share repurchase program involves three important types of costs: a unit *solicitation cost* and a unit *transaction cost*, which were discussed in a previous section, plus a *tender premium* over the current market price, which gives holders an incentive to tender their shares. If a *response fraction* of the accounts and shares tendered for respond favorably to the offer, then the cost of the repurchase program is

$$
\text{Cost} = \frac{\text{solicitation}}{\text{cost}} \times \frac{\text{number of}}{\text{accounts}} + \frac{\text{transaction}}{\text{cost}} \times \frac{\text{response}}{\text{fraction}}
$$

$$
\times \frac{\text{number of}}{\text{accounts}} + \frac{\text{tender}}{\text{premium}} \times \frac{\text{response}}{\text{fraction}} \times \frac{\text{number of}}{\text{shares}} \quad (14\text{-}4)
$$

The number of accounts that are eliminated by the repurchase program is represented by response fraction × number of accounts. Each account eliminated results in a stream of future savings. Let *service cost* denote the average cost per annum of servicing each account containing threshold size or fewer shares, net of any tax savings realized thereon. As a practical matter, service cost is roughly the same for all accounts and so can be estimated by dividing total annual shareholder servicing costs by the total number of shareholder accounts. Suppose the company expects service cost to increase at an annual *escalation rate* and that the company's shareholders discount future payments at *discount rate*. Because the reduction in shareholder servicing costs will increase the earnings available for reinvestment or distribution as dividends, their time value is probably best calculated by using the company's cost of equity capital as the discount rate.

Thus, the repurchase program yields a stream of savings the present value of which amounts to

$$
\text{Benefit} = \frac{\text{response}}{\text{fraction}} \times \frac{\text{number of}}{\text{accounts}} \times \sum_{t=1}^{\infty} \left[\frac{\text{service}}{\text{cost}} \right.
$$

$$
\times \left(1 + \frac{\text{escalation}}{\text{rate}}\right)^{t} \times \left. \left(1 + \frac{\text{discount}}{\text{rate}}\right)^{-t} \right]
$$

$$
= \frac{\text{response}}{\text{fraction}} \times \frac{\text{number of}}{\text{accounts}} \times \frac{\text{service}}{\text{cost}}
$$

$$
\div \left(\frac{\text{discount}}{\text{rate}} - \frac{\text{escalation}}{\text{rate}} \right) \quad (14\text{-}5)
$$

where Formula 4-11 has been used to simplify the sum. The difference between benefit in Formula 14-5 and cost in Formula 14-4 represents the net present value savings, NPV, from repurchasing small shareholdings:

$$NPV = benefit - cost \qquad (14\text{-}6)$$

When NPV is positive, a company can profitably undertake the share repurchase program. By varying the cutoff threshold size and the values of the variables accordingly, a company can determine the scope of the repurchase program that would yield the greatest net present value savings.

Example of Net Present Value Calculation

Offers to repurchase small shareholdings generally involve a price that represents a premium of between $0.50 and $1 per share over the prevailing market price plus a bonus of between $5 and $10 if the entire shareholding is tendered. The bonus typically approximates the annual cost of servicing a shareholder account. The premium price and bonus, together with the opportunity to avoid the disproportionately high brokerage commissions on small odd-lot transactions, provide a strong inducement to sell.

Holding Company is considering whether to tender for all holdings of 50 or fewer shares. Holding Company has 100,000 such accounts, which contain a total of 1 million shares. Holding Company's investment bankers have analyzed similar repurchase programs and have advised Holding Company to offer a premium of $0.50 per share plus $5 to each shareholder who tenders his or her entire account (of 50 or fewer shares). The investment bankers have advised Holding Company to expect 75% of eligible shareholders to tender their entire accounts. Mailing and other solicitation costs will amount to roughly $1 per account.

Each closed account will save Holding Company $5 per annum into the foreseeable future (i.e., to be conservative, escalation rate = 0). Holding Company's cost of equity capital is approximately 20%. Substituting response fraction = 0.75, number of accounts = 100,000, service cost = $5, discount rate = 0.2, escalation rate = 0, solicitation cost = $1, transaction cost = $5, tender premium = $0.50, and number of shares = 1,000,000 gives

$$NPV = \$1,875,000 - 850,000 = \$1,025,000$$

Thus, the company can expect the proposed repurchase program to be advantageous to its shareholders. However, if instead, for example, response fraction = 0.25, transaction cost = $10, and tender premium = $1.50, the repurchase program would not be beneficial to larger shareholders because in that case NPV = −$100,000.

IMPLEMENTING A SHARE REPURCHASE PROGRAM

Having decided that a share repurchase program would be in its shareholders' best interests, a company must then decide how best to implement the program. There are four basic methods.

Open Market Purchases

An open market share repurchase program averages the company's repurchase price during the repurchase period. Approximately two-thirds of the shares repurchased in the United States are bought in open market purchases. Repurchases are made daily subject to SEC regulations governing the timing, price, volume, and coordination of share purchases, which are designed to minimize the impact of the share repurchase program on the company's share price.

Table 14-2
Study of Selected Large Tender Offers

Date	Company	Number of Shares Sought	Dollar Amount, $ (000's)	Number of Shares Outstanding	Number of Shares Sought as % of Outstanding
2/9/76	Teledyne, Inc.	1,000,000	40,000	11,418,004	8.8
2/22/77	International Business Machines Corporation	4,000,000	1,120,000	150,680,685	2.7
6/24/77	Tandy Corporation	3,500,000	101,500	15,464,134	22.6
9/13/77	Boise Cascade Corporation	2,000,000	56,000	29,476,746	6.8
10/3/78	Ashland Oil Inc.	5,000,000	235,000	30,979,982	16.1
1/31/79	Levi Strauss & Co.	2,000,000	87,000	21,887,783	9.1
2/7/79	Georgia-Pacific Corporation	4,500,000	139,500	102,796,315	4.4
7/27/79	The Standard Oil Company (Ohio)	1,700,000	104,550	120,056,269	1.4
2/3/81	The Bendix Corporation	4,000,000	256,000	23,060,763	17.3
9/22/81	Todd Shipyards Corporation	550,000	15,400	5,525,440	10.0
10/14/81	The Seagram Company Ltd.	5,000,000	300,000	35,077,400	14.3
11/23/81	The Firestone Tire & Rubber Co.	10,000,000	115,000	57,723,240	17.3

Source: The Wall Street Journal, various issues.

Private Block Purchases

Privately negotiated purchases of large blocks of shares are most often made in conjunction with, rather than as a substitute for, an open market purchase program. Large blocks can often be purchased at a discount to the prevailing market price, particularly when the transaction is initiated by the seller.

Tender Offer

A company that wishes to purchase a relatively large number of shares can quickly announce a cash tender offer. The company announces the number of shares it seeks and the price it is willing to pay. Such an offer has the advantage of providing an equal opportunity to all shareholders to sell their shares to the company. A tender offer gives widespread public emphasis to the fact that the company is buying a significant amount of its own stock, and there is evidence that, perhaps because of this, tender offers generally have a more significant market impact than open market purchase programs.

Tender Price, $	Premium over Price Prior to Tender, %	Number of Shares Tendered	Number of Shares Tendered as % of Out- standing	Success Ratio, %	Dealer Fee, $	Management Fee, $	% of Price	Stated Minimum/ Maximum Manager Fee
40.00	26.0	2,535,000	22.2	253.5	0.25	None	—	None
280.00	3.7	2,546,000	1.7	63.7	0.75	0.225	0.08	250,000/ None
29.00	19.0	5,426,000	35.1	155.0	None	None	—	None
28.00	14.9	7,000,000	23.7	350.0	None	0.15	0.54	None
47.00	15.3	5,800,000	18.7	116.0	None	None	—	None
43.50	9.8	3,785,614	17.3	189.3	None	0.15	0.34	75,000/ None
31.00	9.7	27,793,200	27.0	617.6	None	0.08	0.26	None
61.50	5.4	2,957,000	2.5	173.9	None	0.21	0.34	50,000/ None
64.00	11.2	5,000,000	21.7	125.0	None	0.23	0.36	150,000/ None
26.50	9.3	397,825	7.2	72.3	0.25	0.25	0.94	None
60.00	16.5	13,600,000	38.8	272.0	0.50	0.15	0.25	150,000/ None
11.50	16.5	600,000	1.0	6.0	0.20	0.07	0.61	200,000/ None

Tender offer programs have two principal drawbacks. Transaction costs for tender offers are generally higher than for other types of repurchase programs. A tender offer would also expose the company to the risk of criticism if too much or too little of its stock were tendered.

The "Dutch auction" tender offer procedure is a seldom-used variation of the general tender offer method that nevertheless does offer a company greater flexibility in determining the price at which the shares are to be purchased. Todd Shipyards Corporation used this procedure in September 1981. Todd specified minimum and maximum amounts of shares it was willing to purchase and minimum and maximum prices it was willing to pay. Each shareholder was asked to specify the minimum price (within the company's range) he or she was willing to accept for the shares tendered. If fewer than the specified minimum number of shares were tendered, Todd would have to pay the maximum price it specified. Otherwise Todd would select a price within the specified range and pay that price for all shares tendered at that price or at a lower price (subject to the requirement that it purchase at least the specified minimum number of shares). The Dutch auction method leads to a lower repurchase cost when the specified maximum price is the price the company would have specified in a fixed-price tender offer and the minimum number of shares is tendered at prices lower than this maximum price.

Tender Offer Considerations. Two of the more important considerations in connection with a tender offer are (1) how to set the tender offer premium and (2) whether to use a soliciting dealer (or group of dealers). Table 14-2 provides information regarding 12 large tender offers. The tender offer premiums vary considerably (from 3.7 to 26.0%) so that simply examining the historical record is not particularly helpful. The premium should be just large enough to attract the desired number of shares. A premium in the range from 10 to 25% is typical. A premium near or below the lower end of this range is usually feasible when large holders have expressed a desire to dispose of their shares or when the daily trading volume is a relatively large fraction of the number of shares sought. Widely dispersed shareholdings and/or very light trading volume and/or an unusually large tender offer normally necessitate an above-average tender premium. However, too great a premium will lead to oversubscription and expose the company to the risk of an unsolicited takeover bid. On the second question, companies tendering for their own shares generally find it advantageous to use dealers in lieu of increasing the tender premium in order to acquire the desired number of shares.

Exchange Offer

Instead of offering cash for shares of its common stock, a company might instead offer securities. The success of such an offer depends on the common stockholders' willingness to exchange a security that enjoys a relatively liquid market for a security for which a liquid market might never develop. Compensating shareholders for this risk might necessitate a large premium. Probably for this reason, the vast majority of common stock repurchase programs have involved cash purchases.

Additional Legal Considerations

A company must determine whether loan agreements or other contracts include any restrictive provisions that might prohibit or limit a stock repurchase program before repurchasing shares. For the same reason, a company should also review its stock exchange listing agreements, its corporate charter, and state law in the state of its incorporation before it institutes a share repurchase program.

SUMMARY

When a company has cash available for distribution to its shareholders, it can repurchase shares in lieu of paying a dividend. Share repurchases are generally more beneficial from a tax standpoint to individual shareholders, but nontaxable institutional shareholders may prefer, and corporate shareholders generally will prefer, a dividend distribution. A company's shareholder mix will determine whether a share repurchase program will be preferable to a dividend distribution—or whether the corporation should use some combination of the two.

Companies have a variety of reasons for repurchasing shares of their own stock in addition to wishing to distribute excess cash, such as a desire to eliminate small shareholdings, increase leverage, buy back "undervalued" shares, neutralize the dilutive impact of employee stock option programs, increase reported earnings per share, consolidate insiders' control, or eliminate market overhang. Not all of these are necessarily consistent with shareholder wealth maximization.

Four basic methods are available for repurchasing shares: open market purchases, privately negotiated block purchases, cash tender offer, or exchange offer. Only the first three would be used by a company wishing to distribute excess cash. A company wishing to eliminate small shareholdings or to buy a relatively large percentage of its outstanding shares would generally use the tender offer method. While it is more expensive than an open market repurchase program, recent evidence indicates that the tender offer method has a more noticeable and more lasting stock market impact.

Working Capital Management and Short-Term Financing

Part 5

The bulk of a financial manager's time is typically devoted to *working capital management*. A firm's *net working capital* equals the amount of its current assets less the amount of its current liabilities. *Current assets*, principally cash and short-term securities, accounts receivable, and inventories, are assets that a company can normally convert into cash within 1 year. *Current liabilities*, principally short-term borrowings, accounts payable, and taxes payable, are obligations that will come due within 1 year. Working capital management involves all aspects of the administration of current assets and current liabilities.

Working capital management can, in theory at least, be treated in the overall context of the analysis of capital investments and the analysis of capital structure discussed in Parts 2 and 3. Capital investment projects typically require additional investments in accounts receivable and inventories, and we included the cash flows associated with these investments in the capital budgeting analysis. Also, it was noted in Chapter 10 that the permanent component of short-term borrowings should be taken into account when evaluating the degree of leverage in a firm's capital structure. Accordingly, a company should expand its investments in current assets up to the point where the marginal rate of return just equals the risk-adjusted marginal cost of capital so invested, and it should also substitute current liabilities for long-term sources of capital up to the point where the firm's overall cost of capital reaches a minimum. The most widely followed approaches to working capital management are not nearly this rigorous, however.

The following example illustrates the fundamental problem in working capital management. The president of Diversified Chemical Company has asked the company's treasurer to study the appropriateness of that company's policy of maintaining its ratio of current assets to current liabilities (its current ratio) at 2.0 times. Diversified Chemical has already established a total-debt-to-adjusted-capitalization objective of 1 : 3. In addition, Diversified Chemical's president would like the company's commercial paper to continue to qualify for an A-1 rating because Diversified Chemical's investment banker has informed him that lower-rated commercial paper is not as readily marketable. After developing a few basic concepts in Chapter 15, we will help Diversified's treasurer evaluate the appropriateness of Diversified's choice of current ratio objective.

Working Capital Management

It is useful to break down the working capital management problem into two basic types of decisions: (1) the relative levels of current assets and current liabilities and (2) the mix of current assets and the mix of current liabilities. This chapter deals with the first issue. Chapters 16 and 17 deal with the second issue.

OVERVIEW OF WORKING CAPITAL MANAGEMENT

Working capital management is governed by the firm's need to maintain adequate liquidity. To avoid technical insolvency, the firm must ensure that it will have sufficient cash on hand to meet its cash obligations as they come due.

Hedging Approach to Working Capital Management

The firm's assets have differing degrees of liquidity. *Liquidity* refers to the relative ease with which a company can convert an asset into cash without loss of value. For example, a security that is actively traded in a well-organized market is more liquid than a specialized piece of equipment. Liquidity considerations are important because of market imperfections; a firm that tries to sell inventory or receivables quickly to raise cash may find that it must accept "distress" prices that are significantly below the true economic value of these assets.

If the firm adopted a hedging approach to working capital management, it would try to match the maturities of its assets and liabilities. In particular, it would finance seasonal variations in current assets by taking on current liabilities of matching maturity, and it would finance long-term assets by issuing long-term debt and equity securities. In addition, in most cases there is a permanent component of current assets; inventories and receivables will remain above some minimum level. This permanent component of current assets would be financed from long-term capital. Under this approach, the borrowing and repayment schedule for short-term borrowing would be set so as to mirror the seasonal swings in current assets. As illustrated in Figure 15-1, short-term borrowings under this sort of policy would fall to zero at the seasonal troughs.

Margin of Safety

The situation is actually more complicated than that depicted in Figure 15-1. Cash inflows and outflows cannot be synchronized perfectly. The firm will therefore try to build some *margin of safety* into its debt maturity schedule. In general, the shorter the maturity schedule, the greater the risk that the firm will be unable to meet its debt service obligations. The firm can reduce this risk by lengthening the maturity schedule of its debt. As illustrated by the margin in Figure 15-2, the firm can accomplish this by financing a portion of its seasonal funds needs on a long-term basis. Near the cyclical troughs (e.g., between points A and B), the firm will have excess cash that it can invest on a short-term basis. Near the cyclical peaks (e.g., between points B and

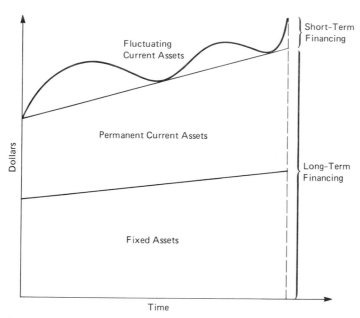

Figure 15-1. Mix of short-term debt and long-term sources of capital.

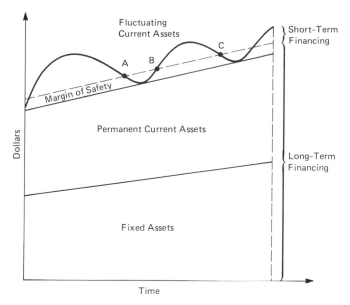

Figure 15-2. Margin of safety.

C), the firm will have net short-term borrowing requirements. As the point B approaches, the firm can liquidate its short-term investments as required to meet its funds requirements. This is likely to be of greater value to the firm when funds needs accelerate rapidly and there is a time lag involved in arranging additional short-term borrowings. In this way, the margin of safety provides a liquidity reserve.

The working capital management policy illustrated in Figure 15-2 is a very conservative one. In particular, the margin of safety results in a higher level of net working capital and a higher current ratio than would be the case without it. Many firms, particularly smaller ones, may operate with a negative margin of safety; the dashed line in Figure 15-2 would lie below rather than above the solid line. In that case, firms utilize short-term borrowings to finance a portion of permanent current assets and perhaps also fixed assets. As a result, they operate with lower net working capital and lower current ratios than firms that follow more conservative policies. The negative margin of safety would increase the firm's exposure to the risk of illiquidity if, among other possibilities, loan agreements should not be renewed. Nevertheless, smaller firms may have to rely heavily on short-term borrowings because market imperfections limit their access to the long-term capital markets.

Management's choice of an appropriate margin of safety depends on the cost and risk-reducing value of the margin of safety and management's trade-off between these two factors. In general, the explicit cost of long-term financing will exceed the cost of short-term borrowings (although the reverse may be true during periods of high interest rates). In that case, a positive margin of safety involves a net cost equal to the difference between the actual cost of long-term financing and the lower cost of short-term borrowing that was foregone. In addition, over the long term, the cost of long-term debt will probably exceed the returns the firm can realize on short-term investments. In that case, the firm would have to cover the excess of interest expense over interest income between points A and B in Figure 15-2 out of operating earnings, which will reduce the cash available for dividends or for other purposes. Management must weigh these costs against the value of reducing the risk of illiquidity in order to select the appropriate margin of safety.

INDUSTRY DIFFERENCES IN LIQUIDITY

The decision concerning the appropriate current ratio and the appropriate margin of safety will also depend on the basic profitability of a company's business and the liquidity of the company's assets. A company's liquid assets provide protection against insolvency. The higher the level of profitability and the more stable the company's profitability and cash flow, the smaller the amount of current assets the company needs to maintain in order to achieve any desired degree of protection against insolvency. Similarly, the more liquid a company's longer-term assets, that is, the easier it would be for a company to dispose of them on short notice without significant loss in value, the higher the degree of insolvency protection they afford and the smaller the required level of current assets required to achieve the same degree of protection.

There are significant differences in liquidity among industries. A study by Petty and Scott found that among the 13 industries they studied, there were significant differences among industry fluctuations in liquidity during both the relatively buoyant 1970 to 1971 period and the comparatively severe 1973 to 1974 period.[1] Companies in the textile products, paper, domestic integrated oil, tire and rubber goods, and building materials industries experienced relatively large swings in liquidity between 1970 and 1974, whereas companies in the crude oil production, meat packing, apparel manufacturing, and retail department store industries experienced relatively mild fluctuations in liquidity over the same period.

There are also significant differences across industries in the liquidity of long-term assets. For example, proven oil and gas reserves are more liquid than limited-purpose fixed plant and equipment. There is a fairly active market in proven oil and gas reserves, which accounts for the relatively greater liquidity of these assets.

Because there are differences in industry liquidity, it is important that any analysis of the alternative values for the current ratio or alternative margins of safety for any particular company start with an analysis of how comparable firms within the same industry have set their current ratios and margins of safety. As in the case of capital structure choice in Chapter 11 and dividend policy choice in Chapter 13, the policy decisions of comparable firms provide useful benchmarks.

DEBT RATINGS AND LIQUIDITY

The firms within any single industry will not all agree on the appropriate choice of current ratio or choice of the appropriate margin of safety, just as they do not all agree on the appropriate degree of leverage or the appropriate dividend policy. Not only do their circumstances and prospects differ, but their relative aversion to risk, including the risk of insolvency, will also differ. Accordingly, some will adopt more conservative working capital management policies than others.

We found in Chapter 11 that the professional rating services assign ratings to a company's debt securities that reflect their assessment of the financial risks investors bear in holding them. The rating services rate commercial paper as well as long-term debt securities. Commercial paper is a short-lived security—the maturity of publicly issued commercial paper cannot exceed 270 days without registering it with the SEC, but the maturity is typically 90 days or less—and the commercial paper rating reflects principally the agencies' assessment of the relative liquidity and financial flexibility of the issuer over the next 2 years or so.[2] The financial ratios of companies whose commercial paper bears a particular rating thus indicate the financial structure consistent with the relative degree of liquidity implicit in the particular commercial paper rating.

Table 15-1 illustrates how certain key financial ratios vary from one commercial paper rating category to another. Only the three highest rating categories assigned by Standard & Poor's Corporation are shown, but the financial ratios also vary systematically for lower-rated commercial paper. More important, only commercial paper rated in one of the categories indicated in Table 15-1 can be marketed broadly.

The companies whose commercial paper enjoys the highest rating are generally the most profitable, least leveraged, and most liquid. Interest and fixed charge coverage is highest, and cash flow relative to debt is strongest.[3]

As with the senior debt rating, a company can view the different commercial paper ratings as surrogates for differing levels of financial risk, in this case liquidity risk. The company can establish the degree of liquidity risk it will have to bear by selecting the risk level (i.e., rating category) most consistent

Table 15-1
Commercial Paper Ratings as Indicators
of Relative Liquidity*

Commercial Paper Rating†	A–1+	A–1	A–2
Definition†	The degree of safety regarding timely payment is "overwhelming."	The degree of safety regarding timely payment is "very strong."	Capacity for timely payment is "strong."
Interest coverage ratio	8.16×	5.31×	3.52×
Fixed charge coverage ratio‡	4.60	3.33	2.42
Cash flow/long-term debt	117.80%	74.57%	47.97%
Cash flow/total debt	89.51	59.89	39.50
Pretax return on average long-term capital employed	25.83	20.22	16.85
Operating income/sales	14.79	13.19	9.48
Long-term debt/capitalization	17.30	24.66	30.58
Total debt/capitalization including short-term debt	21.61	28.94	35.03

*Median of the 3-year simple arithmetic averages for the period 1980–1982 for companies whose commercial paper had the indicated rating.

†As assigned and defined by Standard & Poor's Corporation. Standard & Poor's also has four additional commercial paper rating categories, which are designated A-3, B, C, and D in descending order of relative liquidity.

‡Based on full rental charges, rather than the one-third of rental charges used in the SEC fixed charge coverage calculation.

Source: Credit Overview: Industrial Ratings, Standard & Poor's Corporation, New York, November 1983, pp. 39, 99.

with its objectives and aversion to risk. It can then look to the range within which each of the ratios in Table 15-1 and each of the key liquidity ratios (particularly the current ratio) vary across companies within the chosen commercial paper rating category in order to find a "reasonable range" for each. Also, as in the case of the choice of capital structure, this same basic approach is useful whether or not the company has rated securities outstanding. The objective is to use the information embodied in the professional rating agencies' assessments together with the company's own objectives and risk tolerances to formulate a specific financial policy in terms of quantifiable targets.

CHOICE OF CURRENT RATIO OBJECTIVE

Working capital management involves a number of related decisions. First, the corporation must determine appropriate levels of receivables and inventories consistent with the company's sales objectives. Each will contain a fixed component and a variable component. Second, it must establish the appropriate levels of cash and marketable securities consistent with (1) the continual maintenance of adequate liquidity and (2) the compensating balances required under the company's bank loan agreements. Third, the corporation must decide upon the appropriate levels of payables consistent with the company's maintaining an acceptable credit record. This too will involve fixed and variable components. Fourth, the company must then determine the mix of short-term and long-term financing for its fluctuating current assets consistent with maintaining an acceptable current ratio (and by implication an acceptable level of net working capital and an appropriate margin of safety).

These four sets of decisions are interrelated. For example, the maximum desired level of bank borrowings will determine the amount of bank lines the firm must have available and, therefore, its compensating balance requirements. As a second example, the mix of receivables and comparatively less liquid inventories will affect the overall liquidity of the portfolio of current assets and, therefore, the amount of cash and marketable securities the firm will want to maintain.

In planning and managing its working capital position, the firm will actually use a variety of liquidity measures to guide it. Of the liquidity ratios discussed in Chapter 2, the current ratio is certainly among the more important:

$$\text{Current ratio} = \text{current assets} \div \text{current liabilities} \qquad (15\text{-}1)$$

A higher margin of safety implies that, on average, the firm will finance a higher percentage of its working capital requirements on a long-term basis; it thus implies a higher current ratio. The firm can select an appropriate current ratio objective by first studying the current ratios of comparable firms within the same industry and with the desired commercial paper rating. It can then analyze how different values for its current ratio within or near this "reasonable" range might affect its profitability and interest coverage.

Illustration of Choice of Current Ratio Objective

To close this chapter, we return to the task confronting the treasurer of Diversified Chemical Company. Recall that the president of the company has asked its treasurer to study the appropriateness of the company's policy of maintaining a current ratio of 2.0 times. Table 15-2 provides a financial analysis relating to this question that Diversified's financial staff has prepared.

Diversified Chemical's treasurer finds that the average year-end value of the current ratio for the most recent 5-year period for the major diversified chemical companies other than Diversified Chemical has varied within a range from 1.44× to 2.52× with a median value of 2.14× for comparable companies

Table 15-2
Financial Analysis of Alternative Values for the Current Ratio

Commercial Paper Rating*	5-Year Average Current Ratio for Comparable Chemical Companies			5-Year Average Pretax Interest Coverage for Comparable Chemical Companies		
	High	Low	Median	High	Low	Median
A-1+	2.41×	1.82×	2.12×	8.15×	5.42×	6.79×
A-1	2.52	1.44	2.14	7.29	3.92	5.46
A-2	2.26	1.68	2.01	5.14	4.51	4.79

	9% Short-Term Interest Rate			13% Short-Term Interest Rate	17% Short-Term Interest Rate		
	2.50×	2.00×	1.50×		2.50×	2.00×	1.50×
Current assets	$ 90.0	$ 90.0	$ 90.0	$ 90.0	$ 90.0	$ 90.0	$ 90.0
Fixed assets	210.0	210.0	210.0	210.0	210.0	210.0	210.0
Total assets	$300.0	$300.0	$300.0	$300.0	$300.0	$300.0	$300.0
Short-term debt	$ 36.0	$ 45.0	$ 60.0	} $100.0	$ 36.0	$ 45.0	$ 60.0
Long-term debt (at 13%)	64.0	55.0	40.0		64.0	55.0	40.0
Common equity	200.0	200.0	200.0	200.0	200.0	200.0	200.0
Total liabilities and equity	$300.0	$300.0	$300.0	$300.0	$300.0	$300.0	$300.0

Earnings before interest and taxes	$ 60.0	$ 60.0	$ 60.0	$ 60.0	$ 60.0	$ 60.0	$ 60.0
Interest	11.6	11.2	10.6	13.0	14.4	14.8	15.4
Pretax income	48.4	48.8	49.4	47.0	45.6	45.2	44.6
Taxes (at 50%)	24.2	24.4	24.7	23.5	22.8	22.6	22.3
Earnings available for common	$ 24.2	$ 24.4	$ 24.7	$ 23.5	$ 22.8	$ 22.6	$ 22.3
Return on beginning equity	12.1%	12.2%	12.4%	11.8%	11.4%	11.3%	11.2%
Interest coverage	5.17×	5.36×	5.66×	4.62×	4.17×	4.05×	3.90×
Long-term debt/capitalization	24.2%	21.6%	16.7%		24.2%	21.6%	16.7%
Total debt/adjusted capitalization	33.3%	33.3%	33.3%	33.3%	33.3%	33.3%	33.3%
Safety margin†	$ 14.0	$ 5.0	$ (10.0)		$ 14.0	$ 5.0	$ (10.0)

*Rating determined by Standard & Poor's Corporation.
†Assuming $40 million of current assets are "permanent."

whose commercial paper is rated A-1. The median current ratio does not vary substantially from one rating category to another, being slightly above 2.0× in each case. This evidence alone suggests strongly that a current ratio objective of 2.0× is reasonable, but a fuller analysis should take into account the effect of different current ratios on Diversified Chemical's interest coverage. The average year-end value of the pretax interest coverage for the same companies varied within a range from 3.92× to 7.29× with a median value of 5.46× but was significantly lower for commercial paper rated A-2.

Suppose Diversified Chemical believes that long-term interest rates will average 13% and that short-term interest rates will average 9% over the company's planning horizon. On that basis, increasing the current ratio to 2.50× would reduce interest coverage farther below the median value for companies whose commercial paper is rated A-1 and, in addition, would reduce the return on equity. Diversified Chemical might be tempted to reduce the coverage ratio below 2.0×. However, this would expose the company to additional risk from floating interest rates. At short-term interest rates greater than 13%, reducing the current ratio below 2.0× would lead to decreases rather than increases both in interest coverage and in Diversified Chemical's return on equity. Taking into consideration the median values of the current ratio for the industry as well as this risk, the treasurer recommended that the company try to achieve a minimum current ratio of 2.0× but set its planning target at a slightly higher level.

Finally, note that a current ratio of 2.0× implies a safety margin of $5 million if $40 million of the $90 million of current assets are "permanent" [safety margin = $55 + 200 − (40 + 210) = $5].

SUMMARY

Working capital management involves all aspects of the administration of current assets and current liabilities. This involves two classes of problems: (1) what are the appropriate levels of cash, marketable securities, receivables, and inventories, and (2) what is the appropriate level and mix of short-term indebtedness. In managing their working capital, companies normally find it prudent to finance the permanent component of current assets on a long-term basis and to maintain a margin of safety besides.

The degree of liquidity varies from one industry to another. These differences are due to differences in profitability, differing degrees of cyclicality, and differences in the relative liquidity of longer-term assets. In general, the lower its relative profitability and the more cyclical its business and the less liquid its longer-term assets, the greater the amount of liquid assets and the wider the safety margin a company needs to maintain in order to achieve any particular overall degree of liquidity.

A company can select an appropriate current ratio objective by studying comparable companies within the same industry and with the desired commercial paper rating to identify a reasonable range of values for this ratio. It can then evaluate the impact of different values within this range on its reported financial results and on its financial ratios in order to decide which specific current ratio objective is most appropriate.

Managing Current Assets

This chapter discusses analytical techniques to assist in the management of current assets. There are four principal classes of current assets: cash, marketable securities, receivables, and inventories.

MANAGEMENT OF CASH AND MARKETABLE SECURITIES

In recent years, corporations have placed increasing emphasis on cash management. The liquidity crisis of 1974 to 1975 made the need for adequate liquidity painfully clear, while the high short-term interest rates in 1979 to 1981 made the cost of idle cash balances just as painfully evident. Corporations now use increasingly sophisticated cash management systems to try to determine the level of cash and marketable securities that achieves the desired degree of liquidity at minimum cost.

This section deals with firm's management of its cash and marketable securities. It is appropriate to discuss the two together because the firm can convert marketable securities into cash on short notice. The firm's cash management decision involves two closely related decisions. First, what is the appropriate degree of liquidity (cash plus marketable securities)? Second, what is the appropriate distribution of it between cash and marketable securities in view of the cost of converting marketable securities into cash on short notice? Once we have answered the first question, we can answer the second by determining the desired level of cash transactions balances and investing the balance of the corporation's liquid resources in marketable securities.

Motives for Holding Cash

Cash consists of currency and demand deposits. Corporations, like individuals, have three basic motives for holding cash: (1) a *transactions motive,* (2) a *precautionary motive,* and (3) a *speculative motive.* The transactions motive involves the need for cash to make payments in the ordinary course of business, such as wages, taxes, interest, and dividends. Thus, the desired level of transactions balances will depend to a great extent on the size of the firm (because the number of transactions tends to increase with the size of the firm) and the timing of cash inflows and outflows (because the closer the degree of synchronization, the smaller the average level of cash balances required).

The precautionary motive reflects the need to hold cash to meet unexpected contingencies. A corporation holds cash balances because its cash inflows and outflows are subject to some degree of uncertainty. Precautionary balances serve as a buffer.

Finally, the speculative motive arises in connection with the corporation's desire to have cash on hand to be able to take advantage of profitable opportunities that may arise unexpectedly and require a quick investment of cash. This third motive accounts for a smaller percentage of corporate cash holdings than individual cash holdings; for the most part, corporations hold cash for transactions and precautionary reasons.

Short-Term Investment Alternatives

There exist a variety of investment alternatives that serve as near-money substitutes. Corporations invest on a short-term basis (maturity of 1 year or less) principally in the following types of securities:

- *U.S. Treasury bills which have an original maturity of 1 year or less and U.S. Treasury notes and bonds whose remaining life is 1 year or less.* These short-term U.S. Treasury securities offer the lowest risk of default, the greatest liquidity, but generally the lowest yield. Corporations often invest in U.S. Treasury securities for very short periods via repurchase agreements, or "repos," with securities dealers.
- *U.S. federal agency securities.* These are backed to varying degrees by the U.S. government, in many cases enjoy markets nearly as liquid as those for U.S. Treasury securities, and provide a slightly higher yield than U.S. Treasury securities of like maturity.
- *Negotiable certificates of deposit issued by domestic or foreign commercial banks, which evidence time deposits at the respective issuing banks; bankers' acceptances, which are drafts that a commercial bank has "accepted" and that consequently are valued in accordance with the accepting bank's credit standing; and commercial paper, which are unsecured promissory notes that corporations have issued.* These involve some degree of default risk, which varies with the credit standing of the bank or corporation that stands

behind the paper, enjoy less liquid markets than U.S. Treasury securities, and consequently offer higher yields than U.S. Treasury securities of like maturity. In addition, Eurodollar certificates of deposit generally provide higher yields than domestic certificates of deposit.

- *Preferred stock, particularly adjustable rate preferred stock.* A corporation is entitled to exclude from its taxable income 85% of the dividends it receives from a nonaffiliated corporation provided it has owned the shares at least 46 days. Consequently, a 10% pretax dividend yield provides a 9.31% after-tax yield to a 46% corporate taxpayer. A debt instrument would have to provide a 17.24% pretax yield in order to give the same 9.31% after-tax yield. However, preferred stock investments involve greater credit risk and generally enjoy less liquid markets than the available short-term debt alternatives. There are various types of adjustable rate preferred stock that are designed to trade at a price equal to their face amount. These involve substantially less liquidity risk than fixed-rate preferred stock and consequently have become attractive corporate short-term investment vehicles.

- *High-yielding common stocks.* Corporations also receive the 85% exclusion on the common dividends they receive from nonaffiliates. Because of the 46-day-holding-period requirement, a corporation may execute a "dividend roll" by investing a pool of funds in common and preferred stocks prior to their respective dividend record dates, collecting the dividends, selling each position after 46 days, and "rolling" the funds into new equity investments prior to those shares' record dates.

Determining the Desired Degree of Liquidity

A corporation will determine the desired degree of liquidity, i.e., the desired level of cash balances plus investments in marketable securities, with a view to reducing the risk of technical insolvency to an acceptable level. The higher the degree of liquidity, the lower this risk.[1] A financially robust firm will establish a degree of liquidity that makes this risk negligible.[2]

Estimating the Desired Amount of Transaction Cash

One simple yet useful approach to estimating the desired amount of transaction cash balances treats cash management as in inventory management problem. The corporation manages its inventory of cash based on the cost of holding cash (rather than marketable securities) and the cost of converting marketable securities to cash. The optimal policy minimizes the sum of these costs over the applicable time horizon.

The simplest version of this model assumes that the corporation can predict its future cash requirements with certainty; that the corporation will need an *amount* of cash per period (e.g., per month) for transaction purposes spread uniformly over the period; that the interest rate (i.e., the opportunity cost of holding cash) is some *interest rate* per period (expressed as a decimal that corresponds to the same period during which the corporation will spend *amount*); and that it will cost the corporation a fixed *cost* (in dollars) each time it converts securities to cash. Under these assumptions, the cost-minimizing size of each transaction to convert securities to cash is[3]

$$\text{Cash} = \sqrt{2 \times \text{cost} \times \text{amount} \div \text{interest rate}} \qquad (16\text{-}1)$$

Formula 16-1 produces a saw-tooth pattern of cash holdings that run between *cash* and zero. The corporation sells securities to raise *cash*. The cash balance decreases steadily to zero as the corporation spends the cash. The corporation then sells additional securities to raise *cash*, and so on. Consequently, the average cash balance is *cash*/2.

The model is oversimplified because it ignores uncertainty and assumes that the corporation makes cash disbursements at a uniform rate. More sophisticated models exist that do take the random nature of cash flows into account. The following section discusses one such model. Nevertheless, Formula 16-1 does yield some useful insights. For example, a higher interest rate or lower transactions cost will lead the firm to reduce its cash balances. Also, the corporation's desired cash balances will decrease if it can take actions, such as expediting collections from customers, slowing disbursements to suppliers, or installing an efficient lock-box system, that will reduce its future cash needs.

Illustration of Calculation of Transaction Cash Balance

A corporation projects a need for $1 million of cash per month. It believes it can invest funds on a 30-day basis at an annualized rate of 12% and that converting marketable securities to cash will involve a cost of $200 per transaction.

Substituting into Formula 16-1 with cost = 200, amount = 1,000,000, and interest rate = 0.12/12 gives:

$$\text{Cash} = \sqrt{\frac{2 \times 200 \times 1,000,000}{0.01}} = \$200,000$$

The corporation should sell securities five times per month, or roughly once every 6 calendar days (on average), to raise $200,000 each time. In that case, its average cash balances would be $100,000.

Optimal Amounts of Cash and Marketable Securities

Formula 16-1 indicates the desired level of cash transactions balances. However, the corporation may also have to satisfy compensating balance requirements under its bank loan agreements. Particularly during periods of tight money, commercial banks can insist that borrowers keep some percentage of the loan in a demand deposit account with the lender. When a corporation faces such requirements, its optimal average level of cash balances is the greater of its desired level of cash balances (e.g., cash/2) and the aggregate compensating balance requirement. In most cases, the latter will be the larger of the two.

The optimal amount of marketable securities is the difference between the desired degree of liquidity and the optimal level of cash balances. The firm would then invest this amount in some or all of the alternatives listed above by taking into account its possible future cash needs as well as the riskiness, maturities, and yields involved in these various investments.

The amount of marketable securities might exceed the amount just determined. Firms with large profitable foreign operations located in countries that tax certain types of income at low rates, such as Ireland and Puerto Rico, can benefit by investing the cash abroad rather than by repatriating it and paying U.S. income tax on it. Consequently, companies such as pharmaceutical companies maintain what would appear to be unusually large portfolios of marketable securities. These companies can apply the procedures discussed in this section to determine the liquidity and cash balance requirements of their U.S. operations and then reduce the domestic liquidity needs by the amount of cash they would be willing to repatriate in an emergency.

CASH MANAGEMENT WITH UNCERTAIN CASH FLOWS

When there is a high degree of uncertainty regarding future cash flows, the corporation needs more sophisticated models than Formula 16-1 to handle this uncertainty adequately. The Miller-Orr model offers a useful approach.[4]

The Miller-Orr model determines control limits consisting of an *upper control limit* and a *lower control limit*. When the firm's cash balance reaches the upper control limit, it purchases an amount of marketable securities equal to upper control limit − lower control limit. When the cash balance hits zero, the corporation converts an amount of marketable securities equal to lower control limit to cash. Both actions restore the firm's cash balances to the lower control limit.[5]

The values of the upper control limit and the lower control limit depend on the cost per transaction, the interest rate per period, and the *variance* of the net cash flows (expressed in terms of the same period as the interest rate):

$$\frac{\text{Lower}}{\text{control limit}} = \sqrt[3]{3 \times \text{cost} \times \text{variance} \div (4 \times \text{interest rate})}$$

(16-2a)

$$\frac{\text{Upper}}{\text{control limit}} = 3 \times \text{lower control limit} \tag{16-2b}$$

where $\sqrt[3]{}$ denotes cube root. Because the corporation should meet its cash obligations on a daily basis, the interest rate and variance are normally expressed in terms of a 1-day time period.

Illustration of the Use of the Miller-Orr Model

Returning to the example discussed earlier in this chapter, suppose the corporation has estimated the variance of its daily net cash flows (outflows minus inflows for the day) to be variance = 2.1918 billion. Substituting into Formula 16-2, the control limits are:

$$\frac{\text{Lower}}{\text{control limit}} = \sqrt[3]{\frac{3 \times 200 \times 2,191,800,000}{4 \times 0.12/365}} = \$100,000$$

$$\frac{\text{Upper}}{\text{control limit}} = 3 \times 100,000 = \$300,000$$

The corporation's cash balance will vary between zero and $300,000. Mathematically, the average cash balance will approximate

$$\frac{\text{Upper control limit} + \text{lower control limit}}{3} = \frac{\$400,000}{3} = \$133,333$$

This represents a one-third increase over the average cash balance when future cash requirements are known with certainty. This increase is reasonable: The corporation will generally react to increased uncertainty as to the timing of cash inflows and outflows by increasing the level of cash balances it maintains.

MANAGEMENT OF RECEIVABLES

The two remaining classes of current assets are receivables and inventories. Firms typically have substantial sums tied up in both.

Important Aspects of Receivables Management

Receivables management involves a number of important decisions, the most critical of which concerns which customers the firm will sell to on credit. The firm must also set its basic terms of sale, decide whether to sell on open account or ask customers to sign IOUs, and establish a procedure for deciding to which customers to extend credit (i.e., which are most likely to pay up). The first is generally determined by the terms of sale that are customary for the industry in question. With regard to the second, repeat sales to domestic customers are normally made on open account; corporations generally ask for IOUs only in special cases, e.g., special orders of large value from a new customer, customers requesting an extended repayment period, or export sales. The third area, deciding which customers are likely to repay, is normally handled through credit grading. A corporation can rely on Dun and Bradstreet's ratings of its customers' credit standing or it can form its own credit grading system based on its own collection experience.[6] This section assumes the firm has made the first two decisions and focuses on the question concerning to which customers the company should extend credit.

Receivables Management Model

A company should extend credit to a customer only if its expected profit from doing so is positive. Suppose that the likelihood of the customer making payment if the corporation grants him or her credit is *probability of payment* and that the customer will buy the product only if he or she is granted credit. Further suppose that if credit is granted and repaid, the customer will make repeat purchases with an expected present value of *PV* (*future profit*) but will not make any repeat purchases with probability 1 − *probability of repeat purchases*.

If the company does not extend credit, there is no sale and hence no profit. If the company does extend credit:

$$
\begin{aligned}
\text{Expected PV(profit)} = \ & \text{probability of payment} \times \text{PV(revenue} - \text{cost)} \\
& - (1 - \text{probability of payment}) \times \text{PV(cost)} \\
& + \text{probability of payment} \\
& \times \text{probability of repeat purchases} \\
& \times \text{PV(future profit)} \qquad\qquad (16\text{-}3)
\end{aligned}
$$

The expected present value profit equals (1) the present value of the profit the firm will realize, *PV*(*revenue − cost*), if credit is repaid multiplied by the probability of payment, *less* (2) the present value cost, *PV*(*cost*), that results if it is not repaid multiplied by the probability 1 − probability of payment that it is not, *plus* (3) the present value of future profit if repeat sales occur multiplied by the probability that the customer will wish to make repeat purchases *and* that the firm will indeed be willing to make them (i.e., only if the customer repays the trade credit). *PV*(*cost*) denotes the present value of variable costs, including collection costs. This approach can be used to develop more sophisticated models that incorporate additional contingencies, if so desired.

Illustration of Application of Receivables Management Model

Marion Minicomputer Manufacturing sells its new M III personal computer to dealers for $5000 per machine. The machines cost $4000 each to manufacture.

Marion's prior experience with new direct order customers similar to the one who has just placed an order indicates that they pay 90% of the time and in an average of 30 days. Roughly one out of four new credit customers makes repeat purchases. Marion projects the expected future profitability of such purchases to be $1800. Collection costs average $50 per account, and Marion's required rate of return on receivables is 18% per annum (or 1.5% per month).

Substituting into Formula 16-3, the expected present value profitability of extending credit is

$$
\begin{aligned}
\text{Expected PV(profit)} &= 0.9 \times \left(\frac{5000}{1.015} - 4000 - \frac{50}{1.015} \right) \\
&\quad - 0.1 \times \left(4000 + \frac{50}{1.015} \right) + 0.9 \times 0.25 \times 1800 \\
&= \$789.24
\end{aligned}
$$

Because the expected value is positive, the firm can expect to profit by extending credit and should therefore do so. Note that Marion could expect to profit by extending credit so long as the probability of payment is no less than 0.75 [at which point *expected PV(profit)* is zero]. Thus, Marion could extend credit to the new customer even if the chance of repayment was as little as three out of four (or perhaps a higher percentage depending on how averse to risk Marion's owners are).

MANAGEMENT OF INVENTORIES

Manufacturing companies generally carry three types of inventory: raw materials, work in process, and finished goods. The sizes of the raw materials inventories depend principally on the anticipated level of production, the seasonality of production, and the reliability of the sources of supply. The sizes of the work in process inventories depend mainly on the overall length of each production run and the number of distinct stages in the production cycle. The sizes of the finished goods inventories depend primarily on the rate of sales (units of product per unit of time), the cost of carrying the inventory, the cost of ordering replacement stocks, and the cost of having run out of an item when an order comes in (in the extreme case, the cost of losing the sale and perhaps also the customer).

Inventory Management Model

A simple though still useful inventory management model is the economic order quantity (EOQ) model. Suppose that units are removed from inventory at the constant rate of *sales per period* (the rate at which goods are sold in the case of finished goods inventories); that there is a fixed *reordering cost* (in dollars) per order regardless of the number of units reordered; and that it costs *carrying cost* (in dollars per period) to carry a unit in inventory for an entire period. Under these assumptions, the *economic order quantity* is

$$\text{Economic order quantity} = \sqrt{\frac{2 \times \text{reordering cost} \times \text{sales per period}}{\text{carrying cost}}} \qquad (16\text{-}4)$$

The reader will undoubtedly recognize that Formula 16-4 looks very similar to Formula 16-1. That is so because the two models were derived under parallel assumptions. As in the case of Formula 16-1, Formula 16-4 results in a sawtooth pattern for the inventory level, and the average inventory level over time is economic order quantity $\div$ 2.

Illustration of Application of Inventory Management Model

Marion Manufacturing's largest dealer is selling Marion's new M III personal computer at the rate of 1800 units per year. The dealer's cost of placing an order with Marion is $529 per order (including insurance and shipping charges), and its cost of carrying an M III machine in inventory for a year is $400.

Substituting into Formula 16-4:

$$\text{Economic order quantity} = \sqrt{\frac{2 \times 529 \times 1800}{400}} = 69$$

This economic order quantity implies a reorder roughly 26 (= 1800/69) times per year, or every other week, for 69 machines per order. The average inventory level over time is 34.5 machines.

Like Formula 16-1, Formula 16-4 makes certain simplifying assumptions: Future demand is known with certainty, inventory is utilized at a constant rate, and delivery lead times are constant. In fact, each of these factors is subject to uncertainty. A corporation can compensate for this uncertainty by maintaining *safety stocks*, that is, a buffer inventory. In that case, the average inventory level is roughly ($1/2$ economic order quantity) + *buffer*, where *buffer* denotes the amount of safety stocks.

Safety stocks add to the cost of holding inventories but reduce the likelihood that an item will not be available in inventory when it is needed. The appropriate buffer level is that amount which minimizes the combined cost of stockouts and carrying the additional inventory.

Illustration of Calculation of Safety Stocks

Marion Manufacturing's largest dealer has found that if it is out of stock when a customer arrives, it will make the eventual sale only 50% of the time. For each lost sale, the dealer loses the gross margin of $600 per machine plus the opportunity to earn profit of $300 from the sale of ancillary items. Lost sales as well as back orders (orders the dealer fills when the next shipment arrives) involve record-keeping costs of $50 per stockout. Thus, each stockout costs $0.5 \times (950) + 0.5 \times (50) = \$500$ on average. It costs the dealer $400 to keep a machine in inventory for a year. The dealer estimates that a buffer of 10 units will result in 40 stockouts per year, a buffer of 15 units will result in 25 stockouts per year, and a buffer of 22 units will result in 22 stockouts per year. These buffer levels would result in combined stockout and holding costs amounting to:

$$
\begin{aligned}
10 \text{ units}: \quad & \$400 \times 10 + 500 \times 40 = \$24{,}000 \\
15 \text{ units}: \quad & \$400 \times 15 + 500 \times 25 = \$18{,}500 \\
22 \text{ units}: \quad & \$400 \times 22 + 500 \times 22 = \$19{,}800
\end{aligned}
$$

Thus the dealer should maintain a buffer of 15 machines.

SUMMARY

A company should select a degree of liquidity that will minimize the risk of technical insolvency. It can then employ an inventory approach to estimate the optimal level of transaction cash balances. The firm would hold the remainder of its desired level of liquid resources in the form of marketable securities. The firm chooses the desired level of receivables by balancing the incremental revenues against the incremental costs. It chooses the desired levels of inventories by minimizing the combined cost of inventory and reordering the materials and goods it needs to operate its business.

Chapter 17
Short-Term Financing

This chapter discusses the principal sources of short-term funds, describes how to estimate the cost of funds from each source, and provides a framework for comparing these costs on a consistent basis.

OVERVIEW OF SHORT-TERM FINANCING

A variety of factors affect the level and mix of short-term indebtedness and, more generally, the overall maturity structure of the firm's debt, among them:

- The desired level of current assets, the seasonal component of current assets, the extent of hedging employed in the firm's debt structure, and the desired margin of safety determine the target current ratio and, by implication, the target level of short-term debt.
- Economies of scale in issuing long-term debt securities lead to infrequent, relatively large, long-term debt issues. In the interim, companies borrow on a short-term basis.
- Firms will postpone securities issues and instead borrow short-term funds when they expect long-term interest rates to fall and do the opposite when they expect interest rates to increase.
- Legal restrictions limit the types of loans that institutional investors can make. Companies whose debt is rated below investment grade may be unable to sell debt securities on acceptable terms and therefore have to rely on short-term borrowing.
- Bank loan agreements typically provide greater prepayment flexibility than long-term debt agreements. In addition, banks may be willing to take certain

risks that institutional lenders are not willing to take, and so firms frequently borrow from commercial banks in connection with project-specific financings.

- The existence of bankruptcy costs creates a bias in favor of longer maturities.
- The more averse management is to the risk that interest rates will rise and to the risk that short-term borrowings may not be refunded, the smaller the proportion of (floating rate) short-term borrowings.

Sources of Short-Term Funds

There are three principal sources of short-term funds. A company can arrange trade credit from its suppliers. Alternatively, it can borrow funds from a bank or credit company. Third, if it is sufficiently creditworthy, it can sell short-term IOUs, called commercial paper.

Commercial banks are also the principal traditional source of intermediate-term funds. The terms *short-term funds* and *intermediate-term funds* are used to refer to the original maturity of the debt obligation. Short-term funds are debt obligations that were originally scheduled for repayment within 1 year.[1] Intermediate-term funds are debt obligations that were originally scheduled to mature in between 1 and perhaps as many as 10 years. These definitions are somewhat arbitrary. A more useful distinction involves the source of funds out of which the borrower will repay the loan. Short-term loans are typically arranged to finance seasonal or temporary needs. Intermediate-term loans are to be repaid over a period of years. Accordingly, short-term lenders are principally concerned with the firm's working capital position and its ability to liquidate current assets—collecting on receivables and reducing inventories according to seasonal patterns—to generate cash to meet the firm's current debt service obligations. Intermediate-term lenders are more concerned with the longer-term profitability of the firm's operations. 2pt

TRADE CREDIT

Trade credit is credit firms extend to other firms. Trade credit arises in the ordinary course of business; purchasers of raw materials and supplies are typically permitted to wait until after the goods are delivered to pay for them. Trade credit is the largest single source of short-term funds for business collectively, representing approximately 40% of the current liabilities of nonfinancial corporations. Because suppliers are generally more liberal in extending credit than financial institutions, trade credit is a particularly important source of funds for small companies.

When extending trade credit, the seller specifies the period of time allowed for payment and, in addition, often offers a *cash discount* if payment is made more quickly. For example, the terms "$2/10$, net 30" means the buyer can take a 2% cash discount if it pays within 10 days (referred to as the *discount period*). Otherwise, the full amount is due within 30 days (referred to as the *net period*).

The following example serves to illustrate the importance of trade credit. Suppose that a firm purchases $50,000 worth of supplies each day on terms of $^2/_{10}$, net 30 and that the firm always pays in exactly 10 days. In that case, the firm will owe its suppliers 10 times $50,000, or $500,000, but it can still take the 2% discount on each purchase; that is, suppliers are providing $500,000 of funds at zero cost that the firm can use in its business.

Cost of Trade Credit

If no discount is offered or if payment is made soon enough that the discount can be taken, there is no cost to the firm for the use of the supplier's credit. When cash discounts are offered but not taken, however, trade credit involves an explicit cost. To continue the example, if the firm does not pay its bill within 10 days, it forgoes the 2% discount. If the invoice was for $100, the firm effectively has the use of $98 (the amount net of discount it could have paid on the 10th day) for up to an additional 20 days. The firm effectively pays $2 (the amount of the discount foregone) for the use of the money during this period.

The annualized cost of trade credit can be calculated by applying the following formula:

$$\begin{array}{c} \text{Annualized cost} \\ \text{of trade credit} \end{array} = \left[\begin{array}{c} \text{percentage} \\ \text{discount} \end{array} \div \left(100 - \begin{array}{c} \text{percentage} \\ \text{discount} \end{array} \right) \right]$$
$$\times \left[365 \div \left(\begin{array}{c} \text{net} \\ \text{period} \end{array} - \begin{array}{c} \text{discount} \\ \text{period} \end{array} \right) \right] \qquad (17\text{-}1)$$

It is assumed in Formula 17-1 that the buyer makes payment on the last day of the net period. For the above example,

$$\begin{array}{c} \text{Annualized cost} \\ \text{of trade credit} \end{array} = \frac{2}{100 - 2} \times \frac{365}{30 - 10} = 0.3724, \text{ or } 37.24\%$$

As this example illustrates, trade credit can be very expensive when a cash discount is offered but not taken. The cost increases as the discount increases and as the difference between the net period and the discount period decreases.[2]

Effective Use of Trade Credit

Trade credit offers certain advantages as a source of short-term funds. It is readily available, at least to firms who regularly discharge their obligations to suppliers on schedule. It is informal; if the firm is now paying its bills within the discount period, additional credit can be obtained simply by delaying the payment until the end of the net period or perhaps later (but at the cost of forgoing the discount). Trade credit is also more flexible than other means of short-term financing because the firm does not have to negotiate a loan agreement, pledge collateral, or adhere to a rigid repayment schedule and because the consequences of delaying a payment beyond the net period are much less onerous than those resulting from failure to repay a bank on schedule.

To use trade credit effectively, the firm must weigh these advantages against the associated costs. Delaying payment beyond the discount period involves an explicit cost, as just illustrated. Firms may also "stretch" accounts payable by postponing payment beyond the end of the net period. However, the buyer must be careful to avoid excessive stretching of accounts payable because it can jeopardize the buyer's credit rating and can strain relations with suppliers. This in turn can lead to less attractive repayment terms in the future and perhaps also to higher prices as suppliers attempt to pass through to the buyer the cost of financing the buyer's delinquent payments. These implicit costs of trade credit, while difficult to estimate, should be carefully considered by firms that make extensive use of trade credit.

SECURED AND UNSECURED LOANS

Commercial bank lending is second in importance to trade credit as a source of short-term financing. Banks provide loans in a wide variety of forms that are tailored to the specific needs of the borrower. Banks generally lend to their most creditworthy customers on an unsecured basis. When a borrower represents a significant credit risk, the bank may ask it to provide some form of security, such as a lien on receivables or inventory. Finance companies also lend on a secured basis.

Short-Term Unsecured Loans

Short-term unsecured bank loans take three basic forms: a *line of credit*, a *revolving credit*, or a specific *transaction loan*. Such loans are generally regarded as "self-liquidating": the lender expects that the assets the company purchases with the loan proceeds will generate sufficient cash to repay the loan within a year. Short-term unsecured loans typically bear interest at a floating rate.

A *line of credit* is an arrangement between a bank and a customer concerning the maximum loan balance the bank will permit the borrower at any one time. Banks normally extend credit lines for a 1-year period subject to 1-year renewals as long as the bank continues to find the borrower's credit acceptable. Most credit lines are informal arrangements; if the prospective borrower's credit deteriorates, the bank is not legally obligated to advance funds.

A *revolving credit* agreement represents a legal commitment to lend up to a specified maximum amount any time during a specified period. In return for this legal commitment, the borrower must pay a *commitment fee*, typically between 0.25 and 0.5%, on the difference between the permitted maximum and the amount actually borrowed. Revolving credits often extend beyond 1 year, and the borrower often has the option to convert the revolving credit to a term loan when the revolving credit expires.

A *transaction loan* (also often referred to as *bridge financing*) is a loan the bank extends for a specific purpose. For example, a bank may lend a home builder funds to pay for construction. The loan agreement will require the builder to repay the bank when she or he sells the house.

Term Loan

Bank term loans represent intermediate-term debt, but the similarity between their pricing and the pricing of short-term bank loans makes it appropriate to discuss them in this chapter. A bank *term loan* is a loan for a specified amount that requires the borrower to repay it according to a specified schedule. A term loan generally matures within between 1 and 10 years, but banks have permitted longer maturities under special circumstances. Repayment is normally at regular intervals in equal installments, but in some cases the loan may provide for a larger final payment, called a "balloon" payment, or simply repayment at maturity in one lump sum, call a "bullet" maturity. Term loans may carry a fixed rate of interest but more commonly carry a floating interest rate.

Cost of Bank Financing

Except for a rather small percentage of loans that bear interest at a fixed rate, commercial banks charge interest at a rate that floats. Normally, the interest rate floats with the bank's *prime rate*, but it may float instead with some other interest rate that represents the bank's cost of funding the loan. Commercial banks often offer their larger, more creditworthy customers the option of selecting interest rates based on (1) one of the London Interbank Offer Rates (LIBOR), the rates at which prime banks offer one another deposits in the London market, or (2) the interest rate the bank pays on large certificates of deposit.

A bank will adjust its prime rate to reflect changes in its cost of funds. The prime rate is the interest rate the bank charges its largest, most financially sound customers. Banks charge less creditworthy customers a higher rate, typically expressed as a percentage over prime, depending on the customer's credit standing. For example, if a bank's prime rate is 12%, it might lend to a local manufacturing company at prime plus 0.5%, or 12.5%. The interest rate on the loan would change with changes in the bank's prime rate. If the bank raises its prime rate to 12.5%, the interest rate on the manufacturing company's loan would automatically become 13%.

In addition to charging interest, banks often require borrowers to maintain a fraction of the loan, typically between 10 and 20%, on deposit with the bank in the form of *compensating balances*. This requirement may take the form of a required minimum but more commonly takes the form of a required average deposit balance during a particular interest period. Compensating balances add to the cost of a loan in those instances where the firm's cash balances are higher than they would normally be in the absence of this requirement.

True Interest Cost. When interest is paid in arrears, i.e., at the end of an interest period, and the bank requires the borrower to maintain compensating balances, the *true interest cost* of the loan bearing interest at a *stated rate of interest* is

$$\text{True interest cost} = \left(\text{amount} \times \frac{\text{stated rate}}{\text{of interest}}\right) \div \left(\text{amount} - \frac{\text{average cash}}{\text{balance}}\right)$$

$$(17\text{-}2)$$

where *amount* denotes the amount of the loan and *average cash balance* denotes the increase in the firm's average cash balances that results from the compensating balance requirement. In Formula 17-2, the corporation pays interest of amount × stated rate of interest (on an annualized basis) but can only use *amount − average cash balance* of the loan proceeds in its business.

Formula 17-2 assumes that the compensating balances do not earn interest, which is generally the case. But if the compensating balances earn some yield, the interest so earned, yield × average cash balance, reduces the cost of the loan:

$$\text{True interest cost} = \left[\left(\text{amount} \times \frac{\text{stated rate}}{\text{of interest}}\right) - \left(\text{yield} \times \frac{\text{average cash}}{\text{balance}}\right)\right]$$

$$\div \left(\text{amount} - \frac{\text{average cash}}{\text{balance}}\right) \qquad (17\text{-}3)$$

Illustration of Calculation of True Interest Cost. A company borrows $100,000. The bank charges interest at prime rate plus 0.50 and requires 20% compensating balances, none of which the borrower would otherwise have kept. If the prime rate averages 11.50% during the initial quarter, the true interest cost for that period expressed on an annualized basis is

$$\text{True interest cost} = \frac{100,000 \times 0.12}{80,000} = 0.15, \text{ or } 15\%$$

In the absence of any compensating balance requirements, the true interest cost is simply 12%.

If the borrower could deposit the compensating balances in a time deposit account earning 5% interest, the true interest cost is

$$\text{True interest cost} = \frac{100,000 \times 0.12 - 20,000 \times 0.05}{80,000} = 0.1375, \text{ or } 13.75\%$$

True Interest Cost of Discount Notes. In Formulas 17-2 and 17-3, the borrower pays interest in arrears. Alternatively, the bank may require the borrower to pay interest in advance. It accomplishes this by *discounting* the borrower's note: The borrower signs a promissory note for some *amount* but receives only amount − amount × stated rate of interest × *fraction of year*, the amount of the loan less the interest, where the amount of interest is figured for the fraction of the year the note is to be outstanding. In this case, the company pays interest expense of amount × stated rate of interest × fraction of year but only has the use of amount less the amount of interest. Thus, its true interest cost expressed on an annualized basis is:

$$
\begin{aligned}
\text{True interest} \atop \text{cost} &= \left(\text{amount} \times {\text{stated rate} \atop \text{of interest}}\right) \\[2mm]
&\div \left(\text{amount} - \text{amount} \times {\text{stated rate} \atop \text{of interest}} \times {\text{fraction} \atop \text{of year}}\right) \\[2mm]
&= {\text{stated rate} \atop \text{of interest}} \div \left(1 - {\text{stated rate} \atop \text{of interest}} \times {\text{fraction} \atop \text{of year}}\right) \quad (17\text{-}4)
\end{aligned}
$$

Thus, the true interest cost is higher when interest is paid in advance than when it is paid in arrears. Should the bank also require compensating balances, then adjustments like those in Formulas 17-2 and 17-3 can be made to Formula 17-4.

Illustration of Calculation of True Interest Cost of Discount Note. If the borrower in the preceding illustration has to pay interest on a discount basis at the rate of 12% per annum but has no compensating balance requirements, the true interest cost for a 90-day loan is

$$
\text{True interest cost} = \frac{0.12}{1 - 0.12 \times 0.25} = 0.1237, \text{ or } 12.37\%
$$

True Interest Cost of Installment Loan. Finally, the bank may require the borrower to pay the loan on an installment basis. The true interest cost of such loans is found by calculating the internal rate of return of the relevant cash flows and converting the resulting number to an annualized basis (or whatever other basis is desired).

Illustration of Calculation of True Interest Cost of Installment Loan. Suppose the borrower had to repay the $100,000 loan in three installments of $25,000 each at the end of the first 2 months and $50,000 at the end of 3 months. The company borrows $97,000 (= $100,000 − 100,000 × 0.12 × 0.25) at a true interest cost that solves

$$0 = -97,000 + \frac{25,000}{1 + \text{cost}} + \frac{25,000}{(1 + \text{cost})^2} + \frac{50,000}{(1 + \text{cost})^3}$$

The cost = 1.3658% is expressed in terms of a monthly unit of time so that the true interest cost on an annualized basis is

$$\text{True interest cost} = 12 \times 1.3658\% = 16.39\%$$

The preceding illustrations indicate why it is very important for the analyst to check the terms of the loan agreement to determine how interest is calculated and when the loan has to be repaid. Two loans with the same nominal interest rate may involve substantially different true interest costs because of differences in how interest is calculated or differences in the timing of repayment.

Security

Commercial banks often ask less creditworthy borrowers to pledge security for their loans. When the bank is lending on a short-term basis, it may ask the borrower to pledge liquid assets, that is, receivables, inventories, or securities. Depending on the quality of the receivables it pledges, a company can usually borrow between 50 and 80% of the face value of the receivables. Depending on the quality of the inventories it pledges, with readily marketable finished goods possessing the highest collateral value, a company might be able to borrow up to 90% of their fair market value. The principal benefit a company derives from pledging security is the opportunity to borrow a greater sum than it could obtain on an unsecured basis. In return, the borrower normally sacrifices some degree of control over the assets it pledges.

COMMERCIAL PAPER

The largest, most creditworthy companies are able to borrow on a short-term basis by selling *commercial paper*. Currently more than 1000 companies issue this form of security. Commercial paper consists of unsecured promissory notes that generally have a maturity of up to 270 days.[3] The commercial paper market in the United States grew rapidly during the 1970s and early 1980s to well over $200 billion at year-end 1984, most of it maturing within 30 days. In the early 1980s, a Euro-commercial paper market began to develop rapidly.

Commercial paper is sold either directly or through dealers. Large industrial firms, utilities, and medium-sized finance companies generally sell their paper through dealers, who typically charge a commission of $\frac{1}{8}$ of 1% on an annualized basis. Large finance companies, such as General Motors Acceptance Corporation, typically sell their paper directly. They tailor the maturities and the amounts of the notes to fit the needs of investors, who consist principally of corporations investing excess cash on a short-term basis. In contrast to most industrial firms, the large finance companies use the commercial paper market as a permanent source of funds. This is so because of the more liquid nature and greater interest-rate sensitivity of the finance companies' assets and the lower cost of commercial paper relative to bank financing.

Computing the True Interest Cost of Commercial Paper

Interest on commercial paper is paid on a *discount basis*. The *discount rate* is the rate, expressed on an annualized basis, used to calculate the amount of the discount. For example, if the discount rate for 90-day prime commercial paper is 12%, the issuer of a $1,000,000 promissory note would face an interest obligation (based on a 360-day year) of $30,000 (= $1,000,000 × 0.12 × $90/_{360}$) and would receive net proceeds of $970,000 (= $1,000,000 − 30,000) upon the sale of the note. Since the issuer has the use of only $970,000, its true interest cost is greater than 10%:

$$\text{True interest} \atop \text{cost} = \frac{30,000}{970,000} \times \frac{360}{90} = 0.1237, \text{ or } 12.37\%$$

on an annualized basis. More generally,

$$\begin{array}{l} \text{True interest} \\ \text{cost} \end{array} = \begin{array}{l} \text{discount} \\ \text{rate} \end{array} \div \left(1 - \frac{\text{discount rate} \times \text{maturity}}{360}\right) \quad (17\text{-}5a)$$

where *maturity* is measured in days. Formula 17-5a, which is identical to Formula 17-4 when stated rate of interest is measured in terms of a 360-day year, is needed when comparing the cost of commercial paper to the cost of a bank loan that calls for interest payments in arrears. True interest cost calculated in accordance with Formula 17-5 is also known as the *bond equivalent yield*.

Formula 17-5a assumes that interest is paid on the basis of a 360-day year, as in the case of corporate bonds. Some financial instruments, such as U.S. Treasury bonds and notes, earn interest on the basis of a 365-day year. The true interest cost when interest is paid on the basis of a 365-day year is called the *coupon equivalent yield* and is calculated by multiplying Formula 17-5a by $365/_{360}$:

$$\begin{array}{l} \text{Coupon} \\ \text{equivalent yield} \end{array} = \begin{array}{l} \text{discount} \\ \text{rate} \end{array} \times 365 \div \left[360 - \left(\begin{array}{l} \text{discount} \\ \text{rate} \end{array} \times \text{maturity}\right)\right]$$

$$(17\text{-}5b)$$

Computing the Cost of Borrowing

Issuers of commercial paper generally find it prudent to maintain a backup line of credit with one or more commercial banks to provide insurance against temporary difficulties in selling commercial paper. For example, for several weeks following the bankruptcy of the Penn Central Railroad in 1970, some large issuers of commercial paper, most notably Chrysler Financial Corporation, found it impossible to market new issues to refund maturing issues. Banks typically charge a fee of $1/4$ to $1/2$ of 1% for such backup lines. This cost together with any commissions paid to dealers must be recognized in the cost of borrowing calculation. Incorporating these costs, Formula 17-5a becomes

$$
\begin{array}{l}
\text{Annualized cost} \\
\text{of borrowing}
\end{array} = \left[\frac{\text{discount}}{\text{rate}} \div \left(1 - \text{commission} \right.\right.
$$

$$
\left.\left. - \frac{\text{discount rate} \times \text{maturity}}{360} \right) \right]
$$

$$
+ \text{commitment fee} \qquad (17\text{-}6)
$$

Illustration of Calculation of Annualized Cost of Borrowing

The issuer of the $1,000,000 note discussed earlier typically sells commercial paper through a dealer who charges a commission of $1/8$ of 1%. The issuer also maintains a backup line of credit requiring a commitment fee of $1/2$ of 1%. The issuer's cost of borrowing is thus

$$
\begin{array}{l}
\text{Annualized cost} \\
\text{of borrowing}
\end{array} = \frac{0.12}{1 - (0.00125 \times 90/360) - (0.12 \times 90/360)}
$$

$$
+ 0.005 = 0.1288, \text{ or } 12.88\%
$$

Thus, for example, the firm is better off selling commercial paper if it expects the cost of bank borrowing and the cost of trade credit over the next 90 days to exceed 12.88% on an annualized basis.

Rating Considerations

Investors rely upon the commercial paper ratings assigned by Moody's Investors Service and Standard & Poor's Corporation to assess the creditworthiness of an issuer's commercial paper. Issuers whose commercial paper is rated (Moody's/Standard & Poor's) P-1/A-1+ enjoy the lowest cost of borrowing and the least interrupted access to the market. For example, at times the yield differential between commercial paper rated P-1/A-1+ and commercial paper rated P-3/A-3 has exceeded 2 full percentage points. In addition, there is normally no market for commercial paper rated lower than P-3/A-3, and the market for commercial paper rated P-3/A-3 is generally very limited.

Credit Enhancement

A company whose commercial paper is rated P-3/A-3, and in some cases a company whose commercial paper is rated P-2/A-2, can lower its cost of borrowing by arranging for a first-class commercial bank to provide credit support in the form of an irrevocable letter of credit. A bank typically charges a fee of between $^{1}/_{2}$ and $^{3}/_{4}$ of 1%. There are also legal fees. As a rule of thumb, a letter of credit arrangement can reduce the cost of issuing commercial paper when the issuer's cost without a letter of credit support exceeds the prevailing P-1/A-1 commercial paper rate by roughly 75 to 100 basis points.

COMPARING THE COSTS OF SHORT-TERM
FUNDS FROM DIFFERENT SOURCES

There are other sources of short-term funds, which are less important than those just discussed. For example, bank trust departments will purchase *demand master notes*, which are redeemable upon demand. These typically bear interest at a rate that varies with some readily available benchmark, as for example, the maximum of the 30-, 60-, and 90-day commercial paper rates quoted by General Motors Acceptance Corporation. *Bankers' acceptances*, which are drafts that commercial banks have agreed to honor for payment, are used to finance foreign and domestic trade. They are actively traded and are priced on a discount basis at discounts that approximate the discounts on high-grade commercial paper of like maturity. In addition, finance companies provide lines of credit, generally to less creditworthy companies that might have difficulty borrowing from commercial banks. In most cases, the interest rates on these loans float with the prime rate charged by the largest banks or with the commercial paper rate for "prime quality" commercial paper.

Table 17-1 compares the average annual interest rate on dealer-placed 90-day prime commercial paper, the average annual prime rate charged by money center banks, and the average annual value of 3-month LIBOR for the period 1975 to 1984. Except for brief periods, the prime rate exceeded the other two rates. Over the 10-year period 1975 to 1984, the prime rate exceeded the dealer-placed 90-day prime commercial paper rate by an average of 173 basis points (or 1.73%), but beginning in 1980 the average annual difference averaged more than 2 full percentage points (and at times the differential was considerably greater). In general, the differential tends to widen, with commercial paper becoming even cheaper relative to bank loans, during periods of easy money because market forces tend to force commercial paper rates down more rapidly than banks reduce their prime lending rates. Thus, even after allowing for the roughly 50-basis-point cost of a backup line of credit, commercial paper has generally proven to be a significantly cheaper source of funds than short-term bank loans for companies that are able to borrow in the commercial paper market. Nevertheless, many commercial paper issuers still find it advantageous to maintain at least some minimum level of bank borrowing. There is always the danger, except for the strongest credits, that the market for the issuer's

Table 17-1
Comparison of Commercial Paper Rate,
Prime Rate, and Eurodollar Rate

Year	Commercial Paper Rate,*%	3-Month LIBOR,†%	Prime Rate,‡%	Discount to Prime Rate	
				Commercial Paper Rate,§b.p.	3-Month LIBOR,¶b.p.
1975	6.45	7.02	7.86	141	84
1976	5.38	5.63	6.84	146	121
1977	5.70	6.07	6.82	112	75
1978	8.21	8.85	9.06	85	21
1979	11.44	12.09	12.67	123	58
1980	13.26	14.19	15.27	201	108
1981	16.15	16.78	18.87	272	209
1982	12.42	13.16	14.86	244	170
1983	9.21	9.61	10.79	158	118
1984	10.51	10.85	12.93	242	208
10-year average	9.87	10.43	11.60	173	117

*Average interest rate on dealer-placed 90-day prime commercial paper converted to a coupon-equivalent-yield basis.
†Average of end-of-month values.
‡Annual average.
§Prime rate less coupon-equivalent-yield commercial paper rate (measured in basis points).
¶Prime rate less 3-month LIBOR (measured in basis points).
Sources: *Federal Reserve Bulletin, Financial Times,* International Monetary Fund, *The Wall Street Journal.*

commercial paper could dry up unexpectedly. Also, commercial banks are more likely than the commercial paper market to help a company that is experiencing temporary financial difficulties.

The comparison involving 3-month LIBOR and the prime rate in Table 17-1 is also interesting. The LIBOR rates serve as the benchmarks for pricing Eurodollar loans. On average, over the 10-year period, prime exceeded 3-month LIBOR by 117 basis points. Thus, if a company that would normally borrow at prime has the opportunity to borrow at LIBOR plus a spread that does not exceed 1.17%, the LIBOR-based loan should prove cheaper based on recent experience. More important, banks have, to an increasing extent, offered their U.S. customers the opportunity to select from among several options, as for example prime, 3-month LIBOR plus 0.5%, and 6-month LIBOR plus 0.5%, at the beginning of each interest period. The rate comparison provided in Table 17-1 demonstrates that having this flexibility can lead to significant cost savings.

HEDGING FLOATING INTEREST RATE RISK

A company that borrows floating rate funds will suffer an increase in its interest expense if interest rates rise. To protect against this risk, a company can arrange an interest rate hedge. *Hedging* interest rate risk involves selling and later buying back carefully selected numbers and types of interest rate futures contracts so as to offset an increase in interest expense with a corresponding profit from the futures transaction. This effectively fixes the borrower's interest rate.[4]

What Are Interest Rate Futures?

An *interest rate futures* contract is a transferable agreement between two parties that calls for the delivery of a *standardized financial instrument* during a *specific month* at a price that is established when the futures contract is initiated. For example, an individual who believes that interest rates are about to decrease may buy a U.S. Treasury bond futures contract, which requires only a modest deposit (called the *initial margin* requirement) rather than purchasing U.S. Treasury bonds outright for cash. The U.S. Treasury bond futures contract calls for the delivery of U.S. Treasury bonds with at least 15 years to the earlier of call or maturity with a value as of the delivery date equivalent to $100,000 face amount of an 8% U.S. Treasury bond with 20 years to maturity (the standardized financial instrument).

Hedging with Interest Rate Futures

The price of an interest rate futures contract will fluctuate with changes in interest rates. If interest rates rise, the value of a fixed rate U.S. Treasury bond will decrease. So will the value of the U.S. Treasury bond futures contract because it calls for delivery of a specified amount of a fixed-rate instrument. Each 1-point fluctuation in that contract is worth $1000. So, for example, if the interest rate on long-term U.S. Treasury bonds rises and causes the price of long-term U.S. Treasury bonds to decrease by 1 full point, the holder of $100,000 face amount of the bonds would lose $1000 (= $100,000 × 0.01). But if the holder has sold a U.S. Treasury bonds futures contract, and if the price of that contract had also fallen by 1 full point, the bond holder could realize a $1000 profit by repurchasing the contract at the lower price. The profit on the interest rate futures contract would offset the loss on the cash position. This is the essence of hedging.

Structuring the Hedge

A prospective borrower can hedge against a rise in interest rates between the time it decides to borrow and the time it arranges the loan or against a rise in short-term interest rates while it has floating rate debt outstanding by selling interest rate futures contracts. First, the hedger must select the most appropriate interest rate futures contract to sell. Generally, it is advisable to select the contract that provides the highest correlation between the interest rate (or yield) of the futures instrument and the interest rate against which the hedger seeks protection. Second, the hedger must calculate the appropriate number of contracts to offset the exposure to rising interest rates:

$$\begin{aligned} \text{Number of} \atop \text{contract} &= \begin{bmatrix} \text{amount of loan} & \div & \text{size of contract} \\ \text{(in millions)} & & \text{(in millions)} \end{bmatrix} \\ &\times \begin{bmatrix} \text{interest rate} & & \text{yield sensitivity} \\ \text{sensitivity} & \div & \text{of hedge} \\ \text{of loan} & & \text{vehicle} \end{bmatrix} \times \text{beta} \quad (17\text{-}7) \end{aligned}$$

where *amount of loan* (in millions of dollars) denotes the principal amount of the loan the borrower seeks to hedge; *size of contract* denotes the face amount (in millions of dollars) of the futures contract; *interest rate sensitivity of loan* denotes the present value (in dollars per million) of the increase in future interest obligations that would result from a change of 1 percentage point in the interest rate on the loan being hedged; *yield sensitivity of hedge vehicle* represents the change in the value of the futures contract (in dollars per million) that would result from a change of 1 percentage point in the yield of the underlying financial instrument; and *beta* measures the correlation between changes in interest rate sensitivity and yield sensitivity:

$$\text{Interest rate} = \text{alpha} + \text{beta} \times \text{yield} \quad (17\text{-}8)$$

Illustration of Interest Rate Hedge

Hudson Foods needs to borrow $20 million to meet seasonal cash requirements. The loan will bear interest at prime rate, payable monthly in arrears, and will remain outstanding for 2 months. Prime rate is currently 12%, but Hudson Foods' treasurer is concerned about a forecasted increase in short-term interest rates. Because there is no prime rate futures contract, she decides to initiate a hedge using 90-day Treasury bill futures.

An analysis of historical data reveals:

$$\text{Prime rate} = 1.53 + 0.91 \times \text{T-bill futures rate}$$

where *T-bill futures rate* denotes the discount rate on 90-day Treasury bills. Thus, beta = 0.91. Each 90-day Treasury bill contract has a face amount of $1 million, and a change of 1 percentage point in the discount rate leads to a change in value of $2500 (= $1,000,000 \times 0.01 \times {}^{90}/_{360}$). Each percentage point change in prime rate will increase Hudson Foods' interest bill by $833.33 (= $1,000,000 × 0.01 × $^1/_{12}$) per month per $1,000,000. Discounting 2 months' interest at a 12% annual rate gives interest rate sensitivity of loan = $1641.99.

$$\text{Number of contracts} = \frac{20}{1} \times \frac{1641.99}{2500} \times 0.91 = 11.95 \cong 12$$

Consequently, Hudson Foods decided to sell short twelve 90-day Treasury bill contracts initially.

Hudson Foods sold 12 contracts at a price of 90.00% and drew down the loan. Immediately thereafter, prime rate increased to 13%. At the end of the month, Hudson Foods paid interest of $216,666.67 (= $20,000,000 × $^{0.13}/_{12}$) and closed out its futures position by buying back the 12 contracts at a price of 89.01% for a profit of $29,700 (= $2500 × 0.99 × 12), which more or less offset the effect of the increase in prime rate to 13%.

Hudson Foods then sold

$$\text{Number of contracts} = \frac{20}{1} \times \frac{825.08}{2500} \times 0.91 = 6.01 \cong 6$$

new contracts with 90 days to expiration at a price of 88.80 to hedge against a further increase in prime rate. Coincidentally, prime rate increased another 50 basis points immediately thereafter.

At the end of the second month, Hudson Foods paid interest of $225,000.00 (= $20,000,000 × 0.135/12), repaid the loan, and closed out its futures position by buying back the six contracts at a price of 88.20% for a profit of $9000 (= $2500 × 0.60 × 6). In the absence of hedging, Hudson Foods would have incurred an annualized cost of borrowing of 13.25%. But the profits from the futures transactions reduced the company's debt service obligations to $186,966.67 (= $216,666.67 − 29,700) the first month and $20,216,000 (= $20,225,000 − 9,000) the second month for a cost of borrowing of only 12.08% (before allowing for the commission charges and other costs of hedging). By hedging, Hudson Foods effectively locked in the 12% prime rate at the time it initiated the hedge.

SUMMARY

There are three principal sources of short-term funds: trade credit, bank loans, and commercial paper. Trade credit is the most prevalent but also generally the most expensive. Commercial paper is the cheapest for those companies who can access this market and is growing very rapidly in importance. Nevertheless, companies who can issue commercial paper normally continue to borrow from commercial banks in order to maintain ready access to this source of funds.

This chapter described techniques for estimating the cost of short-term funds from each of these sources. A prospective borrower who has access to more than one source of short-term funds can use Formulas 17-1, 17-3, and 17-6 to compare the costs and determine which source affords the required funds at the lowest cost. A company that borrows on a floating-rate basis can ensure against an increase in its interest expense by hedging.

Part 6

Long-Term Financing

The capital budgeting, capital structure, dividend, and working capital management decisions interact to determine a company's external financing requirements. Part 6 discusses how the firm can satisfy these requirements. This involves a variety of important considerations. For example, flotation costs generally make it uneconomic to fund each new project in accordance with the firm's target capitalization ratios. Thus, the firm must decide which type of security to issue each time it needs funds. As a second example, a company can raise new common equity through a rights offering to its existing shareholders or through a public offering to the whole investment community, but the two methods are not perfect substitutes for one another. Third, because of special tax considerations, it is more economic under certain circumstances for a company to lease an asset rather than to borrow funds and buy it. Finally, project financing an asset can, under certain circumstances, benefit a company's shareholders by effectively expanding the firm's debt capacity, for example, by facilitating a higher degree of leverage than the firm customarily maintains.

To help place the long-term financing decision in perspective, consider the following problem confronting Western Metals and Mining Corporation. Western plans to undertake a mining project that it expects will cost $100 million. The project involves the purchase of mining rights for $10 million, mine development costs of $15 million, and the purchase of mining equipment such as large electric shovels, off-road haulers, bulldozers, and conveyor systems for $75 million. Western's board of directors has directed Western's vice president of finance to prepare a financing plan and, in particular, to explore asset-based financing techniques because of first, the uncertainty regarding Western's future tax position and, second, the possibility that Western might be able to negotiate successfully a long-term purchase contract for the mine's output with an electric utility company. Part 6 is dedicated to helping Western's vice president of finance prepare a financing recommendation for Western's board of directors.

Sources of Long-Term Funds

Chapter 18

There are a number of facets to the long-term external financing decision. What type of security should the firm issue? Should it sell the issue through a registered underwritten public offering or should it instead sell the issue privately to institutional investors? Which market is likely to offer more attractive terms, the domestic capital market or the Eurobond market? How should the terms of the issue be tailored to suit best the issuer's particular circumstances?

OVERVIEW OF SOURCES OF LONG-TERM FUNDS

Table 18-1 provides a breakdown of the principal sources of external long-term financing corporations utilized during the period 1968 to 1982. Over the 15-year period, corporations met roughly 21.6% of their external funds needs by issuing common stock, roughly 5.8% through the issuance of preferred stock, and roughly 72.6% through the issuance of intermediate-term and long-term debt.

Table 18-1 reveals that the aggregate sale of common stock is sensitive to stock market conditions. Corporate issuers try to take advantage of rising markets when the demand for common stock is relatively strong. New issue activity tends to increase during periods of rising share prices, such as 1971 to 1972 and 1980 to 1983. Correspondingly, common stock new issue activity tends to diminish during periods of depressed or falling share prices, such as 1973 to 1974.

Similarly, the volume of fixed income security issues (i.e., preferred stock and debt) tends to vary with the level of long-term interest rates. During periods

Table 18-1
Breakdown of Principal Sources of Domestic External
Long-Term Financing by U.S. Corporations, 1968–1982
(Dollar Amounts in Millions)

Year	Aggregate Domestic External Financing*	Percentage Represented by			Percent Change in S&P 500 Index during Year, %	Moody's Average of Yields on Aa-Rated Corporate Bonds, %
		Common Stock, %	Preferred Stock, %†	Debt, %‡		
1968	$ 21,261	18.3	3.0	78.7	7.66	6.38
1969	25,995	29.4	2.7	67.9	−11.36	7.20
1970	37,450	18.8	3.7	77.5	0.10	8.32
1971	43,227	21.9	8.5	69.6	10.79	7.78
1972	39,716	27.0	8.5	64.5	15.63	7.48
1973	31,694	24.1	10.6	65.3	−17.37	7.66
1974	37,732	10.5	6.0	83.5	−29.72	8.84
1975	53,637	13.8	6.4	79.8	31.55	9.17
1976	53,319	15.6	5.3	79.1	19.15	8.75
1977	54,233	14.8	7.2	78.0	−11.50	8.24
1978	48,212	16.5	5.9	77.6	1.06	8.92
1979	53,090	16.4	6.6	77.0	12.31	9.94
1980	78,896	24.1	4.6	71.3	25.77	12.50
1981	73,142	34.7	2.4	62.9	−9.73	14.75
1982	83,734	28.4	6.1	65.5	14.76	14.41
Total	$735,338	21.6%	5.8%	72.6%		

*Aggregate amount raised through the issuance of common stock, nonconvertible preferred stock, nonconvertible debt, and convertible securities.
†Includes convertible preferred and preference stock.
‡Includes convertible debt.

Sources: "SEC Monthly Statistical Review," U.S. Securities and Exchange Commission, vol. 42, June 1983, pp. 5, 6, 10; *Daily Stock Price Record: New York Stock Exchange*, Standard & Poor's Corporation, New York, various issues; and *Moody's Industrial Manual*, Moody's Investors Service, Inc., New York, 1983, p. a30.

of rising long-term interest rates, such as 1979 to 1981, corporations tend to favor short-term borrowing in the hope that long-term interest rates will fall. When long-term interest rates do fall, as during 1982, corporations begin to fund out this short-term debt.

DEBT VERSUS EQUITY FINANCING

Each time a corporation needs to raise funds externally, it must decide which type of securities to issue. Because of the economies of scale involved in issuing securities and because of the interest rate (or dividend rate) penalties issuers must pay in order to sell small debt or preferred stock issues in the public market, a corporation cannot economically sell a package of securities that contains the same proportions of debt and equity securities as its target capital structure each time it needs funds.

Pro Forma Analysis of Debt versus Equity

Consider a corporation whose target senior debt rating is Aa/AA and whose target capital structure contains one-fourth nonconvertible debt and three-fourths common equity. Suppose the corporation wishes to raise $50 million and that the corporation's investment bankers have advised it that under prevailing market conditions it could sell either (1) $50 million principal amount of debt at par bearing a 12% coupon rate or (2) 2 million shares of common stock at a price of $25 per share. Table 18-2 provides a pro forma analysis of the financial effects of these two alternatives.

The pro forma analysis assumes that the issuer uses the proceeds of the long-term issue to repay $50 million of short-term debt that bears interest at the rate of 10% per annum. As one would expect, issuing common stock has a more severe impact on earnings per share but a more favorable impact on the issuer's credit statistics. Indeed, issuing long-term debt actually results in deterioration of the issuer's credit statistics because it would replace lower-cost short-term debt. More important, because of the issuer's relatively low dividend rate, issuing common stock rather than long-term debt results in an improvement in cash flow net of common dividends.

The pro forma analysis in Table 18-2 is intended to show whether issuing $50 million of long-term debt bearing a 12% coupon rate would cause deterioration of the issuer's credit statistics severe enough to place the issuer's Aa/AA senior debt rating in jeopardy. It does not. The pro forma debt ratios and fixed charge coverage are slightly better than Aa/AA levels, but cash flow as a percentage of long-term debt and total debt is in each case slightly worse than the average for Aa/AA-rated companies. Thus, the company has the flexibility to issue long-term debt. However, the extent of the deterioration in the company's credit statistics suggests that if it should need a further $50 million following the $50 million 12% debt issue, it might have to issue common stock in order to avoid jeopardizing its debt rating.

Which type of security the company finally decides to issue will depend on a variety of considerations in addition to the pro forma impact illustrated in Table 18-2. In particular, the issuer's interest rate and share price expectations will play an important role. If the company expects interest rates and its share price to increase, it will be inclined to issue long-term debt rather than common stock. The specific terms, such as maturity and redemption provisions, will also influence the issuer's decision. In contrast, if its share price has risen sharply of late, the company would probably be inclined to issue common stock and preserve the flexibility to issue long-term debt at a later date.

PUBLIC VERSUS PRIVATE FINANCING

Companies can sell securities to the public through a registered *public offering* or directly to institutional investors through a *private placement*. Securities to be sold in a public offering must first be registered with the Securities and Exchange Commission.

Table 18-2
Pro Forma Analysis of Debt Versus Equity Financing
(Dollar Amounts in Millions Except Per-Share Amounts)

	Average for AA-Rated Industrial Companies		Projected for 12/31/xx		Pro Forma the Issuance of			
					$50MM of 12% Long-Term Debt		2MM Common Shares at $25	
Book Capitalization								
Short-term debt	$ 75.0	9.4%			$ 25.0	2.9%	$ 25.0	2.9%
Long-term debt	$200.0	25.0%			$250.0	29.4%	$200.0	23.5%
Stockholders' equity	600.0	75.0			600.0	70.6	650.0	76.5
Capitalization	$800.0	100.0%			$850.0	100.0%	$850.0	100.0%
Operating Statistics								
Earnings before interest and taxes	$175.0				$175.0		$175.0	
Interest expense	22.0				23.0		17.0	
Income taxes (50% tax rate)	76.5				76.0		79.0	
Earnings available to common	$ 76.5				$ 76.0		$ 79.0	
Average shares outstanding (000)	30,000				30,000		32,000	
Earnings per share	$ 2.55				$ 2.53		$ 2.47	
Amount of antidilution (dilution)					($ 0.02)		($ 0.08)	
Percent					(0.8%)		(3.1%)	
Cash flow from operations	$146.5				$146.0		$149.0	
Common dividends ($0.60/share)	18.0				18.0		19.2	
Cash flow net of dividends	$128.5				$128.0		$129.8	

Pro Forma Analysis of Debt Versus
Equity Financing *(Continued)*
(Dollar Amounts in Millions Except Per-Share Amounts)

	Average for AA-Rated Industrial Companies	Projected for 12/31/xx	Pro Forma the Issuance of	
			$50MM of 12% Long-Term Debt	2MM Common Shares at $25
		Financial Ratios		
Return on average equity	14.50%	13.40%	13.31%	12.74%
Long-term debt as % of capitalization	29.85	25.00	29.41	23.53
Total debt as % of capitalization plus short-term debt	33.20	31.43	32.35	26.47
Pretax interest coverage	7.74×	7.95×	7.61×	10.29×
Fixed charge coverage*	5.83	6.67	6.43	8.18
Cash flow as % of:				
Long-term debt	71.77%	70.25%	62.40%	79.50%
Total debt	59.25	56.91	56.73	70.67

*Fixed charges include $5 million of imputed interest expense, which represents one-third of projected rental expense.

Features of Privately Placed Securities

Securities that are privately placed are not registered. Consequently, securities regulations require companies to offer securities privately only to investors sophisticated enough to make an independent determination as to their investment merits. Because they are not registered, privately placed securities cannot be traded freely; they are thus less liquid than securities that are sold publicly. Companies sell securities privately, usually with the assistance of a securities firm acting as agent, principally to life insurance companies and, to a lesser extent, to property and casualty insurance companies, credit companies, pension funds, and wealthy individuals.

Only about 2% of all common stock is placed privately. Most private placements involve debt securities. Beginning in 1980, the proportion of nonconvertible debt placed privately has fallen sharply. This is principally the result of the short-form registration statement and the shelf registration process, which have enabled issuers to sell securities in the public securities markets much more quickly than heretofore.

Advantages and Disadvantages of a
Private Placement

A private placement offers the following advantages over a public offering:

- There are lower issuance costs. Placing an issue privately enables the issuer to avoid the costs of registering the securities with the SEC, printing prospectuses, obtaining credit ratings from the major rating agencies, and various other expenses. In addition, the fees securities firms charge in connection with a private placement are less than the fees they would charge in connection with a comparable public offering.
- An issuer can obtain commitments from investors more quickly because the inevitable time lag while the company prepares the registration statement and the SEC reviews it that accompanies a public offering is absent in a private placement. However, the short-form registration statement and the shelf registration process introduced recently have greatly expedited the public offering process.[1] The shelf registration process enables an issuer to register a 2-year supply of securities, which it retains "on the shelf" until market conditions are conducive to an offering.
- The private market is more receptive to smaller issues; issues of only a few million dollars each are not uncommon. Public debt issues of less than $50 million principal amount typically involve a rate penalty because their small size decreases their liquidity and lessens their attractiveness to investors.
- There is greater flexibility with respect to design of security arrangements and other terms. Private investors are capable of analyzing complex security arrangements, such as those that arise in connection with project financing. Private lenders are more comfortable with such arrangements than the major rating agencies so that such financing is typically arranged privately.

A private placement also has the following disadvantages relative to a public offering:

- *Higher yield.* To compensate for the illiquidity of their investments, purchasers of privately placed debt require a higher yield than purchasers of comparable public debt issues, and purchasers of privately placed common stock require a discount from the freely traded price of the stock. During the period 1961 to 1977, the average yield on privately placed corporate bonds exceeded the average yield on comparable public issues by approximately 50 basis points.[2] In addition, each major life insurance company sets a schedule of prime, or minimum, lending rates for different maturities, which it reassesses weekly. The prime rates are tied to the rates at which a company whose senior debt is rated A-2/A could raise debt publicly. Consequently, double-A-rated and triple-A-rated companies will normally find it considerably more expensive to sell their debt privately than publicly.

- *More stringent covenants and more restrictive terms.* Because their invest-ments are illiquid, private bond and preferred stock purchasers insist on tighter convenant restrictions, for example, restricting more severely the is-suer's ability to sell additional bonds, to pay cash dividends or repurchase shares of its common stock, or to refund the issue.
- *Shorter maturity.* At times in recent years, private bond purchasers have not been willing to agree to a maturity greater than 15 years. Issuers could achieve a longer maturity only in the public market.

Public Issue versus Private Issue

Small- and medium-sized companies often find it cheaper to place debt privately rather than to offer it publicly, particularly when the size of the issue is $5 million or less. However, when both markets are available, the relative attractiveness of the two can be evaluated by (1) calculating the direct cost of funds under each alternative and then (2) evaluating these relative direct costs in the light of other differences, such as more restrictive debt covenants under the private placement alternative.

For example, suppose that Western Metals and Mining Corporation has been told by its investment bankers that it can raise $75 million to cover the cost of the mining equipment it needs either by selling publicly a 15-year debt issue bearing a 12% coupon and requiring issuance expenses of $900,000 or by placing privately a 15-year debt issue bearing a $12\frac{1}{4}$% coupon but requiring issuance expenses of only $300,000. Suppose that each issue involves a level sinking fund beginning at the end of the tenth year and that Western's tax rate is 50%. Applying Formula 8-2 gives

$$\text{After-tax cost of public debt issue } = 6.09\%$$
$$\text{After-tax cost of private debt issue } = 6.16\%$$

The higher coupon on the private issue would more than offset the lower issuance expenses. If the private issue also contained more restrictive convenants or permitted less refunding flexibility, those factors would reinforce the decision to sell debt publicly. However, if Western is concerned that interest rates might rise more than 25 basis points before it could effect registration of the debt securities and Western is able to "lock in" the $12\frac{1}{4}$% rate immediately through the private placement, Western might decide in that case to proceed with the private placement.

DOMESTIC VERSUS INTERNATIONAL FINANCING

A company can sell U.S. dollar–denominated bonds to U.S. investors in the domestic bond market or to foreign investors in the Eurobond market. Alternatively, a company can sell bonds denominated in a foreign currency. The latter involves a foreign exchange risk because the issuer must either realize foreign currency from its operations or else purchase foreign currency in order to meet its future debt service obligations on this debt.

Dollar-Denominated Borrowing in the Eurobond Market

A *Eurobond* is a bond issued outside the country in whose currency the bond is denominated. The Eurobond market developed during the 1960s when the U.S. government levied an interest equalization tax on the purchase of foreign securities by U.S. investors and imposed restrictions on capital exports by American companies. A U.S.-imposed withholding tax on interest payments by domestic corporations to foreign investors, which was not eliminated until 1984, discouraged foreign purchases of domestic bond issues and furthered the development of the Eurobond market.

Companies headquartered in the United States issue dollar-denominated Eurobonds to investors in Europe (hence the prefix "Euro") and other areas outside the United States. Eurobonds denominated in other currencies are also issued, but U.S. dollar–denominated bonds represent more than half the total Eurobond market. The Eurobond market remains distinct from the U.S. domestic bond market in spite of the elimination of withholding tax. Eurobonds are not registered with the Securities and Exchange Commission and therefore cannot be issued to U.S. investors. Second, bonds sold in the United States must be issued in registered form, whereas Eurobonds are typically issued in bearer form. This provides holders anonymity, which Eurobond investors appear to value highly.[3]

United States dollar–denominated Eurobond issues are as varied as domestic bond issues. Most are straight debt issues, but convertible Eurobonds and Eurobonds with warrants are not uncommon. Nevertheless, there are important differences between the domestic bond market and the Eurobond market:

- Eurobond investors typically possess assets denominated in several currencies. The relative attractiveness of U.S. dollar–denominated Eurobonds and hence the relationship between bond yields in the domestic bond market and the U.S. dollar–denominated Eurobond market depends on U.S. dollar exchange rates. When the U.S. dollar is appreciating relative to the other major currencies, Eurobond investors tend to increase their purchasing of U.S. dollar–denominated Eurobonds, which can drive Eurobond yields below domestic bond yields and create an attractive borrowing opportunity for U.S. corporations, giving rise to a so-called Eurobond "window."[4] Nevertheless, possibilities for arbitrage exist which ensure that Eurobond yields normally track domestic bond yields fairly closely.

- Because of investors' exchange rate sensitivity, Eurobond maturities are typically shorter and issue sizes are generally smaller than in the domestic market.
- Eurobond investors tend to be more sensitive to the identity of the issuer and less sensitive to the issuer's credit standing than domestic investors. As a result, certain American companies that are very well known in Europe can borrow more cheaply in the Eurobond market than some more highly rated purely domestic U.S. companies.
- Eurobonds are generally bearer bonds that pay interest annually.

Payment of interest on an annual basis makes it necessary to convert the yield to an equivalent semiannually compounded basis when comparing domestic and Eurobond borrowing alternatives. That is, the cost of debt for a Eurobond issue should be calculated from Formula 8-1 and then converted to an *equivalent semiannually compounded basis* by applying the formula:

$$\begin{matrix} \text{Equivalent} \\ \text{semiannually} \\ \text{compounded cost} \end{matrix} = 2 \times \left(\sqrt{1 + \text{annualized cost of debt}} - 1 \right) \quad (18\text{-}1)$$

For example, suppose that Western Metals and Mining Corporation can issue the 12% public debt issue mentioned in the previous section in the domestic market or a $12\frac{1}{4}\%$ Eurobond issue instead. Suppose that the Eurobond issuance expenses are such that the after-tax cost of the issue is 6.20% on an annualized basis. By Formula 18-1, the equivalent semiannually compounded cost of the Eurobond issue is

$$\text{Equivalent semiannually compounded cost} = 6.11\%$$

The domestic issue is slightly cheaper.

Because of the segmentation of the Eurobond market and the domestic bond market, Eurobond borrowing enables a U.S. corporation to expand the market for its debt. Over the past 15 years, U.S. companies have sold approximately 10% of their long-term debt issues in the Eurobond market. The volume of Eurobond financing increased from $4.1 billion in 1980 to $6.2 billion in 1981 and $12.6 billion in 1982 when the strength of the U.S. dollar brought about a sharp increase in the foreign demand for U.S. dollar–denominated bonds.

Foreign Currency–Denominated Borrowing

A company may also choose to issue bonds denominated in a foreign currency. This would be prudent, for example, if the company borrowed funds denominated in the foreign currency of a country in which it holds substantial assets and derives substantial revenues. A full consideration of the issues surrounding such investments and techniques for managing foreign exchange exposure lies beyond the scope of this book.[5] This section is concerned with how a corporation can gauge the relative costs of borrowing in dollars on the one hand or in some other currency on the other.

The relative yields at which a company can issue bonds denominated in different currencies are somewhat deceiving. For example, an American company may be able to issue 10-year U.S. dollar–denominated bonds bearing a 10% coupon or 10-year Swiss franc–denominated bonds bearing a 5% coupon. Is the Swiss franc issue really only half as expensive? Of course not. The American company keeps its accounts in dollars. Consequently, the relative costs of the two alternatives should be compared in dollars. In particular, if the Swiss franc appreciates relative to the dollar, servicing the Swiss franc debt will become more expensive, and the actual *equivalent dollar cost* of the Swiss franc issue will exceed 5%. Indeed, the divergence in yields between U.S. dollar–denominated debt and comparable Swiss franc–denominated debt implies that investors do expect the Swiss franc to appreciate relative to the dollar.

If one could predict future foreign exchange rates, the interest and principal repayment obligations could be converted into dollars at the applicable exchange rates with the resulting amounts used in Formula 8-1 or Formula 8-2, as appropriate. However, future exchange rates are influenced by a variety of factors, which make predictions hazardous. Nevertheless, various econometric forecasting services do provide forecasts of the dollar exchange rate relative to major currencies.

Alternatively, a company might be able to arrange a *currency swap*. Such an arrangement involves two companies who agree to exchange specified amounts of different currencies, to make specified interest payments to each other (or a specified periodic net interest payment from one to the other), and to make repayment at a specified future date according to a specified exchange ratio. Such an arrangement enables the U.S. borrower to figure the equivalent dollar cost of the loan implicit in the currency swap arrangement.

The equivalent dollar cost of a loan denominated in a foreign currency that calls for semiannual interest payments can be calculated by modifying Formula 8-2:

Net proceeds in foreign currency $\times$ initial exchange rate

$$
= \sum_{t=1}^{\substack{\text{number} \\ \text{of periods}}} \frac{\text{exchange}}{\text{rate}(t)} \times \left[\left(1 - \frac{\text{tax}}{\text{rate}} \right) \times \text{interest}(t) \right.
$$

$$
\left. + \frac{\text{sinking}}{\text{fund}(t)} - \frac{\text{tax}}{\text{rate}} \times \text{amortization}(t) \right]
$$

$$
\div \left(1 + \frac{\text{dollar cost}}{2} \right)^t \tag{18-2}
$$

Table 18-3
Calculation of Realized Equivalent Dollar Cost
of Foreign Currency–Denominated Debt
(Dollar Amounts in Thousands)

Period	Dollar Borrowing	After-Tax Interest*	Sinking Fund Payment*	Expense Amortization*	Net Cash Flow
0	−$74,250,000	—	—	—	−$74,250,000
1–19	—	$2,460,938	—	$10,938	2,450,000
20	—	2,460,937	$10,937,500	10,937	13,387,500
21	—	2,050,781	—	10,938	2,039,843
22	—	2,050,781	10,937,500	10,937	12,977,344
23	—	1,640,625	—	10,938	1,629,687
24	—	1,640,625	10,937,500	10,937	12,567,188
25	—	1,230,469	—	10,938	1,219,531
26	—	1,230,469	10,937,500	10,937	12,157,032
27	—	820,313	—	10,938	809,375
28	—	820,312	10,937,500	10,937	11,746,875
29	—	410,156	—	10,938	399,218
30	—	410,156	10,937,500	10,937	11,336,719

Dollar cost = 5.95%

*Calculation assumes an exchange rate of $1.75/£.

where *initial exchange rate* and *exchange rate(t)* represent the cost of a unit of the currency in which the loan is denominated, for example, dollars per pound sterling ($/£), and *interest(t)* and *sinking fund(t)* are expressed in the foreign currency. Formula 8-1 can be modified similarly.

For example, suppose that Western can borrow £37,500,000 from a British institution at a coupon rate of 15%. The *initial exchange rate* is $2.00/£. Suppose further that the British institution is willing to accept debt service payments in dollars at an exchange rate of $1.75/£ and that the issuance expenses amount to £375,000. In that case,

$$\begin{array}{l} \text{Net proceeds} \\ \text{in foreign} \\ \text{currency} \end{array} \times \begin{array}{l} \text{initial} \\ \text{exchange} \\ \text{rate} \end{array} = (£37,500,000 - £375,000) \times \$2.00/£$$

$$= \$74,250,000$$

Table 18-3 illustrates the calculation of the after-tax dollar equivalent cost of servicing the loan:

$$\text{Dollar cost} = 5.95\%$$

Table 18-4
Underwriting Spread and Issuance Expenses As Percentage of Offering Price for Registered Public Offerings, 1973–1982

Issue Size (Millions of Dollars)	Common Stock			Preferred Stock			Convertible Debt			Bonds		
	Under-writing Spread, %	Issuance Expenses, %*	Total, %	Under-writing Spread, %	Issuance Expenses, %*	Total, %	Under-writing Spread, %	Issuance Expenses, %*	Total, %	Under-writing Spread, %	Issuance Expenses, %*	Total, %
Under 10.0	9.26	5.70	14.96	7.94	5.09	13.03	7.35	3.37	10.72	4.14	1.38	5.52
10.0 to 24.9	6.24	1.90	8.14	4.54	1.44	5.98	3.91	1.60	5.51	3.09	0.96	4.05
25.0 to 49.9	5.00	0.93	5.93	2.59	0.55	3.14	2.53	0.75	3.28	1.91	0.72	2.63
50.0 to 99.9	4.05	0.45	4.50	2.99	0.36	3.35	1.87	0.46	2.33	1.23	0.40	1.63
100.0 to 199.9	3.97	0.36	4.33	3.07	0.25	3.32	1.45	0.28	1.73	0.96	0.25	1.21
200.0 to 500.0	3.60	0.37	3.97	2.62	0.10	2.72	1.14	0.13	1.27	0.89	0.14	1.03
Over 500.0	2.31	0.05	2.36	—	—	—	—	—	—	1.41	0.06	1.47
Average	4.92	1.39	6.31	3.96	1.30	5.26	3.04	1.10	4.14	1.95	0.56	2.51

*Includes SEC filing fee, legal fees, accountants' fees, blue sky expenses, printing, engraving, mailing, and miscellaneous out-of-pocket expenses.

Source: Securities Data Company, Inc.

Compared with the 6.09% cost of a comparable domestic public debt issue, the sterling Eurobond debt issue would provide a saving of 14 basis points. However, before deciding to enter into the swap arrangement, Western would have to weigh any differences in the other terms of the two debt alternatives to make sure they did not offset this saving.

UNDERWRITTEN VERSUS NONUNDERWRITTEN SALE OF SECURITIES

A company may choose to market its securities issues itself (as the U.S. government does), but the vast majority seek the assistance of investment bankers because of their expertise and experience in designing and marketing securities issues.

Investment Banking

The *investment banker* serves as an intermediary between the issuer and the ultimate purchasers. Investment bankers provide advice regarding the appropriate security to issue (debt versus equity) and the pricing and other terms of the security to be offered; advice regarding the appropriate market (public or private, domestic or international); and assistance with preparation of the required documentation. They market the securities to investors and, in connection with a *purchase-and-sale* offering, underwrite the issue, which involves purchasing the entire issue from the issuer at an agreed-upon initial public offering price less a fixed *gross underwriting spread* and incurring the risk that the entire issue may not be saleable at the initial public offering price.

Securities firms' compensation represents a significant portion of the cost of floating a new issue. Table 18-4 provides average spread information for public offerings of various types and sizes during the period 1973 to 1982. Information regarding private placement fees is generally not disclosed publicly, but approximate fee levels can be obtained by consulting investment bankers. The private placement fee would normally be much lower than the gross spread for a comparable public offering because (1) the private placement is targeted at a relatively small number of sophisticated investors rather than the broader investing public and thus involves lower selling costs and (2) the private placement involves no underwriting.

Table 18-4 reveals that it is generally most expensive, strictly in terms of the total cost of issuance, to issue common stock and least expensive to issue (nonconvertible) bonds. This reflects the greater risks involved in underwriting common stock issues and also the higher selling commissions required to distribute common stock issues, large portions of which are typically marketed to individual investors. Table 18-4 also reveals the significant economies of scale involved in issuing securities.

Direct Sales of Securities

Several finance companies and certain other issuers have bypassed the investment banking industry and issued securities directly to investors. For example, Sears Roebuck Acceptance Corp. offered $250 million of medium-term notes (maturing in between 2 and 10 years) in December 1981 in a registered public offering. Direct public offerings like the Sears offering are often undertaken by finance companies. Nonfinancial companies seldom offer securities directly to the public. One exception is an innovative offering of "Energy Thrift Certificates" by Green Mountain Power Corporation beginning in 1979.[6]

Most direct sales of securities involve the direct placement of debt securities. Commercial banks and industrial companies often place debt issues directly with institutional investors in private transactions. In addition, new issue dividend reinvestment plans and electric utilities' customer stock purchase plans represent a form of direct sale of common stock. The rapid growth of these plans in recent years has increased the proportion of common equity companies, particularly electric utilities, raise directly from investors.

The direct sale of securities saves the issuer the underwriting spread or private placement fee the investment banker would charge. However, the issuer does not have available the information and underwriting services the investment banker provides. Direct placement may be cheaper when the issuer has a natural market it can exploit—for example, selling common equity to current shareholders or debt or equity securities to an electric utility's ratepayers—or has extensive market information available because the issuer is in frequent direct contact with potential investors, for example, commercial bank direct placements of debt securities.

Competitive versus Negotiated Offering

A company can offer securities publicly using either of two methods: through competitive bidding or through a negotiated offering. Under *competitive bidding*, the issuer specifies the type of securities it wishes to sell and invites securities firms to bid for the issue. In a *negotiated offering*, the issuer selects one or more securities firms to manage the offering and works closely with them to design the terms of the issue and to determine the appropriate time to issue the securities. Currently, registered public utility holding companies are required to offer securities competitively, but other companies are free to choose the most desired offering technique.[7] Other electric utilities tend to offer debt and preferred stock by competitive bid, except during periods of heightened market volatility, but generally sell common stock on a negotiated basis. Railroads frequently sell equipment trust certificates through competitive bidding, but other industrial companies seldom sell securities via competitive bidding.[8]

Which offering method is more likely to facilitate the lower cost of funds has been hotly debated. Empirical evidence is not conclusive. However, a number of recent studies suggest that the competitive process can lead to significant cost savings during stable market periods when there is strong competition among bidding groups.[9] Nevertheless, the negotiated offering process offers greater flexibility as to the design of the securities and the timing of the issue because the issuer has not committed in advance to a specific set of terms (e.g., maturity and redemption terms) and to a particular offering date (in competitive bidding, the date bids are to be received). It also gives securities firms the opportunity to form the most effective selling group for the issue (rather than splitting into competing bidding groups) and provides a stronger incentive for them to assess the demand for and stimulate interest in the issue prior to pricing because, in contrast to a competitive bid, they know that they will have the securities to sell. These advantages can more than offset the reduction in underwriting spread, if any, during periods of heightened market volatility and interest rate uncertainty, particularly if the issuer has few debt issues outstanding to serve as pricing benchmarks, the issuer's financial condition is weak or deteriorating, or its business prospects are changing. In such situations, the negotiated offering process facilitates a more intensive selling effort, which can result in a lower cost of funds.

A recent development in corporate underwriting has had an important effect on the process by which securities are sold. In March 1982, the SEC instituted Rule 415, the so-called "shelf registration rule," which permits an issuer to register an inventory of securities of a particular type sufficient to cover its financing requirements for up to 2 years. The securities remain "on the shelf" until the issuer finds market conditions sufficiently attractive to sell some of them. Rule 415 has effectively extended competitive bidding to issues of securities by the roughly 2000 large corporations that qualify for use of the shelf registration statement. Securities firms and institutional investors can bid for securities that a company has on the shelf. The available evidence suggests that the shelf registration process has enabled the largest, most creditworthy companies to realize a lower cost of funds.[10]

SUMMARY

A company that needs to raise long-term funds externally has a number of alternatives available. The initial decision involves what type of security to sell. The prospective issuer must decide in the light of its capital structure objectives and its current financial condition whether to sell debt or equity securities. Economies of scale and investors' liquidity preferences make it impractical for a company to sell debt and equity securities each time it needs funds in exactly the proportions debt and equity represent in the company's target capital structure.

After deciding what type of security to sell, the company must determine which market offers the most attractive terms. Placing securities privately often involves lower issuance costs, permits the company to secure commitments from investors more quickly, and affords greater flexibility with respect to the size of the issue and the design of security arrangements. But private placements generally must provide a higher yield and, in the case of debt and preferred stock, involve a shorter maturity and more restrictive convenants. The Eurobond market often affords attractive opportunities to borrow, particularly during periods when the dollar is strong relative to other currencies.

Most companies use an investment banker to help them design and then market their issues. Notable exceptions include finance companies who often sell debt securities directly to investors and a variety of companies, particularly public utility companies, who have found it advantageous to sell additional common stock directly to current shareholders through new issue dividend reinvestment plans. The bulk of the securities issued in the United States are sold in negotiated underwritten public offerings.

Raising Additional Common Equity

Larger companies typically raise the bulk of the additional common equity they need internally by reinvesting some portion of earnings. But smaller or rapidly growing companies typically resort to new issues, and even large companies sometimes find it advantageous to raise a large amount of common equity through a public offering. In addition, many companies have instituted dividend reinvestment or employee stock purchase plans that generate additional common equity on a continuing basis.

DISTINGUISHING FEATURES OF COMMON STOCK

A company's common stockholders are the residual claimants to its operating cash flow and assets. Collectively, they own the company and have the right to elect its board of directors and to vote on certain matters specified in the corporation's charter.

Principal Features of Common Stock

A company's corporate charter limits the number of *authorized shares* of common stock. A company cannot issue shares unless it has authorized shares available. Increasing the number of authorized shares is normally noncontroversial, but it does require a shareholder vote. Consequently, it is prudent for management to ensure that it has enough shares authorized but not yet issued to meet any foreseeable corporate needs, and when it does not, to ask shareholders to increase the number of authorized shares at the next annual meeting.

Shares become *issued shares* when a corporation sells them to investors. Issued shares at any balance sheet date consist of *outstanding shares*, which are held by investors, and *treasury shares*, which the corporation has repurchased from investors. Earnings per share and book value per share calculations are based on the number of outstanding shares.

Shares of common stock are issued with or without *par value*. Par value has little economic significance. But because some states do not permit companies to sell shares at a price below par value, par value is generally set at a low value.

Principal Stockholder Rights

The principal rights of a company's common stockholders fall into four categories: (1) dividend rights, (2) voting rights, (3) liquidation rights, and (4) preemptive rights. Common stockholders have the right to receive their respective pro rata shares of common stock dividends when these are declared by the company's board of directors. They also typically are entitled to one vote per share. However, companies sometimes issue multiple classes of common stock, and these may include a class of nonvoting common shares or a class of common stock with more or less than one vote per share. When two or more classes of common shares exist with disproportionate voting rights and the shares of the different classes are publicly traded, the relative share prices will reflect the differences in voting rights.[1] Nevertheless, companies sometimes issue a second class of common stock with limited voting rights in order to preserve insider control.[2]

Common stockholders also have the right to receive their respective pro rata shares of the corporation's net assets upon any winding up or dissolution of its business. However, common stockholders' dividend rights and liquidation rights are junior to the rights of debtholders and preferred stockholders; a company can pay common stock dividends in cash only after it has met its interest, preferred stock dividend, and sinking fund requirements, and common stockholders are entitled to receive payments in the event of liquidation only after the corporation has repaid its debt and preferred stock obligations in full. Finally, common stockholders may possess *preemptive rights*, which give them the right to subscribe for new share issues before the company can offer shares to others. Such offerings to exisiting shareholders, which are called *rights offerings*, are discussed later in this chapter.

SOURCES OF ADDITIONAL COMMON EQUITY

The principal sources of additional common equity capital are:

- Retained earnings

- Public offering to the general investment community of shares of the parent company or of a subsidiary
- Rights offering to the company's shareholders
- Direct placement of shares with institutional investors or, as newer companies have done, with larger companies who wish to make venture capital investments in return for licensing rights or other benefits
- Sale of newly issued common shares through a new issue dividend reinvestment plan, employee stock plan, or a customer stock purchase plan
- Contribution of newly issued common shares to a pension plan in lieu of a cash contribution
- Conversion of convertible securities

In recent years, rights offerings have diminished in importance while dividend reinvestment plans have taken on increased importance, particularly for public utility companies. Also in recent years, companies have contributed sizeable amounts of common stock to their pension plans in lieu of cash.[3]

METHODS AND COST OF A PUBLIC OFFERING

Table 19-1 provides details concerning a representative group of public common stock offerings that took place during the period 1980 to 1984. Included is American Telephone and Telegraph Company's public offering of 16,000,000 shares for $1,060,000,000 on March 10, 1983, the largest public common stock offering in terms of aggregate dollar value done up to that time.

Methods of Offering

There are two principal methods for offering common stock publicly: negotiated offerings and competitive offerings. With the exception of registered public utility holding companies, which are required to sell securities through competitive bidding, common stock is almost always offered on a negotiated basis. The shelf registration process has changed this somewhat. It permits the issuer to register up to a 2-year inventory of shares. After the SEC declares the registration statement effective, the issuer can sell portions of this inventory as market conditions permit, for example, in response to solicited or unsolicited bids from securities firms or investors. One potential drawback to this procedure is that registering shares representing several offerings may adversely affect the company's share price because the registered but unissued shares, which may be offered at any time, overhang the market.

Costs of the Offering

The costs of a public offering consist of three components: (1) the gross spread paid the underwriters, (2) the market impact of the announcement of the offering and subsequent marketing activity, and (3) out-of-pocket expenses, such as lawyers' and accountants' fees, engraving and printing, and mailing. However, out-of-pocket expenses are a significant cost factor only in connection with very small offerings.

Gross Spread. As Table 18-4 illustrates, gross spread as a percentage of the proceeds of the issue tends to vary inversely with the size of the issue because of the economies of scale in issuing securities.

Table 19-1
Study of Selected Public Common
Stock Offerings, 1980–1984

Date of Offering	Issuer	Shares Issued Number (000)	Shares Issued Value ($Millions)	Percentage Increase in Shares Outstanding	Gross Spread Amount	Gross Spread Percent of Offer Price
1/29/80	Cincinnati Gas & Electric	3,400	$ 54.8	12.5	$0.55	3.41
1/30/80	Federal Express	1,083	63.9	13.5	2.20	3.73
4/29/80	Getty Oil	4,000	296.0	4.9	2.00	2.70
8/19/80	Duke Power	4,000	69.5	5.0	0.58	3.34
3/02/81	Trans World Corp.	2,500	50.6	15.5	1.12	5.53
4/07/81	American Electric Power	9,000	146.3	6.1	0.548	3.37
5/27/81	Apple Computer	2,600	81.3	4.7	1.50	4.80
10/29/81	Middle South Utilities	5,000	63.8	4.3	0.348	2.73
3/23/82	Lockheed	2,000	96.8	16.6	1.75	3.62
5/05/82	Florida Power & Light	3,000	97.5	6.6	0.185	0.57
12/01/82	American Telephone & Telegraph	16,500	990.0	1.9	1.35	2.25
12/07/82	RCA	6,000	141.0	7.9	0.85	3.62
3/03/83	Grumman	1,200	59.4	10.2	1.95	3.94
3/10/83	American Telephone & Telegraph	16,000	1060.0	1.8	1.30	1.96
5/12/83	Caterpillar Tractor	5,000	236.3	5.6	1.62	3.43
8/12/83	Apollo Computer	1,600	53.6	8.0	1.50	4.48
8/24/83	Texas Utilities	5,000	123.1	4.3	0.60	2.44
10/04/83	Burroughs	3,000	157.5	7.1	1.75	3.33
11/16/83	Middle South Utilities	7,000	111.3	4.5	0.343	2.16
11/01/84	American President Companies	2,000	66.0	17.2	1.25	3.79

*Calculated as percentage change in share price less percentage change in S&P 500 between the day 30 days prior to the offering date and the offering date. Negative value indicates relative price decrease.
†Calculated as percentage gross spread less market impact of offering.

Market Impact. A company's share price typically declines upon the announcement of a public offering.[4] At first glance this may seem puzzling. If the corporation intends to invest the issue proceeds in a project that will earn a rate of return at least equal to the corporation's hurdle rate, its share price should not fall. Indeed, if the expected return on equity exceeds the corporation's cost of equity capital, the share price should increase. Does the tendency for the share price to fall upon the announcement of a public offering indicate then a tendency for corporations to invest in unprofitable projects?

The share price falls not because investments are generally unprofitable but because the offering will increase the supply of shares of stock that are offered

Public Offering Price	Last Sale before Pricing	Closing Price 30 Days before Pricing	Percentage Change during 30 Days before Pricing		Market Impact of Offering*, %	Effective Spread†, %	Method of Offering‡
			Share Price	S&P 500			
$16.125	$16.125	$16.625	−3.01	5.78	−8.79	12.20	N
59.000	59.000	46.625	26.54	6.73	19.81	−16.08	N
74.000	76.750	70.000	5.71	5.15	0.56	2.14	N
17.375	17.250	18.375	−5.44	0.46	−5.90	9.24	N
20.250	20.250	20.125	0.62	1.90	−1.28	6.81	N
16.250	16.250	16.125	0.78	3.13	−2.35	5.72	C
31.250	31.250	28.750	8.70	−1.26	9.96	−5.16	N
12.750	12.250	11.875	7.37	2.69	4.68	−1.95	C
48.375	48.500	51.375	−5.84	0.29	−6.13	9.75	N
32.500	32.500	30.875	5.26	2.56	2.70	−2.13	N
60.000	59.875	59.625	0.63	2.40	−1.77	4.02	N
23.500	23.750	26.375	−10.90	0.39	−11.29	14.91	N
49.500	49.500	50.250	−1.49	7.36	−8.85	12.79	N
66.250	66.250	68.750	−3.64	4.19	−7.83	9.79	N
47.250	47.250	39.750	18.87	5.41	13.46	−10.03	N
33.500	33.750	45.750	−26.78	−1.99	−24.79	29.27	N
24.625	24.500	25.500	−3.43	−4.88	1.45	0.99	N
52.500	51.625	53.625	−2.10	0.77	−2.87	6.20	N
15.900	15.750	16.000	−0.63	−2.55	1.92	0.24	C
33.000	33.000	33.500	−1.49	2.38	−3.87	7.66	N

‡C denotes a competitive offering. N denotes a negotiated offering.

Sources: Prospectuses and *Daily Stock Price Record: New York Stock Exchange*, Standard & Poor's Corporation, New York, various issues.

for sale in the market. As illustrated in Figure 19-1, the demand curve for a company's shares at any particular point in time is downward-sloping. Prior to the announcement of the offering, the share price is P_0 and the quantity of the shares traded (say, average monthly turnover) is Q_0. Investors who believe the company's stock is worth at least as much as P_0 hold the stock in their portfolios. Those who do not own it must think that a share is worth no more than P_0 (otherwise they would puchase shares). In order to entice investors to buy the newly issued shares, a lower price would be required, P_1 in Figure 19-1, if the company simply offered the shares for sale and let the market "find its own level."

New share issues are not handled in this manner, however. A company typically engages a syndicate of securities firms to market the new issue. This selling effort increases the demand for the company's shares. Just how much it increases demand depends on the intensity and degree of success of the selling effort. If the proceeds from the new issue will be invested profitably, the company's share price will "recover" as information regarding this becomes more widely disseminated in the marketplace. If the expected return on equity exceeds the company's cost of equity capital and if the new issue is marketed successfully, it should be expected that the company's share price at the time of the offering (adjusted for movements in the general market since the announcement date) should exceed the preannouncement share price. This is illustrated by $P_2 > P_0$ in Figure 19-1.

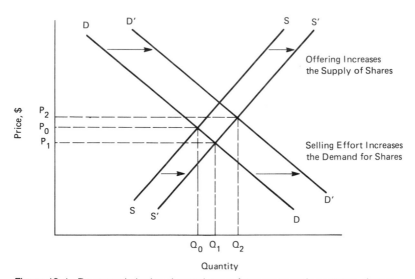

Figure 19-1. Downward-sloping demand curve for a company's common shares.

The *market impact* of a new share issue can be measured as the relative percentage change in the issuer's share price:

$$
\begin{aligned}
\text{Market} \atop \text{impact} \;=\; & \left[\left(\begin{array}{c} \text{initial public} \\ \text{offering} \\ \text{price} \end{array} - \begin{array}{c} \text{closing price} \\ \text{on day prior to} \\ \text{announcement} \\ \text{of offering} \end{array} \right) \div \begin{array}{c} \text{closing price} \\ \text{on day prior to} \\ \text{announcement} \\ \text{of offering} \end{array} \right] \\[2ex]
& - \left[\left(\begin{array}{c} \text{value of S\&P 500} \\ \text{at time of} \\ \text{pricing} \end{array} - \begin{array}{c} \text{closing S\&P 500} \\ \text{on day prior to} \\ \text{announcement} \\ \text{of offering} \end{array} \right) \div \begin{array}{c} \text{closing S\&P 500} \\ \text{on day prior to} \\ \text{announcement} \\ \text{of offering} \end{array} \right]
\end{aligned}
$$

Alternatively, 30 days prior to the offering date might be used in place of the announcement date. In Formula 19-1, the percentage change is adjusted for the change in the S&P 500 index to reflect the movement of the overall market during the same period. Table 19-1 indicates that the market impact can vary substantially from issue to issue. But market impact will tend to be greater the greater the percentage increase in the number of shares outstanding.[5]

Effective Spread. When an issuer's share price declines relative to the market because of an offering, the true spread the issuer pays is the *gross spread* adjusted for this market impact:

$$\text{Effective spread} \;=\; \text{gross spread} \;-\; \text{market impact} \qquad (19\text{-}2)$$

On the other hand, if the market impact of the issue is favorable, for example, because of particularly effective marketing, the effective spread is less than the gross spread by the amount of the favorable market impact. This distinction is important because, for example, an issuer who pays a 5% gross spread but whose stock rises 2% relative to the market (for a 3% effective spread) is better off than another issuer who pays a 4% gross spread but whose share price falls 2% relative to the market (for a 6% effective spread). Issuers who compare gross spreads and fail to take market impact into account are not comparing the true issuance costs.

How to Lower the Cost of a New Issue

In general, companies should sell new issues of common stock to those purchasers from whom they can realize the greatest net proceeds per share. Opportunities may arise for issuers to reduce costs of issuance and thereby realize greater net proceeds. One such opportunity that may present itself is increased institutional demand for an issue.[6] Institutional commission charges are substantially lower than retail commission charges. Thus, an issue targeted to institutional investors requires a smaller selling concession and hence gross spread than one targeted to retail purchasers. Table 19-2 illustrates the savings that are possible, based on a sample of 20 electric utility common stock offerings that were targeted to institutional investors in 1982 and 1983. On average, the percentage gross spread was 1.40% lower and the effective spread was 3.32% lower than in prior offerings by these companies during the 1977 to 1982 period. Consequently, if a company's shares are particularly attractive to institutional investors, targeting an issue, or even just a part of an issue, to that segment of the market can reduce issuance costs.

Timing

Issuers and their investment bankers typically spend a great deal of effort trying to time an offering appropriately. The objective, of course, is to realize the best possible price for the shares. But correct timing requires not only expert judgment but also a certain amount of luck because of the vagaries of the marketplace. Nevertheless, there are certain steps an issuer can take to minimize the timing risk:

- It is best not to offer shares too near an expiration date for options on the company's shares. Option-related buying and selling of the company's shares may affect the company's share price.
- It is generally preferable to issue during periods when the calendar of competing issues is relatively light. During periods in which there is temporarily a short supply of new issues, the sales forces of the leading securities firms can focus a greater proportion of their selling effort on each new issue.
- It is generally better to offer higher yielding common stocks just before rather than just after the ex-dividend date so as to take advantage of investor

Table 19-2
Cost Savings Realized by Targeting a Common
Stock Offering to Institutional Investors

	Institutional Offerings, %	Prior Offerings, %	Difference, %
Average percentage gross spread	1.94	3.34	−1.40*
Average market impact†	0.61	−1.09	1.70‡
Average effective spread§	1.34	4.66	−3.32*
Average percentage net proceeds	98.44	97.24	1.20*

*Statistically significant at the .005 level.

†Measured as the percentage change in share price relative to the percentage change in the Dow Jones Utility Index between the day prior to the announcement of the offering and the offering date. Negative value indicates a decrease in share price relative to the Dow Jones Utility Index.

‡Statistically significant at the .05 level.

§Calculated as the percentage gross spread less the market impact.

Source: John D. Finnerty, "How to Lower the Cost of Floating a New Stock Issue," *Public Utilities Fortnightly,* vol. 111, March 17, 1983, p. 29. Reprinted by permission.

dividend preferences, which can boost a company's share price above its equilibrium level just prior to the ex-dividend date but which can also depress the share price below its equilibrium level just after that date.[7]

■ It is generally better to offer common stock during periods of heightened demand for common stocks when investors are realigning their portfolios to increase the percentage of funds invested in common stocks, as occurred during 1982 to 1983.

■ Companies, like utilities, that have heavy common stock financing needs often find it advantageous to make two smaller offerings in lieu of one larger one. This enables them to hedge their price risk and reduces the potential market impact of the offering. The shelf registration process has reduced the cost of splitting an offering into multiple smaller offerings.

METHOD AND COST OF
A RIGHTS OFFERING

Instead of offering common stock to the general public, a company may instead restrict the offering to its current shareholders on a privileged-subscription basis. Such offerings are called *rights offerings* because the company distributes to its shareholders *rights* to *subscribe* for additional shares at a specified price. The corporate charters of many companies give current shareholders the *preemptive right* to subscribe for new issues of the company's common stock or of securities convertible into shares of the company's common stock. This is often the case when one narrow shareholder group controls a large percentage of the company's shares; preemptive rights give the shareholder group the right to maintain their respective ownership percentages of the company's common stock. However, in recent years, most large companies with widely dispersed shareholdings have received shareholder approval to eliminate preeemptive rights. Companies outside the United States tend to rely on rights offerings to raise additional equity capital to a greater extent than U.S. companies.

How a Rights Offering Works

In a rights offering, the company distributes to each shareholder one *right* for each share the holder owns as of the specified *record date* for the rights offering. Rights are exercisable prior to some stated *expiration date* on the basis of a specified number of rights and the payment of a stated amount of cash for each new share of common stock subscribed for. The length of the *subscription period* during which rights may be exercised typically varies between 14 and 24 days. For example, on October 18, 1978, Long Island Lighting Company offered 6,402,515 additional shares of its common stock to its current shareholders on the basis of one new share for seven rights (i.e., each seven shares already owned) plus a *subscription price* of $17.15 per new share during the 18-day subscription period. Shareholders can either (1) exercise the rights and subscribe for shares or (2) sell the rights, if they are transferable (they usually are); otherwise the rights will expire worthless at the close of business on the expiration date. In the 1978 Long Island Lighting Company rights offering, investors subscribed for 6,178,777 shares, representing 96.5% of the shares offered.

Value of Rights

To encourage shareholders to subscribe, the issuer establishes a subscription price that is less than the market price of its stock on the record date. This discount makes the rights valuable. Investment bankers generally recommend setting the subscription price so that each right will have an initial value of no less than $0.15 to $0.20. Establishing this minimum rights value is intended to induce nonsubscribing shareholders to sell their rights rather than let them expire.

The initial value of each right just after the offering is announced and when the stock is trading rights-on (i.e., when a purchaser is entitled to receive rights when they are distributed) is:

$$
\begin{aligned}
\text{Initial market value of one right} = & \left(\begin{array}{c} \text{market value} \\ \text{of share trading} \\ \text{rights-on} \end{array} - \begin{array}{c} \text{subscription} \\ \text{price} \end{array} \right) \\
& \div \left(\begin{array}{c} \text{number of rights} \\ \text{required to purchase} + 1 \\ \text{one share} \end{array} \right) \quad (19\text{-}3)
\end{aligned}
$$

The divisor in Formula 19-3 reflects the fact that for every *number of rights required to purchase one share* outstanding prior to the offering, there will be that number of shares plus 1 following the offering. For example, the initial value of each right issued in connection with the 1978 Long Island Lighting Company rights offering was:

$$
\text{Initial market value of one right} = \frac{\$18.375 - \$17.15}{7 + 1} = \$0.15
$$

when rounded to the nearest penny.

As soon as the stock begins trading ex-rights, buyers are no longer entitled to receive rights to subscribe for shares. The share price decreases by the value of the right to which it is no longer entitled:

$$
\begin{aligned}
\text{Share price ex-rights} = & \begin{array}{c} \text{market value} \\ \text{of share trading} \\ \text{rights-on} \end{array} - \begin{array}{c} \text{market value} \\ \text{of one right} \end{array} \quad (19\text{-}4)
\end{aligned}
$$

In the case of the 1978 Long Island Lighting Company rights offering,

$$\frac{\text{Share price}}{\text{ex-rights}} = \$18.375 - 0.15 = \$18.22$$

The offering of rights does not affect shareholder wealth; the value of a right plus the value of a share ex-rights should equal the value of a share rights-on. Prior to the rights offering, seven shares were worth $7 \times \$18.375 = \$128.625$. For every seven shares outstanding, the company issues one new share and receives $17.15. On the ex-date, each share is thus worth $(\$128.625 + 17.15)/(7 + 1) = \$18.22$.

Immediately thereafter, the market value of each right will vary with the price of the company's common stock:

$$\begin{array}{c}\text{Subsequent}\\ \text{market value}\\ \text{of one right}\end{array} = \left(\begin{array}{c}\text{share price}\\ \text{ex-rights}\end{array} - \begin{array}{c}\text{subscription}\\ \text{price}\end{array}\right) \div \begin{array}{c}\text{number of rights}\\ \text{required to purchase}\\ \text{one share}\end{array}$$

$$(19\text{-}5)$$

To continue the Long Island Lighting Company example, the market value of a right when the company's share price decreases to $18 should be

$$\begin{array}{c}\text{Subsequent}\\ \text{market value}\\ \text{of one right}\end{array} = \frac{\$18.00 - 17.15}{7} = \$0.12$$

when rounded to the nearest penny.

The valuation Formulas 19-3 and 19-5 provide the theoretical value of a right. The actual value may deviate from the theoretical value because of transaction costs, speculation, or concentrated selling of rights by nonsubscribers or concentrated buying of rights by subscribers during the subscription period.[8]

Setting the Subscription Price

The issuer should set the subscription price low enough so that there is little likelihood that its share price will fall below the subscription price during the subscription period. If the market price falls below the subscription price, shareholders will not exercise rights and subscribe for shares; they will be able to purchase shares more cheaply in the open market. The risk of this happening will depend to a great extent on the volatility of the company's share price and on the direction of movement of share prices generally during the subscription period.

Setting a lower subscription price does not affect shareholder wealth, but it does result in greater dilution in reported earnings per share because the company must issue a greater number of shares. In addition, the issuer will probably wish to preserve its current dividend rate because reducing the dividend rate to compensate for the larger issue size might signal a deterioration in the company's prospects and adversely affect the company's share price. But if the company maintains its dividend rate, the larger issue will mean greater dividend requirements. In order to minimize both dilution and the required increase in dividend requirements, companies generally prefer to engage securities firms to "stand by" to purchase unsubscribed shares on an underwritten basis rather than to reduce the subscription price in order to ensure a successful offering. Roughly two-thirds of all rights offerings are underwritten.

Establishing the Terms of a Rights Offering

Suppose that an issuer wishes to raise an amount *proceeds* via a rights offering to its shareholders. It must determine the appropriate *subscription price* and *subscription ratio*, the number of rights required to purchase one share, so as to achieve a target minimum *initial market value of one right* and realize its desired *proceeds*. Assuming the announcement of the offering will have no market impact, its current share price can serve as *market value of share trading rights-on*. The company should set the *subscription price* and *subscription ratio* so that:

$$
\begin{aligned}
\text{Subscription price} &= \left(\begin{array}{c} \text{market value} \\ \text{of share trading} \\ \text{rights-on} \end{array} - \begin{array}{c} \text{initial} \\ \text{market value} \\ \text{of one right} \end{array} \right) \\
&\div \left(1 + \frac{\begin{array}{c}\text{initial market} \\ \text{value of one right}\end{array} \times \begin{array}{c}\text{shares} \\ \text{outstanding}\end{array}}{\text{proceeds}} \right) \quad (19\text{-}6a)
\end{aligned}
$$

$$
\begin{aligned}
\text{Subscription ratio} &= \text{subscription price} \times \text{shares outstanding} \\
&\div \text{ proceeds} \quad\quad\quad\quad\quad\quad\quad (19\text{-}6b)
\end{aligned}
$$

First solve Formula 19-6a for subscription price. Then substitute that value into Formula 19-6b to solve for subscription ratio.

For example, suppose that a company has 30,000,000 shares outstanding that are trading at a price of $25 per share. Suppose further that it wishes to raise $50 million and that its investment banker has recommended a minimum rights value of $0.20 per right. Substituting into Formulas 19-6a and 19-6b gives

$$
\text{Subscription price} = \frac{\$25.00 - 0.20}{1 + (0.20 \times 30{,}000{,}000/50{,}000{,}000)} = \$22.14
$$

$$
\text{Subscription ratio} = \frac{\$22.14 \times 30{,}000{,}000}{\$50{,}000{,}000} = \$13.28
$$

One further step is required. The subscription ratio should be an integer value. The value obtained from Formula 19-6b should be *rounded down* to the nearest integer, in this case 13, because the initial value of the right should not be less than the desired minimum, in this case $0.20. A subscription ratio of one new share for each 13 outstanding requires a subscription price of $21.67 [= $50,000,000/(30,000,000/13)]. Rounding the subscription price to a convenient price, the company should offer its shareholders the right to subscribe for one new share for each 13 shares held at a price of $21.75 per share. Note that the initial market value of each right will be

$$\text{Initial market value of one right} = \frac{\$25.00 - 21.75}{14} = \$0.23$$

Advantages and Disadvantages of a Rights Offering

A rights offering preserves for shareholders the option of retaining their proportionate ownership and voting interests in a company when it sells additional common shares. But this is really beneficial only to shareholders with large holdings; a small shareholder can easily preserve his or her proportionate ownership and voting interest in a public offering simply by purchasing additional shares from the underwriters or in the open market.

A rights offering may also be more beneficial than a public offering to a company that does not have broad market appeal or that has concentrated stock ownership because it enables the selling effort to be focused on investors who already own shares and who are therefore familiar with the company. In addition, common stock issued in a rights offering can be purchased on margin whereas common stock issued in a public offering cannot.

It is also often argued that a rights offering is beneficial to shareholders because they can buy shares at a "bargain price" or because they perceive the rights as a "dividend." But as already noted, a stockholder receives no benefits from the rights; the company's share price falls following the ex-date and the decrease in price offsets the value of a right, as in the case of a stock dividend. The shareholder is just as well off following the rights offering as she or he was before it, provided she or he either sells the right or exercises it but, of course, is worse off is she or he fails to sell or exercise it.

On the other hand, there are three principal disadvantages to a rights offering. First, a rights offering generally takes longer to complete, which can be a serious disadvantage during periods of heightened market volatility. Second, the rights offering results in greater dilution in earnings per share and greater cash dividend requirements than a general public offering because of the need to set the subscription price below the market price in order to give the rights value and reduce the risk of an unsuccessful offering. Third, shares are not necessarily being sold to those investors who are willing to pay the highest price, as for example, a large institution that does not currently own shares but would like to and is willing to pay more than the prevailing market price but is prevented from accumulating a satisfactory share position because the stock is very thinly traded.

Rights Offering versus Public Offering

A company should issue new shares through a rights offering rather than an offering to the general public if the rights offering will afford a lower cost of equity capital. Financial textbooks typically argue that a rights offering provides a lower cost of funds. But, in practice, companies raise substantially more funds through public offerings than through rights offerings.

Issuance expenses are often lower in a rights offering. However, a recent study by Hansen and Pinkerton calculated the flotation costs associated with the sale of shares through nonunderwritten rights offerings to shareholders other than the parent company or some other holder of a large block of centrally controlled common stock and found that these costs were proportionately higher than the flotation costs in an underwritten public offering of the same size.[9] A rights offering is likely to involve lower issuance expenses if there is a small group that holds a large percentage of the shares *and* that small group agrees to exercise its rights. In addition, a recent study by White and Lusztig found that the announcement of a rights offering tends to have a significant negative impact on the issuer's share price.[10]

A nonunderwritten rights offering will generally involve lower issuance expenses than an underwritten rights offering. However, the issuer must be willing to bear the risk of market changes and there are other implicit costs to consider. Bearing the risk that the share price might fall below the subscription price and cause the offering to be unsuccessful imposes a cost. The Hansen and Pinkerton study thus suggests that unless a company has a major shareholder group that will agree to exercise its rights, it is in the issuer's shareholders' best interest to use the underwritten public offering method to distribute the offering.

DIVIDEND REINVESTMENT PLANS AND EMPLOYEE STOCK PLANS

Many companies have instituted *dividend reinvestment plans* that give shareholders the opportunity to reinvest dividends plus supplementary cash plus, in some cases, interest payments on the company's bonds and/or dividend payments on the company's preferred stock in newly issued shares of the company's common stock. To an increasing extent, companies are permitting shareholders to reinvest dividends and, in some cases, to invest other cash payments in shares at a discount from the prevailing price of the stock. When offered, this discount is typically 5%, which is intended to approximate the proportionate issuance expenses and market impact of a public offering. Companies also often provide *employee stock plans* that give their employees the right to subscribe for shares of the company's stock, often at a discount from the prevailing market price of the stock.

Dividend reinvestment plans and employee stock plans can represent a significant source of additional common equity to a company. Dividend reinvestment plans raised approximately $4.6 billion in 1983, representing more than 10% of the amount raised through sales of additional common shares that year.

New Issue Dividend Reinvestment Plans

A new issue dividend reinvestment plan is very similar to a rights offering. In general, only existing shareholders are entitled to participate.[11] They represent an alternative to a public offering of shares or a conventional rights offering as a source of additional common equity. New issue plans provide a more or less regular quarterly infusion of additional common equity. The amount of capital a company can raise depends, of course, on the amount of dividends it pays and on the percentage of dividends and the amount of supplementary cash its shareholders decide to reinvest. Utility companies, which have the highest payout ratio of any industry group, have been the most active proponents of new issue dividend reinvestment plans.

In general, even for electric utilities, new issue plans will not be able to produce sufficient funds over the course of the year to replace a public offering. However, because such sales are spread over the year and the purchasers are shareholders who have previously indicated a desire to purchase, there is probably little, if any, market impact. In addition, companies do not have to pay any underwriting commission or standby fee to investment bankers, and offering shares through a new issue plan requires at most a minimal commitment of management time. Consequently, new issue plans will generally yield common equity capital at a lower cost than a public offering.

The administrative costs of a new issue dividend reinvestment plan make such plans a more expensive source of additional common equity than retained earnings. Nevertheless, when shareholders have a net preference for dividends over capital gains, as electric utility shareholders appear to, introducing a new issue plan reduces the cost of raising the payout ratio. Thus, the increase in electric utility company payout ratios that occurred during the 1970s, as new issue plans proliferated in that industry, can be attributed in part to the narrowing of the differential between the cost of retained earnings and the cost of common equity from other sources.

COMPARATIVE COST OF COMMON EQUITY FROM DIFFERENT SOURCES

Formulas 8-6 and 8-7 give the cost of retained earnings and the cost of a new common stock issue (sold via public offering), respectively. The only difference between the two formulas is that the denominator in Formula 8-7 contains an adjustment factor, which reflects the fact that the net proceeds per share in a public offering are less than the share price. We can generalize on this result:

$$
\begin{Bmatrix} \text{Cost of} \\ \text{additional} \\ \text{common equity} \end{Bmatrix} = \left\{ \begin{Bmatrix} \text{indicated} \\ \text{annual} \\ \text{dividend rate} \end{Bmatrix} \div \left[\begin{matrix} \text{current} \\ \text{share price} \end{matrix} \times \left(1 - \begin{matrix} \text{issuance} \\ \text{costs} \end{matrix} \right) \right] \right\}
$$

$$
+ \begin{matrix} \text{projected} \\ \text{dividend} \\ \text{growth rate} \end{matrix} \qquad\qquad (19\text{-}7)
$$

The issuance costs associated with each source of funds determine the relative cost of funds from that source. Retained earnings are generally cheapest because *issuance costs* = 0. Public offerings and rights offerings are generally most expensive. Dividend reinvestment plans and employee stock plans fall in between: There are no underwriting fees; there is little, if any, market impact; and out-of-pocket expenses are much lower than in a public offering or a rights offering.

It is important to note that *issuance costs* in connection with dividend reinvestment plans, rights offerings, and employee stock plans do *not* include the discount, if any, on the shares offered. In the case of dividend reinvestment plans and rights offerings, shareholders effectively offer the discount to themselves. In the case of employee stock plans, the discount is more appropriately treated as an employee compensation expense. Issuance costs in Formula 19-7 consist of expenses that shareholders must pay to third parties.

SUMMARY

There are seven principal sources of additional common equity capital: retained earnings, public offering of new shares, rights offering of new shares to current shareholders, private placement of new shares, sale of new shares through a dividend reinvestment or employee stock plan, contribution of shares in lieu of cash to the company's pension plan, or conversion of convertible securities. Public offerings account for most of the new common equity capital companies raise from external sources. In evaluating the cost of common equity associated with a public offering, it is important to consider the effective spread rather than simply the gross spread paid to the underwriters.

Instead of offering new shares to the general public, a company can restrict the offering to existing shareholders on a privileged-subscription basis. Rights offerings, at least in the United States, are typically made by companies controlled by a narrow shareholder group that wishes to retain its percentage ownership interest. A rights offering can also be advantageous to a company that does not enjoy broad market appeal or whose shareholders might be particularly receptive to a new share offering. However, rights offerings take longer to complete and so involve greater market exposure than a public offering, cause offering, cause greater dilution, lead to greater cash dividend requirements, and permit the company and its underwriters less control over marketing strategy. When all the costs associated with each method of offering are properly allowed for, the underwritten public offering is cheaper than a rights offering for most companies. It is not surprising, therefore, that the underwritten public offering is the more widely used technique for raising large amounts of new common equity capital.

Many companies have introduced new issue dividend reinvestment plans and employee stock plans. Such programs represent a continuing source of additional equity capital at a lower cost than a public offering. A new issue dividend reinvestment plan supplemented by occasional public offerings is the most cost-effective strategy for raising new common equity capital externally for companies, such as utilities, that maintain a high payout ratio.

Chapter 20

Issuing Long-Term Debt and Preferred Stock

This chapter reviews the principal features of long-term debt and preferred stock and describes a series of analytical models a company can use to decide how to tailor the terms of a long-term debt or preferred stock issue to fit its particular circumstances. The chapter also describes how to determine when preferred stock is cheaper to issue than debt.

FEATURES OF LONG-TERM DEBT

This section characterizes the principal features of long-term debt. Subsequent sections explore the implications of each of these features for the cost of debt and the issuer's overall financial flexibility.

Principal Classes of Long-Term Debt

There are five principal classes of long-term corporate debt instruments: unsecured debt, secured debt, income bonds, tax-exempt debt, and convertible debt. Convertible bonds are discussed in the next chapter.

Unsecured Debt. Unsecured long-term debt consists of notes and debentures. By securities industry convention, the term *notes* is normally used to describe unsecured bonds with an original maturity of 10 years or less and the term *debentures* is normally used when the original maturity exceeds 10 years. Notes and debentures are issued on the strength of the issuer's general credit; they are not secured by specific property. If the issuer goes bankrupt, note holders and debenture holders become general creditors. Consequently, note and debenture holders look to covenant restrictions in the contracts governing their loans for protection.

331

Debentures may be issued in different levels of seniority. *Subordinated debentures* rank behind (unsubordinated) debentures in terms of the payment of interest and principal and the distribution of the company's assets in the event of liquidation. Consequently, subordinated debentures carry a higher interest rate than senior debt of the same company.

Secured Debt. There are several types of secured debt: mortgage bonds, collateral trust bonds, collateralized mortgage obligations (CMOs), equipment trust certificates, and conditional sales contracts are the most common. An issue of *mortgage bonds* is secured by a lien on specific assets of the issuer, which are described in detail in the legal document, called a *mortgage*, that conveys the lien. *Collateral trust bonds* are similar to mortgage bonds except that the lien is against securities. If the issuer defaults in the payment of principal or interest or in the performance of some other provision of the loan contract, lenders (or the trustee acting on their behalf) can seize the assets securing the bonds and sell them to pay off the debt obligation. If the proceeds are insufficient to satisfy the claims of bond holders in full, they become general creditors alongside debenture holders for the balance of their claim. The mortgage thus provides extra protection not available to debenture holders, and this extra protection facilitates a lower interest rate. However, the issuer sacrifices flexibility in selling assets because mortgaged assets can be removed from the asset pool only with mortgage bond holders' permission or if suitable substitute collateral is provided. *Collateralized mortgage obligations* are similar to collateral trust bonds except that the CMOs are secured by a pool of mortgages and the debt service on the CMOs depends on the flow of interest and principal payments from the mortgage pool.

Equipment trust certificates are frequently issued to finance the purchase of railroad rolling stock, aircraft, and certain other types of equipment that is readily saleable. A trust is formed to purchase the equipment and lease it to the user. The trust issues the certificates to finance 75 to 85% of the purchase price and holds title to the equipment until the last of the certificates has been fully repaid, at which time title passes to the lessee. Because the trustee can immediately repossess the property and resell it in the event of bankruptcy, equipment trust certificates provide good security, and accordingly typically carry a rating one full category higher than the lessee's senior debt rating. Consequently, they afford relatively low-cost debt. *Conditional sales contracts* are similar to equipment trust certificates except that the lender is either the equipment manufacturer or a bank or finance company to whom the manufacturer has sold the conditional sales contract (rather than a third-party trust).

Income Bonds. Some, or in many cases all, of the interest on an *income bond* is contingent on the issuer's income (hence the bond's name). The bond indenture specifies an earnings test, and interest must be paid if the company has sufficient income under the test. In contrast, preferred stock dividends are paid at the discretion of the company's board of directors. Thus, investors should prefer income bonds over preferred stocks. Because the contingent nature of interest payments reduces the risk of bankruptcy, issuers should find both securities to be of comparable riskiness. Moreover, the fixed formula has, until recently, enabled issuers to deduct interest payments on income bonds for tax purposes, giving a significant cost advantage over preferred stock. One of the great puzzles in finance has been why so many companies issued preferred stock rather than income bonds when income bonds seemed to offer greater advantages for both the issuer and investors.[1]

Income bonds are less attractive to corporate investors than preferred stock because of the 85% dividends received deduction. They are less attractive to highly risk averse lenders than straight debt because of the contingent nature of interest payments. Income bonds may have also suffered an image problem because they have most frequently been issued in connection with railroad reorganizations. In addition, as a result of a recent tax change, there is the risk that the Internal Revenue Service will recharacterize an income "bond" as equity if the contingent payments are responsible for 50% or more of the bond's value.

Tax-Exempt Corporate Debt. Corporations are permitted under the Internal Revenue Code to issue tax-exempt bonds for certain specified purposes. Bond holders do not have to pay federal income tax on the interest payments they receive and so they are willing to accept a lower interest rate than on taxable debt. As a general rule, if a company plans to construct facilities that qualify for tax-exempt financing, it should use such financing to the maximum extent possible.

Principal Features of Long-Term Debt
The preceding discussion highlighted the principal differences among the various classes of long-term debt. More important from an analytical standpoint, long-term debt instruments share certain common features:

- A stated *maturity* by which time the borrowed funds must be fully repaid. In contrast, common stock does not have a stated maturity and preferred stock issues often do not have stated maturities.
- A stated *principal (or face) amount*, which represents the borrower's repayment obligation.
- A stated *coupon rate of interest* (possibly zero). Long-term debt issues pay interest at regular intervals, semiannually on domestic issues, and annually on Eurobond issues, typically at a *fixed rate* but sometimes on a *floating-rate basis*.
- A *mandatory redemption* (or *sinking fund*) *schedule*, which calls for a sequence of *mandatory redemption payments* (i.e., principal repayments)

prior to the maturity date. Bonds are generally redeemed through the sinking fund at their face amount (i.e., *at par*).

Instead of incorporating a sinking fund provision, a corporation can issue *serial bonds*. But even if the redemption schedules are identical, serial bonds and sinking fund bonds involve significant differences. All the bonds of a sinking fund issue are available to meet any particular sinking fund obligation, which provides the issuer the flexibility to repurchase bonds at a discount on the sinking fund date if interest rates rise following issuance. Each series of a serial bond issue is separate so that its price approaches par on the redemption date. Because of the greater refunding flexibility, corporate issuers have generally preferred to incorporate a sinking fund provision over issuing bonds in series.

- An *optional redemption provision*. Issuers of long-term debt typically have the right to *call* the issue (or some portion of it) for early redemption according to a schedule of *optional redemption* (or *call*) *prices* that scales down by equal annual amounts from par plus the coupon the first year to par call for 1 or more years immediately prior to maturity. This option is valuable to the issuer (but disadvantageous to bond holders) if interest rates drop after the debt is issued. Accordingly, the issuer's ability to call bonds for optional redemption is typically restricted during the first several years the bonds are outstanding.

Protective Covenants

A long-term bond is evidenced by a legal contract between the borrower and the lenders. A long-term lender provides funds for an extended period, as long as 40 years in some cases. Consequently, a lender will require that the loan contract contain provisions that will protect the lender and, in particular, that will alert the lender if the borrower's financial condition should deteriorate significantly.

These provisions take the form of certain *negative covenants* which limit the borrower's ability to: (1) incur additional indebtedness (*debt limitation*), (2) use cash to pay dividends or make share repurchases (*dividend limitation*), (3) mortgage assets (*limitation on liens* and/or a *negative pledge clause*), (4) borrow through one of its subsidiaries (*limitation on subsidiary borrowing*), (5) sell major assets (*limitation on asset dispositions*), (6) merge with or into another company or sell substantially all assets to another company (*limitation on merger, consolidation, or sale*), and (7) sell assets and lease them back (*limitation on sale-and-lease-back*); or which require the borrower to maintain a certain minimum current ratio and/or minimum level of working capital (*current ratio test* and *working capital maintenance test*, respectively) and/or to maintain a specified minimum net worth (*net worth maintenance test*). In addition, there are *affirmative covenants*, which impose certain obligations on the borrower. Most are fairly innocuous, for example, requiring the borrower to maintain its properties properly, keep accurate financial records, comply with applicable laws and regulations, pay taxes, and furnish lenders with financial statements quarterly. However, issuers whose financial strength merits a double-A or triple-A rating, and even the stronger single-A-rated issuers, are generally not required to include any debt limitation, dividend limitation, current ratio test, working capital maintenance test, net worth maintenance test, or similar financial restrictions in the indentures for their long-term debt issues. Lenders instead rely on the borrower's continuing financial prudence.

Loan agreements also specify certain *events of default*. If the borrower fails to pay interest or repay principal promptly (subject possibly to a short grace period), defaults on another debt issue, or fails to adhere to one of the covenants, the lenders (or a trustee acting on their behalf) can demand repayment of the debt. But covenants are designed to serve simply as an early warning system; in most cases, the trustee and/or lenders will work with the borrower to make changes to the borrowing company's operating policies or make management changes or take other steps designed to restore the borrower's financial health. Only as a last resort will lenders demand repayment and likely force the company into bankruptcy.

A prospective borrower should seek to negotiate covenant restrictions that do not limit its operating flexibility. Loan agreements for other borrowers whose credit standing is comparable will indicate covenant restrictions lenders have accepted in similar circumstances as well as the covenant trade-offs they are willing to accept. The borrower should also try to achieve covenants that are consistent with and, if possible, not less restrictive than those in its previous long-term debt issues in order to minimize the cost of monitoring its compliance.

CHOICE OF DEBT MATURITY

A corporation that plans to sell a new issue of debt must decide what terms are appropriate in the light of prevailing market conditions.

Principal Considerations

There are four important aspects to the choice of maturity. First, the debt repayment schedule should not bunch the company's debt repayment obligations. Second, during periods of generally rising interest rates, fixed-rate debt with a longer maturity will normally prove cheaper than shorter-term debt that is rolled over at successively higher interest rates. Third, if the company is taking steps to strengthen its credit standing, a maturity somewhat shorter than would otherwise be called for would be appropriate because a company's cost of borrowing will tend to fall as its financial condition strengthens. Fourth, selling longer-term debt typically requires a yield premium.

Shorter-Term Issue versus Longer-Term Issue

The yield curve is said to be upward-sloping when an issue that calls for full repayment on one date requires a higher yield to maturity than an issue of the same credit standing that calls for full repayment on an earlier date. Graphically, the curve linking different maturity-yield combinations moves upward and to the right as in Figure 20-1. For example, a company might be able to issue debt maturing in 7 years at an interest cost of 10% or debt maturing in 20 years at an interest cost of 12%. Which alternative is more attractive? In recent years, issuers' expectations that interest rates would drop back to historical levels coupled with the yield premium that long-term bond investors required for a maturity of 20 years or longer shifted the mix of long-term debt issues toward the 5- to 10-year maturity range.

If a company issues 7-year debt rather than 20-year debt, it will have to refund the 7-year issue. One technique for approaching the choice of maturity is to calculate the break-even refunding rate, that is, the interest cost of a 13-year refunding issue required to make the company indifferent between selling a 7-year issue and a 20-year issue. A corporation will be indifferent between issuing intermediate-term fixed-rate debt and long-term fixed-rate debt only if the two alternatives have the same after-tax cost of borrowing. Flotation costs will not be an important factor in this decision so they can be ignored. The two alternatives will be equally attractive only if the refunding issue carries an interest rate equal to *break-even refunding rate* that satisfies the following equation:

$$
\begin{aligned}
\text{Amount of issue} = & \sum_{t=1}^{2I} \left[\left(1 - \frac{\text{tax}}{\text{rate}}\right) \times \frac{\text{interest}(t) \text{ on}}{\text{intermediate}} + \frac{\text{sinking}}{\text{fund}(t)} \right] \\
& \div \left(1 + \tfrac{1}{2} \begin{array}{c} \text{cost of} \\ \text{long-term} \\ \text{issue} \end{array} \right)^t \\
& + \sum_{t=2I+1}^{2T} \left[\left(1 - \frac{\text{tax}}{\text{rate}}\right) \times \begin{array}{c} \text{interest}(t) \text{ at} \\ \text{break-even} \\ \text{refunding rate} \end{array} + \frac{\text{sinking}}{\text{fund}(t)} \right] \\
& \div \left(1 + \tfrac{1}{2} \begin{array}{c} \text{cost of} \\ \text{long-term} \\ \text{issue} \end{array} \right)^t
\end{aligned}
\tag{20-1}
$$

In Formula 20-1, the intermediate-term issue matures after $2I$ interest periods, and the refunding issue matures when the long-term issue would. The amount

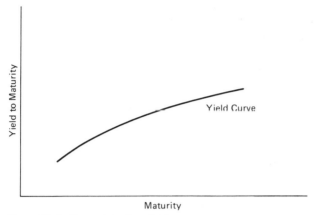

Figure 20-1. Upward-sloping yield curve.

interest(t) at break-even refunding rate represents the amount of interest owing on the refunding issue at the end of period t when the issue carries the *break-even refunding rate*.

Example of Break-Even Refunding
Rate Calculation

Suppose a company faces the two alternatives specified in Table 20-1. If it is assumed that the 7-year issue will not be refunded prior to maturity, the refunding issue would have a 13-year maturity. The debt service requirements are substituted into Formula 20-1 along with *cost of long-term issue* $= 0.06$ and the resulting equation is solved iteratively for

$$\text{Break-even refunding rate} \ = \ 14.15\%$$

If the company expects the interest rate for its 13-year debt to be less than 14.15% at the end of year 7, it should issue the intermediate-term debt. If it expects its 13-year new issue rate to exceed 14.15% at the end of year 7, it should instead sell the long-term issue.

The break-even calculation assumes the intermediate-term issue remains outstanding until it matures. If the intermediate-term issue permits 3 years of par call, the issuer has the flexibility to shorten the issue's maturity to 4 years at no cost. The break-even refunding rate is lower the sooner the intermediate-term issue is refunded.

Finally, the intermediate-term issue affords greater refunding flexibility. If interest rates drop, the intermediate-term issue can be called after the fourth year at par whereas the long-term issue cannot be called until the end of the fifth year and then only at a premium. Because of this, even if the corporation thinks it somewhat more likely that new issue rates will be above the break-even refunding rate, it might nevertheless prefer to issue intermediate-term debt.

SIGNIFICANCE OF INCLUDING A SINKING FUND

When the yield curve is upward-sloping, including a sinking fund should result in a lower interest rate on the debt issue because the debt obligation is repaid,

Table 20-1
Break-Even Analysis for Intermediate-Term Debt Versus Long-Term Debt
(Dollar Amounts in Millions)

I. Issue Terms

	Long-Term Issue	Intermediate-Term Issue	Refunding Issue
Amount	$50 million	$50 million	$50 million
Coupon	12%	10%	Break-even refunding rate
Maturity	20 years	7 years	13 years
Call protection	5 years	4 years	5 years
Sinking fund	$10 million each in years 16–20	none	$10 million each in years 9–13
Years of par call	3 years	3 years	3 years

II. Debt Service on Intermediate-Term Debt/Refunding Issue Package

Interest Period	After-Tax Interest*	Sinking Fund Payment	Interest Period	After-Tax Interest*	Sinking Fund Payment
1–14	$1.25	—	36	$30 × BERR/4	$10.00
15–31	50 × BERR/4	—	37	20 × BERR/4	—
32	50 × BERR/4	$10.00	38	20 × BERR/4	10.00
33	40 × BERR/4	—	39	10 × BERR/4	—
34	40 × BERR/4	10.00	40	10 × BERR/4	10.00
35	30 × BERR/4	—			

III. Sensitivity of Break-Even Refunding Rate to Year of Refunding

	Intermediate-Term Issue Redeemed at End of Year			
	4	5	6	7
Break-even refunding rate	12.95%	13.29%	13.68%	14.15%

**Break-Even Analysis for Intermediate-Term
Debt Versus Long-Term Debt** *(Continued)*

(Dollar Amounts in Millions)

IV. Improvement in Refunding Flexibility Due to Intermediate-Term Issue			
	Break-Even Refunding Rate Assuming Issuance of		
Refunded at End of Year	Long-Term Debt†	Intermediate- Term Debt‡	Difference
5	10.87%	12.00%	113 b.p.§
6	10.95	12.00	105
7	10.94	12.00	106

*Assumes a marginal corporate income tax rate of 50%. BERR denotes the break-even refunding rate.

†Interest rate at which the corporation would be indifferent between refunding the long-term issue and leaving it outstanding.

‡Interest rate at which the net present value of the refunding would be zero.

§Basis points.

on average, more quickly than it would be if it were repaid fully at maturity (a so-called *bullet maturity*).[2]

Average Life

When a debt issue provides for a sinking fund, the issue's maturity overstates the length of the period the original debt remains outstanding. For example, a debt issue that matures in 10 years but involves equal sinking fund payments at the end of years 6 through 10 has what might be thought of as an effective maturity of 8 years. This effective maturity is called *average life*.

Average Life Formula. The average life of a debt issue is calculated by weighting the timing of each sinking fund payment by the proportion of the issue repaid through that sinking fund payment:

$$\text{Average life} = \sum_{t=1}^{\text{maturity}} t \times (\text{sinking fund payment at end of year } t$$

$$\div \text{ aggregate principal amount of issue}) \qquad (20\text{-}2)$$

Illustration of Average Life Calculation. A company issues $50 million principal amount of sinking fund debentures, which call for payments of $4 million each at the end of years 10 through 19 and a balloon payment of $10 million at the end of year 20. Applying Formula 20-2,

$$\text{Average life} = [4 \times (10 + 11 + 12 + 13 + 14 + 15 + 16$$
$$+ 17 + 18 + 19) + (10 \times 20)] \div 50$$
$$= 15.6 \text{ years}$$

Impact of Including a Sinking Fund on Cost of Debt

Incorporating a sinking fund affords three types of potential cost savings. First, the sinking fund shortens the issue's average life, and this results in a lower cost of borrowing when the yield curve is upward-sloping. Second, the sinking fund schedule spreads out the debt repayment obligation, and this reduces the risk of default. Third, if interest rates fall following issuance, a sinking fund issue will have a lower realized cost of debt than a non–sinking fund issue of equal maturity because the sinking fund will enable the issuer to redeem portions of the issue at par and refund them at the lower prevailing interest rates. However, the opposite situation occurs if interest rates rise following issuance. Formula 20-1 can be used to calculate a break-even refunding rate for the rolled over sinking fund payments in order to help an issuer decide whether to include a sinking fund.

Value of the Delivery Option in Public Debt Issues. Rising interest rates also create an opportunity for the issuer of publicly held debt to repurchase bonds at a discount in the open market and deliver them to the trustee in satisfaction of sinking fund requirements. For example, suppose a company issues 2-year debt bearing a 10% coupon rate and amortizing in two equal annual installments. If interest rates rise to 12% one year after issuance and the issue is publicly traded, the price per bond will be $98.21\% = 110/1.12$. The issuer can repurchase bonds in the open market to satisfy the sinking fund requirement. The realized cost of debt (before flotation costs) is just the internal rate of return that equates the present value of the after-tax debt service stream to the gross proceeds (assume $1 for purposes of illustration):

$$1 = \frac{(1 - 0.5) \times 1 \times 0.1}{1 + \text{IRR}} + \frac{0.5 \times 0.9821}{1 + \text{IRR}}$$
$$+ \frac{(1 - 0.5) \times 0.5 \times 0.1}{(1 + \text{IRR})^2} + \frac{0.5}{(1 + \text{IRR})^2} \qquad (20\text{-}3)$$

$$\text{Realized cost of debt} = \text{IRR} = 4.39\%$$

assuming a 50% tax rate. If the issue were privately placed, however, the issuer would not be able to reacquire the bonds in the market. The issuer would have to redeem them at par. As a result, the realized cost of debt would be 5.00%.

Because privately placed debt generally does not grant a delivery option, there is a cost advantage to issuing debt publicly.

SETTING THE INTEREST RATE

Most issuers of long-term debt select the fixed coupon rate of interest that makes the bonds worth par. However, at times issuers have found it advantageous either to set the coupon rate below the applicable prevailing market rate or to let the interest rate float according to some specified formula.

Deep Discount Bonds

In 1981 and 1982, many corporations issued so-called *deep discount bonds*. They carried very low interest rates, in some cases zero, and accordingly were sold at prices representing deep discounts from their principal amounts. Certain investors, particularly pension funds, found the deep discount bonds and zero coupon bonds attractive. They are generally callable at par and so the deep discount offers a high degree of call protection. Of course, this reduces the issuer's refunding flexibility. The discount also reduces the lender's reinvestment risk because the investor's "income" each period is effectively reinvested at the issue's yield to maturity regardless of what interest rates are at the time. In addition, deep discount bonds tend to be more price volatile than full-coupon bonds and thus offer greater potential for price appreciation if interest rates should fall.

Issuers also found the deep discount bonds and zero coupon bonds attractive because they were permitted to deduct for tax purposes a pro rata portion of the original issue discount each period. Interest could be deducted at a faster rate than it accrued, which substantially reduced the effective after-tax cost of the debt. The Tax Equity and Fiscal Responsibility Act of 1982 eliminated this tax advantage. Zero coupon bonds became attractive again in 1984 because certain foreign investors, who were able to realize the discount tax-free, were willing to accept a much lower pretax yield than a comparable full-coupon issue would have required. In general, deep discount bonds represent an attractive borrowing alternative when there is a large enough yield advantage to compensate for the loss of refunding flexibility.

Analytical Procedure. The yield-refunding flexibility trade-off can be analyzed in the following manner:

- Calculate the realized after-tax cost of issuing conventional current coupon debt. Evaluate this cost under alternative interest rate scenarios assuming that the issue is refunded when it is profitable to do so.
- Calculate the realized after-tax cost of issuing comparable deep discount bonds for the same interest rate scenarios.

■ Choose the alternative which is generally cheaper under the interest rate scenarios that are considered the most likely to occur.

Example of Deep Discount Bond Analysis. Figure 20-2 applies this method of analysis to the following two alternatives: (1) a 20-year non–sinking fund bond not callable for five years that is sold at par with a 12% coupon and (2) a 20-year deep discount bond (without sinking fund) that carries a 6% coupon, that provides an 11% yield to maturity, and that consequently is priced at 59.885%, or $598.85 per bond. The curve indicates the year-refunding rate combinations that would make the issuer indifferent between the two alternatives. If interest rates fall within the shaded region in Figure 20-2, the conventional current coupon issue will involve the lower realized after-tax cost.

Fixing the Interest Rate or Letting It Float

A floating interest rate benefits the issuer when market interest rates fall but proves more costly than a fixed interest rate when market interest rates rise. Companies such as banks and finance companies whose return on assets fluctuates with interest rate movements often find it prudent to issue such debt. For example, General Motors Acceptance Corporation issued $250 million principal amount of Adjustable Rate Notes due November 15, 1990 on November 13,

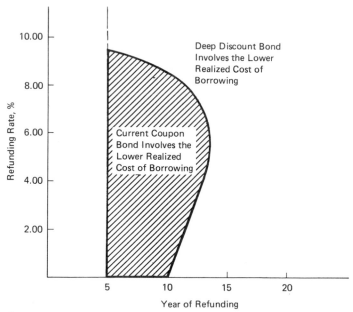

Figure 20-2. Comparison of conventional current coupon bond and deep discount bond.

1980. The interest rate on these notes is adjusted annually beginning 2 years from the date of issue. On each adjustment date, it is set equal to 107.2% of the arithmetic average of the two most recent weekly average yields to maturity of U.S. Treasury securities adjusted to a constant maturity of 10 years.[3]

Before deciding whether to issue floating rate long-term debt, a company should compare the prospective terms for such an issue against the following alternatives:

- Issuing a sequence of shorter-term issues whose successive maturities match the successive interest rate adjustment dates.
- Issuing fixed-rate debt that matures the day the floating-rate issue does.

The sequence of shorter-term issues involves roughly the same degree of interest rate risk as the longer-term floating-rate issue. The sequence of shorter-term issues involves greater issuance expenses but a lower yield premium relative to the yield curve for U.S. Treasury securities because a longer maturity generally requires a greater liquidity premium and a greater credit risk premium. However, companies can achieve the issuance expense savings by issuing *extendible notes*. These securities permit the issuer to reset the interest rate at regular intervals, typically every 3 years, but give holders the right to put the bonds back to the issuer immediately thereafter. As long as the issuer resets the interest rate at a market level, the put option will not be exercised and the debt will thus effectively be rolled over.

In the second case, the floating-rate issue exposes the issuer to the risk that interest rates will change. If the issuer's revenues are not sensitive to interest rate movements, this will increase the firm's financial risk. Companies are generally averse to such risks. Consequently, such an issuer would prefer the floating-rate alternative only if it expects interest rates to fall significantly on average. On the other hand, when the issuer's revenues are sensitive to movements in interest rates, borrowing on a floating-rate basis may actually reduce the company's financial risk by aligning the fluctuations in revenues and interest expense.

Interest Rate Swaps

Interest rate swaps provide a mechanism by which lower-rated issuers can borrow more cheaply than if they sold debt directly to investors in the public or private fixed rate debt markets. In the simplest form of swap, two issuers of different credit standing borrow equal amounts simultaneously: The stronger credit sells fixed-interest-rate bonds, and the weaker credit borrows at a floating interest rate under a loan agreement of matching maturity. The two companies then swap interest rate obligations with the interest rates adjusted so as to compensate the stronger credit for agreeing to enter into the swap arrangement. Thus, no principal changes hands. Because the interest rate differential on short-term loans to the borrowers is less than the interest rate differential on longer-term loans to them, it is mutually advantageous to arbitrage between the fixed rate and floating rate markets. Typically, the stronger credit, often a commercial bank, wishes to borrow on a short-term basis anyway. It simply uses its longer-term credit capacity to reduce its cost of short-term debt.

For example, suppose a triple-B-rated company can borrow on a short-term basis at LIBOR plus 0.5% and on a long-term basis at 12% but that the commercial bank can borrow on a short-term basis at LIBOR and on a long-term basis at 10.50%. Suppose the bank borrows on a long-term basis, the triple-B-rated company borrows on a short-term basis, and the two swap interest payment obligations with the company agreeing to pay the bank 10.50% and the bank agreeing to pay the company LIBOR minus 0.50%. The company saves 150 basis points (12% minus 10.50%) on its fixed-rate obligation but loses 100 basis points on its floating-rate obligation, for a net saving of 50 basis points. The bank also saves 50 basis points because it borrows effectively at LIBOR minus 0.50%.[4]

SETTING THE OPTIONAL REDEMPTION PROVISIONS

The *optional redemption*, or *call, provision* gives the issuer the flexibility to call the issue for redemption if interest rates fall significantly following issuance or if the issuer desires to eliminate troublesome covenant restrictions. Virtually all corporate debt issues include call provisions, and as noted earlier in the chapter, the call provision has become highly standardized. Including a call provision is generally mutually advantageous to the issuer and investors for tax reasons.[5] The issuer can deduct the call premium from ordinary income, whereas a bond investor who has held the bonds long enough pays tax on it at capital gains rates. Also, corporations pay tax at a higher marginal rate than most bond investors (such as pension funds, which are tax-exempt) so that the interest rate premium borrowers pay investors on account of the call option involves a net tax benefit.

FREQUENCY AND TIMING OF DEBT ISSUES

There are economies of scale in issuing long-term debt, and investors are more receptive to issues that are large enough to ensure that a relatively liquid secondary market for the bonds will develop. Consequently, companies issue long-term debt in large, discrete amounts.

As a general rule, a company should sell long-term debt when it finds the market receptive rather than waiting until it absolutely has to. This is particularly true for companies whose senior debt is rated less than investment-grade. During periods of tight money or particularly volatile interest rates, the market for non-investment-grade bonds has shrunk. During such periods, even triple-B-rated issuers have been forced to accept tighter covenant restrictions or shorter maturities than they are accustomed to.

Even under normal market conditions, issuers can sometimes benefit by accelerating or delaying an issue. A variety of factors can affect the debt markets. A large Treasury financing, for example, can temporarily depress the debt market. Issuers must remain flexible with respect to timing in order to prevent temporary factors from adversely affecting their cost of borrowing.

Gauging the Cost of Waiting to Issue Long-Term Debt

A company can use Formula 20-1 to gauge the cost of delaying a long-term debt issue. The short-term debt remains outstanding for $2I$ periods; the interest cost of the short-term debt replaces the interest cost of the intermediate-term issue; and *break-even long-term rate* replaces break-even refunding rate.

For example, suppose a company that contemplates a 20-year bullet maturity issue expects interest rates to decrease over the next 6 months. The company would have to pay a 12% coupon rate to sell such an issue currently but can sell 30-day commercial paper at a 10% discount rate. Its income tax rate is 50%.

Applying Formula 17-5b, the *coupon equivalent yield* of the 30-day commercial paper is

$$\text{Coupon equivalent yield} = \frac{0.1 \times 365}{360 - 0.1 \times 30} = 0.1022, \text{ or } 10.22\%$$

If the company is contemplating waiting six months, it must allow for the compounding effect of rolling over the commercial paper 182.5/30 times during the 6-month period:

$$\begin{array}{l}\text{Effective cost of} \\ \text{short-term debt}\end{array} = \left(1 + \frac{0.1022}{365/30}\right)^{182.5/30} - 1 = 0.0522$$

per 6-month period, or 10.44% expressed on an annualized basis.

Substituting amount of issue = \$1, tax rate = 0.5, interest(t) on short-term debt = 0.0522, cost of long-term issue = $0.5 \times 0.12 = 0.06$, and $I = \frac{1}{2}$ into Formula 20-1 and solving for the unknown gives

$$\text{Break-even long-term rate} = 0.1206, \text{ or } 12.06\%$$

for a 19.5-year bullet maturity issue. If long-term interest rates rise more than 6 basis points over the 6-month period, waiting will prove to have been more expensive.

Prefunding Future Long-Term Borrowing
Requirements

The opposite situation to that just considered arises when the yield curve is inverted. Short-term interest rates exceed long-term interest rates so that an issuer can invest the proceeds of a long-term debt issue in short-term securities at a positive spread. By accelerating a long-term debt issue, the company can realize savings that it can use to offset a portion of future interest expense. But there is an opportunity cost because long-term interest rates might fall in the interim.

A measure of the benefit of prefunding can be obtained in the following manner. Suppose that in the previous example the company had planned to issue 6 months hence and that it could invest the proceeds of a long-term debt issue in 6-month coupon-bearing securities paying interest at a 15% annual rate. The company would realize a positive carry of 3%, or $0.0075 after taxes per dollar of debt, during the 6-month period. Ignoring issuance expenses in order to simplify the example, net proceeds are effectively $1.0075 per dollar of debt "issued" 6 months hence. Applying Formula 8-2, the company's pretax cost of "preborrowing" 19.5-year funds solves

$$1.0075 = \sum_{t=1}^{39} \frac{0.5 \times 0.12/2}{(1 + 0.5 \times \text{pretax cost}/2)^t} + \frac{1 + 0.5 \times 0.12/2}{(1 + 0.5 \times \text{pretax cost}/2)^{40}}$$

so that

$$\text{Pretax cost} = 0.1187, \text{ or } 11.87\%$$

Prefunding lowers the issuer's immediate cost of borrowing by 13 basis points. The risk the company faces in prefunding is that interest rates for 19.5-year debt might fall more than 13 basis points over the next 6 months.

ISSUING PREFERRED STOCK
AND PREFERENCE STOCK

Preferred stock represents a hybrid, combining certain features of common stock and certain features of debt. Preferred stock ranks senior to common stock and junior to debt in terms of both claims on the corporation's operating income and claims on the company's assets in the event of liquidation. Preference stock is essentially identical to preferred stock except that it is junior to preferred stock; dividends must be paid in full on the preferred stock before the company can pay any dividends on its preference stock.[6]

Principal Features of Preferred Stock

Preferred stock has the following principal features:

■ *A par (or stated) value.* Issues that are sold predominantly to institutional investors are typically given a $100 par value, whereas those that are sold to individual investors are typically given a $25 par value because then a round lot (100 shares) would cost only $2500.

- *A stated dividend rate.* Preferred stock pays dividends quarterly, like common stock, but at a stated rate, like debt. Preferred stock dividends are declared at the discretion of the board of directors and are not tax-deductible. Missing a dividend payment does not put the company into default, but preferred stockholders typically have the right to elect a specified number of directors after the issuer has missed a certain number of dividend payments. Preferred stock dividends that are missed must usually be cumulated and paid in full before the company can pay any cash dividends on its common stock.
- *Optional redemption provisions.* Preferred stock typically has optional redemption provisions similar to those that debt issues have.
- *Mandatory redemption provisions. Nonredeemable* preferred stock is perpetual like common stock.[7] *Redeemable* preferred stock contains sinking fund provisions similar to those of sinking fund debentures. The shorter the average life of the preferred stock issue, the more debtlike it is.[8]

Financing with Preferred Stock

The nondeductibility of preferred stock dividends makes preferred stock financing more costly than debt financing for a tax-paying corporation. However, corporate investors are entitled to an 85% dividends received deduction. Because of this, the dividend yield to maturity for a preferred stock issue is normally less than the yield to maturity of a similarly structured debt issue. Thus, preferred stock financing may be cheaper for a company that does not expect to be in a tax-paying position over the life of the issue.

Utility companies have been the heaviest issuers of preferred stock. Preferred stock typically represents between 10 and 15% of an electric utility's capitalization. Utilities are permitted to recover preferred stock dividends but not common stock dividends through the rates they charge their customers. During the 1970s, electric utility market-to-book ratios fell well below 1, indicating that these companies were not earning returns sufficient to cover their cost of common equity, and many utility companies felt it beneficial to their common stockholders to increase the preferred stock component of their capitalizations.

In recent years, the bulk of the fixed-dividend-rate preferred stock issues have contained sinking fund provisions. Previously, most preferred stock issues were perpetual. The change is at least partly the result of a ruling by the National Association of Insurance Commissioners, which permits property and casualty insurance companies to value preferred stock issues for regulatory purposes at their face amount only if the issue's maturity does not exceed 40 years and if it has a sinking fund that begins no later than 10 years from the date of issue and retires at least 2.5% of the issue per year.

Adjustable Rate Preferred Stock

A large market for adjustable rate preferred stock developed beginning in 1982. The principal investors were corporations seeking short-term investment vehicles that would enable them to take advantage of the 85% dividends received deduction without exposing them to the liquidity risk of long-term fixed-rate preferred stock. The basic security has evolved through several generations to a security whose dividend rate is adjusted by Dutch auction every 7 weeks—just long enough to enable corporate purchasers in the previous auction to claim the deduction. Issuers find the security attractive because it is perpetual with a dividend yield substantially below the interest rate on short-term debt. Of course, issuers have to bear the floating-rate risk but a nontaxable company can issue the preferred in lieu of commercial paper or bank borrowings.

Fixing the Terms of an Issue

Because of the similar structures of debt and sinking fund preferred stock, the methods of analysis discussed earlier in this chapter for debt can be used to evaluate alternative maturities and alternative sinking fund structures and the effect of letting the dividend rate float. Basically, only two adjustments are necessary: There are no tax shields because dividend payments are not tax deductible and dividends are paid quarterly.

Whether to Issue Perpetual Preferred

One consideration that arises only in connection with preferred stock is the trade-off between perpetual preferred stock and sinking fund preferred stock. The following break-even model provides the annual dividend yield to maturity for the refunding issue that would make a company indifferent between issuing perpetual preferred stock and issuing sinking fund preferred stock that matures in *maturity* years with a sinking fund that begins after *start of sinker* years:

$$
\begin{aligned}
\text{Break-even} \atop \text{dividend rate} = {\text{annual dividend} \atop \text{rate on sinker}} &+ \left({\text{annual dividend} \atop \text{rate on perpetual}} - {\text{annual dividend} \atop \text{rate on sinker}} \right) \\
&\times \left[(\text{maturity} + 1) - {\text{start of} \atop \text{sinker}} \right] \\
&\times \left[1 - \left(1 + {\text{quarterly dividend} \atop \text{rate on perpetual}} \right)^{-4} \right] \\
&\div \left[\left(1 + {\text{quarterly dividend} \atop \text{rate on perpetual}} \right)^{-4 \times S} \right. \\
&\quad \left. - \left(1 + {\text{quarterly dividend} \atop \text{rate on perpetual}} \right)^{-4 \times (M+1)} \right]
\end{aligned}
$$

(20-4)

where S = start of sinker and M = maturity.

In Formula 20-4, the sinking fund involves equal annual payments and each sinking fund payment is refunded with new preferred stock involving a cost equal to the *break-even dividend rate*. Consequently, the break-even dividend rate should be thought of as the average (over time) after-tax cost of replacement funds that would make the issuer indifferent between the sinking fund issue and the perpetual issue. If the average cost of replacement funds should exceed the break-even dividend rate, the perpetual issue would prove to be the less expensive alternative.

Illustration of Sinking Fund Preferred Versus Perpetual Preferred Analysis

Consider a 25-year sinking fund preferred stock issue that could be sold with an annual dividend yield of 11.50% and a level sinking fund that begins at the end of the tenth year. Suppose a perpetual issue requires an annual dividend yield of 12%. Applying Formula 20-4:

$$\begin{array}{l} \text{Break-even} \\ \text{dividend rate} \end{array} = 0.115 + (0.12 - 0.115)$$

$$\times \frac{[(25 + 1) - 10][1 - (1 + 0.12/4)^{-4}]}{(1 + 0.12/4)^{-40} - (1 + 0.12/4)^{-104}}$$

$$= 0.1493, \text{ or } 14.93\%$$

If the issuer believes its average cost of replacement funds will exceed 14.93%, it should sell the perpetual issue. Otherwise it should sell the sinking fund issue.

The relative attractiveness of the two alternatives depends ultimately on the yield differential between the sinking fund issue and the perpetual issue.

Table 20-2
Break-Even Annual Dividend
Rate for a Refunding Issue

Annual Dividend Rate on Perpetual Issue, %	Yield Differential*			
	Maturity = 25		Maturity = 40	
	50 b.p., %	125 b.p., %	50 b.p., %	125 b.p., %
8	9.37	11.43	10.35	13.88
10	12.04	15.11	13.61	19.02
12	14.93	19.32	17.29	25.22
14	18.08	24.20	21.50	32.75

*Difference between annual dividend yield on perpetual preferred stock issue and annual dividend yield on a sinking fund preferred stock issue with a level sinking fund that begins at the end of the tenth year.

Table 20-3
Calculation of Break-Even
Non-Tax-Paying Period

(Cost of Preferred Equity = 10.894%*)

Company Becomes Taxable in Year	After-Tax Cost of Debt When Interest Tax Shields Are†	
	Carried Forward, %‡	Lost Forever, %
1	6.000	6.000
2	6.026	6.606
3	6.083	7.211
4	6.171	7.803
5	6.288	8.371
6	6.434	8.905
7	6.608	9.399
8	6.812	9.849
9	7.044	10.253
10	7.303	10.612
11	7.587	10.929
12	7.894	11.206
13	8.218	11.448
14	8.554	11.659
15	8.895	11.842
16	9.236	12.000

* Expressed on an equivalent semiannually compounded basis.
† Assumes a 50% marginal income tax rate in the years the company is taxable.
‡ Interest tax shields carried forward and recognized in full the year the company becomes taxable.

Table 20-2 provides values of break-even dividend rate for various yield differentials and for two maturities. Because utility perpetual preferreds have often required a yield premium of 125 basis points or greater, it is not difficult to understand why electric utility companies have to an increasing extent in recent years incorporated sinking fund provisions in their preferred stock issues.

PREFERRED EQUITY VERSUS DEBT

Preferred stock yields to maturity are generally lower than the yields to maturity of comparably structured debt instruments because of the 85% dividends received deduction. Consequently, preferred equity would be cheaper if the issuer never expected to pay income taxes over the life of the issue and believed that it would never be able to utilize the incremental tax loss carry forwards that would result from the interest deductions.

Companies project their tax positions out over their planning horizons. A company might feel reasonably confident that it will not find itself in a tax-paying position over the next, say, 5 years but feel highly uncertain about the period beyond. One approach to dealing with the preferred equity versus debt trade-off is to identify the *break-even non-tax-paying period*, that is, the number of years that the issuer would have to remain nontaxable in order to be indifferent between preferred equity and debt financing.

Table 20-3 illustrates how this analysis might be accomplished. For simplicity, a 15-year non–sinking fund issue is assumed. The preferred stock issue requires a 10.75% annual dividend yield, and the debt issue requires a 12.00% yield to maturity. Any tax shields that cannot be used currently are assumed in one case to be carried forward and recognized fully the first year the company becomes taxable and in the other case to be lost forever.

Assuming a 50% marginal income tax rate, a fully taxable corporation would pay a 6.000% cost of debt and a 10.894% equivalent semiannually compounded cost of preferred stock (before flotation costs in each case). If the company did not expect to become taxable until year 11 and expected to be so marginally profitable that the prior years' tax deductions for incremental interest expense would be lost forever, the after-tax cost of debt would exceed the cost of preferred stock. However, even if the corporation were never taxable during the entire 15-year period the debt is outstanding, debt would still be the cheaper alternative as long as the company could carry the losses forward and recognize them fully within the foreseeable future.

SUMMARY

Debt instruments have certain principal features in common: a stated maturity, a stated principal amount, a stated coupon rate of interest (or interest rate formula, in the case of floating-rate debt), a mandatory redemption schedule, an optional redemption provision, and covenant restrictions designed to protect bondholders.

In choosing maturity, the issuer should avoid bunching its aggregate debt maturity schedule. A company will generally select a shorter maturity if it expects its credit standing to improve or if it expects interest rates to fall. Including a sinking fund will generally reduce the issuer's cost of borrowing when the yield curve is upward-sloping. A sinking fund also spreads out the debt repayment obligation. The delivery option that accompanies the sinking fund provisions of most public debt issues—but is seldom found in privately placed debt—is valuable because it gives the issuer the flexibility to lower its realized cost of debt by repaying at a discount if interest rates rise following issuance. Companies generally issue long-term debt at par on a fixed-rate basis. Companies have at times found it advantageous to issue deep discount bonds, and companies whose revenues are interest rate–sensitive have issued longer-term debt on a floating-rate basis.

Preferred stock represents a hybrid; it combines certain features of debt and certain features of common stock. Because of the similarities between the characteristics of debt and preferred stock, the same analytical techniques can be applied to both with only minor modifications. Preferred stock will be cheaper than debt for a non-tax-paying corporation because of the 85% dividends received deduction available to corporate investors.

Financing with Options

Chapter 21

Companies, particularly smaller ones, often find it more attractive to issue convertible bonds or bonds with warrants than to issue nonconvertible debt. A warrant entitles the holder to buy common stock at a stated price for cash. A convertible bond entitles the holder to exchange the bond for a stated number of shares of the issuing company's common stock. Both types of securities thus incorporate a form of option.

VALUING OPTIONS

An *option* gives the holder the right to buy the underlying security (a *call option*) or sell the underlying security (a *put option*) at a specified price (the *exercise price*) on or before the option's *expiration date*. *European options* can only be exercised on the expiration date, whereas *American options* can be exercised at any time up to and including the expiration date. In most cases, the underlying security is common stock, and call options are more prevalent than put options. For example, an Exxon October 40 call option traded on March 9, 1984 at a price of $1.50 per underlying share. The option would give its holder the right to purchase 100 shares of Exxon Corporation common stock at a price of $40 per share on or before October 20, 1984, and it would cost an option purchaser $150 (= $1.50 × 100) plus commissions to obtain this right. Convertible securities and warrants both represent forms of call options.

Theoretical Value and Actual Value of a Call Option

The solid line in Figure 21-1 illustrates the relationship between the theoretical value of a call option at any point in time and the value of the underlying

353

common stock. A call option's *theoretical value* equals the greater of (1) zero and (2) the difference between the exercise price and the underlying share price times the number of shares per contract. If the share price is less than the option's exercise price, the theoretical value (which would equal the actual value if the option were about to expire) would be zero. At share prices greater than the exercise price, theoretical value increases with the underlying share price. For example, if the exercise price is $50 per share and the shares are worth $75 per share, the option's theoretical value is $25 per underlying share (or $2500 on a standard 100-share contract). But an option involves a right to buy, not an obligation. Even if the option is immediately exercisable, the option holder can continue to hold it in the hope that it will increase further in value. Consequently, an option's actual value will tend to exceed its theoretical value. The dashed line in Figure 21-1 illustrates this relationship. The greater the time to expiration and, most important, the more volatile the underlying share price, the greater the potential for further appreciation in value and, hence, the greater is the actual value of the call option relative to its theoretical value.

Black-Scholes Model for Valuing Options

Fischer Black and Myron Scholes have developed a sophisticated model for valuing a European call option on a stock that does not pay dividends.[1] The Black-Scholes model provides the equilibrium option value that would prevail

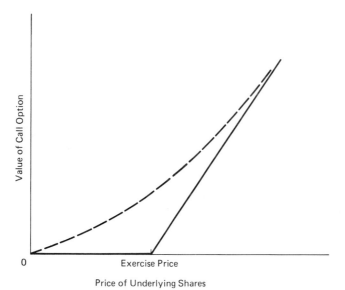

Figure 21-1. Relationship between the value of a call option and the price of the underlying shares.

if investors were able to combine options and shares of the underlying stock into fully hedged, and therefore riskless, portfolios.

The Black-Scholes model leads to the following rather formidable formula for the equilibrium value of a call option:

$$\begin{array}{l} \text{Current value} \\ \text{of call option} \end{array} = \begin{array}{l} \text{current} \\ \text{share price} \end{array} \times N(d_1) - \begin{array}{l} \text{exercise} \\ \text{price} \end{array} \times N(d_2)$$

$$\div \; \exp \left(\begin{array}{l} \text{risk-free} \\ \text{rate} \end{array} \times \begin{array}{l} \text{time to} \\ \text{exercise} \end{array} \right) \qquad \text{(21-1)}$$

where $N(d)$ denotes the probability that the standard normal random variable takes on a value less than or equal to d and where

$$d_1 = \left[\ln \left(\begin{array}{l} \text{current} \\ \text{share price} \end{array} \Big/ \begin{array}{l} \text{exercise} \\ \text{price} \end{array} \right) + \left(\begin{array}{l} \text{risk-free} \\ \text{rate} \end{array} \times \begin{array}{l} \text{time to} \\ \text{exercise} \end{array} \right) \right.$$

$$\left. + \left(\tfrac{1}{2} \text{ variance} \times \begin{array}{l} \text{time to} \\ \text{exercise} \end{array} \right) \right] \div \sqrt{\text{variance} \times \begin{array}{l} \text{time to} \\ \text{exercise} \end{array}}$$

$$\text{(21-2a)}$$

$$d_2 = d_1 - \sqrt{\text{variance} \times \text{time to exercise}} \qquad \text{(21-2b)}$$

The symbol "exp" denotes the function "raise to the power of the number e (approximately 2.71828)," and the symbol "ln" denotes the function "take the natural logarithm of," both of which can be found on many hand-held calculators. The values of $N(d)$ can be found in a table of cumulative normal probabilities. The value of $N(d_1)$ represents the *hedge ratio*, the ratio of the number of shares to purchase to the number of shares against which to sell call options, necessary to maintain a fully hedged position.

The *risk-free rate* (expressed as a decimal) is measured as the continuously compounded short-term risk-free rate of return, e.g., the rate of return on Treasury securities that are about to mature. *Time to exercise* is the length of time until the option is scheduled to expire. The *variance* is measured as the variance of the continuously compounded total rate of return on the underlying stock. Risk-free rate, time to exercise, and variance must all be denominated in terms of the same unit of time.

The *current value of call option* in Formula 21-1 is greater the greater are (1) the volatility of the price of the underlying shares (reflected in variance), (2) the time to exercise, (3) the risk-free rate, and (4) *current share price* relative to exercise price. Volatility is generally the most important but also the most difficult to estimate. It is typically assumed that the volatility of historical returns over some recent period is a reasonable proxy for expected future volatility. But when volatility itself changes from one period to another, it is best to (1) estimate variance for periods of varying lengths, say 1 to 5 years, (2) calculate

Table 21-1
Illustration of the Calculation of the Value of a
Call Option Using the Black-Scholes Formula

Current share price = $33 per share   Time to exercise = 60 days = 0.16438 year
Exercise price = $30 per share   Risk-free rate = 0.10225 per annum on continuously compounded basis

Variance

Month	Ending Share Price	Encing Price/ Beginning Price	Logarithm (Ending Price/ Beginning Price)	Month	Ending Share Price	Ending Price/ Beginning Price	Logarithm (Ending Price/ Beginning Price)
0	$25.50	—	—	7	$23.75	1.06742	0.06524
1	27.00	1.05882	0.05716	8	28.25	1.18947	0.17351
2	31.50	1.16667	0.15415	9	24.50	0.86726	-0.14242
3	28.00	0.88889	-0.11778	10	20.75	0.84694	-0.16613
4	27.75	0.99107	-0.00897	11	26.50	1.27711	0.24460
5	25.00	0.90090	-0.10436	12	33.00	1.24528	0.21936
6	22.25	0.89000	-0.11653		Variance = 0.27284 on annual basis		

$$d_1 = \frac{\ln(33/30) + (0.10225 \times 0.16438) + [(0.27284/2) \times 0.16438]}{\sqrt{0.27284 \times 0.16438}} = 0.63530$$

$$d_2 = d_1 - \sqrt{0.27284 \times 0.16438} = 0.42353$$

$$N(d_1) = N(0.63530) = 0.73738 \qquad N(d_2) = N(0.42353) = 0.66404$$

Current value
of call option $= \$33 \times 0.73738 - \$30 \times 0.66404/\exp(0.10225 \times 0.16438) = \underline{\$4.74}$

current value of call option for each, and (3) work with the resulting range of values or an average of these values.

Illustration of Option Value Calculation

Table 21-1 illustrates the application of the Black-Scholes formula to calculate the value of a call option. Variance is estimated using one year's monthly data to keep the example simple. In practice, either weekly observations for the past year or monthly data for the past few years would be used in order to reduce the sensitivity of the estimate to any single observation. The expression "logarithm (ending price ÷ beginning price)" represents the formula for calculating the total return on the stock expressed on a continuously compounded basis.

Applying Formulas 21-1 and 21-2 gives

$$\text{Current value of call option} = \$4.74$$

The appropriate hedge ratio is $N(d_1) = 0.73738$; the investor should purchase 73.738, or roughly 74 shares, for every 100-share call option she or he sells in order to achieve a perfectly hedged position.

The current value of call option is sensitive to the value calculated for variance. For example, suppose that using 2, 3, 4, and 5 years of data has produced estimates for variance of 0.26291, 0.25321, 0.21320, and 0.23514, respectively. The corresponding values of current value of call option are $4.70, $4.66, $4.48, and $4.58, respectively. Thus, a reasonable range of values for the call option is $4.48 to $4.74 per share. However, if the analyst believes that the relatively high share price volatility over the past year is likely to continue, then the $4.74 value should be used.[2]

Adjustments for Dividend Payments

Most options in the United States, including warrants and the conversion option on convertible bonds, are American options. In addition, options are often written on dividend-paying stocks. An American option, because it can be exercised any time prior to its expiration date, must be worth at least as much as a European option. But Robert Merton has demonstrated that it would be uneconomic for a holder to exercise a call option on a non–dividend-paying stock prior to its expiration date.[3] Thus, Formulas 21-1 and 21-2 are also valid for American options on non–dividend-paying stocks.

A cash dividend represents in essence a partial distribution of the company's assets. Option holders can qualify for the dividend only if they exercise their options prior to the ex-dividend date. The greater the dividends paid prior to the expiration date, the lower the value of a European call option. In the case of an American option, it may prove advantageous to exercise on the last trading day preceding one of the ex-dividend dates so as to qualify for the dividend distribution.

Two adjustments to the Black-Scholes formula are required when the stock pays dividends:

1. Adjust the current share price in Formulas 21-1 and 21-2a by subtracting the present value of the dividends per common share the company is expected to pay on or before the option's expiration date. The appropriate discount rate is the risk-free rate.
2. Reapply Formulas 21-1 and 21-2 for each ex-dividend date prior to the option's expiration date. For each such date, treat the last trading day prior to the ex-dividend date as the option's expiration date. The maximum of the option values so calculated is the best estimate of the current value of call option.

CHARACTERISTICS OF CONVERTIBLE SECURITIES

Companies issue bonds and preferred stock that are convertible at the option of the holder into the common stock of the same corporation. Securities that provide this option are called *convertible bonds* and *convertible preferred stock*, respectively.

Principal Features of the Conversion Option

A convertible bond can be viewed as a package consisting of a straight bond, typically issued in the form of a subordinated debenture, and a long-term call option, or warrant, that is exercisable by tendering the bond in exchange for the issuer's common stock at the specified conversion (i.e., exercise) price. The Hughes Tool Company $8\frac{1}{2}\%$ Convertible Subordinated Debentures due April 1, 2005, which were discussed in Chapter 8, illustrate the features of the conversion option:

- Each bond is convertible at any time prior to maturity into common stock of Hughes Tool Company at a *conversion price* of $\$62\frac{3}{8}$ per common share. That conversion price represents a *conversion premium* of 17.97% over the previous closing price of Hughes Tool Company common stock ($\$52\frac{7}{8}$). Thus, an investor is entitled to receive common shares representing a *conversion ratio* of $\$1000/\$62.375 = 16.0321$ shares of common stock per convertible bond. These conversion terms are fixed for the life of the issue. However, some convertible issues do provide for one or more "step-ups" in the conversion price over time. The conversion premium on convertible debt and convertible preferred stock issues typically falls within the range from 10 to 20%.
- The conversion price will be adjusted for stock splits, stock dividends, rights offerings that involve a discounted offering price, or the distribution of assets (other than cash dividends) or indebtedness to shareholders. The conversion

price will only be adjusted, however, if the adjustment is at least some threshold amount (1% in the case of the Hughes Tool issue).

■ Holders who surrender their bonds for conversion are not entitled to receive accrued interest; in general, it is therefore disadvantageous for a holder to convert just prior to an interest payment date.

■ If the bonds are called for redemption, the conversion option will expire just before (typically between 3 and 10 days) the redemption date. Issuers can use the optional redemption feature to force conversion. To prevent an "unexpectedly early" call, many of the more recent convertible issues have prohibited the issuer from calling the bonds within 3 years of issuance unless the underlying share price equals or exceeds 150% of the stated conversion price over a specified period, typically 20 or 30 consecutive trading days.

The conversion feature of convertible preferred stock is structured similarly.

Convertible Debt versus Convertible Preferred Stock

The principal buyers of convertible securities have typically been individuals and convertible bond funds, neither of whom could benefit from the corporate 85% dividends received deduction. Consequently, under most market conditions, a company could obtain essentially the same terms whether it issued convertible debt or convertible preferred stock. Issuers who are in a tax-paying position therefore find it cheaper to issue convertible debt. On the other hand, issuers who do not expect to be in a tax-paying position for a number of years typically issue convertible preferred stock because that security will not increase the debt ratio and the underlying preferred stock can be perpetual. A company that is uncertain of its future tax position can issue *convertible exchangeable preferred stock*, which consists of convertible preferred stock that is exchangeable at the option of the company (i.e., when it becomes a taxpayer) into convertible debt of the company.

Exchangeable Debentures

Companies have also issued bonds exchangeable for the common stock of other companies. For example, on December 1, 1982, CIGNA Corporation issued $100 million principal amount of 8% Subordinated Exchangeable Debentures due December 1, 2007, which are exchangeable for shares of common stock of Paine Webber Incorporated. CIGNA had previously obtained the Paine Webber shares when it sold its investment banking subsidiary to Paine Webber. An issue of exchangeable debentures is structured like a conventional convertible debenture issue.[4] Exchangeable debenture issues may be attractive to a company that owns a block of another company's common stock when it would like to raise cash and intends eventually to sell the block but wishes to defer the sale—either because it believes the shares will increase in price or because it wishes to defer the capital gains tax liability it will incur upon sale of the shares.

VALUING CONVERTIBLE SECURITIES

A convertible bond derives its value from two sources: its value as a bond and the value of the underlying common stock. The value of the straight bond portion of the package, called the *bond value* of the convertible bond, represents the value the convertible bond would have if it were never converted. The value of the common stock underlying a convertible bond, called the bond's *conversion value*, equals the conversion ratio times the prevailing share price and represents the value the convertible bond would have if the holder had to convert it immediately. A convertible bond cannot sell for less than either its bond value or its conversion value.

Thus, a convertible bond provides a hedge. If interest rates rise but the underlying stock price holds steady or increases, bond value falls but conversion value places a floor under the value of the convertible bond. Similarly, if the price of the underlying stock falls but interest rates hold steady or fall, conversion value falls but bond value places a floor under the value of the convertible bond.

Measuring the Bond Value of a Convertible Bond

The bond value of a convertible bond is measured by discounting the stream of interest and principal payments the company would be obligated to make if the bond were never converted at the yield the market would require on a new issue of debt by the same company with the same bond features but no conversion option. It is convenient in most cases to value the bond on a yield-to-remaining-average-life basis, which assumes that the issue matures in one lump sum on the date that corresponds to the bond issue's average life:

$$\begin{array}{c}\text{Bond value of} \\ \text{convertible bond}\end{array} = \sum_{t=1}^{A} \left[\frac{\text{semiannual interest payment per bond}}{(1 + \frac{1}{2} \text{ required yield to average life})^t} \right]$$

$$+ \frac{\text{principal amount of bond}}{(1 + \frac{1}{2} \text{ required yield to average life})^A} \quad (21\text{-}3)$$

where A = average life and denotes the number of semiannual interest periods in the remaining average life of the bond.

For example, suppose that a new 25-year Hughes Tool straight debt issue with a 19-year average life would have required a 10% yield to average life if offered on April 3, 1980, the day the Hughes Tool convertible debt issue mentioned earlier was sold. In that case, the bond value of each Hughes Tool convertible bond was:

$$\text{Bond value of} \atop \text{convertible bond} = \sum_{t=1}^{38} \frac{\$42.50}{(1.05)^t} + \frac{\$1000}{(1.05)^{38}} = \$873.49$$

at the time of issue. At the same time, the same convertible bond had a

$$\text{Conversion value} \atop \text{of convertible bond} = \text{conversion} \atop \text{ratio} \times \text{current} \atop \text{share price} \qquad (21\text{-}4)$$

$$= 16.0321 \times \$52.875 = \$847.70$$

Premiums Over Bond Value and Conversion Value

The Hughes Tool convertible bonds could not have sold for less than the higher of their bond and conversion values, $873.49. But investors purchased the bonds at par, or $1000 per bond. A convertible bond will generally sell at a premium to both its bond value and its conversion value.

Figure 21-2 illustrates this relationship. The convertible bond's conversion value rises in proportion to the underlying share price. Bond value also increases; the favorable conditions that bring about increases in the share price also enhance the company's credit standing. This reduces the required yield to average life and raises the bond value of the convertible bond. The shape of the bond value curve in Figure 21-2 reflects the fact that as the company's financial condition improves, the successive reductions in yield become smaller and smaller because the yield differential between bonds of

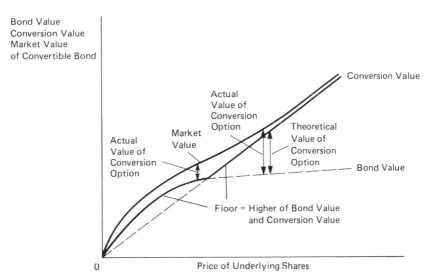

Figure 21-2. Bond value, conversion value, and actual market value.

the same maturity in adjacent rating categories narrows as a bond's rating improves.

For any particular share price, the greater of bond value and conversion value represents the floor. The actual market value tends to exceed this floor. The market value of the convertible bond will exceed the bond value, reflecting the actual value of the conversion option, and will also exceed the conversion value because the convertible bond provides downside protection. If the share price falls, the value of the convertible bond will not fall below the bond value. But for very high common stock prices, the value of this downside protection is small. Moreover, as the conversion value rises above the convertible bond's redemption price, a call in order to force conversion becomes increasingly likely. Thus, at progressively higher share prices, the market value of the convertible bond converges to its conversion value.

Payback Calculations

Convertible securities are typically bought and sold on the basis of a break-even relationship between the conversion premium on the one hand and the difference between the interest (or preferred dividend) income the convertible security provides and the dividend income the underlying common stock would provide on the other. The magnitude of the conversion premium investors are willing to accept depends on the extent to which the convertible security provides a higher level of income on a current basis than an equal dollar investment in the underlying common stock would.

The payback calculation in the case of convertible debt takes on either of the following two basic forms:

$$\begin{matrix} \text{Rule of} \\ \text{thumb} \end{matrix} = \begin{matrix} \text{conversion} \\ \text{premium} \end{matrix} \div \left(\begin{matrix} \text{current annual} \\ \text{interest yield} \end{matrix} - \begin{matrix} \text{indicated annual dividend} \\ \text{yield on common stock} \end{matrix} \right)$$

(21-5)

$$\begin{aligned} \text{Break-even} = & \left(\begin{matrix} \text{dollar} \\ \text{issue price} \end{matrix} - \begin{matrix} \text{conversion} \\ \text{value} \end{matrix} \right) \\ & \div \left(\begin{matrix} \text{annual interest on} \\ \text{convertible bond} \end{matrix} - \begin{matrix} \text{annual dividends on equal} \\ \text{dollar amount of common stock} \end{matrix} \right) \end{aligned}$$

(21-6a)

$$\begin{aligned} = & \frac{\text{conversion premium}}{1 + \text{conversion premium}} \\ & \div \left(\begin{matrix} \text{current annual} \\ \text{interest yield} \end{matrix} - \begin{matrix} \text{indicated annual dividend} \\ \text{yield on common stock} \end{matrix} \right) \end{aligned}$$

(21-6b)

When the convertible bond is not priced at par, conversion premium should be calculated as the premium the bond purchaser effectively agrees to pay:

$$\text{Conversion premium} = (\text{dollar issue price} - \text{conversion value})$$
$$\div \text{conversion value} \qquad (21\text{-}7)$$

Current annual interest yield equals the ratio of the annual interest on the convertible bond to the price paid for the bond. Similar formulas apply to convertible preferred stock.

Break-even is just *rule of thumb* divided by 1 plus the conversion premium. Hence, the two measures of payback will move in parallel although break-even will always be a smaller number. Both have generally varied between 2 and 4 years. The two payback values for the Hughes Tool issue are[5]:

$$\frac{\text{Rule of}}{\text{thumb}} = \frac{0.1797}{0.085 - 0.0159} = 2.60 \text{ years}$$

$$\text{Break-even} = \frac{0.1797/1.1797}{0.085 - 0.0159} = 2.20 \text{ years}$$

Investment bankers set the terms of new issues of convertible securities so that they are consistent with the payback characteristics of outstanding convertible debt issues. In concept, either rule of thumb or break-even could be used; what is most important is that the chosen measure be applied consistently.

FINANCING WITH CONVERTIBLE SECURITIES

Convertible securities are best viewed as delayed common equity financing. Issuers and investors both expect the company's share price to rise enough to stimulate conversion within a period of roughly 2 to 4 years following issuance. Investors are therefore willing to accept an interest rate on a convertible debt issue that is below the rate that they would normally require on a nonconvertible but otherwise identical issue. However, this interest rate must exceed the common stock dividend yield in order to give investors the incentive to buy the convertible security rather than the issuer's common stock. Issuers are willing to provide this higher current level of income to investors in order to be able to sell deferred common equity at a conversion price that exceeds the prevailing common stock price. Investor receptivity will depend to a large extent on the outlook for the stock market and for the prospective issuer. Convertible debt financing has been used most frequently during periods of generally increasing share prices and by smaller, more rapidly growing companies.

Generally, given the indicated annual dividend yield at which its common stock is trading, a company will have the flexibility to trade off higher coupon for higher redemption premium, subject to providing a payback that is competitive under prevailing market conditions. For example, if a break-even of no greater than 2.50 years is dictated by current market conditions and the indicated annual dividend yield of the company's common stock is 2.0%, the following offering yield-conversion premium combinations are possible:

$$\frac{\text{Yield to}}{\text{maturity}} = 5.64\% \qquad \frac{\text{conversion}}{\text{premium}} = 10\% \qquad \text{break-even} = 2.50 \text{ years}$$

$$\frac{\text{Yield to}}{\text{maturity}} = 7.22\% \qquad \frac{\text{conversion}}{\text{premium}} = 15\% \qquad \text{break-even} = 2.50 \text{ years}$$

$$\frac{\text{Yield to}}{\text{maturity}} = 8.67\% \qquad \frac{\text{conversion}}{\text{premium}} = 20\% \qquad \text{break-even} = 2.50 \text{ years}$$

The only exception to the payback restriction is that an issuer may be able to achieve a higher payback by setting the coupon rate "close to" the rate that would be required on a straight debt issue with identical debt features. For example, under market conditions like those that prevailed late in 1982, the issuer just considered might have been able to achieve *conversion premium =* 30% and break-even = 2.88 years by setting *coupon rate =* 10%.

Motives for Financing with Convertible Securities
Convertible securities are perceived by issuers to offer a number of advantages relative to other securities:

- Convertible debt carries a lower coupon rate than straight debt. The coupon rate differential is typically between 200 and 500 basis points.
- A company with a poor credit standing but good growth prospects may not be able to sell a straight debt issue publicly but can sell a convertible debt issue. Companies that issue convertible debt for this reason view convertible debt as "cheap debt."
- Because of the conversion premium, a company will issue fewer shares than it would have to sell at the current share price in order to raise the same amount of cash, and dilution in earnings per share will consequently be less.
- Convertible debt provides tax deductions, which the immediate sale of common stock would not.
- The gross underwriting spread is lower for convertible debt than for common stock. Issuance costs are lower than for either issuing common stock or issuing short-term or intermediate-term debt and refunding it with common stock.
- Issuing convertible securities effectively broadens the market for the company's common stock because life insurance companies, commercial banks, and governmental pension funds generally face tight restrictions on their ability to invest in common stocks but do have considerably greater flexibility to invest in convertible securities.

Dilution in Reported Earnings per Share
The potentially dilutive impact of issuing shares upon conversion must be reflected in the calculation of "fully diluted earnings per share." Under Accounting Principles Board Opinion No. 15, this supplemental earnings-per-share

calculation treats the convertible securities as having been fully converted at the beginning of the accounting period. The company must report fully diluted earnings per share along with primary earnings per share if the fully diluted figure is materially smaller. Nevertheless, dilution in earnings per share will always be less than for a common stock issue that raises the same amount of cash as long as there is a conversion premium.[6]

WHAT IS A WARRANT?

A *warrant* is a special form of call option. Whereas conventional call options are written by investors against outstanding shares of a company's stock, warrants are issued by the company. Warrants thus dilute the issuer's outstanding equity, which conventional call options do not. In addition, warrants typically do not expire for several years, and some companies, such as Allegheny Corporation, have even issued perpetual warrants. In contrast, conventional call options typically expire within a matter of months. The Black-Scholes option valuation formula can be used to value warrants with two modifications to reflect the dilutive impact of issuing warrants and the special computational problems resulting from their long lives.

Principal Features of Warrants

The provisions of a warrant are essentially the same as the provisions of a call option. For example, American Express distributed 932,000 Common Share Purchase Warrants to its common stockholders on February 26, 1982, and sold an additional 900,000 such warrants to the public on March 31, 1982, at a price of $12.625 per warrant. Each warrant entitles the holder to purchase at any time on or before February 28, 1987, one share of American Express common stock at an exercise price of $55 per common share,[7] which represents a premium of 17.0% over the previous closing price of American Express common stock. Warrant premiums customarily fall within the range of 15 to 30%. American Express can accelerate the expiration date if the price of American Express's common stock trades at a price of $95 per share for a period of 10 consecutive trading days. The American Express warrants are also redeemable beginning March 1, 1984, at a price of $40 per warrant. This redemption feature, like the redemption feature on a convertible bond, permits the issuer to force holders to exercise the call option. The exercise, redemption, and acceleration prices are adjusted if American Express pays a dividend in common stock, splits its common stock, distributes some of its assets (other than cash dividends), issues stockholders rights to purchase shares at a discount from the prevailing market price, and in certain other circumstances. However, as is typically the case, American Express warrant holders are not entitled to vote or to receive dividends.

Warrants are often issued along with debt in units. For example, on April 14, 1983, MGM/UA Entertainment Co. issued $400 million of 10% Senior Subordinated Notes due April 15, 1993, along with 5,600,000 Common Stock Purchase Warrants. The warrants are exercisable in cash or in exchange for 10% notes, which would be valued at par in the exchange. The warrants were *detachable* after July 15, 1983, which means that purchasers could sell the warrants for cash after that date and continue to hold the 10% notes. In contrast, a convertible bond effectively has *nondetachable* warrants.

VALUING WARRANTS

Because a warrant is a form of call option, the techniques for valuing options also apply to warrants. Unfortunately, the longer lives of warrants make attempts to project future share price volatility (i.e., variance) even more susceptible to error than in the case of conventional options. Consequently, estimated warrant values are subject to greater uncertainty than the estimated values of conventional options. Because of this uncertainty, it is usually better to (1) estimate a range of warrant values corresponding to a range of variance estimates that correspond to historical periods of varying lengths and then (2) determine a point estimate within this range.

Adjusting for Dilution

In addition to their longer lives, warrants differ from conventional call options in that they are issued by corporations. The new shares issuable upon the exercise of warrants represent a source of dilution. A study by Galai and Schneller has indicated how to take this dilution into account when valuing warrants that are not yet issued: Treat the warrant like a conventional call option; calculate the value of a call option that has the same exercise price, time to exercise, and other characteristics relevant to valuation as the warrant; and divide the option price by

$$
\begin{array}{c}
\text{Dilution} \\
\text{factor}
\end{array} = 1 + \left(\begin{array}{c} \text{number of} \\ \text{warrants} \end{array} \times \begin{array}{c} \text{number of shares} \\ \text{issuable per warrant} \end{array} \right.
$$

$$
\left. \div \begin{array}{c} \text{number of shares} \\ \text{currently outstanding} \end{array} \right) \qquad (21\text{-}8)
$$

that is, 1 plus the proportionate increase in the number of shares that the issuer would have outstanding immediately after all the warrants were exercised.[8] After the firm has issued the warrants, the option valuation formula can be used without further adjustment; the company's share price will already reflect the impact of dilution.

Using the Black-Scholes Formula to Value Warrants

The following procedure can be used to obtain an approximate value for warrants that a firm is contemplating issuing:

1. Estimate the stream of dividends the issuer will pay between the issue date and the expiration date of the warrant.
2. Apply Formulas 21-1 and 21-2 to estimate the option value assuming exercise immediately prior to each ex-dividend date up to the warrant's expiration date. Remember to adjust current share price by subtracting the present value of dividends per common share to be paid up to the ex-dividend date. Current value of call option is the maximum of these values.
3. Divide by the dilution factor and multiply by the number of shares issuable per warrant:

$$\text{Value of warrant} = \frac{\text{number of shares}}{\text{issuable per warrant}} \times \frac{\text{current value}}{\text{of call option}}$$

$$\div \left(1 + \frac{\text{number of warrants} \times \text{number of shares issuable per warrant}}{\text{number of shares currently outstanding}}\right)$$

$$(21\text{-}9)$$

In practice, this procedure can be simplified. The advantage of early exercise depends on the trade-off between the dividends the holder would receive following exercise and the interest the holder could earn on the exercise price if the warrant were not exercised. If the short-term interest rate remains constant, as the Black-Scholes formula assumes, a warrant holder would only exercise just before a dividend increase. Companies generally increase the common dividend no more than once a year. Thus, a warrant expiring after N years can be valued by considering just N possible exercise dates.

Illustration of Warrant Value Calculation

Table 21-2 illustrates the application of the modified Black-Scholes procedure to calculate the approximate value of the MGM/UA warrants. MGM/UA had paid a quarterly cash dividend of $0.05 per share over the preceding 10 quarters, and current share price was adjusted for cash dividends at this rate.

The warrant value was calculated assuming five possible exercise dates. Variance was measured over various historical periods in order to gauge the sensitivity of the value of the warrant to the period selected for estimating variance. Dilution factor = 1.11255.

The MGM/UA warrants are callable at $5 per warrant after April 14, 1986 (3 years from issuance), if MGM/UA's common share price exceeds 150% of the then effective exercise price for 20 trading days within a

Table 21-2
**Illustration of the Calculation of the Value of
a Warrant Using the Black-Scholes Formula**

Current share price = $12.875
Exercise price = $20.00
Risk-free rate = 0.08315
Years to expiration = 5
Dilution factor = 1 + (5,600,000 × 1)/49,753,553 = 1.11255

Time to Exercise	Adjusted Share Price*	Value of Warrant When Variance Is†		
		0.456	0.324	0.288
1 year	$12.685	$1.64	$1.18	$1.04
2 years	12.510	3.09	2.42	2.21
3 years	12.349	4.18	3.41	3.17
4 years	12.201	5.04	4.22	3.96
5 years	12.065	5.74	4.90	4.63

*Calculated as current share price less the present value of cash common dividends at the rate of $0.05 per quarter.
†The 0.456, 0.324, and 0.288 estimates of variance were obtained from historical monthly share prices over the preceding 1-year, 2-year, and $2\frac{3}{4}$-year periods, respectively. The beginning of the $2\frac{3}{4}$-year period is June 1980, the month MGM Grand Hotels, Inc., spun off the predecessor of MGM/UA Entertainment Company to MGM Grand Hotels, Inc.'s shareholders.

30-trading-day period ending not more than 20 days prior to the call date. Assuming exercise in year 3, the modified Black-Scholes procedure produces an estimated range of $3.17 to $4.18 for the value of each warrant. For purposes of comparison, the prospectus for the MGM/UA offering disclosed an estimated value of $12,600,000 for the 5,600,000 warrants, or $2.25 per warrant.[9] A $2.25 value is consistent with a 2-year holding period and expected future share price volatility equal to the share price volatility MGM/UA's stock exhibited over the $2\frac{3}{4}$-year period prior to the offering. It is important to keep in mind that the Black-Scholes model provides only approximate warrant values. If the volatility of MGM/UA's share price were expected to decrease in the future or if MGM/UA were expected to increase its dividend rate within the next 2 or 3 years, the value of the warrant in Table 21-2 would overstate the value investors would attach to the MGM/UA warrants.

FINANCING WITH WARRANTS

Companies sell warrants separately, as American Express Company did, or in combination with other securities, as MGM/UA Entertainment Co. did.

When combined with debt, warrants provide an "equity kicker" that increases the lender's total return if the borrower's share price appreciates. Lenders and borrowers often find a debt-with-warrants package mutually preferable to raising the interest rate on a straight loan because the debt-with-warrants package involves a smaller cash outflow in the early years of the loan but provides the lender greater upside potential to compensate for this.

Accounting for Warrants

When a company issues warrants, it adds the cash proceeds to "additional paid-in capital." When warrants are exercised, the company issues additional common stock at the exercise price per common share plus the amount per common share implicit in the price the company received for the warrants. While the warrants remain outstanding, the issuer must reflect the dilutive impact of the warrants, if any, in a supplemental earnings per share calculation. Under APB Opinion No. 15, the issuer must calculate "fully diluted earnings per share" using the "treasury stock method," which assumes that all warrants are exercised and the company uses the proceeds to repurchase shares of its common stock, and report that number along with "primary earnings per share" if fully diluted earnings per share is materially smaller. There is dilution under this method only if the common stock price exceeds the exercise price of the warrant.

Units

Smaller companies often issue debt and equity securities together in the form of *units*. Each unit typically costs $1000 and consists of one debenture with face amount of $1000, which is effectively sold at original issue discount, plus either (1) a specified number of warrants to buy shares of the issuer's common stock or (2) a specified number of shares of the issuer's common stock, but other combinations are possible.

Bonds with Warrants versus Convertible Bonds.

A convertible bond can be viewed as a package consisting of a straight bond and a nondetachable warrant. It would seem that by making the warrant detachable, the value of the package would be enhanced because the holder would have the flexibility to sell the two components separately. If the convertible bond issue would dilute reported earnings per share, the issuer might have an added incentive to prefer to issue bonds with warrants. However, a convertible debt issue gives a company the flexibility to force conversion of the entire issue to equity. A company can force exercise of the warrants and can redeem the straight bonds (in order to replace them with common stock), but generally only by paying a redemption premium. Thus, warrants are used primarily as "sweeteners" on debt issues rather than as part of a package to replace a convertible debt issue.

Bonds with Common Stock versus Convertible Bonds. Companies also use common stock as the "equity sweetener." If investors could simply purchase the issuer's common stock at the prevailing market price, they could form their own units and there would be only a small cost advantage (to the extent of common stock commission charges) to investors from having the corporation issue units. If the corporation wished to raise debt and equity capital, it could simply sell each type of security separately to those segments of the market that were willing to pay the highest price for each. But the companies that issue units typically have thinly traded stocks. Investors would find forming their own units more costly than buying them from the issuer because of the price pressure of their purchases.

A bond-with-common-stock unit generally offers the investor greater downside protection but less upside potential than a comparable convertible debenture. If the company keeps going but performs poorly so that the convertible debenture is never converted, the redemption value of the unit would exceed the redemption value of the convertible issue by the value of the common stock included in the unit. However, if the company performs well and its share price rises significantly, the value of the convertible debenture will exceed the value of the unit because it can be converted in its entirety to common equity. A company might prefer to issue units rather than convertible debt if it wants to increase its common equity immediately.

Warrants to Purchase Bonds

In recent years, some issuers of debt have issued warrants, typically detachable, to purchase additional bonds with a specified coupon rate, maturity, and other terms. Such warrants enable a frequent issuer of debt to hedge the risk of adverse future interest rate movements. If interest rates rise, the warrant will expire worthless, and the issue price of the warrant will partially offset the impact of the higher interest cost of the future debt issue. However, if interest rates fall, the warrants will be exercised, and the company will be obligated to issue additional debt at what is then an above-market rate of interest.

The Black-Scholes formula can be used to obtain a very rough approximation to the value of a warrant to purchase a bond. However, it is inconsistent to assume that the short-term interest rate is constant, which the Black-Scholes model does, but that the price of the bond underlying the warrant can fluctuate. Efforts are under way to develop more sophisticated versions of the Black-Scholes formula that do not suffer from this deficiency.

SUMMARY

A call option gives its holder the right to buy the underlying security at a specified exercise price on or before the option's expiration date. A warrant is a special long-lived type of call option. A convertible security can be viewed as a package consisting of a nonconvertible security and a special form of call/conversion option. The Black-Scholes model can be used to value conventional call options and, with modifications, to value warrants on dividend-paying stocks that are exercisable prior to expiration.

A convertible bond derives its value from two sources: its value as a straight bond and the value of the underlying common stock into which it is convertible. A convertible bond can never sell for less than the greater of its bond value and its conversion value. In practice, convertible securities are valued on the basis of a payback calculation. This implies a trade-off between coupon rate and the conversion premium. Issuers often find convertible securities to be an attractive financing alternative during periods of generally rising stock market prices. Issuing convertible debt or debt with warrants is also attractive to smaller, less creditworthy companies that are unable to sell straight debt at an acceptable cost.

Asset-Based Financing Techniques

Chapter 22

In Chapters 19 to 21 we discussed *conventional financing* techniques. In connection with such financings, the investor or lender, as the case may be, looks to the cash flow from the issuer's overall business, rather than to any single asset or collection of assets, to provide the return of and a return on his or her investment or loan. In contrast, the investors and lenders involved in an *asset-based financing* look principally to the cash flow from the specific asset or collection or assets in which their funds are invested for these returns. This chapter describes a number of types of asset-based financing and indicates conditions under which each is particularly appropriate.

LEASE FINANCING

The reader may at one time or another have rented an automobile. Such rentals are typically for short periods, perhaps only a few hours. But corporations often rent equipment and real estate for much longer periods.

What Is a Lease?

A *lease* is a rental agreement that extends for 1 year or longer under which the owner of an asset (the *lessor*) grants another party (the *lessee*) the exclusive right to use the asset during the lease period in return for a series of fixed payments. Payments are typically made monthly, quarterly, or semiannually beginning on the date the lease agreement is signed. Payments are normally level, like a homeowner's mortgage payments. Lease agreements often give the lessee the option to renew the lease or to purchase the asset, sometimes at a prespecified fixed price but usually at the asset's fair market value, at the end of the (initial) lease period. Otherwise, the leased asset reverts to the lessor, who is then able to realize the asset's residual value.

Leases differ in terms of the burdens of ownership the lessee must bear. Under a *full-service lease*, the lessor is responsible for maintaining and insuring the asset and paying any property taxes. Under a *net lease*, the lessee is responsible for these costs. Leases also differ with respect to their term and the right of the lessee to cancel the lease during the contract period. *Operating leases* are short-term and are generally cancelable at the lessee's option prior to the end of the contract period. *Financial*, or *capital*, *leases* are long-term, generally extending over most of the estimated useful economic life of the asset, and are generally not cancelable by the lessee before the end of the base lease period. Those financial leases that are so cancelable require the lessee to reimburse the lessor for any losses occasioned by the cancellation. The focus of this chapter is on financial leases.

Types of Lease Financing Arrangements

Virtually all financial leases fall into one of three categories. Under a *direct lease*, the lessee identifies the asset it requires and either leases it directly from the manufacturer or else arranges for a leasing company (or finance company or commercial bank) to buy it from the manufacturer and then enters into a financial lease contract with the lessor. Under a *sale-and-lease-back* arrangement, the owner of an asset sells it, usually at market value, for cash and agrees to lease it back from the purchaser. For example, during the 1974 to 1975 recession, many companies discovered sale-and-lease-back arrangements involving their headquarters buildings an attractive means of long-term financing. Under a *leveraged lease* arrangement, the lessor borrows a substantial portion of the purchase price of the asset, generally up to 80%, and provides the balance of the purchase price as his or her equity investment. To secure the loan, the lessor grants the long-term lender(s) a mortgage on the asset and assigns the lease contract to the lender(s).

Example of a Financial Lease Arrangement

Western Metals and Mining Corporation has entered into discussions with a major finance company regarding the possibility of leasing the mining equipment for its proposed $100 million mining project. Western will need three large electric shovels, each costing $10 million. Suppose that if Western purchases an electric shovel, it would use it for 10 years before selling it. Western expects that each electric shovel will have a market value of approximately $2.0 million after 10 years. The finance company has offered to net lease the electric shovel to Western in return for annual payments of $1.5 million.

Table 22-1 illustrates the direct cash flow consequences to Western of lease financing an electric shovel. The principal benefit Western realizes is the $10 million it does not have to spend to purchase it. This is equivalent

Table 22-1
Direct Cash Flow Consequences to Western of Lease Financing an Electric Shovel
(Dollar Amounts in Millions)

End of Year	Benefit of Leasing — Initial Outlay Avoided	Lease Payments* — Gross	Lease Payments* — Tax Shield†	Lease Payments* — Net	Costs of Leasing — Benefits of Ownership Forgone — Investment Tax Credit	Costs of Leasing — Benefits of Ownership Forgone — Depreciation Tax Shield‡‡	Costs of Leasing — Benefits of Ownership Forgone — Residual Value§	Costs of Leasing — Benefits of Ownership Forgone — Total	Net Cash Flow to Lessee
0	$10.0	$1.5	—	$1.50	$1.0	$0.71	—	$1.71	$8.50
1	—	1.5	$0.75	0.75	—	1.05	—	1.05	(2.46)
2	—	1.5	0.75	0.75	—	1.00	—	1.00	(1.80)
3	—	1.5	0.75	0.75	—	1.00	—	1.00	(1.75)
4	—	1.5	0.75	0.75	—	1.00	—	1.00	(1.75)
5	—	1.5	0.75	0.75	—	1.00	—	1.00	(1.75)
6	—	1.5	0.75	0.75	—	—	—	—	(0.75)
7	—	1.5	0.75	0.75	—	—	—	—	(0.75)
8	—	1.5	0.75	0.75	—	—	—	—	(0.75)
9	—	1.5	0.75	0.75	—	—	—	—	(0.75)
10	—	—	0.75	(0.75)	—	—	$1.0	1.00	(0.25)

*Initial payment due at signing. Lease payments made in advance each year

†Assumes the lessee's marginal income tax rate is 50%.

‡The assumed depreciation schedule involves deductions of 15%, 22%, 21%, 21%, and 21% of 95% of the $10 million purchase price in years 1, 2, 3, 4, and 5, respectively.

§Net of depreciation recapture amounting to $2.0 million × 0.5 = $1.0 million.

to a cash inflow of $10 million. However, Western must make periodic lease payments and must forgo the investment tax credit, depreciation tax shields, and residual value it could realize by owning the electric shovel. Partially offsetting the impact of these cash outflows, the lease payments are tax deductible. The combined effect of these factors is an effective initial net cash inflow of $8.5 million followed by the effective net cash outflows in the rightmost column of Table 22-1.

In Table 22-1, it has been assumed that Western expects to pay taxes at a 50% marginal rate over the next 10 years. If not, the values of the various tax shields would be zero, and the net cash flow column would change accordingly. Lease financing is generally most attractive when the lessee does not expect to be taxable because then the value of the tax benefits foregone is zero.

ADVANTAGES AND DISADVANTAGES OF LEASING

Leasing offers a number of purported advantages. Some are real, but others are probably, for the most part at least, illusory.

Reasons for Leasing

Most leases are short-term operating leases. Such leases provide a convenient means of obtaining the use of an asset for a relatively short period of time. Also, as in the case of computer leases, short-term cancelable leases relieve the lessee of the risk of product obsolescence, which the lessor, such as the equipment manufacturer, might be in a better position to assume. Financial leases typically provide advantages of a different sort.

Reduced Cost of Borrowing. Lease financing often represents a highly cost-effective source of funds for smaller companies. A large leasing company may be able to borrow more cheaply than a smaller operating company. In addition, lessors of readily saleable assets, such as vehicles, do not have to perform credit analyses quite as detailed as those general lenders should conduct, and they are more likely to be able to use "standardized" documentation. This reduces transaction costs.

More Efficient Utilization of Tax Benefits of Ownership. Lease financing provides a mechanism for transferring tax benefits from those who cannot use them to those who can. But in order to do this, the lease must qualify as a "true lease" for tax purposes. The Internal Revenue Service has established guidelines for advance ruling purposes that it applies to distinguish true leases from installment sales agreements and secured loans in a case where the lessor's investment in the property is leveraged. The thrust of the guidelines is to require the lessor to have a specified minimum at-risk investment in the property and to require that the residual have a specified minimum value. Court cases are more generous in treating transactions as leases, notwithstanding the retention of rights by the lessee that would be inconsistent with the guidelines. If the terms of the leasing arrangement satisfy the guidelines, the lessee is entitled to deduct for tax purposes the full amount of each lease payment and the lessor is entitled to the tax benefits of asset ownership and thus can claim the investment tax credit and accelerated depreciation deductions. These guidelines change from time to time, and the case law in the area is also evolving. Consequently, it is important prior to undertaking a financial lease analysis to review the applicable tax standards to verify that a proposed lease arrangement would qualify as a true lease under the tax rules then in effect and to determine whether there might be a more advantageous lease structure that would also so qualify.

New Source of Funds. Lease financing may permit the lessee to tap a new source of funds, for example, finance companies that do not customarily purchase the lessee's securities.

Off-Balance-Sheet Financing. Companies often go to great lengths to design lease structures that achieve off-balance-sheet treatment so as to minimize the impact of the financing on the firm's debt ratio. However, the leasing information disclosed in the footnotes to the firm's financial statements enables securities analysts and the rating agencies to gauge the true financial impact of the leasing arrangements. Indeed, a recent study of the stock market impact of the adoption of FASB 13 found that equity investors had correctly evaluated the financial impact of companies' financial lease obligations prior to the requirement that companies capitalize them on their balance sheets.[1]

Potential Disadvantages of Leasing
The principal disadvantages of leasing are the lessee's forfeiture of the tax benefits of ownership and, in most cases, loss of residual value.

LEASING VERSUS BORROWING AND BUYING

Lease analysis is complex. It also involves some of the more controversial issues in financial management.[2] One cannot hope to deal fully with all the important issues in a single chapter. This section provides but a basic analytical framework for evaluating the lease versus buy alternatives.

Displacement of Debt
Entering into a financial lease agreement is like entering into a loan agreement. There is an immediate cash flow equal to the value of the asset. The lessee realizes this value because it gets the exclusive use of the asset without having

to purchase the asset; it will thus realize the stream of economic benefits (other than tax benefits) that would result if it actually purchased the asset. On the other hand, the lease agreement calls for fixed periodic payments, just like a loan agreement. The lessee must make timely lease payments in order to have uninterrupted use of the asset and so will treat its lease payment obligations just like an interest payment or principal repayment obligation on a loan. Lease financing thus displaces debt. This principle is fundamental to the analysis of lease financing. A company's lease payment obligations belong to the same risk category as the company's interest and principal repayment obligations.

For example, suppose that Western Metals and Mining Corporation currently has $100 million of net assets and a debt-to-equity ratio of 1 : 1. Western's initial capitalization and the impact of different financing alternatives are shown in Table 22-2. If Western financed the $10 million electric shovel on a conventional basis, it would borrow $5 million and invest $5 million of equity funds. That would leave Western with $55 million of debt and $55 million of equity in keeping with its 1 : 1 target debt-to-equity ratio.

If instead Western lease finances the electric shovel and the associated lease obligations have a net present value of $10 million, Western's debt increases to $60 million and its debt-to-equity ratio increases to 1.2 : 1. Western can restore its target debt-to-equity ratio by increasing equity by $5 million and reducing its borrowing for other projects by a like amount. If it does this, its balance sheet will have $45 million of conventional debt plus $10 million of financial lease obligations. Comparing the second and fourth columns of Table 22-2, incurring $10 million of financial lease obligations has displaced $10 million of conventional debt.

Table 22-2
Financial Lease Obligations Displace Debt
(Dollar Amounts in Millions)

	Initial Capitalization	Conventional Financing	Lease Financing	Lease Financing with Target Capitalization Restored
Long-term debt:				
Conventional debt	$ 50	$ 55	$ 50	$ 45
Financial lease obligations	—	—	10	10
Total debt	50	55	60	55
Equity	50	55	50	55
Net assets	$100	$110	$110	$110
Debt-to-equity	1 : 1	1 : 1	1.2 : 1	1 : 1

PRIME IDEAS

APR 27
FORATTEK

MAR 1 / 2

MEADOWS

Cal State

Prime Contractors

MIT

APRIL END

Sept ?

MAR 2 Cancel

→ Designers

BILL
SLACK

MIDLAND
TEXAS

To Lease or to Borrow and Buy

Lease financing often proves less costly than conventional debt financing when a company cannot utilize the tax benefits of ownership; which alternative proves cheaper depends principally on the relative after-tax cash flows required under the lease financing and conventional debt financing alternatives.

The balance of this section assumes that a company has already decided to purchase the asset in question, using the techniques described in Part 2, and is now trying to decide whether asset-based financing would be more economical than conventional financing. The next section deals with how a company can incorporate lease financing analysis directly into its capital budgeting analysis.

Adjusted-Present-Value Approach

The adjusted-present-value approach lends itself very nicely to the lease versus borrow-and-buy decision because the financing is tied to a specific asset. Generalizing from Formula 9-11, the adjusted present value is equal to the sum of (1) the net present value of base case cash flows when discounted at an appropriate rate plus (2) the present value of the tax shields that result from the financing of the project plus (3) the net present value of project-related side effects.

In the case of the lease versus borrow-and-buy decision, the base case cash flows include (1) the cost of the asset plus (2) operating and other expenses, if any, that the lessor bears less (3) the investment tax credit the lessee forgoes less also (4) the pretax lease payments less also (5) the depreciation tax shields the lessee forgoes less also (6) the asset's residual value, if any, that the lessee forgoes. The appropriate discount rate for the lease payments is the lessee's pretax cost of secured debt because a company's lease payments belong to the same risk category as the company's debt service payments and the lease obligations are fully secured (because the lessor retains ownership of the asset). The depreciation tax shields are typically discounted at this rate, but operating expenses and residual value should be discounted at a higher rate, perhaps the company's cost of capital, to reflect their greater riskiness.

The tax shields that result from lease financing are due to the tax deductibility of the lease payments. The appropriate discount rate is thus the lessee's pretax cost of secured debt. The project-related side effects relate to the displaced debt capacity. This factor is particularly important in lease analysis. Overlooking it can lead to serious errors.

Under the adjusted-present-value approach, the *net advantage of leasing* can be calculated according to the following model:

$$\begin{matrix} \text{Net advantage} \\ \text{of leasing} \end{matrix} = \begin{matrix} \text{net present value of} \\ \text{base case cash flows} \end{matrix} + \begin{matrix} \text{present value of lease} \\ \text{payment tax shields} \end{matrix}$$

$$- \begin{matrix} \text{present value of tax shields} \\ \text{lost on displaced debt} \end{matrix} \qquad (22\text{-}1)$$

where

$$\begin{array}{l}\text{Net present value of} \\ \text{base case cash flows}\end{array} = \begin{array}{l}\text{cost of} \\ \text{asset}\end{array} + \begin{array}{l}\text{present value of} \\ \text{expenses lessor bears}\end{array}$$

$$- \begin{array}{l}\text{present value of} \\ \text{investment} \\ \text{tax credit lost}\end{array} - \begin{array}{l}\text{present value of} \\ \text{lease payments}\end{array}$$

$$- \begin{array}{l}\text{present value of} \\ \text{depreciation} \\ \text{tax shields lost}\end{array} - \begin{array}{l}\text{present value of} \\ \text{residual value lost}\end{array} \quad (22\text{-}2)$$

In Formula 22-2, the *present value of expenses lessor bears* refers to expenses (net of related tax deductions) such as maintenance costs that the lessee would have to pay if it owned the asset but that the lessor has agreed to pay. The *present value of residual value lost* depends on whether the lease agreement provides for a purchase option. If it does, the residual value lost is the price the lessee must pay to acquire the asset.

Net Present Value of Base Case Cash Flows. Reconsider the decision confronting Western Metals and Mining Corporation. Suppose that Western's pretax cost of secured debt is 12% and the cost of capital is 15%. Applying Formula 22-2 to the cost figures in Table 22-1 gives

$$\begin{array}{l}\text{Net present value} \\ \text{of base case} \\ \text{cash flows}\end{array} = \$10.0 + 0 - \frac{1.0}{1.12} - \sum_{t=0}^{9} \frac{1.5}{(1.12)^t} - \left[\frac{0.71}{1.12} + \frac{1.05}{(1.12)^2}\right.$$

$$\left. + \frac{1.00}{(1.12)^3} + \frac{1.00}{(1.12)^4} + \frac{1.00}{(1.12)^5}\right] - \frac{1.0}{(1.15)^{10}}$$

$$= -\$4.02 \text{ million} \quad (22\text{-}3)$$

The *net present value of base case cash flows* is negative. On this basis, lease financing does not appear to be advantageous.

Present Value of Lease Payment Tax Shields. The present value of the lease payment tax shields is:

$$\begin{array}{l}\text{Present value of lease} \\ \text{payment tax shields}\end{array} = \sum_{t=1}^{10} \frac{\$0.75}{(1.12)^t} = \$4.24 \text{ million} \quad (22\text{-}4)$$

Western's ability to deduct fully the lease payments would contribute approximately $4.24 million to the value of leasing.

Present Value of Tax Shields Lost on Displaced Debt. Calculating the present value of the tax shields on the debt displaced by the lease financing requires

Table 22-3
Calculation of Equivalent Loan

Year	Funds Available for Debt Service	Debt at Beginning of Following Year	Funds Available to Service Debt to be Repaid*	Debt Repaid at Year-End†	Debt at Beginning of Year‡	Interest Paid
1	$2,460,000	$8,317,595	$1,960,944	$1,849,947	$10,167,542	$1,220,105
2	1,800,000	7,016,651	1,379,001	1,300,944	8,317,595	998,111
3	1,750,000	5,687,650	1,408,741	1,329,001	7,016,651	841,998
4	1,750,000	4,278,908	1,493,266	1,408,742	5,687,650	682,518
5	1,750,000	2,785,643	1,582,861	1,493,265	4,278,908	513,469
6	750,000	2,202,782	617,833	582,861	2,785,643	334,277
7	750,000	1,584,949	654,903	617,833	2,202,782	264,334
8	750,000	930,046	694,197	654,903	1,584,949	190,194
9	750,000	235,849	735,849	694,197	930,046	111,606
10	250,000	—	250,000	235,849	235,849	28,302

*Calculated as funds available for debt service less after-tax interest obligation on debt outstanding as of beginning of following year.
†Calculated in accordance with Formula 22-5.
‡Calculated as debt at beginning of following year plus debt repaid at year-end.

working out exactly how much debt is displaced at each point in time. This involves specifying an *equivalent loan* that requires after-tax debt service each period equal to the net cash flow (base case cash flow less lease payment tax shield) to the lessee under the lease arrangement.

Table 22-3 illustrates the calculation of the equivalent loan. The "net cash flow to lessee" in Table 22-1 for years 1 through 10 represents the available after-tax debt service. The equivalent loan must be fully repaid by the end of year 10. There is $250,000 available to pay debt service at the end of year 10. Each dollar of debt outstanding at the beginning of year 10 requires $1 of principal repayment and $0.06 of after-tax interest because the pretax cost of debt is 12% and the tax rate is 50%. Thus,

$$\$250,000/1.06 = \$235,849$$

of debt can be outstanding at the beginning of year 10.

There is $0.75 million available to pay debt service at the end of year 9. Of this amount, $235,849 \times 0.06 = $14,151 must be used to service debt that will remain outstanding at the beginning of the following year. That leaves $735,849 (= $750,000 − 14,151) to service debt that will be repaid at year-end. Such debt amounts to

$$\$735,849/1.06 = \$694,197$$

Proceeding in this manner, the amount of debt the lessee could repay at the end of the year can be calculated according to the formula

$$\left[\begin{array}{c} \text{Funds available} \\ \text{for debt service} \end{array} - \left(1 - \frac{\text{tax}}{\text{rate}}\right) \times \begin{array}{c} \text{interest} \\ \text{rate} \end{array} \times \begin{array}{c} \text{debt at beginning} \\ \text{of following year} \end{array} \right]$$

$$\div \left[1 + \left(1 - \frac{\text{tax}}{\text{rate}}\right) \times \frac{\text{interest}}{\text{rate}} \right] = \begin{array}{c} \text{debt repaid} \\ \text{at year-end} \end{array}$$

$$(22\text{-}5)$$

Western could have an equivalent loan of \$10,167,542 outstanding at the beginning of year 1.

The interest payments on the equivalent loan are shown in the rightmost column of Table 22-3. The associated tax shields are $1 - tax\ rate = 0.5$ times each payment. Thus,

$$\begin{array}{c} \text{Present value of} \\ \text{tax shields lost} \\ \text{on displaced debt} \end{array} = \$ \frac{0.610}{1.12} + \frac{0.499}{(1.12)^2} + \frac{0.421}{(1.12)^3} + \frac{0.341}{(1.12)^4}$$

$$+ \frac{0.257}{(1.12)^5} + \frac{0.167}{(1.12)^6} + \frac{0.132}{(1.12)^7} + \frac{0.095}{(1.12)^8}$$

$$+ \frac{0.056}{(1.12)^9} + \frac{0.014}{(1.12)^{10}} = \$1.81 \text{ million} \qquad (22\text{-}6)$$

Combining these results

$$\begin{array}{c} \text{Net advantage} \\ \text{of leasing} \end{array} = -\$4.02 + 4.24 - 1.81 = -\$1.59 \text{ million}$$

The *net advantage of leasing* is negative. Western should borrow and buy rather than lease according to this analysis. Western's ability to utilize the tax benefits of ownership fully itself is largely responsible for this negative value.

Equivalent-Loan Approach

A second approach to the lease versus borrow-and-buy decision involves simply comparing the amount of financing provided by the lease to the amount of financing provided by the equivalent loan. The two alternatives involve identical debt service requirements. The alternative that provides the greater amount of financing thus represents the preferred alternative.

In the example under consideration, the lease provides \$8.50 million of financing but the equivalent loan provides \$10.17 million. Thus, borrowing and buying is the more advantageous method of financing.

Net-Present-Value Approach

A study by Lewellen and Emery demonstrates that under reasonable assumptions, discounting the base case cash flows and the lease payment tax shields at the lessee's after-tax cost of secured debt is equivalent to the adjusted-present-value approach reflected in Formula 22-1.[3] Using the after-tax cost of debt automatically takes into account the lease financing's debt capacity side effects.

The net-present-value approach can be summarized in the formula

$$
\begin{aligned}
\text{Net present} \\
\text{value of} \\
\text{leasing}
\end{aligned}
= \frac{\text{cost of}}{\text{asset}} + \sum_{t=1}^{\text{term}} \frac{\text{operating savings}(t)}{(1 + \text{cost of capital})^t}
$$

$$
- \sum_{t=0}^{\text{term}} \left\{ \left[\begin{array}{c} \text{lease} \\ \text{payment}(t) \end{array} - \begin{array}{c} \text{lease tax} \\ \text{shields}(t) \end{array} + \begin{array}{c} \text{benefits of} \\ \text{ownership} \\ \text{forgone}(t) \end{array} \right] \right.
$$

$$
\left. \div \left(1 + \frac{\text{after-tax}}{\text{cost of debt}} \right)^t \right\} - \frac{\text{residual value forgone}}{(1 + \text{cost of capital})^{\text{term}}}
$$

$$(22\text{-}7)$$

where *term* denotes the term of the lease. Applying Formula 22-7 to the net cash flows in Table 22-1 gives

$$
\begin{aligned}
\text{Net present} \\
\text{value of leasing}
\end{aligned}
= \$8.50 - \frac{2.46}{1.06} - \frac{1.80}{(1.06)^2} - \frac{1.75}{(1.06)^3} - \frac{1.75}{(1.06)^4}
$$

$$
- \frac{1.75}{(1.06)^5} - \frac{0.75}{(1.06)^6} - \frac{0.75}{(1.06)^7} - \frac{0.75}{(1.06)^8}
$$

$$
- \frac{0.75}{(1.06)^9} + \frac{0.75}{(1.06)^{10}} - \frac{1.00}{(1.15)^{10}} = -\$1.36 \text{ million}
$$

Internal-Rate-of-Return Approach

As in the case of capital budgeting analysis, the lease versus borrow-and-buy decision can be approached through internal-rate-of-return analysis instead of present-value analysis.[4] The internal-rate-of-return approach involves solving for the internal rate of return of the net cash flow stream:

$$
0 = \frac{\text{cost of}}{\text{asset}} + \sum_{t=1}^{\text{term}} \frac{\text{operating savings}(t)}{(1 + \text{IRR})^t}
$$

$$
- \sum_{t=0}^{\text{term}} \left\{ \left[\begin{array}{c} \text{lease} \\ \text{payment}(t) \end{array} - \begin{array}{c} \text{lease tax} \\ \text{shields}(t) \end{array} + \begin{array}{c} \text{benefits of} \\ \text{ownership forgone}(t) \end{array} \right] \right.
$$

$$
\left. \div (1 + \text{IRR})^t \right\} - \frac{\text{residual value forgone}}{(1 + \text{IRR})^{\text{term}}} \qquad (22\text{-}8)
$$

The internal rate of return, denoted IRR, represents the *cost of lease financing*. It is an after-tax cost. If the cost of lease financing is less than the prospective lessee's after-tax cost of secured debt, the company should lease finance the asset. Otherwise is should borrow funds and buy the asset.

In the case of Western's proposed lease financing, IRR solves the equation

$$
0 = 8.50 - \frac{2.46}{(1 + \text{IRR})} - \frac{1.80}{(1 + \text{IRR})^2} - \frac{1.75}{(1 + \text{IRR})^3} - \frac{1.75}{(1 + \text{IRR})^4}
$$
$$
- \frac{1.75}{(1 + \text{IRR})^5} - \frac{0.75}{(1 + \text{IRR})^6} - \frac{0.75}{(1 + \text{IRR})^7} - \frac{0.75}{(1 + \text{IRR})^8}
$$
$$
- \frac{0.75}{(1 + \text{IRR})^9} - \frac{0.25}{(1 + \text{IRR})^{10}}
$$

$$
\text{Cost of lease financing} = \text{IRR} = 0.1144, \text{ or } 11.44\%
$$

The cost of lease financing is greater than Western's after-tax cost of debt (6.00%) so that Western should borrow funds and buy the asset according to the internal-rate-of-return criterion.

Comparison of Lease Evaluation Techniques

The adjusted-present-value approach, equivalent-loan approach, net-present-value approach, and internal-rate-of-return approach are essentially equivalent approaches. Note that the difference between the amounts of funds the equivalent loan and the lease provide is

$$
\$8.50 - 10.17 = -\$1.67 \text{ million} \cong \frac{\text{net advantage}}{\text{of leasing}} \cong \frac{\text{net present}}{\text{value of leasing}}
$$

The reader can verify that the first three approaches would all indicate a $1.67 million disadvantage to leasing if residual value were discounted at the cost of debt rather than at the cost of capital. However, the net-present-value approach is generally the simplest of the three to apply.

The internal-rate-of-return approach will normally yield decisions consistent with the other three approaches. Financial decision makers may prefer it, however, because it avoids the problem of having to choose a discount rate (or set of discount rates) and because many decision makers feel it is easier to think in terms of percentage costs rather than present values. However, the internal-rate-of-return approach does suffer from two deficiencies. A single discount rate applies to all cash flows regardless of differences in relative risk. Also, there are often two or more changes in sign in the net cash flow stream. In those situations, there may be more than one candidate for "the" internal rate of return. As a practical matter, both problems are typically of little significance. If the decision maker feels more comfortable with the internal-rate-of-return approach, then that method should be employed.

When Is Lease Financing Advantageous?

It should be apparent to the reader that lease financing the electric shovel would be advantageous to Western if (1) Western is not a tax payer, cannot utilize the shield benefits arising out of the proposed mining project as carrybacks, and does not expect to be able to use the benefits as carryforwards and (2) Western can repurchase the shovel at the end of the lease term for an inconsequential sum. (It would be inconsistent with the Internal Revenue Service guidelines and most decided cases, however, for there to be any agreement at the inception of the lease that gives the lessee the right to purchase the property at the end of the lease term for an inconsequential sum.) In that case, the lease arrangement involves solely the sale of tax benefits, which would be worthless to Western if it were not able to claim these tax benefits. The lessee and the lessor can both benefit under the lease arrangement—at the expense of the government, which suffers a reduction in tax revenue.

For a non-tax-paying corporation, Formulas 22-1 and 22-2 reduce to

$$\begin{aligned} \text{Net advantage} \atop \text{of leasing} &= {\text{cost of} \atop \text{asset}} + {\text{present value of} \atop \text{expenses lessor bears}} \\ &- {\text{present value of} \atop \text{lease payments}} - {\text{present value of} \atop \text{residual value lost}} \quad (22\text{-}9) \end{aligned}$$

In the case of Western's contemplated lease financing,[5]

$$\begin{aligned} \text{Net advantage} \atop \text{of leasing} = \$10,000 - \sum_{t=0}^{9} \frac{1500}{(1.12)^t} - \frac{2000}{(1.15)^{10}} = \$13,300 \end{aligned}$$

In general, the net benefits that a lessee and a lessor realize collectively result from the tax efficiency of leasing. These net benefits are greater (1) the higher the lessor's marginal tax rate is relative to the lessee's marginal tax rate and (2) the greater and the more accelerated are the tax deductions available to the owner of an asset.

INTEGRATING LEASING CONSIDERATIONS INTO CAPITAL BUDGETING

Lease financing can effectively reduce a company's cost of capital by enabling a lessee to sell tax benefits that might otherwise go underutilized. It is possible that a project that would be uneconomic if the firm had to finance it on a conventional basis might become economic if lease financed. In addition, bankruptcy considerations may be important. A lessor normally experiences less difficulty and finds it less expensive than a secured lender to seize the asset in the event of bankruptcy because the lessor is the owner of the asset. Suppliers of capital to smaller companies or to less creditworthy companies, for whom the risk of bankruptcy is greater, often prefer to channel funds through a lease rather than a loan.

A capital investment project whose net present value is negative can become economic if the value the non-tax-paying company realizes through the sale of the tax benefits of ownership more than offsets the negative net present value of the project's pretax cash flows. Table 22-4 illustrates the cash flow streams for a project that would be economic if lease financed but uneconomic if financed on a conventional basis. Because lease financing is asset-specific, the adjusted-present-value technique should be used in the capital investment analysis.

It is assumed in Table 22-4 that the company will never be able to claim the tax benefits of ownership. Debt financing would be of no benefit in that case. Assuming a 15% marginal cost of equity capital, the adjusted present value of the project assuming conventional financing is − $2.31 million. The project would not be economic if it were financed on a conventional basis.

Table 22-4
Comparison of Conventional Financing and Lease Financing
(Dollar Amounts in Millions)

Period	Cost of Asset	Net Cash Benefits	Residual Value	Net Cash Flow	Lease Payment	Equivalent Loan Debt Service
0	$50.00	—	—	−$50.00	$8.50	—*
1	—	$12.00	—	12.00	8.50	$ 8.50
2	—	11.50	—	11.50	8.50	8.50
3	—	11.50	—	11.50	8.50	8.50
4	—	11.00	—	11.00	8.50	8.50
5	—	11.00	—	11.00	8.50	8.50
6	—	10.50	—	10.50	8.50	8.50
7	—	10.50	$2.00	12.50	—	2.00†

Adjusted present value of project (conventional)	−$ 2.31
Amount of equivalent loan‡	$35.85
Net advantage of leasing:	
Cost of asset	$50.00
Initial lease payment	8.50
Financing provided by lease	41.50
Amount of equivalent loan	35.85
Net advantage of leasing	$ 5.65

*Initial lease payment decreases the amount of financing provided by the lease.
†Represents residual value forgone.
‡Assumes a new issue rate of 12.00% for the company's debt.

Suppose instead the project were financed under a lease arrangement that calls for lease payments of $8.50 million at the beginning of each year. The calculation of the adjusted present value of the project must take into account project-related side effects in the form of savings (or additional costs, if negative) resulting from the lease financing:

$$\begin{array}{ccc}
\text{Adjusted present value} & = & \text{adjusted present value} \\
\text{of project (leased)} & & \text{of project (conventional)}
\end{array} + \begin{array}{c}
\text{net advantage} \\
\text{of leasing}
\end{array}$$

$$= -\$2.31 + 5.65 = \$3.34 \text{ million}$$

The *net advantage of leasing* is estimated in Table 22-4 using the equivalent-loan approach. The lease rate is low enough that the *net advantage of leasing* outweighs the negative *adjusted present value of project (conventional)*. In effect, the lessor is willing to pay enough for the tax benefits to make the project economic.

Note that the project's residual value also plays an important role in the economics of leasing. If the residual value were, say, $20 million, the adjusted present value of project (conventional) would be $4.46 million and the net advantage of leasing would be $- $2.49 million. The sponsor should finance the project in that case on a conventional basis even though it does not expect to be able to utilize any of the tax benefits of ownership.

PROJECT FINANCING

Companies often find it advantageous to finance large capital investment projects that involve discrete assets on a project, or stand-alone, basis. *Project financing* is generally possible when:

- The project consists of a discrete asset (or a set of assets) that is capable of standing alone as an independent economic unit.
- The economic prospects of the project, combined with commitments from sponsors and/or third parties, assure that the project will generate sufficient cash flow to service project debt.

The development or construction of mines, mineral processing facilities, electric generating facilities, pipelines, dock facilities, paper mills, oil refineries, and chemical plants have been financed on a project basis.

Project Structure
Each project is unique in certain respects, and the project financing arrangements are designed to suit the project's special characteristics. Suppose that Western Metals and Mining Corporation wishes to develop the coal mine property discussed previously in order to obtain coal to sell to Electric Generating Company, and in return for an assured source of coal supply Electric

is willing to enter into a long-term coal purchase contract with Western. The mine will cost $100 million, and Western would like to borrow a portion of this amount. As described below, the terms of the coal purchase contract can be drawn in such a way that the contract will provide credit support for the loans Western will arrange to finance development of the mine. In the extreme case, the loans may be *nonrecourse* to Western so that lenders will look solely to payments under the coal purchase contract to service their loans.

Projects like the mine project are typically financed with between 50 and 75% debt when financed on a stand-alone basis. The level of borrowing is linked directly to the inherent economic value of the project's assets and to the extent of credit support provided by sponsors, suppliers, customers, governments, and other entities related to the project; and the project loan is designed to be self-liquidating from revenues generated by the project. This credit support takes the form of contractual arrangements to supply raw materials or take output, such as the coal purchase contract mentioned earlier; debt guarantees; insurance; and undertakings such as an obligation by Western to *complete* the mine (i.e., to bring it into production). The coal purchase contract, for example, is important to lenders because it guarantees a market for the mine's output. It reduces the risk that the mine will be rendered uneconomic and transfers a portion of the economic risk of the project from Western to Electric.

Security Arrangements in Project Financing
One of the more crucial aspects of project financing involves identifying project risks and then designing contractual arrangements to (1) allocate those risks among the various parties involved with the project and (2) convey the credit strength of creditworthy companies to support project debt. These credit support arrangements typically include the following.

Completion Undertaking.
There is always a risk that a project will not be brought into operation successfully either because there is a technical failure (e.g., it fails to operate at its design capacity) or because cost overruns make it uneconomic to complete construction or impossible for sponsors to raise the additional funds. Lenders are seldom willing to assume completion risk, but banks may be willing to assume it when the sponsor has sufficient equity invested and the economics are so compelling that noncompletion is very unlikely. A completion undertaking obligates the sponsors or other creditworthy entities either (1) to assure that the project will pass certain performance tests by some specified date or (2) to repay the debt. As an example of the former, the coal mine might be required to produce a certain number of tons of coal per month for a certain specified number of months prior to some specified date.

Purchase, Throughput, or Tolling Agreements. These obligate one or more creditworthy entities to purchase the project's output or use its facilities. Purchase agreements that are capable of supporting project financing take the form of *take-or-pay contracts*, which obligate the purchaser to take the project's output or else pay for it if product is offered for delivery (but normally only if product is available for delivery), or *hell-or-high-water contracts*, which obligate the purchaser to pay in all events, that is, whether or not any output is available for delivery. The latter is, of course, stronger and therefore provides greater credit support. *Throughput agreements*, which are often used in pipeline financing, require shippers to put some specified minimum amount of product through the pipeline each period in order to enable the pipeline to generate sufficient cash to cover its operating expenses and its debt service requirements. *Tolling agreements*, which are often used in financing processing facilities, require users to process a certain specified minimum amount of raw material each period.

Raw Material Supply Agreements. These require that the sponsors or other creditworthy entities supply the facility's raw material needs or else make compensatory payments.

Cash Deficiency Agreements. Unless the purchase, throughput, or tolling agreement is of the hell-or-high-water variety, interruptions in availability or deliverability can result in the project realizing insufficient cash to meet its debt service obligations. Sponsors may therefore have to provide supplemental credit support in the form of an *equity contribution agreement*, which obligates them to invest additional cash as equity as required by the project to meet its debt service obligations; a *dividend clawback* or *tax clawback agreement*, which obligates the sponsors to repay cash dividends previously received from the project or to contribute the cash value of project-related tax benefits they realize from their participation in the project; or some other form of *cash deficiency agreement* that will provide cash flow to meet the project's obligations to lenders. The stronger the cash deficiency arrangement, the greater the proportion of economic risk borne by the project's sponsors.

The contractual arrangements will determine how much of the project risks are transferred to other parties. It is important for a project sponsor and its advisors to analyze carefully a proposed set of contractual arrangements to ensure that the risks the sponsor will have to bear are tolerable and that the allocation of the economic rewards of the project is commensurate with the allocation of project risks.

Principal Advantages of Project Financing
When applied appropriately, project financing affords a number of significant advantages relative to financing on the sponsors' general credit.

Risk-Sharing. A sponsor can enlist one or more joint venture partners to share the equity risk. Under certain circumstances, a project sponsor can transfer risks to suppliers, to purchasers, and, to a limited degree, to lenders through contractual arrangements like those just discussed. Risks can be allocated to parties who are best able to bear them.

Expanded Debt Capacity. By financing on a project basis rather than on its general credit, a company can often achieve a higher degree of leverage than would be consistent with its senior debt rating objective. Project-related contractual arrangements transfer portions of the business and financial risk to others, which permits greater leverage. In addition, if a company's joint venture partners own at least 50% of project equity, project debt would not normally appear on the company's balance sheet.[6] The expansion in debt capacity is generally greater when project loans are nonrecourse to project sponsors. Finally, project financings can usually be structured so that they fall outside the debt restrictions contained in the sponsoring company's bond indentures and loan agreements.

Lower Cost of Debt. In some cases, the purchasers of the project's output will have a higher credit standing than project sponsors. In that case, financing on the purchasers' credit rather than on the sponsors' credit can lead to a lower cost of debt.

Principal Disadvantage of Project Financing

Project financing involves costs in addition to those incurred in connection with conventional financing. The contractual arrangements are often complex. Consequently, arranging a project financing generally involves significant legal costs and investment bankers' fees. In addition, lenders generally require a yield premium in return for accepting credit support in the form of contractual undertakings rather than a company's direct promise to pay. Moreover, they require additional yield premiums to compensate for any business risk they assume. One study found that project borrowings generally involved a yield premium of between 1 and 2 percentage points.[7] The higher yield and higher transaction costs can be at least partially offset if project financing permits higher leverage.

When to Consider Project Financing

A company should consider financing a capital investment project on a project basis whenever a project consists of a discrete (set of) asset(s) that is capable of standing alone as an independent economic unit and (1) the project is "too big" for the company to pursue on its own or (2) there is a readily identifiable set of purchasers for the project's output who would be willing to enter into contractual commitments strong enough to support project financing or (3) the project's economics are so attractive that lenders would be willing to advance funds on a nonrecourse basis. A project that can be financed on a project basis should be so financed only if that method of financing leads to a greater adjusted present value. This will generally be the case when the tax shield benefits owing to the higher degree of leverage exceed the costs associated with the yield premium lenders require plus the higher after-tax expenses associated with the financing.

PRODUCTION PAYMENT FINANCING

Projects that involve the development of natural resources, particularly oil and gas projects, are often financed through a special form of nonrecourse asset-based financing known as *production payment financing*. A production payment involves a right to a specified share of the revenue from the production from a particular mineral property. A company normally borrows against a production payment contract by selling the contract to a special purpose trust or corporation, which borrows the purchase price from one or more banks. (Banks are generally not permitted to own mineral interests directly.) This loan is secured by the production payment contract and is repaid exclusively from revenues generated from the production and sale of the minerals.

In order for the production payment contract to be valuable as collateral, the mineral deposit covered by the production payment must contain adequate proven reserves, the reserves must be recoverable at reasonable cost, and there must be an assured market for the production. When the collateral value is deemed adequate and the operator provides a completion undertaking satisfactory to lenders, a company can typically borrow between 50 and 80% of the present value of the future cash flow expected from the sale of production from the reserves.

Production payment financing affords a number of advantages relative to direct financing on a company's general credit:

- Production payment loans are typically nonrecourse, thus expanding the company's debt capacity.
- Debt service is generally tied to production, which enables the company to defer its debt service obligations until production has begun.
- The rating agencies do not view a nonrecourse production payment as debt.[8]

The two potential disadvantages of production payment financing are that lenders typically require a yield premium to compensate for the risk that production may later prove inadequate to cover debt service fully, and that borrowers suffer some reduction in operating flexibility because the production payment contract may require production during periods when production is uneconomic, for example, because of low mineral prices.

LIMITED PARTNERSHIP FINANCING

Leveraged lease financing represents a cost-effective alternative to debt financing when the lessee is unable to utilize fully the tax benefits of asset ownership. Limited partnership financing represents a tax-oriented form of equity financing. Limited partnerships have been formed to finance real estate projects, oil and gas exploration and development, filmmaking, cable television systems, and various other ventures.

Characteristics of Limited Partnerships

A *limited partnership* is a special form of partnership in which certain partners, called *limited partners*, enjoy limited liability; their liability is limited to the funds they have invested or otherwise have put at risk in the limited partnership. The limited partners are passive investors like the stockholders of a corporation. But a limited partnership does not pay taxes; gains or losses for tax purposes flow through to the partners. Thus, a company that plans a tax-intensive investment, such as oil and gas drilling, but believes it will not have sufficient taxable income to utilize fully the tax benefits of the venture, could form a limited partnership to flow the tax benefits through to investors. Particularly in risky projects like oil exploration, these tax benefits can offer a substantial inducement to individual investors to share the investment risks inherent in such projects.

A limited partnership is operated by a *general partner*. The general partner often invests only a small percentage of the total equity of the limited partnership, typically between 1 and 10% for limited partnerships that are sold to individual investors. Profits, losses, tax credits, and cash distributions are allocated among the partners in accordance with a sharing formula specified at the time the limited partnership is formed. Typically, cash is distributed between the general partner and the limited partners in proportion to their respective equity investments until the limited partners have recovered their capital. Thereafter, the percentage of cash allocated to the general partner increases, often substantially. For example, Cinema Group Partners was formed in 1981. The general partner contributed 10% of partnership capital. The limited partners were promised 90% of profits, losses, tax credits, and cash distributions until they had recovered their investment; thereafter, 80% until they had received cash representing in the aggregate 200% of their investment; thereafter, 70% until they had received cash representing in the aggregate 300% of their investment; and 60% of any subsequent cash distributions.[9] In addition, the general partner typically receives a management fee, which was calculated as 4% of the limited partnership's net worth in the case of Cinema Group Partners.

Types of Limited Partnership Structures

There are two basic types of limited partnership structures, depending on whether individual investors or institutional investors are being solicited. These two classes of investors have different investment objectives and exhibit different attitudes toward risk. The economic characteristics of the investment will determine to a large extent whether it is more appropriate for individual or institutional limited partnership financing. In general, individual investors are more tax-motivated than institutional investors. They look for tax deductions in the early years for the return of their investment. They are more willing than institutional investors to wait until the later years for actual cash distributions. Institutional investors exhibit a lower tolerance for bearing economic risk than individual investors and prefer investments that will afford more or less regular cash distributions throughout the life of the project.

Tax-intensive investments, such as oil and gas exploration, filmmaking, or research and development, are marketed almost exclusively to individual investors. The partnerships are designed so that the limited partners realize the bulk of the available tax benefits but also bear a substantial share of the economic risks. Investment projects that do not involve special tax incentives are typically marketed to institutional investors. To gain acceptance among these investors, the limited partnership normally must require a significant equity contribution by the general partner(s), cash distributions over the life of the project comparable to what an institution would earn on a bond investment of the same magnitude as its investment in the limited partnership, and, overall, what the institutions perceive as a "fair sharing" of the economic risks and rewards associated with the investment.

Measuring the Corporation's Incremental Cash Flows

A corporation that sets up a limited partnership and serves as general partner effectively experiences the following cash flow benefits and costs:

- Initial cash inflow equal to the net proceeds from the sale of units of limited partnership interest.
- Annual cash inflows equal to the taxes payable on the portion of partnership taxable income allocated to the limited partners.
- Initial cash outflow equal to the amount of the investment tax credit allocated to the limited partners.
- Annual cash outflows equal to (1) the cash distributions to the limited partners plus (2) the tax shield resulting from the portion of partnership tax losses allocated to the limited partners.
- Terminal cash outflow equal to the residual value net of taxes of the limited partnership's assets allocated to the limited partners.

In addition, if the limited partnership borrows funds and lenders have recourse to the general partner for payment of interest and repayment of principal, such financing impinges upon the general partner's debt capacity.

Table 22-5
Calculation of Cost of Limited Partner Capital
(Dollar Amounts in Millions)

End of Year	Net Proceeds of Financing[a]	Partnership Operating Cash Flow	Partnership Taxable Income[b]	Distribution to Limited Partners[c]	Investment Tax Credit Forgone[d]	Tax on Income (Loss) Forgone[e]	Residual Value Forgone	Net Cash Flow to Sponsor[f]
0	$45.8	—	—	—	—	—	—	$45.80
1	—	($1.5)	($1.50)	—	$1.58	($0.68)	—	–2.26
2	—	(3.0)	(3.00)	—	3.00	(1.35)	—	–4.35
3	—	3.5	0.24	$ 3.15	—	0.11	—	–3.04
4	—	7.0	2.21	6.30	—	1.00	—	–5.30
5	—	10.0	5.43	9.00	—	2.45	—	–6.55
6	—	12.0	7.43	10.80	—	3.35	—	–7.45
7	—	14.0	9.43	12.60	—	4.25	—	–8.35
8	—	16.0	16.00	11.62	—	5.81	—	–5.81
9	—	17.5	17.50	8.75	—	4.38	—	–4.37
10	—	19.0	19.00	9.50	—	4.75	$58.51[g]	–63.26

Cost of limited partner capital[h] = 12.26%

[a] Calculated as gross proceeds of $50 million less 8% selling commission and $200,000 of miscellaneous expenses.

[b] Calculated as operating cash flow less ACRS 5-year depreciation on 95% of asset cost (6.53, 9.57, 9.14, 9.14, and 9.14 in years 3 through 7, respectively).

[c] Calculated as 90% of operating cash flow until limited partners recover their $50 million investment (during year 8) and 50% of operating cash flow thereafter.

[d] Assumes 10% investment tax credit with $15.8 million of limited partners' funds invested in year 1 and $30.0 million invested in year 2.

[e] Taxes payable (credit) by the general partner if the income allocated to the limited partners had instead been included in its income. Calculation assumes a 50% marginal corporate income tax rate.

[f] Calculated as the net proceeds of financing plus tax on income (loss) forgone less distribution to limited partners less also investment tax credit and residual value forgone.

[g] Assumes the cable television system is sold for 9 times year 10 operating cash flow, or $171.0 million. Residual value forgone is net of tax on depreciation recapture of $39.16 ($19.58) forgone and tax on capital gain of $26.45 ($7.41) forgone.

[h] Calculated as the internal rate of return of the net cash flow stream.

This imposes a cost, like that experienced in connection with leasing, equal to the value of the tax shield benefits forgone as a result of this loss of debt capacity.

Table 22-5 illustrates the incremental cash flows associated with financing a new cable television system on an all-equity basis through a limited partnership that the general partner intends to terminate after 10 years. The financing involves the sale of $50 million of units of limited partnership interest that raises $45.8 million net of issuance expenses. The limited partnership agreement calls for the limited partners to contribute 90% of partnership capital; to receive 90% of partnership gains, losses, tax credits, and cash distributions until they have received aggregate cash flows equal to their original $50 million investment; and to receive 50% of partnership gains, losses, tax credits, and cash distributions thereafter. It is assumed in Table 22-5 that the limited partnership sells the cable television system after 10 years for nine times the last year's operating cash flow, or $171 million, half of which it must distribute to the limited partners. The general partner thus foregoes $85.5 million less tax (calculated at the applicable corporate rates) on the depreciation recapture and capital gains tax liabilities that must be borne by the limited partners. This leaves $58.51 million of after-tax forgone residual value.

Measuring the Cost of Limited Partner Capital

The cost of the capital raised from limited partners is just the discount rate that equates the present value of the cash outflows in Table 22-5 to the initial $45.8 million cash inflow:

$$\begin{array}{c} \text{Net proceeds} \\ \text{of financing} \end{array} = \sum_{t=1}^{T} \begin{array}{c} \text{net cash flow} \\ \text{in year } t \end{array} \div \left(1 + \begin{array}{c} \text{cost of limited} \\ \text{partner capital} \end{array} \right)^{t}$$

(22-10)

$$\begin{array}{c} \text{Cost of limited} \\ \text{partner capital} \end{array} = 12.26\%$$

The cost of limited partner capital in this case should be compared with the sponsor's cost of common equity because limited partnership financing represents an alternative to straight common equity financing. For example, if the sponsor of the investment project has a 15% marginal cost of common equity for investment projects of this type, limited partnership financing is cheaper than straight common equity financing.

The cost of limited partner capital depends importantly on the limited partners' tax position and on the asset's residual value. The higher the tax rate on the limited partners' income, the greater the value of the tax shields transferred to them and the lower is likely to be the corporation's cost of raising funds through limited partnership financing. In addition, the lower the portion of residual value that needs to be allocated to limited partners, the less expensive becomes the cost of funds, as was the case with lease financing.

The approach just illustrated, together with Formula 22-10, can also be used to calculate the cost of limited partner capital when the limited partnership borrows. Net cash flow in that case must reflect the cash required to service the partnership's borrowing and the associated interest tax shields.

FINANCING CORPORATE REAL ESTATE

Corporate real estate represents a significant component of companies' asset portfolios yet one that most companies do not manage actively.[10] As many companies discovered during the 1974 to 1975 liquidity crisis, corporate real estate represents a store of value that can provide substantial borrowing power during difficult periods.

Critical Factors in Corporate Real Estate Financing

There are two important aspects to the financing of corporate real estate. First, at the time it builds a facility a company must decide whether to finance the facility on its general credit and own it or instead to lease the facility. The lease versus borrow-and-construct decision involves the same principal considerations as the lease versus borrow-and-buy decision discussed earlier in the chapter in connection with equipment investments.

Second, if the company decides to borrow and construct, it must decide whether to borrow on its general credit or to arrange mortgage financing. Mortgage financing can typically be arranged on a nonrecourse basis to cover up to 70 to 90% of the cost of the facility. Mortgage financing may reduce the company's operating flexibility with respect to the facility, but it may also have a smaller impact on the company's credit capacity than borrowing on the company's general credit. In addition, financing the facility on the company's general credit preserves the company's ability to arrange sale-and-lease-back financing in the future.

Significance of Mortgage Financing

Mortgage financing may facilitate a lower cost of debt and a higher degree of leverage than financing on a company's general credit. In evaluating a proposed capital investment project that contains a significant amount of real estate for which mortgage financing can be arranged on attractive terms, the adjusted-present-value approach discussed in Chapter 9 should be used in order to factor into the evaluation any special benefits attributable to mortgage financing.

SUMMARY

A company can finance a project either on its general credit, by promising investors and/or lenders a share of the future cash flow from its entire portfolio of assets, or on an asset-based basis, by promising providers of capital a share of the future cash flow from a discrete (set of) asset(s). Asset-based financing techniques include leasing, various forms of project financing, production payment financing, limited partnership financing, and real estate mortgage financing.

Lease financing involves an extended rental agreement under which the lessor grants the lessee the exclusive right to use the asset for a specified period in return for a series of fixed lease payments, the right to claim certain tax benefits of ownership, and the right to realize at least a specified portion of the asset's residual value at the end of the lease term. Lease financing can be mutually advantageous to lessor and lessee when the lessor's income is taxed at a higher rate than the lessee's income, when the lessor enjoys a lower cost of borrowing than the lessee, or when the lessor is better able to bear the risks of obsolescence of the leased items than the lessee. But lease financing displaces borrowing and should therefore be analyzed as an alternative to borrowing to buy the asset. Limited partnership financing provides an alternative to leasing as a means of "selling" the tax benefits of ownership.

Project financing may be advantageous when a project involves a discrete (set of) asset(s) that is capable of standing alone as an independent economic unit that promises to generate sufficient cash flow to service project debt. Designing a project financing requires careful financial engineering to allocate the project-related risks among the parties who are best able to bear them, allocating the project's economic rewards in a manner commensurate with the allocation of project risks, and designing contractual arrangements to accomplish this. Under the appropriate circumstances, project financing can lead to more efficient risk-sharing, expanded debt capacity for the project's sponsor(s), and a lower overall cost of funds than conventional financing.

Part 7

Liabilities Management

When a corporation issues debt securities to raise capital, it agrees contractually to make fixed payments over the life of the issue and to repay the final installment of the debt at maturity. The corporation can treat this liability passively, leaving the securities outstanding and meeting each payment obligation as it comes due. Alternatively, it can seek out opportunities to reduce its cost of capital by repurchasing debt securities at a discount, by refunding it with lower-cost debt, or by exchanging other securities for outstanding debt securities. A company can reduce its cost of debt and increase shareholder wealth by managing its liabilities as effectively as it manages its assets.

The following example illustrates the type of problem with which we are concerned in Part 7. In the fall of 1976, New Jersey Bell Telephone Company had an opportunity to redeem its 9.35% Debentures due 2010 and replace the $100 million issue with another issue of 8.00% Debentures. The refunding would save $1,350,000 of pretax interest expense each year.

But the redemption would require New Jersey Bell to pay $1077.40 per $1000 face amount of debt. Would the value of the stream of future interest savings exceed the cost of the redemption premium and make the refunding worthwhile? The answer is yes, and Chapter 23 develops an analytical framework that explains why and measures the net-present-value savings from this refunding.

Refunding Premium Debt and Preferred Stock

Chapter 23

A corporation *refunds* an outstanding issue of its debt by selling a new issue of debt and using the proceeds to redeem, or repay, the outstanding debt.

REFUNDING HIGH-COUPON DEBT

When the coupon rate on the new issue is less than the coupon rate on the old issue, refunding the outstanding issue will reduce the corporation's interest expense. Refundings are not costless, however. The corporation must pay holders of the old issue a redemption premium unless the old issue is about to mature. Also, the corporation must bear the cost of the new issue, and there are tax consequences associated with these expenditures. But when interest rates fall sufficiently below the coupon rate on an outstanding issue, a corporation can benefit its shareholders by *calling* the old issue for redemption and refunding it with a new lower-coupon debt issue.

Other reasons exist for undertaking a refunding. For example, the corporation may wish to eliminate restrictive covenants. Replacing the issue(s) that contain(s) the offensive covenants will accomplish this. Also, the corporation may wish to extend the average maturity of its outstanding debt. Selling a new debt issue that has a longer maturity than the issue that is retired will achieve this. While both motives are valid, this chapter discusses how to analyze the profitability of the most common form of bond refunding: substituting one issue for another because of the interest savings that will result.

Why Refunding High-Coupon Debt Can Be Beneficial

A corporation should refund high-coupon debt only if it can issue new debt that has the same after-tax debt service requirements as the old issue and after paying all costs associated with retiring the old debt and issuing the new debt still have a surplus left over that is available for distribution to its shareholders.

Suppose that a corporation has outstanding a $1000 bond that bears interest at the rate of 10% per period and that matures in one period. Suppose further that the corporation could redeem this issue immediately by paying holders $1010 (implying a *call premium* amounting to 1% of the face amount of the debt) and that the corporation can issue new debt at par bearing a 4% interest rate at a flotation cost of $5 (after taxes). If the corporation's marginal tax rate is 50%, a new issue of debt in the amount of $1029.41 would have the same $1050 after-tax debt service requirement as the old issue. Thus, without altering its after-tax debt service requirements, the corporation can raise $1029.41 through the sale of new debt, pay out $1005 after taxes to redeem the old issue (the corporation can deduct the cost of the call premium for tax purposes) plus an additional $5 to float the new issue, and still have $19.41 left over to distribute to its shareholders. This surplus is the increase in shareholder wealth that results from the refunding.

Note, however, that if the bond was not callable, it would trade in the market at a price of approximately $1057.69 (= $1100/1.04). If the corporation had to pay this price to retire the old issue, it would have to pay $1028.85 (= $1057.69 less tax savings of $28.84) for the debt plus $5 flotation costs. As a result, the proceeds of the new debt issue would fall short of the costs of the refunding operation by $4.44 (= $1028.85 + 5.00 − 1029.41). The refunding would be profitable to the corporation's shareholders only if the after-tax flotation costs were less than $0.56. As this example illustrates, the call option is the factor principally responsible for the profitability of refunding high-coupon debt.

Application of Discounted Cash Flow Analysis

A somewhat simpler procedure is available for calculating the surplus, or net present value, owing to the refunding. Note that if the firm were to issue $1000 of new debt bearing a 4% coupon, it would realize after-tax interest savings of $30 one year hence. Discounting these savings at the 2% after-tax interest cost of the new issue gives $29.41. Subtracting the $5 after-tax cost of the redemption premium and the $5 flotation costs of the new issue gives the same $19.41 surplus calculated earlier. Thus, a corporation can evaluate the profitability of refunding high-coupon debt by discounting the after-tax interest savings at the after-tax cost of money for the new issue and subtracting the after-tax cost of the refunding operation.

The refunding decision is not a capital investment decision even though the methods of analysis are similar. Refunding involves restructuring the firm's liabilities, whereas capital investment involves purchasing physical assets. The distinction between refunding and capital investment is important. Financial analysts who make the mistake of treating the refunding decision as a capital investment decision often use the corporation's cost of capital as the discount rate in the refunding analysis. This is wrong because the corporation finances the retirement of the old debt by issuing a new series of debt. Thus, the cost of debt is the appropriate discount rate in a refunding analysis, rather than the cost of capital (which includes, on a weighted basis, the cost of equity funds).

Analyzing a Proposed Refunding of High-Coupon Debt

The cost of the refunding operation has four components. First, and largest, is the cost of calling the old bonds. Bond indentures typically require the corporation to pay a premium above the principal amount of the bonds. Second, issuing the new bonds involves an underwriting commission and various expenses such as lawyers' and accountants' fees, and printing costs. Third, calling the old issue involves certain expenses, including the cost of printing the redemption notice in newspapers and paying the bond trustee's fees for canceling the old bonds. Fourth, the corporation will generally want to sell the new issue before calling the old issue in order to be sure that it has the funds available to pay holders of the old issue and in order to know beforehand the interest cost of the new issue.

The cash outlays required to meet these expenses are partly offset by certain tax savings. The call premium is tax deductible. Also, the interest expense on the new issue during the overlap period is tax deductible just like any other interest expense. In addition, issuance expenses plus new issue discount if the bonds were sold to investors for less than their par value (or less the new issue premium if the bonds were sold for more than their par value) on an issue cannot be deducted currently but must be amortized for tax purposes over the life of the issue. If the issue is refunded, the unamortized balance as of the refunding date is deductible immediately.

The semiannual savings consist of the reduction in semiannual after-tax interest expense plus the increase (or less the reduction) in the semiannual expense amortization tax shields.

One of the principal steps in the refunding analysis is the specification of the new issue. In order to hold the company's after-tax debt service requirement fixed, the amortization schedule and maturity of the new issue should match the amortization schedule and maturity, respectively, of the old issue.

The interest rate on the new issue should be the interest rate noncallable debt with the same amortization schedule and maturity as the new issue would bear. When a corporation calls an issue for redemption, it exercises the one-time call option. Only if the new issue is noncallable will the corporation have exercised its call option in full and not simply reissued part of it in the form of a new call option on the new issue.

Illustration of Refunding Analysis

The New Jersey Bell example mentioned at the beginning of this part will serve to illustrate the calculation of the net-present-value savings from refunding high-coupon debt. On November 1, 1976, New Jersey Bell Telephone Company redeemed its 9.35% Debentures due 2010 at a price of 107.74%, or $1077.40 per bond. The issue consisted of 100,000 bonds representing $100 million principal amount. Some weeks earlier, on September 21, 1976, New Jersey Bell issued $100 million principal amount of 8.00% Debentures due 2016 in anticipation of this redemption. Table 23-1 illustrates a net-present-value analysis of this refunding.

At the time of the refunding, a 34-year New Jersey Bell issue required roughly the same coupon as a 40-year issue. However, the refunding issue was callable after 5 years, as is customary for Bell System debt issues. Thus, the 8.00% coupon rate overstates the interest rate that a noncallable issue would

Table 23-1
Discounted Cash Flow Analysis of the Economics
of Refunding High-Coupon Debt

Assumptions	Old Issue	New Issue
Amount refunded	$100,000,000	$100,000,000
Coupon rate	9.35%	7.70%
Remaining life	34 years	34 years
Issuance expenses plus original issue discount (or less original issue premium)	$814,300*	$992,000
Cost of repurchase:		
Per bond	107.74%	
Total	$107,740,000	
Debt retirement expenses†	$300,000	
Overlapping interest‡	$962,500	
Issuer's tax rate	50%	

Benefits of Refunding	Pretax	After-Tax
Semiannual interest expense:		
Old issue	$4,675,000	$ 2,337,500
New issue	3,850,000	1,925,000
Savings	825,000	412,500
Semiannual expense amortization:		
New issue	14,588	7,294
Old issue	11,975	5,988
Savings (cost)	2,613	1,306
Semiannual savings	$ 827,613	$ 413,806
Present value of semiannual savings§		$15,617,773

Discounted Cash Flow Analysis of the Economics of Refunding High-Coupon Debt *(Continued)*

Costs of Refunding	Pretax	After-Tax
Redemption premium	$7,740,000	$ 3,870,000
Debt retirement expenses	300,000	150,000
Overlapping interest	962,500	481,250
New issue expenses	992,000	992,000
Less write-off of unamortized expenses plus discount (or less premium) on old issue	(814,300)	(407,150)
Total costs	$9,180,200	$ 5,086,100

Net-Present-Value Analysis

Net present value of refunding	$10,531,673
Break-even refunding rate	8.769%

Sensitivity Analysis

Interest Rate on Now Issue	Net-Present-Value Savings	Interest Rate on New Issue	Net-Present-Value Savings
7.00%	$18,261,964	8.00%	$ 7,428,791
7.25	15,419,368	8.25	4,933,501
7.50	12,668,540	8.50	2,517,227
7.75	10,006,097	8.75	177,088

*Unamortized balance.

†Calculated as $3 per bond.

‡Represents 1.5 months of interest on $100 million at the rate of 7.70% per annum (the interest rate on the new issue).

§Cash flows are discounted at the after-tax interest rate on the new issue (expressed on a semiannual basis).

Source: John D. Finnerty, *An Illustrated Guide to Bond Refunding Analysis*, Financial Analysts Research Foundation, Charlottesville, Va., 1984, pp. 28–29. Reprinted by permission.

have required. One study has estimated that the call option costs Bell System debt issuers an extra 30 basis points.[1] Subtracting this amount from 8.00% implies a 7.70% coupon rate for a noncallable issue.

Refunding the 9.35% issue cost approximately $5,086,100 net of taxes but saved New Jersey Bell $412,500 per semiannual period in after-tax interest expense. Additional expense tax shields added $1306 per semiannual period. Discounting the $413,806 semiannual savings at the after-tax interest rate on the new issue, the present value of the semiannual savings stream was approximately $15,617,773, and the net present value of the refunding was $10,531,673. New Jersey Bell would have realized net-present-value savings as long as the interest rate on a noncallable new issue was below the break-even rate of 8.769% (equivalent to 9.069% for an otherwise identical callable issue).

Discounted Cash Flow Model

The discounted cash flow model underlying Table 23-1 is:

$$
\begin{aligned}
\text{NPV} = \sum_{t=1}^{\text{maturity}} &\left\{ \left[\left(1 - \frac{\text{tax}}{\text{rate}}\right) \times \tfrac{1}{2} \left(\begin{array}{c} \text{interest} \\ \text{rate on} \\ \text{old issue} \end{array} - \begin{array}{c} \text{interest} \\ \text{rate on} \\ \text{new issue} \end{array} \right) \times \begin{array}{c} \text{principal} \\ \text{amount} \\ \text{refunded} \end{array} \right. \right. \\
&\left. + \frac{\text{tax rate} \times (\text{new issue expenses} - \text{unamortized balance})}{\text{maturity}} \right] \\
&\left. \div \left[1 + \tfrac{1}{2}\left(1 - \frac{\text{tax}}{\text{rate}}\right) \times \begin{array}{c} \text{interest rate} \\ \text{on new issue} \end{array} \right]^{t} \right\} \\
&- \left\{ \left(1 - \frac{\text{tax}}{\text{rate}}\right) \times \begin{array}{c} \text{redemption} \\ \text{premium} \end{array} + \left(1 - \frac{\text{tax}}{\text{rate}}\right) \times \begin{array}{c} \text{deductible} \\ \text{expenses} \end{array} \right. \\
&\left. + \begin{array}{c} \text{new issue} \\ \text{expenses} \end{array} - \left(\frac{\text{tax}}{\text{rate}} \times \begin{array}{c} \text{unamortized} \\ \text{balance} \end{array} \right) \right\}
\end{aligned}
\tag{23-1}
$$

NPV denotes the net-present-value savings. *Interest rate on old issue* and *interest rate on new issue* are expressed in decimal form (e.g., 0.1 for 10%). *Tax rate* denotes the corporation's marginal ordinary income tax rate. *Principal amount refunded* is matched by a new issue of equal principal amount (assumed to be sold at par). *New issue expenses* denotes expenses such as underwriting spread and lawyers' and accountants' fees, which are not tax deductible immediately. *Unamortized balance* represents the unamortized balance of the expenses plus original issue discount (or less original issue premium) for the old issue. *Redemption premium* denotes the aggregate redemption premium. *Deductible expenses* denotes the debt retirement expenses plus overlapping interest, which are tax deductible currently. *Maturity* is the number of semiannual periods remaining until the old issue was originally scheduled to mature.

It is important to appreciate that Formula 23-1 assumes that the issuer can fully utilize the interest and amortization expense tax deductions and that the old issue matures in one lump sum. The procedure illustrated in Table 23-1 is modified later in the chapter to accommodate sinking fund issues.

Application to Regulated Companies

The analysis described in this chapter is interpreted differently when applied to public utility companies and to other regulated companies. Regulatory commissions normally pass a utility company's interest expense through to its ratepayers. The net-present-value savings resulting from a refunding will consequently accrue to ratepayers rather than to shareholders. Consequently, the regulated company should make sure that the costs of the refunding will also be passed through to ratepayers so that the refunding operation will not be detrimental to its shareholders. When ratepayers derive the full benefit and bear the full cost of the refunding, Formula 23-1 indicates the net-present-value savings—but to ratepayers instead of shareholders.

Financial Reporting Considerations

Refunding high-coupon debt results in a loss for financial reporting purposes. This loss is equal to the difference between the repurchase price and the book value at the time of reacquisition, after adjusting for the tax deductibility of (1) the premium paid and (2) the unamortized balance of issuance expenses. However, this book "loss" should not stand in the way of a refunding when the net present value is positive. When refunding is economic (NPV > 0), the stock market can be expected to react to this true economic gain rather than to the book loss.

TIMING THE REFUNDING

Just because it is economic to call and refund an issue immediately, it is not necessarily in the shareholders' best interest to do so. Shareholders might realize even greater savings if the corporation postpones the refunding and interest rates decline further. The decision as to whether to refund or to wait thus requires an assessment of the likelihood that interest rates will decrease.

Break-Even Approach

One approach to dealing with this problem is break-even analysis: If the firm can realize net-present-value savings of X by refunding immediately, what future new issue rates will produce the same level of savings after discounting back to the decision point?

For example, consider an electric utility company that is studying whether to refund $50 million principal amount of its 10% debenture issue that is scheduled to mature in 25 years. Suppose the issue is callable currently at a cost of 108.15% per debenture. Suppose also that the utility's new issue rate is currently 9.00% for callable 25-year debt and 8.75% for 25-year noncallable debt and that the utility's tax rate is 50%. Refunding the 10% issue immediately would produce net-present-value savings amounting to $2,684,421. What would the new issue rate have to be in five years, for example, to produce savings of $2,684,421 in today's dollars?

If the utility's 5-year new issue rate for noncallable debt is also 8.75%, this question can be rephrased as: What new issue rate is required in 5 years to pro-

vide net-present-value savings of \$3,332,947 [= 2,684,421 × $(1.021875)^{10}$]?
Suppose that the call price 5 years hence is 106.67%. Solving for the new issue
rate that results in net-present-value savings at that time of \$3,332,947 gives
8.75% (for a 20-year callable issue). Thus, interest rates would only have to
fall 25 basis points over the next 5 years for the firm to be able to realize
greater savings from refunding at that time rather than immediately.

Dynamic Programming Approach

Several writers have suggested a more rigorous approach using a technique
known as dynamic programming to deal with the timing problem.[2] Dynamic
programming takes the nature of interest rate movements explicitly into account.
This subsection outlines the Boyce-Kalotay approach.

The Boyce-Kalotay approach enables the decision maker to compare the
profitability of each refunding opportunity with all possible future refunding
opportunities for the same issue. The primary output of this analysis is a
single curve, called a *stopping curve*, which indicates at each point in time the
refunding rate on the new issue at which the corporation should be indifferent
between waiting and refunding. Figure 23-1 illustrates a stopping curve for
a 30-year debt issue that bears interest at a 10% rate, that is noncallable for

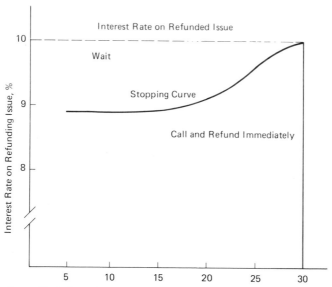

Figure 23-1. Stopping curve for timing the refunding of 30-year
debt issue. (*John D. Finnerty,* An Illustrated Guide to Bond Refunding Analysis, *Financial Analysts Research Foundation, Charlottesville,
Va., 1984, p. 41. Reprinted by permission.*)

5 years, and that is callable at par during the last 3 years. At new issue rates less than those shown on the stopping curve, the firm should call and refund because the savings immediately realizable exceed the savings the firm can expect to realize by waiting.

The dynamic programming approach involves constructing the stopping curve by working backward in time from the maturity date of the issue. The reason for proceeding in this manner is quite simple. At each point in time we wish to calculate the value of the "call and refund" strategy and of the "wait" strategy and compare the two values to determine which strategy is preferable. But the value of the "wait" strategy in turn depends on what happens in the future. By proceeding backward in time, we can use the values of "calling" and "waiting" from the previous step (i.e., one period later in time) to calculate the values for "calling" and "waiting" for the current step. Each calculation thus reflects what might happen in all future periods up to maturity (i.e., at all previous steps in the analytical process). In this manner, dynamic programming simplifies the overall problem to a sequence of one-period decision problems. During each period, the stopping curve helps the decision maker decide whether to "refund immediately" or to "wait one period" (and reach another decision at that time based on where the new issue rate is in relation to the stopping curve).

The procedure for constructing the stopping curve is best illustrated by reconsidering the decision facing the electric utility. To simplify the example, suppose that the utility can call the issue at either of only two points in time: after 5 years or after 10 years.

Working backward in time, first consider what might happen at year 10, the last opportunity to refund. As illustrated by the NPV_{10} curve in Figure 23-2, the utility could refund the 10% issue profitably in year 10 if the new issue rate on a conventional issue is less than the "call point" of 9.73% (9.48% for a noncallable issue) at that time. The curve NPV_{10} provides the net-present-value savings that correspond to the optimal strategy for different possible interest rates. This value is the greater of (1) the net-present-value savings from refunding (which are positive if refunding is economic) and (2) zero (if it is not economic to refund the issue in year 10, it will never be refunded). The net-present-value calculations are performed using the interest rate on a noncallable issue as the refunding rate and assuming that the call feature requires a yield premium of 25 basis points.[3]

Next consider what might happen at year 5. The analysis is more complex than for year 10 because the corporation might wish to pass up a profitable opportunity at year 5 if it expects a more profitable opportunity at year 10. This requires that we calculate explicitly the value attached to the "wait" strategy. The value of waiting depends, however, on how interest rates might change between years 5 and 10.

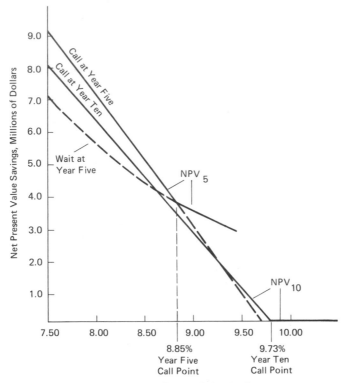

Figure 23-2. Call points for years 5 and 10. (*John D. Finnerty*, An Illustrated Guide to Bond Refunding Analysis, *Financial Analysts Research Foundation, Charlottesville, Va., 1984, p. 43. Reprinted by permission.*)

Suppose that the utility's financial staff has analyzed historical interest rate movements for similarly rated long-term electric utility bonds and discovered that this new issue rate has varied on a month-to-month basis with a standard deviation equal to 2.0% of the prevailing interest rate. Over a 5-year period, the new issue rate would vary with a standard deviation equal to 15.49% of the interest rate at the beginning of the 5-year period.[4]

Boyce and Kalotay suggest treating interest rate changes in the following manner: For each possible interest rate in the current period, the interest rate in the following period is either +1 standard deviation or −1 standard deviation from this period's interest rate, each with probability $\frac{1}{2}$. For example, if the interest rate at year 5 is 9.00%, the interest rate at year 10 is either 10.39% (9 + 0.1549 × 9) or 7.61% (9 − 0.1549 × 9), each with probability $\frac{1}{2}$. But if the interest rate were 7.61%, the 10% issue could be refunded profitably. This would produce net-present-value savings of $7,618,390. Thus, the expected value of the "wait" strategy at year 5 is:

$$\text{Expected value of "wait" strategy} = \frac{1}{2} \times 7,618,390 + \frac{1}{2} \times 0$$

$$= \$3,809,195$$

when the interest rate at year 5 is 9.00%. Discounting these savings back to year 5 at an assumed after-tax 5-year discount rate of 4.375% (i.e., assuming a flat yield curve) gives expected net-present-value savings from waiting as of year 5 amounting to $3,068,001 [= $3,809,195 \times (1.021875)^{-10}$]. Repeating this calculation for the different possible interest rates at year 5 results in the curve labeled "wait at year 5" in Figure 23-2.

Next, the net-present-value savings from refunding immediately are calculated in the usual manner. The greater of (1) the net-present-value savings from refunding immediately and (2) the expected net-present-value savings from waiting determines the optimum strategy. The net-present-value savings corresponding to the optimum strategy are labeled NPV_5 in Figure 23-2. At interest rates less than the 8.85% year 5 call point, the optimum strategy is to call immediately and refund. At interest rates greater than 8.85%, the optimum strategy is to wait. In particular, at interest rates between 8.85% and 9.69% (the break-even rate) in year 5, it is profitable for the utility to refund the 10% issue immediately, but the optimum strategy is to wait. Performing the analysis just illustrated but for monthly intervals between years 5 and 30 would produce the stopping curve in Figure 23-1.

TENDER OFFERS AND OPEN MARKET PURCHASES

Long-term bonds issued by industrial corporations typically provide bondholders 10 years of call protection, and long-term bonds issued by public utility companies typically provide 5 years of call protection. Such provisions generally prohibit a company from calling any portion of the call-protected issue if the company has raised or else intends to raise the cash it needs to do this by selling a new lower-cost issue of debt that ranks on a parity with or is senior to the refunded issue. Nevertheless, a corporation can refund call-protected high-coupon debt by purchasing bonds in the open market or by tendering for outstanding bonds and selling a new issue to raise the cash to do it.

Repurchasing high-coupon debt is generally most profitable when (1) the yield curve is upward-sloping and (2) investors think a call is likely soon after the period of call protection expires. Bell System companies have called debt issues for redemption on several occasions. Consequently, high-coupon

Bell System debt issues tend to trade on a "yield-to-first-call" basis, that is, as if investors expect the issuer to redeem the debt at the earliest opportunity. For example, suppose a 15% debt issue has a remaining life of 37 years but becomes callable at a price of 112.86% in 2 years. Further suppose that the company's new issue rates are 7% for 2-year debt and 10% for 37-year debt. If investors did not expect the company to call the issue ever, its price would be 148.65%. However, if they expect the company to call it in 2 years, its price would be 125.90%. Thus, the prospect of an imminent call serves to hold down a bond's price and make it cheaper to purchase and refund the debt.

With two adjustments, the method of analysis illustrated in Table 23-1 applies also to refundings accomplished through open market purchases or a tender offer. The principal differences are that (1) the issuer must pay the free market price or, in the case of a tender offer, some premium over this price, rather than a fixed optional redemption price and (2) holders are free to accept or reject the issuer's offer. Thus, both the principal amount refunded and the redemption premium in Formula 23-1 are subject to some degree of uncertainty, and the values of the other variables will vary accordingly. The analyst takes this into account by first estimating the amount of the issue that can be reacquired at a presumed redemption premium and then applying the discounted cash flow analysis illustrated in Table 23-1 to this portion of the issue.

The second adjustment involves the added transaction costs of a repurchase program or tender offer. In a repurchase program, the issuer repurchases the bulk of the bonds through securities firms, which add a premium to their cost of acquiring the bonds. This premium can simply be included in the redemption premium. In a tender offer, the issuer will normally find it advantageous to engage securities firms in order to acquire as many bonds as possible at the tender price. If so, the issuer must pay a "soliciting dealer fee," which is typically between $2.50 and $7.50 per bond depending on market conditions and other factors.

Illustration of Tender Offer Analysis

On January 21, 1977, four Bell System subsidiaries, South Central Bell, New England Telephone, Northwestern Bell, and Indiana Bell, each tendered for one of its outstanding high-coupon debt issues. South Central Bell, for example, tendered at a price of 115.75% for its $225 million principal amount of 10% Debentures due September 15, 2014. At the time of the tender, the company could have issued new 37.5-year noncallable debt bearing a $7\frac{3}{4}\%$ coupon. Bondholders tendered $193.9 million principal amount of the issue by February 4, 1977, the expiration date for the tender offer.

As illustrated in Table 23-2, the tender offer made possible $1,086,124 of semiannual after-tax savings with a present value of $42,766,044. The tender offer premium cost the company $15,269,625 after taxes. After allowing for the expense amortization write-off and the other costs of the refunding, the tender produced net-present-value savings of approximately $26,235,214.

Timing the Tender Offer

One of the most critical factors in connection with an open market purchase program or a tender offer concerns timing. Specifically, are the shareholders better off if the company reacquires the bonds now at (or at a slight premium to) the prevailing market price and thereby "locks in" the savings currently obtainable, or are they better off if the company instead waits until the bonds are callable to redeem the bonds at the lower optional redemption price? A "wait and call" strategy subjects the company to the risk that interest rates might rise in the interim and eliminate the savings that the company can realize by reacquiring the bonds now.

Illustration of Tender-Now-versus-
Wait-and-Call Analysis

For the South Central Bell refunding discussed earlier in this section, the initial call price was 108.15%. Thus, waiting to call the bonds the company received in the tender would have saved $76 per bond ($1157.50 tender price less $1081.50 redemption price) in acquisition cost plus soliciting dealer fees of roughly $3.50 per bond, or a total of $7,707,525 after taxes. However, waiting to call the issue would require sacrificing the interest savings over the period spanning the proposed tender offer date and the date of the call. It might also involve an even greater cost if the corporation's new issue rate increases in the interim.

Table 23-2 includes an economic analysis of tendering versus waiting. A reasonable assumption for purposes of analyzing the economics of the call-and-wait strategy is to assume that the corporation's new issue rate is the same on both dates. In that case, the shorter period over which the corporation realizes interest savings reduces the net present value of the benefits of refunding to $37,669,466. After subtracting the net present value of the associated costs, the net present value, as of the date of the proposed tender offer, of waiting to call the bonds was $29,433,289 (versus the $26,235,214 savings realizable by tendering immediately). Thus, waiting would have involved an additional $3,198,075 of net-present-value savings if South Central Bell's new issue rate were the same on the call date as on the tender date. But South Central Bell also had to weigh the risk that its new issue rate might be higher on the call date, perhaps even high enough to make refunding uneconomic. In particular, if South Central Bell's new issue rate were greater than 7.913%, tendering immediately would (in retrospect has proven to) provide greater net-present-value savings. South Central Bell decided to proceed with the tender.

Table 23-2
Discounted Cash Flow Analysis of Tendering Now Versus Waiting to Call a High-Coupon Debt Issue

	Tender	Call
Refunded debt	$193,900,000	$193,900,000
Refunding issue:		
Amount	193,900,000	193,900,000
Coupon rate	7.75%	7.75%
Remaining life	37.5 years	35 years
Issuance expenses	1,946,625	1,946,625
Issuer's tax rate		50%

Benefits of Refunding (After Taxes)

	Tender	Call
Benefits begin	Immediately	After 2.5 years
Semiannual interest savings	$ 1,090,688	$ 1,090,688
Increase (decrease) in semiannual expense amortization	(4,564)	(3,637)
Semiannual savings	$ 1,086,124	$ 1,087,051
Net present value to date of proposed tender*	$42,766,044	$37,669,466

Costs of Refunding (After Taxes)

	Tender	Call
Redemption premium	$15,269,625	$ 7,901,425
Tender offer fees	339,325	—
Other costs	2,237,475	2,237,475
Less write-off of unamortized expenses	(1,315,595)	(1,227,888)
Total costs	$16,530,830	$ 8,911,012
Net present value to date of proposed tender	$16,530,830	$ 8,236,177†

Net-Present-Value Analysis

	Tender	Call
Net present value of refunding	$26,235,214	$29,433,289
Break-even refunding rate for call-and-wait strategy		7.913%

*Discounted at the after-tax cost of a new 37.5-year issue (1.9375% per semiannual period).
†Discounted at the after-tax cost of a new 2.5-year issue (1.5875% per semiannual period).

Source: John D. Finnerty, *An Illustrated Guide to Bond Refunding Analysis*, Financial Analysts Research Foundation, Charlottesville, Va., 1984, p. 32. Reprinted by permission.

Determining the Tender Offer Premium

A second critical issue that arises in connection with a tender offer is the appropriate premium. The appropriate premium will depend on such factors as investors' interest rate expectations, the composition of the bondholder group, and the yields available on alternative investments. The premiums offered in the Bell System subsidiaries' tenders were determined by calculating the respective tender prices that would provide a yield-to-first-call comparable to the yield an investor could realize by investing in U.S government agency issues over the same time horizon. For example, just prior to the tender offer, the South Central Bell issue was trading at a price of 114.25% for a yield-to-first-call of 6.85%. Government agency issues with 2.5 years to maturity were trading at the time at a yield of 6.30%. The tender offer price of 115.75% represented a yield-to-first-call of 6.29% (because once the tender was announced, the market price would increase to the tender price). Hence, by tendering and then reinvesting the proceeds in a government agency issue, a bondholder could have realized the same yield as implied in the tender price but with less credit risk. This accounts for the high percentage (86%) of bonds tendered.

Relative Attractiveness of Tenders and Market Purchases

The open market purchase method will generally be cheaper when the market for the bonds is liquid enough that the repurchase program does not exert much upward pressure on price. Bonds can be repurchased from different holders at the (different) prices they are willing to accept. It is important, however, to handle the program discreetly so as not to alert the market. However, for larger programs, the tender offer method is generally more appropriate, particularly when the issue is widely dispersed among a large number of holders. The tender offer method treats all bondholders equally, in particular, with respect to the price each receives for his or her bonds.

REFUNDING SINKING FUND ISSUES

The method of analysis described earlier in this chapter must be modified in order to apply it to high-coupon sinking fund issues. Bond indentures typically enable the issuer to redeem bonds for sinking fund purposes at their par value but require the issuer to call bonds for optional redemption at prices that represent premiums over the bonds' par value (except in the last few years immediately prior to maturity when optional redemption at par may be possible). When the optional redemption (or call) price exceeds the mandatory redemption (or sinking fund) price, it may be more profitable for a company to call only a portion of the issue for immediate redemption and to wait to redeem the balance at the lower sinking fund price rather than to call the entire issue immediately.

Suppose that a corporation pays tax at a 50% rate and has $2 million principal amount of debt outstanding that bears interest at a 16% coupon rate and that amortizes in two equal installments 6 months and 1 year from now, each of which is paid at par. Further suppose that the optional redemption price is 102.50% and that a new 6-month issue and a new 1-year issue would each require a 12% coupon. Ignoring issuance expenses, the net-present-value savings from refunding an amount representing the first sinking fund payment can be calculated by treating it as a separate debt issue and substituting into Formula 23-1:

$$\text{NPV}_1 = \frac{\$0.5 \times 0.02 \times 1,000,000}{1.03} - (0.5 \times 25,000) = -\$2791$$

The net-present-value savings from refunding the second $1 million sinking fund payment are calculated similarly:

$$\text{NPV}_2 = \frac{\$0.5 \times 0.02 \times 1,000,000}{1.03}$$
$$+ \frac{0.5 \times 0.02 \times 1,000,000}{(1.03)^2} - (0.5 \times 25,000) = \$6635$$

The net-present-value savings from refunding the entire issue is just the sum of NPV_1 and NPV_2, or $3844. However, it is only economic to refund the second sinking fund amount. The company's shareholders are better off if the company calls only $1 million of the issue for immediate redemption and waits 6 months to redeem the balance at par through the operation of the sinking fund. Such a strategy produces net-present-value savings of $6635.

This example also illustrates the correct procedure for evaluating the economics of refunding a sinking fund issue. Bond indentures for publicly distributed sinking fund debt issues typically give the issuing company the option to credit reacquired bonds against a sinking fund obligation and give the issuer the flexibility to call for redemption less than the full amount of the issue then outstanding. In such cases, the issue should be decomposed into a serial debt obligation with each series maturing on one of the sinking fund payment dates. Then Formula 23-1 can be applied separately to each sinking fund amount in order to determine which, if any, the company can refund profitably.

Let *sinking fund amount*(k) denote the sinking fund payment due at the end of k semiannual interest periods [sinking fund amount(k) = 0 when no payment is due], and let *new issue rate*(k) denote the interest rate on a new noncallable debt issue of the company that matures in one lump sum after k periods. Formula 23-1 gives the net-present-value savings from refunding *sinking fund amount(k)* when this amount is substituted for *principal amount refunded, new issue rate(k)* is substituted for *interest rate on new issue,* and a pro rata share of the old issue's unamortized expenses is substituted for *unamortized balance.*

When the yield curve is flat [*new issue rate(k)* is the same for all values of *k*], the more distant sinking fund amounts are the more profitable ones to refund because the interest savings are realized over a longer period. When the yield curve is downward-sloping [*new issue rate(k)* is smaller for longer maturities], the interest savings per period are greater for refunding more distant sinking fund amounts. Thus, the most distant sinking fund amounts are the most profitable to refund. Only if the yield curve is upward-sloping might one of the intermediate sinking funds amounts be the most profitable to refund. In any case, the number of sinking fund amounts that a company can call profitably for immediate redemption on any particular date will be greater (1) the higher the coupon rate on the outstanding issue is relative to the prevailing level of interest rates and (2) the smaller the call premium is. In addition, in recent years many public debt issues have permitted the issuer to as much as double any sinking fund payment. This feature tends to increase the proportion of the issue that the corporation should wait to redeem through the sinking fund.

Illustration of Analysis for Sinking Fund Issue

A company is considering calling its 14% sinking fund debentures that have a remaining life of 10 years and that provide for 10 sinking fund payments of $1 million each at the end of each year. The optional redemption price is 105.60%. The unamortized balance of issuance expenses is $110,000. The corporation pays tax at a 50% marginal rate. The company's new issue rates are 12% for 1-, 2-, or 3-year issues; $12\frac{1}{4}\%$ for 4-, 5-, and 6-year issues; and $12\frac{1}{2}\%$ for longer-term issues. Issuance expenses in each case amount to 1% of an issue's proceeds.

Table 23-3 summarizes the results of the discounted cash flow analysis. The most distant six sinking fund amounts, representing $6 million principal amount of the issue, should be called immediately. Calling this amount will produce net-present-value savings of $69,053. Calling less distant sinking fund amounts is not profitable because the present value of the after-tax interest savings is less than the after-tax redemption premium.

Privately Placed Debt Issues

A complication arises in connection with privately placed debt issues. The indentures for such issues typically require that any bonds purchased from holders (i.e., through private negotiated transactions) or optionally redeemed must be credited against future sinking fund obligations in reverse order. That

Table 23-3
Discounted Cash Flow Analysis of the Economics of Refunding High-Coupon Sinking Fund Debt

Years to Sinking Fund Payment	Amount	After-Tax Interest Savings		Increase (Decrease) in Amortization		After-Tax Cost (Saving)			Net-Present-Value Savings
		Semi-annual Amount	Net Present Value	Semi-annual Amount*	Net Present Value	Redemption Premium	Other Costs†	Write-off of Unamortized Balance	
1	$1,000,000	$5,000	$ 9,567	$(250)	$(478)	$28,000	$11,500	$(5,500)	$(24,911)
2	1,000,000	5,000	18,585	(125)	(465)	28,000	11,500	(5,500)	(15,880)
3	1,000,000	5,000	27,086	(83)	(450)	28,000	11,500	(5,500)	(7,364)
4	1,000,000	4,375	30,630	(63)	(441)	28,000	11,500	(5,500)	(3,811)
5	1,000,000	4,375	37,201	(50)	(425)	28,000	11,500	(5,500)	2,776
6	1,000,000	4,375	43,387	(42)	(417)	28,000	11,500	(5,500)	8,970
7	1,000,000	3,750	42,002	(36)	(403)	28,000	11,500	(5,500)	7,599
8	1,000,000	3,750	46,657	(31)	(386)	28,000	11,500	(5,500)	12,271
9	1,000,000	3,750	51,035	(28)	(381)	28,000	11,500	(5,500)	16,654
10	1,000,000	3,750	55,151	(25)	(368)	28,000	11,500	(5,500)	20,783

*Assumes that unamortized balance is allocated pro rata over the 10 sinking fund payments.

†Assumed to be tax deductible cost of $3 per bond plus 1% of issuance proceeds ($10,000).

Source: John D. Finnerty, *An Illustrated Guide to Bond Refunding Analysis*, Financial Analysts Research Foundation, Charlottesville, VA, 1984, p. 52. Reprinted by permission.

is, the company must meet its continuing sinking fund obligations in cash until there are no longer any bonds outstanding. As a result, cash purchases and optional redemptions serve simply to reduce the maturity of the issue. This restriction does not pose any problems when the yield curve is flat or downward-sloping. But when it is upward-sloping, the most distant sinking fund amounts are no longer necessarily the most profitable to refund. Consequently, in that case, the analyst must evaluate the economics of repurchasing the most distant sinking fund amount, the two most distant as a package, the three most distant as a package, and so on, and if any lead to (positive) net-present-value savings, pick the package of sinking fund amounts that offers the greatest net-present-value savings. If the indenture for the debt issue in the preceding example contained this restriction, the company would still find it economic to redeem the $6 million principal amount of the issue immediately.

FORCED CONVERSIONS

The call provision associated with a convertible debt issue gives the issuer a means to force holders to convert the debt into common stock. Holders may not do this voluntarily even when the market price of the stock exceeds the conversion price by a significant margin if the dividends they would receive after conversion are less than the interest they now receive. When the market value of the common stock they would receive exceeds the optional redemption price, announcing a call of the convertible issue will motivate holders to convert because that is more profitable to them than tendering the bonds for redemption. Forcing conversion in this manner benefits the issuer, of course, by accelerating the conversion of debt into common equity. It can also enhance discretionary cash flow net of all dividends when the increase in common stock dividends is less than the after-tax interest payments on the convertible issue.

Illustration of Forced Conversion Analysis

Time Incorporated called its Series C $4.50 Cumulative Convertible Preferred Stock for redemption on November 3, 1982, at a redemption price, including accrued dividends, of $54.9375. The issue was convertible into 1.5152 shares of Time Incorporated common stock at a conversion price of $33 per share. The market price of the common stock was $46\frac{3}{8}$, representing a 40.5% premium over the conversion price. But because the common stock dividend was only $1 per share per annum, a holder who converted would suffer a decrease in annual dividend income amounting to $2.98 = ($4.50 − 1.5152 × 1.00) per preferred share. Consequently, few holders had converted voluntarily. However, the market value of the common stock represented a significant cushion over the redemption price per share (the redemption price per bond divided by the conversion ratio) amounting to:

$$
\begin{aligned}
\begin{matrix} \text{Forced} \\ \text{conversion} \\ \text{cushion} \end{matrix} &= \left(\begin{matrix} \text{market price} \\ \text{of common stock} \end{matrix} - \begin{matrix} \text{redemption} \\ \text{price per share} \end{matrix} \right) \\
&\div \begin{matrix} \text{redemption} \\ \text{price per share} \end{matrix} \\
&= \frac{46.375 - (54.9375/1.5152)}{54.9375/1.5152} = 27.9\%
\end{aligned}
\tag{23-2}
$$

This naturally gave holders a strong incentive to convert in response to the redemption notice. With the assistance of investment bankers, the entire issue was converted.

Timing the Forced Conversion

Investment bankers generally recommend that a company not call a convertible issue unless the forced conversion cushion is at least 15% in the case of a low-beta stock and at least 20% in the case of a high-beta stock. Bond indentures require a company to give holders advance notice (typically 15 or 30 days) when calling an issue. If the company's share price falls below the redemption price per share during this period, holders will tender the bonds for redemption rather than convert. The greater the cushion, the lower the risk of this occurring.

To eliminate this possibility altogether, most companies engage the services of an investment banker (as Time Incorporated did) to underwrite the redemption. In return for a standby fee (generally between 0.5 and 1.5% of the underwriting commitment), the banker agrees to purchase from the company the number of shares of common stock that would have been issued if bonds that were tendered for redemption had instead been converted. Typically, the banker pays a purchase price equal to the redemption price per share and agrees to remit to the company 80% of the profit the banker realizes by reselling the shares at the higher market price. The banker also normally receives a take-up fee (generally between 2.5 and 5.0% of the redemption price per share) if the standby arrangement results in the banker having to purchase from the company more than 5% of the issue.

REFUNDING PREFERRED STOCK

Preferred stock instruments call for regular periodic payments just like debt. In many cases, they also provide for sinking funds. Preferred stock differs from debt in that missing a preferred stock dividend or sinking fund payment is not an event of default. Nevertheless a company that is financially healthy will treat these payments as fixed obligations. If it is assumed that issuers make preferred stock dividend and sinking fund payments on a timely basis, the methods of refunding analysis discussed in this chapter and the next are easily modified to handle preferred stock refundings.

Relationship to Bond Refunding

Preferred stock dividend payments are not tax deductible, and the redemption premium and issuance expenses for a preferred stock issue are neither deductible immediately nor amortizable for tax purposes over time.[5] Also, because dividends are payable quarterly, the cash flows associated with a preferred stock refunding should be calculated and then discounted on a quarterly basis.

Refunding High-Dividend-Rate Preferred Stock

Incorporating these changes, Formula 23-1 becomes

$$
\begin{aligned}
\text{NPV} = \sum_{t=1}^{\text{maturity}} &\left[\left(\begin{array}{c} \text{$\frac{1}{4}$ dividend rate} \\ \text{on old issue} \end{array} - \begin{array}{c} \text{$\frac{1}{4}$ dividend rate} \\ \text{on new issue} \end{array} \right) \right. \\
&\left. \times \begin{array}{c} \text{amount} \\ \text{refunded} \end{array} \div \left(1 + \begin{array}{c} \text{$\frac{1}{4}$ dividend rate} \\ \text{on new issue} \end{array} \right)^{t} \right] \\
&- \left(\begin{array}{c} \text{redemption} \\ \text{premium} \end{array} + \begin{array}{c} \text{new issue} \\ \text{expenses} \end{array} \right)
\end{aligned}
\tag{23-3}
$$

Dividend rate on old issue and *dividend rate on new issue* are expressed as a fraction of the share price (for example, 0.2 for a $25 share that pays $5 per year) and *dividend rate on new issue* is the new issue rate for a noncallable issue. *Amount refunded* denotes the face amount of preferred stock refunded. *Redemption premium* and *new issue expenses* denote the aggregate redemption premium and the issuance expenses for the new issue, respectively. *Maturity* denotes the number of quarterly periods remaining until the old issue was originally scheduled to mature.

Illustration of Preferred Stock Refunding Analysis

A company proposes to call and refund its 15-year 12% cumulative preferred stock issue with a new 10% issue; $50 million worth is outstanding. The 12% issue matures in one lump sum and has a call price of $115 per share. Issuance expenses will amount to $750,000.

Refunding the 12% issue would yield quarterly dividend savings of $250,000 but require an aggregate redemption premium of $2,500,000. Applying Formula 23-3, the refunding would produce net-present-value savings amounting to $4,477,164.

Perpetual Issues

Preferred stock is often issued in perpetual form. In that case, the discounted cash flow model takes a simpler form than Formula 23.3:

$$
\text{NPV} = \left[\left(\begin{array}{c} \text{dividend rate} \\ \text{on old issue} \end{array} - \begin{array}{c} \text{dividend rate} \\ \text{on new issue} \end{array} \right) \times \begin{array}{c} \text{amount} \\ \text{refunded} \end{array} \right.
$$

$$
\left. \div \begin{array}{c} \text{dividend rate} \\ \text{on new issue} \end{array} \right] - \left(\begin{array}{c} \text{redemption} \\ \text{premium} \end{array} + \begin{array}{c} \text{new issue} \\ \text{expenses} \end{array} \right) \qquad (23\text{-}4)
$$

If the 12% issue just discussed were instead perpetual, the $250,000 quarterly savings could be realized in perpetuity. The refunding would produce dividend savings with a present value of $10 million, resulting in net-present-value savings of $6.75 million.

Timing the Refunding

Questions concerning the timing of a refunding of preferred stock and whether it is beneficial to purchase in the open market or tender for shares of high-dividend-rate preferred stock can be analyzed using the techniques described earlier as long as Formula 23-3 is used in place of Formula 23-1. The break-even annual dividend rate for a perpetual issue can be calculated directly:

$$
\begin{array}{c} \text{Break-even} \\ \text{dividend rate} \end{array} = \begin{array}{c} \text{dividend rate} \\ \text{on old issue} \end{array} \times \begin{array}{c} \text{amount} \\ \text{refunded} \end{array}
$$

$$
\div \left(\begin{array}{c} \text{redemption} \\ \text{price} \end{array} + \begin{array}{c} \text{new issue} \\ \text{expenses} \end{array} \right) \qquad (23\text{-}5)
$$

Redemption price denotes the aggregate price paid to retire the preferred stock, and the other variables are as defined before. The break-even dividend rate for refunding the 12% perpetual issue just described is break-even dividend rate = 11.268%. That is, refunding would be economic as long as the new issue carries an annual dividend rate less than 11.268%.

SUMMARY

A corporation can lower its cost of debt and increase shareholder wealth by managing its liabilities effectively. This involves exploiting profitable opportunities to refund outstanding debt and preferred stock issues and to force conversion of convertible securities.

This chapter described techniques for evaluating the economics of refunding premium debt and preferred stock. The net-present-value savings from refunding high-coupon debt equal the change in after-tax debt service requirements discounted at the after-tax interest cost of the new issue. In order for the analysis to be meaningful, the maturity of the new issue should match the maturity of the old issue and the new issue should be noncallable. With two modifications, the same procedure applies to high-dividend-rate preferred stock. Dividends and the costs associated with the refunding are not tax deductible, and dividends are paid quarterly.

The presence of a sinking fund adds a degree of complexity to the refunding analysis. The analyst should bear in mind that debt issues do not have to be called in their entirety. Thus, in a low-interest-rate environment, it may be more profitable for a corporation to call only a portion of an issue rather than all of it and to retire the balance through the operation of the sinking fund.

Refunding Discounted Debt

Financial experts have long debated whether a company can profitably refund an issue of discounted debt, that is, indebtedness that bears a below-market coupon rate of interest and that is consequently selling in the market at a discount to its face amount.[1] The profitability of such refundings is highly sensitive to tax factors, particularly the tax treatment of the gain a company realizes when it reacquires its debt at a discount.

WHEN IS IT PROFITABLE TO REFUND DISCOUNTED DEBT?

Suppose that a corporation has outstanding a $1000 bond that bears interest at the rate of 5% per period and that matures in one period. Suppose further that a new one-period par value bond would require a 10% coupon and would involve a flotation cost of $5 (after taxes). The discounted issue would be worth $1050/1.10 = $954.55 per bond. If the corporation's marginal tax rate is 50%, a new issue in the amount of $976.19 would have the same $1025 after-tax debt service requirement as the old issue. Thus, without altering its debt service requirements, the corporation can raise $976.19 through the sale of new debt, pay out $959.55 to redeem the old issue and cover the cost of floating the new bond, and still have $16.64 left over to distribute to its shareholders.

Refunding the discounted issue is profitable because it produces additional tax shield benefits. Whereas only $50 (or 4.76%) of the $1050 pretax debt service payment obligations associated with the old issue are tax deductible, $97.62 (or 9.09%) of the $1073.81 pretax debt service payment obligations associated with the new issue are tax deductible. The new issue has tax shield benefits

425

amounting to $48.81 (= 97.62 × 0.5), whereas the old issue has tax shield benefits of only $25.00 (= 50.00 × 0.5). The difference less the cost of flotation is $18.81—more than the $16.64 net present value calculated earlier. Whereas the opportunity to call bonds at a below-market option price accounts chiefly for the profitability of refunding high-coupon debt, the opportunity to increase the proportion of debt service payments that is tax deductible is what accounts for the profitability of refunding discounted debt.

Refunding discounted debt involves one further tax factor: the tax treatment of the gain ($45.45 in the foregoing example) the corporation realizes by extinguishing debt at less than its face amount. Under the Internal Revenue Code, if a corporation repurchases its debt for cash or its common stock, the entire gain would be taxed as ordinary income. However, the Internal Revenue Code permits the corporation to write down certain of its assets by the amount of the gain, thus deferring this tax liability. Depreciable assets must be written down first, which spreads the tax liability over the depreciable lives of the assets that are written down (since the writedown reduces future depreciation deductions).[2]

The tax treatment accorded the gain is crucial to the economics of refunding discounted debt. If the corporation in the foregoing example had to include the gain in its taxable ordinary income, it would face a tax liability of $22.73 (= $45.45 × 0.5). Even if it can defer this liability, the present value of the liability is $21.65 (= $22.73/1.05), which exceeds the $16.64 savings calculated earlier. Tax changes in recent years have eliminated various strategies companies had used to realize a tax-free gain.

EVALUATING THE ECONOMICS OF REFUNDING DISCOUNTED DEBT

A corporation should refund discounted debt only if it can issue new debt that has the same after-tax debt service requirements as the old issue and after paying all costs associated with retiring the old issue and selling the new issue, including any tax owing on the gain, still have a surplus left over to distribute to its shareholders. As in the case of refunding high-coupon debt, a simple procedure is available for calculating this surplus. Note that if the corporation in the preceding example were to issue just enough debt to cover the cost of repurchasing the old debt, its after-tax interest expense would increase from $25.00 (= $1000 × 0.05 × 0.5) to $47.73 (= $954.55 × 0.10 × 0.5), but it would save $45.45 (= $1000 − 954.55) in principal repayment obligations. Its net after-tax savings at the end of the one period would thus be $22.72 (= $25.00 − 47.73 + 45.45). Discounting these savings at the after-tax interest rate on the new issue gives $21.64. Subtracting the $5 flotation cost results in the same $16.64 net-present-value saving calculated earlier. Thus, even though

Assumptions	Old Issue	New Issue
Principal amount	$50,000,000	$33,857,500
Coupon rate	8.00%	15.00%
Remaining life	10 years	10 years
Issuance expenses plus original issue		
discount (less original issue premium)	$ 400,000*	$ 380,000
Debt retirement expenses†	$150,000	
Issuer's tax rate	50%	

Benefits of Refunding	Pretax	After-Tax
Semiannual expense amortization:		
New issue	$ 19,000	$ 9,500
Old issue	20,000	10,000
Savings (cost)	$(1,000)	$(500)
Present value of semiannual savings (cost)‡		$(6,948)
Present value of decrease in principal		
repayment obligation‡		7,730,550
Total benefits		$ 7,723,602

Costs of Refunding	Pretax	After-Tax
Semiannual interest expense:		
New issue	$ 2,539,313	$ 1,269,656
Old issue	2,000,000	1,000,000
Semiannual increase	$ 539,313	$ 269,656
Present value of increase in semiannual		
interest expense‡		$ 3,747,195
Tax on the gain	—	—
New issue expenses	$ 380,000	$ 380,000
Debt retirement expenses	150,000	75,000
Less write-off of unamortized balance of		
issuance expenses on old issue	(400,000)	(200,000)
Total costs		$ 4,002,195
Net present value of refunding	$3,721,407	

*Unamortized balance.
†Calculated as $3 per bond.
‡Discounted at the semiannual after-tax interest rate on a new full-coupon issue (3.75%).

Source: John D. Finnerty, *An Illustrated Guide to Bond Refunding Analysis*, Financial Analysts
Research Foundation, Charlottesville, Va., 1984, p. 63. Reprinted by permission.

the economic motivation for refunding is different in the two cases, the basic analytical procedure is the same: Discount the change in after-tax debt service obligations at the after-tax cost of the refunding issue.

Illustration of Discounted Debt Refunding Analysis

Suppose that a corporation is considering refunding $50 million principal amount of its 8% debentures that mature in 10 years. The 8% issue has a market price of 67.715%, or $677.15 per bond, which implies a yield to maturity of 14.12%. Suppose the corporation can reacquire the discounted debt in such a way that it will not incur any tax liability on the gain. The unamortized balance of issuance and other expenses associated with the portion of the 8% issue to be retired is $400,000. The corporation has been informed by its investment bankers that under prevailing market conditions a 10-year debt issue would require a 15% coupon.

Table 24-1 illustrates the calculation of the net present value of refunding the 8% debentures. The refunding would increase semiannual after-tax interest expense by $269,656. The present value of these additional obligations is $3,747,195. The refunding would also reduce the corporation's principal repayment obligation by $16,142,500, producing net-present-value savings of $7,730,550. Allowing for the other benefits and costs of the refunding, the net-present-value savings are $3,721,407. However, if the gain were taxable immediately, the refunding would create a tax liability of $8,071,250, which would make the refunding uneconomic.

Discounted Cash Flow Model

The foregoing example illustrates the application of the following discounted cash flow model:

$$
\begin{aligned}
\text{NPV} = \sum_{t=1}^{m} \Bigg\{ &\left[\left(1 - \frac{\text{tax}}{\text{rate}} \right) \times \tfrac{1}{2} \left(\begin{matrix} \text{interest rate} \\ \text{on old issue} \end{matrix} \times \begin{matrix} \text{principal} \\ \text{amount refunded} \end{matrix} \right. \right. \\
&\left. - \begin{matrix} \text{interest rate} \\ \text{on new issue} \end{matrix} \times \begin{matrix} \text{principal amount} \\ \text{of new issue} \end{matrix} \right) \\
&\left. + \frac{\text{tax rate} \times (\text{new issue expenses} - \text{unamortized balance})}{m} \right] \\
&\div \left[1 + \tfrac{1}{2} \left(1 - \frac{\text{tax}}{\text{rate}} \right) \times \begin{matrix} \text{interest rate} \\ \text{on new issue} \end{matrix} \right]^{t} \Bigg\} \\
&+ \left(\begin{matrix} \text{principal} \\ \text{amount refunded} \end{matrix} - \begin{matrix} \text{principal amount} \\ \text{of new issue} \end{matrix} \right) \\
&\div \left[1 + \tfrac{1}{2} \left(1 - \frac{\text{tax}}{\text{rate}} \right) \times \begin{matrix} \text{interest rate} \\ \text{on new issue} \end{matrix} \right]^{m}
\end{aligned}
$$

$$- \left\{ \left(\begin{matrix} \text{tax rate} \\ \text{on gain} \end{matrix} \times \text{gain} \right) + \left(1 - \frac{\text{tax}}{\text{rate}} \right) \times \begin{matrix} \text{deductible} \\ \text{expenses} \end{matrix} \right.$$

$$+ \begin{matrix} \text{new issue} \\ \text{expenses} \end{matrix} + \begin{matrix} \text{nondeductible} \\ \text{expenses} \end{matrix} - \left. \left(\frac{\text{tax}}{\text{rate}} \times \begin{matrix} \text{unamortized} \\ \text{balance} \end{matrix} \right) \right\}$$

$$(24\text{-}1)$$

where m denotes the number of semiannual periods until the old debt is scheduled to mature. The new debt is assumed to be issued at par. The *gain* is equal to the difference in principal amounts, *principal amount refunded − principal amount of new issue*. The *tax rate on gain* denotes the effective time-adjusted tax rate on the gain; if the gain is deferred in whole or in part, *tax rate on gain × gain* denotes the present value of the tax payments.

Timing

Timing is as important in the case of refunding discounted debt as it is in the case of refunding high-coupon debt, and the timing problem can be approached in a similar manner in both cases. For example, a price of 67.587% per bond 1 year hence (versus 67.715% currently) would also produce net-present-value savings of $3,721,407 (assuming a flat yield curve, after discounting back 1 year at a 7.50% after-tax rate) if the corporation were to wait to refund the 8% issue in the preceding example. This would imply a yield to maturity on the outstanding issue of 14.58% and a new issue rate of 15.46% assuming the yield at which the bonds trade remains at a discount of 88 basis points to the new issue rate. Consequently, if the corporation believes there is a strong likelihood that interest rates will rise more than 46 basis points during the coming year, it may prefer to postpone the refunding.

Refunding Discounted Convertible Debt

Companies may also refund convertible debt. For example, in October 1977 United Air Lines, Inc., and its parent UAL, Inc. offered to exchange a new issue of 8% convertible subordinated debentures for United Air Line's outstanding $4\frac{1}{4}$% convertible subordinated debentures and 5% convertible subordinated debentures, both of which had been trading at a discount because of their low interest rates and high effective conversion premiums. The 8% issue set a lower conversion price.

A convertible debenture issue represents a package of securities consisting of (1) straight debt and (2) a conversion option the holder can exercise by tendering the debt in exchange for stock. This suggests the following analytical approach. Set the redemption terms and the conversion terms of the new issue so that they have the same respective values as those of the outstanding issue. Then analyze the refunding as though it only involves straight debt. This will indicate whether a "pure" refunding would be profitable. If it is profitable, the corporation can decide whether the value of the refunding to the corporation's shareholders is enhanced by increasing the portion of the refunding package that is attributable to the conversion option. If a pure refunding is not profitable, the corporation must decide whether simply increasing the likelihood of conversion is worth this cost (and whether its shareholders might be better off if instead of refunding the corporation waits and issues common stock at the time debtholders allow their conversion options to expire unexercised).

Financial Reporting Considerations

Under generally accepted accounting principles, refunding discounted debt results in a reported gain equal to the face amount of debt reacquired less the cost of reacquiring it—regardless of whether there is a positive net present value. If the gain is material in an accounting sense, the issuer can include in ordinary income only that portion which is associated with debt that was scheduled to come due within 1 year of the repurchase date; it must report the remaining portion as an extraordinary gain.

SINKING FUND MANAGEMENT

The sinking fund provisions in corporate bond indentures for publicly held debt generally give the corporation the option of either (1) making a cash payment to the trustee for the face amount of the bonds to be retired on the sinking fund date or (2) delivering the required number of bonds that the corporation has previously repurchased from holders. This so-called *delivery option* is valuable when the debt issue is trading in the market at a discount from its face amount. In that event, it is cheaper for the corporation to satisfy the sinking fund requirement through open market purchases. It is worth noting that the trustee is normally not authorized under the indenture to make open market purchases; the corporation itself must make these purchases and deliver the bonds to the trustee. It is also worth noting that the indentures for privately placed bonds generally do not provide a delivery option.

Because of, first, the cash savings that can result from satisfying sinking fund requirements at a discount and, second, uncertainty regarding future interest rates and hence future bond prices, it may be to a corporation's advantage to *prepurchase* sinking fund debt that is currently trading at a discount in anticipation of future sinking fund requirements. In addition, certain institutions have made it a practice to buy up sinking fund issues. By *cornering* the issue, the institution can force the corporation to retire the debt at a price near the debt's face amount. In this way, the institution effectively appropriates for itself the benefits the corporation would have realized had it made the prepurchases. By prepurchasing a large enough portion of the issue, the corporation can stymie the accumulator by lengthening the period of time until the corporation would be obligated to purchase the accumulator's holdings.

The economics of prepurchasing future sinking fund requirements should be analyzed by comparing the after-tax cash flows associated with (1) prepurchasing and (2) leaving the securities outstanding and repurchasing or redeeming them on the sinking fund date. In order to avoid introducing capital structure effects that might bias the analysis, the analyst should assume that the corporation borrows the funds it uses to make the prepurchase. With this assumption, the prepurchase involves the refunding of discounted debt, and Formula 24-1 applies but with one modification. If the sinking fund amount is left outstanding, the corporation might nevertheless be able to purchase it on the sinking fund date for less than its face amount. If the mandatory redemption price is 100%, as is normally the case, the face amount of the debt is the maximum price the corporation would ever have to pay to retire the debt. Using this price will bias the analysis toward prepurchase.

One possible approach in this regard is to assume that the yield to average life of the issue is the same on the sinking fund date as on the proposed prepurchase date. Denote by *price on redemption date* the bond price on the sinking fund date required to produce a yield to remaining average life equal to the issue's current yield to average life. Prepurchasing on the sinking fund date would produce savings equal to the difference between the principal amount refunded and the aggregate *price on redemption date* less the tax, if any, on this gain. Thus, Formula 24-1 can be used to evaluate the economics of prepurchases by treating the sinking fund issue as a serial debt issue and applying Formula 24-1 separately to each sinking fund payment with *price on redemption date − principal amount of new issue* for the sinking fund payment in place of *principal amount refunded − principal amount of new issue*, with the number of semiannual periods until the sinking fund obligation comes due in place of *m*, and with a pro rata share of the issuance expenses of the old issue in place of *unamortized balance*. In this analysis, *interest rate on new issue* is for new debt issued on the prepurchase date that matures on the sinking fund date.

Illustration of Sinking Fund Prepurchase Analysis
A corporation is considering whether to prepurchase some portion of its outstanding 8% sinking fund debentures. It currently has none of the issue in its treasury. The issue contains a sinking fund that requires equal payments at the end of each of the next 9 years in the amount of $5 million each, giving the issue an average life of 5 years. The corporation estimates that it will be able to borrow on a short-term basis over the next year or next 2 years at an average cost of 10% per annum, and the corporation's investment banker estimates that the corporation's new issue rates are 12% for debt with a maturity of between 3 and 5 years and 12.50% for debt with a maturity of between 6 and 9 years. The 8% issue is trading at a price of 86.966%, or $869.66 per bond, imply-

Table 24-2
Discounted Cash Flow Analysis of the Economics of Prepurchasing Sinking Fund Debt

Years to Sinking Fund Payment	As of Sinking Fund Date				Repayment Savings		Semiannual After-Tax Interest Expense*		Increase in Interest Expense		Net Savings (Cost) of Prepurchase§	Net Savings (Cost) Assuming Redemption at Par
	Remaining Average Life	Bond Price†	Current Bond Price		Amount	Present Value‡	Old Issue	New Issue	Semi-annual Amount	Present Value‡		
1	4.5	87.966%	86.966%		$ 50,000	$ 47,591	$100,000	$108,708	$ 8,708	$ 16,784	$ 30,807	$603,513
2	4.0	89.025	86.966		102,950	93,268	100,000	108,708	8,708	32,759	60,509	557,649
3	3.5	90.143	86.966		158,850	133,034	100,000	130,499	30,499	165,219	(32,185)	380,569
4	3.0	91.327	86.966		218,050	172,131	100,000	130,499	30,499	214,094	(41,963)	300,364
5	2.5	92.578	86.966		280,600	208,793	100,000	130,499	30,499	260,163	(51,370)	224,763
6	2.0	93.901	86.966		346,750	239,689	100,000	135,884	35,884	354,539	(114,850)	95,946
7	1.5	95.301	86.966		416,750	270,882	100,000	135,884	35,884	401,916	(131,034)	21,680
8	1.0	96.780	86.966		490,700	299,911	100,000	135,884	35,884	446,465	(146,554)	(48,152)
9	0.5	98.345	86.966		568,950	326,981	100,000	135,884	35,884	488,355	(161,374)	(113,817)

* Assuming 50% tax rate.
† Assuming yield to remaining average life of 11.50%.
‡ Discounting at the semiannual after-tax interest cost (2.500% for years 1–2, 3.000% for years 3–5, and 3.125% for years 6–9).
§ Present value of repayment savings less present value of increase in interest expense.

ing a yield to average life of 11.50%. Table 24-2 summarizes the results of the prepurchase analysis. For purposes of simplification, the example ignores issuance expenses and related tax effects and assumes that the prepurchase transactions are structured so as to avoid any tax on the gain.[3]

Based on the analysis in Table 24-2, the corporation would conclude that is could prepurchase at least the first two sinking fund amounts profitably ($10 million principal amount). If the corporation expects interest rates to fall sharply over the next few years or if it believes that an accumulator has started buying the issue, it might decide to buy as many as seven sinking fund payments ahead ($35 million principal amount). Finally, if the corporation already has a portion of the 8% issue in its treasury (i.e., prepurchased previously and not yet submitted to the trustee), the sinking fund amounts available for prepurchase should be reduced (beginning with the first, continuing with the second, and so on until the amount in the treasury has been exhausted) to take these previous prepurchases into account.

Timing of Prepurchases

The timing problem can be handled as described in the preceding section by treating each sinking fund obligation as a separate debt issue. In this case, the repurchase price and the new issue rate are not as closely tied as in the case of a discounted issue having a bullet maturity. Consequently, break-even analysis involves finding prepurchase-price–new-issue-rate combinations for different points in time that would make the corporation indifferent between prepurchasing a particular sinking fund amount immediately and waiting.[4]

DEFEASANCE

Exxon Corporation announced on July 6, 1982, that it had *defeased*, or eliminated from its balance sheet, six Exxon debt issues representing approximately $515 million principal amount of indebtedness. Exxon accomplished this by depositing irrevocably with a trustee a portfolio containing approximately $312 million worth of U.S. government and federal agency securities the interest and principal payments from which would be sufficient to discharge fully the debt service requirements of the six Exxon debt issues. In addition to eliminating the debt from Exxon's balance sheet, the defeasance operation increased Exxon's earnings by roughly $130 million after provision for taxes that would have to be paid on income generated by the defeasance portfolio. A company may wish to defease outstanding debt in order to restructure its balance sheet and improve its credit standing (as Exxon indicated it did), to free itself of restrictive covenants, or to refund discounted debt.

Defeasing an outstanding debt obligation involves substituting for the issuer's promise to pay a package of U.S. government obligations (consisting of U.S. Treasury securities and/or U.S. government–guaranteed securities) and perhaps also some cash sufficient to discharge the debt obligation in full and in a timely manner. There are two types of defeasance. In a novation, or legal defeasance, the debt issuer's obligations under the indenture are discharged, and the debt is eliminated from the issuer's books for tax as well as financial reporting purposes. In an in-substance, or economic, defeasance, the debt is eliminated for financial reporting purposes only; the debt obligation is neither legally discharged nor removed from the issuer's books for tax purposes.[5] A company can effect a novation only if the bond indenture permits it or if bond-holders grant approval. With but few exceptions, corporate bond indentures do not authorize a defeasance. Consequently, corporate defeasances are generally of the in-substance variety.

Economics of In-Substance Defeasance

When a company defeases outstanding debt, it purchases a stream of U.S. government debt service payment obligations, which it uses to form the defeasance portfolio. The issuer either uses excess cash or raises funds through the issuance of new debt or equity securities to purchase the package of U.S. government obligations. When debt securities are issued, the defeasance operation is tantamount to a bond refunding.

The purchase price of the defeasance portfolio corresponds to the yield at which the U.S. government obligations are trading on the purchase date. Thus, through a defeasance, a company effectively reacquires its debt at a premium price which corresponds to the lower yield at which U.S. government obligations trade relative to the company's debt. In addition, in an in-substance defeasance the company is liable for the tax obligations generated by the defeasance portfolio but continues to deduct interest payments on the defeased debt. This creates an added tax drain when the present value of these tax obligations exceeds the present value of the tax shields on the defeased debt.

Whether a company can undertake an in-substance defeasance profitably depends principally on two factors:

- There must be available U.S. government obligations with sufficiently low coupons so as to permit the company to acquire a defeasance portfolio with a relatively high proportion of capital gain income and relatively low proportion of (ordinary) interest income, thus minimizing the potential added tax drain.
- The company's senior debt must carry a comparatively high rating so that the yield premium the company must effectively pay in order to defease its debt is not so large that it renders the defeasance uneconomic.

Illustration of Defeasance Analysis

The economics of an in-substance defeasance funded with a new issue of debt can be evaluated by modifying Formula 24-1. Two important changes are needed. The *principal amount of new issue* must be large enough to cover the cost of a portfolio that will provide a cash flow stream sufficient by itself to meet each debt service payment on the defeased debt when the payment comes due. In addition, there may be a net additional tax drain, depending on the sign of

$$
\begin{array}{c}
\text{Tax} \\
\text{increase} \\
\text{(decrease)}
\end{array}
= \sum_{t=1}^{m} \left[\begin{array}{cc} \text{portfolio tax} & \text{tax shields on} \\ \text{liability}(t) & \text{defeased debt}(t) \end{array} \right]
$$

$$
\div \ 1 \ + \ \tfrac{1}{2} \left(1 - \frac{\text{tax}}{\text{rate}} \right) \times \frac{\text{interest rate}^t}{\text{on new issue}} \qquad (24\text{-}2)
$$

In-substance defeasance results in a net additional tax drain (a *tax increase*) when the present value of the tax obligations of the defeasance trust exceeds the present value of the tax shields generated by the defeased debt. This occurs unless the trust can be formed in a way that the bulk of its income is taxed at capital gains rates, for example, through the purchase of deep discount full coupon Treasury securities.[6]

Table 24-3 illustrates the method of analysis just described as applied to the $50 million of debt in Table 24-1. The net present value of the

Table 24-3
Discounted Cash Flow Analysis of the Economics
of In-Substance Defeasance

Assumptions	Old Issue	New Issue
Principal amount	$50,000,000	$37,000,000
Coupon rate	8.00%	15.00%
Remaining life	10 years	10 years
Issuance expenses plus original issue discount (less original issue premium)	$ 400,000[a]	$ 380,000
Defeasance trustee's fees[b]	$150,000	
Issuer's tax rate	50%	

Benefits of Defeasance	Pretax	After-Tax
Semiannual expense amortization:		
New issue	$ 19,000	$ 9,500
Old issue	20,000	10,000
Savings (cost)	$(1,000)	$(500)
Present value of semiannual savings (cost)[c]		$(6,948)
Present value of decrease in principal repayment obligation[c]		6,225,600
Total benefits		$ 6,218,652

Discounted Cash Flow Analysis of the Economics of In-Substance Defeasance *(Continued)*

Costs of Defeasance	Pretax	After-Tax
Semiannual interest expense:		
New issue	$ 2,775,000	$ 1,387,500
Old issue	2,000,000	1,000,000
Semiannual increase	$ 775,000	$ 387,500
Present value of increase in semiannual interest expense[c]		$5,384,779
Present value of portfolio tax liability[c]		$14,100,000
Present value of tax shields on defeased debt[c]		14,035,166[d]
Tax increase (decrease)		$ 64,834
Tax on the gain	—	—
New issue expenses	$ 380,000	$ 380,000
Defeasance trustee's fees	150,000	75,000
Less write-off of unamortized balance of issuance expenses on old issue	—	—
Less present value of excess cash released from the defeasance trust[c]	(10,000)	(10,000)[e]
Total costs		$ 5,894,613
Net present value of in-substance defeasance		$ 324,039

[a] Unamortized balance.

[b] Calculated as $3 per bond. Represents the present value of the costs of establishing and maintaining the defeasance trust.

[c] Discounted at the semiannual after-tax interest rate on a new full-coupon issue (3.75%).

[d] Includes interest and amortization tax shields generated by the defeased debt.

[e] Present value of excess cash released by the defeasance trustee.

defeasance is calculated with the aid of Formula 24-1 with the following modifications:

- Principal amount of new issue covers the cost of the defeasance portfolio. It has been assumed in Table 24-3 that the portfolio costs $37 million. Thus, the debt is effectively acquired at a cost of $740 per bond (= $37,000,000/50,000), a premium over the $677.15 cost of reacquiring it for cash.
- There is a slight tax increase. It has been assumed in Table 24-3 that the defeasance portfolio generates tax payment obligations the present value of which is $14,100,000, whereas the defeased debt throws off tax shields the present value of which is $14,035,166.
- Because the defeased debt remains on the issuer's books for tax purposes, there is no amortization write-off associated with in-substance defeasance.

- It is virtually impossible to match the cash flow stream of the defeasance portfolio to the debt service stream of the defeased debt. One is limited by the supply of available Treasury securities. Statement of Financial Accounting Standards No. 76 requires that the defeasance trust provide cash flows that precede and "approximately coincide" with the debt service obligations they are intended to meet. It does not specify a reinvestment rate for cash income realized in advance of a debt service payment date. Accountants generally permit a company to assume a modest reinvestment rate (not more that 5%) provided there is not a "significant" mismatching of cash flows. Table 24-3 assumes, conservatively, a zero reinvestment rate. In that case, interest earned on such income will represent excess cash that the trustee can release to the company. The present value of these cash distributions is subtracted in Table 24-3 because they represent a return to the issuer of a portion of the cash investment in the defeasance portfolio.

Taking all these factors into account, the in-substance defeasance has a net present value of $324,039. Note that this value is particularly sensitive to the magnitude of the tax increase created and to the cost of the defeasance portfolio. A modest increase in either would render the in-substance defeasance uneconomic, at least from the standpoint of the company's shareholders. In contrast, bondholders get a windfall because of the credit backing the defeasance portfolio provides.

The bond indentures for tax-exempt industrial revenue bond and industrial development bond issues typically contain a defeasance provision, which permits the issuer to effect a novation. Unlike in-substance defeasance, a novation is a taxable transaction. Consequently, Formula 24-1 applies but with two modifications. Principal amount of new issue must cover the cost of the defeasance portfolio, and the present value of excess cash released from the defeasance trust should be added back when calculating the net present value of the defeasance.

SUMMARY

It is possible under certain circumstances for a corporation to refund discounted debt profitably. But the factors that are responsible for the profitability of refunding discounted debt are fundamentally different from those that account for the profitability of refunding high-coupon debt. The profitability of refunding discounted debt results from an increase in the proportion of debt service payments that are tax deductible. But even though the source of the profitability is different in the two cases, the basic analytical approach is the same: discount the change in *after-tax* cash flows at the *after-tax* interest cost of a new debt issue.

As in the case of premium debt, the presence of a sinking fund creates an opportunity for profit through effective liability management. Publicly held debt typically gives the issuer a delivery option. Accordingly, in a high-interest-rate environment, it may be more profitable for the corporation to buy bonds at a discount in anticipation of future sinking fund requirements rather than to wait until the sinking fund date to buy bonds or to redeem them at par.

Financial Planning and Strategy

Part 8

Parts 2 through 7 provided separate discussions of six principal aspects of financial policy and analysis. We treated these subjects individually in order to highlight the important concepts associated with each. We pointed out, however, that these various policy decisions interact. In Part 8 we bring these areas together and point out more clearly how these critical decisions affect one another.

Chapter 25 draws on the basic elements of Parts 2 through 7 to develop a unified framework for corporate financial planning. The chapter describes the financial planning process and develops an integrated financial planning model. Careful planning is particularly crucial during the early years in a company's life cycle. Chapter 26 deals with the financing of start-up and early growth, which is referred to as *venture capital financing*. Early growth typically takes place from within a company. But at some point, healthy companies find it more advantageous to grow by acquiring other companies. Chapter 27 describes and illustrates a number of techniques for evaluating the economics of a proposed acquisition, drawing heavily on the capital budgeting techniques introduced in Part 2. In a competitive environment, continued growth and profitability are not inevitable. When its profitability diminishes, a company might decide to sell assets and redeploy the financial resources elsewhere. Chapter 28 develops analytical approaches for evaluating the alternatives available in such situations.

Probably the most exciting of the subjects discussed in Part 8 is corporate acquisitions. To illustrate, suppose Eastern Foods Company, with annual sales of $1.2 billion, is considering acquiring publicly traded Zeus Frozen Foods Company, which has annual sales of $600 million. The acquisition would increase Eastern's sales by 50% and would enable Eastern to enter the frozen foods business more quickly and, Eastern believes, more cheaply than it could on its own. The latter point rests, of course, on how much Eastern must pay to acquire Zeus. Eastern's board of directors has asked the company's financial staff to recommend the price that Eastern should offer to pay Zeus' shareholders for their shares, to determine the maximum price Eastern can afford to pay to acquire Zeus, and to recommend the financial package that Eastern should offer Zeus' shareholders. We will help Eastern's financial staff perform this task in Chapter 27.

Planning for the Future of the Business

Chapter 25

"A company that does not plan for its future may not have one" is an aphorism familiar to chief corporate planning officers. Simply reacting to events as they unfold may not create problems as long as the company's operating environment remains favorable. But when adversity sets in—an unanticipated sharp decline in product sales or an unexpected sharp increase in interest rates—a company that lacks effective contingency plans might find itself hard pressed to cope and, in the extreme case, propelled toward extinction.

WHAT IS FINANCIAL PLANNING?

Financial planning is an integral part of the firm's overall planning process. *Financial planning* might be defined in the following manner. It is a process in which a company:

- Formulates a set of consistent financial objectives for the company
- Projects the financial impact of alternative operating strategies (which are identified in the company's strategic and operating planning processes) under alternative financial policies (capital structure policy, dividend policy, etc.) and under differing assumptions as to the company's future operating environment
- Assesses these consequences in relation to its objectives and decides which financial policies to adopt and what sort of long-term and short-term financing programs to pursue
- Prepares contingency plans to alter its basic financial strategies in the event future developments should differ from those the company now expects

Financial planning involves analyzing the interactions among the capital investment, capital structure, dividend, liquidity, financing, and liability man-

441

agement options available to a company. The whole is not simply the sum of the parts; it is therefore important for a company to consider explicitly the interactions among the various policy decisions. Also, financial planning involves more than forecasting. Forecasting concentrates on the expected outcome. The real value of financial planning is that it helps a company prepare for deviations from the expected outcome.

The emphasis in financial planning is on analysis rather than strict optimization. Financial planning indicates the expected consequences of alternative courses of action. In the end, top management must judge which plan is best. There does not exist a financial planning model that is truly capable of processing the bewildering array of factors that affect firm valuation. The world is too complex. Financial planning helps a company evaluate anticipated returns and risks and determine a reasonable set of strategies and contingencies, which it embodies in its *financial plan*.

Financial planning typically consists of two phases. First, the company prepares a *long-term financial plan*. Most companies have a long-term planning horizon of between 3 and 5 years. However, companies like utilities that are involved in industries that require longer lead times for capital projects often adopt longer planning horizons. Second, the company also prepares a more detailed *short-term financial plan*, which contains a cash budget for the coming year, based on the first year of the long-term plan. The long-term plan reflects the company's strategic choices and financial policy choices over the planning period, and the short-term plan and cash budget reflect the company's operating plan for the coming year. Most companies update their financial plan annually.

COMPONENTS OF A FINANCIAL PLAN

The principal components of an effective financial plan include:

- A clear statement of the corporation's strategic, operating, and financial *objectives*
- A clear statement of the business and economic *assumptions* on which the plan is based
- A description of the *basic business strategies* for each of the company's principal lines of business and a clear statement as to how the managers within each line of business would alter their basic strategies in the event any of the principal contingencies they foresee (e.g., economic adversity and differing responses by competitors) actually occurs
- An outline of the *planned capital expenditure program*, including breakdowns by time period, by division and/or line of business, and by category (e.g., plant expansion and replacement)
- An outline of the *planned financing program*, including breakdowns by time period and by source of funds

- A set of *pro forma statements*, including period-by-period income statements, balance sheets, and flow of funds statements

FINANCIAL LEVERAGE AND OPERATING LEVERAGE

We found in Chapter 10 that as long as a company's return on assets exceeds its cost of debt, increasing the company's *financial leverage*, that is, the ratio of debt to equity in its capital structure, will increase the company's return on equity:

$$\frac{\text{Return on}}{\text{equity}} = \frac{\text{return on}}{\text{assets}} + (\text{debt} \div \text{equity})$$
$$\times \left(\frac{\text{return on}}{\text{assets}} - \frac{\text{cost of}}{\text{debt}}\right) \qquad (25\text{-}1)$$

The greater financial leverage magnifies the impact that an increase in operating income, and hence return on assets, will have on the company's return on equity. The concept of operating leverage is analogous.

Operating Leverage

A simple example in which a company sells a single product will serve to illustrate the concept of operating leverage. The company's *operating income* can be expressed as its total sales revenue less its variable costs and fixed costs of operating its business:

$$\frac{\text{Operating}}{\text{income}} = \frac{\text{unit}}{\text{price}} \times \frac{\text{unit}}{\text{sales}} - \frac{\text{unit variable}}{\text{cost}} \times \frac{\text{unit}}{\text{sales}} - \frac{\text{fixed}}{\text{costs}}$$
$$= \left(\frac{\text{unit}}{\text{price}} - \frac{\text{unit variable}}{\text{cost}}\right) \times \frac{\text{unit}}{\text{sales}} - \frac{\text{fixed}}{\text{costs}} \qquad (25\text{-}2)$$

where *unit price* denotes the price charged for the product; *unit variable cost* denotes the labor, raw material, and other costs that vary with the level of output expressed on a per-unit basis; *unit sales* are measured in physical units; and *fixed costs* consist of depreciation and other operating costs that do not vary with the level of output.

If fixed costs were zero, then operating income would vary in direct proportion to changes in unit sales. Each additional unit of sales would contribute the amount *unit price* less *unit variable cost* to operating income. But when a company has fixed costs, changes in unit sales have a disproportionate impact on operating income. This is what is meant by *operating leverage*.

Table 25-1 illustrates how fixed costs give rise to operating leverage. In the absence of fixed costs, each doubling of unit sales leads to a doubling of operating income. But when fixed costs are $500, doubling unit sales to

Table 25-1
Illustration of Operating Leverage

		Unit price = $10.00		Unit variable cost = $5.00			
		Fixed Costs = 0		Fixed Costs = $250		Fixed Costs = $500	
Unit Sales	Percentage Increase	Operating Income	Percentage Increase	Operating Income	Percentage Increase	Operating Income	Percentage Increase
100	—	$ 500	—	$ 250	—	—	—
200	100	1000	100	750	200	$ 500	Infinite
400	100	2000	100	1750	133	1500	200
800	100	4000	100	3750	114	3500	133
1600	100	8000	100	7750	107	7500	114

200 units from 100 units increases operating income to $500 from zero. Doubling unit sales to 400 units from 200 units leads to a threefold increase in operating income. Further doubling unit sales leads to percentage increases in operating income that exceed 100% though by successively smaller amounts.

Break-Even Level of Sales

Formula 25-2 leads to a second useful concept. The amount of unit sales for which operating income is zero is called the *break-even level of sales*. If unit price and unit variable cost do not vary as the level of output varies, then Formula 25-2 can be solved:

$$\frac{\text{Break-even}}{\text{level of sales}} = \text{fixed costs} \div \left(\text{unit price} - \frac{\text{unit variable}}{\text{cost}}\right) \quad (25\text{-}3)$$

Note that the smaller is *unit variable cost* in relation to *fixed costs* the lower is the *break-even level of sales*.

Figure 25-1 is called a *break-even chart*. It shows how operating income varies with the level of sales and pinpoints the location of the break-even level of sales. For the example presented in Table 25-1, *unit price* = $10.00 for all levels of output so that the *total revenue* curve is a straight line. Similarly, the *total variable costs* curve is a straight line because unit variable cost = $5.00 for all levels of output. The break-even level of sales occurs where *total revenue* equals *total costs*, which is determined by where these two curves intersect:

$$\text{Break-even level of sales} = \frac{\$500}{(\$10 - 5)} = 100 \text{ units}$$

when fixed costs = $500. At unit sales greater than 100 units the company realizes a profit, but at unit sales of less than 100 units it records a loss.

Interaction of Financial Leverage and Operating Leverage

Table 25-1 illustrates the fact that the closer a company's level of sales is to the company's break-even level of sales, the comparatively greater will be the impact on its operating income of any given percentage change in unit sales. In addition, Table 25-1 illustrates that operating leverage increases with the level of fixed costs. In general, companies in capital-intensive industries, such as the airline, machinery, mining, and steel industries, have comparatively high degrees of operating leverage, whereas firms in less capital-intensive industries, such as the service industries, have relatively low degrees of operating leverage.

Increasing leverage in a company's capital structure increases not only the average return on equity but also the riskiness of the company's equity because realized returns on equity become more variable. Consequently, a highly leveraged company in a capital-intensive industry tends to exhibit greater volatility in its profitability and cash flow than comparable companies that have less financial leverage or less operating leverage.

It is important to keep the possible effects of financial leverage and operating leverage in mind when preparing the financial plan for a company. Both are sources of volatility. Thus, to reduce the volatility of, for example, interest coverage or earnings per share, a company can (1) decrease the proportion of debt in its capital structure and thereby reduce financial leverage or (2) reduce

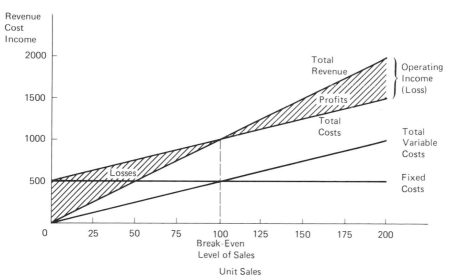

Figure 25-1. Break-even chart.

fixed costs and thereby reduce both the break-even level of sales and operating leverage.

A FINANCIAL PLANNING MODEL

Most large corporations utilize some form of model to assist them in the financial planning process.[1] These models are generally constructed around the sources and uses of the firm's cash resources. They are also typically simulation models, which project the financial impact of alternative commercial strategies and alternative financial policies under specified assumptions regarding the company's future operating environment. The level of detail and degree of sophistication exhibited by these models vary widely, owing in large part to differences in specific user requirements.

The principal output of the financial modeling process is a set of pro forma financial statements for each of the business-environment-commercial-strategy-financial-policy combinations under consideration. Management reviews these in order to select the most preferred commercial-strategy-financial-policy mix. It is important to appreciate that it is the expert judgment of the firm's managers, rather than some sort of optimizing routine contained in the planning model, that ultimately determines which course of action the firm will follow.

Role of Forecasting

Forecasting is a crucial part of the planning process. Typically, each of a company's various business units will formulate its own plan, and these separate plans will be aggregated to form the company's business plan. This may involve, for example, each division forecasting its own unit sales and the prices it will receive for its products. It is important that these various forecasts be consistent; they should be based on a common forecast of inflation, overall level of economic activity, level of interest rates, etc. Achieving consistency requires that top management prepare a forecast of these macroeconomic variables and disseminate this forecast to each of the planning units. It also requires a careful checking of the business unit plans at the corporate level to ensure consistency with the corporate macroeconomic forecast.

The Model

The business enterprise is a dynamic system. Its capital budgeting, capital structure, dividend, liquidity, financing, and liabilities management decisions continually interact. A useful framework for analyzing this interaction is the flow of funds model presented in Chapter 3. The separate policy decisions discussed in Parts 2 through 7 can be overlaid on this framework to develop a planning model.

Table 25-2 lays out a simplified planning model. The model requires various input terms, including a sales forecast (entered as $\Delta revenue$ for each year during the planning period), an interest rate forecast (entered as $\Delta interest\ rate$), a forecast of future levels of selling, general, and administrative expense (entered as $\Delta SG\ \&\ A$), a forecast of annual capital expenditures (entered as $CAPEX$), and specification of critical financial policy variables ($NWC\ ratio,\ payout\ ratio,$ and $debt\ ratio$).

Income Statement Equations. Eight equations generate the projected income statements. Equation E1 projects future net sales revenue as the sum of the preceding year's net sales revenue plus the forecasted year-to-year change from the preceding year, where $revenue(-1)$ denotes the level of net sales revenue in the preceding year. Equations E3 and E5 determine the projected level of selling, general, and administrative expense (SG & A) and the projected average interest rate on the company's outstanding debt ($interest\ rate$), respectively, in the same manner.[2] Equations E2, E4, and E7 determine various items in the income statement under the assumption that the company's gross profit $margin$, book $depreciation\ rate$, and book $tax\ rate$ are fixed over the planning horizon. Equation E6 calculates projected interest expense under the assumption that any debt repayments or new issues take place at year-end; interest expense thus equals the average interest rate for the year in question multiplied by the amount of debt outstanding at the end of the preceding year $[debt(-1)]$. Equation E8 is just an accounting identity, which is used to calculate net income.

Flow of Funds Statement Equations. The next seven equations generate the projected flow of funds statements. Equation E9 is an accounting identity; deferred taxes represent the timing differences between the recognition of tax expense for financial reporting purposes $[depreciation\ (book)]$ and for current cash payment purposes $[depreciation\ (tax)]$.

Equations E10, E13, E14, and E15 are accounting identities. Cash flow equals net income plus noncash charges. The amount of funds that must be raised from external sources ($funds\ required$) equals the amount of funds required for capital expenditure, increased working capital, debt repayment, and dividend purposes less the amount of funds generated internally ($cash\ flow$). These required funds can be raised from either of two sources: a new debt issue or a new common stock issue.[3] The mix of new debt and new equity is determined so as to preserve the company's target debt-to-capitalization ratio ($debt\ ratio$). To preserve this capital structure, the year-end debt level should equal the debt ratio times year-end capitalization [equity(-1) + net income − dividends + debt(-1) − repay + funds required]. The difference between this target level and the amount of debt that carries over from the prior year less

Table 25-2
A Scaled-Down Financial Planning Model

Input Items

I1 Year-to-year changes in net sales revenue (Δrevenue)

I2 Gross profit margin (margin), which is assumed to remain fixed over the planning period

I3 Year-to-year changes in selling, general, and administrative expense (ΔSG & A)

I4 The rate of depreciation of fixed assets for financial reporting purposes (depreciation rate), which is assumed to remain fixed over the planning period

I5 Embedded cost of long-term debt at the beginning of the planning period [interest rate(0)]

I6 Year-to-year changes in the average cost of long-term debt (Δinterest rate)

I7 Average tax rate (tax rate), which is assumed to remain fixed over the planning period and which is also assumed to be the same for both tax payment and financial reporting purposes

I8 A schedule of depreciation rates for tax purposes, which is used together with the amount of planned capital expenditures to determine the amount of depreciation expense for tax purposes for each year during the planning period [depreciation(tax)]

I9 Year-to-year expenditures for new property, plant, and equipment (CAPEX)

I10 Ratio of the increase in net working capital to the increase in net sales revenue (NWC ratio), which is assumed to remain fixed over the planning period

I11 Target payout ratio (payout ratio)

I12 Repayment schedule for the planning period for long-term debt outstanding at the beginning of the period (repay)

I13 Target ratio of long-term debt to total capitalization (debt ratio)

I14 Values of the following principal income statement and balance sheet items as of the beginning of the planning period: net sales revenue (revenue), net working capital (working capital), fixed assets (fixed assets), other long-term assets (other assets), long-term debt (debt), and shareholders' equity (equity)

Income Statement Equations

E1 Revenue = revenue(-1) + Δrevenue

E2 Cost of goods sold = $(1 - \text{margin}) \times$ revenue

E3 SG & A = SG & A(-1) + ΔSG & A

E4 Depreciation(book) = depreciation rate $\times$ fixed assets(-1)

E5 Interest rate = interest rate(-1) + Δinterest rate

E6 Interest = interest rate $\times$ debt(-1)

E7 Tax(book) = tax rate $\times$ [revenue $-$ cost of goods sold $-$ SG & A $-$ depreciation(book) $-$ interest]

E8 Net income = revenue $-$ cost of goods sold $-$ SG & A $-$ depreciation(book) $-$ interest $-$ tax(book)

Flow of Funds Statement Equations

E9 Δdeferred taxes = tax rate $\times$ [depreciation(book) $-$ depreciation(tax)]

E10 Cash flow = net income + depreciation(book) + Δdeferred taxes

E11 ΔNet working capital = NWC ratio $\times$ Δrevenue

E12 Dividends = payout ratio $\times$ net income

E13 Funds required = CAPEX + Δworking capital + repay + dividends $-$ cash flow

E14 Net debt issue = debt ratio $\times$ [equity(-1) + net income $-$ dividends + debt(-1) $-$ repay + funds required] $-$ [debt(-1) $-$ repay]

E15 Net stock issue = funds required $-$ net debt issue

A Scaled-Down Financial Planning Model *(Continued)*

Balance Sheet Equations

E16 Working capital = working capital (-1) + Δworking capital
E17 Fixed assets = fixed assets(-1) + CAPEX − depreciation(book)
E18 Deferred taxes = deferred taxes(-1) + Δdeferred taxes
E19 Net assets = working capital + fixed assets + other assets − deferred taxes
E20 Debt = debt(-1) − repay + net debt issue
E21 Equity = equity(-1) + net income − dividends + net stock issue

Ratio Definitions

E22 Interest coverage = [revenue − cost of goods sold − SG & A − depreciation(book)] ÷ interest
E23 Net margin = net income ÷ revenue
E24 Cash-flow-to-long-term-debt ratio = cash flow ÷ debt

---

repayments [debt(-1) − repay] represents the amount of debt that needs to be issued (or repurchased if *net debt issue* is negative). The balance of external funds requirements is met from a new stock issue or, if net stock issue is negative, shares are repurchased.

Equations E11 and E12 hold by definition. The NWC ratio embodies the firm's current ratio objective, and the payout ratio embodies its dividend policy objective.[4]

Balance Sheet Equations. The remaining six equations generate the projected balance sheets. Equations E16, E17, E18, E20, and E21 project various items as the amount at the end of the prior year plus the change during the year in question. Equation E19 is just an accounting identity for net assets.

Building More Sophisticated Models. It is easy to think of ways to improve the model in order to make it more useful in practical situations.[5] We have already suggested a few ways. But there are others, for example, keeping track of the number of common shares and indicating per-share data and breaking out current assets and current liabilities. Such changes would be useful, but it is important to avoid excessive detail. A financial planning model should provide just enough detail to indicate clearly the financial impact of the different commercial strategies and financial policies the company has under study. Excessive detail is likely to inhibit the planning process by making it more difficult to see these effects clearly.

Illustration of the Application of the Model

To illustrate the use of the model we have just developed, consider the following planning problem. Atlantic Electronics Company is going through its annual planning exercise. Atlantic is forecasting that its net sales revenue will grow at

Table 25-3
Illustration of the Application of the Scaled-Down
Financial Planning Model
(Millions of Dollars)

	Latest Year	Projected Ahead				
		1 Year	2 Years	3 Years	4 Years	5 Years
Income Statement						
Revenue	$ 750.0	$ 825.0	$ 907.5	$ 998.3	$1098.1	$1207.9
Cost of goods sold	450.0	495.0	544.5	599.0	658.9	724.7
SG & A	60.0	63.0	66.2	69.5	72.9	76.6
Depreciation	45.0	50.0	56.5	63.7	71.7	80.2
Interest expense	32.0	40.3	44.7	49.7	55.2	61.0
Income taxes	65.2	70.7	78.2	86.6	95.8	106.2
Net income	$ 97.8	$ 106.0	$ 117.4	$ 129.8	$ 143.6	$ 159.2
Flow of Funds Statement						
Net income	$ 97.8	$ 106.0	$ 117.4	$ 129.8	$ 143.6	$ 159.2
Depreciation	45.0	50.0	56.5	63.7	71.7	80.2
Change in deferred income taxes	20.0	22.0	23.0	25.0	27.0	30.0
Cash flow from operations	162.8	178.0	196.9	218.5	242.3	269.4
Capital expenditures	140.0	180.0	200.0	225.0	240.0	250.0
Increase (decrease) in working capital	14.5	15.0	16.5	18.2	20.0	22.0
Debt repayment	25.0	—	10.0	10.0	20.0	20.0
Dividends	19.6	21.2	23.5	26.0	28.7	31.8
Net funds required	$ 36.3	$ 38.2	$ 53.1	$ 60.7	$ 66.4	$ 54.4
Debt issued (repurchased)	$ 36.3	$ 36.9	$ 51.1	$ 56.4	$ 68.3	$ 68.6
Stock issued (repurchased)	—	1.3	2.0	4.3	(1.9)	(14.2)
Net funds raised (used)	$ 36.3	$ 38.2	$ 53.1	$ 60.7	$ 66.4	$ 54.4

Balance Sheet

Net working capital	$ 150.0	$ 165.0	$ 181.5	$ 199.7	$ 219.7	$ 241.7
Property, plant, and equipment	1000.0	1130.0	1273.5	1434.8	1603.1	1772.9
Other assets	50.0	50.0	50.0	50.0	50.0	50.0
Deferred taxes	(80.0)	(102.0)	(125.0)	(150.0)	(177.0)	(207.0)
Net assets	$1120.0	$1243.0	$1380.0	$1534.5	$1695.8	$1857.6
Long-term debt	$ 336.0	$ 372.9	$ 414.0	$ 460.4	$ 508.7	$ 557.3
Common equity	784.0	870.1	966.0	1074.1	1187.1	1300.3
Capitalization	$1120.0	$1243.0	$1380.0	$1534.5	$1695.8	$1857.6

Ratios

Interest coverage	6.09×	5.38×	5.38×	5.35×	5.34×	5.35×
Net margin	13.0%	12.8%	12.9%	13.0%	13.1%	13.2%
Payout ratio	20.0	20.0	20.0	20.0	20.0	20.0
Debt ratio	30.0	30.0	30.0	30.0	30.0	30.0
Cash-flow-to-long-term-debt	0.49×	0.48×	0.48×	0.47×	0.48×	0.48×

a 10% annual rate. It expects selling, general, and administrative expense to grow at only half this rate. Atlantic expects to maintain its 40% gross profit margin, 5% book depreciation rate, and 40% tax rate (after allowance for investment tax credit) throughout the planning period. Its embedded pretax cost of debt is 10%, but it is concerned that continuing inflation could raise its pretax cost of debt to 12%. Its target financial policies are NWC ratio = 0.2, payout ratio = 0.2, and, in order to maintain its single-A senior debt rating, debt ratio = 0.3.

Table 25-3 shows selected items from Atlantic's financial statements as derived from the planning model in Table 25-2. Consider the projections for 1 year ahead. Net sales revenue increases by 10%, from $750 million to $825 million. The gross profit margin is 40% so that

$$\text{Cost of goods sold} = \$(1 - 0.4) \times 825.0 = \$495.0 \text{ million}$$

Selling, general, and administrative expense increases by 5%, from $60.0 million to $63.0 million. Depreciation expense is calculated as 5% of beginning-of-year property, plant, and equipment ($1000.0 million). The interest rate is 12% so that interest expense is 12% of beginning-of-year long-term debt ($336.0 million).

Turning to the flow of funds statement, the calculation of the increase in net working capital uses the assumed NWC ratio:

$$\frac{\text{Increase (decrease)}}{\text{in net working capital}} = 0.2 \times (\$825.0 - 750.0) = \$15.0 \text{ million}$$

and the dividend calculation uses the assumed payout ratio:

$$\text{Dividends} = 0.2 \times \$106.0 = \$21.2 \text{ million}$$

The amount of net funds required is simply the sum of capital expenditures, the increase in net working capital, and the amount of common dividends (collectively $216.2 million) less the $178.0 million of funds generated internally. Of this amount, $36.9 million must be raised through a new debt issue in order to preserve Atlantic's 30% ratio of long-term debt to capitalization.

Turning to the balance sheet, net working capital increases by $15.0 million. Property, plant, and equipment increases by the $180.0 million of gross spending and decreases by the $50.0 million of depreciation, for a net increase of $130.0 million.

Table 25-3 illustrates but one simple iteration in the planning process. Atlantic would want to "fine tune" the calculations. For example, it would be impractical to issue $1.3 million of common stock and Atlantic would reduce the payout ratio in years 1 to 3 and possibly increase it in later years. But, glancing back at Table 11-3, it appears, in this base case at least, that Atlantic's financial policies are sustainable. The critical financial ratios are consistent with a single-A senior debt rating even under the higher-interest-rate scenario Atlantic is assuming in this iteration, and Atlantic would have enough free cash flow available to sustain, on average, a 20% payout ratio.

Sensitivity Analysis and Alternative Commercial Strategies

Atlantic would also want to repeat this exercise to test the robustness of its financial policies under different assumptions regarding the future operating environment and to evaluate alternative commercial strategies. One of the results of this process might be a set of contingency plans. For example, Atlantic might find it prudent to reduce its leverage if interest rates rise sharply in order to protect its senior debt rating. This might necessitate selling additional common stock rather than debt or reducing the payout ratio. Rather than wait for interest rates to rise before deciding what to do, Atlantic would be wise to plan how to counter this as well as other possible adverse developments in its operating environment.

A Final Note on the Planning Model

As the foregoing example illustrates, corporate financial planning models generate a set of accounting statements rather than perform any sort of optimization analysis, discounted cash flow analysis, or risk analysis. These models do not by themselves determine what constitutes "the" optimal financial policy set; they simply provide a series of snapshots that reveal the accounting impact of certain strategies or financial policy decisions under a specified set of assumptions.[6] But by pointing the "camera" in the right direction and by taking a sufficient number of snapshots, financial managers can see enough of the company's true financial picture to make intelligent financial decisions.

SHORT-TERM PLAN AND CASH BUDGET

The projected financial statements in Table 25-3 are useful for long-term but not for short-term planning purposes. They lack sufficient detail for closely monitoring the business. That requires a more detailed short-term plan, including a cash budget.

Short-Term Financial Plan

The *short-term financial plan* contains a more detailed income statement, flow of funds statement, and balance sheet for each quarter (or, in many cases, for each month) for the coming fiscal year. The short-term plan reflects seasonal factors, which a year-by-year plan cannot. Publicly owned companies must report their results quarterly, and the short-term plan projects these quarterly results. In addition, the short-term plan is useful for control purposes. At the end of each quarter (or month), top management can review the company's performance relative to the short-term plan. Deviations from the short-term plan may suggest the need for changes to the company's operating strategy and/or financial policies.

The short-term plan must be consistent with the projected first year of the long-term financial plan. The quarterly (or monthly) income statements should add up to the income statement for the full year. The flow of funds statements should add similarly. The balance sheet as of the end of the last quarter should agree with the projected year-end balance sheet for the first year of the financial plan.

Cash Budget

The short-term financial plan typically includes a cash budget. The *cash budget* provides a quarterly (or, in many cases, monthly) breakdown of cash receipts and disbursements. As such, it is really a flow of funds statement prepared on a cash basis. It plays a crucial role in firm planning because the company must have cash available when it is needed for payments to employees, suppliers, creditors, etc.

SUMMARY

Financial planning is an integral part of a company's overall planning process. It takes place within a flow of funds framework and involves formulating financial objectives, projecting the financial impact of alternative operating strategies under alternative financial policies and also under alternative operating scenarios, selecting in light of these consequences the "best" financial policies and financing program for the firm, and preparing contingency plans. The completed financial plan outlines the firm's financial strategy and projects the financial consequences of that strategy. It is important to appreciate that it is the judgment of top management—and not some arcane optimization routine contained in a mathematical planning model—that determines the desired financial plan.

While the principal output of the financial planning process is the financial plan, the planning process is also useful in other ways. It forces the firm to articulate its financial objectives, to formulate financial policies to meet those objectives, and to test those policies against different operating environments and alternative commercial strategies. The planning process, if done properly, also forces management to contemplate turns of events that might upset its basic strategy and to devise contingent strategies for dealing with such developments. Finally, the financial plan provides a benchmark against which future financial performance may be evaluated.

Chapter 26

Financing Start-Up and Early Growth

This chapter deals with the most crucial period in a company's financial development: from inception through the initial public offering. Company founders and venture capitalists provide funds initially. But if the company is successful, it will eventually be able to raise common equity through the sale of its shares to the public. A company's initial public offering thus marks a watershed in its financial development.

WHAT IS VENTURE CAPITAL?

The term *venture capital* refers to the funds invested in a business either at its inception or during the high-risk stages that follow. During these early stages, the probability that the business will fail and that investors will lose their entire investment is greater than at any other time in a company's life cycle. Because of these high risks, a venture capital investment typically takes the form of an equity investment, and the investors involved are sophisticated enough to evaluate the attendant risks.

Sources of Venture Capital

Suppliers of venture capital seek to invest in young companies that have exceptional growth prospects. They wish to invest early in a company's life cycle, have the company grow rapidly so that their investment will appreciate quickly, and then liquidate their investment—either through an initial public offering or through the sale of the new venture to another company—after 5 to 7 years (or sooner, if possible) at a substantial multiple of the cash they originally invested. In contrast to other classes of investors, venture capitalists are active investors. They maintain close and frequent contact with the people running each of the companies in which they have invested, and they are prepared to provide management expertise or other forms of direct assistance the new company may require.

Traditionally, wealthy families and successful business executives were the principal source of venture capital. A variety of private financial institutions, some of which are partially subsidized by the government, developed in the 1960s into major sources of venture capital.[1]

Today wealthy individuals are still an important source of venture capital, particularly when it comes to raising "seed" money for new ventures. Many invest through *research and development limited partnerships*, which finance certain specified research and development programs for a company in return for the right to claim the tax benefits and the right to receive royalties or to sell the technology if the research is successful.[2] In addition, the Small Business Investment Company Act of 1958 authorized the establishment of small business investment companies (SBICs) to borrow from the Small Business Administration on a subsidized basis and to make equity investments in and to extend loans to "small businesses"; companies (other than SBICs) and funds have been established specifically to raise venture capital money from passive investors; a number of industrial corporations have become actively involved in venture capital; and insurance companies, pension funds, college endowments, and other traditionally passive institutional investors invest in new ventures, normally indirectly by participating in venture capital funds. Also, while the public equity market is not normally receptive to share issues by new ventures, during periods such as 1967 to 1969 and 1980 to 1983 when there is a "hot" new issues market, companies have found it possible to raise seed money through a public offering. For example, Trilogy Limited, at the time a development stage company, sold 5 million shares of its common stock to the public for $12 each on November 9, 1983, raising net proceeds of $55,848,050. Finally, although not considered among the traditional sources of venture capital, commercial banks, finance companies, and leasing companies also provide financing to companies that may not be quite ready to go public. None of these provide seed financing, but loans or lease financing can often be arranged to supplement traditional venture capital financing in the later venture stages.

RAISING VENTURE CAPITAL

A new enterprise's ability to raise venture capital in the amounts and at the times required depends on a number of factors. Among the more important of these are the general availability of venture capital, the basic technical feasibility and commercial viability of the venture, the projected economics of the venture relative to venture capitalists' required investment returns, the general reputation and track record of the enterprise's management, and the credibility of their business plan.

Availability of Venture Capital

The overall availability of venture capital is very sensitive to the after-tax rates of return that are potentially realizable and, hence, to the marketability of initial public offerings and to the rate at which capital gains are taxed. Table 26-1 illustrates that when the new issues market is hot, as during 1967 to 1969 and 1980 to 1983, this tends to attract capital to the venture capital industry. In addition, the reductions in the capital gains tax rate in 1978 and again in 1981 were followed each time by a substantial increase in the volume of funds flowing into the venture capital industry.

Venture Capitalists' Required Returns

Venture capitalists require expected rates of return that are commensurate with the substantial risks they take. If the venture fails, the venture capitalists can lose

Table 26-1
Volume of Venture Capital Financing and
Initial Public Offerings, 1969–1983
(Dollar Amounts In Millions)

Year	Capital Raised by Venture Capital Firms	Initial Public Offerings			S&P 500 Index	
		Number	Aggregate Value	Average Size	Beginning of Year	Change during Year
1969	$ 171	1026	$ 2605	$ 2.5	103.9	(11.4%)
1970	97	358	780	2.2	92.1	0.1
1971	95	391	1655	4.2	92.2	10.8
1972	62	568	2724	4.8	102.1	15.7
1973	56	100	330	3.3	118.1	(17.4)
1974	57	15	51	3.4	97.6	(29.7)
1975	10	15	265†	17.7	68.6	31.5
1976	50	34	234	6.9	90.2	19.2
1977	39	40	153	3.8	107.5	(11.5)
1978*	600	45	249	5.5	95.1	1.1
1979	300	81	506	6.2	96.1	12.3
1980	700	237	1397	5.9	107.9	25.9
1981*	1300	448	3215	7.2	135.8	(9.7)
1982	1800	222	1446	6.5	122.6	14.7
1983	4500	888	12,600	14.2	140.6	17.3

*Maximum tax rate on capital gains was reduced in 1978 to 28% and in 1981 to 20%
†An initial public offering by Adolph Coors Company accounted for $127.1 million.

Sources: Venture Economics, Inc., Wellesley Hills, Mass., Howard & Company, *GOING PUBLIC: The IPO Reporter* (January 5, 1984), and Standard & Poor's Corporation, *Security Price Index Record*, New York, 1984, p. 4.

their entire investment; if it is successful, the venture capitalists may have to wait 5 years or longer to realize their return of and return on their investment. As a rough rule of thumb, a venture capitalist would normally expect its portfolio of investments to return, on average, a multiple of three times the original investment within 4 years, or multiple of four times the original investment within 5 years.[3] These returns on an annually compounded basis amount to approximately 31 to 32% per annum pretax and, imputing capital gains tax at a 20% rate, approximately 27 to 28% per annum after tax. They would require higher expected returns on individual investments because they know that some will fail. They will also require relatively higher expected returns from relatively riskier investments. Commitments to furnish seed money to get a venture started could conceivably require an expected return of 10 to 20 or more times the original investment.

Table 26-2 illustrates the sequence of venture capital financing leading up to the initial public offering for Apollo Computer Inc. The investments in Apollo would have to be regarded as extraordinarily successful. The first-round venture capital investors realized a multiple of 110 times their investment before taxes within 3 years. Imputing taxes at a 20% capital gains rate, the investment yielded an annually compounded after-tax rate of return of more than 350% per annum.

The returns venture capitalists realized on their investment in Apollo are atypical. A rough rule of thumb quoted by venture capitalists is that one highly successful investment like the Apollo investment out of ten is sufficient to provide an acceptable overall portfolio return. A recent study by Huntsman and Hoban seems to bear out the dependency of portfolio returns on the extraordinary success of a few investments.[4] Huntsman and Hoban evaluated the returns three well-known venture capital firms realized on 110 venture capital investments they made between 1960 and 1975. They found that roughly one in six investments resulted in total failure; that the average annual rate of return on the portfolio was 18.9% (pretax); but that eliminating the 10 most profitable investments would have caused the portfolio return to become negative.

STRUCTURING THE FINANCING

Entrepreneurs wish to give up as small a percentage of the company as possible. They also wish to have as few constraints as possible on their managerial and entrepreneurial discretion. The venture capitalists, who are being asked to make a substantial financial commitment, will not agree to invest unless they can expect to realize an acceptable rate of return in light of the riskiness of the venture *and* unless they are assured of having a significant say in how the venture is developed.

Table 26-2
Illustration of Successive Rounds of Venture
Financing: Apollo Computer Inc.

Date of Sale	Principal Purchaser(s)	Number of Shares	Price per Share	Amount Invested	Date of Purchase to Date of Public Offering	
					Length of Period, yr	Investment Magnified*
February 1980–December 1980	Employees	4,200,000	$ 0.02	$ 84,000	3.1–2.3	1100 times
April 1980	Venture capitalists	7,875,000	0.20	1,575,000	2.9	110
November 1980	Venture capitalists	2,650,000	1.00	2,650,000	2.3	22
August 1981	Venture capitalists	1,200,000	5.00	6,000,000	1.6	4.4
August 1982	Venture capitalists	833,342	6.00	5,000,052	0.6	3.7
March 3, 1983	Initial public offering	2,500,000†	22.00	55,000,000	—	—

*Pretax value calculated as the ratio of the initial public offering price to the investors' purchase price.
†Plus 1.5 million shares offered to the public by shareholders of the company.
Source: Apollo Computer Inc., prospectus, March 3, 1983, pp. 20–21.

Financial Terms

There is no precise formula for determining in any particular situation how much ownership the entrepreneur(s) will have to give up in order to interest venture capitalists. This will be determined through negotiation. But an entrepreneur who is seeking venture financing should propose a deal structure, X dollars for Y percent of the company, that a venture capitalist can reasonably expect to provide an adequate rate of return.

Gauging How Much of the Company to Sell. Consider an entrepreneur who has decided to raise an amount *funds invested* from venture capitalists. Venture capitalists are believed to require a particular after-tax *multiple of investment* based on their estimated future *capital gains tax rate* as of the date they liquidate their investment in the venture. At that date, they estimate that the company will be worth an estimated *price-earnings multiple* of net income. This requires *pretax proceeds* of:

$$\begin{aligned}\text{Pretax}\atop\text{proceeds} = \Bigg[\bigg(\begin{matrix}\text{multiple of}\\ \text{investment}\end{matrix} - \begin{matrix}\text{capital gains}\\ \text{tax rate}\end{matrix}\bigg) \\ \div \bigg(1 - \begin{matrix}\text{capital gains}\\ \text{tax rate}\end{matrix}\bigg)\Bigg] \times \begin{matrix}\text{funds}\\ \text{invested}\end{matrix}\end{aligned} \qquad (26\text{-}1)$$

But at the time they sell their shares, the venture capitalists realize their pro rata share of the company's aggregate value. This pro rata share represents the share they receive when they invest, adjusted for the dilution that will result from future financings before the company goes public. Their percentage ownership must thus be the pretax proceeds given by Formula 26-1 divided by the market value of the company and adjusted for this dilution:

$$
\begin{aligned}
\text{Percentage of} \atop \text{company offered} &= \left[\left(\text{multiple of} \atop \text{investment} - \text{capital gains} \atop \text{tax rate} \right) \div \left(1 - \text{capital gains} \atop \text{tax rate} \right) \right] \\
&\quad \times \left[\text{funds} \atop \text{invested} \div \left(\text{price-earnings} \atop \text{multiple} \times \text{net} \atop \text{income} \right) \right] \\
&\quad \times \left(1 + \text{dilution} \atop \text{factor} \right) \qquad\qquad (26\text{-}2)
\end{aligned}
$$

Illustration of Estimation of the Percentage of a Company to Be Offered to Venture Capitalists.   An entrepreneur has been advised that a return of between five and six times the initial investment on an after-tax basis should be sufficient to interest prospective investors. She needs to raise $2 million. A company comparable to hers has recently "gone public" at a multiple of 12 times earnings. Her 5-year projections indicate aggregate earnings of $3 million in 5 years and that after this financing her company will have to increase its outstanding shares by a further 20% in one more round of venture financing. The capital gains tax rate is 20%.

Applying Formula 26-2 gives a range of

$$
\text{Percentage of} \atop \text{company offered} = \frac{5 - 0.2}{1 - 0.2} \times \frac{2}{12 \times 3} \times (1.2) = 0.400, \text{ or } 40.0\%
$$

and

$$
\text{Percentage of} \atop \text{company offered} = \frac{6 - 0.2}{1 - 0.2} \times \frac{2}{12 \times 3} \times (1.2) = 0.483, \text{ or } 48.3\%
$$

If the venture capitalists accept the entrepreneur's projections and find an after-tax multiple of between five and six times acceptable, they will have to receive between 40.0 and 48.3% of the company. Of course, before they would agree to accept this deal, they would undertake a thorough investigation of the company and its prospects and would test the reasonableness of the 12 times price-earnings multiple.

Other Terms

Venture capitalists normally are given board representation and in many cases also belong to the executive committee. They are also typically given a right-of-first-refusal or some other form of antidilution protection. In addition, the company undertakes to provide regular business reports, financial statements, and, particularly in the case of high technology companies, regular research and development reports.

Form of Investment

Some venture capitalists prefer to stand alongside management in the capital structure and thus purchase common equity. Others prefer to stand ahead of management, in the event the venture fails and must be liquidated, and take either preferred stock or debt. However, because of the substantial risks involved, a fixed income security issued in connection with a venture financing contains a conversion feature, which enables the venture capitalist to share in the upside potential of the business. A frequently used form of venture investment vehicle is zero-dividend-rate preferred stock convertible into common stock on a share-for-share basis at the time the company goes public. The zero dividend rate reflects the fact that the new venture needs its cash principally for product development and capital expenditure purposes.

ADVANTAGES AND DISADVANTAGES OF GOING PUBLIC

The bull market of 1980 to 1983 enabled a large number of companies to go public. *Going public* is a term that refers to the sale of its common stock to the general investing public by a company for the first time. After going public, the company's shares can be publicly traded, but except in certain special situations, the company becomes subject to regular reporting requirements under the federal securities laws.

Advantages of Going Public

Among the more important advantages of going public are:

Raise new capital. Going public enables a company to raise additional capital. Generally, a profitable growing company can sell its shares in the public equity market at a higher price than in the venture capital or private placement markets.

Achieve liquidity for current shareholders. Existing shareholders typically sell portions of their shares as part of the initial public offering in order to realize a cash return on their investment and, in the case of the entrepreneurs, to diversify their investment portfolios. The availability of a public market gives shareholders much greater flexibility to sell shares when they choose to, for example, to create their own "dividend" income stream.

Create a negotiable instrument. Going public makes the common stock negotiable and gives it an ascertainable market value. The company will find it easier to make acquisitions for stock because sellers generally prefer a marketable security over a nonmarketable one.

Increase the company's equity financing flexibility. A publicly traded company is able to raise additional equity more quickly and more cheaply than it could were it not public.

Enhance the company's image. Because of the standards investment bankers apply before agreeing to take a company public, going public represents a milestone in a company's development.

Disadvantages of Going Public

Going public is not without disadvantages, however:

Additional regulations. A public company is subject to regular reporting, proxy solicitation, insider trading, and other regulations under the Securities Act of 1933 and the Securities Exchange Act of 1934.[5] A public company must report publicly on a regular basis information regarding its operating results, financial condition, significant business developments, and other sensitive matters such as officers' salaries and transactions between the company and its management. Complying with these disclosure requirements is expensive and time-consuming.

Accountability to public shareholders and market pressure to perform. Managers of most publicly held companies feel constrained to make decisions that will benefit the company's earnings, and by implication its share price, in the short run. "Managing" quarter-to-quarter earnings can hamper a company's flexibility.

Dilution of ownership interest. Existing shareholders lose a portion of their ownership interest, and if the company sells a sufficiently large voting interest to the public, existing shareholders may lose voting control.

Expense of going public. Going public involves significant expenses, typically from 6 to 13% of the amount of the offering but even larger percentage amounts for very small offerings, and the commitment of substantial management time.

Higher estate valuation. Negotiability increases a stock's value. Estate tax obligations are consequently greater when a stock is publicly traded. But the availability of the public market gives beneficiaries of the estate a means of selling shares to raise cash to pay the tax.

Pressure to pay dividends. The new public shareholders will eventually expect the company to begin paying dividends, even though the company may be able to reinvest the funds more profitably in its business.

DECIDING WHEN TO GO PUBLIC

The decision to go public depends on a number of factors. The principals involved must conclude that the advantages outweigh the disadvantages. Then they must find one or more securities firms who are capable of managing the initial public offering.

Criteria for Going Public

A company's success in (1) finding capable underwriters to sponsor and assist it and (2) completing its offering at an attractive price-earnings multiple will depend to a great extent on how well it has performed and on its future prospects. A company that wishes to go public should have demonstrated sustained profitability over a period of at least the last 3 to 5 years; established a diversified product mix and customer and supplier bases; achieved a strong market position for each of its principal products; and grown to a size large enough to be credible in the public market ($25 million of assets and/or $25 million of sales would normally be considered acceptable). It should also have a capable and stable management team and possess above-average sales *and* profit growth prospects in order to have its stock appeal to capital gains–oriented investors. There should be no major legal threat, such as pending patent or product liability litigation, to the company's ability to continue in its current businesses on its current basis.

The foregoing list represents something of an underwriters' "wish list" of attributes. It is certainly true that not every company that has gone public has exhibited 3 years of uninterrupted profitability, had at least $25 million of assets, and had above-average growth prospects. Some had never earned a profit; some had never even produced a product. But for the most part, a company's chances for a successful initial public offering are enhanced if it possesses all the aforementioned attributes.

Receptivity of the Market

A company that wishes to go public should do so when (1) it has achieved the attributes just discussed and (2) the stock market is most receptive. Table 26-1 shows how the volume of initial public offerings varied during the 15-year period 1969 to 1983. The receptivity of investors depends to a great extent on the overall prospect for capital gains, which depends on the tone of the stock market, and on how they expect these capital gains to be taxed. The new issues boom of 1980 to 1983 accompanied a major stock market rally that increased the S&P 500 index by nearly one-half between year-end 1978 and year-end 1983. It also began soon after the 1978 reduction in the capital gains tax rate and was helped by the 1981 reduction in that rate to a maximum of 20%.[6]

Alternatives to Going Public

A company that needs to raise additional equity capital from outside sources but that does not wish to go public can raise funds through a private placement of its shares or by otherwise restricting the offering so that it qualifies for one of the exemptions from the registration requirements under the Securities Act of 1933. Shares sold exclusively within a company's state of incorporation can qualify under the so-called "intrastate exemption." In addition, Regulation D under the Securities Act of 1933 offers three specific exemptions from registration that are really somewhat liberalized private placement exemptions. Shares sold privately or sold under Regulation D involve restrictions as to resale so that the price the issuer receives is likely to be significantly less, because of the illiquidity of the purchaser's investment, than the issuer could receive in an initial public offering.

THE INITIAL PUBLIC OFFERING PROCESS

To go public, a company must register shares for sale, price them, and effect the offering.[7]

Preparing the Company to Go Public

Before a company can go public, certain business practices may have to be modified in order to put dealings with insiders on an arm's-length basis, and the board of directors will usually have to be reconstituted by adding to the board outside individuals to represent public investors. The company will have to conform its accounting principles to generally accepted accounting principles, if they do not so conform already, and audited financial statements will have to be prepared, if they are not already available. The company may also have to be recapitalized by splitting the common stock so that it can be priced within a suitable range for the offering.

The Offering

A company that wishes to go public must register the shares for sale under the Securities Act of 1933. The basic registration document is the Form S-1 Registration Statement.[8] After the company files the registration statement with the Securities and Exchange Commission, the underwriters distribute the preliminary prospectus and begin the marketing effort. The underwriters will use this effort to gauge investor demand for the new issue. After the SEC has reviewed the registration statement and the underwriters have identified sufficient demand to warrant selling the issue, the company and the managing underwriters revise the registration statement to reflect the SEC's comments, negotiate the public offering price, and file the amended registration statement with the SEC. Once the SEC declares the registration statement "effective," the initial public offering can take place. The public offering process may take either of two basic forms: (1) a purchase-and-sale, in which the underwriters purchase the shares from the issuer and thereby guarantee the sale of a specified number of shares at a specified price, or (2) in the case of riskier offerings, a best-efforts underwriting, in which the underwriters use their "best efforts" to sell a specified number of shares at a specified price but do not guarantee either the price or the number of shares they will be able to sell.

An initial public offering typically involves a combination of a primary offering by the company and a secondary offering by selling shareholders. It is important to avoid having the offering appear to prospective investors as simply a "bail out" of current shareholders. As a rough rule of thumb, an issuer should try to limit the secondary component to no more than one-quarter of the offering.

PRICING THE INITIAL PUBLIC OFFERING

Pricing the new issue is perhaps the most challenging aspect of the initial public offering process.

Basic Pricing Considerations

There are three basic sets of considerations involved in pricing a new issue. The issue should be priced relative to comparable shares. The issue price should fall within, or at least near, the range of $10 to $20 per share. The issue should be underpriced roughly 10 to 15%.

Analysis of Comparable Publicly Traded Companies. The managing underwriters base their pricing recommendation on an analysis of the prices at which comparable companies' shares are trading in the market. They prepare a comparative pricing schedule, which shows pertinent operating and financial data for the issuer and for the most closely comparable publicly owned companies. Managing underwriters use such a schedule to try to determine how the prospective issuer compares to its publicly traded peer group in terms of the operating and financial characteristics that are important to share valuation. The new issue will effectively compete against its peer group for investors' dollars, which is what makes this comparative analysis so important. For an unseasoned company, the price-earnings multiples at which closely comparable companies are trading will reflect investors' growth assessments, risk assessments, and discount rates. Consequently, comparative pricing analysis represents a way of applying market-determined valuation parameters directly to the valuation of shares to be offered to the public for the first time. The managing underwriters also evaluate the present state of the prospective issuer's development, the quality of its management team, and the prospective issuer's projected profitability relative to the profitability of the comparable companies.

The analysis of comparable publicly traded companies will suggest a range of price-earnings multiples and a range of market-to-book ratios within which the prospective issuer's common stock would be likely to trade if the company's shares were already trading publicly. A careful comparison of the prospective issuer with each of the comparable companies will suggest where within each of these ranges the prospective issuer's shares would be likely to trade were the company already public.

**Table 26-3
Ranges of Issue Size, Price, and
Underwriting Spread for Initial
Public Offerings of $10 Million
or Greater, 1981–1983**

Size Range S	Number	Percentage of Total
$10 \leq S < 20$	229	50.2
$20 \leq S < 50$	170	37.3
$50 \leq S < 100$	37	8.1
$100 \leq S$	20	4.4
	456	100.0

Price Range P	Number	Percentage of Total
$P < 10$	36	7.9
$10 \leq P < 15$	210	46.1
$15 \leq P < 20$	147	32.2
$20 \leq P < 25$	53	11.6
$25 \leq P$	10	2.2
	456	100.0

Underwriting Spread Range U	Number	Percentage of Total
$5.0\% \leq U < 6.5\%$	46	10.1
$6.5\% \leq U \leq 7.5\%$	359	78.7
$7.5\% < U \leq 9.0\%$	47	10.3
$9.0\% < U$	4	0.9
	456	100.0

Source: prospectuses.

Pricing within Traditional Range. Underwriters generally like the shares in an initial public offering to be priced within a range from $10 to $20 per share. Table 26-3 shows that 357 of the 456 initial public offerings involving $10 million or more during the period 1981 to 1983, representing more than three-quarters of the offerings in this size range, were priced within the $10 to $20 per share range. If the initial pricing analysis suggests a price well above this customary price range, the managing underwriters will recommend a stock split prior to the offering.

There are two principal justifications for this. First, it makes the value of a 100-share "round lot" fall within a range of $1000 to $2000, which makes it affordable to small investors. Second, the stock split increases the number of shares available for trading, which is important to the development of a liquid secondary market for the stock.

Underpricing. Underwriters generally try to price an initial public offering at a discount of between 10 and 15% to the price at which they expect the shares to trade in the after-market.[9] A number of empirical studies have measured the extent of this underpricing and found that in some cases it is substantially greater than 15%.[10] Underwriters underprice initial public offerings in order to increase the likelihood that the shares will perform well in the after-market. If a new issue were to fall sharply in price just after the offering, investors' confidence in the company could be shaken, and the company could consequently find the stock market less receptive to a follow-on common stock offering.

Illustration of the Pricing of an Unseasoned Issue

Table 26-4 contains a comparative pricing schedule for the initial public offering of Prime Financial Software Corp. Prime would like to raise approximately $30 million. A very rough preliminary analysis suggested a price in the area of $15 per share, so Prime plans to sell 2 million common shares.

The managing underwriters for Prime's initial public offering have identified nine companies that produce software similar to Prime's and that are similar to Prime in terms of size and other operating and financial characteristics. The comparative pricing schedule furnishes selected operating and financial data and various common stock valuation statistics and indicates the pro forma effect of the offering on Prime's balance sheet and projected earnings per share. This is important because the common stock offering will alter Prime's balance sheet and will increase the number of common shares outstanding. Prime plans to repay $2 million of debt bearing a 14% interest rate, and Prime will have 17 million—versus 15 million currently—shares outstanding after the offering.

Prime has exhibited above-average growth and above-average profitability. But its return on average equity has been helped to some extent by its relatively

Table 26-4
Illustration of a Comparative Pricing Schedule
(Dollar Amounts in Millions Except Per-Share Data)

Company	Brief Business Description	Latest 12 Months	
		Net Sales	Net Income
Prime Financial Software Corp. Prime pro forma the offering	Designs and markets proprietary comprehensive financial analysis software packages to corporations and financial institutions.	$ 65.1	$ 6.5
Applied Financial Software, Inc.	Develops and markets tax- and accounting-oriented proprietary software primarily to local and regional accounting firms.	124.7	12.1
Business Software Research Group	Developed and markets the highly successful FINAL proprietary financial analysis software package.	186.5	17.9
Computer Accounting Corporation	Develops and operates proprietary software systems for broad range of accounting applications.	131.8	12.9
Computerized Financial Analysis Inc.	Designs and markets proprietary comprehensive financial analysis software packages to corporations and financial institutions.	68.7	6.9
Financial Computing Corporation	Develops and operates proprietary software systems for broad range of financial, tax, and accounting applications.	114.3	11.7
Financial Management Software Corp.	Develops and markets proprietary software and designs software to suit individual customer specifications.	60.6	5.8
Financial Software Development Corp.	Designs, produces, and markets application software packages for business and professional applications.	63.7	6.0
National Software Corporation	Developed and markets the highly successful TAXPLANNER proprietary individual tax planning software.	178.9	18.4
Software Workshop, Inc.	Develops software for scientific and business applications under contract to corporations and government agencies.	80.1	7.1

Comparables:
High
Low
Mean

	Earnings per Share		Latest 12 Months			
			Operating Margin, %	Net Margin, %	Return on Average	
Latest 12 Months	5-Year Growth, %	Projected Full Year	Operating Margin, %	Net Margin, %	Assets Pretax, %	Equity After-Tax, %
$0.46	25.3	$0.58	20.8	10.1	54.2	48.1
0.50		0.60				
0.80	20.9	1.07	19.9	9.7	37.5	27.8
0.89	22.5	1.10	19.8	9.6	46.8	32.3
1.20	23.4	1.44	20.1	9.8	36.2	26.7
0.52	27.6	0.71	21.0	10.0	34.8	25.8
0.80	28.2	1.00	24.7	10.2	43.1	33.4
0.37	19.7	0.48	20.4	9.6	33.8	24.6
0.44	17.6	0.51	19.3	9.4	34.5	22.3
0.97	31.3	1.30	20.9	10.3	45.6	27.3
0.55	18.3	0.65	18.5	8.9	26.9	17.7
	31.3		24.7	10.3	46.8	33.4
	17.6		18.5	8.9	26.9	17.7
	23.3		20.5	9.7	37.7	26.4

Illustration of a Comparative
Pricing Schedule *(Continued)*
(Dollar Amounts in Millions Except Per-Share Data)

Company	Common Shares Traded	Common Shares Outstanding	52-Week Share Price Range		
			High	Low	Close
Prime Financial Software Corp.	—	15,000,000	—	—	—
Prime pro forma the offering	—	17,000,000	—	—	—
Applied Financial Software, Inc.	OTC	15,500,000	$33 1/2	$27 1/4	$31 1/4
Business Software Research Group	NYSE	20,700,000	34 5/8	24 1/2	31 1/8
Computer Accounting Corporation	OTC	11,080,000	46 1/2	26 1/4	44 5/8
Computerized Financial Analysis Inc.	OTC	14,500,000	26 5/8	15	23 3/8
Financial Computing Corporation	ASE	15,750,000	36 3/4	18	35
Financial Management Software Corp.	OTC	16,250,000	14 1/2	10 3/4	13
Financial Software Development Corp.	OTC	14,120,000	14	10	13 1/4
National Software Corporation	NYSE	18,900,000	51 1/8	29 7/8	48 1/8
Software Workshop, Inc.	OTC	14,620,000	19 5/8	12	16 1/4

Comparables:

High
Low
Mean

high leverage, and the returns on average assets and on average equity have been influenced by a comparatively high ratio of sales to assets. Thus, Prime's operating margin and net margin are probably more reliable indicators of its relative long-run profitability. Both measures are above the respective averages but within the respective ranges exhibited by the comparable group. The group of comparables is trading within a range of price-earnings multiples of 30 to

Total Assets	Total Capital- ization	Percent Pre- ferred	Percent LT Debt	Latest 12 Months EPS	Pro- jected Full- Year EPS	Book Value per Share	Market/ Book Ratio	Indi- cated Annual Divi- dend Rate	Indi- cated Annual Divi- dend Yield
$25.0	$18.0	—	25.0	—	—	$0.90	—	—	—
53.0	46.0	—	5.4			2.56			
67.5	53.2	—	10.0	39×	29×	3.09	10.1×	—	—
80.4	69.7	3.8	13.2	35	28	2.80	11.1	$0.10	0.3%
75.3	60.2	—	8.9	37	31	4.95	9.0	—	—
45.8	34.8	—	13.5	45	33	2.08	11.2	—	—
65.3	52.1	—	23.6	44	35	2.53	13.8	0.20	0.6
37.9	31.2	5.4	14.4	35	27	1.54	8.4	—	—
36.5	30.3	—	7.9	30	26	1.98	6.7	—	—
88.8	76.4	—	6.5	50	37	3.78	12.7	—	—
57.1	47.7	—	10.3	30	25	2.93	5.5	—	—
		5.4	23.6	50	37		13.8		0.6
		—	6.5	30	25		5.5		—
		—	12.0	38	30		9.8		—

50, based on historical earnings per share, and 25 to 37, based on the earnings per share projected for each company for its current fiscal year.

Prime's managing underwriters might reasonably conclude from reviewing the comparative pricing schedule that Prime's shares after the offering should trade toward the upper end of the price-earnings multiple range for comparable companies. They would note that Computerized Financial Analysis, Inc., which is the company most nearly comparable to Prime, is currently trading at a multiple 45 times historical earnings and 33 times projected earnings, which are in line with where the other comparables are trading. These values thus represent good point estimates of where Prime's shares would be expected to trade on a "fully distributed" basis, that is, as if the offering and the heightened trading activity that typically immediately follows had already taken place and the share price had reached an "equilibrium" level.

These price-earnings multiples are then applied to historical and projected earnings. Pro forma earnings per share are also included in the analysis. Prime plans to repay $2 million of debt, to invest a portion of the proceeds in its business, and to invest the balance temporarily in money market instruments. Prime estimates that these temporary investments will add $0.06 per share to its earnings. The market will not apply the same multiple to investment income as to operating earnings. Investment bankers heavily discount, or ignore altogether, these temporary earnings when pricing an initial public offering.[11]

Table 26-5 shows the range of values Prime's managing underwriters estimated for the fully distributed price of Prime's shares: $17.82 to $20.70. The underwriters would price the shares for sale at a discount from this price, say 10%, giving a public offering price in the range of $16 to $18⅝ per share. At the time of pricing, the company and the managing underwriters would agree

Table 26-5
Estimating the Initial Public Offering Price

		Latest 12 Months EPS		Projected Full-Year EPS
Price-earnings multiple		45		33
Actual	Operating EPS	$ 0.46	Operating EPS	$ 0.58
	Operating EPS × multiple	$ 0.46 × 45	Operating EPS × multiple	$ 0.58 × 33
	Share price	$20.70	Share price	$19.14
Pro forma	EPS	$ 0.50	EPS	$ 0.60
	Investment EPS	0.06	Investment EPS	0.06
	Operating EPS	$ 0.44	Operating EPS	$ 0.54
	Operating EPS × multiple	$ 0.44 × 45	Operating EPS × multiple	$ 0.54 × 33
	Share price	$19.80	Share price	$17.82

Fully distributed price range: $17.82–$20.70
Public offering price (net of 10% pricing discount): $16.04–$18.63
Proceeds to issuer (public offering price
 less 7% underwriting spread): $14.92–$17.33

on an underwriting spread to compensate the securities firms for managing the issue, underwriting the offering, and selling the shares. Table 26-3 shows that roughly 80% of the initial public offerings of $10 million or greater during the period 1981 to 1983 involved an underwriting spread of between 6.5 and 7.5%. A spread representing the midpoint of this range would leave Prime with net proceeds of roughly $15 to $17 per share, or $30 million or more in the aggregate, as Prime desires.

As a final note, the actual public offering price cannot, of course, be a range. The managing underwriters would select a price within the range $16 to $18 5/8 in order to begin probing the market but would adjust this price—and set the eventual public offering price—as market conditions dictate.

SUMMARY

Venture capital is the principal source of funding for a company during the early stages of its development. Venture capitalists seek to invest in enterprises that have exceptional growth prospects with the intention of liquidating their investments after 5 to 7 years at a substantial multiple of the funds they committed initially.

When a young company has demonstrated its ability to sustain adequate growth and acceptable profitability, the venture capitalists can "cash out" through public offerings of their shares. *Going public* is a term that refers to the sale of its common stock to the general investing public by a company for the first time. Going public enables a company to raise new equity capital relatively cheaply, achieves liquidity for current shareholders, creates a negotiable instrument for acquisitions, and has certain other advantages. However, it subjects a company to public disclosures and other regulatory requirements and has certain other disadvantages.

The initial public offering process culminates in the pricing of the shares and their offering to the public. The managing underwriters and the issuer negotiate the public offering price by reference to the prices at which comparable stocks are trading. An initial public offering is usually priced at a discount of between 10 and 15% from the shares' "fully distributed" price in order to enhance the new issue's appeal to prospective investors.

Evaluating Corporate Acquisitions

Few financial events attract headlines quite the way a protracted "battle for control" of a very large company does. The 3-month skirmish in mid-1981 over Conoco, at the time the ninth largest oil company in the United States, is an excellent case in point. It involved Seagram, Texaco, Mobil, DuPont, and several leading Wall Street law firms and investment banks, and it culminated in DuPont's acquisition of Conoco for $7.6 billion despite a substantially higher cash bid by Mobil.[1] It was the largest merger to date in U.S. history.

WHAT IS SPECIAL ABOUT A MERGER?

A *merger* involves a combination of two companies in which the *acquiror* absorbs all the assets and liabilities of the *acquiree* and assumes the acquiree's business. The acquiree loses its independent existence, typically becoming a subsidiary of the acquiror. In a *consolidation*, two (or more) companies combine to form an entirely new entity. The distinction between acquiror and acquiree becomes blurred because shares of each of the consolidated companies are exchanged for shares of the new company. Each of the consolidating companies loses its independent existence, typically becoming subsidiaries of the new company.

When two companies of roughly equal size combine, they often choose to consolidate. When they are of unequal size, one (usually but not always the larger of the two) *acquires* the other through merger. While the distinction between a merger and a consolidation is important in a legal sense, the analytical techniques described in this chapter apply to both. Accordingly, it is assumed throughout the chapter that one party to a corporate combination can

475

be identified, or at least treated for analytical purposes, as the acquiror, and we shall use the terms *corporate acquisition* and *merger* interchangeably to refer to corporate combinations generally.

As the foregoing definitions suggest, what distinguishes a merger from other forms of capital investment is its size and scope. The capital investment projects discussed in Part 2 involved specific assets. A merger involves the acquisition of an entire company. Buying a company, with its own portfolio of assets and its own liabilities, is certainly more complicated than buying a new machine or building a new plant. There are a host of special legal, tax, and accounting issues involved.

The size and complexity of the investment pose a challenge analytically. Integrating a going enterprise into another company is more complex than installing a new machine in a factory, particularly if the acquiree's business is outside the acquiror's existing businesses. Estimating the incremental cash flows that an acquiror can expect to result from a merger is therefore inherently more difficult than the measurement problems encountered in Part 2. In addition, the acquisition must normally be large enough to be of consequence to the acquiror. Consequently, the economics of the acquisition and how the company finances the acquisition tend to interact so that selecting the appropriate discount rate is inherently more difficult than in other forms of capital investment. Yet this choice is often crucial because of the amount of corporate funds that the company must commit to the acquisition.

MOTIVES FOR MERGING

There are a number of possible motives a company may have for seeking to merge with a particular company. The ultimate purpose should be to increase the wealth of the acquiring company's shareholders.

Framework for Judging Merger Motives

The shareholders of the acquiring company can benefit from a merger only if the two firms are worth more in combination than they are separately. To provide a framework for discussion, suppose that the acquiror and acquiree are worth *market value of acquiror* and *market value of acquiree*, respectively, prior to merging but would be worth *market value after merging* in combination. As discussed further below, the acquiror will normally have to offer the acquiree's shareholders a *premium* above the market value of the acquiree for their shares. The acquiror will also incur various *costs and expenses* related to the merger transaction. The *net advantage of merging* to the acquiror's shareholders equals the difference between (1) the total value of the firm postmerger and (2) the cost of effecting the acquisition and the value of the firm premerger:

$$\begin{aligned}
\begin{matrix}\text{Net advantage}\\\text{of merging}\end{matrix} &= \begin{matrix}\text{market value}\\\text{after merging}\end{matrix} - \left\{\left(\begin{matrix}\text{market value}\\\text{of acquiree}\end{matrix} + \text{premium}\right)\right. \\
&\left. + \begin{matrix}\text{costs and}\\\text{expenses}\end{matrix}\right\} - \begin{matrix}\text{market value}\\\text{of acquiror}\end{matrix} \\
&= \left[\begin{matrix}\text{market value}\\\text{after merging}\end{matrix} - \left(\begin{matrix}\text{market value}\\\text{of acquiree}\end{matrix} + \begin{matrix}\text{market value}\\\text{of acquiror}\end{matrix}\right)\right] \\
&- \begin{matrix}\text{costs and}\\\text{expenses}\end{matrix} - \text{premium} \qquad\qquad (27\text{-}1)
\end{aligned}$$

The term in brackets in Formula 27-1 represents what is commonly referred to as the *synergistic effect* of a merger; the whole is worth more than the sum of the parts when this expression is positive. But even if it is positive, the acquiror's shareholders will benefit only if the premium plus the costs and expenses do not consume the benefits arising out of the synergy.

Motives

The balance of this section explores various motives for merging in relation to this framework.

Operating Efficiencies and Economies of Scale. Two companies may decide to merge in order to achieve operating efficiencies or to take advantage of economies of scale. The merged companies can eliminate duplicate facilities, duplicate operations, and duplicate departments, for example, when two airlines that have overlapping routes merge. Achieving operating efficiencies is more likely to result from either a *horizontal merger*, which involves two companies in the same line of business, or a *vertical merger*, which involves integrating forward toward the consumer or backward toward the source of supply, than from a *conglomerate merger*, which involves companies in unrelated businesses. However, at least partly for antitrust reasons, most mergers in the United States during the postwar period have been conglomerate mergers. A conglomerate merger will result in improved efficiency only if the managers of the acquiror are able to transfer their knowledge and skills to the (unrelated) business of the acquiree.

Realize Tax Benefits. When a company has tax loss carryforwards that it cannot fully utilize, acquiring a tax-paying company can prove mutually beneficial because the tax loss carryforwards shelter from taxation income of the profitable firm with which it combines.[2] For example, when the Penn Central Corporation emerged from bankruptcy, it was able in effect to monetize its substantial tax loss carryforwards by acquiring taxable companies. In addition, under certain circumstances, a net tax benefit may also result from "stepping up" to market value the tax basis of the acquiree's assets in a taxable acquisition.

Grow More Quickly or More Cheaply. A company may find that it can grow more quickly or more cheaply by acquiring other companies than through internal development. For example, it is generally quicker and it may prove cheaper to acquire new products, new facilities, or a national distribution network by acquiring a company that already has developed them. However, the price the acquiror must pay is crucial. External growth is more likely to prove cheaper for the acquiror than internal growth when the acquiror and acquiree each have specific requirements that the other is particularly well-suited to fulfill because each then contributes to the synergy.

Owners Wish to Sell. The owners wishing to "cash in their chips" is often the principal motive behind the acquisition of a private company.

Diversification. Diversification is typically one of the principal motives behind a conglomerate merger. A company can reduce the cyclicality of its earnings and cash flow by acquiring another company whose earnings and cash flow exhibit a different cyclical pattern. This reduces risk. But diversification benefits the acquiror's shareholders only if they could not achieve such diversification on their own. Because of opportunities for "homemade diversification," the supposed benefits of diversification are largely illusory in many cases.

Suppose market value of acquiree = $50 million and market value of acquiror = $200 million prior to their merger. The two combine in a *pure conglomerate merger*. There are no synergistic effects; shareholders will benefit only if the "diversification" that results from the merger accomplishes something that they cannot do for themselves. Prior to the merger, investors could combine the shares of the two companies in their portfolios in whatever proportions they chose. But when the two merge, their operations will combine in terms of market value in the ratio $4:1$ ($= 200:50$). Only the investors who held shares of both companies in the ratio of $4 worth of the acquiror's stock for each $1 worth of the acquiree's stock would wind up after the merger with the same portfolio they had prior to the merger. Investors who are not comfortable with the new ownership percentages will sell some of the shares they hold in the new entity. Thus, the merger will add to the supply but not to the demand for the shares of the merged firm so that

$$\begin{array}{c} \text{Market value} \\ \text{after merging} \end{array} \leq \begin{array}{c} \text{market value} \\ \text{of acquiree} \end{array} + \begin{array}{c} \text{market value} \\ \text{of acquiror} \end{array} = \$250 \text{ million}$$

Under what conditions will equality hold? Suppose that shares of the acquiror and the acquiree produced rates of return of 20 and 25%, respectively, and that there are two other companies, one of which has the same risk-return characteristics as the acquiror (company X) and the other of which has the same risk-return characteristics as the acquiree (company Y). In that case, investing $80 in company X and $20 in company Y (a ratio of 4 : 1) produces a rate of return of

$$\begin{array}{c}\text{Rate of return}\\(\text{4X TO 1Y})\end{array} = \frac{\$80 \times 0.20 + \$20 \times 0.25}{\$100} = 0.21, \text{ or } 21\%$$

Investing $80 in the acquiror and $20 in the acquiree prior to the merger would have yielded the same rate of return with identical risk. But suppose a $100 investment in the merged firm returns more than 21%. Say it returns 22%, or $22 per $100 invested. If there are no transaction costs or other impediments to trading, an investor could buy $100 worth of the merged firm's shares and realize $22 of income, and sell short $80 worth of company X and $20 worth of company Y and forgo $21 of income. The risks of the investment and short sale would exactly offset one another; so the investor would realize a pure arbitrage profit of $1. The opportunity for arbitrage will vanish only if the shares of the merged firm produce a return of 21%:

$$\begin{array}{c}\text{Rate of return}\\(\text{merged firm})\end{array} = \frac{\$200 \times 0.20 + \$50 \times 0.25}{\text{market value after merging}} = 0.21$$

which implies that market value after merging = $250 million. Diversification per se has not done anything for shareholders that they could not do for themselves.[3] But if the close substitutes, company X and company Y, did not exist, investors would have required a rate of return greater than 21%, resulting in market value after merging of less than $250 million to compensate for the reduction in investment opportunities.

The homemade diversification argument, like the "homemade leverage" argument in Part 3 and the "homemade dividends" argument in Part 4, rests on certain idealized assumptions: no taxes, no transaction costs, no bankruptcy penalties, and no other market imperfections. Similar to what we found in Parts 3 and 4, relaxing these assumptions will show why diversification can indeed create value.

Diversification can increase value in at least three ways. First, diversification can reduce the probability of bankruptcy. Because of the expense that bankruptcy typically involves, reducing this risk has value to shareholders. Second, diversifying at the firm level may be more efficient from a tax standpoint than paying out the excess cash to shareholders as dividends and letting shareholders invest the funds themselves. Of course, the firm could repurchase its own shares if it wishes to have shareholders taxed on the distribution at capital gains rates, but a privately held firm may run the risk of having the IRS treat the share repurchase program as a "constructive dividend." Third, even in the absence of bankruptcy costs, merger can produce a sort of financial synergy. The larger and better diversified firm would be viewed as less risky by creditors and the rating agencies and so would be able to issue more debt than the two firms could separately (given the same senior debt rating for all three).[4]

The Evidence

The two most crucial issues raised in connection with mergers are: (1) whether mergers increase value and, if so, (2) how this increase in value is allocated between the shareholders of the acquiring firm and the shareholders of the acquired firm. The preponderance of the empirical evidence suggests that the stockholders of acquired firms tend to benefit handsomely because of the premium they receive for their shares, whereas the shareholders of acquiring firms tend to realize only very modest gains or to break even.[5]

LEGAL, TAX, AND ACCOUNTING CONSIDERATIONS

This section provides an overview of the more important legal, tax, and accounting considerations relating to mergers. It does not purport to be complete. The issues involved are very complex, and a company that contemplates a merger should seek expert technical assistance.

Legal Considerations

A merger transaction must comply with federal antitrust law, state antitakeover statutes, the corporate charter of each company, and federal and state securities laws.

Antitrust Considerations. Section 7 of the Clayton Act forbids a company to purchase the assets or the stock of another company if the purchase *might substantially lessen competition* or *tends to create a monopoly* in *any line of commerce* or *any section of the country*. This test is potentially very broad. However, the percentage of potential mergers contested on antitrust grounds is small. Many of those that are can survive this challenge by having the acquiror agree to sell assets in the affected market(s) in order to restore competition. Mergers involving very large companies are the most likely to be challenged.

Form of Transaction. There are three basic ways of effecting a corporate acquisition: The acquiror can merge or consolidate with the acquiree; the acquiror can purchase some or all of the common stock of the acquiree; or the acquiror can purchase only the assets of the acquiree.

In a merger or consolidation, the acquiror or new entity, respectively, automatically obtains all the assets and liabilities of the acquiree. This assumption of liabilities makes it prudent for the acquiror to undertake a comprehensive due diligence investigation of the acquiree before the merger to ferret out all significant hidden liabilities. A merger or consolidation must comply with each corporation's charter, which establishes requirements for shareholder approval and normally gives dissenting shareholders the right to demand that they receive the appraised "fair market value" of their shares in cash. However, a merger or consolidation offers the most flexible means of structuring a tax-free acquisition.

If instead the acquiror purchases the acquiree's stock, it still obtains the acquiree's assets *and* liabilities but no shareholders' meetings are involved, and shareholders generally do not have appraisal rights. Any shareholder who does not like the price offered can refuse to sell his or her shares. However, if the acquiror purchases fewer than 80% of the acquiree's voting securities, it will not be able to consolidate the acquiree for tax purposes and 15% of the dividends it receives from the acquiree would be taxable. Indeed, if any of the acquiree's shares remain outstanding, there is a minority interest in the subsidiary that could hamper the acquiror's financial or operating flexibility in the future. Consequently, an acquiror that purchases shares from less than all of the acquiree's shareholders, for example, through a tender offer, typically follows this purchase with a formal merger in order to eliminate the minority interest.

If the acquiror purchases only the selling company's assets, the liabilities of the seller, other than those specifically assumed by the buyer, remain the responsibility of the seller. There is thus substantially less likelihood that hidden liabilities will be discovered after the transaction to the detriment of the buyer, and there is no problem with minority shareholders. In addition, the buyer's shareholders do not normally have to approve the transaction, and most corporate charters require only 50% approval by the seller's shareholders. There are three principal drawbacks to this structure: (1) The conditions necessary to achieve a tax-free transaction are stricter than those for a merger, (2) transferring the ownership of individual assets is costly and time-consuming, and (3) the company rather than its shareholders receives the sale proceeds, and distributing the proceeds to shareholders might trigger a tax liability.

Other Legal Considerations. Any purchases of the acquiree's securities must comply with the federal securities laws and federal disclosure requirements. Securities offered to the acquiree's shareholders will normally have to be registered with the Securities and Exchange Commission. In regulated industries, the acquiror must obtain the approval of the cognizant regulatory authority. Also, state antitakeover statutes and regulations can impede mergers. Finally, indenture covenants generally require that the debt be repaid immediately at par if the acquisition would result in violation of one of the indenture covenants.

Tax Considerations

A company can structure a corporate acquisition so as to qualify it as tax-free; otherwise the transaction is taxable. In a *tax-free acquisition*, the acquiror's tax basis in each asset whose ownership is transferred in the transaction is generally the same as the acquiree's, and each seller who receives only stock does not have to pay any tax on the gain he or she realizes until the shares are sold. In a *taxable transaction*, the acquiror can, if it wants to, increase the tax basis in the assets it acquires to the fair market value of the consideration it pays to acquire them (including the fair market value of the acquiree's liabilities assumed by the acquiror), and unless the sale is an installment sale (i.e., for nontraded debt of the acquiror), each shareholder who sells his or her shares must recognize gain or loss for tax purposes immediately.

Requirements for Tax-Free Treatment. To qualify as tax-free, the Internal Revenue Code requires the transaction to have a business purpose and the acquiror to continue to operate the acquiree's business. The Code also imposes certain requirements on the mode of acquisition and medium of payment.

In the case of a merger or consolidation, the transaction must qualify as a merger or consolidation under applicable state law, and the shareholders of the acquiree must receive at least 50% of the aggregate purchase price in stock of the acquiror, either common or preferred, either voting or nonvoting.[6] This permits a two-step merger: The acquiror can purchase up to 50% of the acquiree through a cash tender offer and then effect a statutory merger in the second step. Any shareholder who receives cash is taxed on the gain immediately; shareholders who receive only stock defer the tax obligation.

Different rules apply to acquisitions other than mergers and consolidations, such as stock-for-stock acquisitions, and in some circumstances to certain mergers or consolidations, but the net result of the rules is that a transaction can be structured as tax-free in most cases so long as the acquiring corporation is willing to issue stock equal to at least 50% of the consideration.

To Be or Not to Be Tax-Free. A tax-free transaction benefits a shareholder who has a gain because it permits her or him to defer tax on the gain until the shares acquired in the acquisition are disposed of. An installment sale of stock of the acquired company for nontraded debt would also accomplish deferral until the debt was repaid; and, unlike a tax-free transaction involving stock, such an acquisition is treated from the acquiror's point of view as a taxable acquisition. A taxable transaction can benefit a shareholder of a closely held company who would have a loss for tax purposes but has sufficient taxable income from other sources to absorb the loss because it creates a tax shield. A taxable acquisition of assets or a taxable acquisition of stock that permits the acquiror to write up the acquiree's assets for tax purposes can be advantageous to the acquiror.

This may happen when the acquiree has substantial depreciable or depletable properties, such as oil and gas reserves, that when written-up to market value will generate increased depreciation and depletion deductions and the present value of these deductions exceeds the immediate tax recapture liability triggered by the write-up. But the interests of the acquiror and the selling shareholders often conflict; the "high" market value of the assets that makes writing up their tax basis advantageous is likely to be reflected in a high share price for the acquiree, which creates a capital gain.

Deciding whether to structure a corporate acquisition as a taxable transaction requires comparing (1) the net present value expected from writing up the acquiree's assets and (2) the increase, if any, in the aggregate acquisition cost necessary to compensate shareholders for the increased tax liability:

$$\begin{array}{l}\text{Net advantage of}\\ \text{taxable transaction}\end{array} = \begin{array}{l}\text{net present value}\\ \text{from write-up}\end{array} - \begin{array}{l}\text{incremental cost}\\ \text{of acquisition}\end{array} \qquad (27\text{-}2)$$

When *net advantage of taxable transaction* is positive, the acquiror should structure the acquisition as a taxable transaction that permits asset write-up. The two terms on the right-hand side of Formula 27-2 are calculated in the following manner:

$$\begin{array}{l}\text{Net present}\\ \text{value from}\\ \text{write-up}\end{array} = \sum_{t=1}^{\substack{\text{depreciable}\\ \text{life}}} \left\{ \begin{array}{l}\text{corporate}\\ \text{tax rate}\end{array} \times \left[\begin{array}{l}\text{depreciation}\\ \text{deduction}(t)\\ \text{after write-up}\end{array} - \begin{array}{l}\text{depreciation}\\ \text{deduction}(t)\\ \text{before write-up}\end{array} \right] \right.$$

$$\left. \div \left(1 + \begin{array}{l}\text{pretax yield}\\ \text{on new debt}\end{array} \right)^{t} \right\} - \begin{array}{l}\text{recapture}\\ \text{tax liability}\end{array} \qquad (27\text{-}3)$$

$$\begin{array}{l}\text{Incremental}\\ \text{cost of}\\ \text{acquisition}\end{array} = \left[\begin{array}{l}\text{shareholders'}\\ \text{capital gains}\\ \text{tax rate}\end{array} \times \left(\begin{array}{l}\text{acquisition cost}\\ \text{per share in}\\ \text{tax-free transaction}\end{array} - \begin{array}{l}\text{shareholders'}\\ \text{average tax}\\ \text{basis per share}\end{array} \right) \right.$$

$$\left. \div \left(1 - \begin{array}{l}\text{shareholders'}\\ \text{capital gains}\\ \text{tax rate}\end{array} \right) \right] \times \begin{array}{l}\text{number}\\ \text{of shares}\\ \text{outstanding}\end{array}$$

$$\times \left\{ 1 - \left[1 \div \left(1 + \begin{array}{l}\text{shareholders'}\\ \text{discount rate}\end{array} \right)^{N} \right] \right\} \qquad (27\text{-}4)$$

In Formula 27-3, *depreciable life* denotes the period over which the written-up assets will be depreciated (or amortized or depleted) for tax purposes. The discount rate in Formula 27-3 is the pretax yield on new debt the firm could issue that would mature when the depreciable life of the written-up assets ends. This assumes that the added depreciation deductions belong to the same risk class as the firm's interest deductions. Finally, the *recapture tax liability* equals the amount of prior years' depreciation and other deductions and prior years' investment tax credits that are recaptured.[7]

The *incremental cost of acquisition* in Formula 27-4 is but a rough estimate; the detailed information required to calculate a precise value is rarely, if ever, available. Nevertheless, a review of the acquiree's shareholder list will indicate the mix of individuals, corporations, pension funds, and other tax-exempt institutions, etc. The acquiror's investment banker can estimate the *acquisition cost per share in tax-free transaction.* A review of the acquiree's share price and trading volume history will provide a rough indication of, first, what proportion of the acquiree's shares are unlikely to qualify for long-term capital gains treatment and, second, the average tax basis of the acquiree's shareholders. The divisor in Formula 27-4 is needed because the incremental cost of acquisition, which is added to the price paid each shareholder, is itself taxable. The last term in brackets is a present value factor, which reflects the fact that the acquiree's shareholders would have to pay tax on their gains at the time they sell their shares. A taxable acquisition accelerates this liability by N years. N might be estimated as the average holding period for the acquiree's shareholders.

Illustration of Net Advantage Calculation. Suppose a corporation has a single asset that it purchased for $1 million 10 years ago. The asset is fully depreciated for tax purposes, and its investment tax credit is fully vested. The asset has a current market value of $3 million. An acquiror in a taxable transaction could write up the asset to the $3 million purchase price, which it could depreciate under the 5-year ACRS system, but would have to pay tax (at the 46% ordinary income tax rate) on the $1 million depreciation recapture. The acquiror's 5-year new issue debt rate is 10%. Applying Formula 27-3,

Net present value from write-up

$$
= \$\frac{0.46 \times (0.15 \times 3,000,000 - 0)}{1.10} + \frac{0.46 \times (0.22 \times 3,000,000 - 0)}{(1.10)^2}
$$

$$
+ \frac{0.46 \times (0.21 \times 3,000,000 - 0)}{(1.10)^3} + \frac{0.46 \times (0.21 \times 3,000,000 - 0)}{(1.10)^4}
$$

$$
+ \frac{0.46 \times (0.21 \times 3,000,000 - 0)}{(1.10)^5} - 0.46 \times 1,000,000
$$

$$
= \$574,702
$$

Also suppose that the corporation has a single shareholder who had planned to work for an additional 10 years, then sell her company and retire. Because of her high income, she invests in high-grade tax-free municipal bonds, which currently yield 8% for a 10-year maturity. Her tax basis in her company stock is her original $1 million investment. To compensate the shareholder for the incremental present value tax liability she will incur in a taxable transaction, the acquiror must pay:

$$\begin{matrix} \text{Incremental} \\ \text{cost of} \\ \text{acquisition} \end{matrix} = \$\frac{0.2 \times (3,000,000 - 1,000,000)}{1 - 0.2} \times \left[1 - \frac{1}{(1.08)^{10}} \right]$$

$$= \$268,403$$

so that

$$\begin{matrix} \text{Net advantage} \\ \text{of taxable} \\ \text{transaction} \end{matrix} = \$574,702 - 268,403 = \$306,299$$

and the acquiror and the acquiree can benefit mutually from a taxable transaction (at the expense of U.S. taxpayers).

Accounting Considerations

Acquisitions often involve difficult accounting issues. One of the most important issues, in practice, is whether to structure the acquisition as a pooling of interests or as a purchase of assets.

Pooling versus Purchase. In a *pooling of interests*, the respective assets, liabilities, and operating results of the companies involved in the merger are added together without adjustments. The financial statements of the companies are combined as though the companies had always been commonly owned, that is, there are no adjustments made to the recorded values of the companies' assets or liabilities. The acquiror's financial statements for the 5 fiscal years preceding the merger must be restated to reflect the pooling (if the impact would be material).

Under the *purchase* accounting method, one of the companies is identified as the acquiror, and the acquiror is treated as having purchased the assets of the other company. The purchase price, after deducting the fair market value of the liabilities the acquiror assumes, is allocated to the assets acquired. Any excess of the purchase price over the fair market value of the net assets acquired is recorded as goodwill, which the acquiror must amortize over a period not exceeding 40 years. This represents a noncash charge against the acquiror's net income. If instead of an excess there is a deficiency, the deficiency is assigned as a reduction in the carrying value of long-term assets. The reported net income of the acquiror includes the net income of the acquiree only from the date of the acquisition.

Illustration of the Different Accounting Impact. Table 27-1 illustrates the different financial reporting impact of pooling versus purchase accounting.

ABC Company acquires XYZ Company for $160 million, paying a multiple of 16 times XYZ Company's earnings. In the first case, to qualify for pooling accounting, XYZ shareholders exchange their shares for shares of ABC. ABC Company's shares are trading at $20, a price-earnings multiple of 10. Thus, ABC Company will have to issue 8 million shares in exchange for XYZ Company's 10 million shares. The respective balance sheets and income statements of ABC Company and XYZ Company are simply added item by item. As a result of the merger, ABC Company will have earnings per share of $1.76, representing dilution of 12% from premerger earnings per share. Such dilution always occurs under the pooling-of-interests method when the acquiror's shares are valued at a lower price-earnings multiple in the exchange of shares than are the acquiree's shares.

In the second case, for purposes of illustration, ABC Company is assumed to effect a two-step tax-free merger. It issues $72 million of common stock at a price of $20 per share and uses the proceeds to tender for 4.5 million of XYZ Company's shares. In the second step, ABC Company issues another 4.4 million shares in a merger. As a result, it issues 8 million shares to acquire XYZ Company for $160 million, as before. But the accounting treatment is

Table 27-1
Illustration of the Differing Impact of Pooling
Accounting and Purchase Accounting
(Dollar Amounts in Millions)

	Before Merger		Pooling Accounting	Purchase Accounting	
	ABC	XYZ		Adjustments	Result
Balance Sheet Impact					
Assets					
Cash and securities	$ 10	$ 5	$ 15	—	$ 15
Inventories	70	40	110	+4[a]	114
Other current assets	20	10	30	—	30
Property, plant, and equipment	200	100	300	+10[b]	310
Goodwill	—	—	—	+40[c]	40
Other long-term assets	20	—	20	—	20
Total assets	$320	$155	$475		$529
Liabilities and Shareholders' Equity					
Current liabilities	$ 50	$ 25	$ 75	—	$ 75
Deferred taxes	50	30	80	−30[d]	50
Long-term debt	70	30	100	−6[e]	94
Equity	150	70	220	−70 + 160[f]	310
Total liabilities and shareholder's equity	$320	$155	$475		$529

Illustration of the Differing Impact of Pooling
Accounting and Purchase Accounting *(Continued)*
(Dollar Amounts in Millions)

	Before Merger		Pooling Accounting	Purchase Accounting	
	ABC	XYZ		Adjustments	Result
Income Statement Impact					
Net revenue	$350	$150	$500	—	$500
Cost of sales	250	112	362	$+1^g$ $+4^h$	367
Selling, general, and administrative	25	15	40	—	40
Interest expense	7	3	10	—	10
Goodwill	—	—	—	$+1^i$	1
Pretax income	68	20	88		82
Income tax expense	34	10	44		44
Net income	$ 34	$ 10	$ 44		$ 38
Average shares outstanding (000)	17,000	10,000	25,000		25,000
Earnings per share	$2.00	$1.00	$1.76		$1.52

Pro forma adjustments:

[a] Revaluation of inventories to fair market value.

[b] Revaluation of property, plant, and equipment to fair market value.

[c] Goodwill calculated as:

Purchase price	$160
Less XYZ Company equity	(70)
Less XYZ Company deferred taxes	(30)
Plus increase (decrease) in XYZ Company liabilities to fair market value	(6)
Excess (deficiency) of fair market value of XYZ Company assets over (under) book value of assets	54
Allocated to inventories	4
Allocated to property, plant, and equipment	10
Allocated to goodwill	$ 40

[d] Elimination of XYZ Company deferred income taxes.

[e] Revaluation of XYZ Company long-term debt to fair market value.

[f] Elimination of XYZ Company equity and addition of new ABC Company equity.

[g] To record the impact of additional book depreciation on property, plant, and equipment, which is assumed to be recorded straight-line over 10 years. (Noncash charge that is not deductible for tax purposes.)

[h] Upward inventory adjustment increases the cost of goods sold. Full impact assumed to occur the first year. (Noncash charge that is not deductible for tax purposes.)

[i] To record the amortization of goodwill over 40 years. (Noncash charge that is not deductible for tax purposes.)

different. ABC Company must revalue XYZ Company's assets and liabilities and record goodwill. ABC Company has paid $160 million for a company whose book value of equity is only $70 million. Also, the acquiree's deferred taxes must be eliminated under purchase accounting. Finally, it is assumed that the acquiree's debt has a fair market value of only $24 million because interest rates have risen since XYZ Company issued the debt and that the fair market value of XYZ Company's inventories and property, plant, and equipment exceeds their respective book values by $4 million and $10 million. Thus:

Purchase price		$160 million
Fair market value of assets	169	
Fair market value of liabilities	49	
Difference of fair market value		120
Goodwill		$ 40 million

Turning to the income statement, three principal adjustments are made. The higher book value of the fixed assets increases the depreciation deduction. The increase in depreciation and the upward inventory adjustment increase the cost of sales by $1 million and $4 million, respectively. In addition, the goodwill must be amortized. As a result of these charges, net income and earnings per share are lower under purchase accounting.[8] But because depreciation and amortization are noncash charges, cash flow decreases only to the extent of the increase in cost of sales due to the inventory adjustment.[9]

Requirements for Pooling. Accounting Principles Board Opinion No. 16 specifies the requirements to qualify a transaction for pooling-of-interests accounting treatment. To qualify, the acquiror must issue stock with rights identical to those of the majority of its outstanding voting common stock in exchange for at least 90% of the acquiree's voting common stock and meet certain other tests. Most important, any treasury stock of the acquiror that was repurchased within the preceding 2 years and not earmarked for specific corporate purposes other than acquisitions is considered "tainted." The number of tainted shares is subtracted from the number of shares issued in the merger when determining whether the acquiror has met the 90% test.

Does the Choice of Accounting Method Matter? In practice, it usually does matter. The two methods affect reported earnings differently. This concerns the managers of publicly traded companies who attach significance to period-to-period earnings comparisons. In reality, however, the choice of accounting method probably has considerably less significance than most managers realize. As Table 27-1 illustrated, the choice of accounting method per se does not affect real cash flow. A study by Hong, Kaplan, and Mandelker of mergers in the 1954 to 1964 period found that the use of pooling-of-interests accounting generally did not lead to superior share price performance even though reported earnings were higher than under purchase accounting.[10]

FINANCIAL ANALYSIS OF COMPARABLE ACQUISITIONS

There are two basic approaches to valuing corporate acquisitions: (1) by inference from the prices paid for companies and for individual assets in comparable transactions and (2) discounted cash flow analysis. Finance textbooks emphasize the discounted-cash-flow approach, but the analysis-of-comparables approach is used more widely in practice.

The two approaches differ in one fundamental respect. The analysis-of-comparables approach is used to determine a "reasonable" price to pay. The discounted-cash-flow approach is used to calculate the impact of an acquisition on shareholder wealth given a particular acquisition cost. It can be used to estimate the maximum price an acquiror could pay without harming the wealth of its shareholders. The two approaches are thus complementary.

The Merger Premium

The acquiror must normally pay a premium over the price at which the acquiree's shares are trading (or would trade) in the market. The analysis-of-comparables approach can be used to determine a reasonable premium. The required premium will vary from one industry to another depending on the industry's prospects and from one company to another within any industry depending on that company's relative financial and business characteristics and relative prospects. The required premium may also depend on the state of the stock market. Companies in high-growth industries like communications and broadcasting will generally command higher multiples than companies in slow-growth industries like steel manufacturing or in cyclical industries like building materials manufacturing. Companies in the retail end of an industry like food products will generally command higher multiples than companies in the wholesale end of the industry because of the value attached to having a strong "consumer franchise." In acquisitions of publicly traded companies between 1974 and 1983, the average premium paid over the acquiree's closing share price 5 business days prior to the initial announcement averaged 45%. The median premium paid was 40% but roughly one premium in six exceeded 80%.[11]

Determining a Reasonable Price to Offer

Investment bankers use a table like Table 27-2 to determine a reasonable price for the acquiror to offer for the acquiree's shares. The table provides the

Table 27-2
Illustration of Analysis-of-Comparables Approach
(Dollar Amounts in Millions Except Per-Share Amounts)

Date Announced	Acquiror/ Acquiree	Information on Acquiree for Latest 12 Months Prior to Acquisition				Purchase Price		Multiple of			Premium Paid Over Market Price 1 Month before Announcement
		Net Revenue (5-yr Growth)	Net Income (5-yr Growth)	Cash Flow (5-yr Growth)	Book Value	Aggregate	Per Share	Earnings Paid	Cash Flow Paid	Book Value Paid	
—	Eastern/ Zeus	$600.0 (12.3%)	$28.3 (11.9%)	$42.3 (12.6%)	$165.9	—	—	—	—	—	—
12/10/85	Northern/ Broadway	630.0 (10.9)	26.9 (10.2)	40.2 (10.3)	176.6	$406.2	$33.75	15.1×	10.1×	2.3×	57.9%
11/5/85	Roberts/ American	435.0 (9.8)	19.6 (10.0)	29.3 (10.1)	142.4	270.5	39.50	13.8	9.2	1.9	46.5
9/7/85	Hunter/ Brighton	465.1 (6.7)	22.7 (7.5)	34.9 (8.7)	129.5	220.2	24.50	9.7	6.3	1.7	38.2
8/3/85	Anderson/ Pacific	833.1 (12.9)	41.7 (12.7)	59.8 (13.1)	280.7	729.8	55.25	17.5	12.2	2.6	68.4
4/30/85	Midwest/ Multi-Star*	600.0 (11.7)	29.4 (12.4)	44.4 (12.7)	196.9	452.8	27.60	15.4	10.2	2.3	53.1
2/1/85	Meat Pro/ Hudson*	720.0 (10.1)	31.7 (9.9)	42.1 (9.2)	209.8	440.6	38.25	13.9	10.5	2.1	49.1

Date										
11/30/84	Frank's/ St. Helen's	412.7 (13.6)	16.5 (12.6)	21.5 (11.1)	120.8	302.0	43.50	18.3	14.0	2.5	62.5
10/19/84	Paul Pan/ DB&S*	440.0 (11.4)	22.0 (11.7)	35.4 (11.0)	161.3	321.2	31.25	14.6	9.1	2.0	51.4
8/4/84	Strand/ Atlantic	514.0 (11.1)	23.7 (8.3)	36.7 (8.2)	160.1	303.4	29.87	12.8	8.3	1.9	48.3
7/16/84	Cardinal/ Empire	550.0 (10.8)	24.8 (8.7)	36.9 (9.0)	160.7	287.7	44.00	11.6	7.8	1.8	44.4
For the comparables:											
High		13.6%	12.7%	13.1%				18.3×	14.0×	2.6×	68.4%
Low		6.7	7.5	8.2				9.7	6.3	1.7	38.2
Average		10.9	10.4	10.3				14.3	9.8	2.1	52.0

*Frozen foods processors.

following pricing benchmarks for a carefully selected group of acquisitions of publicly traded companies:

$$\begin{matrix}\text{Multiple of} \\ \text{earnings paid}\end{matrix} = \begin{matrix}\text{purchase price} \\ \text{per share}\end{matrix} \div \begin{matrix}\text{acquiree's fully diluted} \\ \text{earnings per share} \\ \text{before extraordinary items}\end{matrix} \quad (27\text{-}5)$$

$$\begin{matrix}\text{Multiple of} \\ \text{cash flow paid}\end{matrix} = \begin{matrix}\text{purchase price} \\ \text{per share}\end{matrix} \div \begin{matrix}\text{acquiree's fully diluted} \\ \text{cash flow per share} \\ \text{before extraordinary items}\end{matrix} \quad (27\text{-}6)$$

$$\begin{matrix}\text{Multiple of} \\ \text{book value paid}\end{matrix} = \begin{matrix}\text{purchase price} \\ \text{per share}\end{matrix} \div \begin{matrix}\text{acquiree's book} \\ \text{value per share}\end{matrix} \quad (27\text{-}7)$$

$$\text{Premium paid} = \left(\begin{matrix}\text{purchase price} \\ \text{per share}\end{matrix} - \begin{matrix}\text{acquiree's share} \\ \text{price premerger}\end{matrix} \right)$$
$$\div \begin{matrix}\text{acquiree's share} \\ \text{price premerger}\end{matrix} \quad (27\text{-}8)$$

The following ratio is often useful for companies that have substantial manufacturing facilities:

$$\begin{matrix}\text{Multiple of} \\ \text{replacement} \\ \text{cost paid}\end{matrix} = \left(\begin{matrix}\text{aggregate purchase} \\ \text{price of equity}\end{matrix} + \begin{matrix}\text{market value of} \\ \text{debt assumed}\end{matrix} \right)$$
$$\div \begin{matrix}\text{replacement cost} \\ \text{of acquired assets}\end{matrix} \quad (27\text{-}9)$$

The following ratio is useful for natural resource companies whose assets often enjoy relatively liquid secondary markets (e.g., oil and gas reserves, and timber and timberland):

$$\begin{matrix}\text{Price paid} \\ \text{per unit of} \\ \text{resource}\end{matrix} = \left(\begin{matrix}\text{aggregate purchase} \\ \text{price of equity}\end{matrix} + \begin{matrix}\text{market value of} \\ \text{debt assumed}\end{matrix} \right)$$
$$\div \begin{matrix}\text{number of units} \\ \text{of resource acquired}\end{matrix} \quad (27\text{-}10)$$

In Formulas 27-5 and 27-6, if the company is in a highly cyclical industry, earnings per share and cash flow per share for each company should be averaged over a period that corresponds to the length of one cycle. Also, if projected earnings are available for each company as of its acquisition date, it is useful to calculate the *multiple of earnings paid* on both a historical and a projected basis. In Formula 27-8, *acquiree's share price premerger* is typically measured 30 days before the initial announcement of the acquisition. However, if any of the companies among the set of comparables had been the subject of takeover rumors more than 1 month before its acquisition, its premerger share price may be inflated. If so, the *premium paid* to acquire it will be understated.

In Formula 27-9, *replacement cost of acquired assets* can often be estimated either from the supplemental information on inflation accounting that large companies are required to include in their year-end financial statements or from industry benchmarks, e.g., Douglas fir timberland is worth so many dollars per thousand board feet of timber. In Formula 27-10, *number of units of resource acquired* is measured in physical units. Different resources can be combined by adopting some standard of equivalence. For example, an oil and gas company's hydrocarbon reserves can be expressed on a "net equivalent barrel" basis by calculating the number of barrels of oil that would have the same market value (or energy content) as the company's gas reserves. Then *price paid per unit of resource* would be expressed in terms of dollars per net equivalent barrel.

Illustration of Analysis-of-Comparables Approach

Table 27-2 illustrates the application of the analysis-of-comparables approach to Eastern Foods Company's possible acquisition of Zeus Frozen Foods Company. Zeus currently has 10 million shares outstanding, which are trading at a price of $26.50. This gives Zeus a current market value of $265 million. Eastern's financial staff believes that there has been no merger speculation or other factors that might have inflated Zeus' share price. (If there had been, Eastern's financial staff would have to reduce the premium paid accordingly.)

The analysis-of-comparables table contains data for 10 carefully selected recent acquisitions of food processing companies that are similar to Zeus in terms of size and business and financial characteristics. Three are also frozen food processors.

In terms of its growth (and other characteristics), Zeus compares very favorably with the 10, and reasonable acquisition multiples and a reasonable acquisition price would fall within the upper half of each of their respective ranges. This implies the following value ranges for Zeus' equity:

Multiple of earnings paid	$14.3\times - 18.3\times$	Aggregate purchase price	$404.7 - 517.9$ million
Multiple of cash flow paid	$9.8\times - 14.0\times$	Aggregate purchase price	$414.5 - 592.2$ million
Multiple of book value paid	$2.1\times - 2.6\times$	Aggregate purchase price	$348.4 - 431.3$ million
Premium paid:	$52.0\% - 68.4\%$	Aggregate purchase price	$402.8 - 446.3$ million

   The intersection of the four value ranges is $414.5 million to $431.3 million. This gives a price per share in the range of $41.45 to $43.13 per Zeus share. This range also seems consistent with the multiples and premiums paid for the frozen food processor subgroup. Any price per share within this range would represent a reasonable price in the sense that it would not be out of line with the prices acquirors have paid in comparable situations. If Eastern is very anxious to acquire Zeus and is very concerned about other potential bidders, Eastern will be tempted to bid at the upper end, or perhaps above the upper end, of this range. How high Eastern can afford to bid is determined in the next section.

   Before closing this discussion, it is only fair to point out to the reader that the analysis-of-comparables approach does not always work as smoothly as in the foregoing illustration. In many cases, it is difficult to identify a well-defined group of comparables. For example, the candidates may all be in multiple businesses. In other cases, because of the multiplicity of factors that affect valuation, the various value ranges do not overlap. Then the analyst must use judgment in determining an appropriate value range, for example, by eliminating less closely comparable companies from the table. In yet other cases, some of the comparable companies have significant "hidden assets," as for example land carried on the books at historical cost which may be well under its current market value, or the companies may use significantly different accounting policies that make it difficult to compare their earnings meaningfully. In such cases, the multiples and premiums of these "comparable" companies may be poor guides until they are expressed on a basis that makes them truly comparable—to each other and to the potential acquiree.

Liquidation Approach

The potential liquidation, or break-up, value of a company should also be considered in a merger evaluation. A holding company that operates a number of essentially autonomous companies or a company that owns a number of dissimilar assets can be valued on the following basis:

$$
\begin{aligned}
\begin{matrix} \text{Liquidation} \\ \text{value of} \\ \text{acquiree's} \\ \text{equity} \end{matrix} = \text{cash} &+ \begin{matrix} \text{liquidation value} \\ \text{of receivables,} \\ \text{inventories, and other} \\ \text{current assets} \end{matrix} + \begin{matrix} \text{liquidation} \\ \text{value of} \\ \text{long-term} \\ \text{assets} \end{matrix} \\[2ex]
&- \begin{matrix} \text{repayment} \\ \text{of debt and} \\ \text{capitalized} \\ \text{lease obligations} \end{matrix} - \begin{matrix} \text{cost of} \\ \text{settling} \\ \text{other} \\ \text{liabilities} \end{matrix} - \begin{matrix} \text{cost of} \\ \text{redeeming} \\ \text{preferred} \\ \text{stock} \end{matrix} \\[2ex]
&- \begin{matrix} \text{corporate} \\ \text{liquidation} \\ \text{tax} \\ \text{liability} \end{matrix} - \begin{matrix} \text{transaction} \\ \text{costs} \end{matrix}
\end{aligned}
\tag{27-11}
$$

The liquidation values estimated when applying Formula 27-11 should be based on the values that can be realized within a reasonable time frame, say 1 year, rather than in a "fire sale." Formulas 27-5 to 27-7 and 27-10, and in the case of subsidiaries that are publicly traded, Formula 27-8 can be used to value subsidiaries. Normally, a corporation has value as a going concern; its value exceeds *liquidation value of acquiree's equity*. But this is not always the case. If the corporation is a pure holding company with a number of unrelated businesses, the sum of the parts may exceed the whole. In any case, liquidation value places a floor under the acquisition value of a corporation.

DISCOUNTED CASH FLOW ANALYSIS OF PROPOSED ACQUISITIONS

There are two basic discounted-cash-flow approaches to evaluating corporate acquisitions: the weighted-average-cost-of-capital approach and the adjusted-present-value approach.

Weighted-Average-Cost-of-Capital Approach

Table 27-3 illustrates the application of the weighted-average-cost-of-capital approach to the evaluation of the possible acquisition of Zeus Frozen Foods Company. Eastern Foods Company would actually do a variety of discounted cash flow analyses in order to evaluate the impact of alternative operating assumptions concerning Zeus. It is assumed that Eastern has already decided that it would not be advantageous to elect to step up the tax basis of Zeus' assets. Eastern decided to use a 10-year time horizon in its analysis.

Acquisition Cost. It is assumed in Table 27-3 that Eastern purchases all of Zeus' outstanding stock for cash at a price of $45.25 per share (16 times earnings). Zeus currently has $100 million of debt outstanding, which bears interest at a 10% rate and which matures in one lump sum at the end of 10 years. Eastern will be able to assume this debt at a present value cost to Eastern of

$$\begin{array}{c} \text{Present value} \\ \text{cost of debt} \\ \text{acquiror assumes} \end{array} = \sum_{t=1}^{\overset{\text{maturity}}{}} \begin{array}{c} \text{semiannual} \\ \text{debt service} \end{array} \div \left(1 + \begin{array}{c} \text{discount} \\ \text{rate} \end{array}\right)^t$$

$$= \sum_{t=1}^{20} \frac{5}{(1.065)^t} + \frac{100}{(1.065)^{20}}$$

$$= \$83.5 \text{ million} \tag{27-12}$$

assuming Eastern can issue new 10-year debt at a 13% yield. The gross cost of the acquisition is thus $536 million (= $452.5 + 83.5). However, based

Table 27-3
Discounted Cash Flow Analysis of Acquisition of Zeus Frozen Foods Company: Weighted-Average-Cost-of-Capital Approach
(Dollar Amounts in Millions)

						Year					
	0	1	2	3	4	5	6	7	8	9	10
Purchase of equity[a]	$(452.5)	—	—	—	—	—	—	—	—	—	—
Cost of debt assumed	(83.5)	—	—	—	—	—	—	—	—	—	—
Transaction costs	(5.0)	—	—	—	—	—	—	—	—	—	—
Acquiree's excess cash	35.0	—	—	—	—	—	—	—	—	—	—
Net acquisition cost	$(506.0)	—	—	—	—	—	—	—	—	—	—
Incremental Free Cash Flow:											
Revenue	—	$672	$753	$843	$944	$1057	$1184	$1326	$1486	$1664	$1864
Cost of goods sold[b]	—	500	560	627	702	786	881	987	1106	1238	1387
SG&A	—	82	92	103	116	128	145	162	180	203	227
Depreciation (tax)	—	16	25	35	40	45	50	55	60	65	70
Pretax operating profit	—	74	76	78	86	98	108	122	140	158	180
Income taxes[c]	—	37	38	39	43	49	54	61	70	79	90
Net operating profit	—	37	38	39	43	49	54	61	70	79	90
Depreciation (tax)	—	16	25	35	40	45	54	55	60	65	70
Net operating cash flow	—	53	63	74	83	94	104	116	130	144	160
Net investment in working capital[d]	—	$ (17)	$ (20)	$ (22)	$ (25)	$ (28)	$ (32)	$ (36)	$ (40)	$ (44)	$ (50)
Investment in fixed assets	—	(25)	(25)	(30)	(40)	(50)	(50)	(50)	(50)	(50)	(50)
Synergistic impact net of taxes[e]	—	10	10	10	12	12	12	15	15	15	15
Incremental free cash flow	—	21	28	32	30	28	34	45	55	65	75

496

Terminal Value of Net Assets:										
Going-concern basis[f]	—	—	—	—	—	—	—	—	—	933
Disposition basis[g]	—	—	—	—	—	—	—	—	—	1191
Incremental Net Cash Flow:										
Going-concern basis	$(506.0)	$ 21	$ 28	$ 32	$ 30	$ 28	$ 34	$ 45	$ 55	$ 65
										$1008
Disposition basis	$(506.0)	$ 21	$ 28	$ 32	$ 30	$ 28	$ 34	$ 45	$ 55	$ 65
										$1266

Required return on acquisition equity $= 0.10 + 1.20 \times 0.0595 = 0.1714$

Cost of capital for acquisition $= \frac{1}{3} \times 0.065 + \frac{2}{3} \times 0.1714 = 0.1359$

IRR (going-concern basis) $= 12.02\%$
IRR (disposition basis) $= 14.06$
NPV (going-concern basis) $= \$(54.5)$
NPV (disposition basis) $= 17.6$

---

[a] Estimated as 16 times prior years' earnings ($45.25 per share).

[b] Excluding depreciation.

[c] Assumes a 50% marginal income tax rate.

[d] Increase in inventories and receivables net of increase in payables.

[e] Estimated after-tax savings resulting from eliminating redundant overhead and redundant production facilities and from marketing certain of Eastern's products through Zeus' distribution network.

[f] Calculated as 9.4 times terminal year's earnings ($79.5 million), which represents the price-earnings multiple at which Zeus' shares are currently trading, plus the amount of debt then outstanding ($185.2 million).

[g] Calculated as 16 times terminal year's earnings ($79.5 million) plus the amount of debt then outstanding ($185.2 million) and net of capital gains tax at a 28% rate (with tax basis of $506 million).

on an analysis of Zeus' financial statements, Eastern believes that Zeus has approximately $35 million of excess cash and marketable securities that it will be able to apply toward the purchase price. (This represents a potential pitfall, however. What appears as excess cash may in fact be tied up as compensating balances or may be overseas and repatriating it could trigger a significant tax liability.) Eastern has estimated that investment bankers' fees and other expenses net of taxes will total $5 million. The net acquisition cost to Eastern of acquiring Zeus is thus $506 million. Note that if the acquiree's debt accelerated as a result of the acquisition, the net acquisition cost would increase to $522.5 million.

Financing. Eastern's financial staff has studied the capital structure policies of larger food companies in the manner described in Part 3. On the basis of that analysis, Eastern believes that it could finance the acquisition on a long-term basis with debt and equity in the ratio of $1:2$ without any adverse impact on its senior debt rating or on how it might choose to finance other projects. The amount of new long-term debt Eastern can issue is the amount it can have outstanding after the acquisition less the amount of debt is assumes:

$$\begin{matrix} \text{Amount} & & \text{net} & & \text{target} & & \text{present value} \\ \text{of debt} & = & \text{acquisition} & \times & \text{debt-to-value} & - & \text{cost of debt} \\ \text{issuable} & & \text{cost} & & \text{ratio} & & \text{acquiror assumes} \end{matrix}$$

$$= \$506.0 \times \frac{1}{3} - 83.5 = \$85.2 \text{ million} \qquad (27\text{-}13)$$

Operating Assumptions. Eastern believes that Zeus' revenue will grow at the rate of 12% per annum (the historical growth rate) and that cost of goods sold and selling, general, and administrative expense (SG&A) will also each grow at 12% per annum. Annual depreciation tax deductions are estimated from Zeus' reported tax basis in its assets and from Eastern's estimate of Zeus' required capital expenditure program. The estimated net investment in working capital is designed to maintain fixed receivables-to-sales and inventories-to-sales ratios because Eastern believes that Zeus' credit management and inventory management policies are among the best in the food industry. The capital expenditure forecast is designed to maintain long-run average effective capacity utilization of 87%, which Eastern believes is appropriate. The synergistic impact represents Eastern's estimate of the benefits it will realize by eliminating redundant overhead and redundant production facilities and from marketing certain of Eastern's products through Zeus' distribution network.

Note three important potential pitfalls. It is easy to be too optimistic about the acquiree's growth prospects and about the synergistic benefits from the merger; the more dissimilar the acquiree's and the acquiror's businesses, the more difficult it will be to find true synergies. It is also easy to underestimate the amount of investment that will be required; the older the acquiree's plant and equipment, the higher the required postmerger capital expenditures.

Terminal Value. Terminal value is estimated on two different bases: (1) Eastern continues to own Zeus beyond the investment horizon, and (2) Eastern sells Zeus at the investment horizon. In the first case, Zeus' terminal value is estimated by applying an appropriate multiple—its current price-earnings multiple, 9.4 (= 26.50/2.83), seems reasonable—to Zeus' pro forma earnings in year 10 estimated as though Zeus were on a stand-alone basis. In year 10, Zeus would have $100 million principal amount of 10% debt plus $85.2 million of 13% debt, giving rise to $10.5 million of after-tax interest expense. Subtracting this from Zeus' estimated year 10 net operating profit of $90 million leaves $79.5 million of earnings. Multiplying by 9.4 gives a terminal value of $747.3 million for Zeus' equity. Adding the terminal value of Zeus' debt, $185.2 million, gives:

$$\begin{array}{l} \text{Terminal value} \\ \text{of net assets} \end{array} = \begin{array}{l} \text{terminal} \\ \text{value of} \\ \text{equity} \end{array} + \begin{array}{l} \text{terminal} \\ \text{value of} \\ \text{debt} \end{array} - \begin{array}{l} \text{tax on} \\ \text{gain} \end{array}$$

$$= \$747.3 + 185.2 - 0 = \$932.5 \text{ million} \qquad (27\text{-}14)$$

There is no tax on the increase in the value of Zeus unless Eastern disposes of Zeus.

In the second case, the estimated $79.5 million of earnings are multiplied by the acquisition multiple Eastern assumes it will pay for Zeus, 16, and the amount of debt attributable to Zeus is added to get gross proceeds of $1457 million. But if Eastern sold the Zeus stock, it would incur capital gains tax of $266 [= 0.28 × (1457 − 506)] million, leaving:

$$\begin{array}{l} \text{Terminal value} \\ \text{of net assets} \end{array} = \$1272 + 185 - 266 = \$1191 \text{ million}$$

The calculation of terminal value is often critical. By assuming a high enough future multiple, an acquiror can justify any price. It seems prudent to assume that the future acquisition multiple will be no greater than the current acquisition multiple.

Acquisition Analysis. The analyst can now apply the procedures described in Part 2. The required return on acquisition equity is estimated by applying the capital asset pricing model. The risk-free rate is 10% and an analysis of companies comparable to Zeus indicates a beta of 1.20. Applying Formula 9-6 gives:

$$\begin{array}{l} \text{Required return on} \\ \text{acquisition equity} \end{array} = 0.10 + 1.20 \times 0.0595 = 0.1714, \text{ or } 17.14\%$$

Applying the weighted-average-cost-of-capital formula gives:

$$\begin{array}{c}\text{Cost of capital}\\\text{for acquisition}\end{array} = \text{1/3} \times 0.065 + \text{2/3} \times 0.1714 = 0.1359, \text{ or } 13.59\%$$

This cost of capital figure is then used to calculate the net present value of Eastern's proposed "investment" in Zeus:

$$\begin{array}{c}\text{Net present value}\\\text{of acquisition}\end{array} = -\begin{array}{c}\text{net}\\\text{acquisition}\\\text{cost}\end{array} + \sum_{t=1}^{m} \left[\begin{array}{c}\text{incremental}\\\text{net cash flow}(t)\end{array}\right.$$

$$\div \left.\left(1 + \begin{array}{c}\text{cost of capital}\\\text{for acquisition}\end{array}\right)^{t}\right]$$

$$+ \left[\begin{array}{c}\text{terminal value}\\\text{of net assets}\end{array} \div \left(1 + \begin{array}{c}\text{cost of capital}\\\text{for acquisition}\end{array}\right)^{m}\right]$$

$$(27\text{-}15)$$

where m = investment horizon.

The weighted-average-cost-of-capital approach suggests that the acquisition of Zeus at a price representing 16 times earnings would be unprofitable on a going-concern basis but would be profitable on a disposition basis. The real worth of the business at the end of 10 years is the higher of the two terminal values, which will normally be the value calculated on a disposition basis, provided Eastern would be willing to sell the business if that proves to be the most profitable alternative at that time.

The real value in calculating terminal value on both bases is that it reveals the sensitivity of the acquisition decision to the terminal value, and in this case, to the multiple applied to terminal year's earnings. Because the net present value of the acquisition is negative on a going-concern basis, Eastern's financial staff would be wise to recheck its assumptions to make sure it has avoided the pitfalls discussed in this section. If the assumptions hold up under closer scrutiny, Eastern would probably be well-advised, on the basis of Table 27-3, to offer a price lower than $45.25 per share initially but, on the basis of the net-present-value (disposition basis) calculation, appears able to pay as much as $470.1 (= $452.5 + 17.6) million, or roughly $47.00 per share, to acquire Zeus. At that price, Zeus' shareholders would experience a 77% gain ($47.00 versus $26.50) while Eastern's would expect only, at best, to break even.

Adjusted-Present-Value Approach
Eastern's financial staff has determined that a $1:2$ debt-to-equity ratio is appropriate. This suggests that $85.2 million of the $422.5 million of cash

Eastern needs to finance the acquisition can be raised through the issuance of new debt without altering Eastern's debt capacity. The adjusted-present-value approach facilitates a more accurate determination of the amount of debt Eastern could issue to utilize fully Zeus' debt service capacity.

Table 27-4 illustrates the application of the adjusted-present-value method to the proposed acquisition of Zeus. The incremental net cash flows are taken from the disposition case in Table 27-4. The unleveraged beta for Zeus is calculated by applying Formula 9-9:

$$\text{Unleveraged beta} = \frac{1.20}{1 + (1 - 0.5) \times \frac{1}{2}} = 0.96$$

since the leveraged beta used in Table 27-4 was 1.20. Thus, from Formula 9-6:

$$\begin{array}{l}\text{Required return}\\ \text{on project equity}\end{array} = 0.10 + 0.96 \times 0.0595 = 0.1571, \text{ or } 15.71\%$$

The net present value of the acquisition on an all-equity basis is

$$\begin{array}{l}\text{Net present value}\\ \text{of acquisition on}\\ \text{all-equity basis}\end{array} = -\$506.0 + \sum_{t=1}^{10} \frac{\text{incremental net cash flow}(t)}{(1.1571)^t}$$

$$= -\$56.8 \text{ million}$$

Next, we must calculate the present value of the interest tax shields. By proceeding in the manner illustrated in Chapter 9, we can calculate how much debt Zeus could have outstanding as of the beginning of each year so as to preserve a debt-to-value ratio of $1:3$ and then determine the associated annual interest tax shields and calculate their present value. The result is shown in Table 27-4.

Consider year 10. The present value of the 10% issue as of the beginning of the year is \$97.27 million. The present value of the year 10 incremental net cash flow is \$1094.11 million. Let *year 10 debt* denote the amount of new 13% debt Zeus could have outstanding at the beginning of year 10 if the debt-to-value ratio is $1:3$. Zeus' total value is

$$\text{Total value} = 1094.11 + \frac{5.00}{1.13} + \frac{0.5 \times 0.13 \times \text{year 10 debt}}{1.13}$$

The market value of Zeus' outstanding debt is

$$\text{Value of debt} = 97.27 + \text{year 10 debt}$$

Then *total value = 3 × value of debt* means that

$$\text{Year 10 debt} = \$274.17 \text{ million}$$

Table 27-4
Discounted Cash Flow Analysis of Acquisition of Zeus Frozen Foods Company: Adjusted-Present-Value Approach
(Dollar Amounts in Millions)

Year	Incremental Net Cash Flow*	Present Value of Remaining Cash Flows†	Assumed 10% Debt Beginning-of-Year Debt‡	Interest Paid	Interest Tax Shield*	New 13% Debt Beginning-of-Year Debt	Interest Paid	Interest Tax Shield*
1	$ 21	$ 449.17	$83.47	$10.00	$5.00	$ 93.78	$12.19	$ 6.10
2	28	498.74	84.35	10.00	5.00	109.30	14.21	7.11
3	32	549.09	85.35	10.00	5.00	124.61	16.20	8.10
4	30	603.35	86.48	10.00	5.00	140.71	18.29	9.15
5	28	668.14	87.76	10.00	5.00	159.70	20.76	10.38
6	34	745.11	89.22	10.00	5.00	181.98	23.66	11.83
7	45	828.16	90.87	10.00	5.00	205.37	26.70	13.35
8	55	913.27	92.74	10.00	5.00	228.38	29.69	14.85
9	65	1001.74	94.86	10.00	5.00	251.30	32.67	16.34
10	1266	1094.11	97.27	10.00	5.00	274.17	35.64	17.82

* Assuming a 50% marginal income tax rate.

†Present value of incremental annual net cash flows beginning in the year indicated through the tenth year discounted at 15.71%.

‡Present value at 13% yield (semiannually compounded).

Next consider year 9. The total value of Zeus at the beginning of the year is

$$\text{Total value} = \$1001.74 + \frac{5.00}{1.13} + \frac{5.00}{(1.13)^2} + \frac{17.82}{(1.13)^2}$$
$$+ \frac{0.5 \times 0.13 \times \text{year 9 debt}}{1.13}$$

and the market value of its outstanding debt at that time is

$$\text{Value of debt} = 94.86 + \text{year 9 debt}$$

The $1:3$ debt-to-value standard means that

$$\text{Year 9 debt} = \$251.30 \text{ million}$$

Continuing in this manner, we obtain interest tax shields the present value of which is

$$\text{Present value of acquisition interest tax shields} = \$82.6 \text{ million}$$

and

$$\begin{array}{c}
\text{Adjusted} \\
\text{present value} \\
\text{of acquisition}
\end{array} = \begin{array}{c}
\text{net present value} \\
\text{of acquisition on} \\
\text{all-equity basis}
\end{array} + \begin{array}{c}
\text{present value of} \\
\text{acquisition interest} \\
\text{tax shields}
\end{array}$$
$$+ \begin{array}{c}
\text{net present value of} \\
\text{acquisition-related} \\
\text{side effects}
\end{array}$$
$$= -\$56.8 + 82.6 + 0 = \$25.8 \text{ million} \quad (27\text{-}16)$$

Note that if Eastern had decided, say for tax reasons, to finance the acquisition of Zeus on an all-common-stock basis, there would still have been a positive impact on Eastern's debt capacity. Returning to Table 27-4, the present value of the interest tax shields in the extreme right-hand column would measure this acquisition-related side effect. Formula 27-16 would give

$$\begin{array}{c}
\text{Adjusted present value} \\
\text{of acquisition}
\end{array} = -\$56.8 + 27.1 + 55.5 = \$25.8 \text{ million}$$

It is important to keep in mind when evaluating a proposed acquisition that is to be financed exclusively with common stock that there are important debt-capacity side effects, enough in this latter case to make the adjusted present value positive.

The adjusted-present-value approach makes possible a more precise determination of the debt capacity created through the acquisition. It indicates that

Eastern can actually issue $93.78 million of new debt against Zeus' cash flow initially and, if Eastern's projections are correct, an additional $180.39 (= $274.17 − 93.78) million of debt over the next 9 years. As a result, the adjusted present value of the acquisition is $25.8 million versus the $17.6 million estimated using the weighted-average-cost-of-capital approach. The difference is due to the fact that the weighted-average-cost-of-capital approach fails to pick up the effect of the expansion in Eastern's debt capacity over time.

METHOD OF PAYMENT

The medium of payment is certainly not a matter of indifference to acquirors. They often think it is "cheaper" to pay in common stock than to pay in cash when they think their stock's price is attractive. But whether it is really cheaper depends on how the transaction is structured and on what subsequently happens to the acquiror's share price.

Common Stock and Net Acquisition Cost

Suppose Eastern wished to buy Zeus in an exchange of common stock. If Eastern's management and Zeus' management agreed on a firm price of $452.5 million payable in Eastern common stock, the net acquisition cost would remain $506 million regardless of what happened thereafter to Eastern's share price. But in stock-for-stock acquisitions it is customary to negotiate an exchange ratio, that is, so many shares of Eastern for each share of Zeus. If the acquiror's share price then changes, so does the net acquisition cost.

To continue the Eastern/Zeus example, suppose that Eastern has 30 million shares outstanding that are trading at a price of $22.625 each. Zeus has 10 million shares outstanding. If Eastern offers to pay $45.25 for each Zeus share, it will have to exchange 2 (= 45.25/22.625) of its shares for each Zeus share. Eastern will have to issue 20 million (= 2 × 10,000,000) new shares. As a result, Zeus' former shareholders will own 40% [= 20,000,000/(20,000,000 + 30,000,000)] of Eastern after the acquisition. If the exchange ratio is fixed and if stock market investors believe that the market value of Eastern's equity should be $1157.05 million after the acquisition, which equals Eastern's current market value ($678.75 million) plus what it will pay to acquire Zeus' equity ($452.5 million) plus the adjusted present value in the disposition case ($25.8 million), then Eastern's share price will rise to $23.14 per share ($1157.05/50), and its cost of purchasing Zeus' shares will increase to $462.8 million (= $23.14 × 2 × 10,000,000). The fixed exchange ratio effectively appropriates 40% of the adjusted present value for Zeus' former shareholders. On the other hand, if Eastern's share price falls, Zeus' former shareholders would share the burden.[12]

Dilution in Earnings per Share

A publicly traded acquiror is usually concerned about the impact an acquisition will have on its future reported earnings per share. Table 27-5 illustrates what can happen in a pooling transaction. If there are no synergistic or other benefits, the market value of the combined entity is just the sum of the market values of the acquiror and the acquiree. When the acquiror has the lower price-earnings multiple, its earnings per share are diluted; when the acquiror has the higher price-earnings multiple, the merger increases its earnings per share.

In general, dilution in earnings per share occurs when a company pays a price-earnings multiple that exceeds the price-earnings multiple at which its own shares are trading. But the higher price-earnings multiple paid for the acquiree presumably reflects the acquiree's superior earnings growth prospects. Over time, the acquiror's earnings per share as a result of the merger would catch up with what its earnings per share would have been in the absence of the merger. Figure 27-1 illustrates this for the dilution case in Table 27-5. It is assumed that the acquiror's earnings would grow at 5% per annum without the acquisition and at 10% per annum with it. Dilution is eliminated after a little more than 3 years.

Many companies use the type of "break-even" analysis illustrated in Figure 27-1 to decide whether to proceed with a transaction and how to finance

Table 27-5
Impact of Acquisition on Reported Earnings per Share

	Dilution Case, Exchange Ratio = 0.8 Acquiror Share for Each Acquiree Share		
	Acquiror	Acquiree	Combined
Total earnings	$50,000,000	$10,000,000	$60,000,000
Number of shares	10,000,000	5,000,000	14,000,000
Earnings per share	$5.00	$2.00	$4.29
Share price	$50.00	$40.00	$50.00
Price/earnings ratio	10.0×	20.0×	11.7×

	Antidilution Case, Exchange Ratio = 0.2 Acquiror Share for Each Acquiree Share		
	Acquiror	Acquiree	Combined
Total earnings	$50,000,000	$10,000,000	$60,000,000
Number of shares	10,000,000	5,000,000	11,000,000
Earnings per share	$5.00	$2.00	$5.45
Share price	$100.00	$20.00	$100.00
Price/earnings ratio	20.0×	10.0×	18.3×

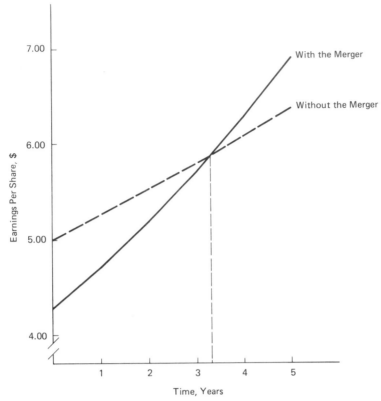

Figure 27-1. Elimination of dilution in earnings per share.

it. Companies are loath to accept "too much" dilution so they set a break-even standard, say 3 years to eliminate dilution, as one of the acquisition restrictions that must be met. Such a standard is analogous to the way in which many companies use the payback period criterion in capital budgeting analysis.

If the dilution standard is violated, acquirors will try to adjust the financing package. This often results in preferred stock being included in the financing package. For example, if the acquiror in the dilution case in Table 27-5 found the initial dilution intolerable, it might issue preferred stock instead. If the preferred stock issue would require a 5% dividend rate, there would be no dilution.

Avoiding Reduction in Acquiree's Dividend Rate

A proposed exchange of the acquiror's common stock for the acquiree's common stock runs a greater than average risk of rejection by the acquiree's stockholders if the acquiree's stock has a relatively high dividend yield and the exchange would result in a substantial reduction in the dividend income of the acquiree's shareholders. In such cases, the acquiror may substitute preferred stock for a portion of its common stock in order to preserve the dividend income level of the acquiree's shareholders and to avoid having to alter its own dividend policy.

TENDER OFFERS

Few events in business pack as much drama—or engender as much bitterness—as a hostile tender offer by one company for the shares of another. A *tender offer* is an offer to purchase shares of stock at a stated price from shareholders who are willing to "tender" shares at that price. A tender offer permits an acquiror to bypass the target company's management in its acquisition effort. In other cases, management may be ambivalent to a merger proposal, and a tender offer lets the shareholders decide for themselves whether they like the offer. Typically, the tender price represents a substantial premium over the target's prevailing share price, and tender offers are almost always made exclusively in cash.

There are a number of potential advantages to a cash tender offer. First, a cash tender offer represents the quickest means of obtaining control of another company. There are no terms to be negotiated and no securities to be registered. Second, it offers greater flexibility than other acquisition strategies. A company can tender for just enough shares to give it effective control and then effect a merger structured as a tax-free reorganization to achieve 100% ownership. Third, a cash tender offer represents the simplest way for a foreign company to buy an American company. American investors would generally be reluctant to swap shares of a U.S. company for securities of a foreign company for legal and other reasons.

Eastern's finance staff has concluded that Eastern should make a cash tender offer for up to 50% of Zeus' shares followed by a tax-free exchange of shares because that would enable Eastern to obtain effective control of Zeus quickly while giving Zeus' shareholders the flexibility to choose either a taxable or a tax-free sale of their shares.

STRUCTURING AND FINANCING A LEVERAGED BUYOUT

A *leveraged buyout* is an acquisition that is financed principally, sometimes more than 90%, by borrowing on a secured basis. Lenders look to the collateral value of the company's assets as security for their loans and to the operating cash flow these assets are expected to generate as the source of cash to service these loans.

Example of Leveraged Buyout Financing

The purchase of Gibson Greeting Cards, Inc. from RCA Corporation in January 1982 is an interesting example of leveraged acquisition financing at work. In January 1982, a group of investors that included members of Gibson's management purchased Gibson from RCA for $58 million plus repayment of indebtedness to an RCA affiliate amounting to $22,566,000. Fees and expenses and other cash requirements totaled $4,019,000. The investor group financed the leveraged buyout in the following manner[13]:

- $39,807,000 of drawings under a $100 million 5-year revolving credit facility secured by a pledge of Gibson's accounts receivable, inventories, and certain other assets and by a subordinated security interest in Gibson's machinery and equipment. The lender was given warrants representing the right to purchase 24.3% of Gibson's equity at a nominal price.
- $13 million of indebtedness secured by a pledge of Gibson's machinery and equipment and by a subordinated security interest in Gibson's accounts receivable, inventories, and certain other assets.
- $30,778,000 of indebtedness related to the sale-and-lease-back of Gibson's three principal properties.
- $1 million equity investment. Gibson's management purchased approximately 20% of the equity in the new company.

Distinguishing Characteristics of a Leveraged Buyout

The Gibson Greetings example illustrates the distinctive features of a leveraged buyout:

- A well-established company (Gibson or its predecessors had been in business since 1850) that, in many cases, is a division or subsidiary of a large publicly traded company that would like to dispose of it.
- Very high leverage.
- Multiple layers of secured debt with the most junior class(es) and/or the class providing the largest portion of the debt financing being given a significant equity interest to induce lenders to take this risk.
- Operating cash flow is dedicated to repaying debt, the senior-most debt first, as quickly as possible.
- Company management is given a substantial equity stake, typically 10 to 20%, to give them a strong economic incentive to operate the business profitably.
- Outside equity investors and lenders who receive an equity interest look to the public offering of their shares within 5 to 7 years for the return on their investment. There are very tight restrictions limiting cash dividend payments.

Ideal Leveraged Buyout Candidate

The ideal leveraged buyout candidate is a company that has:

- Multiple product lines with secure leading market position, strong brand identity, and broad customer base in each (Gibson was the third leading producer of greeting cards and gift wrapping paper in the United States at the time of the buyout).
- Industry characterized by low rate of technological change and not affected by fashion trends.
- Assets with good collateral value (e.g., good quality receivables and readily marketable nonperishable inventory).
- Historical record and projections indicate stable profitability and stable cash flow (i.e., noncyclical business).
- Purchase price represents a relatively low multiple of earnings, preferably no more than eight times (the higher the multiple, the more difficult it will be for the available operating cash flow to service debt incurred to finance a high percentage of the purchase price).
- Minimal capital expenditure requirements (operating cash flow must be used to repay debt).
- Very capable management.
- Low leverage currently (so as to facilitate the maximum use of debt capacity to buy out existing shareholders).

Leveraged Buyout Financing Structure

The aforementioned qualities characterize a company that has relatively low operating risk. It is this low operating risk that permits the company to take on an unusually high degree of financial risk. In addition, layers of subordinated debt provide comfort to senior lenders much like true equity. Since subordinated lenders almost always have an equity interest as well, the subordinated debt really represents a mechanism for getting them an interim flow of cash while creating tax shields for the company. The subordinated debt also is often given a contingent sinking fund, with principal repayments tied to the amount of cash flow left over after senior lenders have been paid, so that bankruptcy risk is lower than the company's capital structure would suggest.

The actual financing structure for a leveraged buyout will depend crucially on the perceived riskiness of the company's business, its cash flow characteristics, and the quality of its assets, all of which determine how much debt the company can support. The following rough parameters characterize the financial structure of many leveraged buyouts:

- Senior debt, typically provided by banks and finance companies, which has a maturity of between 7 and 10 years and carries a floating interest rate. Life insurance companies and pension funds are also often willing to advance a portion of the senior debt on a fixed-rate basis. Senior debt typically represents between 60 and 80% of the total financing.

- Subordinated debt, typically provided by life insurance companies and special leveraged buyout funds (many of which pool moneys invested by pension funds), which typically has a maturity of between 10 and 20 years and carries a fixed interest rate. Subordinated debt typically represents between 10 and 20% of the total financing.
- Preferred equity, typically provided by life insurance companies, which is used when the debt layers exhaust the company's ability to use interest tax shields. Preferred equity carries a dividend rate slightly below the interest rate on subordinated debt because of the 85% dividends received deduction, but its other terms are similar to those of subordinated debt.
- Common equity, which is typically provided by management (10 to 20%), subordinated lenders (40% to 60%), and senior lenders and other classes of equity investors. Subordinated lenders typically require an annual cash return on their aggregate investment, aside from the equity kicker, that is comparable to the yield on Treasury securities with a maturity that matches the period they expect to hold their investment in the leveraged buyout.

Within these parameters, investment bankers try to determine the maximum level of debt the company can support. The analysis-of-comparables approach together with the discounted-cash-flow approaches will suggest a reasonable purchase price. This price together with the company's borrowing capacity will indicate the maximum degree of leverage for the buyout.

SUMMARY

A merger represents a special form of capital investment. One company acquires the entire portfolio of assets and, typically, the liabilities of another company. Such a transaction is larger, more complex, and thus more difficult to analyze than the purchase of a single asset. Companies have a variety of motives for merging, but a merger can benefit the acquiror's and the acquiree's shareholders only if the two companies are worth more together than apart and by an amount large enough to offset the transaction costs involved in merging them.

An acquiror can structure an acquisition so that it is either taxable or tax-free. The tax treatment of the acquisition can have significant cash flow consequences for the acquiror. An acquiror can also structure an acquisition so that it qualifies for purchase accounting treatment or pooling-of-interests accounting treatment. The choice of accounting method can have a significant impact on the acquiror's earnings per share, although the impact on the acquiror's market value is less clear.

There are two basic approaches to valuing corporate acquisitions: the analysis-of-comparables approach and the discounted-cash-flow approach. The former is more widely used in practice, but the two can be used effectively in concert. The analysis-of-comparables approach is used to gauge a reasonable acquisition price. This is done by analyzing the price-earnings multiples, cash flow multiples, book value multiples, and premiums paid in comparable acquisitions and inferring from these reasonable multiples at which to value the acquiree. The discounted-cash-flow approach is designed to measure the net present value of an acquisition to the acquiror's shareholders. The two discounted-cash-flow approaches introduced in Part 2, the weighted-average-cost-of-capital approach and the adjusted-present-value approach, were modified in this chapter to handle corporate acquisitions.

Contraction, Reorganization, and Liquidation

Chapter 28

Chapters 26 and 27 dealt with corporate birth and expansion. This chapter deals with corporate contraction and failure. In a competitive economy, there are forces at work that tend to allocate productive resources to their most efficient uses. Companies that are well-run will periodically review their assets, dispose of those that are not generating adequate profits, and reinvest the sales proceeds in more profitable ventures. But competition also means that some companies that are not managed effectively will fail, and their assets will be sold to others who presumably can utilize them more efficiently.

DISPOSING OF ASSETS OR BUSINESSES

A company that is reviewing the profitability of an asset (or a business) it owns must answer two questions. Should it keep the asset or dispose of it? If disposal is preferable, which method is most beneficial to shareholders?

Deciding Whether to Dispose of an Asset

A company should dispose of an asset whenever it can employ the funds more profitably elsewhere. This depends on what the asset is worth in its present use and what it is worth to someone else. These profitability calculations must reflect the cost and tax consequences of redeploying the funds.

Present Value of Disposing of an Asset. The present value of disposing of an asset or a business can be estimated using the weighted-average-cost-of-capital approach in the following manner:[1]

$$
\begin{aligned}
\text{Present value} \\
\text{of disposing of} \\
\text{asset in year } J
\end{aligned}
= \sum_{t=0}^{J} \frac{\text{incremental free}}{\text{cash flow}(t)} \div \left(1 + \frac{\text{discount}}{\text{rate}}\right)^{t}
$$

$$
+ \frac{\text{disposal value}}{\text{in year } J} \div \left(1 + \frac{\text{discount}}{\text{rate}}\right)^{J} \qquad (28\text{-}1)
$$

Incremental free cash flow(t) measures the asset's contribution to the company's free cash flow during year t if the asset's disposition is postponed beyond year t. *Disposal value in year J* represents the after-tax sales proceeds the company would expect to realize by waiting until year J to dispose of the asset; it reflects the value of the asset to someone else. The relative advantage of waiting will depend on the incremental free cash flows the asset would generate during the holding period and on how the asset's disposal value would change during the holding period. For an individual asset, the discounted value of its after-tax cash flows from time of sale to abandonment will provide a good estimate of the future sale price. For a business, the multiple of earnings paid, multiple of cash flow paid, or multiple of book value paid calculated according to Formulas 27-5, 27-6, and 27-7, respectively, when applied to the appropriate quantity expected in some future year J will provide a good estimate of the future sale price. In each case, these pretax sales proceeds will have to be adjusted for related tax effects to obtain the disposal value.

The discount rate in Formula 28-1 measures the opportunity cost of continuing to tie up funds in the asset until year J. If the company is not capital-constrained, then the comparable-company approach or the surrogate-period-by-period-returns approach can be used to calculate the appropriate weighted average cost of capital to serve as the discount rate. But suppose the company is somehow capital-constrained; leaving funds tied up in the asset in question would force it to eschew projects for which the associated net present value is positive. In that case, discount rate should be measured as the weighted average cost of capital for the most profitable J-year project in order to reflect the profitability of these other alternatives.

The following procedure will indicate whether immediate disposal of the asset is in the shareholders' best interest:

- Select a reasonable time horizon, say, 5 years.[2]
- If *present value of disposing of asset in year J* exceeds the current disposal value (present value of disposing of asset in year 0) for any of $J = 1, J = 2,$ ..., then postpone the decision to dispose of the asset and plan to reconsider the decision the following year.
- If present value of disposing of asset in year J is less than the current disposal value for all $J = 1, J = 2,$ ..., then disposing of the asset is preferable to continuing to hold it.[3]

Illustration of Disposal Analysis

Table 28-1 illustrates the analysis leading to a manufacturing company's decision to dispose of its insurance subsidiary. The manufacturing company calculated a 15% weighted average cost of capital for its insurance investment. Immediate disposal provides the greatest net present value. However, if the manufacturing company instead expected substantial free cash flow in the coming year, say $45 million, then it would postpone the decision to sell.

Deciding How to Dispose of an Asset

There are a variety of alternatives available to a company for disposing of unwanted assets. It can sell the assets for cash and/or securities. If a subsidiary is involved, the parent company can sell the stock or the assets of the subsidiary for cash and/or securities; it can sell the stock of the subsidiary in one or more public offerings; or it can spin the subsidiary off to its shareholders. A company should choose the method of disposal that maximizes the after-tax net present value to its shareholders.

SPINNING OFF A SUBSIDIARY

As an alternative to selling an unwanted business, a company can place the unwanted assets in a subsidiary and distribute all the shares of this subsidiary to its existing shareholders, thereby creating a separate public company. A spin-off can qualify as a tax-free transaction if the parent owned at least 80% of the subsidiary, the parent distributes shares representing at least an 80% voting interest in the subsidiary (and 80% in number of each class of nonvoting

Table 28-1
Illustration of Disposal Analysis
(Dollar Amounts in Millions)

Year	Incremental Free Cash Flow	Earnings	Disposal Value*	Present Value of Disposing of Asset†
0	—	$30.0	$380.0	$380.0
1	$15.0	33.0	412.4	371.7
2	10.0	36.3	448.0	346.3
3	20.0	39.9	486.9	333.3
4	30.0	43.9	530.1	320.2
5	50.0	48.3	577.6	312.0

*Assumes the parent company sells the stock of the subsidiary at a multiple of 15 times the subsidiary's earnings, that the parent company's tax basis in the subsidiary's stock is $200 million, and that the parent company pays tax at a 28% rate on the capital gain.

†Calculated by discounting cash flows at a 15% rate.

stock), the spin-off is not in anticipation of a taxable acquisition of either the company or a subsidiary, and certain other conditions are met. In such a case, no gain (or loss) will be recognized by the company or its shareholders for tax purposes.

Motives for Spin-Offs

Companies have a variety of motives for spinning off subsidiaries:

- Dividing a conglomerate into its constituent businesses reverses the effects of a conglomerate merger, which were discussed in Chapter 27. It can increase shareholder wealth, for example, by increasing opportunities for shareholder diversification. A study by Miles and Rosenfeld investigated the stock market impact of 55 spin-off announcements for the period 1963 to 1980 and found that they had a very significant positive impact on shareholder wealth.[4]

- A large relatively mature dividend-paying company that spins off a relatively small but profitable and rapidly growing subsidiary can benefit shareholders if the spin-off improves the flow of information regarding the subsidiary and causes investors to appreciate better the subsidiary's prospects. In addition, it will give the parent company's shareholders the opportunity to trade capital gains for dividends by selling the former subsidiary's shares and reinvesting in a dividend-paying stock.

- A spin-off can eliminate negative synergy, as occurs when a utility holding company has a "nonregulated" subsidiary but its regulators reduce the utility's permitted rates (and hence profits) because of the profits the non-regulated subsidiary earns.

- Under certain circumstances, a spin-off of a subsidiary that has a market value substantially less than its carrying value on the parent company's books will not involve any loss for financial reporting purposes. Companies that wished to dispose of subsidiaries without reporting a loss have spun them off to their shareholders. However, shareholders may be better off if the company sells the subsidiary.

Evaluating a Potential Spin-Off

Spinning off a subsidiary will benefit a company's shareholders only if (1) their aggregate stock market value if they were separate companies would exceed the stock market value of the company in the absence of a spin-off and (2) the stock market value of the subsidiary following the spin-off would exceed the present value of the after-tax proceeds from disposing of the subsidiary through a sale or by some other means.

The change in aggregate stock market value is measured by:

$$\begin{matrix} \text{Present value} \\ \text{of spin-off} \\ \text{alternative} \end{matrix} = \begin{matrix} \text{stock market} \\ \text{value of parent} \\ \text{ex-subsidiary} \end{matrix} + \begin{matrix} \text{stock market} \\ \text{value of subsidiary} \\ \text{after spin-off} \end{matrix}$$

$$\begin{matrix} - & \text{stock market} \\ & \text{value of company} \\ & \text{before spin-off} \end{matrix} \qquad (28\text{-}2)$$

The analysis of comparable publicly traded companies, as illustrated in Chapter 26, can be used to estimate the separate post-spin-off values of the parent company and of its subsidiary. The present value of the asset sale alternative is

$$\begin{matrix} \text{Present value} \\ \text{of asset sale} \\ \text{alternative} \end{matrix} = \begin{matrix} \text{stock market} \\ \text{value of parent} \\ \text{ex-subsidiary} \end{matrix} + \begin{matrix} \text{present value} \\ \text{of disposing of} \\ \text{subsidiary in year } J \end{matrix}$$

$$\begin{matrix} - & \text{stock market} \\ & \text{value of company} \\ & \text{before sale} \end{matrix} \qquad (28\text{-}3)$$

Formulas 28-2 and 28-3 lead to the requirement that the stock market value of the subsidiary must exceed the after-tax sales proceeds in order for a spin-off to benefit shareholders. To continue the example of the preceding section, suppose the insurance company's equity would be worth 10 times earnings, or $300.0 million, on a freely traded basis. In that case, the manufacturing company's shareholders would be better off if the company sold rather than spun off the insurance subsidiary.

BUSINESS FAILURE

The bankruptcy of the Penn Central Railroad Company and the Wickes Companies, Inc., have made it abundantly clear that even very large corporations can fail. In some cases, failure is only temporary; given time to straighten itself out, a company will be able to repay its debts. At the other extreme are companies that are worth more dead than alive; they are truly failed and should be liquidated. In between are varying degrees of financial distress.

A company that finds itself in financial distress has four basic alternatives. It can seek to sell some of its assets in order to raise cash to pay its lenders; it can ask its lenders to renegotiate the terms of their loans or to exchange voluntarily some portion of their debt holdings for equity instruments of the distressed company; it may seek a merger with a company that is strong financially; or, if the company's situation is acute and the first three alternatives are unavailable or unworkable, the company may have to seek protection from its creditors under the provisions of the bankruptcy code.

Signs of Financial Distress

When financial distress sets in, it typically does so over an extended period. This deterioration eventually reveals itself in the company's published financial statements. As discussed in Chapter 2, it is possible to use discriminant analysis to build predictive models to detect the onset of financial distress. These use a variety of financial ratios to detect the significant deterioration in profitability and liquidity and the significant increase in leverage that typically presage bankruptcy.

Bankruptcy

Bankruptcy is a judicial process through which debtors can obtain relief from their indebtedness.[5] It gives debtors a fresh start, but it also provides for equal treatment of the various creditors. There are two basic forms of bankruptcy: reorganization and liquidation. Under a *reorganization*, as governed by chapter 11 of the U.S. Bankruptcy Code, the creditors are restrained while the debtor works out a plan to settle its debt obligations—usually for less than 100 cents on the dollar—and while the debtor's business continues to operate under the supervision of the bankruptcy trustee. Under a *liquidation*, as governed by chapter 7 of the U.S. Bankruptcy Code, the debtor's business is liquidated in an orderly manner, and the proceeds are distributed first to creditors according to a strict order of priority with any residual proceeds distributed to shareholders.

REORGANIZING VERSUS LIQUIDATING A DISTRESSED FIRM

A company that seeks protection from its creditors under the bankruptcy laws must choose between reorganization and liquidation. If the company's creditors believe that the value of the payments they will realize if the company is liquidated exceeds the present value of the payments they could expect to receive in the future if the company is reorganized, they will seek to have the company liquidated. If the company is liquidated under chapter 7 of the U.S. Bankruptcy Code, the absolute priority rule observed in the distribution of proceeds will normally leave nothing for shareholders. Consequently, shareholders will normally prefer a reorganization under chapter 11 to a liquidation under chapter 7. However, a reorganization can be mutually beneficial to stockholders and creditors if the company's difficulties are only temporary. For example, new management might be able to revitalize the business by correcting the excesses of prior management and by operating the business more efficiently. The voluntary reorganization of Chrysler Corporation is an excellent example.

The fundamental issue with regard to reorganization is whether the company represents a viable business. Certain types of businesses are more difficult to bring out of reorganization than others. For example, a company in a high-technology industry that is dependent on a few critical employees for its competitiveness or a company in an industry like heavy equipment manufacturing that is dependent on a network of independent dealers for distributing its products may cease to be viable if its key personnel and distributors, respectively, leave. On the other hand, a company in a business such as retailing in which competition is based more on price than on technical superiority and in which sales do not require a specialized distribution network is more likely to emerge from reorganization successfully.[6]

Even if a company is viable, liquidation might still be the alternative shareholders prefer. If the liquidation value of their equity exceeds the value of the package of securities the proposed reorganization plan would provide them, they should seek to liquidate the company.

LIQUIDATING A HEALTHY FIRM

Not only distressed firms are liquidated. For example, on December 15, 1980, the Board of Trustees unanimously approved a Plan of Complete Liquidation and Termination of the Franklin Realty Group, a real estate investment trust. The Board of Trustees concluded that "it was unlikely that the Shares [of the Trust] would trade in the stock market at or near the estimated fair market value of its underlying assets ... [and] that shareholders would realize greater benefit from the sale of the Trust's assets and distribution of the proceeds therefrom to shareholders than they would if the Trust continued in existence in its present form."[7] Accordingly, they decided to seek shareholder approval to liquidate the Trust.

Motives for Liquidating a Healthy Firm

Liquidating a going concern can benefit its shareholders when the present value of the liquidating distributions, net of payments to creditors and taxes, exceeds the value of their equity in the company on a going-concern basis. This can happen when:

- A company has substantial readily marketable assets whose market value greatly exceeds the value at which they are recorded on the company's balance sheet and whose returns are principally in the form of capital appreciation that does not show up in the company's reported earnings and cash flow. Real estate investment companies are a prime example, and several publicly traded real estate investment trusts have been liquidated in recent years.
- A holding company owns a number of unrelated businesses; none of the securities analysts who follows the company fully understands all of its businesses; and its proportionate mix of businesses differs significantly from the proportionate weighting of the respective industries in the portfolios of its largest shareholders. The former will lead to impairment in the quality

of information disseminated about the company, and the latter will lead to a "portfolio discount" in the company's share price.

- A corporation has property that has appreciated in value that its shareholders would like to operate in their own names at a stepped-up tax basis. A dividend of the property would be taxed at ordinary income tax rates, but liquidation proceeds (above and beyond recapture) would be taxed at capital gains rates.
- A company has accumulated earnings over a period of years that its stockholders would like to take out of the company on a pro rata basis but in a manner that would make them taxable at capital gains rates rather than at the higher ordinary income tax rates.

Requirements to Avoid Double Taxation

A company that sells off its assets without a plan of liquidation adopted by its shareholders and then distributes the proceeds to its shareholders would subject its shareholders to two layers of taxation. A company can avoid taxation at the corporate level (above and beyond recapture) and qualify the gains its shareholders realize for capital gains tax treatment by adopting a formal plan of liquidation and executing it in compliance with section 337 of the Code. This requires, among other things, distributing all the company's assets, other than assets required to discharge its liabilities, within 12 months of the date the shareholders adopt the plan.

When Is Liquidation Advantageous?

Liquidation is advantageous to a company's shareholders when the value shareholders can realize by selling the company's assets, settling all its debt obligations, and paying their related taxes is greater than (1) the value they can realize by continuing to operate the company and (2) the value they can realize under any other alternative such as selling the company. The *net advantage of liquidating* a company is:

$$
\begin{aligned}
\text{Net advantage of liquidating} = {} & \text{liquidation value of corporate assets} - \text{cost of settling corporate liabilities} - \text{cost of redeeming preferred stock} \\
& - \text{corporate tax liability and transaction costs} \\
& - \text{tax shareholders pay upon liquidation} - \text{expected present value of after-tax proceeds from future sale}
\end{aligned}
\tag{28-4}
$$

In Formula 28-4, the company should liquidate if net advantage of liquidating > 0. In practice, the *expected present value of after-tax proceeds from future sale* is the greater of (1) the value of the company on a going-concern basis and (2) its acquisition sale value.

Table 28-2
Illustration of Calculation of Net
Advantage of Liquidating
(Dollar Amounts in Millions)

Assets	Book Value	Liquidation Value	Liabilities and Shareholders' Equity	Book Value	Cost of Settling
Cash	$ 10	$ 10	Current liabilities	$ 25	$ 25
Other current assets	40	30	Long-term debt	30	35
Machinery	100		Preferred equity	10	11
Less depreciation	30		Capital stock and surplus	10	
Net machinery	70	120	Retained earnings	75	
Land	20	125	Total liabilities and shareholders' equity	$150	
Other long-term assets	10	15			
Total assets	$150	$300			

	Operating Basis	Acquisition Basis
Liquidation value of corporate assets	$300.0	$300.0
Cost of settling corporate liabilities	(60.0)	(60.0)
Cost of redeeming preferred stock	(11.0)	(11.0)
Corporate tax liability	(15.0)	(15.0)
Transaction costs*	(3.0)	(3.0)†
Tax shareholders pay upon liquidation‡	(30.2)	(30.2)
After-tax liquidation proceeds	180.8	180.8
Expected present value of after-tax proceeds from future sale	(148.0)§	(172.0)¶
Net advantage of liquidating	$ 32.8	$ 8.8

*Calculated as 1% of the liquidation value of corporate assets.
†Calculation assumes that the acquiror pays all transaction costs.
‡Calculated in the following manner:

Liquidation value of corporate assets	$300.0
Cost of settling corporate liabilities	60.0
Cost of redeeming preferred stock	11.0
Transaction costs	3.0
Net proceeds	226.0
Recapture ($30 million at 50% tax rate)	15.0
Proceeds to shareholders	211.0
Basis	60.0
Capital gain (taxable at 20% tax rate)	$151.0

§Calculated as two times the book value of common equity adjusted for capital gains taxes of $22.0 [= 0.2 × (2 × 85 − 60)].
¶Calculation assumes capital gains tax rate of 20% and tax basis of $60.0.

Illustration of Liquidation Net Advantage Calculation

Table 28-2 illustrates the application of Formula 28-4 to a proposed liquidation. The company, whose common stock is currently trading at a price representing two times book value per share, has what is commonly termed a "hidden asset." Land, carried on the books at its historical cost of $20 million, has an estimated market value of $125 million. By liquidating, the company's shareholders could realize after-tax proceeds of $180.8 million (proceeds of $211.0 million net of $30.2 million of capital gains taxes), assuming their aggregate tax basis is $60 million and that they have all held their shares long enough to qualify for long-term capital gains tax treatment. In that case, relative to continuing on a going-concern basis, net advantage of liquidating = $32.8 million. Suppose that an acquiror interested principally in acquiring the company's land would pay $200 million for the company's equity and would agree to assume the company's liabilities. In that case, relative to the acquisition alternative, net advantage of liquidating = $8.8 million. The company should seek to liquidate its assets separately rather than to sell the entire asset portfolio to this buyer or to continue operating.

SUMMARY

A company should dispose of an asset or a business whenever it can realize greater profits by reinvesting the after-tax proceeds from the disposition in some other project of comparable risk *and* immediate disposal of the asset is more advantageous than disposing of it in the future. A variety of alternatives are available for disposing of an asset or a business. A company should select the one that maximizes the after-tax net present value to its shareholders.

A company can spin off a subsidiary to its shareholders in lieu of selling it. A spin-off can benefit the company's shareholders only if the two companies are worth more apart than together *and* the stock market value of the subsidiary after the spin-off would exceed the present value of the after-tax proceeds from disposing of it by some other means.

A company that cannot meet its current obligations has four basic alternatives: sell assets to raise cash, try to reach a voluntary settlement with lenders, seek a merger partner, or seek protection from creditors under the bankruptcy laws. There are two basic forms of bankruptcy: reorganization and liquidation. In a reorganization, the company continues to operate while it reorganizes its capital structure and prepares a plan to repay its debts. In a liquidation, the company's assets are sold and claims are settled in order of strict priority. Shareholders typically realize greater value in a reorganization than in a liquidation.

Even healthy companies have at times found it advantageous to liquidate voluntarily. This is advantageous when the present value of the liquidating distributions, net of payments to creditors and taxes, exceeds the value of shareholders' equity in the company on a going-concern basis. Asset-rich companies or conglomerates in which there is little or no synergy among the businesses are examples of companies that have found voluntary liquidation beneficial.

Sources of Financial Information

Part 9

Sources of Financial Information

Chapter 29

Much of the financial analyst's efforts are devoted to evaluating the future impact of alternative courses of action on the performance and financial condition of the business enterprise. To accomplish this, the analyst tries to draw on the most reliable business and financial information available. When the analyst is employed by a company or is engaged by a company to perform a study, he or she normally has access to a wealth of financial information, such as detailed projections, that management has generated for budgetary and control purposes but has not released to the public. But, in many cases, the analyst is limited to information that is publicly available.

FINANCIAL DATA PROVIDED PUBLICLY BY COMPANIES

The primary sources of financial information are the reports that companies make available to their securities holders. Companies subject to the public reporting requirements of the Securities and Exchange Commission publish a number of financial reports. The most useful of these are the annual Form 10-K and quarterly Form 10-Q reports, which contain more detailed information and a more extensive description of the company's business and recent operating performance than that which is normally included in a company's annual and quarterly reports to its shareholders. In addition, Form S-1, Form S-2, Form S-3, and Form S-14 registration statements (or the documents incorporated in them by reference) contain detailed historical financial information.

The principal documents containing the firm's full financial statements and the principal secondary sources that provide either full or condensed financial statements are listed in Table 29-1. In recent years, the SEC has streamlined

Table 29-1
Where to Find a Company's Financial Statements

Primary Sources (Full Financial Statements)

Principal Financial Information Provided

Document	Income Statements	Balance Sheets	Changes in Financial Position	Financial and Operating Summary	Share Price, Dividend History	Business Segment Breakdown	Geographic Segment Breakdown	Impact of Inflation
Annual Report on Form 10-K[a,b]	3 yr[c]	2 yr	3 yr[c]	5 yr	—	3 yr	3 yr	5 yr
Form S-1, Form S-2, Form S-3, Form S-14 Registration Statement[a,d,e]	3 yr and interim[c]	2 yr and interim	3 yr and interim[c]	5 yr	2–5 yr, at least the last 2 by qtr[f]	3 yr	3 yr	5 yr
Annual Report to Shareholders[b,g]	3 yr[c]	2 yr	3 yr[c]	5–10 yr	2 yr by qtr	3 yr	3 yr	5 yr
Quarterly Report on Form 10-Q[a,b]	For qtr and for year-to-date 2 yr	End of qtr and end of most recent fiscal year	For year-to-date 2 yr	—	—	For qtr 0–2 yr	For qtr 0–2 yr	—

Secondary Sources

Organization	Publication(s) or Information Provided	Updating Done
Disclosure, Inc.	Documents filed with the SEC recorded on microfiche	As documents are filed
Moody's Investors Service, Inc.	Moody's Industrial Manual, Moody's OTC Industrial Manual, Moody's Public Utility Manual, Moody's Bank & Financial Manual, Moody's Transportation Manual	Annually
Standard & Poor's Corporation	Compustat	As new information becomes available

[a] Filed with the Securities and Exchange Commission, Washington, D.C. Also normally available directly from the company.

[b] Must be issued by corporations with more than $3 million in total assets *and* 500 or more shareholders of record in a single class of its equity securities as of latest fiscal year-end.

[c] SEC regulations require companies to provide audited income and flow of funds statements for (at least) the most recent 3 years and audited balance sheets for the most recent 2 years. Companies occasionally provide additional years' financial information.

[d] Because of the recent introduction of the abbreviated Form S-3 Registration Statement, which does not require the company to furnish full financial statements, most large companies can incorporate by reference the full financial statements filed as part of their latest Form 10-K annual report and most recent Form 10-Q reports.

[e] The Form S-2 and Form S-3 Registration Statements are abbreviated disclosure documents. The financial statements included in Form S-3 Registration Statements are typically incorporated by reference from the company's most recent Annual Report on Form 10-K or some other document containing them that has been filed with the SEC. The financial statements included in Form S-2 Registration Statements are typically incorporated by attaching the company's most recent Annual Report on Form 10-K or Annual Report to Shareholders.

[f] Registration statements for new issues of common stock.

[g] Many companies also prepare "summary statistical reports," which provide more detailed historical operating and financial statistics. In addition, electric and gas utilities prepare "uniform statistical reports," which they provide to financial analysts, the American Gas Association, and Edison Electric Institute

529

corporate reporting requirements by making the Form 10-K annual report the primary disclosure document and by permitting a large number of issuers to use the abbreviated Form S-3 registration statement. This trend will probably continue and may lead to more detailed disclosure in the Form 10-K, as for example, projections of earnings, capital requirements, and other quantities of interest.

Publicly held companies also distribute proxy statements to their shareholders prior to the annual meeting. This document discloses information concerning compensation paid top executives, the shareholdings of insiders, and the names of top management and directors.

The financial information that is made publicly available is almost exclusively of a purely historical nature. Recently, following a long history of prohibiting companies from including financial forecasts in prospectuses and reports filed with it, the SEC has tried to encourage companies to make earnings forecasts publicly available.[1] Companies have been reluctant to release projections, however, out of fear that inaccurate forecasts might lead to shareholder resentment or, worse, litigation. In many applications, such as the financial analysis of acquisitions and the valuation of common stocks by investors, the lack of projections of earnings, cash flow, and other quantities of interest is a serious handicap. In such instances, one of the most important duties of the financial analyst is to use the publicly available information to formulate a set of projections. A number of research services are in business principally to provide such information to investors. Their major publications are listed later in this chapter.

GENERAL SOURCES OF
FINANCIAL INFORMATION

Financial analysts should be familiar with the major sources of financial information. A number of business publications and research services regularly collect financial information from companies, market organizations, government agencies, and other sources and compile reports that contain information that is useful in a broad variety of situations. Familiarity with these sources can save many hours of searching for information and, more important, save hours that might otherwise be spent duplicating work that has already been done by someone else.

Table 29-2 lists the major business and finance newspapers, periodicals, and journals and indicates some of the special features provided by each. The newspapers represent the best sources of current financial information. This includes price quotations and trading volumes and, in many cases, yield and other data for stocks, bonds, and options traded on the major exchanges and in the over-the-counter market; price quotations for commodity and financial

Table 29-2
Selected Major Business and Finance Newspapers, Periodicals and Journals

---

Newspapers

Barron's (weekly)
  Tabulation of securities prices and economic and financial indicators
Commercial and Financial Chronicle (weekly)
  Stock quotations and foreign exchange rates
Financial Times of London (international daily)
  Articles on European companies
  Stock quotations on major world exchanges
Journal of Commerce
  Commodities, insurance industry, and transportation
M/G Financial Weekly
Money Manager (weekly)
The New York Times
  Widely read business and finance section that includes securities price quotations
  and a variety of articles on business and finance subjects
The Wall Street Journal
  Articles on variety of business subjects
  Comprehensive stock, bond, option, and commodity price quotations
Wall Street Transcript (weekly)
  Extracts of brokerage house reports

Periodicals

Business Conditions Digest	*Fortune**
Business Week	*Harvard Business Review*
Dun's Review	*Institutional Investor*
The Economist (international)	*Investment Dealer's Digest*
Euromoney (international)	*Nation's Business*
Financial Executive	*Sloan Management Review*
Financial World	
Forbes†	

Journals

Financial Analysts Journal	*Journal of Finance*
Financial Management	*Journal of Financial Economics*
The Financial Review	*Journal of Financial and Quantitative*
Journal of Accounting, Auditing	*Analysis*
& Finance	*Journal of Financial Research*
Journal of Accounting Research	*Journal of Money, Credit, and Banking*
Journal of Business	*Journal of Portfolio Management*
Journal of Economics and Business	

---

*Annually provides (1) rankings of 500 largest U.S. industrial corporations by sales and also by a variety of other measures; (2) rankings of 100 largest commercial banking, diversified financial, and diversified service companies; and (3) rankings of 50 largest life insurance, retailing, transportation, and utility companies.
†Annually provides (1) rankings of 500 largest U.S. corporations by sales, profits, assets, and market value and (2) a comparative study of American corporations by industry.

futures; cash prices for commodities; money market and foreign exchange rates; individual company news and earnings and dividend announcements; market averages and trading data; and a variety of domestic and international business and financial news.

The periodicals listed in Table 29-2 are of four principal types. *Business Week, Dun's Review, Financial World, Forbes,* and *Fortune* are chiefly concerned with the past performance and future prospects of individual companies and industries. *Business Conditions Digest, The Economist,* and *Nation's Business* are more concerned with broader economic, political, and business trends. *Euromoney, Institutional Investor* (which publishes both domestic and international editions), and *Investment Dealers' Digest* address themselves to financial market conditions, financings, and related subjects. *Financial Executive, Harvard Business Review,* and *Sloan Management Review* serve as forums for the exchange of management ideas, which often include interesting practical financial insights.

The journals listed in Table 29-2 contain articles of a more esoteric nature, which often demand a high level of mathematical sophistication to appreciate fully. Nevertheless, these journals frequently report the results of significant empirical studies and refinements to existing analytical approaches in a manner that can be readily understood by someone who does not have a highly technical background.

In addition to the newspapers and periodicals listed in Table 29-2, numerous newspapers, newsletters, and journals specific to particular industries provide relevant articles and statistical summaries. Many active industry trade associations produce annual fact books and other reports that contain useful business and financial information about particular industries. The list of such publications is too extensive to be included here but many research libraries maintain lists of these publications. Lorna Daniells' *Business Information Sources* contains an annotated bibliography of domestic and international sources of financial and business information.[2] The U.S. government provides a variety of useful surveys and publications, which are listed in *Guide to U.S. Government Statistics* and in the *American Statistics Index.*

Table 29-3 lists the principal sources of information for each of the subject areas discussed in this book. The major research services that are responsible for these and other useful reports include:

Dow Jones & Company, Inc., 22 Cortlandt Street, New York, N.Y. 10007

Duff and Phelps, Inc., 55 East Monroe Street, Chicago, Ill. 60603

Dun & Bradstreet Inc., Three Century Drive, Parsippany, N.J. 07054

Moody's Investors Service, Inc., 99 Church Street, New York, N.Y. 10007

(Continued on page 538)

Table 29-3
Selected Sources of Financial
Information by Subject Area

Aggregate Business and Economic Information

Economic Report of the President (annual)
Statistical Abstract of the United States (annual)
Survey Research Center, University of Michigan, *Economic Outlook U.S.A.* (quarterly)
U.S. Congress, *Annual Report of the Joint Economic Committee*
U.S. Department of Commerce, *Business Statistics* (biennial)
U.S. Department of Commerce, *U.S. Industrial Outlook* (annual)

Recent Business and Economic Developments

Business Week
Council of Economic Advisers, *Economic Indicators* (monthly)
The Economist
Federal Reserve Bulletin (monthly)
M/G Financial Weekly
Morgan Guaranty Trust Company, *World Financial Markets*
Standard & Poor's *Outlook*
U.S. Department of Commerce, *Business Conditions Digest* (monthly)
The Wall Street Journal

Business and Economic Information by Industry

Dun & Bradstreet, *Key Business Ratios* (annual)
Predicasts F & S Index
Standard & Poor's *Industry Surveys*
Standard & Poor's *Outlook*
Standard & Poor's *Trends & Projections* (monthly)
U.S. Census Bureau, *Annual Survey of Manufactures*
U.S. Department of Commerce, *Business Statistics* (biennial)
U.S. Department of Commerce, *Quarterly Financial Report for Manufacturing, Mining, and Trade Corporations*
U.S. Department of Commerce, *Survey of Current Business* (monthly)
U.S. Department of Commerce, *U.S. Industrial Outlook* (annual)

Business and Financial Information by Company

Dun & Bradstreet, *Europe's Largest 15,000 Companies*
Dun & Bradstreet, *Key British Enterprises*
Dun & Bradstreet, *Million Dollar Directory* (annual)
Dun & Bradstreet, *Principal International Businesses* (annual)
Dun & Bradstreet, *Who Owns Whom*
Financial Post Corporation Service (Canadian)
Jane's Major Companies of Europe
Moody's Manuals (Bank & Finance, Industrial, OTC Industrial, Public Utility, Transportation, International)
Polk's *World Bank Directory*

Standard & Poor's *Compustat*
Standard & Poor's *Register of Corporations, Directors and Executives*
Time Books, *The Times 1000*

Corporate Capital Expenditures and Investment Attitudes

F. W. Dodge Division, McGraw-Hill Information Systems Co.
Federal Reserve Bulletin

Corporate Capital Structure and Credit Analysis

Commerce Clearing House, *Capital Changes Reporter*
Standard & Poor's *Credit Week*

Corporate Long-Term Financing

Federal Reserve Bulletin
Institutional Investor (annual financing directory)
Investment Dealers' Digest (semiannual *Corporate
Financing Directory)*
Securities and Exchange Commission, *Statistical Bulletin* (monthly)

Project Financings

Predicasts F & S Index of Corporate Change
Mergers & Acquisitions: The Journal of Corporate Venture

Liabilities Management Activities

Commerce Clearing House, *Capital Changes Reporter*
Investment Dealers' Digest (exchange offers; repurchase offers)
Moody's *Bond Record*
Standard & Poor's *Called Bond Record*
Value Line, Inc., *Value Line Options & Convertibles*

Dividend Information

Commerce Clearing House, *Capital Changes Reporter*
Moody's *Dividend Record*
Standard & Poor's *Dividend Record*
The Wall Street Journal

Share Repurchases and Stock Splits

Bank & Quotation Record
Commerce Clearing House, *Capital Changes Reporter*
Predicasts F & S Index of Corporate Change
Investment Dealers' Digest
M/G Financial Weekly
The Wall Street Journal

Venture Capital and Business Formations

Economic Report of the President (aggregate historical figures)
Guide to Venture Capital Sources
Venture (magazine)
Venture Capital Journal

Small Business Management and Financing

Going Public
Inc.
Journal of Small Business Management

Mergers and Acquisitions

Acquisition-Divestiture Weekly Report
Commerce Clearing House, *Capital Changes Reporter*
Conference Board, *Announcements of Mergers and Acquisitions*
Federal Trade Commission, *Statistical Report on Mergers and Acquisitions*
Predicasts F & S Index of Corporate Change
W. T. Grimm & Co., *Mergerstat Review* (annual)
Mergers & Acquisitions (quarterly)
National Review of Corporate Acquisitions

Business Failures and Liquidations

Commerce Clearing House, *Capital Changes Reporter*
Economic Report of the President (aggregate statistics)
Predicasts F & S Index of Corporate Change

General Bond Market Developments

Daily Bond Buyer
Public Securities Association, *Municipal Market Developments*
Standard & Poor's *Fixed Income Investor* (weekly)
The Wall Street Journal

General Stock Market Trends and Developments

Barron's
Capital International Perspective (international; monthly)
Investor's Daily
M/G Financial Weekly
Securities and Exchange Commission, *SEC Monthly Statistical Review*
Standard & Poor's *Outlook*
The Wall Street Journal

Securities Price Quotations

Bank & Quotation Record (monthly and year-to-date ranges in each
  issue; annual ranges in January issue)
Barron's
Commercial and Financial Chronicle
Fitch's *Bond Quotations*
Fitch's *Stock Quotations*
Investor's Daily
National Daily Quotation Service
The New York Times
Standard & Poor's *Daily Stock Price Record* (quarterly volumes for
  New York Stock Exchange, American Stock Exchange, and
  Over-the-Counter)
The Wall Street Journal

Principal Terms of Outstanding Securities

Moody's Manuals (Bank & Finance, Industrial, OTC Industrial,
  Municipal and Government, Public Utility, Transportation, International)

Fixed Income Security Ratings and Investment Information

Duff and Phelps, *Bond Ratings* (Industrial/Financial, Utility)
Moodie's International Bond Service
Moody's *Bond Record* (monthly)
Moody's *Bond Survey* (new debt issues)
Moody's *Convertible Bonds*
Standard & Poor's *Bond Guide* (monthly)
Standard & Poor's *Fixed Income Investor* (weekly)
Standard & Poor's *Standard Convertible Bond Reports*
Value Line, Inc., *Value Line Options & Convertibles*
The Wall Street Journal

Commercial Paper Ratings

Moody's *Bond Record* (monthly)
Standard & Poor's *Commercial Paper Ratings Guide* (monthly)

Money Market Rates

Bank & Quotation Record (monthly)
Federal Reserve Bulletin (historical)
Investor's Daily
M/G Financial Weekly
The Wall Street Journal

Table 29-3
Selected Sources of Financial Information
by Subject Area *(Continued)*

Foreign Exchange Rates

Bank & Quotation Record (monthly)
Morgan Guaranty Trust Company, *World Financial Markets*
The Wall Street Journal

Earnings Forecasts

Argus Research Corporation
Duff and Phelps, Inc.
Institutional Brokers Estimate System, *Monthly Summary Data*
Moody's *Handbook of Common Stocks*
Standard & Poor's *Earnings Forecaster* (weekly)
Standard & Poor's *Outlook*
Standard & Poor's *Stock Reports*
Value Line, Inc., *Value Line Investment Survey*
Wall Street Transcript
Zachs Investment Research, Inc., *Corporate Earnings Estimates*
Various publications of brokerage houses and banks

Historical Common Stock Statistics

Bank & Quotation Record (monthly)
Dow Jones *Investor's Handbook*
Moody's *Handbook of Common Stocks*
Moody's *Handbook of OTC Stocks*
Standard & Poor's *Analysts Handbook* (by industry)
Standard & Poor's *International Stock Reports*
Standard & Poor's *Stock Guide*
Standard & Poor's *Stock Reports*

Insider Trading Activity

Information, Inc., *The Insiders' Financial
 Chronicle)*
M/G Financial Weekly
Securities and Exchange Commission, *Official Summary of Security
 Transactions and Holdings* (monthly)
Stock Research Corporation, *Weekly Insider Report*

Institutional Securities Portfolios

Best's Market Guide (common stock, preferred stock, and bond holdings
 of insurance companies)
Spectrum 1, 2, 3, 4, 5, 6 (Investment Company Stock Holdings Survey,
 Investment Company Portfolios, Institutional Stock Holdings Survey,
 Institutional Portfolios, 5% Beneficial Ownership, and Insider Ownership)

537

Table 29-3
Selected Sources of Financial Information
by Subject Area *(Continued)*

Vickers *Facts on the Funds*
Vickers Guide (Insurance Company, Investment Company,
 Bank and Trust Company, College Endowment, and Money Manager Portfolios)

Options Market Developments and Price Quotations

Bank & Quotation Record
Commercial and Financial Chronicle
Investor's Daily
M/G Financial Weekly
Options Letter
Securities and Exchange Commission, *SEC Monthly Statistical Review*
Value Line, Inc., *Value Line Options & Convertibles*
The Wall Street Journal

Commodity Prices (Cash and Futures) and Financial Futures Prices

Journal of Commerce
M/G Financial Weekly
The Wall Street Journal

Standard & Poor's Corporation, 25 Broadway, New York, N.Y. 10004

Value Line, Inc., 711 Third Avenue, New York, N.Y. 10017

In addition to the sources listed in Table 29-3, there are many industry-related publications that are useful. The *Financial Analyst's Handbook* contains an excellent bibliography of such sources. Also, the *Predicasts F & S Index United States* and the *Predicasts F & S Index International* index the periodical literature that would be useful to the financial analyst by product, company, and industry.

SUMMARY

In order to function effectively, the analyst must not only be thoroughly familiar with the techniques of financial analysis but must also have at least a working knowledge of the principal sources of financial information. Tables 29-1 to 29-3 list selected sources of information that financial analysts will find useful when applying the techniques described in this book.

CHAPTER NOTES

CHAPTER 2

[1] The SEC defines fixed charges to include also the preferred stock dividend requirements of consolidated subsidiaries to third parties.

[2] A study of 40 major corporations revealed that including unfunded vested pension liabilities in capitalization as debt raised the average debt-to-equity ratio of these companies by 50%. Patrick J. Regan, "Potential Corporate Liabilities Under ERISA," *Financial Analysts Journal*, vol. 32, March-April 1976, pp. 26–32.

[3] Edward I. Altman, "Financial Ratios, Discriminant Analysis and the Prediction of Corporate Bankruptcy," *Journal of Finance*, vol. 23, September 1968, pp. 589–609.

[4] Formulas 2-25 and 2-27 are very similar in form. A_t grows at a constant average annual rate in both. But A_t is assumed to grow in *discrete amounts* (between the end of one period and the end of the next) in Formula 2-25 and to grow *continuously* in Formula 2-27. This distinction between discrete growth and continuous growth will become clearer in Chapter 4 in the context of the compounding of interest.

CHAPTER 5

[1] In some cases, this definition does not produce a unique value. For example, suppose there are four possible outcomes, 1, 3, 7, and 10, each with probability .25. Any value between 3 and 7 satisfies the definition of a median. By convention, the weighted average of the two outcomes that bracket the range of values, in this case $(3 \times 0.25 + 7 \times 0.25)/0.50 = 5$ is called the median.

[2] It is also possible, in theory, to achieve the same result by adjusting the stream of expected cash flows rather than the discount rate. This is done by subtracting the appropriate amount from each expected cash flow. This produces a set of *certainty equivalents*, which are discounted at the riskless interest rate. This method would, however, be cumbersome in practice because of the difficulty in calculating the certainty equivalents.

CHAPTER 6

[1] Accelerated depreciation, which is permitted under the Internal Revenue Code, would produce greater depreciation expense, and hence greater free cash flow, in the early years in Table 6-2 with corresponding reductions in these amounts in the later years. These and other tax-related factors are discussed in more detail in Chapter 7.

[2] See J. Hirshleifer, *Investment, Interest and Capital*, Prentice-Hall, Inc., Englewood Cliffs, N.J., 1970, pp. 51–56.

CHAPTER 7

[1] The amount of investment tax credit a company can claim in any year is currently limited to $25,000 plus 85% of taxes payable.

[2] The Tax Equity and Fiscal Responsibility Act of 1982 reduced the benefit of the investment tax credit by requiring a company to reduce its depreciable base in an asset by one-half of the amount of any investment tax credit claimed. Thus, in this example the depreciable base decreases to $48,500.

[3] Jack E. Gaumnitz and Douglas R. Emery, "Asset Growth, Abandonment Value and the Replacement Decision of Like-for-Like Capital Assets," *Journal of Financial and Quantitative Analysis*, vol. 15, June 1980, pp. 408–409.

[4] Ibid., p. 411.

[5] For a discussion of multiperiod capital budgeting techniques, see H. Martin Weingartner, *Mathematical Programming and the Analysis of Capital Budgeting Problems*, Markham Publishing Company, Chicago, 1967.

CHAPTER 8

[1] Myron J. Gordon, *The Investment, Financing, and Valuation of the Corporation*, Richard D. Irwin, Inc., Homewood, Ill., 1962.

[2] An interesting way to look at Formula 8-11 is to assume that the convertible debt is redeemed and new common stock is issued simultaneously, but without underwriting or other expenses, on the break-even date. In that case, the cost of convertible debt represents a blending of the cost of debt over the period up to conversion and the cost of retained earnings for the period thereafter.

CHAPTER 9

[1] William F. Sharpe, "Capital Asset Prices: A Theory of Market Equilibrium under Conditions of Risk," *Journal of Finance*, vol. 19, September 1964, pp. 425–442, and John Lintner, "The Valuation of Risk Assets and the Selection of Risky Investments in Stock Portfolios and Capital Budgets," *Review of Economics and Statistics*, vol. 47, February 1965, pp. 13–37.

[2] Richard Brealey and Stewart Myers, *Principles of Corporate Finance*, McGraw-Hill Book Company, New York, 1981, chap. 8, provides a fuller discussion of the CAPM.

[3] Studies indicate that perhaps as few as 10 stocks are sufficient in many cases to eliminate substantially all nonsystematic risk.

[4] Gordon J. Alexander and Norman L. Chervany, "On the Estimation and Stability of Beta," *Journal of Financial and Quantitative Analysis*, vol. 15, March 1980, pp. 123–137, and Nicholas J. Gonedes, "Evidence on the Information Content of Accounting Numbers: Accounting-Based and Market-Based Estimates of Systematic Risk," *Journal of Financial and Quantitative Analysis*, vol. 8, June 1973, pp. 407–443.

[5] Coupon equivalent yield is explained in Chapter 17.

[6] Roger G. Ibbotson and Rex A. Sinquefield, *Stocks, Bonds, Bills, and Inflation: The Past and The Future*, Financial Analysts Research Foundation, Charlottesville, Va., 1982.

[7] The one possible exception to this is that investors tend to require a higher rate of return for smaller companies.

[8] Debt service coverage can be calculated from Formula 11-2.

CHAPTER 10

[1] Franco Modigliani and Merton H. Miller, "The Cost of Capital, Corporation Finance and the Theory of Investment," *American Economic Review*, vol. 48, June 1958, pp. 261–297. In a companion paper, which is discussed in Chapter 12, Modigliani and Miller also demonstrated that under certain assumptions the firm's choice of dividend policy is irrelevant to the stock market value of its equity.

[2] This is the startling conclusion Modigliani and Miller reached when they introduced corporate income taxes in their famous "correction" article. See Franco Modigliani and Merton H. Miller, "Corporate Income Taxes and the Cost of Capital: A Correction," *American Economic Review*, vol. 53, June 1963, pp. 433–443.

[3] "Quarterly Financial Report for Manufacturing, Mining, and Trade Corporations: Fourth Quarter 1982," U.S. Department of Commerce, Washington, D.C., April 1983.

[4] At year-end 1983, long-term capital gains were taxed at 40% of the tax rate applicable to the taxpayer's ordinary income. Interest income, dividend income (exclusive of $100 on an individual return or $200 on a joint return), and short-term capital gains had to be included in ordinary income and hence taxed at the full rate.

[5] Merton H. Miller, "Debt and Taxes," *Journal of Finance*, vol. 32, May 1977, pp. 261–275.

[6] See Roger H. Gordon and Burton G. Malkiel, "Taxation and Corporate Finance," in Henry J. Aaron and Joseph A. Pechman, *How Taxes Affect Economic Behavior*, Brookings Institution, Washington, D.C., 1981, pp. 131–192.

[7] A study by Flath and Knoeber estimates that the net advantage of corporate borrowing varied between $0.23 and $0.26 per dollar of additional debt during the period 1965 to 1972. See David Flath and Charles R. Knoeber, "Taxes, Failure Costs, and Optimal Industry Capital Structure: An Empirical Test," *Journal of Finance*, vol. 35, March 1980, pp. 99–117.

[8] David W. Glenn, "Super Premium Security Prices and Optimal Corporate Financing Decisions," *Journal of Finance*, vol. 31, May 1976, pp. 507–524, argues that institutional restrictions lead to premium market prices for debt securities that qualify as legal investments and that restrictions on short selling activity prevent arbitrageurs from eliminating the premium (by selling high-grade bonds short and using the proceeds to purchase low-grade bonds that do not qualify as legal investments). Glenn concludes that for most firms, the optimal capital structure includes the greatest amount of debt consistent with obtaining an investment-grade rating acceptable to institutional investors. This would imply a senior debt rating in the single-A category.

CHAPTER 11

[1] Robert M. Bowen, Lane A. Daley, and Charles C. Huber, Jr., "Evidence on the Existence and Determinants of Inter-Industry Differences in Leverage," *Financial Management*, vol. 11, winter 1982, pp. 10–20; Eli Schwartz and J. Richard Aronson, "Some Surrogate Evidence in Support of the Concept of Optimal Capital Structure," *Journal of Finance*, vol. 22, March 1967, pp. 10–18; David F. Scott, Jr., "Evidence of the Importance of Financial Structure," *Financial Management*, vol. 1, summer 1972, pp. 45–50; David F. Scott, Jr., and John D. Martin, "Industry Influence on Financial Structure," *Financial Management*, vol. 4, spring 1975, pp. 67–73.

[2] Bowen, Daley, and Huber, op. cit.

[3] See *Credit Overview: Industrial Ratings*, Standard & Poor's Corporation, New York, November 1983, pp. 17–27.

[4] Ibid., p. 22.

[5] For example, a senior debt rating of A-2/A would imply a subordinated debt rating of A-3/A−.

[6] As long as preferred equity represents no more than 5% of a company's capitalization, if it is nonregulated, 10% if it is a natural gas or telephone utility, or 15% if it is an electric utility, the use of preferred equity financing will not normally impair the company's senior debt rating. *Corporate and International Ratings*, Standard & Poor's Corporation, New York, 1982, pp. 83–84.

[7] *Industrial Ratings*, op. cit., p. 35.

CHAPTER 12

[1] Merton H. Miller and Franco Modigliani, "Dividend Policy, Growth and the Valuation of Shares," *Journal of Business*, vol. 34, October 1961, pp. 411–433.

[2] Benjamin Graham, David L. Dodd, and Sidney Cottle, *Security Analysis*, 4th ed., McGraw-Hill Book Company, New York, 1962, p. 518.

[3] Note that share price = price-earnings multiple × earnings per share when the company pays two-thirds of its earnings as dividends.

[4] James E. Walter, "Dividend Policies and Common Stock Prices," *Journal of Finance*, vol. 11, March 1956, pp. 29–41.

[5] Miller and Modigliani did note that dividend policy might affect a company's share price, their "dividend irrelevancy" proposition notwithstanding, if dividend changes convey useful new information regarding the firm's earnings prospects.

[6] A company's share price declines by the amount of the declared but unpaid dividend when it begins trading on the ex-dividend date.

[7] Fischer Black, "The Dividend Puzzle," *Journal of Portfolio Management*, vol. 2, winter 1976, pp. 5–8.

[8] Kenneth M. Eades, "Empirical Evidence on Dividends as a Signal of Firm Value," *Journal of Financial and Quantitative Analysis*, vol. 17, November 1982, pp. 471–500, and references therein.

[9] Wilbur G. Lewellen, Kenneth L. Stanley, Ronald C. Lease, and Gary G. Schlarbaum, "Some Direct Evidence on the Dividend Clientele Phenomenon," *Journal of Finance*, vol. 33, December 1978, pp. 1385–1399, found evidence suggesting that higher-payout firms tend to attract less heavily taxed investors and that lower-payout firms tend to attract more heavily taxed investors, which indicates that the bias the tax system creates in favor of capital gains does affect investor behavior.

[10] Difference in tax liabilities is $0.45 tax on firm 2 dividend + $0.22 tax on firm 2 capital gain − $0.37 tax on firm 1 capital gain.

[11] Between 1955 and 1980, for example, the percentage of New York Stock Exchange–listed common stocks owned by institutional investors increased to 35% from 15% of the aggregate market value of the shares listed there. Nonprofit institutions accounted for 60% of institutional holdings at

year-end 1980. *New York Stock Exchange Fact Book*, New York Stock Exchange, New York, 1982, p. 50.

CHAPTER 13

[1] *New York Stock Exchange Fact Book*, New York Stock Exchange, New York, 1982, p. 70.

[2] For example, in 1979 Western Pacific Industries Inc. declared a $23 special dividend following the sale of its Western Pacific Railroad unit.

[3] Allen Michel, "Industry Influence on Dividend Policy," *Financial Management*, vol. 8, autumn 1979, pp. 22–26. An earlier study came to the same conclusion. See also Edwin P. Harkins and Francis J. Walsh, Jr., *Dividend Policies and Practices*, Conference Board, New York, 1971.

[4] Formula 13-1 is a generalization of the Gordon constant growth rate model, which is widely used in utility regulatory proceedings. See Myron J. Gordon, *The Cost of Capital to a Public Utility*, Michigan State University, East Lansing, Mich., 1974.

[5] In the infinite horizon case, Formula 13-1a becomes $ROE(T) = $ growth $\div (1 - $ payout$)$ when there are no new share issues, which is just the Gordon growth model.

[6] Guy Charest, "Split Information, Stock Returns and Market Efficiency—I," *Journal of Financial Economics*, vol. 6, June-September 1978, pp. 265–296.

[7] Correspondingly, a *reverse stock split*, which reduces the number of shares outstanding and raises the share price proportionately, generally elicits a negative reaction. See J. Randall Woolridge and Donald R. Chambers, "Reverse Splits and Shareholder Wealth," *Financial Management*, vol. 12, autumn 1983, pp. 5–15.

CHAPTER 14

[1] Francis J. Walsh, Jr., *Repurchasing Common Stock*, The Conference Board, Report No. 659, New York, 1975, and Francis A. Lees, *Repurchasing Common Stock*, The Conference Board, Research Bulletin No. 147, New York, 1983.

[2] Under Section 302 of the Internal Revenue Code, the share repurchase must also satisfy one of the following three conditions in order for any gain to qualify for long-term capital gain treatment: (1) The payment is deemed "not essentially equivalent to a dividend," or (2) the repurchase results in a "substantially disproportionate" reduction in the shareholder's interest in the company, or (3) the repurchase completely terminates the stockholder's interest in the company.

[3] Tandy Corporation, 1977 annual report to shareholders, June 30, 1977, pp. 48–54.

[4] Joseph Finnerty, "Insiders and Market Efficiency," *Journal of Finance*, vol. 31, September 1976, pp. 1141–1148, and Jeffrey F. Jaffe, "Special Information and Insider Trading," *Journal of Business*, vol. 52, July 1974, pp. 410–428.

[5] See Kenneth R. Marks, "The Stock Price Performance of Firms Repurchasing Their Own Shares," *The Bulletin*, New York University Graduate School of Business Administration, 1976 (1), pp. 6–7.

[6] Larry Y. Dann, "Common Stock Repurchases: An Analysis of Returns to Bondholders and Stockholders," *Journal of Financial Economics*, vol. 9, June 1981, pp. 113–138; Terry Dielman,

Timothy J. Nantell, and Roger L. Wright, "Price Effects of Stock Repurchasing: A Random Coefficient Regression Approach," *Journal of Financial and Quantitative Analysis*, vol. 15, March 1980, pp. 175–189; Ronald W. Masulis, "Stock Repurchase by Tender Offer: An Analysis of the Causes of Common Stock Price Changes," *Journal of Finance*, vol. 35, May 1980, pp. 305–321; and Theo Vermaelen, "Common Stock Repurchases and Market Signalling: An Empirical Study," *Journal of Financial Economics*, vol. 9, June 1981, pp. 139–183.

[7] Dielman, Nantell, and Wright, op. cit.

[8] Discussions of share repurchases often single out repurchasing as an alternative to capital investment as a separate objective. If a corporation has funds available that it cannot invest in projects that will yield at least the hurdle rate, those funds represent "excess cash." It is really only in this sense that share repurchases represent an "alternative" to capital investment.

[9] Hai Hong, Robert S. Kaplan, and Gershon Mandelker, "Pooling vs. Purchase: The Effects of Accounting for Mergers on Stock Prices," *The Accounting Review*, vol. 53, January 1978, pp. 31–47, furnishes supporting empirical evidence.

[10] The model developed in this section is based on Edwin J. Elton and Martin J. Gruber, "The Effect of Share Repurchase on the Value of the Firm," *Journal of Finance*, vol. 23, March 1968, pp. 135–149. It assumes that all shareholders are identical and that each shareholder sells an equal proportion of his or her holdings back to the company.

[11] The model developed in this section is based on Wayne S. Marshall and Allan E. Young, "A Mathematical Model for Re-Acquisition of Small Shareholdings," *Journal of Financial and Quantitative Analysis*, vol. 3, December 1968, pp. 463–469.

CHAPTER 15

[1] J. William Petty, II, and David F. Scott, Jr., "The Heterogeneity of Corporate Liquidity: Industry and Risk Group Effects," *Journal of Economics and Business*, vol. 32, spring 1980, pp. 206–218.

[2] *Credit Overview: Industrial Ratings*, Standard & Poor's Corporation, New York, November 1983, pp. 38–39.

[3] As one would expect from comparing Table 15-1 with Table 11-3, there is a strong correlation between a company's senior debt rating and its commercial paper rating (assuming, of course, that it has both types of ratings). In general, it would be unusual for a company whose senior debt is rated AA− or higher to have a commercial paper rating lower than A-1+, and it would also be unusual for a company whose senior debt is not rated investment grade (i.e., at least BBB−) to have a commercial paper rating as high as A-3. Ibid., p. 38. Generally, a commercial paper rating of A-1 correlates with a senior debt rating in the single-A range, and a commercial paper rating of A-2 correlates with a senior debt rating in the triple-B range.

CHAPTER 16

[1] Technical insolvency occurs whenever a corporation fails to meet its cash obligations.

[2] Strictly speaking, one can argue that the firm should select the degree of liquidity at which the expected cost of maintaining the optimal degree of liquidity exceeds the expected cost of bankruptcy by a margin large enough to satisfy the corporation's shareholders. As a practical matter, these costs of bankruptcy are probably high enough that the two criteria are equivalent.

[3] William J. Baumol, "The Transactions Demand for Cash: An Inventory Theoretic Approach," *Quarterly Journal of Economics*," vol. 66, November 1952, pp. 545–556.

[4] Merton H. Miller and Daniel Orr, "A Model of the Demand for Money by Firms," *Quarterly Journal of Economics*, vol. 80, August 1966, pp. 413–435.

[5] A trigger point greater than zero for the sale of securities would be appropriate if there were delays between the sale of securities and the receipt of cash proceeds.

[6] P. F. Smith, "Measuring Risk on Consumer Installment Credit," *Management Science*, vol. 11, November 1964, pp. 327–340, offers a practical example of how a company can accomplish this.

CHAPTER 17

[1] Note the important distinction between *short-term funds* and the accounting definition of *short-term debt*. Unless refunded earlier, every debt obligation becomes short-term debt within a year of its scheduled maturity.

[2] For example, terms of $3/10$, net 30 involve a cost of 56.44% and terms of $2/10$, net 20 involve a cost of 74.49%.

[3] It is possible for commercial paper to have a maturity longer than 270 days, but such an issue would have to be placed privately or else registered with the Securities and Exchange Commission.

[4] Nancy H. Rothstein and James M. Little, eds., *The Handbook of Financial Futures*, McGraw-Hill Book Company, New York, 1984, provides a comprehensive guide to financial futures.

CHAPTER 18

[1] A company can register common stock on the abbreviated Form S-3 registration statement if either (1) nonaffiliates own voting shares worth at least $150 million or (2) nonaffiliates own voting shares worth at least $100 million and the annual trading volume in the stock is at least 3 million shares and, in addition to (1) or (2), certain reporting and nondefault requirements are met. A company that fails to meet this "float" test can still register debt securities using the Form S-3 if the debt is rated "investment grade" by at least one of the major rating agencies.

[2] Burton Zwick, "Yields on Privately Placed Corporate Bonds," *Journal of Finance*, vol. 35, March 1980, pp. 23–29. The differential varied considerably during this period, from a quarterly low of 5 basis points to a quarterly high of 94 basis points.

[3] After the elimination of withholding tax, the U.S. Treasury sold an issue of Eurobonds in October 1984 that preserved purchasers' anonymity. The issue offered a yield of 11.10% on a semiannual equivalent basis, which was 32 basis points lower that the 11.42% yield at which bonds of the same issue were sold, in registered form, to U.S. investors.

[4] Joseph E. Finnerty, Thomas Schneeweis, and Shantaram P. Hegde, "Interest Rates in the Eurobond Market," *Journal of Financial and Quantitative Analysis*, vol. 15, September 1980, pp. 743–755, provides an interesting study of the behavior of Eurobond interest rates.

[5] The interested reader is referred to Alan C. Shapiro, *Multinational Financial Management*, Allyn and Bacon, Boston, 1982.

[6] James F. Gatti, John R. Mills, and Peter J. McTague, "The Feasibility of Small Denomination Consumer Note Issues as a Source of Funds for Non-Financial Borrowers," *Financial Management*, vol. 10, autumn 1981, pp. 41–53.

[7] Rule U-50 under the Public Utility Holding Company Act of 1935 requires competitive bidding. However, the SEC has granted exemptions during volatile market periods.

[8] One notable exception is Exxon Corporation's use of the so-called "Dutch auction" competitive bidding process. See "Exxon Plan to Offer Its Notes at Auction Is Gaining Attention," *The Wall Street Journal*, September 21, 1982, p. 43.

[9] For example, Frank J. Fabozzi and Richard R. West, "Negotiated Versus Competitive Underwritings of Public Utility Bonds: Just One More Time," *Journal of Financial and Quantitative Analysis*, vol. 16, September 1981, pp. 323–339. However, they also found that the negotiated process tended to produce lower borrowing costs during volatile market periods, although the difference in borrowing costs was not significant statistically.

[10] David S. Kidwell, M. Wayne Marr, and G. Rodney Thompson, "SEC Rule 415: The Ultimate Competitive Bid," *Journal of Financial and Quantitative Analysis*, vol. 19, June 1984, pp. 183–195, found that debt issues sold under Rule 415 between July 1982 and April 1983 carried offering yields roughly 30 to 40 basis points lower than the yields on comparable negotiated offerings and also involved lower underwriting spreads. They also found that shelf-registered utility debt issues led to cost-of-borrowing savings of roughly 26 basis points in comparison with more traditional utility bond bids.

CHAPTER 19

[1] Haim Levy, "Economic Evaluation of Voting Power of Common Stock," *Journal of Finance*, vol. 38, March 1983, pp. 79–93.

[2] One of the best examples is the Ford Motor Company, which has two classes of common stock. Class B Stock, owned by members of the Ford family, controls 40% of the total voting power of the company but represented only 9% of the total number of common shares Ford had outstanding at year-end 1982.

[3] For example, Eastman Kodak Company contributed $241 million worth of its common stock in September 1982, and Aluminum Company of America contributed $58 million worth of its common stock in July of that year. Other companies have contributed preferred stock or other securities or, in some cases, real estate, timberlands, or other real assets in lieu of cash to their pension funds. Under the 1974 Employee Retirement Income Security Act (ERISA), a corporate pension plan may hold "qualifying" securities of the corporate sponsor but the amount of such securities cannot exceed 10% of the fair market value of the pension plan's assets.

[4] John W. Bowyer, Jr., and Jess B. Yawitz, "The Effect of New Equity Issues on Utility Stock Prices," *Public Utilities Fortnightly*, vol. 105, May 22, 1980, pp. 25–28, found that utility share prices fell relative to the Dow Jones Utility Index upon the announcement of an offering during both periods of generally rising share prices and periods of generally falling share prices.

[5] The negative market impact may also be due, in part, to the reduction in leverage that results from a common stock offering.

[6] John D. Finnerty, "How to Lower the Cost of Floating a New Stock Issue," *Public Utilities Fortnightly*, vol. 111, March 17, 1983, pp. 25–29, discusses how such an opportunity developed during 1982 for certain electric utility common stock issuers.

[7] John D. Finnerty, "The Behavior of Electric Utility Common Stock Prices Near the Ex-Dividend Date," *Financial Management*, vol. 10, winter 1981, pp. 59–69.

[8] Empirical evidence suggests, however, that arbitrage activity is generally successful at keeping the market value of a right close to its theoretical value. See Robert M. Soldofsky and Craig R. Johnson, "Rights Timing," *Financial Analysts Journal*, vol. 23, July-August 1967, pp. 101–114.

[9] Robert S. Hansen and John M. Pinkerton, "Direct Equity Financing: A Resolution of a Paradox," *Journal of Finance*, vol. 37, June 1982, pp. 651–665. For example, suppose a parent company wishes to offer shares of a 90%-owned subsidiary and plans to purchase its pro rata share of the offering. The flotation costs of the issue really apply only to the remaining 10% of the issue.

[10] R. W. White and P. A. Lusztig, "The Price Effects of Rights Offerings," *Journal of Financial and Quantitative Analysis*, vol. 15, March 1980, pp. 25–40.

[11] At least two companies, Control Data Corporation and Orange and Rockland Utilities, do not limit participation to current shareholders.

CHAPTER 20

[1] Bowman Brown, "Why Corporations Should Consider Income Bonds," *Financial Executive*, vol. 35, October 1967, pp. 74–78, and John J. McConnell and Gary G. Schlarbaum, "Returns, Risks, and Pricing of Income Bonds, 1956–76," *Journal of Business*, vol. 54, January 1981, pp. 33–57.

[2] Edward A. Dyl and Michael D. Joehnk, "Sinking Funds and the Cost of Corporate Debt," *Journal of Finance*, vol. 34, September 1979, pp. 887–893, confirms this empirically.

[3] General Motors Acceptance Corporation, prospectus, November 13, 1980, pp. 10–11.

[4] More exotic swap arrangements than the one discussed here are possible. For example, the two parties could borrow in different currencies and swap liabilities. Such transactions can be of mutual benefit to multinational companies each of which has borrowed heavily in a particular (but differing) currency but still has significant borrowing requirements in that currency.

[5] William M. Boyce and Andrew J. Kalotay, "Tax Differentials and Callable Bonds," *Journal of Finance*, vol. 34, September 1979, pp. 825–838.

[6] Companies normally issue preference stock only when charter limitations prevent them from issuing additional preferred stock.

[7] In recognition of this, the SEC permits companies to include only nonredeemable preferred stock in stockholders' equity.

[8] The major rating agencies treat a sinking fund preferred stock issue as debt for purposes of their financial ratio analysis when the issue's average life is 10 years or less.

CHAPTER 21

[1] Fischer Black and Myron Scholes, "The Pricing of Options and Corporate Liabilities," *Journal of Political Economy*, vol. 81, May-June 1973, pp. 637–654. Fischer Black, "Fact and Fantasy in the Use of Options," *Financial Analysts Journal*, vol. 31, July-August 1975, pp. 36–72, provides a practical explanation of the model and its uses.

[2] Perhaps because of the difficulty of estimating variance, James D. MacBeth and Larry J. Merville, "An Empirical Examination of the Black-Scholes Call Option Pricing Model," *Journal of Finance*, vol. 34, December 1979, pp. 1173–1186, found that the Black-Scholes formula prices tended to be less than (greater than) market prices of call options when the exercise price was greater than (less than) the underlying share price. Black, op. cit., reported exactly the opposite results, however. In any case, there is empirical evidence that Black-Scholes formula prices are not exact.

[3] Robert C. Merton, "Theory of Rational Option Pricing," *Bell Journal of Economics and Management Science*, vol. 4, spring 1973, pp. 141–183.

[4] However, unlike conventional convertible debt, any gain or loss a holder realizes upon exchanging debentures for stock would normally be taxable. The issuer of the exchangeable debentures would also recognize gain or loss upon the exchange.

[5] Rule of thumb may be thought of as a "yield payback" calculation because it relates the conversion premium (in percent) to the premium in yield on the convertible bond over the common dividend yield. Break-even may be thought of as a "dollar payback" calculation because it relates the conversion premium (in dollars) to the difference in annual dollar return on equal dollar investments in the convertible debt and in the underlying common stock. If conversion premium in rule of thumb is calculated by dividing by the conversion price, rather than the current share price, conversion premium $= (62.375 - 52.875)/62.375 = 0.1523$, then we get the break-even value: $0.1523/(0.085 - 0.0159) = 2.20$.

[6] There can be immediate dilution in primary earnings per share if the convertible security's yield to maturity is less than $66\frac{2}{3}\%$ of the average Aa corporate bond yield at the time of issuance.

[7] American Express Company, prospectus, March 31, 1982.

[8] Dan Galai and Meir I. Schneller, "Pricing of Warrants and the Value of the Firm," *Journal of Finance*, vol. 33, December 1978, pp. 1333–1342.

[9] MGM/UA Entertainment Co., prospectus, April 14, 1983, p. 7.

CHAPTER 22

[1] John D. Martin, Paul F. Anderson, and Arthur J. Keown, "Lease Capitalization and Stock Price Stability: Implications for Accounting," *Journal of Accounting, Auditing & Finance*, vol. 2, winter 1979, pp. 151–163, found that there was no significant stock market reaction to the announcement of lease capitalizations by a sample of companies each of which announced significant capitalized lease obligations just after FASB 13 became effective.

[2] Richard S. Bower, "Issues in Lease Financing," *Financial Management*, vol. 2, winter 1973, pp. 25–34, and Wilbur G. Lewellen, Michael S. Long, and John J. McConnell, "Asset Leasing in Competitive Capital Markets," *Journal of Finance*, vol. 31, June 1976, pp. 787–798, review the critical issues.

[3] Wilbur G. Lewellen and Douglas R. Emery, "On the Matter of Parity among Financial Obligations," *Journal of Finance*, vol. 36, March 1981, pp. 97–111.

[4] Paul F. Anderson and John D. Martin, "Lease vs. Purchase Decisions: A Survey of Current Practice," *Financial Management*, vol. 6, spring 1977, pp. 41–47, found that the internal-rate-of-return approach is the most widely used approach in practice.

[5] If Western were not a taxpayer, there would be no depreciation recapture. The residual value foregone would be the full $2.0 million.

[6] Footnote disclosure of any contingent liabilities or of any take-or-pay or similar undertakings would normally be required. Nevertheless, there may be some benefit from a debt rating standpoint. The rating agencies generally ignore off-balance-sheet financing obligations that represent less than 5% of a company's capitalization.

[7] Larry Wynant, "Essential Elements of Project Financing," *Harvard Business Review*, vol. 58, May-June 1980, pp. 165–173.

[8] Edward Z. Emmer, "The Impact of Energy Project Financings on Public Utility Ratings," *Standard & Poor's Fixed Income Investor*, January 14, 1978, p. 908.

[9] Cinema Group Partners, prospectus, April 17, 1981, p. 4.

[10] A recent study estimates that real estate represents 25% of the assets of American companies, worth in the aggregate between $700 billion and $1400 billion, but that only 20% of American corporations manage their real estate for profit. See Sally Zeckhauser and Robert Silverman, "Rediscover Your Company's Real Estate," *Harvard Business Review*, vol. 61, January-February 1983, pp. 111–117.

CHAPTER 23

[1] William M. Boyce and Andrew J. Kalotay, "Optimum Bond Calling and Refunding," *Interfaces*, vol. 9, November 1979, pp. 36–49.

[2] *Ibid.*; Alan Kraus, "The Bond Refunding Decision in an Efficient Market," *Journal of Financial and Quantitative Analysis*, vol. 8, December 1973, pp. 793–806; and H. Martin Weingartner, "Optimal Timing of Bond Refunding," *Management Science*, vol. 13, March 1967, pp. 511–524, are among the more useful of these.

[3] The calculations assume redemption prices of 108.15% at year 5 and 106.67% at year 10 and a tax rate of 50%. They also ignore issuance and other expenses in order to simplify the example.

[4] These characteristics conform to what is known as a geometric random walk model. Past studies have found that interest rate movements approximate a geometric random walk. In the geometric random walk model, the percentage 2.0% is found by calculating the standard deviation of the difference of logarithms of new issue rates for successive months.

[5] There are special cases in which dividends and issuance expenses are tax deductible. For example, preferred stock with a very short maturity (e.g., 5 years or less) is treated as debt under the Internal Revenue Code. Consequently, Formula 23-1 applies to such issues.

CHAPTER 24

[1] John D. Finnerty, *An Illustrated Guide to Bond Refunding Analysis*, The Financial Analysts Research Foundation, Charlottesville, Va., 1984, chap. VII, reviews this debate and establishes conditions under which it is profitable for a company to refund discounted debt.

[2] Pending the issuance of new rules by the Internal Revenue Service, a company would normally write down assets in the following decreasing order of priority: (1) depreciable assets secured by the debt, if any; (2) depreciable assets acquired with the proceeds of the debt issue, if any; (3) all other depreciable assets on a pro rata basis; and finally (4) inventories. Since the passage of the Bankruptcy Tax Act of 1980, a company is no longer permitted to write down the tax basis of nondepreciable assets.

[3] Certain types of direct debt-for-debt exchanges result in a tax-free gain.

[4] Andrew J. Kalotay, "On the Management of Sinking Funds," *Financial Management*, vol. 10, summer 1981, pp. 34–40.

[5] Finnerty, *An Illustrated Guide to Bond Refunding Analysis*, chap. X, provides a detailed analysis of the economics of both novation and in-substance defeasance.

[6] Note that acquiring stripped Treasury securities (i.e., the coupons separated from the corpus and vice versa) will not achieve the desired tax treatment. As a result of the Tax Equity and Fiscal Responsibility Act of 1982, the stripped coupons and the corpus are treated as original issue discount bonds. Any discount must be amortized for tax purposes as interest effectively compounds, and this amortization is taxed as ordinary income on a current basis.

CHAPTER 25

[1] Henry I. Meyer, *Corporate Financial Planning Models*, Wiley, New York, 1977, provides a more thorough discussion of corporate financial planning models and of how to construct and use them than is possible in the limited space available here.

[2] The reader might interpret interest rate as the average interest cost of debt for a firm that has only floating rate debt outstanding. A more sophisticated model would allow for fixed rate debt and would distinguish between debt outstanding as of the beginning of the planning period and the debt the firm issues during the planning period.

[3] A more sophisticated model would incorporate the other sources of short-term and long-term capital that are available.

[4] The fixed payout ratio would cause dividends to vary as net income varies. A more sophisticated model would incorporate the constraint that dividends per share should not decrease, at least not for planning purposes, for the reasons discussed in Part 4.

[5] The more sophisticated financial planning models often take the form of several equations that are solved simultaneously. Jack Clark Francis and Dexter R. Rowell, "A Simultaneous Equation Model of the Firm for Financial Analysis and Planning," *Financial Management*, vol. 7, spring 1978, pp. 29–44, describes a general simultaneous linear equation model.

[6] Linear programming has been used to develop more sophisticated optimization models. One such model is described in Steven F. Maier and James H. Vander Weide, "A Practical Approach to Short-Run Financial Planning," *Financial Management*, vol. 7, winter 1978, pp. 10–16. But until someone succeeds in identifying the precise relationship among the multiplicity of factors that affect firm valuation, financial planning models, regardless of their degree of mathematical sophistication, will be able to do no better than to suggest "approximate" solutions to the problem of finding the "best" financial policy mix.

CHAPTER 26

[1] John McKiernan, *Planning & Financing Your New Business: A Guide to Venture Capital*, Technology Management, Inc., Chestnut Hill, Mass., 1978, and Stanley E. Pratt and Jane K. Morris, eds., *Pratt's Guide to Venture Capital Sources*, 8th ed., Venture Economics, Inc., Wellesley Hills, Mass., 1984, provide names, addresses, and investment criteria for a large number of venture capitalists.

[2] Investors typically enjoy additional tax advantages. In many cases, 90% or more of the investment is tax deductible, much of it the first year. Also, if the partnership is properly structured, the technology it develops qualifies as a capital asset, in which case royalty income is taxed at capital gains rates.

[3] McKiernan, *op.cit.*, p. 4.

[4] Blaine Huntsman and James P. Hoban, Jr., "Investment in New Enterprise: Some Empirical Observations on Risk, Return, and Market Structure," *Financial Management*, vol. 9, summer 1980, pp. 44–51.

[5] Carl W. Schneider and Jason M. Shargel, *"Now That You Are Publicly Owned . . . ,"* Bowne & Co., Inc., New York, August 1983, provides an excellent summary of these regulations.

[6] The dollar volume of initial public offerings in 1983 is somewhat inflated because it includes several conversions of large savings banks from mutual to stock form and the initial public offering of shares in large well-established subsidiaries.

[7] Carl W. Schneider, Joseph M. Manko, and Robert S. Kant, *Going Public: Practice, Procedure and Consequences*, Bowne & Co., Inc., New York, August 1983, contains a more detailed discussion than is possible here of the legal and regulatory aspects of going public.

[8] Two shorter-form registration statements are available for small offerings.

[9] John S. R. Shad, "The Advantages, Disadvantages, and Costs of 'Going Public,'" in G. Scott Hutchison, *Why, When and How to Go Public*, Presidents Publishing House, Inc., New York, 1970, pp. 32–33, and Thomas B. Calhoun, "Pricing the Company's New Issue," in Hutchison, pp. 64–65.

[10] See Roger G. Ibbotson, "Price Performance of Common Stock New Issues," *Journal of Financial Economics*, vol. 2, September 1975, pp. 235–272, and Brian M. Neuberger and Chris A. La Chapelle, "Unseasoned New Issue Price Performance on Three Tiers: 1975–1980," *Financial Management*, vol. 12, autumn 1983, pp. 23–28, and the references contained therein. The Ibbotson study found 11.4% underpricing, on average, during the 1960 to 1969 period. The Neuberger and La Chapelle study found substantially greater underpricing during the 1975 to 1980 period, which as Table 26-1 shows, was a period of relatively low initial public offering activity. The Neuberger and La Chapelle study also found, as did earlier studies, that less prestigious underwriters tend to underprice to a greater degree than prestigious underwriters.

[11] Excluding these earnings does not mean that they are ignored in the valuation process. The temporary investments will be liquidated as funds are needed to support the growth of the business. Their value to the issuer is thus reflected in the price-earnings ratio. Without these funds the company could not make the capital expenditures needed to support growth consistent with a 33 price-earnings ratio. To add these temporary earnings to "true" operating earnings and then apply a price-earnings ratio of 33 would represent double counting.

CHAPTER 27

[1] "The Making of the Megamerger," *Fortune*, Sept. 7, 1981, pp. 58–64, chronicles the events surrounding the merger.

[2] The merger must have a legitimate business purpose, however, in order for the Internal Revenue Service to permit the profitable firm to utilize the other firm's tax loss carryforwards. The acquisition of a tax loss company by a profitable company is much more complex, not only

because of the greater difficulty of showing a business purpose for such an acquisition, but also because of the need to structure the acquisition to get the tax loss into the same legal entity as the profitable assets. In general, it is easier to survive the scrutiny of the IRS when the acquiror is the one with the tax loss carryforwards.

[3] The case of Kaiser Industries is often cited as a practical example to support this conclusion. Prior to its dissolution in 1977, Kaiser Industries was organized as a holding company with three publicly traded subsidiaries, Kaiser Aluminum, Kaiser Cement, and Kaiser Steel. But the stock of Kaiser Industries traded at a significant discount from the net asset value of its investments in its three subsidiaries—until Kaiser Industries announced its intention to liquidate, when the discount disappeared.

[4] On the other hand, bondholders tend to benefit at the expense of stockholders because each of the merged firms effectively guarantees the other's debt as a result of the merger.

[5] Michael C. Jensen and Richard S. Ruback, "The Market for Corporate Control: The Scientific Evidence," *Journal of Financial Economics*, vol. 11, April 1983, pp. 5–50, and J. Fred Weston and Kwang S. Chung, "Do Mergers Make Money?" *Mergers & Acquisitions*, vol. 18, fall 1983, pp. 40–48.

[6] If the acquiree is merged into a subsidiary of the acquiror (a so-called *subsidiary merger*), the Code also requires that the subsidiary acquire "substantially all" the assets of the acquiree. Under present IRS guidelines, this means at least 90% of the fair market value of net assets and at least 70% of the fair market value of gross assets. If the acquiror merges one of its subsidiaries into the acquiree (a so-called *reverse subsidiary merger*), the acquiror must gain control of at least 80% of the acquiree in exchange for voting stock.

[7] In the case of plant and equipment, depreciation is recaptured to the extent that assets are written up over their preacquisition tax basis. If fair market value exceeds the original cost basis, all prior depreciation deductions are recaptured. In the case of real property, such as buildings, only the excess of accelerated depreciation over straight-line depreciation is recaptured. Investment tax credit recapture is limited to prior years' ITC that has not yet vested.

[8] The negative impact is generally least when the maximum value can be allocated to the longest-lived assets.

[9] If instead the acquisition were taxable but created no goodwill, cash flow could increase as a result of an increase in depreciation expense for tax purposes with little impact on earnings.

[10] Hai Hong, Robert S. Kaplan, and Gershon Mandelker, "Pooling vs. Purchase: The Effects of Accounting for Mergers on Stock Prices," *Accounting Review*, vol. 53, January 1978, pp. 31–47.

[11] *Mergerstat Review 1983*, W. T. Grimm & Co., Chicago, 1984, pp. 74–75.

[12] Because of this, prospective acquirees often try to negotiate a flexible exchange ratio designed to get them a fixed dollar price for their shares.

[13] Gibson Greetings, Inc., prospectus, May 19, 1983, pp. 3–4.

CHAPTER 28

[1] The adjusted-present-value approach can also be used.

[2] A longer time horizon might be appropriate in the case of timber or other assets whose market value can appreciate quite rapidly over a period of several years.

[3] Gordon J. Alexander, P. George Benson, and Joan M. Kampmeyer, "Investigating the Valuation Effects of Announcements of Voluntary Corporate Selloffs," *Journal of Finance*, vol. 39, June 1984, pp. 503–517, found that the announcement of an impending divestiture has generally had a favorable share price impact.

[4] James A. Miles and James D. Rosenfeld, "The Effect of Voluntary Spin-off Announcements on Shareholder Wealth," *Journal of Finance*, vol. 38, December 1983, pp. 1597–1606. An increase in shareholder wealth is not assured, however, because a spin-off also reverses the potential debt capacity expansion, bankruptcy risk reduction, and tax shield utilization benefits that can result from combining businesses.

[5] Jeff A. Schnepper, *The New Bankruptcy Law*, Addison-Wesley, Reading, Mass., 1981, provides a detailed discussion of the provisions of the U.S. Bankruptcy Code.

[6] An excellent example of a successful retailing reorganization is Toys "R" Us, Inc., which emerged in 1978 from the bankruptcy of Interstate Stores, Inc. Toys "R" Us quickly became very profitable and within just a few years of its emergence from bankruptcy was able to sell debt securities in the public market.

[7] Franklin Realty Group, proxy statement, March 31, 1981, pp. ix–x.

CHAPTER 29

[1] Recent studies by Jaggi and Ruland suggest that forecasts by management are, in general, more accurate than analysts' forecasts. See Bikki Jaggi, "Further Evidence on the Accuracy of Management Forecasts Vis-a-Vis Analysts' Forecasts," *Accounting Review*, vol. 55, January 1980, pp. 96–101, and William Ruland, "The Accuracy of Forecasts by Management and by Financial Analysts," *Accounting Review*, vol. 53, April 1978, pp. 439–447.

[2] Lorna M. Daniells, *Business Information Sources*, University of California Press, Berkeley, Calif., 1985.

Index

ABOUT THE AUTHOR

John D. Finnerty, Ph.D., is a vice president of Lazard
Frères & Co., an associate editor of *Financial Management*,
and a director of the Financial Management Association.
He has worked as an investment banker for eight years,
first with Morgan Stanley & Co. and currently with Lazard Frères & Co. Prior to becoming an investment banker, Dr. Finnerty taught mathematics and economics to
graduate management students at the Naval Postgraduate
School. He is the author of *An Illustrated Guide to Bond Refunding Analysis* as well as many professional articles.